Between Commitment
and Disillusion

By H. Stuart Hughes

Intellectual and Cultural History

Oswald Spengler: A Critical Estimate (1952)
Revised edition (1962)
Consciousness and Society (1958)
Revised edition (1977)
The Obstructed Path (1968)
The Sea Change (1975)
Prisoners of Hope (1983)

General History

The United States and Italy (1953)
Third edition (1979)
Contemporary Europe: A History (1961)
Fifth edition (1981)

Essays

An Essay for Our Times (1950)
An Approach to Peace (1962)
History as Art and as Science (1964)

H. Stuart Hughes

Between Commitment and Disillusion

The Obstructed Path
and
The Sea Change

1930–1965

with a new introduction

Wesleyan University Press
Middletown, Connecticut

Published by arrangement with Harper & Row, Publishers, Inc.
Portions of this work appeared in *American Scholar*.

LIBRARY OF CONGRESS CATALOGING-IN-PUBLICATION DATA

Hughes, H. Stuart (Henry Stuart), 1916-
  Between commitment and disillusion: The obstructed path
and The sea change 1930-1965: with a new introduction / H.
Stuart Hughes. p. cm.
  Reprint (1st work). Originally published: 1st ed. New York:
Harper & Row, 1968.
  Reprint (2nd work). Originally published: 1st ed. New York:
Harper & Row, 1975.
  Twin sequels to: Consciousness and society. 1958.
  Includes bibliographical references and indexes.
  ISBN 0-8195-5136-8 (alk. paper)
  ISBN 0-8195-6193-2 (pbk. : alk. paper)
  1. France—Intellectual life—20th century. 2. Europe—Intel-
lectual life—20th century. 3. United States—Intellectual life—
20th century. 4. United States—Civilization—Foreign influ-
ences. 5. Intellectuals—United States. I. Hughes, H. Stuart
(Henry Stuart). 1916- Obstructed path. 1987. II. Hughes,
H. Stuart (Henry Stuart), 1916- Sea change. 1987. III.
Title. DC33.7.H84 1987
944.08—dc19   87-16841
                                                         CIP

All inquiries and permissions requests should be addressed to the
Publisher, Wesleyan University Press, 110 Mt. Vernon Street,
Middletown, Connecticut 06457

Distributed by Harper & Row, Publishers, Keystone Industrial
Park, Scranton, Pennsylvania 18512

Manufactured in the United States of America

FIRST WESLEYAN EDITION, 1987
WESLEYAN PAPERBACK, 1987

For Judy

Plus tost seront Rhosne, et Saone desjoinctz
Que d'avec toi mon coeur se désassemble. . . .
MAURICE SCÈVE, "Délie"

and

To the memory of Hans Meyerhoff

Contents

Introduction to the Wesleyan Edition

Every author must feel gratified by the resuscitation of one or more of his books that have been out of print. In my case the pleasure is enhanced by the fact that the republication of *The Obstructed Path* and *The Sea Change* restores the unity of my trilogy on early- and mid-twentieth century European intellectual history, which I inaugurated with *Consciousness and Society*. I find the new one-volume format entirely appropriate: the two books in question were conceived as parallel studies with an identical time frame.

The trilogy as a whole belongs to a variety of intellectual history which dominated the field for two decades from the late 1950s to about 1980. This type of writing falls in between two others which have focused primarily on textual analysis—its predecessor being the classic history of ideas associated with A. O. Lovejoy and his school, its successor the contemporary studies deriving from Parisian structuralism and deconstruction. With both these latter, ideas rather than human beings have served as the protagonists of the intellectual drama; in both cases, precision of method has ranked above concern for the context in which ideas have developed.

In contrast, the "school" that my work exemplifies—in common with the work of Peter Gay, Leonard Krieger, Frank E. Manuel, and Carl E. Schorske—has laid heavy stress on context, whether social or psychological. In so doing, it has regarded writers and thinkers themselves as the major protagonists. By the same token, it has focused on intellectual biography, or, possibly more often, on linked vignettes of members of a generation with comparable assumptions and life experiences. It has devoted attention to such writers' class situation and family history, suggesting thereby the extent to which Marxism and psychoanalysis have hovered in the background. And, as opposed to the schools preceding and following it, which have tended to share the concerns and methods of philosophers or literary critics, mine has preferred to deal with "social thought," in the sense of general speculation on the role of human beings in the societies that have formed them and that they in turn have altered.

A taxing assignment: no wonder that, of late, books like mine have been under repeated assault for their metaphorical language and their tendency to sprawl. Yet how can one avoid such pitfalls if one is trying to tackle "big" rather than clearly delimited questions? Imprecision and range are two faces of the same coin: the latter, I trust, still gives my work an abiding relevance.

When my twin books were published, in each case something like a half dozen of their protagonists were still alive. Today this is true of only two, Erik H. Erikson and Claude Lévi-Strauss—both octogenarians. With the others, their last years brought no new writing which might have changed my assessment. Or perhaps I should make one exception: the appearance of André Malraux's *Antimémoires* (plus four shorter sequels). But although this "anthology" took rank as a major literary event, its fracturing of chronological sequence, its maddening alternations between autobiography and extrapolations from Malraux's own novels, its pretentious and sometimes irrelevant conversations with "historic personalities," these taken together failed to clarify the ultimate mystery of the author's personal life. I might add for the record Simone de Beauvoir's *La cérémonie des adieux*, where in her customarily meticulous fashion she chronicled the physical disintegration of Jean-Paul Sartre and the stoic serenity with which he bore his multiple afflictions, notably blindness, in the final phase of his existence.

The first of my two studies, *The Obstructed Path*, was originally published nearly two decades ago, in early 1968. I recall the date in order to explain certain features whose raison d'être might not be readily apparent. For example, in the second chapter, on the major twentieth-century current in historical writing, I did not employ the term "School of the *Annales*," which came into general usage sometime in the 1970s. In the same chapter I ventured a critical judgment on Fernand Braudel, which may strike many readers as excessive in view of the fact that he subsequently became the most honored historian in the Western world. In this case I have not revised my opinion: I still believe that despite his impressive accomplishments, Braudel set a model of sloppy procedure and encouraged an ossification of dogma which Marc Bloch would never have countenanced.

A more curious feature of *The Obstructed Path* is the absence of any reference to the Parisian student insurrection, the "Events of May," which exploded less than four months after its publication. I doubt, however, whether, if I had been able to write of these tumults, my interpretation would have been perceptibly altered; with the exception of Sartre, the figures I was discussing were too old or too detached from public events to have been much moved by the brouhaha of May. Graver in its effect on my book was the fact that I completed it in Paris in the late winter and spring of 1967, when the full force of structuralism was just beginning to impinge on the French intellectual scene. I might well have omitted any mention of what was occurring. But this I found quite impossible: after all, I had already decided to include in my work an extended discussion of the great proto-structuralist Lévi-Strauss; I was also on Sunday mornings laboriously working my way though Michel Foucault's *Les mots et les choses*, which was hot from the press. The result of my tentative musings emerged in a few fragmentary passages at the very end of my book.

One of these, the assessment that structuralism was "difficult to export," proved quite wrong; soon this way of thinking and its heirs began to exert a tyranny over American departments of literature. But I do not retract the reservations I expressed; on the contrary, as the 1970s advanced, my doubts about what struck me as hermetic cultism grew stronger. Had I been writing ten years later, I might have attempted a full-scale reckoning with it. By the mid-1980s, my sense of urgency had dissipated. With the death not only of Foucault but of Roland Barthes and Jacques Lacan in the short span of a half decade, their style of thought and writing was beginning to show signs of having passed its crest. In this new perspective my characterizations ("fragile constructions," "untenable syntheses") may seem closer to the mark than they did shortly after they first saw the light.

For my second book, *The Sea Change*, which appeared seven years after *The Obstructed Path*, I have less in the way of rectification to propose. The chief lacuna readers may notice is in my references to Ludwig Wittgenstein. Since I wrote about him, the "Wittgenstein industry" has poured forth a torrent of special studies which are naturally absent from my footnotes. I am not aware, however, that any of them has substantially altered my conclusions. One other matter deserves comment. I deplored the "neglect" into which the work of Franz Neumann had fallen. In the late 1970s and early 1980s this situation started to change: through the labors of such younger German scholars as Rainer Erd and Alfons Söllner, Neumann's thought was restored to circulation—at least in his native land. I am happy to have contributed to this righting of an intellectual injustice.

I hope that the republication of my two studies may help to do the same for others of my protagonists whose nuanced vision is in danger of being obliterated by the "terrible simplifiers" of today.

—H. STUART HUGHES

Preface

Preface to The Obstructed Path

FOR a long time I was perplexed as to what kind of sequel I should write to my *Consciousness and Society*—published ten years ago—or indeed, as to whether I should follow it with any sequel at all. Certain major tendencies of European social thought in the four decades (1890–1930) covered by that volume had established themselves clearly in my mind: the succeeding era seemed to lack a comparable focus.

As the years passed, matters gradually sorted themselves out until it became apparent that more than one sequel was required. It was only by dividing the intellectual generation 1930–1965 into two distinct groupings that I could make sense of it. The first was limited to the French. The second consisted of the anti-fascist émigrés from Central Europe and Italy who settled in England or the United States. The reasons for treating these two themes separately should emerge from a reading of the first chapter of the present study.

This book forms, then, the second volume of a trilogy, which, after a further pause for reflection, I hope to complete before another ten years have gone by. I should hasten to add that it is a free-standing work in itself and that it is not necessary to read *Consciousness and Society* in order to understand it. It is intended as a contribution both to European intellectual history in the contemporary era and to the study of the culture of modern France. In the latter guise, it marks my first effort to deal explicitly with a French theme. Although I have been acquainted with France for more than forty years and have taught its history, I have

refrained until now from putting on paper any extended
reflections about it; I can only speculate on the origins of
this curious *pudeur*.

Certain portions of the book have previously figured in
the following forms: Chapter 1 was delivered as a lecture on
the occasion of Cornell University's centennial celebration
in April 1965; selections from Chapters 2 and 3 constituted
the Stephen Allan Kaplan Memorial Lectures which I gave
at the University of Pennsylvania in March 1966; parts 1–
4 of Chapter 3 were published in *The American Scholar*,
XXXV (Fall 1966), and part 4 of Chapter 5 in *Ramparts*, V
(March 1967). There are also a few echoes of phraseology
from reviews I wrote of Simone de Beauvoir's *The Mandarins*, of Camus's *The Rebel*, and of Lévi-Strauss' *The
Savage Mind*, when these books first appeared in English
translation.

To maintain a consistent tone, I have uniformly employed
the past tense, even when dealing with authors whose work
at the time of writing was far from finished. The footnotes
are designed to make a bibliography unnecessary. Although I
have almost invariably used the original French version of
the works cited, and I begin each footnote with this version,
I have referred the reader to the pages of the English translation, where such exists, taking care when necessary to correct the passages I have quoted.

Among those to whom I should like to express my grati-
tude, I should first mention François Crouzet and René
Rémond, professors of history at the University of Paris
(Nanterre), who arranged for me to teach at Nanterre as
Bacon Exchange Professor from Harvard University in the
second semester of the academic year 1966–1967, and thereby
to complete my book in the appropriate atmosphere of Paris.
I have also profited from conversations with Jean-Marie
Domenach, Claude Lévi-Strauss, Edouard Morot-Sir, and
Paul Ricoeur. Two of my PhD students, David L. Schalk

and Dominick La Capra, contributed respectively to my understanding of Martin du Gard and Durkheim, while Stephen A. Schuker undertook, on a wholly volunteer basis, the tedious and indispensable task of serving as my representative at home base in Widener Library while I was away in France. I am particularly indebted to Stanley Hoffmann for giving the entire manuscript a reading that was both discerning and heartening. Of my wife, to whom the book is dedicated and who combed it over for errors of fact and logic, I can only say that without her stimulation and encouragement it would have been neither conceived nor carried through to completion.

—1968

Preface to The Sea Change

THIS study concludes the investigation which I began with *Consciousness and Society* and which subsequently, as I explained in the preface to the second volume of the series, *The Obstructed Path*, developed into a trilogy. Like its predecessors, it is a free-standing work that can be read independently of the others. And as with them, I have followed my by now habitual procedure of writing throughout in the past tense and dispensing with a bibliography.

Two portions of Chapter 3 have earlier figured as follows: the section on Salvemini was given as a Lauro De Bosis Memorial Lecture at Harvard University in October 1971 and was repeated the following May (in Italian) before the Circolo Italiano di Boston; the section on Neumann (in slightly different form) was published in 1969 in *The Intellectual Migration*, edited by Donald Fleming and Bernard Bailyn.

My work on this book confronted me with a new and perplexing problem: here, as opposed to the earlier volumes of the trilogy, I was personally and sometimes even closely acquainted with a number of the protagonists. I hope that the survivors among the cast of characters—and they are lamentably few—will not be too grievously wounded by my critical comments.

During my last year of writing, death carried off three people whose reading of the book would have been particularly important to me: George Lichtheim, who so notably enriched my knowledge of Marxism in all its guises; Karl Loewenstein, the last direct link to Max Weber's circle, who first introduced me as a senior at Amherst College to the universe of German social thought; and Inge Werner Neumann Marcuse, the widow of one and the wife of another leading figure in this study, who never allowed friendship to stand in the way of expressing the full vigor of her beliefs.

My gratitude goes first to Dorothy Skelley, who typed the successive installments of the manuscript with meticulousness and unfailing good humor; second, to two of my Ph.D. students, Martin Jay and Paul A. Robinson, whose books *The Dialectical Imagination* and *The Freudian Left* I have tried to acknowledge amply in the footnotes to Chapters 4 and 5; and third, to those whose conversation sustained my spirits and contributed to my thoughts in ways of which I suspect they were mostly unaware—Lewis A. Coser, Henry Hatfield, Gerald N. Izenberg, David S. Luft, and John E. Toews.

My wife, Judy, besides giving me constant intellectual companionship, added to her customary and indispensable critique of my reasoning a more specific contribution to my understanding of ego psychology without which the latter part of Chapter 5 would have come out in a far weaker and more tentative form.

—1975

The Obstructed Path

CHAPTER
I

Introduction:
The Obstructed Path

IN HIS NOVEL *Le Grand Meaulnes*, Alain-Fournier speaks of a search for an "ancient obstructed path, the path to which the weary prince could find no entrance. It is found at last at the most forlorn hour of the morning, when you have long since forgotten that eleven or twelve is about to strike. . . . And suddenly, as one thrusts aside bushes and brier, . . . it appears in sight as a long shadowy avenue, with at its end a small round patch of light."[1]

The words are from 1913—but the sentiment might have been expressed with equal fervor at almost any time over the next forty years of French cultural history. In itself no more than a literary metaphor, it may serve to forecast the insecurities of the decades ahead. The *motif* of an "obstructed path," of blind alleys and blocked vistas, of faltering and stalemate, and of an increasingly desperate search for a way out, pervades the thinking of Frenchmen of all types and intellectual interests through nearly a half century following the outbreak of the First World War. It is as though Alain-Fournier had divined, one year before the conflict, the life-

[1] Translation by Françoise Delisle as *The Wanderer* (Boston and New York, 1928), p. 156.

1

long obsession of his contemporaries who, more fortunate than he, were to survive the terrible year 1914: the sense of one's world as a dark tunnel, beset with vague threats and of uncertain exit.

Besides the wound of the war itself—more grievous in France than elsewhere, since here the loss of youth was irreparable—the four years of bloodshed prompted a wider questioning of traditional French values. Yet this came only slowly: the delayed-action effect that postponed to the 1930's France's social and political examination of conscience was also apparent in the cultural sphere. An Indian summer of glory bedazzled Frenchmen and foreigners alike with an image of primacy that was already threatened on all sides. On the international scene, the first flush of illusion was quickly over: the ambiguous outcome of the Ruhr occupation and the electoral victory of the Left in 1924 marked the beginnings of abdication as a great power and a turning inward of the national energies. But from the narrower standpoint of the assumptions on which social and political life rested, the next half decade remained one of substantial self-satisfaction and self-esteem. It took the great depression and the advent of Hitler to shake the French loose from their inherited securities.

So much is familiar to any student of the period. What is less readily apparent is the extent to which this delayed realization of the war's effect had its parallel—indeed, was reinforced—by a corresponding overestimate of France's cultural situation. The military and diplomatic illusions of the years 1919–1924—the conviction that the French had regained the leadership of Europe and were once more the grande nation to which others would defer—appeared confirmed by the general esteem which France's artists and writers enjoyed. In painting, the prestige of the school of Paris remained unchallenged; in literature, such writers as Proust and Gide and Valéry had suddenly come into their own as the precursors of the avant-garde; in philosophy, Henri Bergson seemed without a rival. Subsequently, from the middle of the decade on, as the French withdrew from foreign commitments to the cultivation of their own garden, the nation's sense of cultural primacy became, if anything, still more pronounced. For an assertion of artistic or philosophical pre-eminence served as psychic compensation for the relinquishment of an active international role. The rest of the civilized world might no longer follow France's diplomatic leadership, but it continued to pay tribute to its creative achievements. Paris might have lost its position as the hub of international doings, but it still ranked as the cultural capital of the West.

Even the more perceptive French were usually unaware of the extent to which their country's artistic and literary primacy rested on an accumulation of past glories. While they realized perfectly well—perhaps overestimated—the benefits they enjoyed from a classical tradition extending in unbroken, orderly succession from the seventeenth century, they did not appreciate how close they were to that tradition's end. By 1930, the original avant-garde experiments had spent their force. Proust was dead, and Gide and Valéry beyond the period of their greatest creativity and influence. With this passing of masters, the perspective on them began to be subtly altered. Their works now figured less as the great innovations of the early twentieth century than as contemporary classics. And as the 1930's passed, and writers of similar scope failed to appear, people began to suspect that theirs might be the last generation for which the classical tradition would be a living reality.

In France, classicism had greater continuity than in other comparable European countries; it also pervaded the national culture more completely. In England, the classical tradition was associated with particular phases of literary history— and those not necessarily the most tenacious or influential. In Germany, it meant the legacy of one great era of achievement whose products had subsequently been embalmed by the schools and the official purveyors of ethical values—and which in the process had become more and more remote

from actual behavior. Neither among the English nor among
the Germans did the classical tradition prompt the dominant
style of thought. England had no single "official" philosopher; Germany had Kant, but by the twentieth century the
Kantian tradition had been interpreted so variously as to
remain only the vaguest point of reference—and besides, few
pedagogues aimed to teach children to write like Kant. In
France, in contrast, Descartes had for nearly three centuries
supplied a ready-made style of thought and of expression;
here Cartesianism suffused the intellectual atmosphere so
thoroughly that much of the time it went unnoticed. The
French not only possessed an official philosopher; they had
in the Cartesian tradition a pass-key that did service for
literature and social thought alike. Across the Rhine, "high"
culture might go one way and social science quite another—
with both of them for the most part irrelevant to the country's public life. In France, all these endeavors shared a
common ancestor and found in Cartesian categories the
guide to the orderly style of thought and the felicity of expression which had long been assumed to constitute the
special excellences of the Gallic mind.

By the 1930's, this ancient confidence was flagging. Or at
the very least a few Frenchmen of particular discernment
were beginning to discover the fragility of their country's
cultural prestige abroad. Claude Lévi-Strauss has related how
on his arrival in Brazil toward the middle of the decade he
found the products of French social science still enjoying
almost universal esteem. But the names held in highest honor
were of a generation that had passed or was passing; their
successors had become the generalizers or popularizers of
earlier discoveries. The national talent had been canalized
toward synthesis and ready explanation; it excelled in exposing with clarity and grace the larger outlines of theories,
which was all that the general public wanted or needed to
know.[2] In broader terms, the French were maintaining a cult

---

[2] *Tristes tropiques* (Paris, 1955), translated (and slightly abridged)
by John Russell under the same title, Atheneum paperback edition
(New York, 1963), p. 105.

of the spoken and written word which might impress the remoter reaches of the Latin world but which was becoming outmoded elsewhere; in France people still tended to assume that an elegant verbal solution to a problem would suffice to settle it. Such was the special vulnerability of the French classical tradition as the second quarter of the twentieth century began.

So it seems to us in retrospect: with the experience of a further generation behind us, we find confirmation for the contemporary suspicions that classicism had reached its end. In this perspective, authors like Proust and Valéry rank as the last of the French classicists (to whom some might add Albert Camus in the role of a dutiful grandson). And we can see the next generation as an era in which one writer after another strove to break the classic mold—not so much in technical experimentation (for that had been the work of the previous quarter century) as in the moral assumptions on which their work was based. The classical tradition had assumed a common psychology and a common standard of artistic excellence; even at its end, when it enlarged the criteria of conscious time, when it discovered the inconsequence of personal motivation or made room for the sexual deviant within the circle of a recognized humanity, it did so with a universal aim and in accordance with a rigorous canon of literary craftsmanship. By the 1930's and 1940's such a purist definition of the writer's aim seemed dated; indeed, the métier as such came under question as ethically insufficient for an apocalyptic era.

Hence the literature of engagement: this also is an old story. In the present context, what is significant is that in the literary as in the political and social field the real reckoning with the First World War arrived a decade late. The end of the classical tradition—and with it the ebbing of the flood of innovation, in the novel, in painting, in music, that the years immediately preceding the war had witnessed— came accompanied and reinforced by the great depression and the fascist onslaught. The result was a crisis of confidence on all sides. Just as the grave malfunctioning of

France's economic and administrative machinery was becoming generally apparent, the foundations of pride in the country's cultural tradition were beginning to be sapped. The years of political and social despair were also years of aesthetic and moral rethinking. What wonder that the prewar era figured in retrospect as the belle époque—that nostalgia for a time of facile pleasures and national confidence should have had its parallel in regret over a waning of cultural self-assurance.

It was to be another generation before both types of confidence were regained. After the Second World War, as in the aftermath of the First, the full social and moral effect of the military ordeal was a long time on the way. Not until the mid-1950's were the tempos and manners of a new kind of society in general evidence. And it was about the same time that the signs of innovation in intellectual and aesthetic interests became widespread. Hence for cultural study, the conventional division of contemporary French history into an interwar and a post-Second World War period makes little sense. The more natural order is to continue the effects of the pre-1914 currents down to the late 1920's, and then to delimit another era—the years of desperation—from the 1930's to the early 1960's. It is this latter era that now needs to be defined.

With the liberation of Paris from Nazi occupation and the end of the Second World War, France seemed once more to have become the cultural center of Europe. The old primacy had apparently been regained—one could even say that it had been reinforced by the almost total abdication of Germany. In the late 1940's, Paris was the focus of general curiosity and attention: the existential philosophy of Jean-Paul Sartre figured as the most discussed intellectual movement in the Western world. Superficially the situation looked much as it had been following the First World War, with the cultural pilgrims returning to France as numerous and as eager as before. But this time their worship at the shrine had a crucial difference: in the 1920's the Parisian novelties had been in evidence for more than a decade—they were extensions before a wider audience of what had previously been the concern of coteries; after 1944, foreigners came to Paris on true voyages of discovery—they wanted to find out what the French had been up to during their years of enforced isolation.

What the Englishman or American discovered often disconcerted him. For it was both novel and curiously familiar; it was both new and at the same time very old. In literature and philosophy, the merging of previously antagonistic systems and a calculated crudity in diction might shock or amuse. But the elements that went into the process were familiar enough. Marxism and phenomenology were far from new—it was only their marriage that came as a surprise. Likewise the modes of thought of men like Sartre and Merleau-Ponty were not as strange as they at first seemed—whether Cartesian or Hegelian or a combination of the two, their antecedents had been the common property of the European educated public long before the occupation of 1940 had cut off the French from intellectual circulation.

Had their imposed isolation been only four years long? This was what the foreign observer began to wonder as he noticed a perplexing provincialism in French cultural responses. Perhaps the separation of France from a wider intellectual exchange had started a good deal earlier, as early as the beginning of the 1930's. It was then that French concentration on indigenous values had assumed a character of prickly defensiveness. In the military sphere, it came to be called the complex of the Maginot Line. From the intellectual standpoint, it bore no such clear label. Yet the phenomenon was obvious enough: as the French had gradually found themselves outclassed in arms, bereft of economic expedients, ideologically torn asunder, and diplomatically beleaguered, their assertions of cultural superiority had quite naturally become more insistent. And this cultural pride was one of the intangible forces that sustained them through the

long ordeal of military occupation. Those who knew the
French on the morrow of victory can recall the patronizing
tone they frequently took toward their American or British
liberators—a tone brought to a perfection of unruffled assurance in the greatest literary classic of the Second World
War, the memoirs of General de Gaulle.

After 1933, the French had been more and more alone.
The only great nation of the Western European continent
that resisted a fascist takeover had paid the price in an increasing isolation of its intellectuals from a wider exchange
of ideas. What had earlier been the misfortune of Italy and
Germany and Austria by the mid-century had revealed an
unsuspected positive aspect. It would be absurd, of course,
to suggest that the exile or death of so many Italian or
German writers during the years of fascist tyranny had been
in any sense a cultural gain; on the contrary, this sort of
persecution impoverished the cultural life of their nations—
and in a fashion which in the German case seemed almost
irremediable. But such a vast displacement of intellectual
personnel could not fail to confer a number of side benefits.
In the case of the emigration of the 1930's and 1940's the
chief gain was a breaking down of the provincialism of national cultural frontiers. The fact that so many German
and Austrian writers (and to a lesser extent Italians) passed
a decade or more in Britain or the United States was of
immeasurable value to both sides in the exchange. The universe of discourse of the Anglo-Saxon and the Central European worlds were for the first time brought into close contact, and each was enriched in the process. Indeed, this
near-symbiosis of two widely contrasting traditions appears
in retrospect as the most important intellectual event of
the era.

There was no reason for the French to emigrate before
1940. After then it was too late—and besides, there was the
deep-seated prejudice, going back to the 1790's, against the
whole idea of self-exile. So the French stayed at home. Only
a handful of leading writers such as Jacques Maritain and

Antoine de Saint-Exupéry lived for any length of time in the United States. Thus the French shared scarcely at all in the great exchange of ideas going on in Britain and America. Their own tradition—which they had always assumed to be the central one—was suddenly cut off from the world outside.

We are back to the theme of confinement, of breaking out of an impasse. Let us turn now to define this process of turning inward in the specific field of social thought.

For the Americans and the émigrés from Central Europe, the masters of twentieth-century social thought were Sigmund Freud and Max Weber. Neither of these was honored in France as he had been in Germany before 1933 and subsequently in the United States. The French were far from being ignorant of what Freud and Weber had taught. But their application of Freudian doctrine was largely confined to imaginative literature or semi-intellectual conversation— the clinical practice of psychoanalysis was far less widespread in France than in Central Europe or America—and it was only a rare French scholar, like the young Raymond Aron, who had fully digested Weber's criteria for a methodology of social science.

The reasons for the French resistance to Freud are not far to seek. Psychoanalysis has always prospered less in a predominantly Catholic milieu than among Protestants or Jews; in this respect Italy in the interwar years was even more resistant than France. But among the French there was a special reason for reluctance to take up Freudianism and for dismay at the appearance of a discipline that claimed to have made a science of introspection. France was, after all, the classic home of the examination of conscience. For three and a half centuries since Montaigne a succession of French moralistes had been subjecting human motivation to a scrutiny that was both precise and disabused. Into this traditional national preserve the foreigner ventured only at his peril; even Freud had experienced his first glimmerings of insight in the hospital of a Frenchman, Charcot. What had a people that had produced Stendhal to learn further about the evasions and prevarications of the human heart? There was presumption in the claim of a mere physician from Vienna that he could reduce to a system what the classics of French literature had left on the level of aphorism or aperçu.

In the interwar years competent French studies of Freudian theories were readily available. As early as 1923 Raymond de Saussure had produced an account of psychoanalytic method which satisfied Freud's close associates (and concomitantly ran afoul of the French police). But in France even a professional understanding of psychoanalysis had a way of turning into something else. The French distrusted Freud's schematizations; they wanted more poetry in their psychology, and they were constantly smuggling in a voluntarist note at which the master would have bridled. Thus beginning in the late 1930's the leading philosopher of science Gaston Bachelard was using the term "psychoanalysis" in a new sense that included the reflective observation of such natural elements as fire and water, and was criticizing classic psychoanalytic theory for converting protean symbols and images into precise concepts; Bachelard envisaged a therapy of return to direct contact with nature and "things," of emotional restoration through work in the world of matter.[3]

Besides all this, the French had produced a contemporary of Freud who before 1914 had been far better known than he and who seemed to have said many of the same things in a more graceful and palatable form. As an explorer of the unconscious, Henri Bergson was in no sense Freud's equal; the adepts of psychoanalytic theory did not even consider him a precursor. But in liberating the study of human behavior from the tyranny of rationalistic, ready-made explanations, he had performed much the same function.

Thus the French possessed on their home ground a

[3] See François Dagognet, *Gaston Bachelard: sa vie, son oeuvre* (Paris, 1965), pp. 29–35, and among Bachelard's own works, *La psychanalyse du feu* (Paris, 1949).

Weltanschauung that was the deceptive mimic of Freudianism. Yet even as such it was far from satisfactory. By 1932, when Bergson's last major work finally appeared, its effect was muted by a protracted delay in its publication and by the fact that its author had been virtually silent during the previous decade. Outside France, *Two Sources of Morality and Religion* evoked little response: Bergson's way of thinking had gone out of fashion. Within France, the book's restrained reception revealed the extent to which the "Bergsonian revolution" in philosophy and social thought had long ago spent its force.

By the 1930's, although Bergson was still held in honor as the French philosopher laureate, it was difficult to find many full-fledged Bergsonians among his country's intellectual elite. The tendency, rather, was toward a selective Bergsonism; each writer chose the particular aspects of the doctrine that fitted his own needs and temperament. And Bergson himself seemed to invite eclectic treatment. He was "one of those philosophers who will always have progeny, because they sow seeds in the mind eternally—but almost no pupils; their system cannot be transmitted."[4] Such was the situation in the literary world. In the lycées and the universities, the official teaching had for the most part fallen back into the familiar neo-Kantian mold.

The failure of the Bergsonian revolution is a perplexing topic: its full explanation would demand a probing into countless individual biographies. At the very least one can say that the slaughter of 1914–1918 had taken the bloom off the philosophy of the élan vital. Tens of thousands of educated young Frenchmen who in the immediate prewar years had intoxicated themselves on Bergson's heady prose had marched off to battle trusting in spiritual fervor to see them through. The ghastly reality had borne almost no resemblance to what they had imagined. Bergson, of course, had not meant his notion of an élan to be taken in an exclusively

[4] Henry Bars, *Maritain en notre temps* (Paris, 1959), p. 197.

or even predominantly military sense. But that was the way the greater part of his young followers had interpreted it. From this standpoint, the Bergsonian ideal was simply another casualty of the First World War.

Beyond that, those who had understood the ideal with the greatest depth and sympathy were nearly all practicing Catholics or converts to Catholicism. At their hands what was left of Bergson's message—and the quiet undercurrent descending from Pascal of which it was the most prominent contemporary manifestation—had passed into the revival of specifically Catholic thinking that distinguished the interwar years. As early as 1913 the young Maritain had published a critique of the Bergsonian philosophy which marked his personal shift toward an allegiance to St. Thomas Aquinas. Two decades later, the cultivation of Thomism was at its peak in Catholic intellectual circles. Neo-scholastic precision had dimmed the prestige of Bergson's anti-intellectualist philosophy. And for those who—as in one aspect of Bergsonism itself—drew sustenance from the American pragmatic tradition, there was a younger Catholic teacher, Gabriel Marcel, to guide them.

Yet enough of Bergson's style of thought lingered among French students of society, more particularly among historians, to make them still aspire to an immersion in the flux of reality. When nearly all the rest had been discarded, this yearning toward a close embrace of social and historical experience remained intact as the core of the Bergsonian inheritance. It implied the rejection of any schematic understanding of the social universe. So far as the concepts of social thought were concerned, it was incompatible with Weber's ideal-type method.

This was one reason why Weber was not accepted in France, as he had been in Germany and was later to be in the United States, as a methodological guide. A more important reason was that in this field also the French already possessed their own master—a contemporary of Bergson's whose influence had held up far better than his.

Emile Durkheim had died in 1917, and many of his ablest young followers had perished in battle. Yet had he lived into the 1930's, he could scarcely have had a prestige greater than that already enjoyed by his students and intellectual heirs. In the interwar years, the systematic study of society in France—and more particularly the linked disciplines of sociology and anthropology—were dominated by Durkheim's precepts. These methodological principles were not always mutually consistent: Claude Lévi-Strauss has complained of their oscillation "between a dull empiricism and an aprioristic frenzy,"[5] and several others have noted how far they traveled in the course of Durkheim's life from their simple positivist origins. The range of Durkheim's interests can be held responsible for some of this diversity of emphasis. The fact that he was starting almost from scratch and that he died before he had time to spell out the final—and more idealist—stage of his thought also help to explain it. But the really troubling aspects of Durkheim's work—and those that created the most difficulty for his heirs—were his philosophical assumptions and the moral view of human society which he had derived from two quite distinct nineteenth-century traditions.

Kant was his master in philosophy, and Comte his great precursor as a systematic sociologist. The wedding of these two in Durkheim's mind already suggested one intellectual problem—a nostalgia for an abstract scheme of ideas which was in implicit contradiction with the empirical labors to which he devoted himself and which he urged on his disciples. Beyond that, it meant a constant search for a moral imperative in the study of society. To the intellectual historian, Kant and Comte may seem to have little in common, but at least they were in agreement in their ethical goal. Kant was unashamedly a moral teacher; Comte believed in a science of morality. Neither would have understood a social theory that aspired to freedom from commitment to specific

[5] "French Sociology," *Twentieth Century Sociology*, edited by Georges Gurvitch and Wilbert E. Moore (New York, 1945), p. 528.

values. Such a "value-free" sociology was what Weber had
proposed and what his German and American disciples were
trying to cultivate. Here, quite apart from differences in
technical methodology, lay a substantial ground for the
divergence of French social thought from the Central European–Anglo American exchange in the 1930's and 1940's.

Durkheim believed with Comte that a moral philosophy
could grow out of "positive science." He himself and the
intellectual tradition he founded were living manifestations
of such a conviction. The values they espoused were secular
and "enlightened"; they were a modernized version of an
eighteenth-century faith. Durkheim and those like him cherished an intense loyalty for the Third French Republic,
which in their minds incarnated the great abstractions of
freedom, democracy, tolerance, and humane behavior.

Hence the school of Durkheim found a reassuring congruence between public values and private morality. The
state in whose educational system they served was also one
to which they could give ethical endorsement. This close
association with the values of the Third Republic presented
no particular problem in the years of growing national confidence before the First World War—although it reduced
critics like Sorel and Péguy to impotent fury. But in the
war's aftermath the Republic's virtues were less apparent;
here also the bloom had disappeared. And by the 1930's—
when nearly every writer of perception, left or right, found
some grievous fault in the Third Republic—a school of social
thought that was so intimately tied to it could not fail to
be threatened also. At the very least, the value system of
Durkheim and his heirs now seemed morally shallow. Indeed,
it sometimes appeared indistinguishable from the "bourgeois
morality" of the ordinary philistine. One cannot understand
the rage—the nausea—of a young philosopher like Jean-Paul
Sartre at France's intellectual establishment on the eve of
the Second World War unless one appreciates how smug
and fatuous the entrenched dignitaries of the Sorbonne
looked to those outside.

Once more the stress is on intellectual confinement and the need of breaking out. French social thought had its own native masters, but they were not the same as those who were held in highest esteem abroad, and their teachings were becoming increasingly irrelevant to the efforts of the younger French thinkers. The ways out of the impasse took a long time to find, and they had little in common with what contemporary writers were doing elsewhere. Neo-Thomism, neo-Marxism, existentialism—these were the paths most frequently followed. No one proved entirely satisfactory: each soon took on specifically French contours which made for difficulties in translation or understanding beyond the confines of French culture. By the 1950's, the modes of thought that had originally been devised as avenues of escape were themselves becoming culs-de-sac.

The 1930's have conventionally been depicted as an era of almost unparalleled squalor in modern French history. The focus has been on diplomatic defeat abroad and on irresponsible partisanship at home—and on that vague complex of unsavory features grouped under the heading of "moral decay." Without question there was much in French politics and society in this decade that was extremely disquieting, and the collapse of 1940 had a long and unhappy prehistory. More especially, the customary warfare among ideological schools mounted to an unprecedented shrillness, as rival intellectual clans threatened to devour each other whole. This merciless, this near-suicidal struggle among France's cultural leaders has been repeatedly chronicled, and with both verve and discernment.[6] While it is an astonishing and en-

[6] See, for example: Jacques Chastenet, *Histoire de la Troisième République*, VI: *Déclin de la Troisième* (Paris, 1962), Chapter 13; David Caute, *Communism and the French Intellectuals 1914–1960* (New York, 1964); Raoul Girardet, "Notes sur l'esprit d'un fascisme français 1934–1939," *Revue française de science politique*, V (July-September 1955), 529–546; Stanley Hoffmann, "Aspects du régime de Vichy," *Revue française de science politique*, VI (January–March 1956), 44–69, "Paradoxes of the French Political Community," *In*

grossing story, it is not the whole record of what French
intellectuals were doing in these years of growing despair.
Nor does the ideological aspect of the succeeding decade—
the schism within France's writers between the Resistance
and the adherents of Vichy, and the apotheosis of the
former at the war's end—exhaust the interpretive possibilities
of that era. An almost exclusive ideological focus on the
1930's and 1940's has made the French intellectuals appear
rather worse than they actually were in the first of these
decades and rather better in the second.

A different perspective emerges if one tries to locate and
analyze what the French wrote in the generation after 1930
that transcended the warfare of ideological schools—the more
lasting achievements of French social thought in these decades when the voices of disinterested investigation came so
near to being stifled in a cacophony of abuse. Those who
tried to lift the level of the debate did so under circumstances of unprecedented difficulty, and their work is all the
more impressive for the obstacles it encountered along the
way.

Such obstacles were not only the perils of partisanship.
They were inherent in the French literary tradition and
French educational practice. Here once again the tendency
to take words for actualities is crucial to our understanding
of the epoch. It helps explain why most of the ideological
rhetoric of the 1930's rings so hollow today: besides its
inflation and its striving after literary effect, it seems to hover
beyond reality in a special atmosphere of its own. In earlier
decades the French knew how to decode the rhetorical
flights of their statesmen and publicists; sometime in the
interwar years they lost the knack. One by one, the honest
and rigorous social thinkers began to realize that a new kind
of discourse was necessary—a discourse which would give a
surer grasp on reality and would translate more easily into

Search of France (Cambridge, Mass., 1963), pp. 21–60; Eugen Weber,
*Action Française: Royalism and Reaction in Twentieth-Century
France* (Stanford, Calif., 1962).

the vocabularies in use outside France. In this perspective, the task of purifying the language from ideological bombast was simply another aspect of the general effort to cast off what was confining in the traditional patterns of thought and expression.

Thus regarded, the activities of intellectuals single-mindedly committed to a political cause must take second rank. The apologists for the extra-parliamentary Leagues or the Popular Front of the 1930's, even the writers who in the next decade were Resistance figures and nothing besides, begin to recede into the background. Yet this background is by no means irrelevant to the wider story. Only a bloodless—and hence uninteresting—writer could remain totally unaffected by the clash of rival doctrines around him; every intellectual of stature necessarily had some moral commitment which could not fail to become more articulate as external threats closed in upon it. The fact that the disinterested study of society was pursued in an atmosphere so charged with ideological passion gave it a particular responsibility of tone. The very isolation under which French intellectual life labored, suffused it with a special intensity, as in the case of a tormented Catholic spokesman like Georges Bernanos or in the thought emerging from the Resistance experience.

In this light, the period from 1930 to the early 1960's appears as one in which desperate and fratricidal passion could in a few privileged instances be harnessed to work of high seriousness and universal scope. The arc of such writing extends all the way from the new social history of Marc Bloch and Lucien Febvre to the imaginative creations of novelists as diverse as Martin du Gard and Malraux—or, at the end of the period and at the farthest reaches of "respectable" inquiry, the cosmological speculations of Teilhard de Chardin. Examples like these mark the range and boldness of French thought in this era; they also suggest its tentativeness and its fragmentary character. The literature and the social thought of some periods bear the stamp of classical self-assurance: this had earlier been the French norm. In contrast, the work of the 1930's and 1940's appears shot through with self-doubt. Such was its special vulnerability, and such its special claim to our esteem. The way out of the impasse could never quite be found; the obstructed path still glimmered only obscurely ahead.

CHAPTER
2

The Historians and the Social Order

I n 1929—the year of Poincaré's retirement and the stock-market crash in the United States, the year in which (as it appeared in retrospect) France's renewed time of troubles began—two French historians, already established scholars in their middle years, inaugurated a journal that in the next decade was to become the single most important forum for the revitalization of historical studies in the Western world. The foundation of the *Annales d'histoire économique et sociale* by Lucien Febvre and Marc Bloch showed that a new generation of historical thinkers had come to maturity—that the neo-idealist precepts of men like Croce and Meinecke no longer remained unchallenged in the imaginative investigation of the past. And for the first time since the eighteenth century, this newly constituted school of economic and social research put France in the forefront of European historical scholarship.

It was characteristic of Bloch and of Febvre that they should have launched their experimental venture at a time when so many of their countrymen were either gripped or about to be gripped by skepticism and despair. They were robust-spirited men, confident of themselves and of the professional discipline they served. Both sons of professors, they had come to their calling with an assurance derived from hereditary familiarity with France's academic elite. Although scarred by four years of combat service, they had suffered from the shock of the First World War less profoundly than had men a few years their juniors; Febvre was thirty-six when the conflict began, Bloch twenty-eight. Their values were already formed: the war stimulated their historical imaginations by making them aware of an incipient new society, but it did not threaten their own moral certainties. These remained "enlightened," democratic, and strictly secular—Third Republican in the most favorable meaning of the term. Something of this ethical security—this good conscience—passed over into their professional labors to sustain them with a happy sense of scholarly integrity and a mountainous volume of work well done.

Such are the reasons for dealing with the historians of society at the very start of the present study. Among their contemporaries in other pursuits, they were the closest to the generations of France's past. In their inmost being, men like Febvre and Bloch lived in a pre-catastrophe world. They also lived rooted in French patriotism, deep and unquestioned—just as they taught their pupils to seek in France's soil and in the tangible evidence of France's monuments the key to the riddles of historical interpretation that had eluded their predecessors. Febvre and Bloch never pretended to know all the answers: they emphasized again and again that the historian was more a "searcher" than a propounder of explanations. But in their restless search they were sure at least of their own point of departure—and in this they were more fortunate (or more limited) than those in other fields who took years or decades to find a solid footing. At the hands of a Febvre or a Bloch the study of history became more flexible, more pluralist, more self-questioning than it had ever been before—and it became so partly because its practitioners lived both in the old universe of certainty and in the new universe of flux, and could exploit the dis-

continuities between the two to the maximum benefit of
their historical understanding.

1. *From Michelet via Durkheim to Henri Berr*

At the death of Lucien Febvre, his leading academic successor referred to him as "since Michelet . . . the greatest, perhaps the only great historian writing in the French language."[1] Outside France such an accolade may sound odd. In
Germany or the Anglo American world until very recently
Michelet did not rank as a great historian at all. He seemed
too careless, too "literary"—too romantic in style and spirit.
The first to rehabilitate Michelet was Edmund Wilson, who
discovered in him the heir of Vico and the precursor of
historical writing harnessed to revolutionary ends. But even
for Wilson he remained primarily a littérateur, a man with
a "novelist's social interest and grasp of character," a "poet's
imagination and passion."[2]

For the French—and particularly for French professional
historians—the polemical stimulus to exhuming Michelet
was rather more pointed. To hold up as an example the
writer whose most celebrated pages were hymns to the vast
anonymous force of the French people was to assault head-on
the established cult of Germanic methodology. Lucien Febvre
knew exactly what he was doing when he claimed Michelet
as his master. "Do you know Michelet?" he asked his readers, with his characteristic verve and irony. "We know him
all too well," he had them answering:

> Between you and me he wasn't that good at history!
> He didn't get to the bottom of his sources. Far better
> scholars than he . . . have proved it. His bibliography,
> . . . not worth speaking of: he didn't even keep his

[1] Fernand Braudel, "Lucien Febvre et l'histoire," *Cahiers inter-
nationaux de sociologie*, XXII (1957), 15.
[2] *To the Finland Station* (Garden City, N.Y., 1940), p. 13.

notes in a filing box. And his history, rotted through
with errors . . . : one can't trust it. Besides, an old
fogey, a humanitarian, a professional patriot, a liberal.[3]

Such criticisms were no news to a man like Febvre: for two
generations they had been the staples of French historical
scholarship. He knew Michelet's weaknesses—what he wanted
to do, as an older associate interpreted his aims, was to be
"another Michelet—but better equipped, with a more critical spirit, . . . intuitive like him, yet not letting himself be
carried away by his creative genius."[4]

As opposed to the dominant fetish of the "documents and
nothing but the documents" and its accompanying emphasis
on strictly political history, Febvre and his associates saw in
Michelet the historian who had tried to "resurrect" the past
in all its variety and complexity, who had viewed a civilization like that of France as the work not merely of its kings
and statesmen but of the untutored strivings of its entire
people. For Michelet all realms of thought and action had
been continuous and all types of historical evidence worthy
of examination; the historian's task was to understand and
describe the "common climate" that underlay them.[5] Most
of these lessons had been forgotten since Michelet's death.
The last quarter of the nineteenth century had witnessed the
triumph of professional scholarship on the Teutonic model;
the study of history offered a prime example of the prestige
of German methods of scientific investigation that had followed France's defeat in the War of 1870.

Yet one of Michelet's precepts stood fast as a basic tenet
of French pedagogy. In the preface to the 1869 reissue of his
History of France, he had warned of the indispensability of
geographical knowledge to historical study: "Without a geo-

[3] Introduction to a volume of selections entitled *Michelet* (in the
series *Les classiques de la liberté*) (Geneva and Paris, 1946), p. 11.
[4] Preface by Henri Berr to Febvre's *Le problème de l'incroyance au
XVIe siècle: la religion de Rabelais* (Paris, 1942), p. viii.
[5] Lucien Febvre, "Vivre l'histoire. Propos d'initiation" (1941),
Combats pour l'histoire (Paris, 1953), pp. 25–26.

graphical basis, the people, the makers of history, seem to be walking on air, as in those Chinese pictures where the ground is wanting. The soil, too, must not be looked upon only as the scene of action. Its influence appears in a hundred ways, such as food, climate, etc."[6] The eighteenth-century philosophes had already argued the practical merits of the linked disciplines of history and geography as antidotes to an exclusive diet of the classics. The educational reformers of the Third Republic had reinforced the association of the two. Just as in Germany philosophy was considered the natural ally and support of historical studies, so in France a geographical foundation for such endeavors came to be assumed. In addition, the alliance of history and geography had a republican flavor; the classics were associated with reaction.[7] By the twentieth century, the characteristic French university professor of history was a convinced republican; a historian of conservative or royalist bent was far more likely to be an amateur man of letters.

At the turn of the century, the masters of French historical scholarship were professional universitaires whose interests were overwhelmingly political and institutional—Charles Langlois for the Middle Ages, Ernest Lavisse for the seventeenth and eighteenth centuries, Charles Seignobos for the contemporary period. Men like these might in a loose sense be called "positivists"; that at least was how Febvre and Bloch referred to them when they made their own appeal for a "broader and more human" definition of historical studies. In an unsophisticated understanding of scientific method and a conviction that "the facts" of history could speak for themselves without the intrusion of hypothesis or theory, Langlois and Lavisse and Seignobos ran true to form

[6] Quoted by H. C. Darby in "Historical Geography," *Approaches to History: A Symposium*, edited by H. P. R. Finberg (London, 1962), pp. 152–153.
[7] Felix Gilbert, "Three Twentieth Century Historians: Meinecke, Bloch, Chabod," *History*, edited by John Higham (Englewood Cliffs, N.J., 1965), p. 367.

as children of the late nineteenth century. But their particular brand of positivism proved comparatively benign. Aided by the grace and fluency of the language in which they wrote, the French professional historians of the early twentieth century were far from being pedants or antiquaries: they organized their works impeccably, and their style ran with a bright clarity. Bergsonians before the fact, they had a talent for working themselves into the historical movement they were studying, for "recapturing the rhythm of this movement by an act of imaginative sympathy."[8] It is noteworthy that the eighteen-volume history of France to the Revolution which Lavisse directed maintained its authority longer than any similar collaborative work of national history published in another country; it was also characteristic of the French historical tradition that the introductory volume to the series, which appeared in 1903, should have been a "tableau" by France's leading geographer, P. Vidal de la Blache.

Such are some of the reasons why a revolt against positivism in historical studies came later in France than in Germany and Italy and in rather different form.[9] The professional landscape in France gave less cause for radical dissatisfaction. Hence the neo-idealist movement associated with such names as Croce and Meinecke largely passed the French by. When the revolt did materialize—a generation after it happened in Germany and Italy—it was less explicitly idealist in tone and less afraid of scientific terminology and associations.

Two further peculiarities of the French historical scene contributed to the scientific cast of methodological innovation. The first was the prestige of Emile Durkheim. Febvre respected Durkheim—and feared the imperialist aims of a school of sociology that threatened to "annex" the study of

---

[8] R. G. Collingwood, *The Idea of History* (Oxford, 1946), p. 189.
[9] For an analysis of this revolt, see my *Consciousness and Society* (New York, 1958), Chapter 6.

history for its own purposes.[10] But Febvre had already completed most of his professional training before 1902, when
Durkheim began to teach in Paris; the direct sociological
influence never dominated his thought. Bloch, eight years
younger than Febvre, came to his historical training when
Durkheim's fame was at its height. He was powerfully attracted to the reigning school of French sociology. Three
decades later he was still citing Durkheim, along with
Michelet, as one of the masters who had taught him that in
order to understand his own time he must avert his eyes from
it and look to the past.[11]

The second special feature of the French historiographic
configuration was the quiet but tenacious work of Henri
Berr. Now nearly forgotten, Berr left behind him a lasting
monument in the form of the multi-volume series entitled
L'évolution de l'humanité. If it is unquestionable that the
French have excelled all others in such collaborative historical enterprises, it is also clear that among the French
collective studies Berr's was the very best. Two generations
after the work of Lavisse and one generation removed from
that of Berr, it is instructive to contrast the two. The former
kept severely to a chronological ordering of data; its sections
were demarcated by the reigns of kings; within the sections
the bulk of the chapters were devoted to politics, war, and
diplomacy, with social and cultural life relegated to "topical"
chapters tacked on to the end. Berr's series established society
and culture as the central focus: although the author of each
volume had license to proceed as he chose, most elected an
analytical scheme in which the emphasis was on transnational
comparisons and the integration of the various aspects of a
given period into a comprehensible synthesis.

[10] "Vers une autre histoire" (first published in *Revue de méta-physique et de morale*, LVIII [1949]), *Combats*, p. 422.
[11] "Que demander à l'histoire?" (address to the *Centre polytech-nicien d'études économiques*, 1937), *Mélanges historiques*, edited by Charles-Edmond Perrin (Paris, 1963), I, 12.

L'évolution de l'humanité, originally planned for a hundred volumes, began appearing in 1920; by 1954—at the death of Berr, past ninety in age—the number published stood at 65. Among them were works of Marc Bloch and Lucien Febvre that had become historical classics overnight. The series continues—in this sense Berr is still a living presence, more than a century after his birth. *L'évolution de l'humanité,* however, was the product of his already established influence. What had originally set him in polemical opposition to his colleagues—and profoundly appealed to a handful of younger men like Febvre—was the foundation two decades earlier, in 1900, of the *Revue de synthèse historique.*

The aim of the new review, in its founder's words, was to overcome the fear of "premature generalizations" that had narrowed the range of French historical scholarship since the 1870's, and to induce specialized scholars in the various branches of history "to be of greater mutual assistance through a clearer conception of the common task." Struck by the sudden popularity of sociology in the Durkheim manner, Berr argued that this had come about through a default on the part of the historians; in renouncing the task of philosophical synthesis, they had left a void that the sociologists had been eager to fill. Among these latter, the example of Durkheim had proved the most helpful; his "great merit" was "to have applied a precise, experimental, comparative method to historical facts." Yet sociology, for all its "importance and legitimacy," was not "the whole of history." Beyond it, Berr found still greater significance in the psychology of individuals and of groups. "The comparative study of societies," he explained, "must lead to social psychology and to a knowledge of the basic needs to which institutions and their changing manifestations are the response." And this study would in turn direct attention to "the psychology of great men of thought and action, of ethnic groups, and of historical crises." At the end of his injunction, Berr urged his colleagues to grapple with the "delicate psychological problem" of arriving "at a clear picture of the role of the intellectual element in history"—an early warning signal of the pitfalls that lay in wait for the twentieth-century historian of ideas.[12]

Such, in schematic outline, was the program to which Berr's friend Lucien Febvre, a half generation younger than he, was to devote nearly fifty years of scholarly endeavor. At the turn of the century the ground had been already staked out that would be formally occupied two or three decades later. In this sense one can equate Berr's projected revolution in French historical studies with the contemporary efforts of the neo-idealists in Germany and Italy. But in this sense alone: although Berr was of an age with Croce and Mcinecke, his mentality was very different. His epistemological canon might be idealist—he held that the historical past existed "only to the extent" that it was "re-created by the mind"— but he was far more science-oriented than the historians who usually bore that label. Much of his language carries the ring of nineteenth-century positivism. In his long life Berr began his studies with the scientific certainties of the first positivist age; he closed them in the more sophisticated idea-world of contemporary neo-positivism; the high-flown philosophizing of the idealists apparently left him cold. In reading the nearly octogenarian Berr's introduction to Febvre's master-piece, published in 1942, we can clearly detect the disparities in historical temperament between the two: more sanguine than the author himself, Berr gently chides his younger friend for claiming less than his due as a reinterpreter of the sixteenth century.

This contrast makes it difficult to assess the part of each in the summary article on history that they jointly wrote for the *Encyclopaedia of the Social Sciences* in the early 1930's. (That the American editors should have chosen two insurgent Frenchmen for this assignment was of historical

[12] The program of the *Revue de synthèse historique* has been translated by Deborah H. Roberts for *The Varieties of History*, edited by Fritz Stern (New York, 1956), pp. 250–255.

significance in itself.) The prose sounds more like Berr than like Febvre. There is a pat, positivist tone to the discussion of historical causality, which, the authors claim, "may be divided into three categories: contingency, necessity and logic." A similar easy confidence seems to underlie the assertion that "the laws of history will most certainly eventually be established." Yet in the same breath Berr and Febvre hasten to inform us that "laws" must be understood rather differently from the way they have been "conceived by some who have pretended to formulate them or by others who deny such a possibility." They should not be thought of as "necessarily universal and eternal"—they should be treated, rather, as "generalities, similarities, uniformities." What begins as an echo of a late nineteenth-century faith ends in a formulation that is impeccable from the standpoint of the up-to-date scientific method of the interwar years. Such is the character of the article as a whole: it suffers from a split personality, as though Berr had written the original draft in a mood of sweeping self-assurance and Febvre had subsequently added the qualifications and sophistications that professional scruple prompted. And so the essay promises more than it performs: the crucial discussion of the place of sociology and psychology in historical study peters out in little more than a general typology. At the end, of course, comes the anticipated call for universal, comparative history. But with an unexpected twist—this new type of historical study will solve the age-old problems of "bias" and "objectivity":

> The ideas of discipline, of subordination of individual view in a general direction, of internal organization of the work—these ideas inherent in every efficacious work of science will penetrate in their turn into history, will . . . assure its gradual transformation into a science conscious of its goal and of its means and notably will solve a capital problem, that of the objectivity of the historian. The various studies, all tainted . . . by an important coefficient of error, of illusion and of personal blindness,

will constantly control each other; the "involuntary biases" too will correct each other and to a large measure cancel out.[13]

We shall of necessity return to these formulations. As answers to the perennial question of value judgments in history, they are transparently inadequate. Meantime it may suffice to suggest that the very inconclusiveness of this effort marks it as a transition document. When the *Encyclopaedia of the Social Sciences* commissioned the article on history, Berr was an elderly man and Febvre only just arrived at a position of mastery in the French historical profession. His foundation of a school of historians in his own image still lay in the future.

In an affectionate memoir of Henri Berr composed for his eightieth birthday, Lucien Febvre traced the qualities that had made the older man so effective a propagandist—cordiality, grace of manner, respect for the ideas of others, above all, an unfailing optimism.[14] Febvre himself was less ingratiating: his own notion of advancing his intellectual cause was unremitting struggle—as "combats" was the title he chose for his collected essays. He and his younger ally Bloch saw Berr as their precursor. There was a hint of patronizing in the way they spoke of him and his work—customarily referring to the *Revue de synthèse historique* as their "Trojan horse" in the enemy's camp. At the end of the 1920's they decided that the era of caution had come to an end: they were now ready for a full-scale assault on the citadels of French historiography.

II. *From Strasbourg to Paris: The Collaboration of Lucien Febvre and Marc Bloch*

The two first came together in the autumn of 1920 in newly liberated Alsace. The conversion of the University of Stras-

---

[13] The article is in volume VII of the *Encyclopaedia* (New York, 1932), pp. 357–368.

[14] "Hommage à Henri Berr" (first published in *Annales: économies—sociétés—civilisations*, VII [1952]), *Combats*, pp. 339–342.

bourg from a German to a French institution had created a
unique opportunity for the recruitment *de novo* of a faculty
of distinction. Febvre arrived as professor of history, Bloch as
a maître de conférences soon to receive a regular chair. Both
had attained the rank of captain in the war—both had won
the citations and decorations that were "the required baggage
of a French gentleman in these years." The mood was of
"joyous spontaneity": the exhilaration of their unprecedented
venture broke down the barriers of distrust and rivalry
ordinarily characteristic of French faculty life.[15] Febvre and
Bloch quickly became friends: they began a collaboration
whose untroubled intensity was to surprise them both. As "a
human achievement"—the younger man put it—in which
they could justly take pride, they "succeeded in pedaling
their tandem together, thanks to the major ideas they held
in common and the great affection they had for each other—
despite strong contrasts in temperament and little taste on
either side for diplomatic cunning."[16]

The senior partner was already a fully accredited historian
when he came to Strasbourg. The French historical profession is well-known for its extended incubation period, and it
was a sign of rapid advance that Lucien Febvre should have
received his doctorate in 1911, at the age of thirty-three, a
safe margin of time before his long years of combat service.
Born in the Franche-Comté, Febvre had spent his childhood
and youth in Nancy, the capital of Lorraine. Both of these
much-fought-over border provinces appealed to the young
man's feeling for the French past, but it was the Franche-
Comté that he considered his "vraie patrie." As a boy he had
discovered in the rugged Jura the sights and sounds and
smells of an earlier era which here lingered on until the close
of the nineteenth century; such direct contact with the
countryside and its living history fired his imagination and

---

[15] Lucien Febvre, "Souvenirs d'une grande histoire: Marc Bloch et
Strasbourg," *Combats*, pp. 391–393.
[16] Letter of Bloch to Febvre, March 11, 1942: "Marc Bloch:
témoignages sur la période 1939–1940," *Annales d'histoire sociale,*
VII (1945), 27.

distinguished his childhood from the more usual atmosphere of confined bookishness in a French intellectual upbringing. As a mature man, Febvre escaped as often as he could from the exhaustion of Paris to the therapy of pastoral life at his country home in the Jura.

In Nancy, a longing to wipe out the shame of 1870 suffused the atmosphere; it was not easy to forget that Metz and the other half of the province lay in German hands. Born eight years after the catastrophe, Febvre came to his historical studies in a mood of patriotic insurgency; the scholarly caution of his older colleagues he saw as a specific case of the more general timidity of the vanquished. Yet to be a historian was not his original intention: his father was a grammarian, and the young Febvre's earlier bent was toward literature. At the same time, he had a historian uncle, and his father read history as an avocation; it was in his father's library that he first came across Michelet.

Much later he added Jacob Burckhardt and Jean Jaurès as masters of imaginative history—and Stendhal, less as a novelist than as a guide to the urban charms of Italy. Meantime Febvre had gone to Paris to seek his intellectual fortune. And this was the best that the capital offered—the elite Lycée Louis-le-Grand and, in 1898, that forcing-house of French academic talent, the Ecole Normale Supérieure. But as opposed to the younger Lorrainers in Barrès' *Les déracinés* —published the previous year—Febvre did not let the blandishments of Paris sap his native ruggedness and rectitude. However sophisticated he later became, he remained a provincial by temperament. His own memories of his early Paris years were of constant discovery—of Wagner and Zola and Rodin at the start, and then, at the turn of the century, the vast explosion of political passion in the Dreyfus Case, and the Exposition of 1900, with its sudden revelation to the young historian's dazzled eyes of the glories of French Impressionist painting. Throughout his life Febvre tried to keep abreast of aesthetic innovation, and he had among his friends the painter Adrien Marquet.

After Normale, the agrégation, and four years of research

under the auspices of the Fondation Thiers, Febvre completed his doctoral thesis on *Philippe II et la Franche-Comté*. This work established his intellectual direction for the future: its major theme was social conflict, and its framework a detailed analysis of the geography of the region. It was fitting that Febvre's first teaching position should have been close to the Franche-Comté in the old Duchy of Burgundy, at the University of Dijon. It was from here that he set out in 1914 to show through four years of armed combat how "passionately French" he was.

Febvre's intellectual heir, Fernand Braudel, has written of him that he was launched into historical scholarship with three exceptional advantages—first, a home in which the classics and humanist culture became so familiar to him that as a mature man he could speak about someone like Montaigne in as informal a tone as he would use in discussing a good friend; then, the "erudite accumulation" of the generation of historians between himself and Michelet, who, however he might rail against their example, taught him to balance the latter's literary "ardor" with patience and documentary care; finally, his arrival on the French academic scene in the "springtime" of the social sciences, and with it the chance to profit by all of them and to develop his faculties along with them.[17] Febvre knew Durkheim's successors as intellectual colleagues; he was also well acquainted with the work of Weber and Sombart—and Marx. His own attitude, however, was always less solemn than theirs. He liked association with younger men, and identified not with

[17] "Lucien Febvre et l'histoire," pp. 16–17; see also by Braudel, "Présence de Lucien Febvre" in the volume of essays written by his friends entitled *Hommage à Lucien Febvre: éventail de l'histoire vivante* (Paris, 1953), I, 1–7; further biographical information may be found in two essays by Febvre himself: the preface to his *Combats*, pp. v–ix, and "La Vie, cette enquête continue" (originally published as the Conclusion to the *Encyclopédie française*, XVII [1935]), *Combats*, pp. 44–49; in Robert Mandrou, "Lucien Febvre 1878–1956," *Revue universitaire*, LXVI (January–February 1957), 3–7; and in Palmer A. Throop, "Lucien Febvre 1878–1956," *Some Twentieth-Century Historians*, edited by S. William Halperin (Chicago, 1961), pp. 277–298.

the generation of Croce and Meinecke, born in the 1860's, and whose intellectual course had been established before 1914, but with those such as Bloch who found their way only after the war was over.

Marc Bloch, on the contrary, identified "up" with those slightly older than he. (This in itself offers one explanation for the harmonious relationship between the two.) He and his classmates at Normale considered themselves "as the last of the generation of the Dreyfus Affair."[18] In so doing they parted company with what came to be called the "generation of 1905"—the post-Dreyfusard youth which inclined toward religion, scorned the parliamentary republic, and preached the mystique of action.[19] Although only twelve years old when the Affair erupted, Bloch had good reason to take it to heart: he sprang from the assimilated Jewish intellectual milieu which discovered to its grief and horror the anti-Semitic hatred that had lain barely concealed under the polite surface of French society. Such people thought of themselves as just as good Frenchmen as any others: the conflict of 1914 gave them a chance to prove it. The fact that he was a Jew is relevant to our appreciation of why Bloch risked his life for his country once more in the second war and why he finally lost it under circumstances of exemplary heroism.

As a young man, however, Bloch scarcely seemed cut to heroic dimensions. The more robust Febvre recalled having encountered him one day in 1902 at his father's house in Paris: "a slender adolescent, his eyes bright with intelligence, his face timid, a bit overshadowed by his older brother, who was to be a physician of distinction."[20] The father, Gustave Bloch, professor of ancient history at the Ecole Normale

[18] *Apologie pour l'histoire ou métier d'historien* (Paris, 1952), translated by Peter Putnam as *The Historian's Craft* (New York, 1953), p. 186.

[19] See my *Consciousness and Society*, pp. 337–344.

[20] "Marc Bloch et Strasbourg," *Combats*, p. 392; see also the essay on Bloch by Febvre in *Architects and Craftsmen in History: Festschrift für Abbott Payson Usher* (Tübingen, 1956), pp. 75–76.

Supérieure, was one of the stern masters who had done their
best to discipline Febvre's youthful enthusiasm. He also
taught his son, who entered Normale in 1904. "I owe to my
father," Marc Bloch wrote, "the best part of my formation
as a historian."[21] The tribute suggests both intellectual gratitude and deep affection. It also shows that the younger Bloch
fully realized what a privileged upbringing he had enjoyed:
in later years he was to give "particularly attentive care . . .
to young researchers who had reached . . . intellectual
heights despite the handicaps of commonplace circumstances
in their youth, as though he wanted . . . to compensate for
the favor fate had granted him."[22]

His own early professional career had proceeded with swift,
untroubled efficiency—the agrégation in 1908 was followed by
a year of study at Leipzig and Berlin, where he attended the
courses of the great historian of religion Adolf von Harnack.
Then after three years at the Fondation Thiers and two of
teaching in provincial lycées, the war caught Bloch in the
midst of research for his doctorate. In this case for once the
French educational system showed itself compassionate: a
special provision for doctoral candidates who had served in
the war allowed him to submit as a thesis only a fragment of
the large work he had originally planned. The result—a study
of the enfranchisement of royal serfs in the Ile-de-France,
completed in 1920—was sufficient to establish Bloch as a
recognized medievalist. It also led him toward the research
topics that were to occupy him for the next two decades,
rural history and the psychological basis of kingship.

The latter interest proved the more transitory. Among
Bloch's three major books, the first, *Les rois thaumaturges,*
published in 1924, initially seems unrelated to the others. A
study of the power of touch—the miraculous ability to heal
scrofula attributed to the kings of France and England—the
book grew directly out of conversations with the author's

21 Preface to *Les rois thaumaturges,* new edition (Paris, 1961), p. vii.
22 Charles-Edmond Perrin, "L'oeuvre historique de Marc Bloch,"
Revue historique, CXCIX (April–June 1948), 162.

physician brother. Hence the medical expertise it displayed: Bloch very sensibly pointed out that scrofulous infections were by nature intermittent; a diminution, even an apparent cure of the disease was completely admissible from a scientific standpoint. But to explain in terms of modern science what had earlier passed as a miracle was not Bloch's chief concern. He was interested, rather, in the aspect of folklore, of popular belief, of what the men of the Middle Ages and early modern times meant when they spoke of the miraculous. In the nineteenth or twentieth century, people held all-or-nothing views of such an event; they asked for unambiguous results—and witnessed few, if any, miracles. The men of an earlier age were not so "intransigent"; they did not expect a constantly reliable performance from their thaumaturges; a quasi-miracle from time to time sufficed. Thus they were psychologically prepared to stretch their belief as circumstances required: "What created faith in a miracle was the idea that a miracle was going to take place"—in short, a "collective illusion."[23]

The phrase sounds like Durkheim, and *Les rois thaumaturges* quite apparently springs from Durkheim's spirit and method. Bloch shared with the master of French sociology the quality of being a Jew who had lost the faith yet remained fascinated by religious experience. More particularly they had in common a concern for religion as the source and primary manifestation of social cohesion. This intellectual absorption Bloch never forsook; while his subsequent work was cast primarily in the framework of economic history, his economic interpretations—as in the case of Weber—were constantly illuminated by material drawn from the history of religion. Still more, the second and major focus of his mature scholarship—the historical sociology of the peasantry—bore directly on the class in which traditional religious values had proved most tenacious.

As early as 1913 Bloch had published a little study of the

[23] *Rois thaumaturges*, pp. 19, 420–423, 426–429.

Ile-de-France in a series of provincial monographs initiated by
the ever-active Henri Berr. (Febvre had quite naturally
written the corresponding book about the Franche-Comté.)
Thus when in the mid-1920's Bloch turned his attention to
rural history, he was not a total stranger to the subject. But
this early work, like his doctor's thesis, had been based on
conventional documentary sources, primarily legal in character. By origin and upbringing, Bloch was anything but a
country dweller: although born in Lyons, he had been taken
to Paris as a small child, and a Parisian he remained. Even
his rural monograph dealt with the region immediately sur-
rounding the capital!

All this began to change when he moved to Strasbourg.
Perhaps it is not too farfetched to suggest that here he began
to discover some long-buried provincial roots. His family had
originally come from Alsace, and Bloch was not above tracing
his unquestioning patriotism to a great-grandfather who had
fought against the Prussians in 1793. In any case, beginning
with the Strasbourg years, we hear of excursions to the
country and tramps in the Vosges. Here Febvre possessed the
previous experience that could "open windows . . . onto the
living countryside." The older man strenuously encouraged
the younger along the path toward which he was already
groping his way. And—whether through self-abnegation or
need of mental change, it is hard to say—Febvre in effect
turned over to Bloch the rural department of their common
enterprise and directed his own future researches toward
religious and psychological history.[24]

A curious game of musical chairs ensued: Bloch took over
Febvre's assignment; Febvre pushed forward the work that
Bloch had begun in his *Rois thaumaturges*. This double
change once again suggests their harmonious working relations. It also suggests self-understanding on both sides: the
cooler-headed Bloch was the better suited to economics and
the history of technology; the fiery Febvre was more at home
in the theological battles of the Reformation.

[24] Febvre, "Marc Bloch et Strasbourg," *Combats*, pp. 394–395.

The first fruit of Febvre's new interest was the study of Luther he published in 1928. Avowedly written for the general public, it was brief, discursive, and in the animated, contentious style that had become his hallmark. Yet it was more than a summary of earlier writing on the subject: as he was to do so often in the future, Febvre took off from the work of a previous scholar, in this case the Catholic historian Father Heinrich Denifle, and then went on to stake out his own interpretation. While welcoming the thoroughness with which Denifle had demolished the conventional image built up over the centuries by Protestant hagiographers, Febvre was far from satisfied with his polemical conclusion—that the Reformation had sprung from Luther's emotional weakness, from "the sorry predicament . . . of a soul so evilly disposed, so wholly a prey of concupiscence that, confessing defeat, it threw down its weapons and evolved a new system of thought from its own undoing." To Febvre all this sounded dangerously simple—"reductive," to use the contemporary expression. In placing the emphasis almost exclusively on Luther's sexual obsessions, Denifle had composed a "pre-Freudian" work of fiction. The truth was rather less sensational· in his early life as a monk Luther's conviction of guilt betrayed no actual transgression but rather an excessive scrupulousness in the performance of his religious duties.[25]

Unquestionably Febvre was on the right track in rejecting his predecessor's work of denigration. Page after page of his *Luther* shows the touch of a master: in the swift sketch of a German society racked with pent-up grievances, ready to break forth into open protest once the word is spoken; in his delineation of Luther's literary style and the way it crystallized a new German language; in his analysis of the great reformer's failure to convey his own vision to the church founded in his name and how that church became the vehicle for what was routine and submissive in his countrymen's mentality. Febvre was at his best in tracing the inter-

[25] *Un destin: Martin Luther* (Paris, 1928), translated by Roberts Tapley as *Martin Luther: a Destiny* (New York, 1929), pp. 28–29.

play of social conflict with religious and metaphysical ideas; he handled both elements as independent variables, treating neither as a function of the other. But in respect to what was becoming his major aim—psychological history—Febvre's *Luther* remained embryonic. Its author saw the potentialities of a psychological biography whose implications would extend beyond the career of a single great figure; he also recognized that the discipline of psychology in France in the 1920's was not yet equipped for such an assignment. "Later," he surmised, "when the science of psychology is sufficiently developed to be applied without hesitation, it will doubtless be possible to discern in the individual whose personal effort precipitates a revolution the clearly and strongly marked representative of a group or family of like yet diversified minds recurring again and again down through the ages."[26]

Febvre predicted better than he knew. Thirty years later—and two years after his own death—a psychiatrist widely read in history and with a long experience of talented and troubled young men produced the psychological biography in depth that Febvre had foreseen.[27] Its tone was Freudian—but Freudian in a sense that Febvre could scarcely have imagined. Like most cultivated Frenchmen of his day, he understood psychoanalytic theory in terms of unidimensional sexual explanations. From this standpoint he was quite correct in questioning Father Denifle's reduction of a great man's inspiration to despair at his ungovernable lust. What Febvre was unprepared for was a post-Freudian canon of interpretation, as flexible and perceptive as his own, in which sexual drives and ideal aspirations would be seen as tightly bound together in an overwhelming longing for divine forgiveness.

The year following the publication of *Luther*, Febvre and Bloch founded their *Annales*. The new review had precisely the effect that its editors had hoped for. Encouraged by the advice of the leading Belgian historian Henri Pirenne and by

26 *Ibid.*, pp. 73–74.
27 Erik H. Erikson, *Young Man Luther* (New York, 1958).

the cooperation of a few contemporaries in France itself, such as Georges Lefebvre, soon to become the greatest of the historians of the French Revolution, Febvre and Bloch made the *Annales* the forum for a broadly-based history that was economic and social, geographical and psychological, all in one. The times were menacing: a review which stressed economics and the historian's concern for his own era fitted the public atmosphere of mounting crisis. Lefebvre in particular offered an example of meticulous scholarship in alliance with social commitment that gathered around him an unusually gifted generation of left-oriented students of the Revolution. Already by the turn of the decade the *Annales* group had begun to exert a perceptible influence within the closely-knit structure of French university life. The external rewards were on the way—for Febvre and Bloch were of that peculiarly fortunate breed of innovators who know how to work inside the established system and attain official recognition while they are still alive to enjoy it. By the early thirties, Strasbourg was becoming too small for their talents. The inevitable move was to Paris.

In 1933, Febvre was called to a newly established chair of the history of modern civilization at the Collège de France. This position provided exactly the setting he needed— prestigious, centrally located, yet outside the regular degree-granting faculties. (We may recall that the Collège de France had similarly given Bergson a platform for reaching a public far beyond the professional confines of philosophy.) Moreover, the chair itself, as Febvre interpreted its stipulations, seemed designed to fit his talents. In his inaugural address, he called attention to the fact that it was in effect a restoration of the professorship which Michelet had held and which had been abolished in 1892. The lesson was manifest: four decades of compartmentalized, "positivist" history had come to an end; France was ready once more to listen to the voice of the "general" historian.[28]

[28] "De 1892 à 1933. Examen de conscience d'une histoire et d'un historien," *Combats*, pp. 3–4.

The move to Paris drew Febvre into a maelstrom of public activities. He served as general editor of the *Encyclopédie française,* he repeatedly lectured abroad, he harried his colleagues and urged on the young with a cascade of short articles and book reviews. Of necessity his major writing proceeded more slowly. Although Febvre's capacity for work was awesome, he was in the classic situation of the scholar who has taken on too much. The completion of his greatest endeavor had to await the dismal quiet of German occupation.

A few years after Febvre, Bloch also came to Paris as professor of economic history at the Sorbonne. Here his working time was rather better protected. Economic history lay outside the mainstream of French academic historiography—indeed, economics as a whole was in a retrograde and neglected state. In another country, it might have occasioned surprise that a medievalist like Bloch should have been named to such a chair with so little previous preparation. In France it was only to be expected: no one else was better qualified.

Moreover, ever since Febvre had spurred him in the direction of rural history, Bloch had been laboring to give himself the technical equipment he required. He had studied land allotments, crop rotation, the different methods of plowing and of harvesting—the realities of traditional agrarian life that one could still detect by observation on the spot. Nor did he limit himself to France. Inspired, like his older friend, with a vision of comparative history, he tried to become equally proficient in the rural techniques and sociology of other Western countries. He plunged into the study of foreign languages; he added Scandinavia to England and Germany as areas whose history he knew at first hand. On a visit to Oslo in 1928 he had sketched the possibilities of the comparative method. The following year he was invited to return for a series of lectures that firmly established his international reputation.

The book that resulted from them, *Les caractères originaux de l'histoire rurale française,* ranks as the first of Bloch's two classic works.[29] Blessedly brief and clear, its scope was wider than its title indicated. Although the focus was on France, the comparative material it presented was drawn from the whole of Western Europe. Beyond that, it marked the first major application of what its author called the "regressive method" in the study of the European countryside. Here, Bloch argued, it was impossible to proceed in the usual chronological fashion. Since the history of rural societies did not enter the written record until the eighteenth century, its investigation demanded that one begin with the present, or perhaps with "a past very close to the present," and then work one's way backward toward the primeval mist. The countryside changed only very slowly; much of its outline remained as it had been in the Middle Ages; the task of the historian was to extrapolate into the past from the direct observation he could make in his own day. Here place names, the look of the fields, folklore—even aerial photographs—showed the historian how to go about his work of reconstruction.

The result was a masterpiece of historical detection. *Les caractères originaux* combined meticulousness in procedure and phraseology with a rare self-assurance in generalization. Bloch's primary effort was directed toward the geographical delimitation of two basic areas of contrasting technique, neither exactly coextensive with the other, each remarkably stable through the centuries—the area of triennial rotation of crops as against regions on a two-year cycle, the area of the wheeled plow as opposed to that of the plow guided by hand —the former in each pair associated with the plains of the north, the latter with the Mediterranean. Distinctions such as these bore no relation to national frontiers; France lay in both areas, which in each case extended far beyond its

[29] Originally published in Oslo in 1931, *Les caractères originaux* was reissued in Paris in 1952, with a supplementary volume of Bloch's subsequent notes and expansions on the same theme. An English translation by Janet Sondheimer, entitled *French Rural History: An Essay on its Basic Characteristics*, was published in Berkeley, Calif., in 1966,

borders. And the same transnational sweep characterized
Bloch's subsequent analyses of community solidarity, the
structure of the family, and the changing nature of the
seigneurie. With *Les caractères originaux* Bloch rescued the
study of rural history from the clutch of antiquaries and
legalists and made it a model of imaginative deduction from
scanty and unorthodox evidence.

Throughout the 1930's Bloch kept at work on the theme
that had emerged as central to his rural investigations—the
relation of popular mentality to technological change. The
example of the water mill became his favorite: the ancients
had known the principle of this invention, but they had
given it little practical application; then, with the decline of
the Roman Empire and a manpower scarcity deriving from
the Christian Church's injunction against holding fellow
Christians as slaves, such mills became an economic necessity; finally, as medieval seigneurs began to enforce a monopoly for their own mills, the primitive hand implements of
the peasantry were driven from use. The entire sequence
could be called a triumph of technology—that and much besides: "In a word, a very old invention which from the start
had almost reached its highest point of perfection secured
. . . its conquests only through the successive action of
factors quite alien to its intrinsic merits: the defeat of an
Empire; a religious belief; a new structure of public authority."[30]

Bloch's writings "are most illuminating when they analyze
the sensitive point at which purposeful, rational action is
limited by accepted customs and beliefs."[31] Just as Febvre
brought his talents to bear at the intersection between religion
and social class, so Bloch sought out the popular attitudes
and practices, the vestiges of an earlier rationality, that put
technical and emotional constraints on innovation. As a

[30] "Technique et évolution sociale: réflexions d'un historien" (first
published in *Europe: revue mensuelle*, XLVII [1938]), *Mélanges*, II,
838.
[31] Gilbert, "Three Twentieth Century Historians," p. 369.

medievalist by training, Bloch had a thorough acquaintance
with the literature of community sentiment; in his later role
as an economic historian, he had learned how to make the
crucial demarcations and distinctions in the realm of technology. The conjunction of these two lines of investigation
produced the second major book for which he was subsequently to be remembered, his study of feudal society.

Bloch's work of synthesis quite naturally took its place in
Berr's *L'évolution de l'humanité*, a first volume appearing in
1939, a second volume a year later.[32] In its discussion of
feudal relationships alone it outclassed its predecessors.
Where these had been legal and schematic, Bloch tried to
retrace the medieval pattern of authority in all its sprawling
inconsistency. Nor was he so much concerned with an
"organization chart" of how the feudal system worked as with
the spirit in which its institutions had been understood.
Hence what was most original in his book was not about
feudalism at all in the usual meaning of the term. It consisted rather of the most curious inquiries into such topics
as place names, difficulties in overland communications,
fluctuations and uncertainties in the sense of time, the role of
"collective memory" in distorting the image of the past to
suit present needs, and the ambiguities with which the
bilingualism of the educated afflicted the discussion of feudal
arrangements. Such apparent preliminaries—which Bloch
grouped under the title "the milieu"—in fact gave the key
to his whole interpretation. And he could cope with them
only because, in addition to the method of direct observation
which he had applied to so good effect in his agrarian studies,
he had exploited a variety of unconventional sources—epic
poems, works of theology, and the like—to enrich his account.

By the time the second volume of his *Feudal Society* was
published, Bloch was once more in military service and his
country in desperate peril. During the years in which he had

[32] A translation of *La société féodale* by L. A. Manyon, entitled
Feudal Society, was published in London in 1961.

been bringing this work to completion, his friend Febvre was
making slower progress. Febvre knew exactly what he wanted
to do with his new program of psychological history, but his
multiple distractions kept postponing its realization. Meantime he made a number of programmatic statements which
showed where he was heading.

By now the rubric "economic and social history" under
which the *Annales* had been launched had become too confining for the type of work at which he aimed. "Properly
speaking," Febvre argued, there was no such thing as economic and social history; there was only history tout court,
in its full "unity"—that is, "the study, carried out in scientific
fashion, of the various activities and various creations of the
men of another day."[33] Such a study was by definition
"social" in character. Febvre never wavered in his attacks on
the chroniclers of politics and diplomacy who wrote of the
high policy of rulers as though it bore no relation to the
deeper and more permanent needs of the ruled. He was almost equally severe with the historians of ideas: these too
handled abstract concepts in a vacuum without reference to
the emotional climate in which they had originated.
"Milieu," "mentality," "climate"—such were the umbrella
terms under which Bloch and Febvre gathered both their
impatience with the work of their predecessors and their
specification of the task ahead.

By Febvre's definition, then, "psychological history" was
not a specialized branch of historical study. It was rather his
particular way of getting at history tout court—just as another
might have chosen an economic or sociological approach. At
the same time Febvre stressed psychology because he found
here the biggest gap in the historian's knowledge of the past.
"We have no history of Love," he complained. "We have no
history of Death. We have no history of Pity nor of Cruelty.
We have no history of Joy." The whole realm of man's
"sensibility" lay virtually untouched by scholarly hands.

[33] "Vivre l'histoire. Propos d'initiation" (lecture to the students of
the Ecole Normale Supérieure, 1941), *Combats,* pp. 19–20.

Febvre himself guessed that the best way to proceed was by tracing the pulsations of emotion—the alternations, gradual or violent, between the predominance of love over hate, or of intellect over affect—in a given era of the past. Every human sentiment, he surmised, was of necessity ambivalent; each was both "itself and its opposite." For the historian, such a line of investigation was at once "extremely enticing and frightfully difficult." But he was not totally without resources: etymologies, iconography, the close study of works of literature—these were some of the instruments at the historian's command in charting the course of human sensibility.[34]

During the war years Febvre finally published in quick succession three studies of religious and intellectual life in the sixteenth century which gave tangible evidence of the new method in practice. The chief of these, *Le problème de l'incroyance au XVIe siècle*, is generally known as his finest achievement. It had been a decade in the making, and its author was over sixty when it appeared. Into it he had poured his rich humanistic scholarship, his almost professional understanding of theology, and the sense for emotional "climate" that he had been cultivating and refining ever since the publication of his book on Luther.

Like Bloch's *Feudal Society*, Febvre's volume on sixteenth-century "disbelief" found a place in *L'évolution de l'humanité*. At first glance, however, it did not look like a work of synthesis. As its subtitle, *La religion de Rabelais*, suggested, its narrower theme was the attitude of François Rabelais toward the Christianity of his day. The idea of such a study had first occurred to Febvre in the Strasbourg years when he had encountered in the work of a certain Abel Lefranc the assertion that Rabelais was an atheist. The accusation sounded odd: total disbelief in the modern sense, Febvre knew, was scarcely conceivable in the idea-world of the six-

[34] "Comment reconstituer la vie affective d'autrefois? La sensibilité et l'histoire" (first published in *Annales d'histoire sociale*, III [1941]), *Combats*, pp. 228–236.

teenth century. And so, as he had earlier done with Luther, but this time more explicitly and thoroughly, he set out to correct the work of a predecessor. His specific purpose was to put the record straight on Rabelais; his wider goal was to determine the limits of credulity and skepticism within which the speculations of Rabelais's contemporaries were confined.

The initial question, then, that Febvre asked himself was not the conventional "Is it true?" but rather "Is it possible?"[35] The answer proceeded in three stages. First came an examination of the evidence against Rabelais—the innuendoes of fellow humanists—which on closer inspection proved to be contradictory and inconclusive. Then Febvre took up the question of what Rabelais himself had said about Christianity—and here he discovered that the attitudes expressed by the good-humored giants Gargantua and Pantagruel, far from being rationalist or freethinking, were actually more acceptable to the Catholic Church than those of the Reformers. Moreover, that the "creed of the giants" was Rabelais's own emerged from a study of his letters and occasional writings: in the early stages of the Reformation he had found himself close in spirit to Luther's followers, but as Calvin turned the movement toward guilt and gloom, Rabelais had broken with him and taken his stand with the aging Erasmus. The conclusion was inescapable: Rabelais was no *libertin*, two centuries ahead of his time; he was typical rather of his educated contemporaries in combining a broad-minded, a personal and "internal," understanding of religion with a total lack of critical sense about miracles, the Scriptures, and the efficacy of prayer.

With this work of clarification behind him, Febvre was ready for his third task—the delineation of the metaphysical and scientific universe of the sixteenth century. For Bloch and Febvre, the supreme sin of the historian was to fall into anachronism—and such, the latter found, had been the way in which writers like Lefranc had dealt with Rabelais and his

[35] *Le problème de l'incroyance*, p. 18.

contemporaries. The men of the sixteenth century, Febvre contended, could not possibly have been atheists in any twentieth-century meaning of the term: their existence was enclosed by the atmosphere and paraphernalia of religion; their notion of science was a compound of childlike curiosity and occult experimentation; they were innocent of the concept of a single truth or of radical choice between contradictory assertions. In brief, they lived in a century which "wanted to believe"—a century which "sought in everything . . . a reflection of the divine."[36]

Most readers found this third aspect of Febvre's work by far the most interesting, and they regretted, as Bloch did, that he had left so much of his "Rabelaisian scaffolding" around it.[37] But Febvre had never intended to proceed otherwise: in the form in which he offered it, his book exposed to professional historians and to the general public alike the method he had adopted and which by implication he was urging on others. Febvre's purpose had been doubly polemical: besides settling a question of substance, he had introduced a new genre of historical study. To this day, historians divide their products into "monographs" and "general works"; they make a similar distinction between social and intellectual history. Febvre's *Rabelais* bridged both these divisions. It was a work of original scholarship on a highly specific theme which had broadened out to encompass a historical question of major dimensions. It was also a study of intellectual monuments— literary and theological—which never lost sight of the social realities and the psychological atmosphere in which those writings had been conceived. After the publication of *Rabelais*, the "history of ideas" could never be quite the same again.

Within two years of each other, Febvre and Bloch had

36 *Ibid.*, p. 500.
37 Letter of Bloch to Febvre, February 13, 1943: "Témoignages," pp. 28–29. Contrast Febvre's statement: *Le problème de l'incroyance*, p. 10.

reached the summit of their achievement. With the appearance of the second volume of *Feudal Society* in 1940 and of *Rabelais* in 1942, the corpus of their larger studies was complete: their two decades of collaboration had produced the best that either had to offer. In the case of the older man, age and new responsibilities now intervened. The younger was cut off in his intellectual prime. After 1939 Bloch and Febvre were unable to continue their joint endeavors. Circumstances parted them: the former went off to the volunteer service that brought martyrdom in his country's cause; the latter lived on, finally gathering in the honors and acclaim that had accrued to the labors of both.

III. *The War Years and Bloch's Three Testaments*

Although he was fifty-three years old and the father of six minor children, Bloch chose to reactivate his reserve commission and to enroll for service on the outbreak of war. He was, he joked, the "oldest captain in the French army." Assigned to staff duties, he fretted at his routine tasks and felt that his talents could have been better employed as a liaison officer with the British. At the beginning of the winter of the "phony war" something more interesting came his way—the responsible but incongruous duty of managing a vast gasoline dump.

Thus Bloch was in a position to appreciate what had gone wrong with French staff procedure when the Germans struck in May. Caught up in the great retreat, and evacuated from Dunkirk to England, he was shipped back to the Brittany peninsula just in time to witness his nation's utter defeat. It is not hard to imagine the grief it caused him. Yet from the boredom and tragedy of his military experience, Bloch—ever the historian—was able to distill a series of reflections which he hoped might someday be of benefit to his countrymen. The little book *Strange Defeat* in which he outlined what he had learned was published only after his death; it was the first of three wartime testaments that he left behind him.[38]

After the liberation of France, when the book appeared, people were surprised that a mere historian—and a medievalist at that—should have understood so well the technicalities of troop deployment. *Strange Defeat* quickly became accepted as one of the first—perhaps the very first—work in which the collapse of 1940 was adequately explained. To those who knew Bloch's earlier writings, the reasons were apparent: his feeling for the interplay between geography and psychology illuminated his whole account. He understood terrain at least as well as most professional officers; he appreciated far better than they did the way in which mechanized warfare had changed the relationship of space to time. He judged his staff colleagues severely: their minds had been too rigid to learn the lessons that Blitzkrieg had taught. But his harshest strictures Bloch reserved for France's economic and governing elite—for its narrowness and egoism and its lack of feeling for "la patrie en danger." On the little people his verdict was milder: the average Frenchman had been caught psychologically unprepared, and his rulers had made the catastrophic error of not taking him into their confidence. Bloch's wartime letters confirm the impression that emerges from his book: although far from being a militant of the Left, his sympathies lay with the common people, and he found in them reserves of good sense and humanity that the upper classes had almost entirely lost.[39]

Yet the over-all effect of *Strange Defeat* is not as depressing as one might suppose. Like Bloch's more strictly historical writings, it has a tone of serenity and of quiet confidence in the future. Such was Bloch's attitude during the German occupation. Reunited with his family near his country place in the Massif Central, he tried to resume his university teaching, although as a Jew he knew the threat that hung

[38] *L'étrange défaite* (Paris, 1946), translated by Gerard Hopkins as *Strange Defeat* (London, 1949).

[39] Letter of Bloch to Febvre, May 3, 1940: "Témoignages," p. 19.

over him. In fact, Bloch was one of the few professors of
Jewish origin whom the Vichy government kept on the rolls.
But only by a subterfuge: he was transferred from Paris to his
old university of Strasbourg, which had been evacuated to
Clermont-Ferrand in the Unoccupied Zone. Here he remained for a year, then shifted south to Montpellier when
his wife's health required a milder climate. His versatility and
capacity for work were unimpaired: at Montpellier he gave a
course on the economic history of the United States, and he
was projecting a history of the Second Reich that would explain Germany's subsequent aberrations. In his Strasbourg
days, Bloch had profited from the university library's extensive German holdings to become thoroughly familiar with
Central European history; it was the Germans who prevented
him from completing his studies.

Bloch's older sons had crossed the Pyrenees to join the
Free French. Their father was soon to follow them into the
Resistance. In the autumn of 1942, when the Germans occupied the whole of France, he was obliged to give up his
teaching. The safe course would have been to go into hiding
and await the liberation. Bloch chose to move to Lyons—his
birthplace and the capital of the Resistance—and to sign up
a third time for active service. He joined the group *Franc-
Tireur*, in which he quickly rose to a position of leadership.
A Resistance colleague has described how a twenty-year-old
résistant arrived proudly at headquarters with his "new
recruit, a gentleman of fifty, wearing the legion of honor,
with a refined face below silver-gray hair and a penetrating
gaze behind his glasses, his briefcase in one hand, a cane in
the other." There was also "mischievous gaiety" in those
eyes, and Bloch thrived on the adventurous side of his new
profession. His co-workers appreciated the "taste for precision,
for punctuality, for logic which gave his calm courage . . . a
kind of absurd charm" that "enchanted" them. Bloch certainly took too many risks: he went through three different
noms de guerre as he circulated about the country trying to

maintain liaison among the disparate groups that had come together as the Mouvements Unis de Résistance. On one of his furtive trips to Paris he saw Febvre for the last time. His older friend found him unchanged: "lucid, optimistic, active." . . . "Be careful! We need you so much afterward," Febvre warned him. Bloch replied: "Yes. I know what's in store for me, if . . . Death? not only that . . . A horrible death . . .", and he vanished down the staircase.

In the spring of 1944, just a few weeks before the landing in Normandy, the Gestapo caught up with him. He was tortured and refused to speak. In mid-June his tormentors took him with twenty-six others to a field north of Lyons, where they were all shot. Alongside Bloch a boy of sixteen "was trembling: 'It's going to hurt. . . .' Marc Bloch took him affectionately by the arm and told him: 'No, *petit*, it won't hurt,' and was the first to cry 'Vive la France!' as he fell."[40]

He left behind him a "spiritual testament" which he had written in Clermont-Ferrand more than three years before. In it he explained why he did not want read at his grave the "Hebrew prayers, whose cadences . . . accompanied so many of my ancestors and my father himself to their last rest." He refused them because he valued above all a "total sincerity in expression and spirit," and it would be dishonest to have recourse to the rites of a religion in which he did not believe. But—like Bergson in similar circumstances—he found it "still more odious that anyone might see in this act of probity something resembling the cowardly behavior of a renegade. . . . Face to face with death," he affirmed that he was born a Jew. "Above all," however, he felt himself "very simply French"; he was so attached to his country and so "nourished by its spiritual heritage and history" that he was "incapable

[40] This account of Bloch in the Resistance is drawn from Febvre's "Marc Bloch et Strasbourg," *Combats*, pp. 405–407, and Georges Altman, "Notre 'Narbonne' de la Résistance," *Annales d'histoire sociale*, VII (1945), 11–14.

. . . of conceiving another" in which he could "breathe easily."[41]

The third of Bloch's posthumously-published writings from the years of occupation and resistance was a book of precepts for historians. The author himself never settled on a definitive title for this unfinished mélange of technical methodology and general reflections, known to the English-speaking public as *The Historian's Craft*. It is hard to tell what its full content would have been if Bloch had lived to complete it; the only indication is a very brief outline which Febvre found among his papers. Yet unsatisfactory as the book is in its fragmentary state, it is the last thing he wrote on the subject and all we have to go on in making a final assessment of his thought.

The Historian's Craft codified a number of the procedures that Bloch had already applied in his major works—notably the method of extrapolating back from present-day observation developed in *Les caractères originaux,* and the detection of the psychological reality behind an apparent untruth as in the case of *Les rois thaumaturges*. On concrete matters such as these, Bloch's little volume was probing and unambiguous. It was also quite clear in its demands on the historian: "What a curious contradiction there is in the successive attitudes of so many historians: when it is a question of ascertaining whether or not some human act has really taken place, they cannot be sufficiently painstaking. If they proceed to the reasons for that act, they are content with the merest appearance, ordinarily founded upon one of those maxims of commonplace psychology which are neither more nor less true than their opposites."[42] Such, in capsule form, was the reproach that Bloch and Febvre had so long directed against their colleagues—the latters' hopeless amateurishness in the matter of historical explanation.

[41] "Testament spirituel de Marc Bloch," *Annales d'histoire sociale,* VII (1945), i–ii.
[42] *Historian's Craft,* p. 195.

Yet here also lay the difficulty with Bloch's handbook. It pointed out what was wrong with the practices of his predecessors and contemporaries, but it did not go very far in specifying how to correct them. Strong on procedure, *The Historian's Craft* offered only tantalizing hints about the philosophical problems confronting the work of historical explanation. The sections missing from the manuscript were precisely those which might have been most helpful on this score: they were to have dealt with cause and chance—including the matter of unconscious motive—"the problem of 'determinant' acts or facts," and "prevision, a mental necessity."[43] Had he lived to write these, Bloch might have settled some of the unresolved difficulties that burden his intellectual legacy. But possibly not: to judge from his earlier writings and the parts of *The Historian's Craft* that he did finish, Bloch preferred to leave his methodological advice fluid and flexible and shied away from a philosophical specification of what he meant.

Much in his little book recalled the neo-idealists. Bloch echoed Croce in protesting against the notion that "Clio's chastity" should be spared the "profanation of present controversy"; he agreed that the questions the historian asked himself were those posed by his own time. He also aligned himself with Dilthey and Weber in arguing that history (like any science) necessarily had recourse to "abstractions" and that one must dissect reality "in order to observe it better"; only then could the work of synthesis begin.[44] Precisely how this synthesis proceeded remained unclear: Bloch limited himself to figures of speech such as "delicate network" and "converging searchlights." Hence a further difficulty: Bloch's colored and metaphorical language makes it almost impossible to give an unambiguous account of his criteria of explanation.

Such an objection might have struck Bloch himself as purist and excessive. Although he had doubtless read the

[43] *Ibid.*, "Note on the manuscripts" by Febvre, p. xvi.
[44] *Ibid.*, pp. 37, 147, 150–151, 155.

standard works in the analytic philosophy of history, he seldom referred to them. His strength, he knew, was his skill as a "craftsman"; some of the greatest of those who presumed to give philosophical direction to historians had no idea of the métier. Yet not all: men like Croce and Collingwood were both eminent philosophers and fully-accredited members of the historian's guild. It is a matter for everlasting regret that Bloch, who was in so many respects the best craftsman of all, should have had no time (or inclination?) to spell out the philosophical basis of his practical precepts.

Consequently it is difficult to locate him in reference to contemporary schools of historical thought. I have elsewhere speculated that Bloch was heading beyond the neo-idealists toward a sophisticated brand of latter-day positivism in the spirit of a skeptical and pluralistic natural science.[45] In the completed portion of *The Historian's Craft* he played with the idea of using the calculus of probabilities to determine whether events were actually or only coincidentally connected. At the beginning of the unwritten sections there was to have been a discussion of "the generation of skeptics (and scientists)." We can also call to witness the gravest lacuna of all, the section on prevision and regularities, which promised to be the most original part of the whole work. What Bloch would have done with these we can only guess; his temperament suggests that he would have restricted them to a mere outline of possibilities.

Compared to Febvre, however, Bloch's notion of procedure was a model of order. It is symptomatic of the difference between the two that Bloch tried at least to put his thoughts into some coherent shape while Febvre simply scattered his advice along the way in the form of polemical articles. To *The Historian's Craft* the older man gave his "unreserved" approval. Bloch himself was less sure: while he recognized that a great deal of what he had written was their common property, he predicted that his friend would "sometimes re-

[45] See my *History as Art and as Science* (New York, 1964), pp. 14–17.

buke" him.[46] That this never happened—that Febvre un-
swervingly maintained a cult of Bloch's work until his own
death—was only natural in view of the tragic fashion in which
the younger man's life had been cut off. It did not mean that
there were no significant matters at issue between them. It
suggested rather that Bloch understood better than Febvre
where their minds diverged.

From the start there had been an anomaly in their relationship that apparently never came into the open. The junior
partner was the greater historian of the two—or at least he
developed into such as he gradually gained mastery over his
novel techniques. Within France, Febvre might be the better
known; abroad Bloch has gained a larger reputation. (Four
of his books, for example, have been translated into English,
and only two by Febvre.) We may suspect that their relationship was held together by more in the way of diplomatic
deference on the part of the younger man than either was
willing to admit. Where Bloch's mind was careful and disciplined, Febvre's was explosive; the latter's categories of
thought were spongier, and his enthusiasms less discriminating. All this, which had lain concealed for two decades, became amply apparent during the years when Febvre carried
on alone, after Bloch's death and the liberation of his country.

IV. *The Postwar and the Febvre Pontificate*

In the natural order of events Bloch could have been expected to outlive Febvre. That the reverse happened was
fateful for the future of historical studies in France. For in
the postwar era Febvre assumed a position of chef d'école—a
quasi-pontificate—which was quite foreign to Bloch's temperament and working methods.

Too old for military service, Febvre passed the war years
in his regular scholarly pursuits, alternating as before be-

---

[46] "Vers une autre histoire," *Combats*, p. 426; dedication to *Historian's Craft*, pp. v–vi.

tween his apartment in Paris and his country home in the
Jura. "Have patience, . . . last it out," he advised his
friends, and so far as possible he adopted a business-as-usual
attitude. He completed his *Rabelais* and the two further
books related to it; he had long ago discovered that burying
himself under a mountain of work was the most reliable
antidote to depressing thoughts. Yet life in fact was desperately changed: even to reach his country retreat he had
to cross the demarcation line between the Occupied and Unoccupied Zones clandestinely and on foot (in itself a sign of
his undiminished vigor). Then there was the question of the
Annales. As a Jew, Bloch could no longer serve on its editorial
board, and he personally wanted to concede nothing to
Vichy's requirements. Febvre counseled a minimum of accommodation: leave Bloch's name off the cover but change
nothing of the content inside. To him the continuity of the
Annales took precedence over everything else. A painful disagreement threatened—the first, apparently, to trouble the
long collaboration of the two. In the end Bloch let Febvre
have his way.[47]

When in the late summer of 1944, the American troops
swept in to liberate the Franche-Comté, one of Febvre's sons
had taken to the hills to help the Resistance and he himself
had received the crushing news of Bloch's death. He returned
to Paris, overwhelmed by the conviction of a vast labor to be
performed and the sense that there were too few men of his
generation left who were qualified to do it. A few months
later he resumed his everlasting round of public commitments, including several new ones. From 1945 to 1950 Febvre
served as a French delegate to UNESCO—a position which
entailed numerous trips abroad—and in 1947 he had the
enormous satisfaction of seeing established under his direction the "Sixth Section" of the Ecole Pratique des Hautes

[47] For this disagreement, see the correspondence in "Témoignages,"
pp. 22–24; further material on Febvre's attitudes and activities during
the war years may be found in Braudel, "Présence de Lucien Febvre,"
pp. 2, 7–15.

Etudes, a center for intellectual cooperation among the social sciences, in which historians were to play the most influential role.

This new responsibility put the official seal on the position of leadership among historians with a concern for social science which Febvre had so long exerted in practice. His intellectual heir has maintained that he could not imagine Febvre as the authoritarian founder of a "school."[48] Perhaps such was not his conscious wish. But in fact Febvre's activities and writings in the postwar period all worked in that direction, reinforcing a primacy which he no longer shared with Bloch. His articles from these years have a more than customarily peremptory and hortatory tone; they sound like bugles marshaling the historical battalions for the "combats" that lie ahead. Besides the familiar attacks on the sins of the profession and the call for comparative history, these essays are both specific and visionary in projecting the great collective enterprises, the teamwork of the future; some of Febvre's postwar prose could have been written by an American foundation executive.[49]

After 1950, when he retired from the Collège de France, Febvre's life was quieter. Perhaps he even became less fearsome. Although his articles and reviews had always been savage, he had lived enclosed in family warmth and in the respect of disciples that eventually grew into affection. "Attentive, charming, passionate, . . . dazzling, scattering about him ideas and memories, happy to see everything, to discuss everything": so one of them has described him. Another has told how Febvre looked at his visitor brightly and straight in the eye—like a "prince of history"—as he sat behind his desk in his large library, with its serene view of the dome of the Val-de-Grâce.[50]

---

[48] Braudel, "Lucien Febvre et l'histoire," p. 20.
[49] See particularly the statements in "Vers une autre histoire," *Combats*, pp. 427, 434.
[50] Braudel, "Présence de Lucien Febvre," p. 5; Mandrou, "Lucien Febvre," p. 7.

Death overtook him, as he would have preferred, in the Franche-Comté, in September 1956. Although he had suffered a heart attack the previous winter, he had apparently made a complete recovery. He had returned with joy to his familiar tasks—above all to the *Annales*, which to the end remained the responsibility he cherished most. One final detail may sum up the rest: very early one morning the old historian, now nearly eighty, had been discovered chopping down a tree which was interfering with the growth of a new one he had planted.

Febvre's successor at the Collège de France, whose doctoral thesis on the sixteenth-century Mediterranean world he had acclaimed as a masterpiece, was Fernand Braudel. If Febvre's primacy had already marked a falling off from the discrimination of Bloch's method, the succession of Braudel to Febvre marked a further step away from clarity of thought and presentation. For the work which the new master had written and which the old master held up as a model to be followed was sprawling and invertebrate. Although fascinating in detail and alive with fresh observations on the relation of geography to history, it lacked a discernible focus. It had taken twenty years to complete; its bulk was enormous; into it its author had apparently tumbled all the miscellaneous lore he had acquired in the course of two decades of study about a region he "passionately loved."[51] The result was to reinforce a tendency toward the gigantic which was already the curse of French historical scholarship.

Braudel claimed to have absorbed the thought of Marc Bloch. But his book showed little of Bloch's talent for establishing a tight relationship among the various strands of his account. In Braudel's work the three major sections—

[51] *La Méditerranée et le monde méditerranéen à l'époque de Philippe II* (Paris, 1949), p. ix; see the critique of Bernard Bailyn: "Braudel's Geohistory—a Reconsideration," *Journal of Economic History*, XI (Summer 1951), 278–282.

dealing successively with geography, with society, and with "events"—never quite came together. And its tone was subject to disconcerting shifts, oscillating erratically between the statistical and the poetic. Such was to be the character of a number of subsequent studies by younger historians who looked to Febvre and Braudel as guides. Romantic flights of rich prose alternating with long stretches of merciless quantification—this was apparently the fashion in which the new generation had understood Febvre's method.

Part of the trouble lay in the predictable exaggeration by epigoni of the lessons they had learned too well. But the fault was also Febvre's own—and to a lesser extent that of Bloch besides. Febvre had not bothered to put his thoughts in order: the nearest thing to a systematic presentation he left behind him was the article he had written with Berr for the *Encyclopaedia of the Social Sciences* a quarter century earlier, and this, as we have seen, was cryptic and unsatisfactory on the crucial issues. Like his master Michelet, Febvre was intoxicated by the pulse of living. He also stayed sufficiently close to the tradition of Berr to be infatuated with science and scientific method: hence his emphasis on team work and on the converging action of the different social sciences. These two aspects of his writing remained distinct and sometimes in contradiction.

On the one hand there were the manifestations of Febvre's expansive temperament—the reiteration of the word "human" (which at his hands, as at Bloch's, gradually degenerated into a historical truism) and the constant resort to figurative, colorful language. At all costs, Febvre and Bloch wanted their prose to be "alive." And perhaps when they began their labors nothing less would have sufficed to shake the French historical profession out of its complacency. Yet the price was a heavy one: reading Febvre today is sometimes a downright embarrassing experience, and the imprecision of his language makes it even harder than with Bloch to discover exactly what he means. The true historian, Febvre claimed, must throw himself into life totally, with the sense that in plunging into it, bathing in it, suffusing himself with human presence, he is increasing tenfold his powers of investigating and of resurrecting the past—a past which . . . gives him back in return the secret meaning of human destiny.[52]

This flight of Bergsonian prose requires little comment; it may suffice to observe that in Febvre's programmatic statements of the postwar years it grew increasingly difficult to recognize the meticulous scholar whose *Rabelais* had become a model of intellectual-history method for a whole generation of younger historians.

Which is all to say that Febvre—like Bloch—was almost invariably more impressive as a practitioner of his craft than as a theorist of it. And this in turn is explicable by the reluctance of both to adopt any terminology that might seem to limit the flow of history itself. Febvre disliked the term "structure"; he preferred to speak of "rhythms," "pulsations," and "currents." But was there so much difference between the two types of expression? Both were merely metaphors—both no more than verbal devices for conveying something of what the historian had finally understood of the thoughts and actions he had studied. The flow metaphors might be aesthetically the more satisfying, but structural explanations would have brought the discipline of history closer to the vocabulary of the other social sciences.

The second aspect—the "scientific" guise of Febvre's thought—was less authentic than the first. He himself strove mightily to keep up with both the social science and the natural science of his day. Almost his last angry word to his professional colleagues—written on the occasion of Einstein's death—was a long rebuke for their failure to acquaint themselves with contemporary scientific method.[53] But the very tone in which he reproved them betrayed him as an

[52] "Face au vent" (first published in *Annales: économies—sociétés—civilisations*, I [1946]), *Combats*, p. 43.
[53] "Sur Einstein et sur l'histoire: méditation de circonstance," *Annales*, X (July–September 1955), 305–312.

amateur. Febvre knew that most historians were grossly ignorant of natural science. He also knew that the way to make the study of history itself more scientific was by refining its techniques of interpretation—by improving its conceptual armory. But he never succeeded in demonstrating how this could be done.

We have seen that in his earlier writings his notion of sociology did not extend much beyond comparisons among social "types" and that his understanding of the psychology of the unconscious was inadequate for exploration in depth. By the time he published his study of sixteenth-century disbelief, his grasp had become surer. But what he had acquired in the meantime had not been any specific new method: there was no evidence in *Rabelais* that its author's theoretical equipment in psychology (or indeed that of the psychological profession in France as a whole) had improved during the decade and a half which had intervened since the appearance of his *Luther*. It was rather that Febvre's "feel" for the subject had been enhanced. And this, as any teacher of history knows, is an intangible that is extremely difficult to impart to others.

So Febvre the expansive heir of Michelet and Febvre the apostle of scientific historiography failed to fuse. Had they done so, he might have understood better than he in fact did the relation of his own value system to his "scientific" labors. We have noted that on this score the article for the *Encyclopaedia of the Social Sciences* merely touched the surface of the problem. The idea that in collaborative history the "involuntary biases" of the different writers would cancel each other out was both ingenious and comforting, but it was far from proved, and it said nothing about how the individual historian might come to terms with his own emotions and loyalties. Nor did Febvre subsequently offer a fuller explanation. His treatment of the perennial question of values made no advance over that of men senior to him— notably Max Weber and Benedetto Croce. On the contrary, it marked a step backward from them.

Croce and Weber had known, as Febvre did, that great

historical writing of necessity derived from some passionate commitment on the part of the historian himself. They had added—and this was the nub of the matter—that the historian could rise above mere partisanship only if he examined his own values with sufficient "objectivity" and discernment to recognize their place in a long succession of opposed or comparable commitments. This process of "self-relativization" Bloch and Febvre never quite accomplished. The life-choices they faced were not sufficiently ambiguous; they had too clear a conscience. Their patriotism carried the force of the self-evident: they were in the peculiarly fortunate position of being untroubled by doubt in two world wars as to the justice of their country's cause. Even the murkier aspects of these conflicts did not worry them unduly. They never seemed to notice that the gain for France in the acquisition of the University of Strasbourg was also the loss to German scholarship of the great institution at which Friedrich Meinecke had taught and Albert Schweitzer had studied. What attitude would Bloch and Febvre have taken toward the brutal struggle that raged in Algeria at the end of the 1950's? Would they have conformed to what their government expected of them or would they have aligned themselves with the dissenters of the Left? Fortunately for their peace of mind, Bloch was no longer alive when the Algerian War broke out, and Febvre died before its bitterest phase began—before an eruption of indignation on the part of his fellow-intellectuals not unlike that aroused by the Dreyfus Case, which had provided the ideological coming of age for both of them.

Despite their knowledge of foreign languages and their international renown, both Bloch and Febvre remained curiously provincial in their stubborn adherence to French norms. Even their lack of interest in the philosophical analysis of their working methods had about it a Gallic quality of the self-contained. This type of inquiry has not been particularly at home in the French-speaking world: with certain notable exceptions such as Raymond Aron and Henri-Irénée

Marrou, its main contemporary proponents have been Germans and Italians, Englishmen and Americans. Not until the mid-1950's, with the publication of a treatise by Marrou on the problem of historical knowledge,[54] did the French historical profession come fully abreast of the work of criticism that for more than a generation past had been in progress abroad.

We are left with a perplexing contrast. From one standpoint, Bloch and Febvre and the school they founded was intransigently French, turned inward and cut off from co-workers in other countries. From another and more permanently significant standpoint, theirs was the most original and fruitful of any such attempt at the renewal of historical writing in the second quarter of the twentieth century. For they had endowed social history—in the widest meaning of the term—with a new standing and a new consciousness of its possibilities. It was not merely that in quantitative terms their example had swept all before it. (By 1961 more than two fifths of the modern history theses being prepared in France were in the economic and social field.)[55] It was also that their successors as social historians, despite the literary flaws and the inordinate length of what they wrote, were setting the model for the rest of the world in combining imaginative sweep with close attention to detail.

Bloch and Febvre had undertaken to give—and in part had succeeded in giving—a new unity to the study of man, which the nineteenth century had fragmented. As against the heterogeneity of explanation in terms of ideal types, they sought a central core of meaning. History they redefined as "retrospective cultural anthropology,"[56] putting their emphasis on the expressions and usages, the styles of thought and

[54] *De la connaissance historique* (Paris, 1954).

[55] See Jean Glénisson, "L'historiographie française contemporaine: tendances et réalisations," Comité français des sciences historiques, *Vingt-cinq ans de recherche historique en France* (1940–1965) (Paris, 1965), I, xi, xxiv–xxv, lxiii.

[56] The term is mine, not theirs.

emotion, that distinguished a given society from its neighbors in space and time.

Through most of human history, they well knew, such life styles had been couched primarily in religious terms. Again and again Bloch and Febvre returned to religion as the base point of their researches. Marc Bloch, his friend recalled, had no real sympathy for religious emotion; he was obliged "to circle rather than truly to penetrate religious problems."[57] Febvre was right in suspecting that in this field—and perhaps in this field alone—he himself was the superior historian. Neither, however, had experienced religion at first hand. When they wrote of it, it was to evoke something from the vanished past—the aspect of life that most clearly marked off the Middle Ages or the sixteenth century from their own era. Yet at the very time they were writing, the faith whose historical significance they had so accurately assessed was experiencing an intellectual revival—and a revival whose leading exponents were Frenchmen of their generation. Bloch and Febvre's renewal of historical studies might have religion as its central focus, but it was not itself inspired by religious belief. To rephrase that faith in terms which would carry conviction to the twentieth century was a wholly distinct line of investigation, pursued by philosophers and imaginative writers whose work met that of the historians only in tragic circumstances when ultimate social commitments were laid bare.

---

[57] *Architects and Craftsmen in History*, p. 79.

CHAPTER

3

The Catholics
and the Human Condition

IN March 1929 the philosopher Gabriel Marcel joined the Catholic Church. It was the last of the great conversions which in the course of forty years had brought to Catholicism so distinguished a roster of France's literary and intellectual spokesmen. First had come the poet Claudel a decade and a half before the turn of the century, then Maritain twenty years later, Péguy on the eve of the First World War, and during and after the war a succession of essayists and imaginative writers. If Marcel's conversion closed the series, its emotional tone also differed from most of the others. It came without painful struggle, without the sense of forcing a stubborn will, without any sacrifice of intellectual independence or agnostic friendships. Its quiet effortlessness was consonant with Marcel's own harmonious personality. It was likewise a sign that by the end of the 1920's the enrollment of a leading thinker in the ranks of Catholicism no longer gave cause for public scandal of jubilation; the new position of religious faith among France's intellectual elite had become accepted as a normal feature of literary life in the interwar years.[1]

[1] For a survey of the Catholic members of this elite, see Gonzague Truc, *Histoire de la littérature catholique contemporaine* (Tournai, 1961).

Yet it was normal in France alone. Elsewhere in the Western world, the situation of Catholicism—or of Christianity in general—was not much different from what it had been in the late nineteenth century; it was marginal to the main course of intellectual endeavor. In a country like Italy, which resembled France in being nominally Catholic, nearly all the dominant thinkers remained outside the Church. In countries of mixed religion such as Germany and the United States, the Protestants held a clear lead over their Catholic fellow citizens. Indeed, the revival of Protestant theology in Germany was the only movement of the 1920's comparable to what was taking place within French Catholicism. But its range was narrower: the neo-orthodoxy of Karl Barth was more austere than French neo-Thomism and had fewer aesthetic connections and affiliations. Only in France did Catholic thinkers—in large proportion converts to the faith—succeed in establishing their view of the universe at the center of intellectual and literary discourse.

Why did this happen in France alone? Or perhaps better, why did a revival of Catholic thought appear first among the French? In France, as elsewhere on the European continent, the last generation of the nineteenth century had been dominated by the defiantly irreligious; the first generation of the twentieth—the generation that came to intellectual maturity in the 1890's—had reacted against the bleak skepticism of their fathers by a rediscovery of religious values. But this return to religious concerns had been detached and impersonal. While Durkheim and Bergson and their American counterpart William James had demonstrated the indispensability of faith for ideal aspiration and social solidarity, they had refrained (at least until the very end of Bergson's life) from proclaiming a religious commitment of their own. They had been fascinated by the works of belief, but they had not become the advocates of any particular belief themselves. That was to be the calling of men a generation younger, born in the 1880's, in whom their elders' abstract will to believe had been translated into a longing for the infinite that gradually suffused their whole being and led them to find in the Catholic Church the inevitable and unchallengeable vessel of transcendance in the secular world.

The Church that welcomed them was far from typical of twentieth-century Catholicism. We may find in the very special situation of the Catholic Church in France—its public humiliation and weakness, its hidden wellsprings of spiritual energy, its desperate factional quarrels and spectacular mutual condemnations—the signs of a vitality that offers a preliminary answer to the question why so many men of intellectual and aesthetic distinction sought shelter within its fold.

1. The Decade of Choice

The events of the decade from 1926 to 1936 faced French Catholics with a set of unavoidable choices. The ten years that stretched from the Papal condemnation of the Action Française to the outbreak of the Spanish Civil War made it impossible for Catholics to remain neutral observers of the social and ideological struggle. These were the years when there began what Marcel called a process of "laying utterly bare . . . our human condition."[2] Thinkers who through training or temperament had adopted a stance of detachment were forced to take sides; others who had already committed themselves were obliged to revise or repudiate their earlier allegiances.

From our post-Johannine vantage point—from our perspective on the far side of Pope John's pontificate and the Second Vatican Council—it requires a mighty effort of imagination to appreciate the shock that ran through French Catholicism when Pius XI put on the Index the works of Charles Maurras and the newspaper that was his mouthpiece. To us the condemnation seems only natural; our question

[2] *Les hommes contre l'humain* (Paris, 1951), translated by G. S. Fraser as *Men against Humanity* (London, 1952), p. 73.

would rather be why it was not done earlier. For Maurras had made no secret of his own disbelief and positivist philosophy; he was quite frank in stating that the Action Française favored the Catholic Church for instrumental reasons—as spiritual support for political reaction. But most of the French Catholic elite had been blind to such distinctions. Obsessed with the sins of the godless Republic, they had given thanks to heaven for ideological support from however suspect a source. The Action Française had grown up in the wake of the Dreyfus Case and the separation of church and state that had been its sequel. In *this* perspective, Maurras and his co-workers appeared as avenging angels, come to rescue French Catholicism from intellectual scorn and material spoliation. To the great majority of the bien-pensants, it seemed incredible that the Holy Father himself should have repudiated the gallant defender of the Church in France. For them the association of Catholicism with royalism and reaction was simply assumed as the normal order of things human and divine.[3]

Before 1926, nearly all the chief figures in the Catholic intellectual revival—with rare exceptions such as Claudel and the novelist François Mauriac—had been either members of the Action Française or within its ideological orbit. After the Papal condemnation, such an association could no longer be automatic. Each individual was obliged to examine his conscience and to make his personal decision. After 1926, the French Catholic was on his own in a fashion almost without precedent. Two decades earlier the act of separation had cut him off from the material reassurance of state support; now he was required to break a further tie—either with Rome or with the secular organization that had long appeared his strongest bulwark. Most conservative Catholics, quite predict-

[3] For general accounts of this crisis, see Adrien Dansette, *Histoire religieuse de la France contemporaine* (Paris, 1948), translated by John Dingle as *Religious History of Modern France* (New York, 1961), II, 378–413, and Eugen Weber, *Action Française: Royalism and Reaction in Twentieth-Century France* (Stanford, Calif., 1962), pp. 230–255.

ably, tried to avoid the choice: they made formal submission to the Papal ban while sabotaging it in practice. Such was the path of a number of the literary mediocrities who populated the French Academy. The more rigorous thinkers scorned so slippery an evasion. Very few defied Rome openly: it took the exceptional ruggedness of a Georges Bernanos to go for years without the sacraments as witness to his political allegiance. It happened much more frequently—as in the case of Jacques Maritain—that the condemnation reinforced doubts which had earlier been held just under the surface of consciousness and pointed the way to a radical rethinking of positions which had had behind them little besides mental inertia and the approval of literary peers.

The French Catholic community was far from recovered from the controversy over the Action Française when the eruption of civil war in Spain faced it with a new and contradictory dilemma. This time the Pope and the bien-pensants were on the same side; in France, as nearly everywhere else in the Catholic world, the overwhelming preponderance of Catholic opinion favored Franco and the Nationalist forces. Once more the adherents of the Action Française found that they and the Vatican had the same enemies. The renewed alignment of the Pope and the French reactionaries in their attitude toward Spain could not fail to encourage friendlier feelings in both parties. The turn to the right in Papal policy which the Spanish War entailed almost inevitably prompted second thoughts on the condemnation of 1926. When Eugenio Pacelli was elevated to the Papal throne as Pius XII at the beginning of 1939, one of his first acts was to accept the submission of Maurras and to lift his predecessor's ban on the Action Française.

By the outbreak of the Second World War, then, it might seem that French Catholicism's position in the secular world had come full circle—that its authoritarian wing was once more dominant. But in fact a return to the *status quo ante* was out of the question. Too much had happened in the meantime: too many consciences had been torn and shaken during the decade of ideological uncertainty. The majority of French Catholics might still acclaim Franco as the strong right arm of the Church—but in France, almost alone in the Catholic world, a scrupulous and well-informed minority refused to accept the legend of the Spanish Nationalist insurrection as a holy crusade. Some of these, like Maritain, were men whose eyes had already been opened by the events of 1926. More surprising was the case of Bernanos, who without denying his reactionary sympathies could not refrain from telling the truth about Nationalist atrocities. By 1936, a certain independence of mind had become characteristic of French Catholic intellectuals. And increasingly this independence expressed itself in social consciousness and in a political evolution toward the Left. The years of disarray in the ranks of the Action Française had also been years of economic depression and fascist advance. In the first half of the 1930's the Catholic trade unions and workers' youth organizations had met these new dangers in a mood of militancy and self-confidence. At the same time and with the same sense of social peril, leading intellectuals were more and more inclined to throw their support to the Catholic Left. The end of the decade found French Catholicism at least as divided as before: on balance, however, the conservatives had lost ground; the forces of social and intellectual renovation now felt that they had the future on their side.

After the Second World War, the French Church—both laymen and clergy—emerged as the most "left" and reformist among the major national branches of Catholicism. This situation was already implicit in the evolution of the 1930's. Still more, it had been latent since the early years of the century. After the separation of 1905, the most promising course for French Catholics was to find virtue in the state of penury to which their Church had been reduced—to cut their remaining links with the established powers and set out to rechristianize the poorer classes. Such had been the contention of Marc Sangnier and the other founders of the French

Catholic Left. But the circumstances of the time had made this impossible: Sangnier's movement, the Sillon, incurred Papal disapproval for a mixture of reasons that the Vatican never disentangled: to the valid charge of organizational indiscipline it had added the less justifiable accusation that the Sillon was tainted with doctrinal "Modernism."[4] In 1910, Saint Pius X had formally condemned it. The parallel action against Maurras—which had been prepared as early as 1914—was allowed to lie buried in the Vatican archives.

Not until the Liberation of 1944 did Sangnier and the younger men who had followed his lead receive the ecclesiastical sympathy he had been denied a generation earlier. French Catholicism of the post-Liberation period was very different in tone from the faith of those who had supported the Action Française. It had shed its conformism and authoritarianism; it had become "both more personal and more social."[5] In its openness of mind, in its willingness to experiment, the Church in France stood as the model for progressives and reformers throughout the Catholic world. That it had become so was in great part the work of obscure men— of Christian trade-union leaders and parish priests who had labored among the poor. It was also the result of a mighty effort of intellectual restatement. One aspect of this renewal had been expressed in imaginative literature, as in the novels of Bernanos and Mauriac. Another aspect was the work of historical scholars such as Daniel-Rops and Etienne Gilson. But the voices of French Catholicism which carried farthest were those of its philosophers—more particularly the exemplary and sharply contrasting figures of Jacques Maritain and Gabriel Marcel.

[4] Charles Breunig, "The Condemnation of the *Sillon:* an Episode in the History of Christian-Democracy in France," *Church History*, XXVI (September 1957), 8–10.

[5] Dansette, *Religious History*, II, 375; see also by the same author, *Destin du catholicisme français 1926–1956* (Paris, 1957), and Livre VII (by René Rémond) in Andre Latreille *et. al.*, *Histoire du catholicisme en France*, III: *La période contemporaine* (Paris, 1962).

ii. *Jacques Maritain in the Ideological Arena*

"What am I?" Maritain wrote to Jean Cocteau. "A convert. A man God has turned inside out like a glove."[6] Of all the great conversions of the twentieth century's opening years, Maritain's was to become the most celebrated. It concentrated in a single personal experience the full range of characteristic influences on a sensitive man of his generation —an impeccably republican and freethinking upbringing, a period of growing despair with the mentality of bleak "scientism" that ruled the Sorbonne, a marriage based on deep sympathy rather than social considerations or closeness of milieu, the friendship of Péguy and the tonic of Bergson's lectures, finally the shock of meeting in the person of Léon Bloy a secular saint manqué who took his Catholicism with total seriousness.

By 1906, when he was baptized into the Church, the twenty-three-year-old Maritain had already behind him the most severe emotional trials of his life. Each element in his adolescence and youth seemed calculated to bring to maximum lucidity his anguished search for spiritual shelter. His mother—separated from his father and almost solely responsible for his education—was a strong-willed woman, the daughter of the elder republican statesman Jules Favre, formally a Protestant but in practice an adept of the strenuous Kantian ethic of the late nineteenth century which found no need for divine sanction. His closest friend was Ernest Psichari, whose similarly freethinking antecedents were suggested by the fact that his grandfather was Ernest Renan. Together the two had discovered Péguy, who had taken them to hear Bergson. And along the way the young Maritain had also found his life companion—a fellow-student, Raïssa Oumansoff, whose Russian Jewish parents had fled

---

[6] *Réponse à Jean Cocteau* (Paris, 1926), translated by John Coleman as *Art and Faith* (New York, 1948).

from Tsarist persecution when she was ten years old and who like her future husband was desolated by the positivist tone of the teaching imparted to her.

In the case of Jacques Maritain, this scientism impinged in a form that was depressing to the point of caricature. His chosen field was biology, and his mentor, Félix Le Dantec, seriously proposed to fabricate human life by synthesis in his own laboratory. As against such an influence, the teachings of Bergson could not have been more appropriate: for young men of Maritain's generation, they came just at the point they were needed most. But unlike the run of his contemporaries, Maritain did not remain content with the Bergsonian philosophy: for him it served as no more than an avenue of approach to an unsuspected world of the spirit. For his initiation into the Catholic faith he sought out the neglected, impoverished, and totally authentic Bloy. For the intellectual formulation of his new commitment he went directly to St. Thomas Aquinas.

Curiously enough, the man who was to become the most prominent exponent of contemporary Thomism originally believed that his conversion to Catholicism entailed renouncing philosophical speculation. He went off to Germany to continue his biological studies, and it was not until his return to France and nearly three years after his conversion that he began a serious reading of St. Thomas. Once launched in this direction, however, Maritain's progress was both rapid and sure-footed: he had discovered in Thomism a method so congenial to his nature that it sufficed him for more than half a century of intellectual endeavor. By 1910 he had published his first essay on Aquinas; two years later he began to teach Thomism at the Collège Stanislas in Paris. And after two further years he was called to the Institut Catholique, the greatest center of French Catholic learning. By the outbreak of the First World War, Maritain—just over thirty—was an established influence in the literary life of his country. Still more, he had clearly marked out his own differences with Bergson and unequivocally broken with the philosophy of the élan vital. His first book, published in 1913, was a thoroughgoing critique of his earlier allegiance; in his *Bergsonian Philosophy* Maritain rejected intuition as a way to metaphysical understanding, proposing in its stead the severe intellectualism that was to become the hallmark of his thought.[7]

The first war marked less of a hiatus in Maritain's career than one might suppose. Himself rejected for military service on physical grounds, he lost his friends Péguy and Psichari in the first months of combat. But the war as such figured only marginally in his published writing. At this stage in his life his commitment to Thomist study was so intense that it left little mental energy for the affairs of the secular world. And he maintained the same critical detachment into the immediate postwar years. By the mid-1920's, a permanent impression of Maritain seemed fixed in the public mind: his writing was austere, difficult, and mercilessly abstract; his personal polemic could be devastating, as his break with Bergson had shown; his own predilection was against nearly all the manifestations of the modern world—in brief, reactionary. In 1922 he had published a little book, *Antimoderne,* whose title gave sufficient evidence of its contents, and in 1925 *Three Reformers,* whose targets, predictably enough, were Luther, Descartes, and Rousseau.

Had the great explosion over the Action Française not intervened, Maritain might never have attained to the serenity and humanity that were characteristic of his later judgments. Nor would he have figured in a prominent place in the history of contemporary French social thought. Maritain himself was fully aware of the significance of this turning point. Several years later he noted in his diary:

[7] For the chronology of Maritain's early years, besides the autobiographical writings of Raïssa Maritain, see Henry Bars, *Maritain en notre temps* (Paris, 1959), pp. 367–373; Charles A. Fecher, *The Philosophy of Jacques Maritain* (Westminster, Md., 1953), pp. 3–35; and Donald and Idella Gallagher, *The Achievement of Jacques and Raïssa Maritain: A Bibliography 1906–1961* (Garden City, N.Y., 1962), pp. 37–38.

Today more than ever, I bless the liberating intervention
of the Church which . . . exposed the errors of the
Action Française, following which I finally examined
Maurras' doctrines and saw what they were worth. There
began for me then a period of reflection devoted to
moral and political philosophy in which I tried to work
out the character of authentically Christian politics and
to establish, in the light of a philosophy of history and
of culture, the true significance of democratic inspiration
and the nature of the new humanism for which we are
waiting.[8]

Before 1926, Maritain had never formally adhered to the
Action Française. But the influence of the priest who was his
spiritual director and his own polemic against the modern
world had led him to extend to it his sympathy and to write
on occasion for its journals. Among the wider public many
assumed him to be *the* philosopher of the movement. His
"apostasy"—as Maurras's adherents called it—surprised both
ideological wings of French Catholicism; to the democratic
and social Catholics it brought welcome reinforcement in the
struggles that lay ahead.

The condemnation of the Action Française impelled
Maritain into the public arena. Here he was to remain for
the next quarter century, gradually establishing himself as the
most widely listened-to spokesman for Catholic social principles, first in France and subsequently in the United States.
By the end of the 1920's his home in Meudon near Paris had
become the gathering place for an extensive circle of
Christian artists and writers, which included the painter
Georges Rouault and the exiled Russian philosopher Nicholas
Berdyaev. The range of these associations seems to have
broadened Maritain's sympathies: his prose became less arid,
and his intellectual exchanges more forgiving; in 1937 he was
reconciled to Bergson, now old and sick and moving toward
Catholicism.

[8] Quoted in *The Social and Political Philosophy of Jacques Maritain*,
edited by Joseph W. Evans and Leo R. Ward, Image edition (Garden
City, N.Y., 1965), p. 9.

By 1934, Maritain was ready to formulate his new view of the social universe. *True Humanism*, based on lectures he delivered in that year in Spain and published as the Spanish Civil War was breaking out, became the cornerstone of everything further he was to write on the subject. All his subsequent volumes of polemic and public philosophy were footnotes to or expansions on the themes that *True Humanism* had announced.

The course of recent history, Maritain now recognized, could not be undone: democracy and its stepchild, socialism, had come to stay. What *True Humanism* set out to do was to suggest how the heroic and saintly values of the Middle Ages could be translated into terms applicable to the contemporary world. Basing himself, as always, on the method of Aquinas, and proceeding in the architectonic order of his master, Maritain traced the historical origins of the kind of humanism he proposed and projected into the future his vision of a Christian society. One would be greatly mistaken, he argued, to see in the popular political faiths of the last two centuries no more than the work of atheist corrosion. The historical roles had been reversed: the purveyors of apparent evil had in fact become the heralds of beneficent change. Such a one was Marx—whose "cynicism," like that of Freud, had unveiled a number of important truths. More precisely, Marx had exposed the materialism and heartlessness of capitalist values—its treatment of human beings as tools rather than persons—and had awakened the working class to a consciousness of its dignity and humiliation. For a Christian, the answer to Marxism was clear. It was to make a reality of the teaching in the gospels.[9] The encyclicals *Rerum Novarum* and *Quadragesimo Anno*—the latter having appeared just three years before Maritain's own lectures— had already pointed the way.

Within this ideological framework, Maritain only lightly sketched the outlines of the future democratic society he had

---

[9] *Humanisme intégral* (Paris, 1936), translated by M. R. Adamson as *True Humanism*, 4th ed. (London, 1946), pp. 42, 86, 108, 223–225.

in mind. Its emphasis would be on fraternity and understanding among the classes rather than on a fictitious equality.
Its institutions would be pluralist and permissive: while
Christian values would give the lead, the Catholic element
would not attempt to impose its will on fellow citizens of
other faiths or no faith at all. This was the view that Maritain developed more fully in the works he subsequently published in the United States, *Christianity and Democracy*, of
1942, and *Man and the State*, which appeared in 1951 and
closed the ideological phase of his career.

The first of these suggested why its author had so long
hesitated to use the word "democracy" at all. As his polemic
against Rousseau had implied, Maritain had earlier considered the term almost irremediably corrupted by sentimentality, intellectual confusion, and a general failure to live
up to its professions. "The tragedy of the modern democracies," he now explained, was that they had "not yet succeeded in realizing democracy": its political accomplishments
had no sufficient counterpart in the social realm; modern
society had proved itself impotent "in the face of poverty
and the dehumanization of work."[10] Such had been the
melancholy balance sheet of more than a century of ideological struggle in Western and Central Europe at the time that
the great democracies had succumbed to fascist domination.

Across the Atlantic Maritain found greater reason for
confidence in democratic values. "The very name democracy," he discovered, had "a different ring in America and
in Europe." In the United States, "despite the influence
wielded by the great economic interests," it had "penetrated
more profoundly into existence, and . . . never lost sight of
its Christian origin."[11] Logically enough, it was in an American setting and in lectures delivered in the English language
that Maritain succeeded in completing the definition of the

[10] *Christianisme et démocratie* (New York, 1943), translated by
Doris C. Anson as *Christianity and Democracy* (New York, 1944), pp.
25, 27.
[11] *Ibid.*, p. 31.

democratic society he had projected in his earlier writings. In
Man and the State he finally reconciled his previous insistence on authority with his subsequent belief in popular
government. A democratic ruler, he surmised, in trying to
rise above the passions of the moment, might well incur "the
disfavor of the people"—yet such a leader could still be acting "in communion with the people, in the truest sense of
this expression." And if he were "a great ruler," he might
"perhaps convert that disfavor into a renewed and more profound trust." Here, as throughout Maritain's political and
social writings, the emphasis was on the mutual responsibility
between rulers and ruled, and of each individual to his fellow
citizens. And—as at the very start of his ideological inquiry—
the key term was "pluralism," to which he now added the
"personalist" note that a younger Catholic thinker, Emmanuel Mounier, had in the meantime brought into general
currency.[12]

When these final lectures were delivered, Maritain had become a stranger in his own country. The high tide of his influence in France had been suddenly and brutally interrupted
by an involuntary exile that was gradually to extend into two
decades of absence from home and a growing alienation from
the French intellectual scene.

On the eve of the Second World War, Maritain's position
in France seemed assured: to his earlier role as the greatest
contemporary interpreter of St. Thomas, he had added that
of a militant spokesman for social Catholicism. Abroad, he
was becoming almost equally famous. He had lectured
throughout Europe and in Canada and South America as
well. He had made three lecture trips to the United States.
On a fourth such journey events overtook him: the fall of
France left him stranded in the country that was to become
his second home.

Here he adjusted rapidly to his new surroundings. He

[12] *Man and the State* (Chicago, 1951), pp. 109, 137. In this case
the English version is the original.

taught at Columbia and at Princeton. Together with Raïssa he made his apartment in Greenwich Village an intellectual and social haven for others similarly exiled from France. Toward his own country his attitude was unequivocal: he had refused to back Franco in 1936; he extended the same refusal to Pétain in 1940. Maritain's wartime writings were a series of appeals to his countrymen to stand fast for the values of liberty and humanity; they were briefer, simpler, more direct than what came before and after. Although he never formally rallied to De Gaulle, Maritain's Free French sympathies were amply apparent. It was only natural that after the Liberation the General should have called on him for assistance in the task of rebuilding the moral confidence of his countrymen. De Gaulle asked Maritain to go to Rome as ambassador to the Vatican, and the philosopher—now sixty-two—felt obliged to accept.

This second exile (and this time self-imposed) lasted until 1948. There followed a third and more puzzling period of life abroad. On resigning his embassy—having done what public duty seemed to demand—Maritain did not return to France to resume his old life as a teacher and writer which had been interrupted for nearly a decade. He went instead to the United States, to take up for five years a professorship at Princeton and then to live in retirement in New York. Not until the death of his wife at the end of 1960 did he resolve to go back to France. And when he did so, it was as an old man, with "a great thirst for silence," come home not for a public role but to prepare himself for death.[13]

By 1961, Maritain's ideological phase was far behind him. He now spoke of his political and social writings as though they were past history. He had no wish to return to the theater of intellectual encounter. France's old intelligentsia pleased him "less than ever"; the young intelligentsia of the new society, which was closer to the world of reality and of manual labor, did not need him as a guide. In these young

[13] Preface to Henry Bars, *La politique selon Jacques Maritain* (Paris, 1961), p. 13.

people, whose way of thinking struck him as "healthier and better ventilated" than that of their immediate forebears, Maritain vested his hopes for the future of Thomism in France.[14] As for himself, he had come full circle: he had returned to the longing for quiet contemplation that had first led him into the Church more than half a century ago.

No doubt we can find in Maritain's disgust with the intellectuals who were holding the front of the stage—the "mandarinate" of the immediate postwar years—a clue to his reluctance to go home in 1948. A France in which Jean-Paul Sartre was the philosophical star could scarcely be to Maritain's liking. Under the influence of writers close to Sartre, Marxism had become the standard pattern of thought for the segment of the French intelligentsia that considered itself ideologically advanced: to Maritain Marxism was an atheist counterfeit of the eternal criteria for a just society. Similarly Sartre and his school had popularized (while misunderstanding them) the works of Freud on French soil: Maritain saw in psychoanalytic theory no more than a fragment of the truth, "a punishment inflicted upon the pride of that conceited, pharisaic personality, which rationalism had built up as an end supreme in itself."[15] By 1948, French Catholics had already absorbed what Maritain had to teach them. The others were not prepared to listen.

In America the situation was reversed. Here the intellectual revival among Catholics had just begun. And there were few of the native-born who could hold their own in an exchange with the irreligious. The Church in the United States desperately needed a spokesman like Maritain. Although the American hierarchy pretended most of the time that he did not exist, the growing reform element among the clergy and laity were eager for his message. Just at the time that Maritain was being neglected in France, he was becoming in-

---

[14] *Ibid.*, pp. 10–11, 14.

[15] *Scholasticism and Politics*, Image edition (Garden City, N.Y., 1960), p. 158. These lectures were originally delivered in English in the United States in 1938.

tensely relevant in the United States. The wisdom of his choice of where to spend the last decade of his active life became apparent only after his return to his own country. In the early 1960's the response of American Catholics to Pope John and the Vatican Council vindicated Maritain's efforts in his final years of teaching.

III. *The Spiritual Journey of Gabriel Marcel*

Born in 1889 and seven years younger than Maritain, Gabriel Marcel from the start seemed to live in a different mental universe. Where Maritain prized clear formulations, Marcel saw in words and in reasoning no more than the external trappings of the mysteries of being. While Maritain very early in life discovered his philosophical master, Marcel groped his way for two decades among contradictory influences and inspirations. The fact that both found a spiritual home in Catholicism was evidence in itself of the permissive range within the French Church. Marcel was anything but a Thomist. Most frequently he is referred to as an existentialist, but the label is not particularly helpful in assessing his social thought. Although he was the first French writer to use the term—as early as 1925—he was not simply the disciple of Karl Jaspers, the man who transplanted a German doctrine to French soil, that he has sometimes been called. By the time he read Jaspers, Marcel had already arrived at his own highly personal philosophy of existence.[16] By that time, by the opening of the 1930's, his philosophical and religious course had finally been set.

For Marcel the central metaphors of his endeavor were "search" or "journey"—or better still, the response to a "call." Born, like Maritain, of a prominent and relatively prosperous family, Marcel experienced even earlier than he had a sense of desolation at the mental world within which he was con-

16 Seymour Cain, *Gabriel Marcel* (London, 1963), pp. 29–30; Paul Ricoeur, *Gabriel Marcel et Karl Jaspers* (Paris, 1947), pp. 435–436.

fined. His childhood was inordinately protected; his family took enormous care over his schooling, and the little Gabriel had no recourse but to be the model student they expected of him. His father, who held the rank of Councilor of State and was later administrator of France's museums, was a man of disciplined mind and impressive cultural equipment. "Imbued with the ideas of Taine, Spencer and Renan, his position was that of the late nineteenth-century agnostics; acutely and gratefully aware of all that . . . art owes to Catholicism, he regarded Catholic thought itself as obsolete and tainted with absurd superstitions." The elder Marcel was a widower. His deceased wife's sister, who brought the boy up, although Jewish by origin, had converted to an ultra-liberal form of Protestantism. In his conscious mind, the boy Gabriel loved and respected his father and his aunt. Deeper down, he felt that he lived in a "desert universe," and even as a child he was haunted by unexpressed thoughts about death.[17]

His "whole childhood" and, he suspected, his "whole life" had been overshadowed by his mother's death when he was four years old. This figure, whom he scarcely remembered, "remained . . . mysteriously . . . present" to him. In the boy's secret cult of his mother's memory lay the origin of his later emphasis on fidelity—on a loyalty extending beyond the grave. It was also responsible for his sense of a "hidden polarity between the seen and the unseen" and for his interest in meta-psychic experiments and in extra-sensory perception.[18]

At the age of eight Marcel went to Stockholm, where his father had been appointed French minister. Although his stay in Sweden was only brief, it revealed to him that other ways of life were possible besides the austere intellectualism of his home, and it opened vistas on the adventurous and the exotic. From this point on, Marcel was to have a passion for travel; his longing to discover and to explore was of a

[17] Gabriel Marcel, "Regard en arrière," *Existentialisme chrétien: Gabriel Marcel*, edited by Étienne Gilson (Paris, 1947), translated as "An Essay in Autobiography" by Manya Harari, *The Philosophy of Existence* (London, 1948), pp. 81–82.

[18] *Ibid.*, pp. 83–84.

Proustian intensity. And when he finally came to read Proust himself, it was with the sharp emotion of discovering an abiding affinity between the novelist's search for a lost past and his own quest for a world beyond that of everyday things to which the memory of his mother beckoned him.

Perhaps it was inevitable that such a boy should become a philosopher—but of a very special and unsystematic variety. He might also have been a musician or an imaginative writer. Music was one expression of the infinite that Marcel cultivated as a gifted amateur; the drama was another. In the dialogue of the stage he found the ideal vehicle for the exchange between the "I" and the "thou" which was central to his view of human relations. As a child playing in the Parc Monceau or in the gardens along the Champs-Elysées, Marcel, lonely and constrained, had invented imaginary characters to people his solitude. "The richness of his thought on the relations between himself and another" may have been "born of this suffering at an isolation too heavy for a child's heart to bear."[19] As a man in his mid-twenties, chance handed Marcel an opportunity to touch the lives of others under tragic circumstances. On the outbreak of the war, too frail for combat service, Marcel found appropriate employment as head of the information service organized by the Red Cross. Here his job was to deal with the constant requests for news of soldiers listed as missing in action. Every day he "received personal visits from the unfortunate relatives who implored" him to find out what he could; "so that in the end every index card" became "a heart-rending personal appeal."[20]

The war was the first great shock to Marcel's life. It broke up the security of the grand bourgeois universe within which he had earlier been both protected and confined. It was responsible for a new tone of anguish in the *Metaphysical Journal* to which he was confiding his search for ultimate

[19] M. M. Davy, *Un philosophe itinérant: Gabriel Marcel* (Paris, 1959), p. 20.
[20] "Essay in Autobiography," p. 90.

reality. At the same time he was grateful for the state of illusion in which he had earlier lived, since it had enabled him to get over the most difficult part of his apprenticeship as a philosopher.

By 1910—at the almost unbelievably early age of twenty— Marcel had passed the agrégation in philosophy, but he never went on to the doctorate or to become a university professor. Instead he taught from time to time at various lycées, as inclination or necessity dictated. Just after the war he married into a leading Protestant family. Although his wife was a woman of talent to whom he was totally devoted, the idea of conversion to her faith never occurred to him. The contrary happened: three years before her death in 1947, she followed him into the Catholic Church. Their life together displayed the harmony that Marcel brought to all his concerns. A Parisian by birth, but far from convinced of the virtues of a great city, he finally found the quarter that suited him, between the Luxembourg and the Sorbonne. He also bought a small château near the Dordogne, which served as his refuge during the Vichy era. A luminous conversationalist, widely read and on terms of easy familiarity with the arts, going almost nightly to the theater, such was this worldly philosopher whose technical specialty was ontology and whose aspiration was for the infinite.[21]

His philosophical antecendents similarly put him into no clear category. First he had turned his attention to the Romantics—especially to Coleridge and Schelling—then to Americans like Josiah Royce and William James and William Ernest Hocking. Quite predictably he followed Bergson's lectures "with passionate interest," and he remained faithful throughout his life to the inspiration Bergson had given him. But his debt to American philosophy was primary. It enabled him to shake himself clear of German abstractions and more particularly of the "idealism based on the impersonal or the

[21] Davy, *Un philosophe itinérant*, pp. 12–14, 20–24, 41, 50.

immanent" which became his bête noire.[22] In the Americans he discovered that pragmatism and a feeling for transcendence—which conventional academic philosophy kept apart —could live comfortably together. He was searching for a kind of understanding which would be both transcendent and tangible; and such a conjunction, he gradually realized, could come only through an intense focus on the interpersonal. This was what he meant when he gave one of his essays the extraordinary title "Position of and Concrete Approaches to the Ontological Mystery."

Marcel preferred to think of himself as a Christian Socratic. He liked to make explorations rather than to propound final answers. His *Metaphysical Journal* did not appear in print until he was in his late thirties. He waited another eight years before publishing his second major philosophical work, *Being and Having*, in 1935. Meantime he had become a Catholic. Yet in a sense he had been a believer all along. His concern for fidelity, for trust, for hope, for witness and promise and natural piety had led him effortlessly toward the Church. One day he received a friendly letter from François Mauriac who asked him quite simply: "Why aren't you one of us?"—to which he reacted, equally simply, with the realization that it was among the Catholics that he belonged.[23] Once more, as so often in his life, he responded to a call. His conversion changed his definition of his métier scarcely at all. He became in no sense a polemicist or an official apologist for the Church. He had always resisted and continued to detest the theatrical attitude toward religion— the giddy sense of a desperate wager—characteristic of Pascal or of so many contemporary converts. Marcel remained a

[22] Gabriel Marcel, *Homo Viator: Prolégomènes à une métaphysique de l'espérance* (Paris, 1945), translated by Emma Craufurd as *Homo Viator: Introduction to a Metaphysic of Hope* (London, 1951), p. 137; on Marcel's debt to American thought, see the lectures he gave at Harvard in 1961: *The Existential Background of Human Dignity* (Cambridge, Mass., 1963), pp. 1–3.
[23] Davy, *Un philosophe itinérant*, pp. 42–43, 48.

philosopher writing primarily for the irreligious and deeply embedded in the secular world.

If Marcel arrived only slowly at his articulate philosophy, he came more slowly still to the formulation of his social thought. In this realm, according to his own account, the key date was the year 1936. But the events of what in retrospect was to appear the decisive spring and summer in the advent of the Second World War impinged on him with less explosive force than in the case of Maritain or Bernanos. They entailed no radical revision of his earlier convictions. He did not feel it necessary to take sides in the Spanish Civil War; on the contrary, he believed it wrong for a Frenchman (as an outsider) to do so. The events of 1936 confirmed, rather, the sense that had been growing on him of a "broken world"—which was the title of a play he had written three years earlier. Such a world was like a watch that had ceased to tell time, or a heart that had stopped beating. Externally things went on as before; within, the human soul was empty.[24]

In 1936, what impressed Marcel most of all was not the Spanish Civil War or the Popular Front government of Léon Blum—which he dismissed as a "failure"—but the pervasive "spirit of surrender . . . concealed . . . by an anti-Fascist rhetoric in which no clear intelligence could place any trust."[25] The defeat of 1940 turned these forebodings into bitter reality. Like the good Frenchman he was—and for all his foreign travel Marcel was strictly faithful to his national heritage—he suffered profoundly from the distress and humiliation of his country. Yet in another sense the experience of German occupation gave Marcel's philosophy a topical relevance that it had never had before. In this context, themes that might once have seemed the disembodied musings of a gentle spirit took on an anguished urgency. It is significant that the first of Marcel's books to deal even

[24] Cain, *Marcel*, pp. 60–61.
[25] *Existential Background of Human Dignity*, pp. 114–115.

tangentially with current problems was a collection of his essays and lectures dating from the years of occupation. Its title, *Homo Viator*—"man the voyager"—sounded a note that was to recur throughout his later thought; its contents stressed the themes of exile, of separation, of captivity, and of hope—above all, of hope—which his audience or his readers did not need to be told how to interpret.[26]

The publication of only one of these wartime essays was actually forbidden by the Vichy censor. In this case the reason was quite apparent: in distinguishing between the concepts of "obedience" and "fidelity," Marcel had come too close to a direct attack on the cult of "systematic docility" that Pétain's government was fostering. Most of the time he restricted his critique to less transparent abstractions. Yet even in discussing a theme ostensibly as inoffensive as "a phenomenology and a metaphysic of hope," Marcel deftly slipped in a series of unmistakable references to his countrymen's current perplexities. A quasi-theological demarcation of the confines of hope and despair imperceptibly passed over into quiet defiance of the Vichy orthodoxy of passive acceptance. "Must not the true believer," Marcel innocently inquired, "be ready to accept the death and ruin of his dear ones, the temporal destruction of his country, as possibilities against which it is forbidden to rebel? . . . If these things come about, must he not be ready to adore the divine will in them?" Having put the matter in terms of a situation at the limits of human endurance, Marcel could readily reject the bien-pensant affirmative answer and proceed to a condemnation of the "softening processes" that made such a chain of reasoning possible. And two paragraphs later he was ready to go over to the counterattack:

> Here I take the example . . . of the patriot who refuses
> to despair of the liberation of his native land. . . . Even
> if he recognises that there is no chance that he will him-
> self witness the hoped-for liberation, . . . he refuses

[26] Cain, *Marcel*, p. 75.

with all his being to admit that the darkness which has
fallen upon his country can be enduring. . . . Still
more: it is not enough to say that he cannot believe in
the death of his country, the truth is much more that he
does not even consider he has *the right* to believe in it,
and that it would seem to him that he was committing
a real act of treason in admitting this possibility.[27]

When he reissued these essays almost two decades later,
Marcel found that the passage of time and the "radical transformation of the historical context" had not brought much
change in his "general perspectives." Yet his tone had become more somber. He now believed that the results of the
second war had been even worse than he had feared.[28] Most
pointedly, he saw contemporary life as "dehumanized" on a
frightening scale.

His anxieties about his own era Marcel had conveyed in
another series of informal essays entitled *Men against Humanity*, which he had published in 1951. Now at last applied
to contemporary society, Marcel's ideas conformed no better
to conventional demarcations than they had while they remained on the level of philosophical speculation. His temperamental reactions were conservative: he was unimpressed
with the ideology of the Resistance and appalled at the in-
justices committed in the purge of suspected collaborationists;
he doubted whether wars of colonial repression were as in-
iquitous as most intellectuals thought; he distrusted the
dominance of a technology that he believed could *"end only
in despair."*[29] At the same time he coupled these counsels of
prudence with other ideological stands ordinarily associated
with the French Left: he spoke out uneqivocally against all
forms of racial or religious intolerance, and he found *"anything"*—even "capitulation"—preferable to the universal
havoc of thermonuclear war.[30]

[27] *Homo Viator* (English translation), pp. 47–48, 125.
[28] Preface to new edition of *Homo Viator* (Paris, 1962), pp. i–ii.
[29] *Men against Humanity*, pp. 23–25, 71, 80–83, 113, 184–185.
[30] Preface to new edition of *Homo Viator*, p. i.

Such apparent inconsistencies troubled Marcel not at all. He was unconcerned about whether a particular attitude he adopted might give temporary comfort to one or another of the contestants in his country's ideological battles. What did concern him was to keep from being the "vassal" of any organized political allegiance—and by the same token to resist "the spirit of abstraction" which he found responsible for the violence in the contemporary world. Against the spirit of abstraction, Marcel pitted the force of love. His plea was for a restoration of simple human values—for the introduction of a social and political order which would rescue "the greatest number of beings possible" from a state of mass "abasement or alienation."[31]

Whether one called such a goal conservative or leftist was quite immaterial to him. Marcel rejected the terms as the source of "frightful confusion,"[32] although in practice he usually came down on the conservative side. His social philosophy, however fragmentary and amateurish, was of a piece with his speculative writings. It sprang from grief at human distress and a longing to give meaning and depth to concrete personal relationships. In this sense it had the eternal validity to which Marcel aspired. It was also conditioned and limited by the era of its composition. Like George Orwell's *1984*, for which Marcel expressed his unqualified admiration, it conveyed an atmosphere of impending catastrophe—a tone better suited to the tormented Europe of the 1940's than to the complacent Continent of two decades later.[33] The anguished, almost hysterical character of Marcel's social writings had begun to date while their author was still alive. This is one of the major problems that confronts us in

[31] *Men against Humanity*, pp. 8, 94, 117.

[32] *Homo Viator*, French edition of 1962, p. 364 (this passage is not in the translated edition).

[33] *Men against Humanity*, pp. 140, 173. Marcel returned to similar themes in *Le déclin de la sagesse* (Paris, 1954), translated by Manya Harari as *The Decline of Wisdom* (London, 1954). On Marcel's condemnation of "fanaticism," see Roger Troisfontaines, *De l'existence à l'être: la philosophie de Gabriel Marcel* (Namur, 1953), II, 131–136.

trying to assess the enduring viability of the independent
Catholic style of thought for which he stood.

IV. *"Philosophers Who Were Catholics"*

"Gabriel Marcel . . . has his Left where Maritain has his
Right and vice-versa." Thus one of the latter's most subtle
and sympathetic expositors has epitomized the difference between the two.[34] Marcel was the more permissive on matters
of faith, Maritain the more "advanced" in his social philosophy. Readers who were exhilarated by the flexibility and
openness of Marcel's speculative writings might find certain
of his political attitudes reactionary. Those who admired
Maritain's ideological stands were frequently repelled by
his uncompromising adherence to the Thomist method. At
one time or other both combated the works of the modern
world, but from the 1930's on, Maritain became more at
home in it, while Marcel grew less reconciled to mass industrial society.

One winter they saw a great deal of each other at the
Versailles home of a fellow convert, Charles du Bos. But
the experience failed to bring them intellectually closer together. Maritain, after trying in vain to persuade Marcel of
the merits of Thomism, simply refrained from mentioning
him in his own writings. Marcel referred periodically to
Maritain, and usually in disparaging terms. On one occasion
he went so far as to call him a "fanatic."[35] Apparently the
temperamental difference between the two was too great to be
bridged. One had been a philosophical prodigy, who at the
age of thirty had done battle with the great Bergson himself: the other had spent nearly two decades struggling toward the light. One was rigorous in his use of language and
unsparing toward his readers: the other wrote in a relaxed,

[34] Bars, *Maritain en notre temps*, p. 100.
[35] *Existential Background of Human Dignity*, pp. 80–81; *Les hommes
contre l'humain*, p. 112 (this passage is omitted from the English
translation).

conversational style. One cultivated a severe intellectualism: the other distrusted the usual paths of the intellect and searched out epiphanies and vistas on the infinite. One was the leading spokesman of the most prestigious variety of Catholic thought: the other held his religious faith half veiled within a texture of discourse to which a nonbeliever might well subscribe.

The listing of contrasts between Maritain and Marcel could be extended further. Enough has already been said to suggest why they remained so far apart. Yet if we shift our focus from their philosophical differences and direct it toward human sympathies and life styles, a new series of parallels—and this time suggesting a latent understanding—begins to emerge. Both Maritain and Marcel came of mixed religious backgrounds; in both cases a liberal Protestant influence entered through the woman responsible for the boy's upbringing; in both cases there was also a Jewish aspect which each took pains to emphasize—Marcel, the antecedents of his mother, Maritain, the parentage of his wife. In this matter of origins, it is notable that each came to Catholicism quite innocent of any previous family association with the Church: each made a radically free choice. Both had been brought up by a strong-willed and intelligent woman; both selected a remarkable wife; both marriages were unusually close.

Perhaps one can do no more with such parallels than to align them in bare outline. A number of emotional affinities readily spring to mind. The high valuation both Maritain and Marcel put on warm personal relations is one. The kindness with which they reached out to near-strangers is another. Rather surprisingly, in view of Maritain's intellectualism and Marcel's absorption with human anguish and the dread of death, both were notable for their cheerfulness of manner. One is tempted to refer to them as merry philosophers. Although they cherished their own country, they were quite at home abroad. Each was an enthusiastic traveler, and each had ties to the United States that were far closer and more understanding than was usual with Frenchmen of their generation.

Even from the more strictly philosophical standpoint, Maritain and Marcel had in common a distaste for both idealism and positivism in their familiar late nineteenth-century forms. Both were equally opposed to the tradition of Descartes. Indeed, they can be thought of as offering the first examples of French thinkers of our time to work quite outside the tradition of Cartesian classicism. Bergson had earlier tried to found a non-Cartesian school of philosophy— but his prose had remained in the French classic mold. Bergson wrote graceful and skillfully organized books. Maritain and Marcel published collections of essays. In the case of the latter, the informal cast of his thought was thoroughly consonant with the essay form. In Maritain's case, the jumbled heterogeneity of his writings is more surprising: his individual books overlap and repeat each other endlessly. If a man whose mental processes were as disciplined as Maritain's could take so little care with the ordering of his literary production, there arises a basic question as to the nature and applicability of such thought in our own time.

Neither Marcel nor Maritain considered himself a *Catholic* philosopher—that is, in the sense of an official expositor of the teachings of the Church. Even the latter, although he stood for a way of thought to which Leo XIII had given Papal endorsement, remained primarily in a secular context. After all, when he settled in the United States, it was at Princeton rather than a Catholic university that he chose to teach. Both, then, could more properly be described as "philosophers who were Catholics." And as such, their life situation was of necessity ambiguous. They lived enmeshed in a society to whose central values they were radically opposed. They wrote in large part for an audience which could neither share nor even understand their religious beliefs. Maritain offered an intellectual method which the majority of his readers refused to embrace; Marcel's method— if such it can be called—was too personal and elusive to be

transmitted to others. Hence of necessity they wrote in fragments. They offered evocations and possibilities rather than
a full exposition of an alternative way of life and of thought.
In the 1930's and 1940's they had shown their countrymen
a way out of an intellectual and moral impasse. At that
point only a few had been prepared to follow them. A quarter
century later, when they were old and tired, their words
found an echo in Rome itself. But this was in a very different
historical context and on the level of applied social philosophy rather than of abstract thought.

   As a formal philosopher, Maritain had been acutely aware
of the incomplete and tentative nature of his own writings.
He had known that he would never write a summa; that task
had been performed once and for all by his master Aquinas.
Nor did he believe he lived in an era whose philosophy bore
the stamp of classical confidence. If one was looking for *that,*
one might as well go back to Descartes—and this was the
last thing Maritain would have urged on his readers. Superficially regarded, Maritain's lifelong hostility to the Cartesian
tradition sounds odd; the two seem to have in common a
schematic order and a penchant for lapidary formulations.
But in Maritain's case the intellectualism was no more than
the scaffolding of his thought; in Descartes it was the thought
itself. What the former could never forgive Cartesianism was
its radical separation of mind and body—of the process of
thinking from the world of external reality. And he conceived his own role less as that of a systematizer or mod-
ernizer of Thomism than as that of a liberator of philosophy
from the deadening influence of Cartesian categories. He
thought of himself as a realist whose work was necessarily
changing and growing under the pressure of historical actuality—a man ceaselessly rethinking the eternal verities in
terms of a consciousness of time and its fluctuations that
was thoroughly contemporary.[36]

   All the above is almost equally applicable to Marcel. In
this final guise of philosophers embedded in the history of

[36] Bars, *Maritain en notre temps,* pp. 20–22.

their own time and yearning to unite metaphysical certainty
with a down-to-earth awareness of actual human relationships, Maritain and Marcel pushed one stage further the
revolution in French thought that Bergson had projected;
they gave twentieth-century anti-Cartesianism a new concreteness, and they did not hesitate to apply it to specific
historical situations. In *this* perspective, the fragmentary
character of their thought had its unsuspected advantages:
it meant that these philosophers "who were Catholics" could
not be dismissed as mere dogmatists; it left their readers free
to make a choice among the different aspects of their work.
In their contrasting personal styles, Maritain and Marcel had
set out in search of an intellectual method: what they had
found had been a series of ethical formulations which spoke
to the condition of a wide variety of men.

By the end of the 1950's these moral injunctions were
again becoming of topical relevance. Although their methodol-
ogies had begun to look quaint, Maritain and Marcel's words
of paternal counsel were being taken up not only in Rome
but still more widely among those Catholics and non-Catholics, both in France and abroad, who had become quite suddenly conscious of the ethical goals they held in common.

v. *Toward the Council*

Most of the time circumstances and temperament had kept
Maritain and Marcel apart. On at least one occasion, however, they had been aligned together. In 1934—the year of
the February riots in front of the Chamber of Deputies, the
year that began France's half decade of intense ideological
strife—they had joined fifty other Catholic intellectuals in
signing a manifesto entitled *Pour le bien commun,* "for the
common good." An appeal to the conscience of Christians,
this document laid down their responsibilities in face of the
unprecedented circumstances of the moment. The political
order it defined was pluralist, the social order one inspired

by the encyclicals of Leo XIII and Pius XI. On basic principles such as these, Maritain and Marcel saw alike. They
were also in agreement in giving to the word "liberty" the
broadest interpretation consonant with the Catholic faith—
an understanding of the concept of religious freedom which
was to receive official endorsement at the Second Vatican
Council in 1965.

Their approach to the common needs and aspirations of
humanity was similarly reflected in the decisions of the
Council. In 1962—the year in which that body convened—
Marcel had drawn attention to the progress of the ecumenical
movement as one of the very few aspects of the contemporary
world in which he could rejoice.[37] The previous year Maritain had condemned once again anti-Semitism in all its forms.
Earlier in his career Maritain had repeatedly discussed the
historical sufferings of the Jewish people: ever mindful of
his wife's religious origins, he had urged on his fellow
Christians an attitude of cordial and sympathetic understanding. The "racial" persecutions of the Nazi era converted this
gentle sympathy into passionate indignation. In the years
immediately preceding the Second World War and during
the war itself, Maritain again and again expressed his moral
solidarity with the Jews. Yet he still felt that he had not
done enough. On returning to France in 1961, he stressed
the need of a "serious examination of conscience" among
Catholics on the entire subject of anti-Semitism, and he noted
with approval the preparatory steps that Pope John XXIII
had already taken in purging the Church's liturgy and teaching of anti-Semitic residues. "Of Israel," Maritain concluded, "we shall never speak with sufficient thoughtfulness
and tenderness. . . . There is a certain exquisite refinement
of sensibility and spiritual delicacy which is found only
among the chosen people. . . . In comparison with the
Jews, we shall always remain half-civilized barbarians."[38]

[37] Preface to new edition of *Homo Viator*, p. ii.
[38] Preface to Bars, *La politique selon Jacques Maritain*, pp. 8–9. In
1965 Maritain published his collected writings on the Jews (dating back
to 1926) under the title *Le mystère d'Israël et autres essais*.

At the Council, echoes of the writings of Maritain and
Marcel—on freedom, on ecumenicism, on the Jews—were
omnipresent, even when the names of the French philosophers were not specifically cited. And from his contemplative
retreat in southern France, Maritain rejoiced at what had
occurred. He gave thanks to heaven that the "idea of freedom
—of that freedom to which man aspires with what is most
profound in his being, and which is one of the privileges of
the spirit—" had been "recognized and put in a place of honor
among the great directing ideas of Christian wisdom," and
that along with it the dignity of the human person had been
similarly consecrated. He was grateful for the vigorous fashion in which the Church now enjoined an attitude of
brotherhood toward non-Catholic Christians, toward those
of other religions, and even toward atheists. From the
theological standpoint, he regretted that alongside the work
of the Council there had sprung up a new version of doctrinal Modernism—a latitudinarian interpretation of dogma
which made the innovations of the early part of the century
look mild indeed. Yet his dominant impression was that the
Church had at last transcended the Counter-Reformation—
that its Age of the Baroque had come to an end.[39]

There was another Frenchman, younger than Maritain
and Marcel, whose memory was also in people's minds as the
progressive wing among the assembled Church fathers began
to gather confidence in its strength—Emmanuel Mounier,
the founder of "personalism" and of the review *Esprit*. Born
in 1905—the same year as Jean-Paul Sartre—Mounier was
even less than he an academic philosopher. Bergson's generation of philosophers had consisted almost exclusively of universitaires; in the next generation Maritain and Marcel had
taught philosophy even though they had passed the greater
part of their mature lives outside the French educational
system; with Mounier—who was of an age to be Bergson's
grandchild—there was no question of philosophy as an academic discipline. His purpose, rather, was to bring philo-

[39] *Le paysan de la Garonne* (Paris, 1966), pp. 9–11, 13, 16.

sophical inquiry to bear on the urgent social questions of his own time. And it was with this aim that in 1932, at the age of twenty-seven, he founded *Esprit*, which until his premature death in 1950 served as the most persuasive voice of the French Catholic Left.

Quite consciously taking up the legacy of Péguy, Mounier wrote like his master abundantly and without system. And like Péguy, he ranks more as a public "educator," or as the conscience of his generation, than as a figure in the formal history of philosophy; similarly, his own writing was virtually indistinguishable from the review he directed, and he inspired a heartfelt loyalty among those who worked with him. This close sense of an équipe of like-minded spirits was implicit in his philosphy: he thought of personalism as a reawakening of the human personality through participation in a living community.

Although Mounier began with the individual personality as the base point of his reflections, it was always at the social group beyond the individual that he aimed. Like Marcel, he was appalled by the dehumanization of industrial society; in common with Maritain, he strove to make a reality of the teaching in the Gospels. The way he chose to do so was more revolutionary by far: Mounier never wavered in his hostility to the capitalist order, and he was unsparing in his criticism of parliamentary democracy and bourgeois values.

In the 1930's, such an attitude, however offensive to the bien-pensants, gave rise to no serious problems of conscience. After the war—and after a spell in Vichy's prisons—when Mounier revived *Esprit*, he faced a radically altered ideological landscape; the strength of organized Communism presented him with a desperate dilemma. On the one hand, he believed it essential to maintain contact with the French working classes; at the same time he knew that the Communist party had become the only political body whose efficacy they recognized. Hence Mounier refused to adopt a conventional anti-Communist stand; he also disdained to remain silent when Communist outrages in Eastern Europe

forced themselves on his attention. At almost any cost he
wanted to keep up a dialogue with the spokesmen of French
Communism—but not at the price of sacrificing his central
principle of respect for the human personality. In Mounier's
last years—and with the Cold War at its height—*Esprit*
was very nearly alone among publicly committed French
intellectual groupings in avoiding enrollment in the ideological camp of the embattled West while simultaneously
eschewing the line of the communisants.[40]

A similar dilemma faced the most militant wing of the
socially-conscious clergy. In 1944 Cardinal Suhard, Archbishop of Paris, had authorized the formation of a Mission of
Paris to evangelize the dechristianized workers of the capital
and its industrial suburbs. At first the young priests who
volunteered for service among the poor concentrated their
attention on pastoral activity and the establishment of community centers for mutual help. Such activities, they soon
found, while bringing comfort and support to derelicts of the
"sub-proletariat" and to women and children, failed to reach
the mass of the workers. To gain the confidence of working-
men themselves, the priests saw no alternative to going into
the factories and taking up manual labor; only by adopting
the way of life of French workers could they persuade men
who had grown up to regard the clergy as class enemies of
the genuineness of their commitment to social change. In
1946, a handful of priests were authorized to work in the factories of the Paris area; five years later their number
(throughout France) had risen to ninety.

Then the difficulties began. In the meantime Cardinal
Suhard had died, and his successor, Cardinal Feltin, although he continued the worker-priest experiment, was more
cautious and skeptical than his predecessor; the same was

[40] On the intellectual and moral legacy of Mounier, see the special
issue of *Esprit*, XVIII (December 1950), more particularly the articles
by Jean-Marie Domenach, François Goguel, and Paul Ricoeur. For an
over-all assessment of Mounier as a political thinker, see Roy Pierce,
Contemporary French Political Thought (London and New York,
1966), Chapter 3.

true of the other members of the French episcopate who were beginning to have worker-priests under their jurisdiction. And increasingly there was ground for doubt: working a full day at heavy manual labor, the priests were finding it difficult to keep up their normal religious observances; they were also undergoing a change of mentality themselves, as their working-class friendships and style of life bred in them a strong sense of solidarity with their new associates; unschooled in modern social theory of any sort, a number of them embraced a crude and sentimental variety of Marxism. The hierarchy could tolerate members of their clergy co-operating with Communist militants in Communist-dominated trade unions; they drew the line at worker-priest participation in Communist-led political demonstrations.

This was what happened in 1952 when two of them were arrested by the police. Shortly thereafter—and quite predictably—the Vatican intervened. In the previous years complaints about the worker-priests from conservative French Catholics had been pouring into Rome, which in 1951 had forbidden their further recruitment. Two years later, the Vatican decided that the worker-priest experiment had gotten out of hand and that the French episcopate had proved unable to control it. In July a new nuncio arrived in Paris bringing instructions to suspend the training and activities of the worker-priests. A public outcry ensued: both progressive Catholics, who had followed the experiment with growing sympathy, and the hierarchy itself attributed the hostility of the Curia to the shortsightedness of Italians unfamiliar with the real situation of Catholicism in France. In November, three out of the six French cardinals, including Feltin of Paris, went to Rome to plead with Pius XII. They received only meager satisfaction: the Pope agreed to permit the resumption of the experiment on a reduced scale, but on what the French regarded as the key question—whether the priests would be allowed to be in the factories for the full working day—Pius XII and his advisers were adamant; they limited manual labor to three hours, which in the view of the French was insufficient to give the priests a truly working-class character.[41]

The altercation between Rome and France sputtered along for another half decade until in 1959 the activities of the worker-priests were halted entirely. The irony of the whole succession of events was that the Pope under whose auspices the final ban was issued—John XXIII—was the same Angelo Roncalli who as nuncio in France from 1944 to 1953 had shown an open-minded appreciation of what the worker-priests were trying to accomplish, and whose brief pontificate was to steer Catholicism as a whole toward the positions that the reformers within the French Church had long been advocating. The future Pope John had received a belated political education in France: during the immediate postwar years, when he was serving in Paris in the corresponding capacity to that of Maritain in Rome, he had witnessed the revival of democratic political life in a context that was militantly leftist; his experience of cooperation between Catholic leaders and Socialists in France in the late 1940's prepared him for the understanding attitude he adopted as Pope toward the "opening to the Left" in Italian politics a decade and a half later.[42]

Despite their disappointment in the case of the worker-priests, the progressive wing of French Catholics had good reason to take comfort from the pontificate of John. His great encyclicals—*Mater et Magister* of 1961, *Pacem in Terris* of 1963—and the Council he summoned in the months between the two vindicated nearly everything the French had stood for over the past generation. And by the same token the message of Pope John and the Council began to resolve the

[41] On the worker-priests, contrast the judicious and moderately critical tone of Dansette's *Destin du catholicisme français*, Chapters 3–6, with the whole-hearted endorsement (including a few misstatements of fact) in the influential novel by Gilbert Cesbron, *Les saints vont en enfer* (Paris, 1952), translated by John Russell as *Saints in Hell* (London, 1953).

[42] E. E. Y. Hales, *Pope John and His Revolution* (Garden City, N.Y., 1965), pp. 175–176.

dilemma with which Mounier had been contending at the time of his death and which had brought the worker-priests to disaster.[43] By the 1960's the Cold War in Europe had spent its force; the Communists were shedding their dogmatism; the old ideological hatreds were losing their virulence. In the new France that was emerging it was possible at last for Catholics and unbelievers, Marxists and liberal democrats, to take up once more—and under vastly more favorable circumstances than in the past—their eternal dialogue on the human condition.

[43] See Marcel David, "Catholicisme et action syndicale ouvrière," *Forces religieuses et attitudes politiques dans la France contemporaine* (Cahiers de la Fondation Nationale des Sciences Politiques, No. 130), edited by René Rémond (Paris, 1965), pp. 177–201, and Jean-Marie Domenach and Robert de Montvalon, *The Catholic Avant-Garde* (New York, 1967). In 1966 Pope Paul VI permitted the resumption—under close supervision—of the worker-priest experiment.

CHAPTER

4

The Quest for Heroism

"THERE is nothing man desires more than a heroic life: there is nothing less common to men than heroism. . . . Is a heroic humanism possible?"[1] Such were the reflections that a reading of André Malraux had prompted in Jacques Maritain. In the new tones that were coming to dominate the novel of the 1930's, Maritain had caught an echo of his own concerns. A heightened sense of tragedy, a longing for heroic endeavor, were bringing the spiritual world of imaginative writers closer to that of the Catholics, even in the case of novelists who prided themselves on their uncompromising denial of God. Over the new literature there also brooded an obsession with death: to die with dignity and in full consciousness of the end—again and again we find a theme that suggests a latent, more tortured understanding of what Gabriel Marcel was seeking in his extended meditation on human mortality.

The new seriousness of tone in the novel of the 1930's was only to be expected in view of the gravity of the times. The interlocking series of crises—economic, diplomatic, ideological—that gripped France and the Western world

[1] *Humanisme intégral* (Paris, 1936), translated by M. R. Adamson as *True Humanism*, 4th ed. (London, 1946), pp. xi, xiv.

could not fail to have a sobering effect. In Britain or the United States the reaction of writers was much the same. But in France it came with particular vehemence: in France alone the assertion and counterassertion of opposed heroic values took on the dimensions of an intellectual civil war. There was also in France a sharper awareness of both history and religion: the French writer characteristically felt obliged to explain his own and his countrymen's place in the tumults that De Gaulle would speak of as the "surf" of history; he was similarly impelled to draw up his reckoning with the religion of his ancestors—which all about him was giving signs of a renewed vitality—and he found himself unable to pass it by, as was common practice in Protestant lands or in countries where a semblance of conformity gave the tone to Catholic life. In France, history and religion were living realities: no novelist who hoped to interest the educated reading public could afford to neglect them.

As early as 1931 Roger Martin du Gard had written: "The future appears laden with catastrophic events. Our fiftieth birthday will doubtless give us a chance to see the beginning of a vast social upheaval in Europe. What then will remain of our . . . books? How shall we adapt ourselves, with our cumbersome baggage, to this new order . . . ?"[2] Martin du Gard had always been distinguished among the established writers for his ethical scruple and sensitivity to history; he was also slightly younger than his literary peers. Hence he could discern rather better than they the questioning of accepted humanist—or classical—attitudes that the new temper implied. The literary generation of which Martin du Gard was a junior member had been inordinately confident of its aesthetic standards (which was still another reason for the intensity of the challenge to it). Writers such as Gide and Valéry, however shaken by personal self-doubt, had no hesitation when it came to the values and procedures of their chosen craft.

---

[2] Quoted in Réjean Robidoux, *Roger Martin du Gard et la religion* (Paris, 1964), p. 276.

Both were humanists—as Proust had been and Claudel and all the rest. That is, they believed in the continuity of something called human nature and in the human mind or spirit as transcending and ruling the realm of corporeal matter. Such was the assumption—frequently unstated—which had linked the most diverse writers in the French classical tradition. Catholics and nonbelievers, revolutionaries and conservatives had alike trusted in the human spirit and expressed a measured confidence in the voice of reason. Frequently skeptical or disabused, they had seldom been totally despairing. They had nearly aways succeeded in detecting some inner logic in human events, and they had only rarely doubted that their fellowmen were masters of their history. After the turn of the decade, all this began to change. Where their elders had found order in the social universe, the younger writers saw incoherence—a world dominated by brute force and the illogic of a tragedy too vast for the human mind to comprehend. "Wallowing in fatality," they considered "history as irremediably absurd, delivered over not to a secret law of progress, still less to the designs of providence, but to pure contingency and chance." Hence a "fundamental pessimism," an "anguish of the individual consciousness" bound to a collective adventure without meaning or final goal"[3]— hence a literature of anxiety which bridged the gap between the Catholic intellectual renewal and the existentialist writing that lay ahead.

The note of anguish had already marked the Catholic version of existentialism which Marcel had propounded. It would appear again in the atheist existentialism of Sartre. It was manifest in the atmosphere of tension and urgency that permeated the literature of the 1930's. For what all these expressions had in common was a consciousness of moral forlornness and a desperate search for the symbolic formulas that might hold it at bay.

The revival of interest in Péguy was one sign of the new

[3] Pierre-Henri Simon, *L'homme en procès: Malraux—Sartre—Camus—Saint-Exupéry*, 3rd ed. (Neuchâtel, 1950), pp. 7–11.

temper. It was also manifest in such sharply contrasting forms as the preaching of rural anarchism in the novels of Jean Giono or the recurring theme of despair in the plays of Armand Salacrou. Sometimes it took the guise of revolutionary protest. More often it found expression in an ethic of the stern performance of duty. In this perspective, the older generation, unimpeachable as literary craftsmen, were found morally wanting: after 1930, an intense contemplation of one's own ego seemed irredeemably frivolous. Face to face with desperation, the younger writers chose heroism.

Of the new themes of the 1930's and 1940's, the quest for heroism was the most pervasive. It gave unity to a variety of strivings that to the casual observer might seem to have little in common. The heroic ideal was nothing new in French literature (there was always Corneille) or in the Western tradition as a whole; what was unusual in the years of depression and war was its simultaneous revival in all quarters of the ideological landscape. At the time, certain of the figures who loomed largest were adherents of the philo-fascist Right: in the works of Henri de Montherlant or Pierre Drieu La Rochelle the young enthusiasts of the extra-parliamentary leagues could find endorsement for their aristocratic longings and disdain for the morality of the run of mankind. Drieu La Rochelle was a casualty of the Second World War: it was only gradually that his reputation began to recover from his record of collaboration and despairing suicide. Montherlant survived the conflict and even enhanced his position with his postwar dramas in verse. Yet even in Montherlant there was a cynical undertone, a fastidious nihilism, which disqualified him as a model for the young. After the Liberation, those who emerged as the incarnations of the heroic ideal were men who had participated in or expressed their solidarity with the Resistance—Bernanos from the older generation, Malraux and Saint-Exupéry among those in their middle years—these and Martin du Gard, the diffident precursor of the roman engagé.

There was another of Martin du Gard's contemporaries who had aspired to write the great symptomatic novel of the century's second quarter. Jules Romains's *Men of Good Will* was certainly the most ambitious work of fiction of the whole era; published in twenty-seven volumes between 1932 and 1946, it aimed to present an all-inclusive panorama of French society. Yet already its opening volumes seemed curiously dated. Whatever its literary defects—and they were many— the attitude of universal benevolence that its title implied no longer suited the tormented epoch in which it appeared. Romains had tried to write of much besides heroism; but the showpiece of the entire work, the volumes on which the public pounced most eagerly, were the two of *Verdun*, published in 1938. Although widely acclaimed as the finest French novel of the late war, *Verdun* failed to convey the ghastly shock of combat: its atmosphere was of heartbroken reminiscence rather than living actuality; the heroism it depicted was of stoic suffering and not of anguished endeavor. Significantly enough, Romains never really recounted the Battle of Verdun: he wrote of preparations and excursions, of peripheral conflicts and life on the home front; the center of the tragedy eluded him.

If there was any other candidate for the great novel of the era, it was unquestionably Martin du Gard's *The Thibaults*. Yet—as we shall very shortly observe—this work, in its efforts to come to terms with the circumstances in which it was composed, suffered what its author himself regarded as irreparable damage. For there was something about the 1930's that escaped the novelists' grasp: no one matched the achievement of Marcel Proust; all blundered in one fashion or another into a blind alley from which they could find no exit. Their historical environment changed too fast; the link between their work and the events around them slipped through their fingers. All of those we shall be considering—Martin du Gard, Bernanos, Saint-Exupéry, Malraux—eventually ceased to write novels. With all of them there came a point where they could only fall silent—or live their own imaginative creations. The more attractive alternative was action—the path shown them by the leader they all respected or served,

General de Gaulle, who in the quiet of retirement was himself to become the classic memorialist of the heroic years.

1. Roger Martin du Gard and the Unattainable Epic

I've had three black moments in my career. . . . The first changed the whole course of my youth; the second bowled me over in my middle years; the third . . . will play the devil with my old age. . . .

The first was when the pious, provincial-minded youngster I was then found out one night, after reading the four Gospels in succession, that they were a tissue of inconsistencies. The second was when I realized that a certain poisonous fellow named Esterhazy had done a piece of dirty work known as the Dreyfus *bordereau*, and that instead of punishing the culprit the French authorities were torturing a wretched man whose only crime was to have been born a Jew. . . .

The third . . . came a week ago when the papers published the text of the ultimatum, and I saw the billiard-stroke that was being prepared for . . . at the expense of millions of lives. . . .[4]

Thus one of Roger Martin du Gard's exemplary characters vents his bitterness on the outbreak of the First World War. The enumeration of successive "black moments" sharply delineates the author's own abiding concerns—his loss of religion, as epitomized by the Modernist crisis in the Catholic Church; the thirst for justice which the Dreyfus Case had awakened among his countrymen; a hatred of war, the residue of more than four years of front-line service that in recollection seemed a meaningless void. With Martin du Gard the religious question came first in time and in personal depth; a feeling for history grew on him as one baffling

[4] Roger Martin du Gard, *Les Thibault: L'été 1914* (Paris, 1936), translated by Stuart Gilbert as *Summer 1914* (New York, 1941), p. 592.

decade followed another; his devotion to a specific ideology was nearly always hesitant and reserved. It is in terms of these three types of involvement—at bottom all moral in nature—that we can best assess his place as critic and exponent of French public values in the years of desperation.

Roger Martin du Gard was in more than one sense a transition figure. A young recruit to the band of lively talents which just before the First World War had gathered around the *Nouvelle revue française*, a longtime friend and counselor of André Gide, he could be considered both a member of the last classic generation and a herald of the literature of engagement to come. If his themes announced the future, his notion of the novelist's function was old-fashioned even among his contemporaries. Tolstoy was his master—rather than the more "twentieth-century" Dostoyevsky—and he twice tried to write an "epic" on the scale of *War and Peace*. There was something backward-looking also in the way he held on to a faith in scientific positivism at a time when imaginative Europeans were breaking away from this legacy of the nineteenth century's waning years. Martin du Gard distrusted the unbridled imagination and severely disciplined his own. His literary canon was what Georg Lukács calls "critical realism": while admiring and following the great realists of the previous century, he refused to accept his own society as a given and wrote of it in a "socialist perspective."[5]

Born in 1881—one year before Maritain, and five before Marc Bloch—Roger Martin du Gard had made the kind of total commitment to literary craftsmanship that these had given to religious philosophy and the study of history. There was in his family no trace of literary tradition: they were men of the law for generations back—a most respectable and conservative subgroup among the French bourgeoisie. And it was not until he had proved that he was sérieux through training as a professional medievalist at the Ecole des Chartes

[5] *Wider den missverstandenen Realismus* (Hamburg, 1958), translated by John and Necke Mander as *The Meaning of Contemporary Realism* (London, 1963), pp. 58–60.

that the young Roger broke to his parents the news that he intended to be a novelist. His experience with historical documents reinforced Martin du Gard's scientific definition of his craft. It also made him ultra-scrupulous in the long years of research with which he preceded the writing of his novels. And it was perhaps responsible for a certain heaviness of manner that he could never totally shed.

In 1913, Martin du Gard had made his reputation with *Jean Barois*. A book whose central and most compelling episode was the Dreyfus Case, *Jean Barois* was in fact more intensely concerned with the conflict of science and religion; it was, as Albert Camus put it, "the only great novel of the 'scientistic' age."[6] Already its author was looking both forward and back: in a mood of nostalgia for the era of scientific certainty which was drawing to a close, he had produced the first of the major ideological novels of the twentieth century.

During the bleak war years—when he served as a non-commissioned officer with a motorized group supplying the front—Martin du Gard also cherished the recollection of the "unforgettable" winter of 1914, the last months of the belle époque, when he himself, ordinarily shy and retiring, had suddenly become at home in the literary and theatrical world of Paris. Life for him, as for so many of his generation, would never be the same again. After a brief postwar venture with work for the theater, to which he would return at intervals to refresh himself from his more extended labors, he withdrew to the country. The rest of his life he was to pass in semi-retirement, mostly in the south of France, far from the literary cliques of the capital and faithful to the point of self-torture to his exacting definition of his craft.

It took twelve years, however, for what the war had cost him to find a reflection in his writing. With Martin du Gard, as with his countrymen at large, the full emotional effect of the slaughter was postponed for more than a decade. Like

[6] Introduction to *Oeuvres complètes de Roger Martin du Gard*, Pléiade edition (Paris, 1955), I, xv.

them, he had at first sought refuge from tragic memories. Sufficiently content in his series of rural retreats, he had thrown himself into a new work—far larger than its predecessor, more psychological in emphasis, and only tangentially touching on public affairs. The new multi-volume novel, *The Thibaults*, was to be the story of two brothers of very different temperaments, "as divergent as possible, but deeply marked by the obscure similarities created by . . . a very strong common heredity." Such a subject allowed the author "to express simultaneously two contradictory tendencies" in his own nature: "the instinct for independence, escape, and revolt, the refusal of all types of conformity; and the instinct for order and proportion, the refusal of extremes," which he owed to his family origin.[7] The result was a substantial succès d'estime. By 1929 the first six parts had appeared; the quality of their literary workmanship and their psychological perception were undeniable. The narrative had reached the eve of the First World War; the volumes announced for the future would enlarge the account of family relationships into that wider depiction of contemporary history that Martin du Gard had only temporarily abandoned. His ideal seemed within his grasp, the Tolstoyan epic on the verge of realization.

On the first day of the year 1931, Martin du Gard and his wife were severely injured in an automobile accident. The two months of hospitalization that followed gave him an opportunity to rethink his writing in progress. This examination of conscience drastically altered the scheme of *The Thibaults*. Still more, it brought about in its author a spiritual change of course that broke his life's work in two.

On the surface all that Martin du Gard had decided to do was to reduce the scale of his novel—which he feared was losing its momentum—and to alter its conclusion. As a technical job alone this was difficult enough: it involved the

---

[7] Roger Martin du Gard, "Souvenirs autobiographiques et littéraires," *Oeuvres complètes*, I, lxxviii.

delicate process of attaching a new ending to the volumes already in print, while "trying to make the graft as unobtrusive as possible."[8] Beyond that—and not fully recognized by the author himself—there had occurred a shift in his own interests which was bound to alter the character and tone of the novel. History was crowding in upon him: the years of permanent crisis had begun. Events were forcing him back toward his prewar concern with ideology. And by the same process Martin du Gard himself—the diffident literary craftsman who had spent the decade of the 1920's almost totally removed from public controversy—was being pushed, like Maritain a few years earlier, into the arena of political debate. Toward the end of the twenties, he had made the acquaintance of André Malraux; the example of Gide was similarly drawing him to the left. The result was that the concluding volumes of *The Thibaults*, while they had the same cast of characters as their predecessors, became in effect a new novel, a novel of ideological engagement.

Seven years had elapsed since the publication of the last volume of the initial series. It was not until 1936—the climactic year of the Popular Front, the Spanish Civil War, and Maritain's *True Humanism*—that the sequel, *Summer 1914*, appeared. The three volumes which composed it were longer than their predecessors; they were more densely packed with events and, most notably, with political conversation. Their central plot concerned the unavailing effort of a group of international Socialists to stop the relentless course toward war in the weeks following the assassination at Sarajevo. At the end of *Summer 1914* one of the Thibault brothers was dead; the other was to perish in the *Epilogue* which closed the novel four years later. By that time their individual fate had become a matter of secondary importance: the war had dissolved their personal experience into that of Europe as a whole, whose disintegration had now taken over from them as the final dominant theme of the entire work.

With the "initial numbing effect" of combat service a

[8] *Ibid.*, p. xcvi.

decade and a half behind him, Martin du Gard had "felt able, even impelled, to use war as his subject matter."[9] *Summer 1914* reached a wider audience than its predecessors. Like Romains's *Verdun*, which appeared two years later, it spoke to the anxieties of Frenchmen who had survived one world conflict and now were living in dread of another. Its international fame was established when it won its author the Nobel Prize for literature in 1937. At the end of that year, when Martin du Gard went to Stockholm to accept his award, his ambitions might well have seemed attained: he was only fifty-six years old, he had almost completed his epic, and the world had recognized his achievement in the most spectacular and satisfying fashion.

Whatever his public success, in private Martin du Gard was racked by anxiety. He returned to Paris by way of Berlin, where he was "overwhelmed" by a "hideous" atmosphere of hatred and lies, of terror and submission.[10] To his intimates he admitted that *Summer 1914* was an aesthetic disappointment, and it seemed clear that it had won the Nobel Prize more for the current relevance of its subject matter than for its literary qualities, which were inferior to those of the earlier volumes of *The Thibaults*. In the course of its metamorphosis, the novel had very nearly turned into an anti-war tract: overstuffed with the rhetoric of the political Left, it had come close to foundering under its ideological freight.

Quietly, somberly, as the second war approached, Martin du Gard worked away at his *Epilogue*. Finished a few months before Hitler attacked Poland, it appeared in print during the winter of the "phony war." Its tone could scarcely have been more appropriate: the novel closed in unrelieved tragedy, with a barely perceptible glimmer of hope for the generation that lay ahead. Sparser in construction and style than *Summer 1914*, it resolved the themes of the earlier volumes, it balanced and reconciled what had come before,

[9] Denis Boak, *Roger Martin du Gard* (Oxford, 1963), p. 129.
[10] Robidoux, *Martin du Gard et la religion*, p. 305.

through a "judicious harmony" that hovered on the edge of despair.[11]

Despite this recovery of his aesthetic equilibrium, Martin du Gard must have known that *The Thibaults* had fallen short of being the epic he had imagined. So he tried once more. In 1941, in the treacherous calm of Vichy rule, he conceived what he called his "summa," an omnibus work into which he could pour the enormous stock of notes on real or imagined people and events he had accumulated over a quarter of a century. The *Souvenirs du Colonel de Maumort* was to consist of the memories and current reflections of an elderly army officer living in retirement under the German occupation—a figure sufficiently close to Martin du Gard himself to provide a congenial vehicle for his own observations, but more of a grand seigneur, a freethinking spirit in the eighteenth-century manner, with a touch about him of Marshal Lyautey. At first *Maumort* seemed to be proceeding at a brisk pace; it gave precisely the stimulus its author needed to get him through the years of suspense and deprivation after the Germans had taken over the full occupation of the country. But this progress was deceptive: it did not go much beyond the preliminary organizational labor on which Martin du Gard always put such stress. When it came to the actual writing, the book failed to advance. By the end of 1943, Martin du Gard was admitting to himself and to Gide that he was engaged in little more than an elaborate game of literary therapy: the novel as such would never see the light.[12]

By this time, however, its author had reached a point in his own self-awareness at which his failure to carry through his second abortive epic had become a matter of secondary concern. His lagging progress on *Maumort* had gradually merged into a realization of the early waning of his creative powers. At the end of the German occupation and in the immediate postwar years, Martin du Gard's mind became

[11] *Ibid.*, p. 310.
[12] On the composition of *Maumort*, see "Souvenirs," pp. ciii–cxl.

more and more absorbed by his own aging and dissolution. As early as *Jean Barois*, he had been fascinated by the course of a premature senescence; now he was witnessing and meditating on his own. In *The Thibaults* he had twice described in clinical detail the processes of dying. The final decade and a half of his life he spent in a long preparation for death. His only remaining goal, he now saw, was to make a good end—to die with dignity and in control of his fears. And it happened, as he had wished, in August 1958, after eighteen years of nearly total silence. He saw himself in his last months as a traveler *"with no baggage,"* and without interest in his past achievements, awaiting the "night train, which does not come at a regular hour, but *which always passes through* before the end of the night."[13]

What are we to make of this truncated career? Was Martin du Gard, as he sometimes wondered himself, not really a novelist at all? He entertained the highest aspirations—as high as those of any French writer of the twentieth century. In the literary histories his reputation hovers between that of the immortals and that of the solid craftsmen who have not quite reached the summits at which they aimed. The very breadth and complexity of his interests condemned his efforts: he never found a literary form flexible enough to encompass all he wanted to say. History and religion—the twin obsessions of the 1930's and 1940's—defeated him: these and the pressure of the ideological themes with which he had been a pioneer but which he always handled with a certain awkwardness.

Martin du Gard had begun his mature life as a professional student of history, and a historian he in part remained. As a chronicler of contemporary society he had the qualities and the defects of that expert French training in documentary analysis to which Bloch and Febvre had reacted with alter-

13 Letter to Marcel de Coppet, March 18, 1958, "Textes inédits," *Hommage à Roger Martin du Gard: Nouvelle revue française,* VI (December 1958), 1162–1163.

nating respect and rebellion. His experience at the Ecole des
Chartes had so molded his mind that it "became impossible"
for him "to conceive a modern personality detached . . .
from the society and history of its time." Such a conception
helped to give his characters the substance and density his
critics applauded. But it was dependent on the availability
—and the digestibility—of a solid documentation. The
method had worked admirably with *Jean Barois* and the
Dreyfus Case: here Martin du Gard was dealing with events
which as a very young man he had viewed only from a
distance, and he could bring to them an optimum combination of sympathy and detachment. With *Summer 1914* he
began to get into difficulties: he had almost no firsthand
knowledge of Socialism, and no matter how hard he worked
over his international ideologists, their conversations never
quite came off; they remained contrived and externally observed. Finally, with *Maumort*, Martin du Gard was obliged
to give up completely: he could breathe life and reality into
the recollections of the Colonel's youth, but when it came to
topical reflections on the Second World War and the occupation, he was at a loss; after the passage of a few months, he
complained, everything he had written seemed platitudinous.
Hence his stubborn refusal to deliver himself of the messages
to his countrymen that were constantly being requested of
him in the euphoria of liberation.[14]

Which is all to say that when he was personally thrown
into the surf of history, he quickly lost his bearings. A similar
difficulty perplexed his repeated efforts to delineate religious
emotion. He himself had at first gone through the same succession of attitudes toward religion that he traced in his fictional protagonist Jean Barois. Having passed his childhood
in a conventionally Catholic family environment, he had
begun in adolescence to reject the literal truth of the Scrip-

[14] "Souvenirs," pp. xlviii–xlix, cxxiii–cxxvi; on this entire subject, see
David L. Schalk, *Roger Martin du Gard: The Novelist and History*
(Ithaca, N.Y., 1967). I have differed with a number of Schalk's
conclusions.

tures and had learned to reinterpret the dogmas of the
Church in terms of aesthetic and moral symbolism, that is, in
the terms suggested by the turn-of-the-century theological
movement which came to be known as Modernism. But with
Martin du Gard this "symbolist compromise" had never given
intellectual satisfaction: by the age of twenty at the very
latest—far earlier than the imaginary Barois—he had lost his
religious faith entirely. And by his mid-twenties, he had subscribed to the atheism and materialism of Félix Le Dantec,
the same Le Dantec who had occasioned such profound
spiritual distress in Jacques and Raïssa Maritain. Nor—
again in contrast to Barois—did he ever return to Catholicism or relent in his hostility toward it. A quarter century
after his original conflict with religion and at a time when
most intellectually sophisticated Frenchmen had called off
their war against the Church, André Gide found him "en-
sconced in his materialism like a wild boar in its wallow"
and still obsessed with the teachings of Le Dantec.[15] And,
after another quarter century had passed, one of his last
public acts was to protest "vehemently" against the prayers
that a Protestant pastor had read at the interment of Gide
himself.[16]

Had this been all, Martin du Gard's attitude toward religion could be readily described as that of a belated nineteenth-century positivist. But there was also his personal
kindness—on which both Gide and Camus laid stress—and
the concern and respect he had for religious emotion. Unlike
Barois, who left his Catholic wife, Martin du Gard remained
closely attached to his own through more than forty years of
a marriage in which their solitary manner of life made them
unusually dependent on each other's company. Still more
significant, he cherished the memory of his former teacher,
the Abbé Marcel Hébert, who had introduced him to "Mod-

[15] Entry for March 1, 1927, André Gide, *Journal 1889–1939* (Paris,
1948), translated and edited by Justin O'Brien as *The Journals of
André Gide* (New York, 1947–1949), II, 394.
[16] Robidoux, *Martin du Gard et la religion*, p. 367.

ernism" and had suffered cruelly when Pius X had condemned his stand. Throughout the writing of *Jean Barois*, Hébert served as Martin du Gard's counselor, although as the author noted in dedicating the novel to his teacher and friend, the latter could not fail to be wounded by its contents. When Hébert died in 1916, Martin du Gard wrote a memorial essay about him—the only finished writing he did during the empty war years. But it was to the "moral stature" of Hébert, to his "exemplary life," and not to his thought that Martin du Gard "gave his admiration"; perhaps the "key to his soul" was that he tried "to live like Hébert and . . . to think like Le Dantec."[17]

When Martin du Gard wrote of the Dreyfus Case, he described it in terms of an ethical ideal that had subsequently been perverted to partisan ends—which was the interpretation of the Affair that Péguy had propounded. And when two decades later in *Summer 1914* he told of the death of Jacques Thibault, it was as a moral sacrifice in the cause of peace and human fraternity. Similarly in the *Epilogue* to the story of the Thibaults, Martin du Gard's account—in diary form—of the physical decline and final stoic suicide of the older brother, Antoine, was an effort to show how an unbeliever could have as edifying a death as any Christian. Such was to be Martin du Gard's own end. In the last part of his life one of the rare new friendships he made was with another priest, this time a cleric with a solid intellectual regard for Catholic dogma, whose courageous death five years before that of Martin du Gard himself helped to give him strength to face the inevitable passing of the "night train."

This unremitting moral search, this ability to win the friendship of members of the clergy whose metaphysic was radically opposed to his, have persuaded Martin du Gard's Catholic interpreter to see in his writings the "under side" or mirror image of a religious attitude.[18] Martin du Gard never truly understood religion: throughout his literary career

[17] *Ibid.*, pp. 108, 113.
[18] *Ibid.*, p. 270.

he was handicapped by his inability to enter into the emotional universe of a believer. Yet he never gave up trying. Nor did he ever depart from a rooted conviction—against which his friend Gide strenuously protested—that outside religious faith there was no grounding for morality.[19]

"In the name of what?" Could there be a secular sanction for moral behavior? The question Martin du Gard ascribed to Antoine Thibault he never answered himself. Intellectually he was an ethical nihilist: in practice he was a man of exquisite moral sensibility. And similarly, when it came to the ideological commitments to which he felt drawn, he was unable to find a stance that suited his temperament. He alternated between an insistence that his business was to write novels and nothing else and sudden passionate plunges into controversy. During his years of military training, which he performed in the Norman capital of Rouen just after the turn of the century, he had become converted to the political Left by a group of young friends who followed the columns the Radical philosopher Alain published in the local newspaper. And throughout his life Martin du Gard remained a man of the Left in his nonconformist turn of mind and in the causes he espoused. Yet even here his attitude was not entirely coherent. While he professed his sympathy for Socialism and the Popular Front, there was nothing of the Socialist militant about him: his natural temper was conservative, and his way of life incorrigibly grand bourgeois.

His experiences in the First World War—about which he was as reticent as most sensitive Frenchmen of his generation—reinforced his leftward leanings. And a hatred of war remained the most abiding of his public attitudes. At first he could not bear the thought of a second major conflict. The unstated purpose of his *Summer 1914,* whose didacticism had undercut its aesthetic qualities, was to prevent a recurrence of mass slaughter. Two months before it appeared he had written of the Spanish Civil War: "I am hard as steel *for neutrality.* My principle: anything, *rather than war! Any-*

[19] Entry for October 20, 1927, *Journals of André Gide,* II, 415–416.

thing, anything! Even fascism in Spain! . . . even fascism in France! . . . *Anything:* Hitler, rather than war!"[20] And in his Nobel Prize acceptance address he expressed the hope that his writings might serve the cause of peace. Yet eventually, in common with so many of his pacifist-minded contemporaries, he was forced to admit that armed resistance to Nazi Germany was unavoidable. And after the Second World War began, he even voiced his regret that he had written *Summer 1914,* since it was now in danger of confusing the minds of young men leaving for military service.

Martin du Gard's public pronouncements, then, although sporadic and occasionally contradictory, had an underlying unity. It was not true, as a number of commentators have stated, that he broke silence "only once" on a matter of public controversy; a careful checking of the facts has proved that he spoke out not infrequently, and that the single occasion noted by one individual is different from that recalled by another. Besides his interventions in the cause of peace, he pleaded in behalf of social justice and human rights. During the occupation he sent a message of solidarity to the clandestine organization of Resistance writers, and four months before his death he joined Malraux, Mauriac, and Sartre in protesting to the President of the Republic against the use of torture in the Algerian War.[21]

By that time, with Gide and Valéry and Claudel all gone, Martin du Gard had become France's senior literary figure. Among the rising generation, Albert Camus in particular had generously recognized what his contemporaries owed to the author of *Jean Barois* and *The Thibaults.* The tragic pessimism of these novels had prepared the way for the new literature of heroism. Yet Martin du Gard himself never quite succeeded in striking the heroic note that came so naturally to his juniors. His characters hovered in a limbo of futile sacrifice: one Thibault brother, as the author himself explained,

[20] Letter to Marcel Lallemand, September 9, 1936, "Textes inédits," p. 1150.
[21] Schalk, *Martin du Gard,* Chapter 6.

died the death of an "imbecile" in quixotic protest against war;[22] the other asphyxiated by slow degrees through an unpardonable neglect of routine precautions against a gas attack. Both died bravely; both died uselessly; both died in failure and disappointment—as their creator had been disappointed in his aspiration to write an epic.

II. *Georges Bernanos and the Chivalric Ideal*

In the 1930's and early 1940's the spokesmen of the French literary Right excluded themselves almost automatically from the roster of writers whose work went beyond mere partisanship. Figures as divergent as Maritain and Martin du Gard—and subsequently Sartre and Camus and Merleau-Ponty—might all be classed as "men of the Left," but their political commitment was not the most interesting or permanently significant thing about them. On the Right it was otherwise: here partisanship set the tone that even in the finest literary craftsmen or most persuasive thinkers drowned out nearly everything else. Hence with the passing of the issues which once seemed of catastrophic urgency, their work has lost its relevance; it has been reduced to rhetoric and little more. The polemicists of the Right were masters of the French language; their prose had a drive and bite that few of their ideological opponents could match. By the same token, it offered the classic examples of the penchant toward verbal inflation, toward taking words for actualities, that was the central weakness of French political exchange throughout the era. Stripped of its topical interest, this prose rings hollow: its intellectual inconsequence and the ignorance of the contemporary world it betrays are exposed in all their glaring inadequacy.

One of these polemicists, however, stood apart from the others in the independence of his way of life and in the utter

[22] Letter to Marcel Lallemand, February 1, 1945, "Textes inédits," p. 1145.

integrity of what he wrote. Georges Bernanos is almost as difficult to classify as Gabriel Marcel. Like Marcel, he was a Catholic, but born in the faith, not converted to it. He shared with François Mauriac the distinction of being one of the two most influential Catholic novelists of the interwar years. And in addition to his novels he wrote a series of extended essays—couched in the form of appeals to his countrymen—which together give the most eloquent expression of the heroic ideal that these years produced.

Bernanos was thirty-eight when his first novel appeared, and over forty when he wrote the first of his major polemics. This long incubation period, reminiscent of Marcel's, suggests a life burdened by material difficulties and unremitting anxiety. Unlike nearly all the rest of his literary peers, Bernanos did not spring from a highly cultivated family. His parents were prosperous enough to give him a good education —his father was an upholsterer and interior decorator—but their origins were simple, and although they lived in Paris, where their son was born in 1888, they remained provincials at heart. Generations back, the Bernanos family had come from Spain; subsequently they had settled in Lorraine; but it was in Artois in the north of France that Georges's father bought the country house which was to become far more real to the boy than his Parisian home and was to put an indelible stamp on his subsequent literary creations.

If there was something Spanish about Bernanos in his vehemence and pride, his sense of honor and his love of risk, the sober, gray Artois countryside provided him with the setting for his novels and the image of the traditional France for which he stood. The local peasants remembered him as a "strong-limbed little boy, . . . with fragile nerves," delighting in rural adventures, but also given to sitting in a pine tree "to read or . . . to say mass and to address interminable sermons to an imaginary congregation."[23] For a boy of such a restless disposition, education was bound to be a spotty affair: he changed schools frequently, and never completed a

[23] Albert Béguin, *Bernanos par lui-même* (Paris, 1954), p. 28.

course of professional training. By the age of eighteen—in 1906—he had espoused the monarchist faith, and two years later he enrolled in the Action Française, in whose noisy ranks he distinguished himself by his zeal for rioting. Already he was making a small reputation as a journalist. In 1913 the Action Française sent him to Rouen to edit the local monarchist newspaper—an assignment that gave him a chance to pit his talents against those of the formidable Alain.

On the outbreak of war, although he had been classified as physically unfit for military service, Bernanos persuaded his way into a cavalry regiment, where, like Martin du Gard, despite numerous wounds and citations, he remained an enlisted man. But for Bernanos the war was something more than empty slaughter. Not that he followed the jaunty line of the professional patriots—in common with most front-line soldiers, he found such effusions nauseating. Yet he could not dismiss as meaningless the sacrament of misery he had shared with his fellow Frenchmen—the war fought "without hatred and without anger" which had marked him for life as a man who carried about within him a daily familiarity with death.

Before it was over he had married, appropriately enough, a direct descendant of the brother of Joan of Arc, who was to bear him six children. To support his growing family he decided that he required something more stable than journalism and characteristically jumped to the opposite extreme, the safe but incongruous life of inspector for an insurance company. Meantime, however, he had discovered that writing was his vocation. The war had changed him from a reactionary brawler into a man of tragic seriousness who felt obliged to "bear witness" to the suffering he had seen about him.[24] Caught up in the postwar literary ferment, he had come across Pirandello and Freud—required reading for a man as subject as he was to devastating attacks of anxiety— and he had steeped himself in the writing of Péguy. The last of these, Bernanos found, never failed to respond to his need,

[24] *Ibid.*, p. 70.

and there was much in the younger writer's style that recalled Péguy—the conversational tone, the obsessive repetitions, the outbursts of cosmic anger, and the notion of religion as at once earthy, familiar, and infinitely majestic.

Immediately after the war Bernanos had began working on his first novel. And during the next few years he wrote away at it in cafés and railroad carriages as he pursued a harassed and nomadic life, sometimes alone and sometimes with his family. When *Under the Sun of Satan* finally appeared in 1926, it was an immediate critical success. It was followed over the next decade by four further novels, culminating in his most popular book, *The Diary of a Country Priest.* Mauriac had already accustomed the reading public to novels that were Catholic in inspiration, but he had kept them within the framework of secular bourgeois society. Bernanos broke more sharply with the literary past. With Mauriac religion was the presupposition behind the novels: with Bernanos it became the stuff of which they were made. They were dramas of sin and degradation, of Christian love and divine grace, and priests were frequently their leading characters. Indeed, the very writing of his novels was for Bernanos the spiritual equivalent of priesthood. Their incomparable power lay "in the gravity of a voice resounding with the echoes of a supernatural storm, in the strange light of a hidden sun which will burst forth only in death."[25]

The Diary of a Country Priest appeared four months before the outbreak of the Spanish Civil War. For reasons of economy, Bernanos was living at the time on the island of Majorca. The war in Spain interrupted his most productive period, tearing him away from his career as a novelist and drawing him into a passionate polemic that would continue unabated until his death.

"I have sworn to move you—with friendship or anger, does it matter which?" With the same phrase Bernanos began the

[25] Gaëtan Picon, Preface to *Bernanos: Oeuvres romanesques,* Pléiade edition (Paris, 1961), p. xxx.

two most powerful of his controversial essays, *La grande peur des bien-pensants* and *Les grands cimetières sous la lune*. The first of these, published in 1931, reflected his highly personal and ambivalent relationship to Charles Maurras and the Action Francaise. In 1919, Bernanos had ended his affiliation with this group: loyal to the idea of a monarchist seizure of power, he disapproved of Maurras's drift toward legal opposition within the framework of the parliamentary regime. But when the Papal condemnation of 1926 descended, it had on Bernanos exactly the opposite of its effect on Maritain. It made him rally behind his old comrades, who now appeared the victims of clerical treachery. Quixotic as always, Bernanos suffered agonies of soul in behalf of a movement in which he no longer fully believed. Not until 1932, when the worst of the storm was over, did he finally break with Maurras—and this time forever.

No wonder, then, that his *Grande peur des bien-pensants* was a puzzling and upsetting book. Its argument outraged nearly everyone. Cast in the form of a rambling and laudatory biography of the founder of French political anti-Semitism, Edouard Drumont, it assaulted not only the cherished values of the Left but the most influential attitude among the Catholic constituency to which Bernanos himself belonged. The Catholic voters of France, he maintained, had become timorous and prone to compromise. Deprecating their wondrous past, feeble in defense of their inherited faith, for thirty years they had looked for nothing better than to enjoy a safe lodging in bourgeois society, to adapt as unobstrusively as possible to the institutions and practices of the parliamentary republic. The bien-pensants, Bernanos argued, had lost the "heroic sentiment of justice and injustice."[26] They had forsworn the legacy of the embattled anti-Dreyfusards.

Such a bare sketch can convey little of the rhetorical force of Bernanos' tract. Its prose swept on in mighty gusts: its bravura passages against the Jews were studded with bizarre images, such as likening them to embalmers patiently pump-

[26] *La grande peur des bien-pensants* (Paris, 1931), p. 409.

ing out by the nostrils the gray matter of France itself.[27] But this was not the Bernanos that a subsequent generation would remember. His call to his fellow-Catholics went unheeded: the bien-pensants who did regain their militancy wasted it on a philo-fascism which was never truly Catholic in inspiration and which by the end of the decade Bernanos had come to detest. His first major polemic, for all its literary power, is now only a period piece, and its anti-Semitism an embarrassment to his admirers. Not so its successor, which decades after the Spanish Civil War was still being cited, along with George Orwell's *Homage to Catalonia,* as among the most telling accounts of the tragedy by a foreign observer.

Writing away in a fine frenzy in his Balearic retreat—his publishers were now keeping Bernanos alive by paying him immediately for each page of manuscript delivered—he found himself in the middle of the Nationalist insurrection that had rapidly taken over the island. Initially Bernanos was inclined to favor Franco's cause: this, after all, was the Catholic side, and one of his sons had even become a member of the Falange. But when he saw the atrocities that were being perpetrated in the name of religion, Bernanos could not hold his tongue. The mass shooting of suspected Republican sympathizers turned his stomach. He had seen, he reported, the lorries go by, laden with men marked for execution:

They rumbled like thunder on a level with the many-coloured terraces, freshly washed and running with water, gay with the murmur of country fairs. The lorries were grey with road-dust, the men too were grey, sitting four by four, grey caps slung on crosswise, hands spread over their tent-cloth trousers, patiently. They were kidnapping them every day from lost villages, at the time when they came in from the fields. They set off for their last journey, shirts still clinging to their shoulders with perspiration, arms still full of the day's toil, leaving the

[27] *Ibid.,* p. 137.

soup untouched on the table, and a woman, breathless, a minute too late, at the garden wall, with the little bundle of belongings hastily twisted into a bright new napkin: *A Dios! Recuerdos!*[28]

But what revolted Bernanos beyond anything else was the part the Spanish Church clergy played in these massacres. He had heard no word of protest from them. In a little town near his, "two hundred inhabitants . . . had been dragged from their beds in the middle of the night, driven in batches to the cemetery, and shot down and burnt in a heap a little further on. The personage whom good manners require that I should refer to as Archbishop, had sent a priest round, who stood with his boots paddling in blood, distributing absolutions between the shootings." All Christian pity seemed forgotten. The world was "ripe for every kind of cruelty." Soon the Stalinists, Bernanos predicted, would get used to burning Trotsky's followers in public, and the Germans would be doing the same to their Jews.[29]

Was this last a sign of regret for what Bernanos had written six years before? Although he never fully recanted his anti-Semitism, he left Spain deeply shaken by the horrors he had seen and appalled by the spectacle of violence that writings like his own had helped to unleash. Once more the experience of war at first hand had checked his polemical fury. Back in France after three years' absence—it was the spring of 1937—he found his country unrecognizable: here also he detected an atmosphere of civil war.[30] From this point on, Bernanos became less partisan in his polemic: he was more concerned to aid in the reconciliation of the French in preparation for the trials that he now knew lay ahead.

At home, however, he could find no ideological comfort. He had quarreled with his former allies, whom his *Grands*

---

[28] *Les grands cimetières sous la lune* (Paris, 1938), translated and abridged by Pamela Morris as *A Diary of My Times* (New York, 1938), pp. 66–67.

[29] *Ibid.*, pp. 90, 144.

[30] *Grand cimetières*, p. 116. This passage is omitted in the translation.

cimetières had scandalized, and he had no use for the Left, which in turn wanted nothing of him. In the summer of 1938 he migrated to South America. The reasons for this move were mixed and obscure: Bernanos was driven to despair by his government's failure to stand up to Hitler; he hoped that by turning to large-scale farming in the New World he would at last be able to support his family; he also apparently longed to carry out an exotic dream of childhood. First in Paraguay and subsequently—and more permanently—in Brazil, Bernanos took up the new trade of ranching. His material success was limited: he had never been good at the mechanics of living. But he became attached to Brazil and soon felt at home there. The endless wastes and the sparse scrub growth of the Brazilian interior gave him a second "metaphysical" landscape for his writings; he had always felt drawn to scenes of desolation, while the charms of the Mediterranean had scarcely touched him.

On the outbreak of the Second World War, isolated in a ramshackle house open to wind and weather, straining his ears for the scraps of news that came over a flickering radio, Bernanos began to keep a diary of his reflections. "We are going back to war," he wrote, "as to the house of our youth." With a heartbroken sensation of déjà vu, he contemplated the ordeal that was beginning. For Bernanos the idea of a second war was harder to bear than the first: this time he had no friends or comrades to sustain his courage. He was totally without illusion: his country was in no shape to fight, and the slaughter of ten or twenty million would make no difference at all. Only at the very end of his observations did Bernanos permit himself the glimmer of a hope that when the carnage was over the meek might at last inherit the earth.[31]

The diary concluded in the spring of 1940 just before the Germans struck in the West. It was not published until after Bernanos' death, under the title *Les enfants humiliés*—the

[31] *Les enfants humiliés: Journal 1939–1940* (Paris, 1949), pp. 9, 130–131, 210, 252.

children of humiliation—which Emmanuel Mounier had chosen for it. In the intervening years, its author had regained his combative spirit. The defeat of his country had resolved his ideological uncertainties. Like Maritain in New York, Bernanos in Brazil rallied his strength and pledged his allegiance to the Free French. His wartime messages, more particularly his *Lettre aux anglais,* joined the corpus of clandestine documents that circulated among the French Resistance. After the Liberation, however, Bernanos was tempted to remain in Brazil. It took a summons from De Gaulle himself —"your place is with us"—to bring him home. He had been back only six months when the General fell from power. Once more Bernanos found himself alone, tilting against the politicians of the Fourth Republic whom he liked no better than those of the Third. His health was also failing. In March 1948—he had just turned sixty—he was taken to the hospital for an operation *in extremis.* He was fully aware of his condition: "I am seized with the holy agony of death," he declared, almost with joy. At his funeral the only prominent writer present was André Malraux, who in the last three years of Bernanos' life had become his friend.

"I have dreamed of saints and of heroes, neglecting the intermediate forms of our species, and I perceive that these intermediate forms scarcely exist, that only the saints and the heroes count." Bernanos was impatient with every sort of moral mediocrity—an attitude entirely compatible with his recognition that his own talents were not extraordinary and that his life had been far from a model of good conduct; le bon dieu, he knew, would understand him in the end. Had he had his way, Bernanos would have liked "to sit down to table every day . . . with old monks or young officers in love with their job."[32] His notion of human greatness was archaic, medieval, chivalric. It was because he had found a quality of chivalry in the anti-Semite Drumont that he picked so odd

[32] *Ibid.,* p. 199; *Diary of My Times,* p. 233.

a political hero, and the loss of this quality was what he bemoaned among his countrymen.

To an attitude that an earlier or later period would have dismissed as merely quaint, the years of desperation gave topical relevance. In the two decades from the publication of his first novel until his death, Bernanos' writing spoke directly to his era. During his lifetime he thought of himself as neglected and misunderstood: today he appears representative of his age. But there was no lack of others who were also striking the heroic chord. What gave Bernanos his special appeal was the total simplicity with which he voiced sentiments that could so easily have turned into theatrical posturing.

The initial clue to an understanding of Bernanos is his absorption with death. During the First World War, he had experienced death all around him: he had seen men die; death had become almost a banality. The war had made saints of the patient, suffering soldiers—saints of "low quality," it was true, who would no more have aspired to true sainthood than to sleeping with the colonel's daughter.[33] (Such was the tone of tender gallows humor that Bernanos fell into when he wrote of his combat service.) In him, however, the war had merely confirmed a disposition with which he had been well acquainted since childhood: at the age of seventeen he had told his confessor that for many years he had been possessed by the fear of death, and that he had come to terms with it only by making the discovery that one might accept death as the "fortunate . . . close" to a life one had loved profoundly.[34] Thus Bernanos had begun the long and painful process—which by its very nature could never be complete—of turning into a source of creation the anguish that held him in its grip.

The other pole of his emotional universe was his image of childhood. There were "two periods in life," he knew, "when

---

[33] *Grande peur,* p. 74; *Enfants humiliés,* p. 11.
[34] Picon, Preface to *Bernanos: Oeuvres romanesques,* pp. xxvi–xxvii.

sincerity" could "be expected, childhood and the death agony," and these alone he found absolutely authenic. Both his novels and his essays were strewn with references to the world of childhood and to the demand he made of himself to remain faithful to what he had been as a child. "I write to justify myself," he once declared, "in the eyes of the child that I was."[35] Hence the world of grownups never seemed to him quite real. The actions of those generally considered responsible men struck him as without merit—or, in his more forgiving moments, no better than comical.

To think like a child was a great source of strength in an era such as the 1930's, when political rhetoric exuded hypocrisy and self-righteousness. Bernanos had a talent for blurting out the simple truths that the ordinary commentator on public affairs would have blushed to utter. But the fact that the world of responsible decision remained a mystery to him severely limited his grasp of contemporary history. He was nearly fifty when he began to discover the unworthiness of his ideological allies, and he never appreciated that there might be other ways of understanding Catholism besides the saintly and chivalric ideal he cherished. He had no comprehension of the social mission of the Church in its twentieth-century guise: he wrote mockingly of *Rerum Novarum*, of Marc Sangnier, and of Jacques Maritain. What he would have thought of the Second Vatican Council is only too easy to imagine.

Hence his version of the quest for heroism lacked a content that could be transmitted to others. He himself did no more than bear witness to the evil of his era—and evil to Bernanos always meant an inability to love. His archaic notion of rectitude might awaken glorious memories, but it could provide guidance only in the simplest of moral situations. His prose might be magnificent, but it had about it traces of conventional bombast which clashed with the honesty of his own thought. To the end—like a child lost in a strange city—

[35] Peter Hebblethwaite, *Bernanos: An Introduction* (London, 1965), p. 87; *Enfants humiliés*, p. 195.

Bernanos remained bewildered by the contemporary world. Two years before his death, in a sudden flash of self-knowledge, he had written a letter that might well stand as his epitaph:

> I cannot bear having lost the image of [my country] which I had formed . . . in childhood. Yet I shall not offer this suffering as an example to anyone. It is like . . . that of a dog who doesn't understand . . . what it misses, but who looks for its dead master everywhere and finally goes off to die on his tomb.[36]

III. *Antoine de Saint-Exupéry as Technician-Adventurer*

Antoine de Saint-Exupéry was frequently called a knight-errant. Yet the way he lived the chivalric ideal was twentieth-century through and through. With Saint-Exupéry we find ourselves in a new world of experience. All the figures we have been considering up to now were already mature men when the First World War broke out; though their period of achievement and fame came after the war, their minds had been formed during the long peace that preceded it, and they continued to treat as abnormal the era of tumult into which they had been thrown. With Saint-Exupéry and those still younger than he, such tumults were assumed as the givens of the human situation. Nostalgia for the past was out of the question: the point now was to rescue or to redefine whatever there was of human value that could be saved from the wreckage.

Although he was only twelve years younger than Bernanos —he was born in 1900—Saint Exupéry belonged to a different spiritual generation, the generation of those just too young to have had the experience of combat service. Had he been a year or two older, there seems little doubt that Saint-Exupéry would have rushed to enlist. His antecedents were aristocratic; he had been educated in elite Catholic schools

[36] Quoted in Béguin, *Bernanos par lui-même*, p. 144.

to a lofty conception of manliness and self-discipline; and while he had lost his faith, he retained from his religious up-bringing an ideal of heroism whose Christian origin was unmistakable. His first intention was to attend the French naval academy; then, having failed the admission examination, he began to study architecture—a passing interest but one which left a permanent mark on his thought. In the early 1920's he took up aviation: here he found the métier that fitted him perfectly, and a flier he remained, with only brief interludes in other occupations, until his death two decades later.

When Saint-Exupéry became a commercial aviator, there was nothing routine about flying. Indeed, it was to escape the safety and tedium of bourgeois society that he and his companions chose to be pilots. They were by necessity pioneers and adventurers, the men who staked out the air routes that subsequent generations would take for granted. First in West Africa, later in South America, Saint-Exupéry risked his life as part of his daily task; he was in two bad crashes, and his friend Mermoz perished in another. Such dangers and the exhilaration of surmounting them provided him with the themes for his books, only two of which, including the one which established his reputation, *Night Flight*, published in 1931, could be called novels. The rest consisted of reminiscences of comradeship and loneliness, of deserts and mountains and exotic settlements, and of the unearthly landscape above the clouds that no previous generation of writers had witnessed.

The Second World War gave Saint-Exupéry a chance to fly for his country. After the defeat of 1940, he made his way to New York, where he spent more than two years writing and nursing his impatience. With the Allied landing in North Africa, he grasped the opportunity to return to combat. Over-age and so stiff from his earlier injuries that he could not get into a cockpit unaided, he insisted on going out on further missions beyond the quota his superiors had grudgingly granted him. He became the despair of his squadron; only a

man bent on challenging death could be as stubborn as he.
His last flight was in late July 1944, six weeks after the execution of Marc Bloch and at the very moment when the
liberation of France had become a certainty.

When Saint-Exupéry's plane disappeared to the north of
Corsica—neither the aircraft nor his body was ever found—
the manner of his death seemed to fit the life he had led.
But in fact he had never cultivated the fascination with
death which gripped Martin du Gard with icy horror, which
nourished the religious faith of Bernanos, and which
prompted men such as Malraux to hurl themselves against
danger in order to be convinced of their own courage. With
Saint-Exupéry risking one's life was simply part of the job.
He glorified neither death nor a career of action for its own
sake. Risk was no more than the unavoidable accompaniment
of a task well performed.

This matter-of-fact, twentieth-century technician's attitude
toward his métier was at least what Saint-Exupéry professed.
But if that was all, why had he picked so hazardous an occupation? It was quite apparent that what appealed to him
about flying was the extra moral effort, the possibilities of
surpassing the human norm, that it called forth. For him, as
for Bernanos, mankind's mediocrities scarcely existed. "A man
was a mere lump of wax to be kneaded into shape." One had
"to furnish this dead matter with a soul, to inject will-power
into it," even at the cost of cruel sacrifice.[37] Thus Saint-
Exupéry wrote of his superior Daurat, the real hero of *Night
Flight*, who put the needs of his new air service above considerations of humanity and believed it his duty to send a
pilot to his death by ordering him to fly in bad weather. And
it was with a similar admiration that Saint-Exupéry related
how his friend Guillaumet, forced down in the high Andes,
had struggled through snow and ice for five days and four
nights until at last he told his rescuers: "I swear that what I

[37] *Vol de nuit* (Paris, 1931), translated by Stuart Gilbert as *Night
Flight*, Signet paperback edition (New York, 1945), p. 39.

went through, no animal would have gone through"—the "noblest sentence," Saint-Exupéry thought, that he had ever heard.[38]

Thus besides being a technically exacting profession which demanded of the pilot an intense self-discipline and concentration of energy, flying was an avenue toward the understanding of men and nature. A plane was a tool, but it was a tool like a peasant's plow which made of him who handled it something beyond a "dry technician"—a man in touch with "universal truth":

> The airplane is a means, not an end. One doesn't risk one's life for a plane any more than a farmer ploughs for the sake of the plough. But the airplane is a means of getting away from towns and their book-keeping and rediscovering a farmer's reality.
>
> Flying is a man's job and its worries are a man's worries. A pilot's business is with the wind, with the stars, with night, with sand, with the sea. He strives to outwit the forces of nature. He awaits the dawn as a gardener awaits the spring. He looks forward to his next landing as to a promised land, and he seeks his truth in the stars.[39]

Flying was also an exercise in comradeship. The greatness of the profession was that it bound men together, teaching them that the true luxury of life was not material goods but relations between human beings. Saint-Exupéry's passages about comradeship focus on the experience of participation with an intensity reminiscent of Marcel's.[40] But the kind of friendships which Saint-Exupéry described were restricted to men: women and children could have little place in the universe of adventure he celebrated; the most pathetic figure in his writing is that of a pilot's wife waiting in vain for her husband's return. It is true that Saint-Exupéry had the same

[38] *Terre des hommes* (Paris, 1939), translated (and rearranged) by Lewis Galantière as *Wind, Sand and Stars* (New York, 1939), p. 58.
[39] *Ibid.*, p. 227. I have altered the translation slightly.
[40] Simon, *L'homme en procès*, pp. 133–134.

grave respect for childhood as Bernanos, and during his years of inactivity in New York he wrote a children's book, *The Little Prince*. But children—and more particularly the figures of young girls who suddenly appear as though by a magic spell at intervals throughout his recollections—could never give more than a reprieve in a life of strenuous exertion; they offered the rare and privileged moments that showed the flier the alternative path, the way of living he had forsworn. For the life of action and individual happiness could not coexist; they were "eternally at war."[41]

There was, then, in flying itself, as in the chief who dispatched his pilots on desperate missions, a necessary cruelty. This was part of the eternal wisdom that Saint-Exupéry believed he had learned from his encounters with nature. One of the curious features of his writing was the way it accepted a type of suffering which most men of comparable sensitivity would find justified only in time of war or revolution. Saint-Exupéry could write without flinching about the practice of certain African desert tribes of leaving an old slave to die in the sand when he was past the age of useful employment, and he argued that one should try to understand those who made war before jumping to the conclusion that they were barbarians. On a temporary assignment as a newspaper reporter, he had a chance to witness the Spanish Civil War at first hand, and he came away from it with the conviction that the sacrifices each side offered to its version of the truth meant much more than the content of the ideology which either professed.

"What's the use of discussing ideologies? If all of them can be proved correct, all of them are also in opposition to the others, and such discussions make one despair of the salvation of man—when actually man everywhere . . . has the same needs."[42] Saint-Exupéry's basic attitude was non-ideological, even anti-ideological. In this respect once again

[41] *Night Flight*, p. 93.
[42] *Terre des hommes, Oeuvres d'Antoine de Saint-Exupéry*, Pléiade edition (Paris, 1959), pp. 252–254. These passages are omitted in the translation.

he recalls Gabriel Marcel. But in Saint-Exupéry there was less human warmth than in Marcel, and still more of a fastidious elitism. Saint-Exupéry's ideal, for all his long residence abroad, was not man the spiritual voyager but man the builder of civilization. An image of construction keeps recurring in his writings, the figure of speech of a technician who had once thought of being an architect. And the builders that Saint-Exupéry evidently had in mind were wielders of authority, convinced that they knew better than the run of mankind what was for humanity's own benefit, and quite prepared—like the founder of an airline—to sacrifice the individual's life or liberty to the great task at hand.

Such an attitude hovered dangerously close to what the fascists were saying. Despite Saint-Exupéry's hatred of fascism and his detachment from any specific ideology, his elitist sympathies and his aloofness toward his fellow-exiles in New York after the defeat of 1940 suggest a mentality not too far removed from that of the moderates at Vichy or the military men in North Africa who looked to Giraud rather than to De Gaulle—a mentality which drew a bitter rebuke from Jacques Maritain. Saint-Exupéry's grasp of political reality was never very solid; it was as precarious as his philosophical center of gravity, which oscillated between the visionary and the technocratic. This was notably true of his longest and most disputed work, *Citadelle*, which remained unfinished at the time of his death: some readers have found in it the final ripe statement of his wisdom; others—and more convincingly —dismiss it as a "bulky collection of oracular utterances, grave maxims, mystical aphorisms, and meditations on man" that adds nothing to his stature.[43] Saint-Exupéry's earlier writing had been stripped and supple; in *Citadelle* it acquired biblical or koranic cadences which left the course of the author's thought irremediably clouded.

When Saint-Exupéry disappeared over the Mediterranean, his friends discovered in his baggage certain typed pages of

[43] Henri Peyre, *The Contemporary French Novel* (New York, 1955), p. 180n.

Teilhard de Chardin that they at first assumed to be his.[44] The confusion was only natural. Both were men whose mysticism had its point of departure and its justification in scientific or technical concerns; both were in the tradition of Pascal. Saint-Exupéry always took a volume of Pascal with him on his travels—in itself a sign that he belonged to a new generation of French writers. A Maritain or a Marcel had tried to escape the cavern of spiritual desolation he found in Pascal: Saint-Exupéry and his contemporaries welcomed it as the bedrock on which they could ground their own efforts at ethical reconstruction.

It was partly for this reason—because his thought echoed the metaphysical questionings of his era—that Saint-Exupéry enjoyed so large a reputation in his lifetime and immediately after his death. What was known of his biography made him an exemplary figure and gave his writings a significance disproportionate to their intrinsic worth. His concept of heroism was purer—in the sense of being less theatrical—than that of Bernanos or Malraux, but it also lacked the demonic force that suffused their novels with the torment of an unbearable anxiety. At its best Saint-Exupéry's writing was finely chiseled: it contributed notably to the process of freeing French discursive prose from the grip of traditional rhetoric, and it translated readily into the English version in which so many of his readers first encountered it. All too often, however, its content was either platitudinous or obscure: it could offer little help in establishing a new style of thought for the postwar era.

iv. *André Malraux as Artist-Adventurer*

As early as his second novel, *The Royal Way*, André Malraux had clearly posed his own ethical problem: "What is one to do with one's soul if neither God nor Christ exists?"

---

[44] Clément Borgal, *Saint-Exupéry: mystique sans la foi* (Paris, 1964), p. 8.

And the answer had come back no less clearly: "Heroism."[45]
Malraux had no doubt that God was dead; he suspected that
in the twentieth century the concept of man might be dead
also. In origin his thought was Nietzschean—in his last novel
Nietzsche himself made a brief appearance—and he likewise
acknowledged debts to Dostoyevsky and Barrès, Stendhal
and Michelet. And of course to Pascal: Malraux's finest
novel, *Man's Fate*, was a Pascalian exercise in human grand-
eur and misery. Besides all this, there was the world of fine
art; Malraux began studying the plastic arts at the age of
eighteen, and the editing of art books was the one regular
profession he ever pursued. Only those unacquainted with
his biography could be surprised when after the Second
World War he shifted his attention from fiction to the writing of essays on painting and sculpture.

About this biography, however, he remained strangely
reticent. He came of a family of ship outfitters in Dunkirk,
but he was born and educated in Paris, and he broke his ties
with home early in life. The dominating figure in his childhood seems to have been a grandfather, who in transposed
form appeared in two of his novels, *The Royal Way* and *The
Walnut Trees of Altenburg*, with his native Flanders first
shifted to Brittany and in the subsequent work to Alsace. It
was only in the latter—his final novel—that Malraux brought
himself to write at any length of family associations. But
beginning with *Man's Fate* the relationship between father
and son began to move into the center of his consciousness:
in 1930, three years before it was published, his own father
had committed suicide.

Whatever the reason, Malraux preferred to keep his early
life a mystery, and he apparently enjoyed the legend that
gathered around it.[46] Many of the details still remain un-
verified. Yet enough is authentic to suggest that nearly all
his novels grew out of his own forays into adventure. *The*

[45] Simon, *L'homme en procès*, p. 35.
[46] W. M. Frohock has skillfully separated fact from legend in the
first chapter of his *André Malraux and the Tragic Imagination* (Stanford, Calif., 1952).

Royal Way drew on his expedition in 1923 in search of ancient bas-reliefs lost in the Cambodian jungle; *The Conquerors* and *Man's Fate* reflected his work with Chinese revolutionists in the middle years of the decade; *Man's Hope* similarly—and much more immediately—derived from his experience as commander of a Republican air squadron in the Spanish Civil War; even *The Walnut Trees of Altenburg* began and ended with fictionalized reminiscences of his service with a tank division at the start of the Second World War. Only after that did legend cease to blend with fiction, and Malraux emerge as an indubitably historical character—as a colonel in the Resistance and in the final campaigns of the war, as Minister of Information in De Gaulle's provisional government of November 1945, and in his last and most protracted incarnation as Minister for Cultural Affairs after the General's return to power thirteen years later.

Malraux, born in 1901, was a year younger than Saint-Exupéry, having also just missed the experience of the First World War. And like Saint-Exupéry's, Malraux's novels celebrated the life of action as a means of defying death. But there was far more of anguish in the way his characters contemplated their own extinction and almost none of the resignation in confronting the forces of nature that permitted Saint-Exupéry's fictional pilots—and perhaps himself—to accept their end. There was rather the tragic conviction, which Malraux held in common with Martin du Gard and Bernanos, but in his case without religious tonality, that one's death delivered the verdict on all that had gone before and that the manner of a man's passing held the key to his courage and dignity. Malraux inaugurated in the French novel the stress on situations of trial at the limit of human endurance which was to become a central theme of Resistance literature; in this perspective, death posed the ultimate test.

"It is easy to die when one does not die alone."[47] If Malraux really intended to say something that his own view of

---

[47] *La condition humaine* (Paris, 1933), translated by Haakon M. Chevalier as *Man's Fate* (New York, 1934), p. 323.

man flatly contradicted, he meant it in the sense that comradeship alone might make the thought of death bearable.
For him, as for Saint-Exupéry, male friendships illumined and
justified the life of action he had freely chosen. But in Malraux's case the cult of comradeship was not restricted to an
elite of the daring. As one novel of adventure followed another, their cast of characters grew and their range of sympathy broadened. And by the same process the theme of
fraternity began to take over from a gratuitous defiance
of death. Malraux's most celebrated scenes were depictions of
the human solidarity forged in extreme situations—a group of
revolutionists awaiting their turn for execution at the end
of *Man's Fate*; peasants bearing down a mountainside on
stretchers the wounded aviators of *Man's Hope*; German
soldiers carrying on their backs to safety the Russian
"enemies" felled by their own gas attack, which was the
central episode of *The Walnut Trees of Altenburg*.[48] If Malraux became a semi-professional revolutionary and for more
than a decade worked in alliance with the Communist party,
it was not through any theoretical allegiance to the doctrine
of Marx: it was because the Communists seemed to offer the
most potent contemporary manifestation of the longing for
human fraternity.

One last comparison with Saint-Exupéry may suggest how
Malraux deepened and intellectualized the fictional material
that in the former's writing had remained no more than a
sequence of evocations. For Saint-Exupéry residence in exotic
places—and in particular his relationships with Moslems—
had prompted ethical relativism and a tolerance for behavior
which the West condemned as inhumane. This was a response that by the 1930's had become classic among educated
Europeans who had lived in Asia or Africa. Malraux readily
understood all that. But he was more concerned about the
intellectual effect—the cultural shock—which hit Europeans
when they realized that their own values depended on a sense
of history which was unique to their culture and which barred
them from the idea-world of the timeless cultures of the East.

[48] Joseph Hoffmann, *L'humanisme de Malraux* (Paris, 1963), p. 221.

The notion of cultural plurality that the anthropologists had introduced was spreading rapidly in the 1920's; everywhere it met resistance of varying intensity. But the French were perhaps the least ready to accept the idea of giving equal dignity to value systems radically different from their own: in the role they had assumed as custodians of the classic and humanist tradition for the entire West, they could not fail to react on this front also with a prickly defensiveness.

Here the attitude of the young Malraux was in notable contrast to that of most of his countrymen. He opted neither for cultural conservatism nor for a relativist irony or despair. His earliest essay—*The Temptation of the West*, published in 1926—was cast in the form of an exchange of philosophical letters between an Asian and a European. A decade and a half later, in *The Walnut Trees of Altenburg*, he gave eloquent expression to his personal reckoning with the theories of Oswald Spengler. Finally, in his studies of the fine arts, the "imaginary museum" he held before his reader's eyes was an effort to show that despite the diversity he recognized and valued, the masterpieces of painting and sculpture from all continents and ages could respond one to another and thereby re-establish a unified notion of mankind.[49]

Malraux lived contemporary history, both in the Far East and at home, not so much for the sake of the "surf" itself, as in an effort to dominate it by absorbing it into his own consciousness. Hence the paradox which threw so many of his readers off the track. If his novels were some of the bloodiest and most frenetic that the interwar years produced, they were also among the most cerebral. Nearly all their leading characters were intellectuals quite prepared to take time out from a scene of battle to speculate on the human condition.[50] From one of these conversations there emerged the clearest single formulation of what Malraux himself was

[49] *Ibid.*, pp. 60–61, 64–66.
[50] On this whole subject, see Victor Brombert, *The Intellectual Hero: Studies in the French Novel 1880–1955* (Philadelphia and New York, 1961), pp. 169–174.

after—and, significantly enough, from the lips of a historian of art: "To transform into consciousness as wide an experience as possible."[51] Exotic adventure, revolution, the defiance of death—these opened avenues to understanding, but they were not the main business at hand. This was to become fully conscious of what man was, and in the end the lessons of a life of action paled before what the monuments of man's art could teach.

Once again, if his readers had followed with sufficient care the deeper-running concerns that underlay the ideological surface of Malraux's novels, they would not have been surprised by his rupture with Communism. This "apostasy" was "slow, subterranean and imperceptible to all but the closest observers."[52] Malraux had never submitted to the confining discipline of party membership. But in the mid-1920's he had worked with Communist revolutionaries in China; in the early thirties he had stood side by side with Gide among France's leading literary fellow travelers as the French Communist party moved toward the Popular Front; in the Spanish Civil War he had accepted Stalinist direction as the only force efficient enough to hold at bay the intervention of the fascist powers. Yet this necessity had troubled him profoundly: in *Man's Hope* he exposed his own emotional struggle between the iron demands of wartime and his moral revulsion at Communist ruthlessness. It is possible that the Spanish Civil War, with the imperative call it made on Malraux's organizing energies, merely delayed a rupture which was already in the making. Sometime after 1938—perhaps in the wake of the Nazi-Soviet Pact—Malraux broke with Communism entirely.

Had Malraux been killed in the campaign of 1940, he would have remained a hero to the French Left, and to

[51] *L'espoir* (Paris, 1937), translated by Stuart Gilbert and Alastair Macdonald as *Man's Hope* (New York, 1938), p. 396. I have altered the translation.

[52] David Caute, *Communism and the French Intellectuals 1914–1960* (New York, 1964), p. 242.

Catholics the "despairing soul," the activist for his own sport, that Gabriel Marcel called him.[53] The image the more conservative public had of him was of an adventurer who was also something of a poseur and whose heroes—as his most famous phrase had it—wanted to put a "scar on the map." During the years of occupation and liberation, a new Malraux began to emerge. In terms of ideology, he had apparently made a volte-face; he had become a strenuous Gaullist—although the incompatibility between his earlier and his later allegiance was at first obscured by the fact that the Communists were cooperating with De Gaulle's provisional government. In terms of aesthetics, he was turning from fiction to the discussion of art, and his tendency to philosophize was growing more pronounced. Even his style was changing: what in his earlier novels had been staccato, nervous, overcharged, by *The Walnut Trees of Altenburg* had become cleaner and more static.

If this, his last, truncated novel (the Gestapo had carried off two thirds of it) most clearly marked the turning point, traces of a new evaluation of humanity had already been apparent in Malraux's novels of the 1930's. The revolutionists of *Man's Fate* were more fully presented than those of *The Conquerors*, and in this second work in a Chinese setting the struggle for human dignity replaced the theme of revolution for its own sake or as a test of man's courage. Still more pronouncedly in *Man's Hope*, the agony of an entire people was now what concerned the author most: the doings of extraordinary individuals were still in the foreground, but the Spanish peasants and workers were also visible, as opposed to the ordinary Chinese whose presence in the earlier novels had been insignificant. The autobiographical origin of this difference seems clear enough: Malraux's experience with Chinese Communism in the 1920's had been in great part play-acting; in Spain it was very real and very close to home. And along with this new feeling for human actuality had come the chastening effect of learning how revolutionists be-

[53] Quoted in Simon, *L'homme en procès*, p. 36.

haved when they were in power. If Malraux had ever subscribed to Marxism at all, it had been in the sense of a
generous vision, as the ethical myth into which Georges Sorel
had redefined it. When the vision became brutal reality,
the myth collapsed.[54]

Unfortunately, however, this ethical progression damaged
the quality of Malraux's novels. As his sympathies broadened,
his literary grasp grew less sure. *Man's Fate*, published in
1933, marked a point of optimum development between the
crudities of his earlier work and the aesthetic difficulties that
arose later on. In 1937, when *Man's Hope* appeared, the de-
terioration was already apparent: despite its majestic sweep
and the occasional glory of its set pieces, it was sprawling,
talky, and overcrowded with characters, with much of it so
close to the vocabulary of journalism and propaganda as to
be incomprehensible today. *The Walnut Trees of Altenburg*,
which was published in Switzerland in 1943, suffered from an
opposite set of defects: while its style had been notably disciplined, its plot was indiscernible, and the series of episodes
which constituted it were only tenuously related one to another. Its eccentricities suggested that what Malraux now
wanted to say no longer fitted the form of the novel.

For all its aesthetic faults, *The Walnut Trees of Altenburg* was in an intellectual sense the most interesting and
significant thing Malraux ever wrote. A fragmentary account
of the careers of an Alsatian father and son called Berger—
which was the name the author himself adopted as a Resistance leader—it was organized as a triptych within a triptych. The two outer panels told of the younger Berger's
tank service and his capture by the Germans in the campaign
of 1940. The central panel (set a generation earlier) dealt
with his father and was itself divided into three free-standing
episodes—the elder Berger's career of adventure as a Near
Eastern specialist in the service of the Young Turk leader
Enver Pasha; his attendance on his return to Europe at a
gathering of intellectuals in a medieval abbey, the Altenburg,
sponsored by his scholar uncle; finally, as an officer serving

[54] Hoffmann, *L'humanisme de Malraux*, pp. 212–213, 244.

in the German Army on the Eastern Front, his witnessing the gas attack already mentioned which was to turn into a manifestation of human fraternity across the barriers of national enmity. That Malraux should have written such a novel at all was remarkable enough. That it should have been almost totally free from anti-German feeling or ideological passion was more noteworthy still.

In Malraux's account both the elder and the younger Berger were seeking what was basic to human beings below their merely individual characteristics or their role as participants in "militant mobs": they wanted to discover what men were like when stripped of their cultural and ideological raiment. The father never quite found the answer: in the colloquy at the Altenburg he had replied with spirit to the Spengler-figure—or rather, the character modeled on Spengler's own guide to speculative anthropology, Leo Frobenius—who had argued that it was impossible to generalize about humanity; the elder Berger had held that under the cultural differences which were all that intellectuals were equipped to notice, there could be found something "fundamental" that made mankind one. He had not lived to complete this understanding—although the response of the German soldiers to the agony of the Russians facing them had given him the clue to what he was after. It was left for his son, in another world war and in the euphoria of escape from death, to learn at dawn, in the peace of a nearly deserted village and from the smile of an old peasant woman, the primeval joy in life that gave it meaning:

Let the mystery of man . . . emerge from that enigmatic smile. . . .

I now know the meaning of the ancient myths about the living snatched from the dead. I can scarcely remember what fear is like; what I carry within me is the discovery of a simple, sacred secret.

Thus, perhaps, did God look on the first man . . .[55]

[55] *Les noyers de l'Altenburg,* French edition (Paris, 1948), translated by A W. Fielding as *The Walnut Trees of Altenburg* (London, 1952), pp. 23–24, 110, 224.

The greatest mystery is not that we have been flung at random between the profusion of the earth and the galaxy of the stars, but that in this prison we can fashion images . . . sufficiently powerful to deny our nothingness.

Thus Walter Berger, the great-uncle of the narrator and the host of the Altenburg, recalled what he had learned more than twenty years before in helping to bring back from Italy his friend Nietzsche, stricken with madness, who in the darkness of the St. Gothard tunnel had suddenly burst into sublime song—a song "as strong as life itself."[56] Nietzsche's inspired singing had seemed to cancel out his own insanity and degradation; such, Malraux concluded, had been the power of all great art since man first began to fashion images in stone or clay. After 1945, laden with glory and weary of adventure, he no longer sought in action the key to the knowledge of man: he looked for it in the masterpieces of art. The fictional colloquy at the Altenburg marked the transition.

Here the author had enlarged the vision of fraternity that had possessed him since the writing of *Man's Fate* into an even more sweeping aspiration toward the "humanization of the world."[57] To elucidate this process was the underlying purpose of his postwar volumes on the fine arts. And similarly he was back to his old problem of cultural pluralism. "We sense every great style," he specified, "as the symbol of a fundamental relationship of man with the universe, of a civilization with the value it holds to be supreme." Each one spoke to the others with an equal dignity and timelessness. The imaginary museum that it was now possible to put together from photographs of the art of all civilizations and all eras gave mankind a mirror for self-knowledge it had never before possessed. Perhaps it would not yet be possible to discover the "fundamental" which bound men together—

[56] *Ibid.*, pp. 72–74.
[57] *Ibid.*, p. 97.

but at least the search could begin. The old museums of Europe's capital cities had been "affirmations" of the aesthetic standards of a single culture. The new imaginary museum would be a cosmic "interrogation."[58]

Once again, however, Malraux's endeavor proved too great for the literary means at his disposal. Although his essays on art were splendid in conception, they were endlessly repetitive, and their style was clotted and portentous, elliptical and frequently obscure. Nor did he present his argument in an intellectually convincing form. His comments on the parallels and interactions among works of art were not the carefully-studied comparisons that the specialists would make but rather his own arbitrary reaction to his aesthetic experiences. He offered peremptory assertions, which the reader might accept or deny, but with which it was hard to engage in fruitful discussion. Such had always been Malraux's weakness. His writings overflowed with ideas: he displayed his cultural wares with the naïveté of a collegian anxious to receive full value from everything he has learned. Yet these ideas bore no clear relation to one another: they jostled each other on the page. Nobody denied that Malraux had a brilliant mind—but brilliance was a commodity of which his countrymen had never suffered a shortage. In his last and most ambitious incarnation—the one in which he tried to pull all his earlier interests together into a celebration of art as the redemption of humanity—Malraux remained a prestidigitator.[59]

However he strove to define a twentieth-century conception of man—however he reiterated the assertions on the far side of despair that he called his "tragic humanism"—his

[58] *Le musée imaginaire* (Paris, 1965), pp. 161–162. This is the third version of Malraux's initial book in his series on the fine arts. The first version was published in Geneva in 1947. The second formed Part I of *Les voix du silence* (Paris, 1951), translated by Stuart Gilbert as *The Voices of Silence* (New York, 1953).

[59] See Claude-Edmonde Magny, "Malraux le fascinateur," *Esprit*, XVI (October 1948), translated by Beth Archer for *Malraux: A Collection of Critical Essays*, edited by R. W. B. Lewis (Englewood Cliffs, N.J., 1964), pp. 125–127.

prose remained abstract and his creative world a solitude. In Malraux's universe women found little place and children none, while ordinary people figured as metaphysical symbols; his belated discovery of common humanity never became flesh and blood.

After the Second World War, despite his change of political allegiance, Malraux was honored as the great precursor of the novel of engagement and the literature of existentialism. After 1958, he served as France's official purveyor of culture. But the esteem he enjoyed was one of isolation, and his addresses to his countrymen became cloudier as he settled into his role of enchanter laureate. The old Malraux of death-defying heroism had been left far behind.

v. *Charles de Gaulle and the Epic as History*

With Charles de Gaulle we return to the generation of Bernanos—indeed the latter was one of the remarkable pupils whom the General's father had taught. Born in 1890, De Gaulle was a classic example of the patriotic young Frenchmen who came of age after 1905. Nourished on the literary imagery of Bergson, Barrès, and Péguy, yearning to find in action an outlet for his impassioned love of country, he entered the First World War with the fervor characteristic of his contemporaries—and survived. He survived, moreover, emotionally intact: his was not the profoundly wounded postwar existence of a Martin du Gard or a Bernanos. Like them, De Gaulle carried about within him the ineradicable sadness which the years in the trenches had instilled. But it was far from being a sadness of resignation. From his first day under fire—from his sudden horrified awareness that courage alone could not stand up to shells and machine-gun bullets—he had known that something was wrong with the way his generation had been prepared for combat. And after the war was over, unlike his fellow survivors who settled into lives of routine and forgetfulness, he resolved to think through the new methods of warfare that would spare his country another invasion and another sacrifice of its youth.

This search led him to the technique of armored warfare and the world of the machine—to the world of Saint-Exupéry. Despite the archaisms of his historical vision and his literary style, De Gaulle educated himself to be a modern man. And his long years of frustration reserved his energies for the future and made him seem younger than he actually was. A few months short of fifty in June 1940 when he assumed his role as national savior, he was sixty-seven when he returned to power—and the France he was to govern thenceforth was the new France of the twentieth century's third quarter. To the historian of social ideas De Gaulle bridges the gap between the generation of the First World War and the one which fought the Second, as his career links literature and the life of action.

Already the young De Gaulle was more sérieux about his patriotism than the run of his contemporaries. There was depth and independence to what he believed beyond a merely conventional respect for tradition. De Gaulle's religious life has remained a mystery: all that is certain is that he was a practicing Catholic; but his respect for Maritain suggests a concern for intellectual definition and the social teachings of the contemporary Church. His family sprang from the north of France—the countryside of Bernanos and of Malraux's ancestors—dignified people, part noble and part bourgeois, their northern gravity now and then enlivened by a streak of fantasy. Charles de Gaulle's grandmother had been a writer and editor, and his father was a teacher with a verve that made a lasting impression on the boys of good Catholic family who were his pupils. The elder De Gaulle's notion of French history was chivalric in the extreme; but he broke sufficiently with the prejudices of his milieu to allow himself to be convinced of the innocence of Captain Dreyfus. A half century later his son emerged as the one Frenchman who could hope to close the emotional fissure in French society that the Affair had left behind it.[60]

Charles de Gaulle celebrated no cult of death. Yet in the First World War he risked his life repeatedly, and it is unlikely that this model officer would have survived the conflict had it not been for the lucky accident that handed him, wounded and unconscious, into German captivity. There was also a fortunate symbolism in where he fell, at the supreme moment of the Battle of Verdun, in the defense of Fort Douaumont. In retrospect, the initial stages of De Gaulle's career seemed appropriately devised for the role ahead.

In the interwar years, however, little of this future was apparent. When in the early 1930's he wrote in the tones of a Vigny of the severe consolations of the professional military life, when he offered his self-portrait as a natural leader of men, steeling himself against career disappointments by cultivating his own ideas in the "secrecy" of his inner life, when he assured his readers that the sword was the "axis of the world," few among his countrymen were prepared to listen.[61] "No voice could seem stranger, more anachronistic than that of this austere, somewhat Jansenist young officer, whose historical pessimism refused to put up with the intellectual slackness that surrounded him. He who saw History as a perpetual and tragic confrontation of nations, how could he fail to feel the bitter joy of a solitary thinker?"[62] There was also something anachronistic in De Gaulle's fidelity to the teaching of Bergson, whom he cited repeatedly in his first book on military strategy. By the time his second such work, *The Army of the Future*, appeared, heroism was coming back into fashion. But it was a heroic ideal that required an exotic setting, or at the very least the stimulus of ideology. De Gaulle's particular combination of an old-fashioned military ethic with a modern technique of warfare cut

[60] On De Gaulle's youth and family background, see Paul-Marie de la Gorce, *De Gaulle entre deux mondes* (Paris, 1964), pp. 8–29, 40.
[61] *Vers l'armée de métier* (Paris, 1934), translated as *The Army of the Future* (London, n.d.), pp. 153, 158.
[62] La Gorce, *De Gaulle entre deux mondes*, p. 60.

across too many entrenched prejudices. The very fact that it was precisely what France required seemed to condemn it to neglect.

Nineteen-forty changed all that. The defeat of his own country had given De Gaulle the somber satisfaction of being proved right. In similar fashion the wager on the future which he offered from London had within three years established itself as the course that combined patriotic devotion with common sense. One by one his country's intellectual spokesmen rallied to his cause. Bloch worked for the Resistance; Maritain and Bernanos sent in their adherence from overseas; Saint-Exupéry overcame his hesitations when he heard De Gaulle speak in Algiers in the winter of 1943-1944; Malraux found his "ideal-type" hero, "made real but enlarged," the hero of "active intelligence, . . . combining mind and will."[63] The unattainable epic had become history.

But in order to fulfill their historic function great deeds must be celebrated. De Gaulle's conviction, dating back to before the First World War, that he would one day perform a service which would be "noted" by his countrymen—a conviction expressed in the very first paragraphs of his memoirs —made it inevitable that he would write those memoirs. Among the national leaders in the second war De Gaulle alone wrote a set of recollections which also rank as literature. Even Churchill's are not comparable to them. For, as the General himself remarked, the British statesman put his memoirs together in piecemeal fashion with the help of a team of researchers; his own were "composed" all by himself, with careful attention to conciseness of thought and to the balance of phrase and structure.

When the first volume appeared in 1954, France's senior historian recognized a kindred mind. Lucien Febvre found in De Gaulle's writing a tone of orgueil—of haughtiness in its old and worthy sense of holding the head high. Greeting the General as a poet, Febvre declared that the author of the

[63] David Wilkinson, "Malraux, Revolutionist and Minister," *Journal of Contemporary History*, I, No. 2 (1966), p. 49.

memoirs had "rediscovered, recreated" the "harmony . . .
of the purest French style."[64] Such might be the verdict of
most older readers. But the younger generation could not
refrain from a smile at the seventeenth-century turns of
phrase, the studied figures of speech, with which De Gaulle
had adorned his account. Even the soldier-historian had not
shed the trappings of an inherited rhetoric.

There was also in the memoirs a curious quality of optical
illusion. Begun in the quiet of De Gaulle's retirement from
politics after 1953, they were not completed until he was
back in power. Yet the aesthetics of their composition demanded that they close on an elegiac note of "bitter serenity."
"The end of an enterprise, the end of an epoch, the end of a
life"—everything returned to the "great adventure of the
war," and the memoirs themselves were cast in the form
of a "monument . . . to the glory of that privileged era."[65]
So, as inevitably as he had begun, De Gaulle was obliged to
finish with a picture of himself patiently waiting in his
garden at Colombey-les-Deux-Eglises:

> Old Earth, worn by the ages, wracked by rain and
> storm, exhausted yet ever ready to produce what life
> must have to go on!
> Old France, weighed down with history, prostrated
> by wars and revolutions, endlessly vacillating from great-
> ness to decline, but revived, century after century, by the
> genius of renewal!
> Old man, exhausted by ordeal, detached from human
> deeds, feeling the approach of the eternal cold, but
> always watching in the shadows for the gleam of hope.[66]

[64] "Psychologie de chef: Charles de Gaulle et ses mémoires," *Annales*, X (July-September 1955), 375–377.
[65] La Gorce, *De Gaulle entre deux mondes*, p. 516.
[66] *Mémoires de guerre*, III: *Le salut 1944–1946* (Paris, 1959), translated by Richard Howard as *The War Memoirs of Charles de Gaulle*,
III: *Salvation 1944–1946* (New York, 1960), p. 330.

5

The Marriage
of Phenomenology and Marxism

THE DEFIANCE OF DEATH, the imprint of one's passage through history by the recording of lofty deeds—these were not the only manifestations of the heroic ideal in the years of war, occupation, and Resistance. There was also the thirst for social justice. As the war went on and the rigors of Nazi rule deepened, the forces opposing it drew closer together and became more conscious of the moral goals they had in common. As the moment of France's liberation approached, the question of how new this new France would be took on a bitter urgency. Under the menace of deportation, torture, or summary execution, the activists of the Resistance began to cross the barriers that had separated class from class; sharing similar fears and hardships, they talked of a republic which would at last make real the word "fraternity" that had figured so long and so platonically in the national motto —a republic "pure et dure," honest and compassionate, but implacable toward traitors and the exploiters of the poor.

Thus regarded, the Resistance ranked along with the Dreyfus Case and the First World War as the third great spiritual revolution which the French had traversed in a half century. And like its two predecessors, the experience disappointed those who had hoped that the nation as a whole would be transfigured by it. Quite predictably its effect was restricted to an elite drawn in disproportionate numbers from intellectuals and militants of the working class. On these, however—and more particularly on intellectuals—its effect was decisive; like the Dreyfus Case two generations earlier, the Resistance provided a criterion of reference, the base point from which to judge past and future. Under this kind of scrutiny, the ideologies of the Right collapsed, and with them the verbal elegance that their leading spokesmen had cultivated. In the perspective of the Resistance, such refinements had a suspicious ring: they seemed calculated to obscure with polite turns of phrase a world of misery and social strife. The writing that emerged from the Resistance tried to mirror in all its crudeness and horror a human reality which the sufferings of war had disclosed.

For at least a half decade after the war's end, the writers who had been résistants dominated the literary and philosophical landscape. In their minds and in the minds of their followers, an anti-fascist record alone counted; the parallel and contemporaneous experience of service at Vichy had best be forgotten as a shameful hiatus in the nation's history. In such circumstances fair-mindedness could hardly be expected. Yet to lump together as unprincipled reactionaries *all* the intellectuals who had rallied to Marshal Pétain was to refuse to understand the special kind of self-abnegation which had led a minority of men of good will to serve a cause that in the end brought them only disrepute. At Vichy there was a little of everything, even of Socialism in its pacifist guise. More especially in the period in which the Marshal had enjoyed a quasi-independence from German control—the beginning of 1941 to the spring of 1942—there had flourished a style of corporative or technocratic thinking which was to be revived (and in part vindicated) with the advent of the Fifth Republic sixteen years later. None of such theorizing, however, occupies a very large place in the history of French social thought: it was neither notably original nor of major influence on public policy. The most charitable judges of Vichy's would-be reformers have characterized them as a heterogeneous collection of malcontents, united only by a conviction that parliamentary democracy was the root of all evil, and condemned by internecine discord to inefficacy and historical neglect.[1]

Yet the apparent triumph of the Resistance way of thought was also the source of its undoing. In France, the memory of the Resistance was celebrated at least as intensively as elsewhere on the Western European continent; it became a cult, a social myth in the style of Georges Sorel, whose majestic features would be tarnished by confrontation with subsequent reality. Out of the Resistance, directly or indirectly, came nearly every "advanced" social movement or current of ideas that stirred French opinion from the end of the war to the mid-1950's. Within the confines of the intellectual avant-garde, its victory shielded it from self-criticism and from an examination of the assumptions on which that victory had been based. So once again provincialism threatened: a self-righteous rigidity settled on the veterans of the Resistance as they became aware of a growing incomprehension and hostility among their fellow citizens or their intellectual counterparts abroad. The result was renewed isolation: the curious combination of neo-Marxism and phenomenological abstraction that set the tone for post-Resistance social thought was eventually to figure as at once the last, the most eccentric, and the most influential of the moral explorations on which the French intellectuals had embarked over the course of a crowded generation.

I. The Intellectual Legacy of the Resistance

The pride of the Resistance can only be understood in terms of the humiliation that had gone before. The collapse of 1940

[1] See Robert Aron, *Histoire de Vichy 1940–1944* (Paris, 1954), translated (in slightly abridged form) by Humphrey Hare as *The Vichy Regime 1940–44* (London, 1958), pp. 145–158; Stanley Hoffmann, "Aspects du régime de Vichy," *Revue française de science politique*, VI (January-March 1956), 46–48; René Rémond, *La droite en France de 1815 à nos jours* (Paris, 1954), pp. 227–230. Compare the more severe judgment in Henri Michel's authoritative *Vichy: année 40* (Paris, 1966).

was without precedent: not even in 1870 had the national self-esteem been so cruelly wounded. Marc Bloch's *Strange Defeat* tried to explain it in terms of a failure of nerve and technical imagination on the part of France's governing classes. André Malraux's *The Walnut Trees of Altenburg* similarly depicted the moral disarray of the crowds of leaderless soldiers whom the Germans had gathered in as prisoners, an account echoed in harsher detail in the third volume of his *Roads to Freedom* that Jean-Paul Sartre published in 1949. Such was the verdict of the résistant writers: France's old elite had abdicated through a failure to live up to its public responsibilities.

It was only gradually, however, that the militants of the Resistance began to think of themselves as an alternative elite. Initially the mood was one of elegy and meditation, of reserving one's energies for an uncertain future. Thus André Chamson, who was subsequently to emerge as a maquisard major, reflected in the treacherous quiet that followed the defeat:

> I hate this silence that servitude imposes on us, but to-day it alone can shelter the truth. We must bear our country's misfortunes as our own private sorrows, . . . in the silence of our meditations. . . . The drama of France has thus become, as it were, a personal drama which each of us carries about within himself, according to his merit and his strength. But the meditation of a people that wants to rediscover its greatness cannot forever remain silent. It needs a thousand voices to attain . . . the conviction of a liberation to come. I hope that these voices will be prepared in this same silence. . . .
>
> To live only in the spirit, yet in fidelity, in memory, and in hope—that is still to serve. . . . My sole purpose is to maintain within me the potential for a greatness that lies beyond me, and to be ready to fulfill what the future may bring.[2]

[2] *Ecrit en 1940* . . . (Paris, 1940), pp. 10, 18.

Less than four years later, the same Chamson reported to the headquarters of his former commanding officer, General de Lattre de Tassigny, now once more in France at the head of the army that was liberating the South. The Resistance major had been ordered to bring back with him the irregular troops he had collected in the region of the Dordogne. On the way he had encountered another writer turned guerrilla chief, and they had merged their forces. De Lattre was curious as to the identity of this new Resistance commander: the name "Colonel Berger" meant nothing to him. "There is no Colonel Berger," he objected, "in the French Army." "But there is an . . . André Malraux in French literature," Chamson answered triumphantly.[3] Thus began the last of Malraux's adventures in the pursuit of his heroic ideal.

Those such as Chamson and Malraux who had enrolled for active military service, first in the irregular formations of the maquis and after the summer of 1944 in De Lattre's liberating army, had neither time nor inclination for the ideological writing that was to give the Resistance its characteristic stamp. The task of clarifying the objectives for the future devolved on the editors of clandestine newspapers and on a handful of older men whose appeals circulated surreptitiously among the résistants. For Catholics the work of Bernanos and Maritain enjoyed a prestige compounded of moral sympathy and literary esteem; the latter in particular became a spiritual adviser *in partibus* to young men and women who were interpreting their faith in terms of an active social mission. Similar injunctions could be found in the personalist message of Emmanuel Mounier.[4] This kind of teaching met in mid-course the new tendencies that the Socialists were expressing. For like the Catholics, the Socialists in the Resistance were shedding their political dogmatism and their

[3] Robert Aron, *Histoire de la libération de la France* (Paris, 1959), pp. 666–668. This passage appears neither in the English nor in the American translation of Aron's book.

[4] Henri Michel, *Les courants de pensée de la Résistance* (Paris, 1962), pp. 151n., 387.

distrust of those whom the ideological quarrels of the past
had relegated to the opposite side of an invisible barricade.
From the prison in which the Marshal's government had confined him, Léon Blum had given his followers the cue. The
critique of his own and his party's conduct that he composed
in 1941 offered friendship to the Catholics and all others
among his countrymen who shared Socialism's humanist
goals. For the future Blum envisaged that his own party
would dissolve itself into a wider grouping in which Marxist
doctrine would be virtually forgotten.[5]

Two months after he had completed his ideological examination of conscience, Blum was brought to trial. With his
own thoughts clarified, he felt free to turn the tables on his
accusers. Blum's defense at Riom combined logic with passion, and personal charm with polemical dexterity: summoned to answer for the defeat of his country, he transformed
the proceedings into a rehabilitation of French democracy.
Even those who had opposed Blum when he headed the Popular Front government of 1936 could not refrain from admiring the bravery of a frail and elderly statesman whose religious
origin exposed him to particular dangers: once more, as in
the case of Captain Dreyfus, a Jew was on trial, and once
more he had justice on his side.[6] The text of Blum's defense
joined the writings of Maritain among the corpus of clandestine documents that gave courage to the Resistance.

However exalted their tone, older men such as these
offered counsels of moderation. Of necessity they clashed with
the more activist policy which the Communists espoused.
The latter were proud of their role as the "parti des fusillés"
—the party whose militants suffered the greatest losses because they took the greatest risks. As the liberation drew near,
the strength and prestige of the Communists grew steadily.

[5] A *l'échelle humaine*, *L'oeuvre de Léon Blum*, V (Paris, 1955),
translated by W. Pickles as *For All Mankind* (London, 1946), pp.
136–138.
[6] See the spirited description in Joel Colton, *Léon Blum: Humanist
in Politics* (New York, 1966), Chapter 15.

Jealous of their organizational independence, they kept their own formations only loosely linked to the rest of the Resistance and to De Gaulle's provisional government in Algiers. Some intellectuals found these tactics annoying; a larger number were willing to give the Communists the benefit of the doubt. Even Bernanos argued that the popularity of Communism was due to a moral default on the part of those who were supposed to stand for spiritual values: people had "become Communists in the same way as the young priests and the young French nobles of the eighteenth century were enraptured with *The Social Contract* and Jean-Jacques Rousseau." The best way to check the spread of Communism, a number of Resistance writers agreed, was "to go beyond it" by offering an ideal that would have an even greater moral appeal. The goal should be to build alongside Communism "a social edifice as revolutionary as its own, but fraternal and authentically French."[7]

Inspired by similar considerations, many of France's leading men of letters were willing to associate themselves for a time with the Communist-led Comité National des Ecrivains, which proved the most successful of the front organizations that Communism launched during the Resistance years.[8] Some apparently joined because they were unaware of the committee's ideological guidance; others agreed to affiliate because they knew of no competing group that covered so wide an intellectual spectrum. The case of Jean-Paul Sartre is instructive: as early as 1941 he had tried to form his own circle of Resistance writers; lacking specific tasks and in the face of Communist hostility, the group had failed to make headway and had eventually been dissolved; three years later, when the Communists changed their tack and asked Sartre to join the committee they were launching, he was happy to

[7] Cited in Michel, *Pensée de la Résistance*, pp. 280–281.
[8] David Caute, *Communism and the French Intellectuals 1914–1960* (New York, 1964), pp. 150–152.

associate himself with people who gave some promise of efficient performance.[9]

Reinforcing the argument from effectiveness which was the Communists' most telling point, was the fact that the non-Communist writers were racked by self-doubt. The majority were sufficiently schooled in the examination of their own motives to realize that they were far from being heroes. For the most part they continued to lead lives in which danger and sacrifice had only a small place. As Merleau-Ponty recalled this era:

> How many heroes are there among the men who today take pride in . . . having resisted? Some were civil servants and continued to draw their salary, swearing in writing—since they had to—that they were neither Jews nor Masons. Others . . . agreed to seek authorization for what they wrote or staged from a censorship which let nothing pass which did not serve its purpose. Each in his own way marked out the frontier of the permissible. "Don't publish anything," said one. "Don't publish anything in the newspapers or magazines," said another. "Just publish your books." And a third said, "I will let this theater have my play if the director is a good man, but if he is a servant of the government, I will withdraw it." The truth is that each of them settled with outward necessity, all except a few who gave their lives.[10]

The result was a settled conviction of ethical ambiguity. In the poisoned atmosphere of German occupation, the Communists alone seemed sure of their course. Risking more and more certain of their ideological goals, they enjoyed a clearer conscience. The lack of self-assurance which so many non-

[9] On this sequence of events see the second volume of Simone de Beauvoir's memoirs, *La force de l'âge* (Paris, 1960), translated by Peter Green as *The Prime of Life* (Cleveland and New York, 1962), pp. 382–383, 396–397, 424–425.
[10] "La guerre a eu lieu" (originally published in June 1945), *Sens et non-sens* (Paris, 1948), translated by Hubert L. Dreyfus and Patricia Allen Dreyfus as *Sense and Non-Sense* (Evanston, Ill., 1964), p. 146.

Communists felt vis-à-vis their Communist Resistance comrades may help explain the enormous reluctance to separate from them—amounting in some cases to a psychological impossibility—that such writers experienced after the inauguration of the Cold War.

For all the heroism and sacrifice that went into it, the social thought of the Resistance lacked specific content. Most of the time, it did not go beyond a reiteration of the principles of fraternity, moral regeneration, and the transcending of factional quarrels. The economic policy the Resistance writers advocated lay somewhere between a nondogmatic socialism and the techniques of the welfare state; in this sphere alone their thought left a visible trace on official practice in the postwar years. Elsewhere the social doctrine of the Resistance was more a state of mind—a mystique—than a tangible program.

To find the permanent legacy of the Resistance in French intellectual life, one has to look rather at its effect on ideological or philosophical tendencies which were already present in the prewar years. Here the wartime experience emphasized or gave prominence to earlier attitudes that now took on a new relevance. Such was particularly the case with social Catholicism, Marxism, and the complex of philosophical teachings that came to be known as existentialism.

The comradeship of the Resistance notably reinforced the leftward course of French Catholic thought. And it added to this tendency a tolerant understanding of Marxism which had earlier been restricted to the circle around Emmanuel Mounier. In the wake of the liberation, Mounier's review *Esprit* emerged from its prewar isolation: its following among Catholics increased; non-Catholics read it with a new sympathy. Indeed there began to appear an ecumenicism of the Left, what hostile critics called a new bien-pensant attitude, a conformism of shared ideological assumptions. Thus Jean Lacroix, an associate of Mounier, could write in terms of a friendly three-way exchange among Marxism, existentialism, and Catholic personalism. And in comparing the three, he treated Marxism with comradely respect: he took the tortuous reasoning of the Leninists at its face value; he stressed in the Marxist canon the principles most congenial to the religiously inclined—its ethical definition of the class struggle, its hatred of disorder, its conviction of the dignity of labor, and its unremitting endeavor to "humanize" the raw material which nature offered. The proper course for those outside the Marxian fold, Lacroix concluded, was not "to refute Marxism" but "to ask that it recognize" the transcendent element in human history "without which its own basic intention could not be accomplished."[11]

Although Léon Blum might be ready to dismiss the Marxian teachings as useless and outmoded, his attitude was not shared by most intellectuals of the Left. To Blum and the older generation Marxism brought back distasteful memories of sectarian quarrels with the Communist party. To the younger generation it was a new intellectual experience, whose inspirational virtues they had learned at first hand during the Resistance years. Marxism in France was preponderantly, though not exclusively, the ideological preserve of the Communists. These had interpreted the doctrine in varying fashion as the tactical requirements of the moment dictated. But the reading of Marx that had proved most rewarding was in terms of a patriotic tradition of strong popular authority—a tradition descending from Auguste Blanqui in the mid-nineteenth century and ultimately from the Jacobins of the Great Revolution. This interpretation had the advantage of being recognizably French.[12] And it coincided admirably with the combination of patriotic and ideological appeals that was the characteristic language of the Resistance. The Resistance gave Marxism in its idiosyncratic French form an intense topical relevance.

[11] *Marxisme, existentialisme, personnalisme: présence de l'éternité dans le temps* (Paris, 1949), pp. 15, 19, 26, 28–29, 47–48.
[12] George Lichtheim, *Marxism in Modern France* (New York, 1966), pp. 11, 17, 23.

As for the third member of the ideological panel—existentialism—its intellectual link with the Resistance was clearly delineated in its own literature. The existentialist emphasis on situations of moral extremity and on the need for personal commitment in ambiguous circumstances had already been present in the philosophy of Gabriel Marcel and in the novel of the 1930's; themes such as these had given the work of André Malraux its tone of anguished urgency. But what in Malraux had been the frenetic gamble of a band of adventurers, the clandestine struggle against the Nazi occupation had made the daily routine of thousands of men and women who had never thought of themselves as heroes. There was pungent irony in the fact that it took the experience of German rule to give living actuality to an austere and intellectually difficult pattern of thought which was itself an import from Germany.

Among the new bien-pensants of the Left, nostalgia for the Resistance dominated the first postwar decade. Along with it went a sense of overwhelming disappointment that the nation as a whole had failed to respond to the breath of change. After a few months of economic experiment—after the nationalization of public services and a vast extension of the social security system—France returned to the familiar procedures of middle-class parliamentary democracy. General de Gaulle relinquished his authority at the beginning of 1946; the quasi-dictatorship he had wielded as the residuary legatee of the Resistance came to an end in a collision with the old political parties. Sixteen months later De Gaulle's most formidable Resistance rivals—the Communists—were less ceremoniously evicted from the government. The Cold War had begun: for seven years the French were to live under American protection, with the threat of a third world conflict hanging over them and their economy precariously supported by aid from the United States.

Realistically considered, it was not surprising that the majority of the nation refused to follow the Resistance lead.

The latter, after all, had never been more than a devoted minority: most people, in common with the run of mankind throughout history, had adopted an attitude of attentisme—of wait-and-see. The final victory had proved the résistants right—but this did not necessarily endear them to the rest of their countrymen. Indeed, it was perhaps this historical vindication itself that made the veterans of the Resistance distasteful to their fellow citizens: the apathetic majority could not forgive the heroic minority for the air of moral superiority with which their triumph in 1944 and 1945 had endowed them. And such an air seemed doubly unjustified in view of the political incompetence so many of the résistants had displayed.

By 1947—or by 1950 at the very latest, when a bitter controversy erupted over forced labor in the Soviet Union and the Korean War broke out—the Resistance writers had irremediably split. A few, of whom Malraux was the shining example, followed De Gaulle in protest against the ineffectiveness of parliamentary government. A larger number, of whom Albert Camus was to become the most celebrated, adjusted more or less grudgingly to the rule of the political Center and to dependence on the United States. But the characteristic intellectuals of the Resistance-inspired Left opted neither for Gaullism nor for parliamentary democracy; they similarly tried to avoid a clear choice between East and West. Those who most punctiliously cherished the Resistance inheritance advocated a neutralist policy, which in practice leaned toward the Soviet Union, since its proponents refused to break their ties with the Communist writers and strenuously combated the governmental line of political moderation and Western solidarity. Such a stand could not fail to alienate the greater part of the intellectual community in Great Britain and the United States: as the 1950's opened, the French once more seemed to be retiring into cultural isolation.

Nineteen-fifty to 1953 were the years of most severe ideological tension. With the outbreak of the Korean War, it was not too farfetched to predict a Russian occupation of Western Europe, and many French writers asked themselves in desperation how they would behave in a situation whose ambiguity made that of the Second World War look childishly simple: their ideological sympathies inclined them toward the Soviet Union; their love of liberty and middle-class way of life bound them to the United States—and they certainly had no intention of becoming "collaborationists." At a later date such moral dilemmas were to sound ridiculous; at the time they were perfectly serious and responsible. Fortunately for the peace of mind of the French intellectuals, in early 1953 Stalin died; the following summer the war in Korea came to an end; and by the mid-1950's the beginnings of economic expansion and prosperity were already apparent. France in fact was over the worst of its postwar difficulties; the new society was on the way. But it took another seven or eight years to liquidate the inheritance of a generation of ideological strife: the intellectuals remained embattled until well into the 1960's.

In the middle years of the previous decade there had appeared two books which from radically contrasting standpoints summed up the ideological conflicts of the immediate postwar era. Simone de Beauvoir's *The Mandarins* and Raymond Aron's *The Opium of the Intellectuals* both dealt with the politics of the French literati—and more particularly with the attitude of the literary Left toward Marxism and the Soviet Union. Their authors had in common a self-confident rationalism, a taste for polemic, and a close acquaintance with Jean-Paul Sartre, whose activities, whether directly reported or in thinly disguised form, provided the central focus for both accounts.

The Mandarins, published in 1954, was an *apologia pro vita sua,* cast in the form of a novel, by Sartre's lifetime companion. As a work of art, it was disappointing—cumbersome, contrived, and repetitious. The intellectual exchange in its dialogue was frequently dazzling, but just as often wordy and self-conscious. *The Mandarins* succeeded most where it tried least—not as a novel, but as journalism of a high order, an imaginative rendering of a milieu that had been observed with both sympathy and penetration. As a portraiture of intellectuals in postwar France, it had no equal.

The comparison with traditional Chinese society its title implied had long been a staple in the game of cross-cultural comparisons—fine cooking, the cultivation of one's garden, a disabused philosophy of life: the elements of the parallel were thoroughly familiar. The stress in this case was on the similarity between the two societies in ascribing the supreme personal status to a self-perpetuating literary intelligentsia. But the ironic promise of the title was never fulfilled: Simone de Beauvoir reserved her humor for the rich and their hangers-on who stood outside the privileged circle. Within— toward the world of the mandarins themselves—her tone was one of muted respect. Indeed, the author herself apparently failed to realize the full force of a title which had been suggested at the last moment by a friend. The protagonists of her novel did not picture themselves as the heirs of an ancient cultural tradition: they figured in their own minds as revolutionaries of the pen.

Yet the subjects they discussed were those over which French intellectuals had been battling for two and a half centuries: the presumed general principles of mankind that found their embodiment in public ethics. And the manner of discussion was irreproachably Cartesian—that is, in terms of sharply defined opposites and lapidary formulations. Nor did Simone de Beauvoir question the validity of a type of abstract reasoning which could lead by apparently rigorous steps to the curious conclusion that the United States was about to "subjugate" the European continent. She never challenged the central assumptions of the leftward-oriented mandarinate among whom she lived. Her unremitting conversational exercises went on within a circle which was both personally and intellectually self-contained.

Hence the pedantic solemnity with which it took its most trivial doings—hence its conviction that what it had to say was of supreme importance for the rest of humanity. In the mental universe of *The Mandarins* there opened a widening gap between expectation and actuality: the aim was as universalist as ever, but in the particular circumstances of the postwar era its result was parochialism. Simone de Beauvoir's novel was at its best in depicting the pathos of French intellectuals cut off from their counterparts elsewhere in the Western world. In the early 1950's cultural communication was breaking down: to the British and Americans the French seemed unrepentantly doctrinaire and intellectualist —they themselves accused the "Anglo-Saxons" of slipping ever deeper into the quicksands of adaptability and empiricism. For Simone de Beauvoir the choice was clear: while giving her ideological opponents their due as men of good will striving for peace and justice according to their lights, her support of necessity went to a neutralist position tinged with philo-Communism.

Raymond Aron made the opposite choice. His Resistance credentials were as good as Simone de Beauvoir's—he had spent the war years as a Free French journalist in London— and his experience was considerably more cosmopolitan. In the early 1930's he had been the first of his generation of intellectuals to go to Germany for philosophical study: out of this experience he had produced two basic works which had introduced the French public to contemporary German sociology and to the neo-idealist philosophy of history.[13] In the following decade his long residence in Britain had given him fluency in English and a ready familiarity with Anglo-American thought. Sartre had been his friend at the Ecole Normale Supérieure; immediately after the liberation the two were once again closely associated. But by 1947 the Cold War

[13] *La sociologie allemande contemporaine* (Paris, 1936), translated from the second edition (1950) by Mary and Thomas Bottomore as *German Sociology* (Glencoe, Ill., 1957); *Introduction à la philosophie de l'histoire* (Paris, 1938), translated by George J. Irwin as *Introduction to the Philosophy of History* (Boston, 1961). For an over-all assessment of Aron as a political thinker, see Roy Pierce, *Contemporary French Political Thought* (London and New York, 1966), Chapter 8.

had driven them apart. Predictably enough, Aron sided with
the English and Americans. Still more, he cut his ties completely with the French Left, attacking as a dangerous
"mystification" the Marxist assumptions of his former friends.

At the very start of his *Opium of the Intellectuals*, published in 1955, Aron signaled his break with the ideological
"family" within which he had come to intellectual maturity;
under current conditions he questioned whether the terms
"Right" and "Left" any longer conveyed a clear meaning,
and he was quite sure that Marxism was having the soporific
effect on the French intellectuals which its creator had a century earlier attributed to religious faith among the masses. In
France—or perhaps better, in Paris—or still more narrowly,
in the neighborhood of Saint-Germain-des-Prés, where the
intellectuals of the Left had their headquarters—a shared
Marxist faith inspired a type of family quarrel that was incomprehensible across the Channel or the Atlantic: in Britain
or the United States people discussed Marx's sociology or
economics "without much passion, as . . . important works"
marking a certain stage "in the development of scientific
knowledge"; in France the same theories were treated as
gospel. More especially—and in Aron's view, most noxiously
—the result of such ideological bemusement was an "idolatry
of history." To the intellectuals of the Left, history had a goal
—the triumph of the proletariat; in its name the most revolt-
ing crimes could be pardoned or condoned; the vision of an
"inevitable future" had blunted the French critical sense and
turned abstract philosophers into "fanatics."[14]

Aron was on firm ground when he reproached his fellow
intellectuals with attributing to "history" a course and an
aim that ideological faith could descry. His own studies had
tried to bring his countrymen abreast of a critical philosophy
of history—German, Italian, or English in origin—which renounced such aspirations, relegating them to the realm of

[14] *L'opium des intellectuels* (Paris, 1955), translated by Terence
Kilmartin as *The Opium of the Intellectuals* (London, 1957), pp. xi,
57, 135, 156–157, 190.

poetic insight or moral uplift. Aron was also quite correct in suggesting that the French intellectuals, "accustomed to speaking for the whole of mankind, ambitious for a role on a planetary scale," were trying "to camouflage the provincialism of their controversies under the debris of the nineteenth-century philosophies of history"—in brief, that their attitude was a curious compound of "nostalgia for a universal idea" and "national pride." Yet in explaining why these intellectuals behaved as they did, he in effect found a justification for them. In the "frozen" state of French society, Aron surmised, France's writers could take little comfort from the external circumstances of life about them. Not until those circumstances became more "worthy of their ideal" would they be reconciled, like their counterparts in Britain and America, to the society in which they lived.[15]

But precisely this had been the point of disagreement all along. In the early 1950's, French society offered a discouraging prospect to anyone who yearned for social justice and human fraternity: the good things of life were still in short supply; the class struggle was very real. True, the signs of change were already apparent: at the very time that Aron and Simone de Beauvoir were writing, the great transformation was beginning. Yet few were able to discern it: in the opening years of the 1950's the most penetrating students of contemporary France were still describing its society in terms of stagnation;[16] even Aron, who had every reason to stress the change, referred only glancingly to the "forces of regeneration . . . ripening under the crust of conservatism." In the late 1940's and early 1950's, it was very difficult for a morally sensitive Frenchman to accept the conditions he saw around him; it was only a step from this to sharing the anger of working people against a government that seemed invariably to side with the propertied classes and was holding in a state

[15] *Ibid.*, pp. 64, 247, 318.
[16] See, for example, Herbert Lüthy, *Frankreichs Uhren gehen anders* (Zürich, 1954), translated by Eric Mosbacher as *The State of France* (London, 1955).

of political quarantine the party that alone inspired much confidence among the poor. And the way in which intellectuals translated their anger was by subscribing with wholehearted recklessness to the doctrine of Karl Marx.

Moreover, from some standpoints the French writers were more farsighted than their compeers in Britain or America who on economic matters or the state of affairs in the Soviet Union seemed so much better informed than they. The French were more alert to the threat of a thermonuclear conflict, and they had a far better appreciation of the horrors of colonial warfare and of the explosive potential within the movements of liberation in Asia and Africa. Taught by their country's experience of eight years of fruitless repression in Indochina—which was to be followed almost immediately by an equally long and even more distressing war in Algeria—the French intellectuals early awoke to the importance of what was just beginning to be called the underdeveloped world. At home, their ideological pronouncements might sound more and more old-fashioned; in the colonies and the ex-colonies they could still evoke a response. As the French intellectuals of the Left sank into obsolescence in their own land, their words gained a new relevance overseas. Such was notably the case with the most talented and influential of them all, Jean-Paul Sartre.

II. *Jean-Paul Sartre: The Idealist Phase*

Shortly after the liberation, Sartre and the existentialist philosophy that was associated with his name suddenly mushroomed into a colossal intellectual fad. The term "existentialism" began to be applied in all kinds of inappropriate contexts, as a word of scorn for the conservatives, as a badge of pride for the young. Sartre himself had every reason to be surprised by his new-found fame. Before the war he had lived only on the margin of the influential cliques that dominated French literary life. However prodigious his talents might appear later on, he had never been acclaimed as a boy genius, and public recognition had been slow in coming; most of his time he had spent as an obscure lycée professor—he was thirty-three when he enjoyed his first literary success. This was just a year before the war broke out, and it was not until the occupation period that he became the center of a circle of like-minded friends and admirers. In these years he and Simone de Beauvoir and a few others would gather at the Café de Flore near Saint-Germain-des-Prés—to exchange opinions, to keep warm in winter, but chiefly to write, to write with an indefatigable single-mindedness that epitomized their commitment to their craft. To his younger friends Sartre ranked as a great "awakener": he spoke to them in direct and colloquial language, eliciting from them what they "really were" under the veneer of their education as civilized Frenchmen. Sartre's manner might be blunt: he refused to take refuge in the polite formulas that usually covered over basic disagreements. But he was also very kind: a wealth of testimony from this period concurs in stressing his generosity. Subsequently, when the tourists and sensation-seekers had driven Sartre and his friends from the Café de Flore, the latter were to recall these first years with nostalgia as a "time of purity."[17]

Sartre was only four years younger than Malraux—he was born in 1905—and the themes of their fictional work had much in common. But their contrasting rates of intellectual maturation set them worlds apart. By the time Sartre began to produce the books that brought him fame and influence, Malraux had already spent a decade and a half at the very center of the French literary scene; when Sartre was finally ready to launch his ideological adventures, Malraux was about to renounce his own and to retire into aesthetic contemplation. Jean-Paul Sartre was slow in recognizing where his

[17] Jacques Guicharnaud, "Those Years: Existentialism 1943–1945," *Yale French Studies*, No. 16 (Winter 1955–1956), translated by Kevin Neilson for *Sartre: A Collection of Critical Essays*, edited by Edith Kern (Englewood Cliffs, N.J., 1962), pp. 16–19.

thought was leading him. His intellectual and emotional biography was both unusual and complex, and he required a long time to sort out its elements. When he was almost fifty, he reached the conclusion that his previous work had been based on a misapprehension; a few years later, he decided to write of his childhood and to try to explain to himself and others how it had all come about.

This was a novelty in French literature—an autobiography that went only to the age of ten and was unashamedly psychoanalytic in inspiration. Sartre's understanding of psychoanalysis had its serious gaps (more of that shortly), but at least he did his best to confront his childhood and to find in it the origin of the ambiguity which was to figure so prominently in his published work. Thus he could write of his early years that they were "paradise" and that he "loathed" everything about them. He also ascribed his lack of a super-ego to the fact that he had never known his father.[18] The latter statement deserves to be treated with skepticism: examples of self-punishment are strewn wholesale throughout Sartre's career. He may have grown up with only one parent—his father, a naval officer worn out by a tropical ailment, died two years after his birth—but he had a maternal grandfather whose image dominated his early years.

A majestic figure, this Charles (or Karl) Schweitzer, a retired Alsatian professor and the uncle of Albert Schweitzer. His full beard made him look like God the Father: he summed up in his person the good conscience of the intellectual class, the sentimental humanism which was to be the butt of his grandson's sharpest attacks. The ideology of the Schweitzer household was behind the times even for its own era; Sartre later complained that he had spent his childhood in the intellectual atmosphere of the reign of Louis-Philippe, and that he had had to jump over eighty years in order to get abreast of his own generation. This highmindedness, however, was without religious tonality: Charles Schweitzer was a Prot-

[18] *Les mots* (Paris, 1964), translated by Bernard Frechtman as *The Words* (New York, 1964), pp. 19, 34, 164.

estant and his wife a Catholic; the two influences canceled out, leaving the boy Jean-Paul with the conviction that religion was of no particular importance—he came by his atheism quite painlessly. At least that is what he later claimed: his writings, on the contrary, suggest a long, unconscious, subterranean struggle with a hidden deity.

The household gods were, rather, the masters of literature and the arts; it was their priesthood to which the young Sartre found himself already consecrated by right of birth. Charles Schweitzer decreed that his grandson should become a writer, and this the latter dutifully did. The one injunction he never rebelled against was the precept "Thou shalt write"; still more, he "internalized" it and made it his own. Words ruled his childhood, as they did his mature years. The inevitable title for his autobiography was *Les mots—The Words* —as his "natural habitat" was a Parisian apartment with a view over the roofs of the city: only here could he breathe the "rarefied air of belles-lettres." As for the world of nature, it meant absolutely nothing to him.[19]

Charles Schweitzer was also something of an actor: he found satisfaction in his noble poses. And in the atmosphere of adoration with which his grandparents and his mother enveloped the boy, the little Jean-Paul was virtually forced to be a comedian also. He felt obliged to produce the charming actions or turns of phrase his "audience" expected of him. When he finally realized that he was an "impostor," his world became a desolation.[20] It is curious that Sartre himself did not stress more explicitly in his memoirs the origin of an obsession with "bad faith" which was to become the central feature of his philosophy.

Here literature stepped in to save him. Shy and bookish, Sartre found few other children to play with in the Luxembourg Gardens. Years later, when his mother had remarried and the family moved to La Rochelle, he felt similarly cut

[19] *Ibid.*, pp. 22–24, 33, 49, 51, 59–63, 98–103, 154–156, 163–165, 178.
[20] *Ibid.*, pp. 83–86.

off from his more robust schoolmates. At home he had discovered that he was de trop—superfluous—another concept which joined his special philosophical vocabulary. Writing gave him a reason for living—forgiveness for the fact of his existence; it was a mask for the grace that others would ask of death or religion, a way to wrench his life free from the play of chance.[21] Behind the strenuous pace of literary exertion which Sartre imposed on himself lay what one of his closest associates called the "calm" and "secret horror" his childhood had left with him. It was responsible for the dark side of his writing, the insistence on the distasteful aspects of existence, that made so many of his readers think of him as irritable and pessimistic rather than the gay, enterprising, universally curious man his intimates knew and loved.[22]

One more element in Sartre's childhood deserves mention. As Alsatians the Schweitzers were bilingual. In his incarnation as Karl, Charles Schweitzer occupied his academic retirement by running a language school which specialized in teaching French to visiting Germans. These students, hearty and sentimental like their teacher, were frequent guests at the family table. Thus the young Jean-Paul was familiar with the sound of German from his earliest years. By childhood exposure he seemed predestined to translate the German philosophical speculation of the first postwar period into terms that would make sense to Frenchmen just emerging from a second world conflict.

By that time—by the time he became a celebrated philosopher in his own right—he had returned to Paris from La Rochelle; he had prepared for the Ecole Normale Supérieure at one of the capital's elite lycées; he had passed the agrégation in 1929—having failed it, significantly enough, on his first time round; he had met in Simone de Beauvoir the

---

[21] *Ibid.*, pp. 96, 134–135, 193, 251.
[22] Francis Jeanson, "Un quidam nommé Sartre," *postface* to new edition of *Le problème moral et la pensée de Sartre* (Paris, 1965), p. 325.

partner who shared his life and thought and to whom he could pour out his half-formed reflections; and in 1933, a few months after Hitler came to power, he had gone off for a year to Germany as Aron's successor at the French Institute of Berlin.

Here he plunged with characteristic energy into the phenomenology of Eduard Husserl. Aron had brought back from Berlin tidings of a type of speculation which seemed to be precisely what Sartre was seeking—a philosophy of the concrete, which focused intensively on appearances themselves without regard for conventional abstract categories. One night the two were drinking together at a bar in Montparnasse. " 'You see,' " said Aron, pointing to his glass, " 'if you are a phenomenologist, you can talk about this cocktail and make philosophy out of it!' Sartre turned pale with emotion. . . . Here was just the thing he had been longing to achieve for years."[23] With the discovery of Husserl, he was launched at last. In Berlin Sartre also read Scheler and the rival existentialists Jaspers and Heidegger. But a close study of the last of these did not come until 1939, when he was preparing himself to compose the major work that was to adapt Heidegger's thought to the French intellectual context.

Sartre's reading of Freud was more spotty. According to Simone de Beauvoir's account, he knew only *The Interpretation of Dreams* and *The Psychopathology of Everyday Life*. What he had understood of psychoanalytic theory attracted him at the same time as it aroused in him a deeply rooted resistance. While admiring in Freud an expert explorer of human conduct, Sartre rejected Freud's formulation of the unconscious as a threat to the metaphysical freedom which was at the heart of the philosophy he was himself elaborating; in its place he put his own concept of bad faith. For the next decade and a half Sartre was to remain an unreconstructed rationalist, ready to find an intellectual affinity in the "poetic" version of psychoanalysis propounded by Gaston Bachelard, but for the most part faithful to the "lucidity" of

[23] Beauvoir, *Prime of Life*, p. 112.

his Cartesian inheritance.[24] Not until the mid-1950's, in the gravest crisis of his entire intellectual life, did he return more humbly to Freud for guidance.

It never seemed to occur to Sartre that he might himself have benefited by psychoanalytic therapy. Yet the evidence of unresolved childhood suffering was amply apparent. As a young man Sartre remained profoundly wounded—wounded by his mother's remarriage when he was eleven years old and by the almost simultaneous and "brutal" discovery that he was far from handsome. He was also haunted by fantasies of illegitimate birth which were to appear again and again in his imaginative writings: one of Sartre's younger friends found in this absorption with "bastardy" the hook on which he could hang his own effort at an amateur psychoanalysis.[25] At the age of thirty Sartre was troubled by hallucinations of lobsters pursuing him.[26] Eventually the lobsters disappeared—lucidity triumphed—but the emotional vulnerability remained.

As Heidegger had followed Husserl in Sartre's intellectual biography—with Freud trailing considerably behind—so Marx arrived later still. By the 1930's Sartre had acquired a few summary notions of Marxian theory, but until the war he remained basically nonpolitical and ideologically uninvolved. While he had rejected with scorn the facile rationalizations of the bourgeoise, he had nothing to put in their place beyond a highly individual form of intellectual anarchism. In 1936 he cheered for the Popular Front—but strictly as an outsider: he did not even bother to vote. Then came Munich to shake him into an awareness that armed resistance to Hitler was unavoidable.[27] And a year later, when the war broke out, he was called up for military service.

During the winter of the phony war, which he spent in enforced idleness with a noncombatant unit in Alsace, Sartre

[24] *Ibid.*, pp. 23, 106–107, 425.
[25] Francis Jeanson, *Sartre par lui-même* (Paris, 1955), pp. 61–62.
[26] Beauvoir, *Prime of Life*, pp. 169–170, 177–178.
[27] *Ibid.*, pp. 211, 268.

had time to think through what he would do when the conflict was over. He determined that he could no longer stand aside from politics: he must "assume his situation" by engaging himself in ideological action; any other conduct would be an evasion, a flight into bad faith. Within less than a year, Sartre had an opportunity to put this new understanding into practice. Captured by the Germans in the great defeat, he threw himself with enthusiasm into the totally novel experience of a prisoner-of-war camp. He was exhilarated by the taste of community living; he stimulated the flagging morale of his fellow prisoners, organizing the production of an anti-German play he had written.[28] When he was released a few months later, he similarly did his best to bring together his literary friends in one of the earliest of the Parisian Resistance groups; later, as we have already observed, he worked with the Communist writers. After the liberation, Sartre established a new review—*Les temps modernes*—that combined literature and politics; and as the Cold War opened, he helped to found a neutralist political movement. This venture—which aimed at aligning the intellectual Left both alongside the Communists and independent of them—succeeded no better than Sartre's first wartime effort; in just over a year it had collapsed utterly, torn apart by its own internal inconsistencies. The experience had a sobering effect: Sartre realized that as a neophyte in politics he had acted precipitately and with insufficient ideological preparation. It was only then that he was ready for a full-scale encounter with Marx as a guide to the second phase of his public career.

Meantime Sartre had become famous as the grand master of French existentialism. It is odd that the identification which was to adhere to him most closely was not applied until late in the war, when he had already been publishing philosophical studies for seven years, and then almost

[28] *Ibid.*, p. 342; Simone de Beauvoir, *La force des choses* (Paris, 1963), translated by Richard Howard as *Force of Circumstance* (New York, 1965), pp. 5–6.

casually. Gabriel Marcel, who had preceded Sartre along a similar path, seems to have been the first to refer to the latter as an existentialist. Sartre thought of himself, rather—to the extent that he was willing to accept a label at all—as a phenomenologist, and only after the war did he issue anything resembling an existentialist manifesto. His fifth and most influential philosophical work, published under the occupation in 1943, was, as its subtitle put it, no more than an "essay in phenomenological ontology."

Being and Nothingness was read straight through by very few of Sartre's contemporaries. When it first appeared, it made little impression on the public, and the reviewers and professional philosophers took their time about discussing it. It was not until Sartre had found a general audience with his plays and novels that people turned back to his philosophical treatise in search of the abstract assumptions which lay behind his imaginative work. What they discovered most of the time only confused them. To readers accustomed to the graceful, limpid style of a Bergson, *Being and Nothingness* was hard going: it was portentously long, and its author had not hesitated "to create new expressions, to do violence to syntax," to weigh down his prose by "piling words on top of each other," and to pursue his argument long after he had made his main point.[29] Still more, the book was so idiosyncratic both in conception and in execution that the French public might be pardoned if it found little connection between Sartre's philosophical speculations and what existentialism had come to mean as a literary movement.

Throughout *Being and Nothingness* Sartre gave full credit to his German masters Husserl and Heidegger—and to Hegel, who was only later to move to the center of his thought. He made passing reference to Bergson and Proust as having gotten into insoluble difficulties through their inadequate theories of memory, and, among his near-contemporaries, to Malraux and Saint-Exupéry; in the former he admired the

[29] Jeanson, *Problème moral*, pp. 136–137.

union of thought and action which was most fully expressed in *Man's Hope*; in the latter he believed he had discovered a concrete illustration of Heidegger's effort to fuse subject and object in a totality of human endeavor.[30] But in Sartre's work there was none of the fascination with death that had gripped the generation of novelists only a few years his senior. For Sartre death was something merely external: it was—to use one of his favorite expressions—"absurd."

His whole elaborate ontological structure rested on the radical distinction he drew between consciousness, which he identified as for-itself (pour soi), and the phenomenal world, including the existence of the individuals who experienced such consciousness, which he consigned to the realm of being-in-itself (en soi). The eccentricity of this distinction lay in the fact that although the for-itself enjoyed all the philosophical prestige imaginable, it had no attributes of its own: consciousness as such was a negative quantity—hence the word "nothingness" in the book's title. Being-in-itself might constitute the totality of the universe, but by its density and massiveness it was always threatening to drag down the for-itself to the level of a routine and depressing existence. Thus Sartre's major assertions all referred back to a single source. Everything he valued—"for-itself, nothingness, human consciousness, freedom, free choice"—was ultimately, in his system, "one and the same thing."[31]

It was Sartre's deepest conviction that the for-itself was radically free. He admitted only grudgingly the limitations imposed on human actions by external circumstances, and he found the true barrier to one person's liberty of choice in the freedom of someone else. The result was a concept of human relations whose bleakness was almost without precedent. Each individual consciousness pursued its existence in isola-

---

[30] *L'être et le néant* (Paris, 1943), translated by Hazel E. Barnes as *Being and Nothingness* (New York, 1956), pp. 131, 170, 431.
[31] Wilfrid Desan, *The Tragic Finale: An Essay on the Philosophy of Jean-Paul Sartre*, Torchbook paperback edition (New York, 1960), p. 101.

tion from the others. Each was prey to an "anguish" which Sartre defined not as fear of what others might do, but as dread of one's own potential for good or evil. Anguish was man's recognition of his freedom: it was the simplest and most profound of his self-definitions. The majority of mankind could not stand such an awareness: they fled for refuge to a state of bad faith, which again needed to be distinguished from untruth or falsehood, since it meant lying to oneself rather than to others. But even the minority who tried to become fully aware of their condition could not manage to live with what the conventional moralists called sincerity. Sincerity was an illusion, an "impossible task." For how could a man remain true to what he had been in the past without converting himself into a fixed "thing" which the very definition of consciousness denied?[32]

In a universe thus constituted, relations between human beings could be only those of conflict—of one freedom pitted against another. Love was as much an illusion as sincerity: what the lover was really after was to subjugate his partner. Similarly the experience of community—of "we"—was never direct: it had always to be mediated by a third relationship. In the conflict of rival freedoms that was the texture of human existence, there could be no more than temporary truces and understandings; respect for the freedom of another was an "empty word," since every attitude one might adopt to express such respect would end by being a violation of the freedom in question.[33]

Far from regarding each other with mutual respect, human beings cast baleful glances which stripped one another of their comfortable disguises. Man's characteristic reaction to the "look" that someone else turned upon him was to feel naked and ashamed.[34] In the Sartrian universe shame was the token and measure of human inadequacy; it suggested the

[32] *Being and Nothingness*, pp. 29, 43, 47–50, 62–63, 525.
[33] *Ibid.*, pp. 364, 366, 375, 409, 429.
[34] *Ibid.*, pp. 288–289.

impossibility of living, as the bourgeois humanists had thought they were doing, at peace with one's fellow men and in the enjoyment of a good conscience.

A concept of being which was so unsparing in its dissection of motives, an ontology which gave no quarter to ethical evasions, had obvious affinities to classic psychoanalysis. Yet when at the end of his long study Sartre defined his own concept of "existential psychoanalysis," it became apparent that his philosophy was irreconcilable with Freud's central insight. Sartre gave the Freudian school full credit for being the only one among his predecessors to start from the "same original evidence" and to try to get at the "more profound structures" of human consciousness. But this search, Sartre contended, had stopped in mid-course: Freud had limited himself to the exploration of his patients' past; he had not gone on to examine the future toward which their emotional configurations were directed. More specifically he had not tried to understand the "fundamental project" that gave meaning to the life of each of them—and man's "project" was to loom ever larger in Sartre's thought as he became increasingly absorbed with the social realm.

Freud had failed to recognize this orientation toward the future, Sartre argued, because he had remained absorbed by the unconscious. He had not sufficiently examined what he meant by the "censorship" that prevented intolerable thoughts from arising to full awareness. More closely examined, the censorship itself proved to be a conscious self-deception—an aspect of bad faith. Sartre's concept of bad faith, as we have already observed, virtually forced him to reject the Freudian "hypothesis of the unconscious": the unconscious gave human beings an alibi for failing to accept the consequences of their inner dishonesty.[35]

In the Sartrian moral universe there was no room for excuses—as there was none for remorse or regret. There was only a sense of "overwhelming . . . responsibility"—the

[35] *Ibid.*, pp. 52–53, 458, 564, 570, 573.

sense that man, "condemned to be free," carried the "weight of the whole world on his shoulders."[36]

Such, in broad outline, was the argument of *Being and Nothingness*. Under its ponderous manner, it was in fact a highly personal self-revelation. Its very vocabulary betrayed the author's anxieties and his unremitting effort to resolve them through literary or philosophical formulations. Sartre, as one of his younger admirers described him, was an obsessive who delivered himself of his obsessions for his readers' profit or expense.[37] He was an intellectual who turned the full force of his intellect upon his own person, who was driven by his inner furies to play a "hellish game with consciousness."[38] Throughout his work lurked the fear of being entrapped, imprisoned, confined. The most pervasive of his metaphors was the viscosity or stickiness of being-in-itself in which the weightless, transparent for-itself was forever in danger of foundering. To such contamination Sartre's characteristic reaction was nausea—as *Nausea* had been the title of the novel with which he had first come to the attention of the reading public. This metaphysical disgust could on occasion extend to the entire corporeal aspect of existence; at one point in *Being and Nothingness* Sartre referred almost casually to the "nauseous character of all flesh."[39]

As the mythic carriers of fleshly values, women thus became automatically suspect: Sartre's critics have repeatedly drawn attention to the harsh treatment he dealt them in his plays and novels, where they figured as soft, damp, porous, and once even as a "swamp." If the flesh (or life, or existence) was dense and viscous—in short, female—the intellect was hard and sharp and male. Between these two realms, there could be neither emotional nor intellectual understanding. "A mind which thinks in Cartesian geometrical terms,

[36] *Ibid.*, pp. 553, 555–556.
[37] Jeanson, "Un quidam," p. 307.
[38] Victor Brombert, *The Intellectual Hero: Studies in the French Novel 1880–1955* (Philadelphia and New York, 1961), p. 197.
[39] P. 357.

which fixes all life in concepts that have the brittle clarity of crystal, . . . can designate the transcendent force of life only as Not-Being, Nothingness."[40]

Sartre had welcomed the density and concreteness of phenomenological speculation as an antidote to the intellectualism of his French philosophical upbringing. But in the course of converting to his own uses what Husserl had taught, he had landed himself in an intellectualism of another kind. In seeking to break out of an old and familiar prison, he had confined himself in a new one of his own construction. This was what Gabriel Marcel—who was uniquely qualified to judge the viability of Sartre's philosophical venture—concluded after a reading of *Being and Nothingness*. While expressing his admiration for the fashion in which its author had delineated the phenomenon of bad faith, Marcel wondered whether Sartre had not in the name of freedom itself condemned his thought "to move in an infernal circle." Beyond that—and this for Marcel was the "most serious question" the book raised—how could a work that set out "from premises which in another age would have been called idealistic" have reached "conclusions which a materialist would not disclaim?"[41] Under Sartre's novel formulations, Marcel, as an obstinate "spiritualist," had detected a crypto-materialism. By the time *Being and Nothingness* was written, the old dichotomy between idealism and materialism (or perhaps better, positivism) had been largely overcome: both philosophers and social scientists had tried to go beyond such nineteenth-century distinctions by focusing on practical procedures that might furnish provisional verification to the constructions of the intellect. In this perspective, Sartre's method marked a step backward: the radical distinction he drew between the for-itself and being-in-itself split apart once

[40] Theophil Spoerri, *Die Struktur der Existenz* (Zürich, 1951), a selection from the chapter on Sartre translated as "The Structure of Existence: *The Flies*" for *Sartre: A Collection of Critical Essays*, p. 59.
[41] *Homo Viator: Prolégomènes à une métaphysique de l'espérance* (Paris, 1945), translated by Emma Craufurd as *Homo Viator: Introduction to a Metaphysic of Hope* (London, 1951), pp. 179, 183.

more the realm of existence and the realm of pure thought.

In Cartesian fashion, Sartre offered his readers an either-or choice. If they found the notion of consciousness without attributes too much for them, they could always opt for the viscosity of corporeal existence. It was here, after all, that life and action went on. The other face of Sartre's ultra-idealism was a concept of being which readily lent itself to the most extreme materialist interpretations.

The Sartrian for-itself was something totally new. Although it might at first glance resemble the mind or the soul or the ego or the consciousness of the Western philosophical and psychological tradition, it was actually distinct from them all, since it lacked definition—or rather, was defined in terms of nothingness. Hence it was necessarily impersonal. It had to be so—for to give it "the slightest granule of being" would mean to "provide something for deterministic influence to take hold of" and thereby to destroy the freedom of "pure and translucid consciousness." Sartre's uncompromising search for freedom ended in its own negation. "In his absolute process of emptying the for-itself" of all content, he "killed it."[42] With conciousness reduced to nothingness, materialism was the only remaining recourse.

Yet in fact Sartre did not succeed in holding to his own philosophical definitions. Ostensibly he had abolished the individual ego, but under a series of transparent disguises it crept back into his prose. Without an ego, without a notion of human individuality, his whole idea of "existential psychoanalysis" would have been impossible. Quite apparently the still-undiscovered Freud of the new discipline would have to work on something more tangible than a negative quantity. This was an aspect of his reflections that Sartre had not yet thought through: his discussion of existential psychoanalysis read like a dangling addendum to his finished work.

Sartre was quite right in discovering an affinity between his own speculations and the procedures of psychoanalysis.

[42] Desan, *Tragic Finale*, pp. 153, 158.

But he had the matter turned around. It was not that he needed to define a new kind of psychoanalytic procedure; Freud's successors were already doing that by sending out investigations in the directions he had simultaneously discovered. It was rather that Sartre—and the other writers who dealt in existential categories—could reveal to the more sophisticated of the post-Freudians their own implicit philosophical assumptions, how without knowing it they had been "unofficial existentialists all along." Sartre's teaching had in common with classic psychoanalysis an insistence on the "unsparing truths" that confronted human beings with the necessity for decision. Both stressed the "anxiety about existence itself" which might go under many names—clinical or philosophical—as one or another symptom cried out for attention. Whether one called it "anomie, estrangement, dread, despair, depersonalization, alienation, abandonment," or anything else, it invariably referred back to an emotional state in which the "darkness of the world" caused "even shadows to disappear."[43] This Sartre had understood: the most telling passages in his whole long book gave it eloquent expression. And this was what his readers retained after they had given up wrestling with his special vocabulary.

Thus what was viable in Sartre's rendering of psychoanalysis had little or nothing to do with his newly-coined abstractions. The same was true of the moral and political implications of his philosophy. From the start there had been something arbitrary about Sartre's ontological categories. And they became more arbitrary still when he began to extend them to the realm of ideology.

There was no necessary connection between Sartre's philosophy of being and any specific political faith. Nor were his readers on the right track when they tried to pick out of his plays and novels a coherent sequence of moral declarations. Sartre had originally made his reputation with his novel

[43] Avery D. Weisman, M.D., *The Existential Core of Psychoanalysis: Reality Sense and Responsibility* (Boston, 1965), pp. vii, 215, 231–233.

Nausea in 1938. Then after the publication of *Being and Nothingness* he had returned to imaginative literature—with plays such as *The Flies* and *No Exit* which were produced in Paris during the final months of the German occupation, and with the first two volumes of his novel *Roads to Freedom*. Like Gabriel Marcel, Sartre found emotional stimulus in shuttling back and forth between philosophy and the theater. Some of his plays carried an implicit message: in *The Flies* an audience trained to the special alertness of the oppressed could detect an undertone of Resistance rhetoric. But there was no one-to-one correlation between what Sartre said in his philosophical works and the lines the actors delivered in his plays. In his imaginative writings Sartre was concerned, rather, to show his characters "in situation," to demonstrate how they forged their own reality at the moment of choice.[44] The Resistance had provided the maximum and unrepeatable example of such testing. Yet even in the plays or novels where it was not evoked at all, Sartre left his characteristic mark in the delineation of a situation of moral extremity: his protagonists were heroes of "the impossible," who walked straight into an "impasse with tragic honesty."[45]

At the end of *Being and Nothingness*, Sartre undertook to follow it with an ethical sequel. And in the last few pages of this book he sketched out the themes that the subsequent work would discuss. But the second treatise never materialized. As happened with the final volume of *Roads to Freedom* for which the public waited year after year in vain, Sartre neglected his promise to his readers in favor of topics that seemed of greater current urgency. In both cases, a gradual shift in his thought made it impossible for him to redeem his earlier pledge. By the mid-1950's, Sartre was no longer in the mood to give a systematic account of the existentialist ethic.

In its absence, a lecture he delivered in the autumn of 1945 had to suffice. This ethical sketch—which was subse-

44 Jeanson, *Sartre par lui-même*, p. 12.
45 Brombert, *Intellectual Hero*, pp. 202–203.

quently published under the title *Existentialism is a Humanism*—was Sartre's response to the awkward situation in which his sudden fame had placed him. As the war ended, existentialism became the topic of the hour. The word was bandied about everywhere; it was, Sartre protested, even turned to purposes of cultural nationalism, as evidence that a much-tormented France was once again in the literary vanguard. At first Sartre tried to refuse the epithet "existentialist" that Gabriel Marcel had applied to him; he was quite ready to grant that his was a "philosophy of existence," but he failed to understand what it meant to be an existentialist. Eventually, however, since everyone else pretended to know—most of them mistakenly—the only recourse seemed to be to accept the label and to try to explain in the simplest possible terms its application to human conduct.[46]

Sartre's lecture, then, was an effort to set straight those who had distorted his thought. According to his most authoritative expositor, Francis Jeanson, Sartre subsequently decided that he had made an "error" in staking out a moral position which was not yet firmly established in his mind. And Jeanson himself, with the older man's blessing, undertook to rectify the situation by stressing in an analysis of his own the openness, the ambiguity, and the total lack of a moral imperative in the existentialist ethic.[47] At the time, however, it is hard to see how Sartre could have avoided some kind of reply to his critics and vulgarizers. By 1945 he had become a public figure; he had been torn from the sanctified obscurity in which his grandfather had taught him that the masters of literature dwelt. His words were now common property; the best that he could do was to join in the process of vulgarization.

Existentialism, Sartre explained, was not a humanism in the old sense of a categorical imperative and the good conscience of the bourgeoisie. It could be called such, however,

[46] See Simone de Beauvoir's account in *Force of Circumstance*, pp. 38–42.
[47] *Problème moral*, pp. 36, 284–285.

in the more basic meaning of a doctrine which made "human life possible" by awakening men to their responsibilities. Starting from a total denial—of God, of conventional morality, of "human nature"—the existential ethic refused to embrace a comfortable skepticism. It taught, rather, that every man was responsible not merely for himself but for all his fellowmen—and that each of the unavoidable choices one made was also a choice for all humanity, since it participated in the creation of the still-undefined entity known as man. Such choices, if "authentic," were necessarily good: the only true evil was bad faith. And they were also choices for freedom: men of good faith could not fail to choose freedom. There might be no such thing as human nature, but there was a "human condition" that made mankind one. Thus every man of good faith must necessarily seek the freedom of everyone else.[48]

This was a long way from the bleak world of universal conflict which *Being and Nothingness* had described. Although Sartre continued to assert that his doctrine was pessimistic in origin and that hope was not necessary to ethical engagement, he now discovered an "optimistic toughness" at the bottom of his despair.[49] *Being and Nothingness* had insisted on the futility of existence: in passages which were to become catchwords, Sartre had declared that man was a "useless passion" and that to "get drunk alone" or to be a "leader of nations" was equally vain.[50] Yet at the very time he was putting these thoughts on paper, Sartre was deeply committed to the ethical goals of the literary Resistance. His abstract reflections and his practical activity were going in separate directions. In his lecture of 1945, Sartre tried to bridge the gap between the two, to establish a philosophical justification for the new imperative which had inspired his Resistance work. But he succeeded only in part. Sartre's moral

[48] *L'existentialisme est un humanisme* (Paris, 1946), translated by Bernard Frechtman as *Existentialism* (New York, 1947), pp. 12, 18–21, 25–26, 45, 53–54.
[49] *Ibid.*, pp. 37, 39–40.
[50] *Being and Nothingness*, pp. 615, 627.

statements lacked the intellectual power of his ontology and had the effect of blunting the harsh outlines of what he had written earlier. In the world of practical action, he was still adrift.

Sartre's emotional sympathies, his doctrine of universal freedom, inclined him toward the Left—and toward a Left which professed its revolutionary character. But this leftism lacked content: it was a temper of mind rather than a fully developed ideology. Sartre's grapplings with Marx were still in the future. And he was to come to Marx not by the ordinary route of party activity, but through the mediation of another philosopher, younger and less well-known than he, Maurice Merleau-Ponty.

iii. *Maurice Merleau-Ponty: From Meditation to Ideology and Back*

Until the Second World War, the intellectual appreciation of Marx in France lagged notably behind what it had been in Germany in the Weimar period or in Italy before the advent of Mussolini. The leaders of the French Socialist and Communist parties had satisfied themselves with summary notions of Marxian theory and felt free to interpret that theory in a characteristically French fashion. For the Socialists this meant a generous, nondogmatic humanism in the style of Jean Jaurès—a way of thought to which Léon Blum remained true throughout his life. The corresponding Communist interpretation was in the Jacobin-Blanquist vein which proved so appealing during the Resistance years. The Socialist party included many professors and littérateurs, but almost no theoreticians of Marxism. The Communists had begun with a number of adherents or sympathizers who professed to be such, but by the end of the 1920's most of these had dropped out, and none had risen to a position of leadership in the party. In France there was no counterpart to the Torinese circle around Antonio Gramsci that gave Italian Communism its characteristic openness and intellectual tone. This lack of an intellectual tradition in France helps explain why the French Communists became so woodenly Stalinist and why they were so much slower than the Italians to inaugurate an ideological "thaw" after Stalin's death. To the extent that the French—either inside or outside the Communist party—had an intellectual understanding of Marxism, it was predominantly Leninist with a Stalinist gloss.[51]

At the turn of the century, the French had participated only slightly in the philosophical and sociological critique of Marxism which was to end in the absorption of a "relativized" Marx into the mainstream of Western thought. While Pareto and Croce among the Italians, and in Germany Max Weber, had offered analyses of Marxism that were widely read and accepted, in France Sorel had remained intellectually isolated and Durkheim had never gotten beyond a few pregnant references to Marx's emotional appeal.[52] It was to be a full generation before the French began to catch up with the Germans and Italians. Predictably enough, the process was inaugurated in 1936 with the lectures on Hegel of an émigré, the Russian Alexandre Kojève, to an audience that included some of France's most influential future intellectuals. Thus the young French of the 1930's came to Marx in the authentic chronological and philosophical sequence; they did not go directly to him, skipping over Hegel as irrelevant to the times, as was so often the case in this period of economic depression in Britain or the United States. Concomitantly, however, the approach via Hegel made the French understanding of Marxism excessively abstract and, in philosophical terms, idealist. And the penchant for Germanic abstraction was reinforced when a few years later, and more particularly during the occupation period, a reading of the thoroughly non-Marxist Husserl and Heidegger prompted an interpretation of Marxism in existential terms.[53]

All this might have ended in the tender-minded under-

[51] Lichtheim, *Marxism in Modern France*, pp. 34, 80.
[52] See my *Consciousness and Society* (New York, 1958), Chapter 3.
[53] Lichtheim, *Marxism in Modern France*, pp. 84–85.

standing of Marx based on his own early manuscripts of a Hegelian cast that was to attain such popularity in America in the 1960's, had it not been for the intrusion of still a third foreign influence. Antonio Gramsci's writings became known only slowly in France; but the work of his rival as the greatest of Lenin's heirs, Georg Lukács, joined the Central European philosophical onslaught that was shaking up the French in the war and postwar years. The book the French read was Lukács' essay of 1923, *Geschichte und Klassenbewusstsein*—history and class consciousness—which had displeased the leadership of the Third International and which its author had subsequently repudiated. In it Lukács had extended Marxism in two directions: he had simultaneously gone back to Hegel in his idealist and literary conceptualization and had moved forward into his own time in an effort to push Leninism to its logical consequences. The result was a view of Marxist action which was even more forthrightly elitist than Lenin's. In Lukács' view the position of greatest prestige and responsibility in a revolutionary situation devolved on the "intellectual workers"; for it was up to them to instill into an inert proletariat an authentic class consciousness—and, if all else failed, by a resort to terror.[54]

Thus Lukács' book of a quarter century earlier suggested how the French could combine the Hegelian source and the Leninist derivative of Marxism into an understanding of that theory which was both idealist and revolutionary, humanist in tone, but with a tolerance for terror. Such an eclectic doctrine was not what the French Communist party taught. But it provided an optimum meeting ground for writers formally affiliated with the party and those who stood outside it in an attitude of sympathy. Its lofty philosophical vocabulary made it intellectually respectable; its "toughness" gave the party, in practice, the last word; in the meantime it offered the writers themselves a key role in the revolution to come.

Among those who had attended Kojève's lectures on Hegel

[54] See the analysis of Victor Zitta, *Georg Lukács' Marxism: Alienation, Dialectics, Revolution* (The Hague, 1964), pp. 183–193.

and studied Lukács with the greatest care was Maurice Merleau-Ponty. One of the curious features of the vicissitudes of
Marxism in postwar France was that its most sophisticated
interpreter and critic should have been an heir of the phenomenological tradition whose original writings seemed to have
nothing to do with ideology.

Merleau-Ponty, by his own account, had never gotten over
an inordinately happy childhood. Like Sartre, he had felt
himself adored by his mother, and he apparently escaped the
need that Sartre experienced later on to reconsider this idyllic
memory. The social origins of the two were also divergent:
Merleau-Ponty came of the grande bourgeoisie and retained
the manners of the gently-bred, while Sartre insisted on the
modesty of his own middle-class milieu and on his independence from polite conventions. It was characteristic of
Merleau-Ponty that he performed his combat service as an
officer—something that was less common among French intellectuals in the Second World War than it had been in
the First. And he likewise differed from most of his counterparts in his attitude toward religion: although he shared
their atheism, he had lost his Catholic faith only in late
adolescence, and he subsequently refrained from the aggressive or insulting tone toward the Church that was normal
among his acquaintance; the rare occasions on which he
referred to religious matters revealed a thorough familiarity
with the Catholic tradition and an awareness of the intellectual changes that were taking place within French Catholicism.[55]

Merleau-Ponty, born in 1908, was three years younger than
Sartre, but their careers at the Ecole Normale Supérieure
had overlapped. Here they had known each other only at a
distance. Subsequently Merleau-Ponty had started out, as

[55] Remy C. Kwant, *The Phenomenological Philosophy of Merleau-
Ponty* (Pittsburgh, 1963), pp. 128–129; Maurice Merleau-Ponty,
"L'homme et l'adversité" (originally published in 1952), *Signes*
(Paris, 1960), translated by Richard C. McCleary as *Signs* (Evanston,
Ill., 1964), p. 242.

Sartre did, teaching philosophy in a succession of lycées. The difference between them—again in character—was that while Sartre never submitted a doctor's thesis and after the war gave up teaching to concentrate exclusively on his writing, Merleau-Ponty followed the normal French pattern of academic advancement, eventually reaching the very top of the country's intellectual establishment. In 1945 he was appointed professor at the University of Lyons; four years later he was called to Paris; and after only three years at the Sorbonne, he received in 1952 a chair at the Collège de France—where Bergson and Febvre had lectured before him, and where Lévi-Strauss was to arrive a few years later—a recognition of the extraordinary position in French intellectual life he had attained in just over half a decade.

From the philosophical standpoint, he and Sartre had followed parallel paths. During the 1930's, they had pursued a similar course of reading and reflection quite independently of one another. Not until the war and Sartre's release from German captivity did they become once more acquainted, and as co-workers in Sartre's original abortive effort at a Resistance organization discover that they had in common the words "phenomenology" and "existence." "Too individualist to . . . pool" their research, they "became reciprocal while remaining separate"; the influence of Husserl was both what divided them and what made them friends. The result was a mixture of sympathy and ineradicable difference in their philosophical approaches which perplexed their students and admirers. In this early period of their association it was Merleau-Ponty rather than Sartre who was mainly responsible for the distance between the two. The younger man preferred to keep his reflections to himself and was thrown off his track by extended discussion. Sartre, on the contrary, loved talking with Merleau-Ponty, as "ventilation" for his own thought, and had a way of referring to their relationship as a team which the latter subsequently resented.[56]

[56] Jean-Paul Sartre, "Merleau-Ponty" (originally published August–September 1961), *Situations*, IV (Paris, 1964), translated by Benita Eisler as *Situations* (New York, 1965), pp. 230–232.

In terms of technical philosophy, Merleau-Ponty's reputation rested on two substantial works, *La structure du comportement*, published in 1942, and his doctor's thesis, *Phéno-
ménologie de la perception*, which followed three years later.
In the latter work in particular he traced the view of human
existence that lay behind his subsequent social thought—a
view that considered mind and body as inseparable and
stressed the preconscious origin of man's conscious activity.
A foe of both rationalism and empiricism in the forms in
which he had encountered them in his own philosophical
training, Merleau-Ponty was in no sense an apologist for
unreason. It was rather that he had been impressed early in
life with the inability of any formulation—whether abstract
or experimental—to give an even remotely adequate account
of the infinite complexity of interpersonal relationships. Like
Marcel, Merleau-Ponty felt that he was groping his way in a
universe which gave up few of its secrets—but in his case
a universe in which religious faith offered no guidance. The
human world was the sphere of contingence, of ambiguity:
in ultimate terms it was unintelligible. Existence was suffused
with meanings—but these were human meanings devoid of
absolute truth. Such a philosophy combined an extreme sub-
jectivism with a radical objectivity in the delineation of
phenomena: its basic attitude was wonder at the marvelous
variety of man's adventure. To the end of his life Merleau-
Ponty remained hostile to any philosophical or historical
theory that tried to climb above the phenomenal world and
attain a bird's-eye view; his own final position has been
summed up in the single expression "en-être"—which can
be translated quite literally by the American colloquialism
"being with it."[57]

Merleau-Ponty had become a Pascalian in adolescence before he had read a word of Pascal himself.[58] This affiliation

[57] Introduction to *Signs*, p. 21; Remy C. Kwant, *From Phenomenology to Metaphysics: An Inquiry into the Last Period of Merleau-
Ponty's Philosophical Life* (Pittsburgh, 1966), p. 227.
[58] Sartre, "Merleau-Ponty," *Situations*, p. 228.

implied a negative attitude toward Descartes and at least a beginning of sympathy for Bergson. In Merleau-Ponty's view, as in that of Maritain, Descartes's great mistake had been to consign mind and body to two distinct realms of being: in his own philosophy they were one; man was a "body subject," both spiritual and material, whose "soul" was no more than the "higher level of the subject's self-organization" and whose conscious activity was marginal in importance to what went on at the preconscious stage. For such a philosophy language offered the clue to all the levels of human existence; man as "speaking subject" epitomized the unity of mind and body in a single movement of self-expression.[59]

This unity Bergson had understood. What Merleau-Ponty prized in Bergson was the boldness of the innovator who had rejected the standard notion of philosophy as a panoramic world-view and had redefined it as thought inherent to the matter at hand; he had no taste for the official "Bergsonism" of his own youth, the master's teaching that had been half-accepted by the Catholic Church and watered down almost beyond recognition.[60] Merleau-Ponty's abiding concern was to find an intellectual method which would attain to an inner understanding of the human world.

Such had also been the aim of the German philosophers and social theorists of the turn of the century. And in purpose, if not in vocabulary, Merleau-Ponty was their legitimate heir. He shunned the word "idealism," which to him, as to Sartre, had a narrower meaning than it did in Germany, recalling unpleasant memories of neo-Kantian teachings in the French lycées. But his work in fact linked up with German twentieth-century idealism in its emphasis on "comprehension"—Verstehen—a method that found "amid the multiplicity of facts a few intentions or decisive aims." Merleau-Ponty had little use for the conventional French notion of

[59] Kwant, *Phenomenological Philosophy of Merleau-Ponty*, pp. 11–13, 18, 47, 50, 61.
[60] "Bergson se faisant" (originally published in 1960), *Signs*, pp. 182–184.

sociology: he was critical of the Durkheim tradition and scornful of a "myth about scientific knowledge" which expected wonders from the "mere recording of facts." His own idea of sociological study was close to how Dilthey and Weber had defined it: it should be expressed in terms of "ideal variables," intellectual constructions which would reflect the vast interrelatedness of human experience, and it should be made continually aware of its limitations through the vigilance of philosophical method. As opposed to the pretensions of the sociologists, Merleau-Ponty found the French historians more modest and realistic in their aims, and he expressed his admiration for the reconstitution of the mentality of a vanished age that he had found in Lucien Febvre's study of sixteenth-century disbelief.[61]

Merleau-Ponty's interest in the social psychology of the past, his concern for the phenomenon of language and for preconscious processes, led him effortlessly to Freud. Like Freud, he found in the pathological and the disturbed a key to the functioning of "normal" humanity. But his chief philosophical tie to psychoanalytic theory was his concept of the "body subject"; in this respect he went farther than Freud in breaking down the old dualism between mind and body. For Merleau-Ponty, Freud was the pathfinder who had inaugurated a new and ampler view of man's relation to his physical equipment; in place of the nineteenth-century idea of the body as a "bit of matter" or a "network of mechanisms," he had substituted the notion of a body that was "lived in," where spirit and matter were engaged in a never-ending process of mutual exchange. This new sense for the life of the flesh was the first aspect of contemporaneity that Merleau-Ponty called to mind when just after the half-century mark he was asked to delineate the characteristic philosophical attitudes that the past fifty years had brought into currency.[62]

[61] "La métaphysique dans l'homme" (originally published in 1947), *Sense and Non-Sense*, pp. 88–93; "Le philosophe et la sociologie" (originally published in 1951), *Signs*, pp. 99, 110.
[62] "L'homme et l'adversité," *Signs*, pp. 226–229.

Marxism was not one of these: it was a legacy from the previous century. But for Merleau-Ponty, as for so many French intellectuals of his generation, Marxism in a nuanced and modernized form was the presupposition that lay behind his speculations about the social world. In this case also, as in that of psychoanalysis, his phenomenological interest in the human body had a direct connection with the theory of a respected predecessor. For in Marxism Merleau-Ponty discovered an understanding of what he called the "flesh of history," the interaction between the material infrastructure of existence and the ideas which human beings had formed about it, a relationship which had escaped nearly all of Marx's intellectual competitors.[63] Reduced to its essentials, Marxism simply meant that "nothing can be isolated in the total context of history, . . . with, in addition, the idea that because of their greater generality economic phenomena make a greater contribution to historical discourse." Or—to put the matter in terms of human action—while Marxism was not in principle an optimistic philosophy, its central idea was that "another history" was "possible," that there was "no such thing as fate," and that man was free—indeed, should strive —to build a future which "no one in the world or out of the world" could know whether or what it would be.[64]

For Merleau-Ponty, then, Marxism was a way of thought that remained open to man's infinite possibilities. And far more clearly than Sartre, he established its connection with what he was perfectly willing to call an "existential philosophy." Hegel and Marx, he argued, had been proto-existentialists without knowing it: the former had founded his "militant philosophy" not on the passive subjectivity of the idealists but on the dynamic idea of intersubjectivity; the latter had gone beyond his explicit system to posit a concept of human relations in which men made their own meanings as they engaged their lives in liberating actions. Properly understood, Marxism had nothing abstract about it: it dealt

[63] Introduction to *Signs*, p. 20.
[64] "Autour du marxisme" (originally published in 1946), *Sense and Non-Sense*, pp. 112, 119.

in concrete relationships among men and social classes, and the morality it taught was one of authentic responsibility and passion as opposed to the formal ethics of the schools.[65]

Thus defined, Merleau-Ponty's Marxism was quite capable of a wide and nonsectarian appeal. Yet alongside formulations that were irreproachably permissive, he allowed himself to interject a scattering of lapidary expressions that conceded nothing to the skeptical. Until very late in his philosophical career, Merleau-Ponty invariably referred to a "proletariat" whose existence and ethical value stood unquestioned: it is curious to find a man ordinarily so critical of abstract entities applying this word in almost as crude a sense as would a party believer. Still more, he whose notion of historical interpretation was usually so refined could on occasion speak of Marxism not as one philosophy of history among others but as *the* philosophy of history—a philosophy so indispensable that if one should have to abandon it, reason in history would cease to exist, leaving "only dreams or adventures."[66]

Apparently Merleau-Ponty was initially unaware of the extent of the cleavage within his own thought. It became apparent to him under conditions of maximum ideological tension five years after he began to apply his Marxist reasoning to the world of political action.

In the months following the liberation, Merleau-Ponty was much sought after by the French Communist intellectuals. They knew very well that at that time he was not one of their kind. Before the war, Sartre surmised, he may have been closer to their way of thinking, until the Moscow purge trials, which were to figure prominently in his subsequent writings, raised awkward questions in his mind.

[65] "La querelle de l'existentialisme" (originally published in 1945–1946), *Sense and Non-Sense*, p. 82; "Marxisme et philosophie" (originally published in 1947), *Sense and Non-Sense*, pp. 133–134; *Humanisme et terreur: essai sur le problème communiste* (Paris, 1947), pp. 118–119.

[66] *Humanisme et terreur*, p. 165.

Evidently the Communists respected in Merleau-Ponty the rigor of an intellectual method impervious to shifts in the party line—a "severe and disillusioned" Marxism of expectant waiting.[67]

This ideological expertise became a precious asset when in 1945 Sartre and his friends founded *Les temps modernes*. As editor, Sartre knew that he needed political guidance; and Merleau-Ponty was willing to furnish it, on the condition that his own role be left undefined. In effect, he served as co-editor of the new review, charged with responsibility for its ideological orientation. In theory, he was merely an ordinary member of the editorial board: he courteously rejected Sartre's repeated offers to place his name alongside his own on the cover of the magazine, and he insisted that Sartre approve everything he wrote. In this fashion the younger man provided himself with an escape hatch for the future: more conscious than Sartre of their deep-running temperamental differences, he apparently already feared the rupture that was to come a half decade later, and he took his precautions in advance.[68]

The book which according to Sartre's own account gave him the "push" that tore him loose from his political "immobility" was Merleau-Ponty's *Humanisme et terreur*.[69] Published in 1947, just as the Cold War, already latent for two years, was becoming manifest, it angered nearly all ideological camps. The Communists disliked its cool and realistic analysis of Stalinism; the democratic Center objected to its attitude of neutrality between East and West and the preference it gave to the goals of the Soviet leaders, if not to their current practice—*Humanisme et terreur* was one of the prime targets of Raymond Aron's *Opium of the Intellectuals*. Reread in the less charged atmosphere of two decades later, Merleau-Ponty's tract—for such it unashamedly was—may seem not nearly so provocative as it did when it

[67] Sartre, "Merleau-Ponty," *Situations*, pp. 237, 242–244.
[68] *Ibid.*, pp. 248–252.
[69] *Ibid.*, p. 253.

first appeared. Basically, it was the most sophisticated
apologia for Soviet Communism to come out of the late
1940's in any Western country: as a plea for suspended judgment, for giving the Soviet Union the benefit of the doubt,
it was to accord far better with the European temper of the
1960's than with the era of maximum political passion which
immediately followed it publication.

In the series of loosely-joined essays that made it up,
Merleau-Ponty pursued three related arguments of steadily
widening scope. The narrow and immediate purpose of
Humanisme et terreur was to answer Koestler's *Darkness at
Noon*. The Moscow purge trials, Merleau-Ponty contended,
were not the crude dramas of sensitive intellectuals pitted
against brutal commissars that Koestler had depicted. More
particularly in the case of Bukharin, whose testimony Merleau-Ponty analyzed in detail, such a trial was the confrontation of two clashing interpretations of Marxism, in which
prosecutor and defendant recognized the common ground on
which they stood and in which the latter was given a chance
to "save his revolutionary honor" by phrasing his recantation
in Marxist terms. Both parties knew that terror was essential
to the making of a revolution, as to its preservation. Beyond
that—and here Merleau-Ponty's argument broadened into its
second phase—the Soviet leaders were more honest than
those of the West in admitting to their own terrorist practices. In their colonies the British and the French pursued
without saying so a policy of repression comparable to Stalin's.
Even at home—and this was Merleau-Ponty's cleverest and
most resented thrust at his compatriots—the trials of French
collaborationists after the war had borne a disquieting resemblance to the harsh political justice that the Soviet courts
had handed out in the 1930's. "To know and to judge a
society," Merleau-Ponty argued, "one must reach to its
depths, to the human tie which binds it together and which
depends not only on juridical relationships but also on the
forms of labor and on the way people love, live, and die.
. . . A regime that is liberal in name may in fact be oppres-

sive. A regime which recognizes its own violence *might* contain more true humanity."[70]

All this being so, the best attitude to adopt toward Communism was a "practical" one of "understanding without adherence and of free examination without belittling." Its aim should be to make clear what the ideological situation actually was, "to underline the real terms of the human problem, beyond the paradoxes and contingencies of current history, to recall to the Marxists their humanist inspiration, . . . and to the democracies their fundamental hypocrisy" —in short, to take advantage of the margin of safety, the "minimum of play" that was still left in the course of events, in the hope of finally saving the peace of Europe.[71]

Such was the third and widest circle of argument in *Humanisme et terreur*. Three years after its publication, the "minimum of play" vanished, and Merleau-Ponty began to regret his own work. By the mid-1950's, he was ready to grant that his "Marxism of expectant waiting" had erred in directing all its attention at the excesses of anti-Communism and in neglecting to attack the "crypto-Communism" which was so prevalent among Merleau-Ponty's own acquaintance.[72] This was certainly the book's major weakness: it loaded the dice against the Western democracies while trying to "understand" the crimes of Stalin; it equated Britain's timid and heartless policy of keeping Jews out of Palestine—a policy that was about to be abandoned—with the systematic terror practiced in the Soviet Union. When he finished *Humanisme et terreur*, Merleau-Ponty had failed to answer a fourth question he had set himself—the extent to which Communism still lived up to its "humanist intentions"—and he had failed to do so because in the terms of "expectant waiting" in which he had put the problem, it was in fact unanswerable.[73]

What had changed Merleau-Ponty's attitude was the out-

---

[70] *Humanisme et terreur*, pp. x, 40–44, 51.
[71] *Ibid.*, pp. 159–160, 196, 202.
[72] *Les aventures de la dialectique* (Paris, 1955), pp. 306–309.
[73] *Humanisme et terreur*, pp. xiv, 200.

break of the Korean War. His reaction to this event, like that of so many other French intellectuals, in retrospect seems disproportionate. He went into a deep depression and made bitter jokes about a future life of exile in which he would work as an elevator man in New York. Too honest to take refuge in the comforting rationalization that the North Korean attack was only a surface appearance and that the real aggressors were the American puppets in the South, Merleau-Ponty recognized that the launching of a military offensive by a Communist state had knocked out a major prop from under his earlier argument. In *Humanisme et terreur* he had pleaded for an attitude of understanding toward the Communist regimes on the grounds that they had not in fact attacked their neighbors; now one of them, with the apparent blessing of the Soviet Union, had done just that. Communism's humanist "mask" had been torn away: Stalin's Russia stood revealed as a "Bonapartist" tyranny.[74]

For months on end Merleau-Ponty nursed his chagrin and disillusionment, turning his anger in upon himself and shaken by remorse for what he had earlier written. *Les temps modernes* ceased to publish articles on politics—which was inevitable, since its two directing spirits differed on the meaning of the war (Sartre had quickly come around to the standard interpretation of the French Left that the South Koreans and the Americans were the guilty parties). In long, inconclusive conversations they tried to save their friendship and their collaboration on the review; Merleau-Ponty's role sank to that of a self-effacing partner whom delicacy of feeling and personal loyalty alone kept from resigning outright. In 1952 he swallowed in gloomy silence the series of articles entitled "Les Communistes et la paix"—the Communists and the peace—with which Sartre announced his conversion to a thoroughgoing sympathy with the party. It was not until a few months later that a minor editorial disagreement between the two at length induced Merleau-Ponty to abandon *Les temps modernes* entirely. Shortly thereafter his mother died.

[74] Sartre, "Merleau-Ponty," *Situations*, pp. 275, 279.

By 1953—the year of dawning hope for the peace of Europe and the world—Merleau-Ponty seemed almost totally bereft, delivered over to a slow internal self-destruction.[75]

Two years earlier, at the height of his post-Korean discouragement, he had written of the contemporary world that it was becoming inexplicable in terms of conventional ideology. Hovering in a limbo that was neither quite peace nor quite war, it was a prey "less to the antagonism of two ideologies than to their common disarray" before a situation of which neither one could give an adequate account; international affairs were confused because the ideas on which they were ostensibly based were "too narrow to cover" their "field of action."[76] The implication was that Merleau-Ponty had relinquished every vestige of Marxist faith and had found nothing to put in its place. In 1955, however, he pulled together his courage for another try. He published a second collection of Marxian essays, entitled *Les aventures de la dialectique*, in which he tried to salvage what he could of his earlier allegiance while defining Marxism in an even more skeptical and relativist fashion than he had in *Humanisme et terreur*.

If this earlier work was the most expert Marxian polemic to appear in postwar France, *Les aventures de la dialectique* was the ablest recapitulation of the intellectual catching-up process which had gone on among French Marxists in the 1940's and early 1950's. Its publication marked the fact that the "French discussion had recovered the level of the earlier German one"—and "with the advantage of additional political experience."[77] Its author did not announce it as a systematic treatise; it was rather a collection of "samples," of "soundings," a "continual rumination" on the problems which Marxism raised. This body of political theory, Merleau-Ponty explained, was as impossible to verify as any other; the only difference was that it knew it was such and that it had

[75] *Ibid.*, pp. 273–274, 276, 279–298.
[76] "L'homme et l'adversité," *Signs*, pp. 238–239.
[77] Lichtheim, *Marxism in Modern France*, p. 80n.

"explored the labyrinth" of human affairs more thoroughly than had its rivals.[78]

The sequence from one to another of the essays which made up *Les aventures de la dialectique* was half left to the reader's imagination; Merleau-Ponty's "rumination" was characteristically elusive. But there gradually emerged the underlying theme of the need to understand Marxism in radically relativist terms as a theory of the consciousness of events rather than a truth immanent in those events themselves. Thus it was indicative of what was to follow that Merleau-Ponty began with an essay on a non-Marxist, Max Weber, singling him out as a new type of liberal who had recognized the material and emotional limits within which liberal principles operated, and who had taught the "best" among the Marxists to understand their theory with rigor and consistency.[79] Merleau-Ponty's discovery of Weber seems to have come just at the time he needed him most to help him over the transition from his earlier to his later political views. A footnote in *Humanisme et terreur* suggests that in the mid-1940's his knowledge was limited to Aron's secondhand account. By the time he came to write *Les aventures de la dialectique*, however, he had studied Weber's writings thoroughly and with transparent sympathy. Merleau-Ponty's essay, entitled "The Crisis of Understanding," is one of the most perceptive brief treatments of Weber there is. In his moment of maximum ideological perplexity he had evidently found comfort in encountering a kindred mind as scrupulous and tormented as his own.

From Weber, Merleau-Ponty went on to Lukács—the early Lukács of *History and Class Consciousness* who still remembered that he had been Weber's pupil. In Merleau-Ponty's interpretation, Lukács had gone a step beyond Weber: he had abandoned the lingering nostalgia for unconditional truth which had haunted his former teacher and had propounded a method which asked nothing beyond the

[78] *Aventures de la dialectique*, pp. 7, 11.
[79] *Ibid.*, pp. 15, 42.

meanings that events themselves prompted. But this subjectivist "Western Marxism" had been stifled in embryo; the leaders of the Third International, after forcing Lukács to recant his errors, had retreated to the safer ground of the rough-and-ready positivism that Engels and Lenin had bequeathed to them. *History and Class Consciousness*—"this cheerful and vigorous essay," which had revived the "youth of the Revolution and of Marxism"—marked the measure of what Communism had given up, the extent of its subsequent resignation.[80]

After such a promising beginning, *Les aventures de la dialectique* diverged, rather disappointingly, into an unnecessarily exhaustive refutation of Sartre's essays on the Communists and peace, which occupied nearly half the volume. The subterranean "ruin" of dialectical reasoning begun by Lukács' recantation and which Merleau-Ponty had subsequently traced through the conflict between Stalin and Trotsky, he now found out in the open in the attitude of Sartre. His former friend, Merleau-Ponty argued, had abandoned all pretense to Marxian method: he took on faith that the Communist party represented the oppressed of the earth —whose status he was unable to define as that of any recognizable proletariat; he turned history into a "melodrama daubed in crude colors" in which the only criterion for political judgment was the anguished expression on the faces of the poor; he blurred all previous intellectual distinctions in a reckless "ultra-Bolshevism" where the extremes of realism and idealism met and merged. If Sartre was serious in his skepticism of Marxist dialectics, then the logic of his position would be just the opposite of the subordination of his own judgment to the party line that he seemed to be proposing—it would be to evaluate Communist behavior step by step, in an agnostic and nominalistic temper. And this was how Merleau-Ponty himself concluded his book: in an epilogue which tried in vain to tie together its heterogeneous

80 *Ibid.*, pp. 44, 61, 80.

predecessors, he outlined the politics of a "new liberalism," a "non-Communist Left" which would renounce revolution as an end in itself while making practical progress toward social equality at home and ideological coexistence abroad.[81]

A tame ending for a philosopher who had once been so pungent an ideologist and one marked by the disabused good sense that nearly always characterized Merleau-Ponty's later political writings. But it was not quite so tame as it might appear in bald résumé: Merleau-Ponty specified that the new liberalism he proposed had nowhere yet been put into practice; when it did materialize, it would follow Weber's "heroic" practice of respecting ideological enemies and treating them as equals. To the end of his life—as Sartre himself generously granted—Merleau-Ponty refused to subscribe to the conventional anti-Communism of the 1950's. And he continued to find, along with Sartre, the new horizon of ideology and social thought in the awakening of Asia and Africa.

Did he remain, then, in any sense a Marxist? One can certainly find a number of nostalgic references to Marxian theory—notably the use of the term "proletariat"—scattered through *Les aventures de la dialectique*. And it is also worth recalling that even in *Humanisme et terreur* Merleau-Ponty had kept his ideological distance from Marxian dogmatics. But the difference between the two books was unquestionable: while the first was sure-footed and almost cocky, the second was tentative and "ruminating." Nor was this change limited to a re-evaluation of Communist practice: it entailed also a rethinking of Marxian theory. His own earlier attitude, Merleau-Ponty now recognized, had been based on a priori moralizing; it had propounded a concept of revolution as "absolute action" which had smacked of "Kant in disguise." It had not been a genuine philosophy of history—not even a Marxist philosophy of history properly understood. By 1960, as Merleau-Ponty explained in one of the very last of his

[81] *Ibid.*, pp. 134–135, 138, 198, 207, 225, 227, 246, 248–249, 279, 302–304.

published essays, Marxism had entered a "new phase" in which it could still "orient analyses and retain a real heuristic value," but in which it was "no longer true *in the sense in which it believed itself true.*" In the course of a century it had "inspired so many theoretical and practical undertakings," had been the "laboratory for so many . . . experiments," even among its enemies, that it would be "simply barbarous" to speak of it in terms of "refutation" or "verification." In the second half of the twentieth century, the works of Marx had become "classics," which like other such classic writings were not to be taken literally, but in relativist terms, as a "second order of truth." Under these conditions it was pointless to ask a man or for a man to ask himself whether he was still a Marxist, since the question was incapable of a yes or no response.[82]

That was as much light on the subject as Merleau-Ponty ever dispensed. We can go no further with it until we examine the last phase of this thought, a phase of return to meditation.

Les aventures de la dialectique stood isolated among Merleau-Ponty's later reflections. It marked a final weary effort to dispose of a bundle of concerns that now lay far behind him. His first period of intellectual effort had been one of intense phenomenological reflection which had produced his two major technical works. This had been followed by a half decade in which he had plunged into the ideological controversies of postwar society and in which he had been strongly engaged by Marxist theory and practice. After 1950 —and still more markedly after the death of his mother in 1953—Merleau-Ponty withdrew once more to a life of reflection and to a growing interest in metaphysics. From this third period of his philosophical life there remain the collected essays he published under the title *Signs* in 1960, just a year before his sudden and totally unexpected death, and

---

[82] *Ibid.,* p. 312; Introduction to *Signs*, pp. 9–11. I have altered the translation slightly.

the posthumous and unfinished volume *The Visible and the Invisible*, which offered the outline of his final meditations.

In his last phase, Merleau-Ponty's writing became even more subtle and elusive than it had been before. Rejecting surface clarity—he detested what he called Sartre's "cursed lucidity"—he had always given his work the "character of a living search" rather than of a finished production; when he began writing a book, he was never quite certain where he was coming out.[83] Perhaps he had read too much German in his youth: his sentences went on endlessly, and it was sometimes impossible to distinguish the main statement from the qualifications that surrounded it. These eccentricities grew more marked as his intellectual self-confidence waned. A "calculated inexactitude," an "enveloping complexity," a "glittering density" of expression—such, in the view of one of Merleau-Ponty's younger associates, were the special attributes of his late style.[84]

Yet among these complexities of his last phase we can discern at the very least a steadily growing interest in the unconscious. Toward the end of his life Merleau-Ponty drew closer to psychoanalytic theory: at the Sorbonne he lectured on child psychology; at the Collège de France he gave a course on "passivity" which included a detailed treatment of memory and dreams. For "classic" phenomenology, as for Sartre, the unconscious was an inadmissible concept. Merleau-Ponty admitted it, although he preferred to call it by other names. And so with the rest of the psychoanalytic vocabulary: again and again we find that a term of Merleau-Ponty's translates readily into Freudian language. But a final, irreducible difference remained: for Freud the body was primarily libidinal—for Merleau-Ponty libido was only an additional aspect of corporality; Freud began with an internal perception of emotional processes—Merleau-Ponty, despite his quarrel

[83] *Ibid.*, p. 24; Kwant, *Phenomenological Philosophy*, p. 9; *From Phenomenology to Metaphysics*, p. 229.

[84] Paul Ricoeur, "Hommage à Merleau-Ponty," *Esprit*, XXIX (June 1961), 1115.

with Descartes, remained sufficiently rooted in the French philosophical tradition to start his reflections with the perception of the external world. Beyond that, it would have gone against his temperament to become too closely identified with any single school; he preferred to situate himself at a crossroads of social thought, leaving his own allegiances veiled in enigma until the last.[85]

To be with it—en-être—this final definition of his metaphysical understanding was perfectly compatible with psychoanalytic method. So was the emphasis he placed on internal comprehension in his reflections on history and in his new respect for the work of Max Weber. Indeed, in Merleau-Ponty's late formulations, Weber tended to blend with a Marx understood in the French philosopher's own categories. Both were depicted as waging an unremitting two-front war against idealism and positivism. Both were applauded as social thinkers almost unique in their understanding of the coherence of body, mind, and external world in a totality of human experience. Not all of this celebration was free of ambiguity: the "relativism beyond relativism"—and beyond both Marx and Weber—which Merleau-Ponty had found in Lukács was never adequately explained; the implication was that the events of history themselves vouchsafed meanings to those who scrutinized them with sufficient care and skepticism. But this was to ask a great deal of history—far more than a professional historian would be inclined to demand. Perhaps the weakest point of Merleau-Ponty's social thought was a lingering tendency to write of history in awestruck terms, an ineradicable penchant, despite his philosophical sophistication, to look for an immanent logic in the course of human affairs.

Sartre was quite sure that such a logic existed—and just before Merleau-Ponty's death he published a large book to prove it. The latter never had a chance to comment on

[85] André Green, "Du comportement à la chair: itinéraire de Merleau-Ponty," *Critique*, XX (December 1964), 1017–1018, 1032–1034, 1036–1037, 1040, 1046.

Sartre's *Critique of Dialectical Reason*. But unquestionably
he would have objected to most of it. The perplexing thing
about the relationship between the two was not that they
parted, but that they managed to hold together so long. Although both had come out of the school of Husserl, what
they had drawn from the German phenomenological tradition was very different: to Merleau-Ponty, who thought of
experience in a dense net of interrelationships, the radical
distinction Sartre drew between the for-itself and being-in-
itself was totally unacceptable. Moreover, their personal and
philosophical temperaments had little in common: where
Sartre, by his own admission, was dogmatic, Merleau-Ponty
was nuancé. It would be tempting, but quite incorrect, to
regard them as a team in the style of Febvre and Bloch; it
would be more accurate to say that they served as half-
friendly, half-antagonistic foils to each other's intelligence.
The only valid parallel to the Febvre-Bloch relationship was
that in each case the younger man was both the better
thinker and the less well known in his own country. There
was a monstrous injustice—against which Sartre himself was
the first to protest—in the widespread impression among the
general public that Merleau-Ponty was his junior partner or
possibly even his disciple.

When Merleau-Ponty was stricken by a fatal heart attack
in early 1961, he and Sartre were in the course of arriving at
a careful reconciliation. The younger man's energetic critique
in *Les aventures de la dialectique*, far from making matters
worse, had cleared the atmosphere, since he had finally
delivered himself of the personal and intellectual resentments he had kept suppressed for a full decade. On the
Algerian War, the two former friends stood once more together in condemning the official policy of repression.[86]
Whether they could have become close again is more than
doubtful—or perhaps it is better to say that they had never
been truly close at all.

[86] Sartre, "Merleau-Ponty," *Situations*, pp. 244, 318–320.

When Merleau-Ponty was struck down, his friends could scarcely believe the news. At the funeral no one gave a memorial address, and "no one . . . regretted it," since no eulogy would have been adequate to lament a philosophical voice irremediably cut off in full speech.[87] There was no question that Merleau-Ponty had much left to say; but there was doubt as to whether he still had the desire to say it. His death was tragic; but precisely what kind of tragedy it was remained unclear. Had he died in the plenitude of intellectual vigor, or had he rather, as Sartre suspected, been succumbing for more than ten years to a slow process of internal destruction? Discouraged he unquestionably was, but the nature and extent of his weariness remained locked in his own heart.

Whatever the answer, Merleau-Ponty after the mid-1950's was lost to French social thought. Whether or not he recovered from his ideological disappointments, he almost entirely abandoned the field of political and methodological criticism. The result was a catastrophe for French intellectual life. The best speculative intelligence that France possessed —the philosopher who had almost "broken through" to a new comprehension of the social universe—removed himself from the scene just at the moment he could have been of greatest help in guiding his countrymen to an understanding of the unfamiliar society they were entering.

IV. *Jean-Paul Sartre: The Marxist Phase*

With Merleau-Ponty out of the way, Sartre was left in *de facto* control of the ideological field they once had shared. Just as the former's confidence was faltering, the latter came into full possession of his own; at the very time that Merleau-Ponty hesitated and withdrew, Sartre overcame his previous scruples and hurtled headlong into the political struggle. He who had once been his younger friend's pupil in matters ideological now felt qualified to pronounce on all subjects

[87] Ricoeur, "Hommage à Merleau-Ponty," p. 1115.

of public controversy. Thus in the early 1950's the political paths of the two crossed each other bound in opposite directions: as Merleau-Ponty declared his disillusionment with Communism, Sartre vowed eternal hatred for the bourgeoisie. And the irony of the matter was that Sartre was "less of a Marxist than Merleau-Ponty: indeed in a fundamental sense no Marxist at all."[88]

For Sartre the decisive year was 1952—the year in which he began to publish his essays on the Communists and peace. The course of events since the outbreak of the Korean War had convinced him that the United States alone threatened to drag humanity into a third world war; the Soviet Union and its dependent Communist parties were striving to preserve the peace—hence it was only logical for him to urge the working people of France to trust in their Communist leaders (although he himself would continue to maintain his personal freedom from party discipline). This line of action had been anticipated the previous year in one of the most influential of Sartre's plays, *The Devil and the Good Lord*, in which it was apparent that the spokesman of revolutionary violence and ruthlessness was expressing the sentiments of the author himself. Three years before in another ideological play, *Dirty Hands*, the moral verdict had been left unclear.

It would be quite wrong, however, to suggest that Sartre had in any sense sold out to Communism. He had always disliked and continued to protest against the Communist practice of twisting reality to party ends, and he remained as stubborn as in the past about telling unpleasant truths; in 1956 he jeopardized his whole rapprochement with the party by denouncing the Soviet suppression of the Hungarian revolt. Nor was his judgment of events in the early 1950's as extravagant as it might appear later on: in the United States, with Senator McCarthy leading the pack, the forces of know-nothing nationalism were in full cry; in France, by virtue of a tricky new electoral law, the Left had been reduced to im-

[88] Lichtheim, *Marxism in Modern France*, p. 98.

potence, while the institutions and personnel of the Fourth Republic were sinking into political squalor. By the middle of the decade, of course, the international outlook had improved: with Stalin dead, and the Korean War and the French war in Indochina both at an end, the peace of Europe was no longer in danger; in 1956 the Americans made no move to aid the Hungarians who had taken up arms. At this point, when Sartre's scruples over Hungary might have tempted him to reconsider his alignment with Communism, events outside Europe supervened, confirming his earlier choice and prompting a rapid reconciliation with his Communist friends.

Like Lenin before him, Sartre discovered the underdeveloped world when he needed it most to buttress a faith that seemed increasingly inapplicable to European conditions. Beginning in 1951, when he made his first trip to the Soviet Union, he systematically visited the lands under revolutionary regimes—more particularly Cuba and China—and other non-European nations with a high revolutionary potential such as Brazil. Here his "ultra-Bolshevism" expressed a bitter reality: the anguished look of the poor was patent for all to see. Moreover, the neo-colonial wars waged by the Western powers provided ample reason for indignation. From 1954 to 1962, the question of Algerian independence mobilized Sartre's ideological energies; after 1965 it was the turn of the American war in Vietnam. Throughout the 1950's and 1960's, and wherever he went in the non-European world, Sartre pledged his solidarity to the revolutionary struggle.

In 1958 he was with the demonstrators in the streets of Paris, singing out the *Marseillaise* in protest against the return to power of De Gaulle. Two years later he was a leading figure among the "121"—the intellectuals who announced their support of the Algerian rebels and asserted the right of French citizens to civil and military disobedience in an unjust war. Summoned before his country's courts, he sent back an answer that turned the charge on his accusers; he refused to cut short his stay in Brazil, where he was committed to a

lecture tour, and he denied the moral legitimacy of the
French government, defying it to impose whatever sanctions
it chose. This was the moment at which Sartre came closest
to political greatness, as he voiced the shame and anger of
professors and writers, of pastors and priests, revolted by the
tortures and barbarities that France's war of repression had
entailed.

Back home at the end of 1960, Sartre found himself
officially unmolested: De Gaulle's government had quite
sensibly decided that it would be folly to make a martyr of
him. But the unofficial violence of the right-wing extremists
was mounting: in 1961, Sartre was obliged to change his
residence repeatedly, and his apartment was devastated by a
plastic bomb. In February of the following year he was again
in the streets, joining his voice to those protesting the callous-
ness of the police toward anti-war demonstrators and the
government's delays in bringing the Algerian conflict to an
end. This was the last and largest of the ideological displays
that had punctuated the postwar years; a million Parisians
had turned out. And then, just at the moment of greatest
bitterness, peace descended. The spring of 1962 brought the
liberation of Algeria and the end of France's three decades
of political strife.

It all happened so fast that the French themselves failed
to understand how an atmosphere of latent civil war could
have changed almost overnight into one of ideological torpor.
In fact such a demobilization of spirits had long been in the
making. For the better part of a decade the French had
been enjoying the most extended period of prosperity they
had known since 1914: the old antagonisms were dissolving;
the traditional political cleavages were losing their relevance.
But the Algerian War had masked the change, prolonging
France's civil hostilities into an era which was basically alien
to them. With the war over, the new France was suddenly
revealed.

Yet Sartre carried on as though nothing had occurred. He
now considered himself as enrolled for life in the worldwide

struggle for freedom, and he had no intention of desisting merely because his countrymen at home had grown more satisfied. In 1964 he declined the Nobel Prize for literature on the ground that a writer should not allow himself "to be turned into an institution"—although he added that if the Algerian War had still been in progress, he would have accepted the award as honoring the cause to which he was pledged. On the verge of sixty, Sartre was too old to reconsider his assumptions or to learn a new ideological language. This fidelity to the established direction of his political thought was manifest in the bulky treatise with which he rounded out the inner dialogue that *Being and Nothingness* had begun—his *Critique of Dialectical Reason*.[89]

In the *Critique* Sartre finally engaged himself with Marxism as an intellectual discipline. Earlier, when he had taken ideological lessons from Merleau-Ponty, his convictions had been more passionate than reasoned, and his declaration of sympathy with the Communists, as his former mentor had pointed out, was insufficiently buttressed by logical argument. His *Critique* was not announced as an answer to Merleau-Ponty's essays on Marxism; but the word "dialectics" in both titles suggested that Sartre intended to defend his "ultra-Bolshevism" against the most subtle and competent of its detractors.

Although the full *Critique* was not published until 1960, its origins dated back to 1957, when a Polish review—inspired by the new intellectual freedom that Poland had won in the previous year—asked Sartre to write an account of the state of existentialism in France after more than a decade of public notoriety. This invitation gave Sartre a chance to think through the relationship between his earlier ontology and his later ideological allegiance. The result of his reflections, sub-

---

[89] For this sequence of events see Simone de Beauvoir's account in *Force of Circumstance*, Chapters 7–11, and the judicious analysis in Caute, *Communism and the French Intellectuals*, pp. 249–257; Michel-Antoine Burnier, *Les existentialistes et la politique* (Paris, 1966), is far more partial to Sartre.

sequently published in slightly altered form in *Les temps modernes*, figured in a third guise under the title "Search for a Method" as an extended preface to the *Critique* itself.[90]

This work apparently gave Sartre more difficulty than any of its predecessors. It involved him in what he called writing "against himself"—presumably meaning against his own inclination—and he complained that he had to "break bones in his head" to bring his thought around to where he wanted it to come out. He wrote the book at a dizzy pace: abandoning his usual practice of pausing and making corrections as he went along, he sat writing for hours and days on end, jumping from page to page without taking time to reread what he had written. He cut short his sleep and kept himself going with a variety of pep pills until his health began to buckle under the strain. His eyes were veiled with weariness; his speech became confused; on occasion he went nearly deaf. Finally his doctor sounded the alarm, and Sartre consented to take some rest.[91] The impression he gave was of a man forcing himself to complete a burdensome task and writing as fast as he could to get it over with. And the style of the book betrayed the effort it had cost. It was incomparably more cumbrous than anything Sartre had written earlier: reviewer after reviewer declared it unreadable.

If its execution was labored, its purpose was simple and direct—to fit Marxism and existentialism together. The former, Sartre declared at the very start, was the "one philosophy of our time which we cannot go beyond," and the latter no more than an "enclave" within it. Marxism figured as the third and last of the classic philosophies of the modern era—the first two having been the rationalism that had sprung from Descartes and Locke, and the German idealist tradition of Kant and Hegel. After these great "moments" had come the time of the epigoni, whose work deserved to be

[90] This is the only part of the *Critique de la raison dialectique*, I, *Théorie des ensembles pratiques*, which is available in English: *Search for a Method*, translated by Hazel E. Barnes (New York, 1963).

[91] Beauvoir, *Force of Circumstance*, pp. 385, 451–453.

called "ideology" rather than true philosophy. Such was existentialism. Yet existentialism ranked as an ideology with a pressing claim to attention, since its purpose was to rejuvenate the teaching of Marx.

In substance, Sartre claimed, Marxism was a very young philosophy: its implications had only begun to be developed. But under the ministrations of the orthodox it had stopped in mid-passage: the Stalinists had turned it into a cult of fixed ideas. The task for existentialism, then, was to restore to the Marxist method its feeling for the specific and the actual—to rediscover a "supple, patient dialectic" that would cling to the contours of human events. Such a dialectic would follow a "progressive-regressive" course not unlike that pursued in psychoanalysis: it would first discover the "project" which gave an individual life its meaning and then trace that project to its remote sources in the past. This method of "comprehension"—Verstehen—would convert Marxism into a new "anthropology" which would be "historical and structural" at the same time. And when the conversion had been completed, existentialism, having done its work, could simply disappear—a process of self-dissolution that Sartre's own book was intended to hasten.[92]

So much for the methodological preface. The bulk of the *Critique* itself consisted of an exhaustive account of the struggle of man's ontological freedom against the resistance of matter and circumstance, of the vast realm of the "practical-inert" which was eternally dragging it down. For Sartre the fact of scarcity gave the key to human history. It was the origin of violence, in that it explained why men killed each other or permitted each other to die. Violence was "interiorized scarcity, . . . that by which everyone sees in everyone else the Other and the principle of Evil."[93] Against the

[92] *Search for a Method*, pp. xxxiv, 7–8, 22–23, 30, 126, 133–134, 150–153, 175, 181.

[93] *Critique*, p. 221; I am following the translation of Wilfrid Desan (p. 94), whose meticulous analyses in *The Marxism of Jean-Paul Sartre*, Anchor paperback edition (Garden City, N.Y., 1966), are indispensable for finding one's way in Sartre's inordinately difficult book.

brute fact of scarcity, men as individuals were powerless. Try as he might—and the *Critique* was the laborious record of his efforts—Sartre could not avoid recognizing that human freedom was less complete than he had imagined when he had written *Being and Nothingness*.

He now saw that such freedom became actual only when men grouped themselves together for mutual assistance. The group, then, furnished the bridge between his earlier and his later view of man, and he strove desperately to keep the individual in the center of his account as he traced the growing complexity of human organizations. Such bodies, he found, had an inevitable tendency to ossify: only an unremitting vigilance could protect them against succumbing to the inert. And among them political parties were by their very nature particularly exposed to degeneration. One of the most curious features of Sartre's reasoning was that while he made no effort to deny the ravages of bureaucracy where Communism was in control—while he readily granted that a Western-type society was preferable from the standpoint of spontaneity—an idealized image of a Communist party such as history had never seen provided the underlying theme for the whole latter part of his book.

It was here that Sartre's congenital passion burst the dikes of dialectical reasoning within which he had tried to confine it. As the *Critique* advanced, the revolutionary romanticism which the public knew from his more journalistic writings came tumbling back in. Some passages breathed a Jacobin fervor: true to the rhetoric of 1793, Sartre spoke of terror as "the very bond of fraternity." Elsewhere, borrowing a term of Malraux's from *Man's Hope*, he celebrated the moment of "apocalypse" when a series of isolated individuals fused into a group inspired by a single aim. Hope and terror, freedom and violence, Sartre explained, were not the antitheses which reactionary authors made of them: they were dialectically linked together in a relationship so complex that it took him more than twenty pages to explain it; the tortured character of the prose itself suggested a strenuous effort at rationalization.[94] For in Sartre's view, revolutionary violence was both inevitable and moral—that is, in conformity with "history." Far more than Merleau-Ponty, Sartre delivered himself over to the illusion that there was such a thing as an underlying course of human events and that he was capable of charting it. Hence the equanimity with which he envisaged the sacrifice of life or liberty in the service of a promised future; he apparently felt that his rooted convictions about the inalienability of man's ontological freedom grave him a special license to condone the terroristic practices of the revolutionary Left.

In a similar flood of passion, Sartre poured out once more his old hatred of the bourgeoisie. It was a class, he declared, forever guilty of "massacres"—"avorteuse, affameuse et diviseuse"—the alliteration suggesting the linked crimes of reducing the birth rate and starving and dividing the poor. Such charges might still carry weight in the world of former colonies; in France itself they had lost touch with reality. And the same was true of the magnificent passage—in a literary sense one of the few in which the old Sartrian verve came through—that sketched the portrait of the bourgeois of "distinction," cultivating a set of tastes as divergent as possible from those of ordinary men, down to and including the well-displayed frigidity of his wife! A judgment so transparently personal can readily be ascribed to the particular quirks of the author's emotional biography—but what are we to do with the parallel assertion that the analytic method itself is as characteristic of bourgeois humanism as the dialectic is by definition anti-bourgeois?[95]

No more than his Marxist predecessors who wrote an equally complicated prose did Sartre ever make clear what he meant by dialectical reason. Nor was he much more precise about the related term "praxis"—which might refer simply to pragmatic behavior or might function in a more sinister fashion as a polite term for amorality. If dialectics

94 *Critique*, pp. 391, 429–450, 689.
95 *Ibid.*, pp. 717, 727, 741.

meant a supple method, which refused to be limited by either-or alternatives and which took account of the ramifying interrelatedness of human emotions and actions, all well and good. But this was no discovery requiring special congratulation. For more than a generation it had been the common coin of social study everywhere in the West—everywhere, that is, except possibly in France. Here the "lucidity" of Cartesian reasoning had never really relinquished its hold, and Sartre himself in his earlier writings had been faithful to that tradition. By the time he composed the *Critique* he had come up against the limitations of Cartesian thought. But it was one thing to recognize in the mind the inadequacy of a certain style of reasoning and something far more difficult to apply that recognition in his own work. When the style of Sartre's *Critique* was not merely turgid—which was most of the time—it displayed the same "cursed lucidity" as in the past. His treatise suggested an extended lecture to himself about being less Cartesian, and one to little avail, since the formulas of this self-correction remained as categorical as before.

It was curious that Sartre failed to recognize a predecessor in Georges Sorel, whose polemic against the literal-mindedness of orthodox Marxism had anticipated his own, and whose apologia for violence had been similarly phrased in terms of a liberating myth. Perhaps Sartre could never forgive Sorel his flirtations with the political Right and his admiration for Mussolini. In any case, the twentieth-century writers he cited with the greatest esteem were for the most part of a younger generation and more respectable from the standpoint of social science. Among sociologists there was Max Weber, among anthropologists Claude Lévi-Strauss, and along with them a distinguished roster of French historians including Georges Lefebvre, Marc Bloch, and Fernand Braudel.[96] Such were the contemporary students of human society in whose work Sartre found anticipations or reflections of his own concerns. But his references to them were confined to a

[96] *Ibid.*, pp. 116, 187, 236–238, 246, 381–382, 487–490, 743.

passing comment or an unnecessarily lengthy paraphrase; they failed to establish any intrinsic connection between twentieth-century social science as its most perceptive practitioners had understood it and the venture on which Sartre himself was embarked. These bows to contemporary scholarship figured as highly un-Sartrian endeavors to legitimate his *Critique*—to prove that it had an impeccable pedigree. At their worst, they were simply dragged in; at their best, they indicated that Sartre, like Merleau-Ponty a few years before, was participating in the generalized French experience of catching up with social study abroad (and with the progress of historical writing in France itself). But Sartre's digestion of the new material was incomplete. He never satisfactorily integrated it with his personal synthesis of Marx and Descartes.

Even this latter was tenuous in the extreme. Sartre's marriage of Marxism to his earlier philosophy entailed a number of sacrifices. It meant tacitly abandoning his former distinction between the for-itself and being-in-itself; it implied a denigration of the contemplative life in favor of revolutionary action; and it made impossible the writing of the work on ethics he had earlier announced—since the claims of praxis now overrode everything else.[97] If Frenchmen of the generation preceding Sartre's—men like Bloch and Febvre—had lived with too good a conscience to question their own values, in his case the process had been just the reverse: he had become so obsessed with the concept of bad faith, he had delivered himself over so totally to his conviction that he, like every other bourgeois intellectual, was ultimately at fault, that in the end he found no norm to live by beyond a desperate commitment to the cause of the oppressed—a commitment which left little scope for intellectual nuances. And by the same emotional imperative Sartre had been driven to compose a whole bulky treatise to rationalize his choice.

In the end the *Critique* boiled down to a "complicated way of talking *about* phenomena with which historians and

[97] Desan, *Marxism of Sartre*, pp. 251, 255, 282.

sociologists" were "perfectly familiar."[98] It was neither Marxism nor social science—nor did it offer the prolegomena to a new understanding of man. Both amateurish and old-fashioned, it closed rather than inaugurated a major phase in French intellectual history.

If this is the case—if Sartre's greatest ideological effort can be written off as a pretentious failure—it may seem pointless to spend so much time on him, indeed to devote more extended attention to him than to any other French intellectual who wrote in the years of desperation. Such is the conclusion of most Anglo-American commentators, who are quite ready to dismiss Sartre with a few patronizing references to a confused mind. But to do so is to miss the point entirely—at least to the historian of ideas. For Sartre had in no sense a second-rate intellect. His interests were as wide as those of any man of his era; he wrote successfully in at least four different genres—the novel, the drama, the essay, and formal philosophy; with a different temperament he could have become a French Goethe. The point, rather, is to ask what there was in his emotional constitution and his relationship to society that made a man of such extraordinary gifts take the road he did.

At the start one needs to insist—again with Anglo-American detractors in mind—that there was nothing base or self-interested about Sartre's alignment with Communism. It brought him little credit and much abuse. The only tangible benefit he derived from it was the pleasure of being royally entertained in Moscow or Havana or Peking. In return he received an unending stream of calumny, sarcasm, and distortion of his thought—not all of which came from the political Right. When the 1950's opened and Sartre set out on his ideological adventures, he was just entering middle life and his fame was securely established; his subsequent forays abroad only damaged the reputation he had already won.

[98] George Lichtheim in *The New York Review of Books*, VI (January 28, 1965), 9.

The conclusion seems inescapable: Sartre's relation to Communism and revolution was inspired by an inner need for atonement—a need to take upon himself the sins of the French bourgeoisie. Whether one chooses to call this attitude heroic or masochistic is immaterial: the evidence of self-punishment remains. The agonies he underwent in composing his *Critique of Dialectical Reason* may stand for all the rest. And even when he was not writing "against himself," Sartre behaved as a man driven by an inner compulsion toward words: he wryly admitted that he went on working at a furious pace decades after he had lost all conscious sense that anyone was ordering him to do so. If Sartre attacked so savagely the crypto-Puritanism of the traditional French bourgeois, it was certainly in part because he knew (and detested) the tyranny of such sentiments in his own heart.

Eventually the words themselves became vehicles of his moral asceticism. In the mid-1950's, Sartre's literary efforts bifurcated. After a struggle with his conscience which the recollections of his associates leave obscure, he evidently determined that literature—in the sense of style and composition—was no longer so important as he had once thought. In effect, he chose to sacrifice his position as a writer to what he regarded as his role in history. Hence the careless, utilitarian cast of his later writings; hence the crabbed style of his *Critique*. But at the same time—and most fortunately for posterity—he kept intact a corner of his literary pasture, which he tended rather more carefully than he had before. If he now devoted the bulk of his writing to polemical ends, he preserved a smaller segment of it as the domain of that "pure" literature which had originally started him on his way. It was to the second category that his autobiography of childhood, *The Words*, belonged—in the sense of craftsmanship as fine a work as he had ever composed.

This little book, published just four years after the *Critique*, seemed to take back or refute much that his Marxian treatise had asserted. After speaking with bemused irony of his "idealist" phase as a "long, bitter-sweet madness" from which he had recovered a decade before, Sartre went on to question the ideological commitment that had succeeded it. His pen, he now recognized, was not really a sword; he was well aware that intellectuals like himself were powerless; he no longer quite knew what to do with his life. But he was resolved to go on writing. It was, after all, his métier: there was no other way in which he was equipped to live.[99]

It is possibly unfair to judge an author by the moment of self-abandonment in which he delivers himself over to the mercy of his readers. Yet in Sartre's case, as in that of so many others, we have no more direct evidence available. Perhaps we can put the matter most charitably by suggesting that the whole ideological phase of Sartre's life—the *Critique* and all the rest—was based on a fundamental skepticism to which the autobiography finally gave expression. As a young man Sartre had thought in terms of the absolute: that had vanished with his idealist style of thinking, and no corresponding imperative had taken its place. There had come instead a more particularist and down-to-earth conviction that even in the absence of any fixed ethical norm, "innumerable tasks" remained to be performed. Alternatively—this time in terms of Sartre's self-definition—he had once thought of himself as a very special kind of person: a mandarin by hereditary right. Now he was cured of that illusion: he was ready to take his place in the ranks of mankind along with other men. But the only way in which he could serve his fellows was by writing in their behalf; and so he would continue to write—and in the fashion that had become habitual to him, in the tone of a peremptory summons to duty.

Thus absolutist thinking went out by the door and came in again through the window.[100] The result, while illogical, had an undeniable dignity and even charm. Sartre meant quite literally what he had said in his lecture on existentialist ethics two decades before—that he (in common with everyone else) bore a responsibility for all his fellowmen. However suspect the emotional origins of so cosmic a sense

99 *The Words*, pp. 253–254.
100 Jeanson, "Un quidam," p. 345.

of responsibility—however it might lend itself to the urbane mockery of his educated countrymen—this sense was the legitimate heir of that aspiration to universal values that had long been the characteristic mark of the French intellectual. In expressing it Sartre aligned himself with the tradition of the great moralistes; he took his place in the lineage of French classicism. Yet he did so with a difference which to him was capital: Sartre thought of the universalism he espoused as something quite new, as an articulation of the longings of the non-European world, only very lately released from the domination of Westerners like himself.

Herein lay the pathos of Sartre's position. For all the generosity of his gestures to the world overseas, he himself remained incorrigibly Cartesian-French. The very manner in which he espoused the cause of the oppressed in Asia or Africa or Latin America betrayed him to be an old-style European intellectual, perhaps the last truly great one that the twentieth century was to see. At bottom he belonged with the ideologists of the previous century—although he angrily rejected the identification—pronouncing as an amateur on the variegated subjects his restless mind encountered. In the second phase of his intellectual endeavors, Sartre succeeded in illuminating no significant facet of human society; his "search for a method" ran into the sands. Sartre's striving toward universalism had the opposite of the effect he had desired: his impassioned revolutionary rhetoric, far from opening up new vistas, cut him off from the mainstream of contemporary social thought.

Sartre's analysis of ethical ambiguity had liberated a whole intellectual generation from facile moralizing. Yet the philosopher "who could unmask the deep bad faith behind the complicated network of individual motives with flawless lucidity, became paradoxically naïve each time he dealt with institutions, political parties, techniques of organization or social structure. . . . On the level of structures, Sartre made the black and white judgments that he—more than anyone— eliminated on the individual level. The subtle, complicated,

supremely comprehensive man that he tried to become . . .
reverted to an ideological bourgeois, peremptorily distinguishing between good and evil."[101] If the premature death of
Merleau-Ponty was a tragedy for French intellectual life, the
ideological adventures of the later Sartre reinforced the loss.
After the mid-1950's Sartre "brutalized" his own thought to
the point of caricature. He turned it to ends that were far
removed from disinterested inquiry. The fact that the most
powerful and original among the French thinkers of the midcentury chose to pursue so eccentric a course could not fail
to retard the efforts of his countrymen to break out of their
self-imposed confinement.

---

[101] Michel Crozier, "The Cultural Revolution: Notes on the Changes
in the Intellectual Climate of France," *A New Europe?* edited by
Stephen R. Graubard (Boston, 1964), pp. 614–615.

CHAPTER
6

The Way Out

IN THE DECADE and a half following the war, France experienced three intellectual enthusiasms that both paralleled and contradicted the continuing influence of Jean-Paul Sartre. In intrinsic terms the successive recipients of the public's favor—Albert Camus, Pierre Teilhard de Chardin, and Claude Lévi-Strauss—had little in common. The first was a man of letters in the classical tradition, the second a scientist-priest and cosmological visionary, the third an anthropologist with irreproachable technical credentials; their writings were in totally different genres, and their explicit ideas seldom met. As social thinkers, their influence was equally diverse: while Camus and Teilhard were exemplary figures rather than rigorous theorists, Lévi-Strauss was a social scientist of major international influence, the first of such stature France had produced since Durkheim. Initially it might seem that the only attribute the three shared was the acclaim their work inspired, their situation at the origin of a cult which went far beyond what they themselves had written.

In addition to this, however, and directly relevant to the conclusions of the present study, Camus and Teilhard and Lévi-Strauss had in common an exotic strain that in itself was responsible for much of their popularity. No one of them conformed to the standard model of the French intellectual;

each drew his material and inspiration from outside France. And all enjoyed at least as great a reputation abroad as at home. This atypical quality, this ability to speak to the concerns of Frenchmen and foreigners alike, suggests the role they shared in the contemporary intellectual history of their country: they were the champions of France's return to a wider community, the men who reached out beyond the confines of their countrymen's cultural fortress. What Camus had discovered in North Africa, or Teilhard in China, or Lévi-Strauss in Brazil became the point of departure for a renewed search for a frame of social discourse wide enough to accommodate the French alongside and in sympathy with their counterparts abroad.

1. *Albert Camus: Sunlight and Exile*

To Camus most of his mature life was exile—exile from the Algerian sun that had nourished him. It was a familiar experience in France for a boy from the provinces to go to Paris to make his intellectual fortune. It was something quite new that a young man born across the Mediterranean should become a major figure in French cultural life: in France there were few parallels to the familiar British practice of assimilating promising "colonials" from overseas. During the period of his worldwide fame Camus might seem to have become a Parisian like any other. Yet what was deepest within him refused to be assimilated to the French norm; to the end of his life a nostalgia for North Africa dominated his thought, giving the key both to his philosophical pessimism and to his unshakable conviction that life was worth living.

Like most of the three-quarter million Europeans who once lived in Algeria, Camus was of mixed origin—his mother Spanish, his father descended from Alsatians who had left their native province on its annexation to Germany in 1871. The family was of the working class: besides his exotic birth,

Camus, in common with Péguy, was distinguished from the intellectuals with whom he was later to associate by the poverty in which he grew up. Born in 1913 in a village near the city of Constantine, Camus never knew his father, who died of wounds he had suffered at the Battle of the Marne. After her husband's death, his mother moved to Algiers, which from then on was to be the boy's home. Deaf, inarticulate, worn down by the domestic service with which she kept the family alive, Camus's silently suffering mother was one pole of the emotional experience that Algiers became for him; the other was the freedom and the joy of life under the Algerian sun—the "pagan" delights of young people tanning themselves on the beaches or splashing in the sea during a summer that stretched on almost without an end. Here lay the earliest and simplest of Camus's ethical dilemmas—how to reconcile his exultation in life itself with his sense of solidarity for the miseries of the poor.

From one standpoint—from the standpoint of European settlement—Algeria was a new, almost a frontier community comparable in its society, as it was in its climate, to California or Australia. Camus spoke of the beautiful city in which he grew up, and of Oran, its ugly sister, the home town of his wife and the setting for his most influential novel, *The Plague*, as cities without a past. Certainly the Algerian youth whom Camus knew, absorbed in physical pleasure, were as untroubled by history as they were by religion. But behind them were the Moslem masses, who had been in the land for centuries or millennia before the Europeans and who far outnumbered them, and behind the tradition of Islam the memory of Rome and Carthage—and more distant still, to the east and across the Mediterranean, Greece itself. As a young man, Camus was to extend his definition of Algeria's meaning for him beyond the beauty of landscapes and young bodies under the eternal sun to embrace the "North African" variant of Greek wisdom exemplified in the Neo-Platonism of Plotinus.

Whether he would have gotten that far without the experience of personal suffering is certainly open to doubt. In his early adolescence, although Camus had been discovered by his teachers and was being given the moral and financial encouragement that enabled him to go on to the lycée and the university, his dominant concerns remained those of the young people he knew: his greatest pride was his skill as the goalie of his soccer team. Then at the age of seventeen he was stricken by tuberculosis; months of enforced inactivity and the menace hanging over him prompted long reflections on the tragedy and absurdities of man's lot. For the rest of his life, although he led a very active existence and seldom spared himself, Camus's health was to be precarious. His illness also barred him from the career of teaching in the French educational system for which he had earlier been destined.

In the end, this disappointment may have been for the best. For a man whose gravest intellectual weakness was a tendency to moralize it was perhaps fortunate that he never became a pedagogue. He had instead an opportunity to explore several different paths and to make his own mistakes. Among the latter were a brief marriage at the age of twenty and a somewhat longer period of membership in the Communist party. From 1934 to the outbreak of the war, Camus led an extraordinarily varied and dynamic life, whose focal points were journalism, directing an experimental theater, and a share in founding a new review, *Rivages*, which was intended to be the voice of "Mediterranean culture." In this last venture Camus found himself associated with the small but congenial literary elite of his native city—men who were just becoming conscious of their special cultural situation as Algerian-French and who recognized in him a leader and companion of surpassing talent.[1] Again it may have been

[1] On Camus's Algerian youth, see Germaine Brée, *Camus*, revised, Harbinger paperback edition (New York, 1964), Chapters 2 and 3, and two articles in the special edition of *La table ronde*, No. 146 (February 1960), published on the occasion of his death: Jacques Heurgon, "Jeunesse de la Méditerranée," pp. 16–21; Armand Guibert, "Limpide et ravagé . . . ," pp. 26–29.

fortunate that Camus spent his early twenties in a milieu
where he was appreciated and encouraged to the full, far
from the literary cliques and the ruthless intellectual competition of Paris. In Algiers he had a chance to write as he
chose and to absorb the example of his French predecessors
—Gide, Malraux, and the rest—through a screen of protective
distance. Hence a characteristic detachment and abstraction
in his writings, hence the severe classicism of a prose he had
purged of local eccentricity.

Two events brought to a sudden and brutal close this
passionate idyll under the Algerian sun. First there was the
approaching war. In the summer of 1939, the twenty-five-
year-old Camus, who thus far had traveled only as far as
Marseilles and Spain and Italy, was obliged to give up his
cherished dream of a trip to Greece.

> I had planned to make the voyage of Ulysses again . . .
> but I did as everyone else did: I did not sail. I took my
> place in the shuffling queue standing in front of the open
> door of hell. Little by little we entered. And at the first
> scream of assassinated innocence, the door slammed shut
> behind us. We were in hell, we have never quite come
> out of it again.[2]

When the war broke out in September, Camus tried to
enlist, not for reasons of patriotism or ideological conviction
but through a simple sense of solidarity. Quite predictably
he was rejected on grounds of health. Meantime his personal
situation in Algiers had become impossible. The second
painful sequence of events in this grievous year was the
reaction to a series of articles that Camus had published on
conditions among the Kabyle population of the neighboring
mountains: totally without racial and religious prejudice himself, he had described in unsparing terms the misery of the
native people and had proposed a set of reforms leading to

[2] "Prométhée aux enfers" (originally published in 1947), *L'été*
(1954), *Essais,* Pléiade edition (Paris, 1965), p. 842. I have quoted
Germaine Brée's translation.

self-administration. The result was something of a local scandal: the authorities in Algiers gave Camus to understand that his presence there was no longer appreciated. Camus took the hint: he moved first to Oran, later, during the winter of the phony war, to Paris. Ironically enough, he had arrived at last in the French capital only just in time to witness the great defeat.

Evacuated to the Unoccupied Zone with the Parisian newspaper for which he was currently working, Camus stood the fogs and gloom of France as long as he could. In company with the girl from Oran whom he had married—and who was to bear him twin children after the war—he returned to Algeria in early 1941. For one more year, the Indian summer of Camus's happiness, the idyll resumed. Then his tuberculosis flared up: in the summer of 1942 he was obliged to go to the mountains of central France to take care of his health; the following November the full occupation of the country cut him off from his wife and from North Africa. Although he was to revisit his homeland more than once after the war, the Algerian phase of his career had come to an end.

By the same token the "historic" period of Camus's life began, as he enrolled in the Resistance, working first in Lyons and later in Paris. As editor of the clandestine newspaper *Combat*, Camus became one of the most influential of the Resistance journalists. In the last months of the German occupation, he led the double life peculiar to the underground: besides his perilous activity as a résistant, he carried on a perfectly open existence in the literary and theatrical milieu of Paris, installed in Gide's apartment and already well known as the author of two noteworthy books, his first novel, *The Stranger*, published in 1942, and a collection of essays, *The Myth of Sisyphus*, which had followed a year later. Not until the end of August 1944, as Paris rose in revolt and the clandestine press came out into the open, did the general public learn that the successful young novelist and the author of the nobly phrased editorials in

Combat were one and the same person. From that moment on, Camus's fame was established; he was only just over thirty, and his name was already a byword throughout the Western world—the first of his generation of writers to achieve international renown.

Camus's experience in the Resistance was the origin of much subsequent misunderstanding—a misunderstanding which clouded his memory even after his death. The commanding position he had won and the editorship of *Combat* that he continued to hold for three years after the liberation made him a public figure. Against his natural inclination, he felt obliged to pronounce on all topics of public controversy, many of which lay far outside the sphere of his natural interests. By temperament and training, Camus was anything but an ideologist or political commentator: he was primarily a literary craftsman, and after that a philosopher, but of the poetic and intuitive type. His ethical generosity had naturally drawn him to the Left, an inclination reinforced by his firsthand experience of discrimination against the native peoples of his homeland. The crimes of the Nazis had turned to passionate revolt this latent anger and hatred of oppression: the scandal of "assassinated innocence" had mobilized his energies for the underground struggle. But his sense of moral outrage gave him few cues for a political program: most of the time it found its outlet in categorical condemnation of cruelty and injustice.

As though unable to believe that Camus's ethical reasoning was in fact that simple, the public searched his writings for an attitude to which a philosophical label could be attached. Unaware that he himself thought of these works as a series of experiments with human and literary material, no one of which fully expressed his own views, his readers found in them a logical progression from a detached to a committed morality. *The Stranger,* the story of an unmotivated murder and of the murderer's indifference to his own crime, seemed to epitomize Camus's original philosophical universe of the absurd. *The Myth of Sisyphus* could similarly be interpreted as a celebration of the value of human existence pitted against despair. Finally, when Camus's greatest novel, *The Plague*, the account of a long, heartbreaking, virtually hopeless struggle against disease and death, appeared in 1947, the public was only too happy to discover in its author a lay saint, a man of modest but surpassing virtue. Unquestionably *The Plague* could be read as an allegory of fascism, the German occupation, and the quiet heroism of the Resistance, but in point of fact Camus had begun to write it in 1941 before his return to France, and its theme had a universal quality that eluded any single line of interpretation.

The most tenacious of the legends which gathered around Camus in the period immediately following the liberation was that he was an existentialist and the comrade-in-arms of Sartre. True, the two had become friends in 1944 and had subsequently seen a great deal of each other. And in some very broad, nonsectarian sense of the word "existentialism," Camus's writings, more particularly his essay on Sisyphus, might fit under the rubric—although he himself later insisted that this very essay was explicitly directed against the reigning philosophy. The almost universal coupling of his name with that of Sartre was based on little more than the personal association of the two and the fact that they were the most prominent pair of writers to have emerged from the French Resistance.

Sartre himself well understood the temperamental differences that separated them. In his own mind the Resistance had inaugurated a lifelong struggle on behalf of the oppressed: there would never be such a thing as a postwar situation of normalcy; the worldwide battle for freedom and equality had only begun. To Camus the experience of war, occupation, and Resistance was something hellish beyond the human norm; he yearned to find his way back to the universe of light from which he had been exiled. To commit oneself totally to an ideological cause he thought of as an emergency expedient, justified and even required in extreme circum-

stances, but in no sense the way to realize man's full capacities. In the war and immediate postwar period, Camus had
of necessity become a political militant, but he hoped that
he would not have to remain one forever. Those of his countrymen who were disappointed by his definition of ideological commitment as a limited liability failed to appreciate
that for Camus, however profound his compassion for the
poor, the joy of living remained the supreme human value.

Thus as Sartre grew more militant and peremptory—and
concomitantly drew closer to the Communist party—Camus
began to relax the either-or fashion in which on the morrow
of the liberation he had separated the just from the unjust
and to rediscover the Western tradition of tolerance and free
institutions. To Sartre the terrorist practices of Stalin's last
years were phenomena that had to be "understood" in terms
of the Soviet Union's beleaguered situation; this was the
lesson that Merleau-Ponty—the original Merleau-Ponty of
Humanisme et terreur—had taught him. To Camus such
political devices were identical with what he and Sartre and
their comrades of the Resistance had loathed and combated in
Hitlerism; when applied by the Russians they deserved exactly
the same reprobation. As early as 1947, he had quarreled with
Merleau-Ponty on this very score. Sartre had tried in vain
to prevent the rupture: as he recalled the incident with
bitter resignation fourteen years later:

I was to the right of Merleau, . . . to the left of Camus.
What perverse humor prompted me to become the
mediator between two friends, both of whom, a little
later, were to reproach me for my friendship for the
Communists, and who are both dead, unreconciled?[3]

By 1949, the issue of forced labor camps in the Soviet
Union was splitting apart the left-oriented writers of Resistance origin. While the Communists blandly lauded the

[3] Jean-Paul Sartre, "Merleau-Ponty" (originally published August-
September 1961), *Situations*, IV (Paris, 1964), translated by Benita
Eisler as *Situations* (New York, 1965), p. 254.

educational merits of such penal service, Merleau-Ponty and Sartre followed an intermediate line: they recognized the abuse but deplored its exploitation in the service of anti-Soviet propaganda. Camus took his stand with those who believed that the camps were an outrage against humanity deserving the fullest publicity, and in so doing he further strained his already precarious relations with Sartre. Then came the Korean War, in which he and Sartre chose opposite sides. By 1952, scarcely anything of their former friendship remained. In that year it vanished entirely, with an angry exchange of open letters prompted by the publication of Camus's *The Rebel*, the longest and most important of his speculative essays.

This book, on which Camus—constantly interrupted by the pressure of his public role—had worked slowly and painfully for a full half decade, was both a philosophical and a political tract. On the level of ethics it tried to formulate more precisely the Stoic protest against mass suffering that had been the central theme of *The Plague*. As a political polemic, Camus's book dealt with the two characteristic attitudes of the French Left which were also the targets of Aron's *Opium of the Intellectuals*—its worship of history and the absolutist intransigence it brought to its ideological concerns.

As the writing of *The Rebel* progressed and the Cold War grew more intense, the past crimes of Hitler began to take second place to the present and now quite visible crimes of Stalin. In its simplest form, Camus's essay was an attempt to convince his fellow intellectuals that the great revolution of the twentieth century had been perverted to ends nearly the opposite of those its progenitors had had in view. For an English-speaking public, with its tradition of philosophical empiricism and common-sense argument, a citation of the bare facts of Stalinist terror and oppression would have sufficed. For the French, a more elaborate train of reasoning was required; Sartre and his like had to be answered on their own philosophical grounds and in their own vocabulary.

So Camus chose to begin his argument in typically Gallic fashion with a Cartesian formula—"I rebel—therefore we exist." The experience of personal rebellion against oppression, Camus argued, founded "its first value on the whole human race."[4] From Rousseau through the regicides of the French Revolution to Marx and Lenin, he outlined the thought of the great rebels who had tried to extend to all humanity their personal vision of a new universe. This was familiar ground. It was only in his parallel account of "metaphysical" rebels that Camus introduced his special abstract twist.

Among the latter he numbered the Marquis de Sade—whose fantasies of torture in closely guarded fortresses offered a microcosm of the future world of the concentration camp—the Romantic poets, Nietzsche, and the French Surrealists. The metaphysical current, he found, fused with the earlier "historical" one in the Russian terrorist of the late nineteenth century, "the cruel high priest of a desperate revolution." And from there it was only a step to "state terrorism"—the "irrational terror" of the Nazis, a "primitive impulse" whose ravages had been "greater than its real ambitions," and the still more fearful "rational terror" of Communism, under which "slavery . . . becomes the general condition, and the gates of heaven remain locked."[5]

By this double route, Camus arrived at a surprisingly mild conclusion. Since rebellion had reached an extreme point of nihilist self-contradiction, its tradition must either disappear or find a "new impetus." Yet when Camus came to define the new source of moral energy, it proved to be very old and very familiar. It was, he asserted, simply moderation—

[4] *L'homme révolté* (Paris, 1951), translated by Anthony Bower as *The Rebel: An Essay on Man in Revolt*, Vintage paperback edition (New York, 1956), p. 22.
[5] *Ibid.*, pp. 160, 186, 219.

mesure—something that was second nature in the Mediterranean world, where he had discovered through his own experience that intelligence was "intimately related to the blinding light of the sun." Moderation, Camus hastened to add, was not "the opposite of rebellion. Rebellion in itself" was the moderation which held the excesses of mankind in tense equilibrium. In the "savage, formless movement of history," moderation alone could dethrone nihilism and restore respect for the value of human life.[6]

Such was the weary, live-and-let-live wisdom that Camus had derived from nearly a decade of participation in his country's ideological struggles. Stated in bald terms, it would have sounded commonplace and, still worse, conservative. So Camus was virtually obliged to dress up his results for the benefit of his public. Living as he did in an intellectual community in which some brand of leftism was de rigueur, he could save his standing and self-respect only by the gymnastic feat of equating ancient common sense with the new imperative of rebellion. And the same was true of the more formal aspects of his presentation: for intellectuals of a special sort a specialized literary argument was required. Hence Camus grafted on to his unexceptionable but routine account of "historical" rebellion the "metaphysical" branch that gave it a loftier look—and in so doing failed to establish any real link from the Marquis de Sade and his spiritual descendants to the world revolution of the twentieth century. By this literary device, Camus rescued his essay from banality. But he also weighed it down with philosophical paraphernalia which barely escaped pretentiousness.

In taking a political stand that was unpopular among most of his associates—however orthodox it might be in the rest of the Western world—Camus apparently felt under a compulsion to vindicate his own position as an intellectual. And at the same time he tried to prove his unshaken loyalty to the tradition of revolt. The result was a disappointing

[6] *Ibid.*, pp. 300–301.

work. Despite the eloquence of its concluding pages and the moral passion that had gone into it, Camus's most extended effort at discursive prose only proved his inaptitude for such a venture. He had already given his personal ethic a classic formulation in *The Plague*. As a novel, *The Plague* had kept the moral precept on the level of metaphor—which was where it belonged. Camus's attempt to explain his meaning more precisely simply weakened the effect of what he had written earlier and brought down upon him a host of critics.

Most of the French read *The Rebel* in terms of their own presuppositions and judged Camus's work accordingly. It was more often outside France that the book was assessed without prejudice: in Britain and America, in fact, it was generally overpraised. In situating *The Rebel* in its intellectual context at home, it is instructive to juxtapose the contrasting objections that Gabriel Marcel and Jean-Paul Sartre lodged against it.

Marcel, while generous in extending his personal respect to the stand Camus had taken, could not accept certain of his formulations, which he found "soft and insufficient." He refused to endorse Camus's contention that risking one's life in rebellion "purified" such an action. For a Christian, Marcel asserted, revolt and the violence that went with it were by their very nature morally equivocal. Nor was the attitude of passive resistance a satisfactory response: under contemporary conditions, it was little better than "hypocrisy" in the face of evil. To the ethical problems Camus had raised, no simple answer could be given; each successive movement on behalf of freedom or humane behavior had to be judged on its own merits. To the Christian conscience, Marcel concluded, revolt could never have "the last word": it would remain a "crucifying" dilemma through all time.[7]

[7] Marcel's essay, entitled simply "L'homme révolté," after being delivered as a lecture in 1951, was subsequently published in the special number of *La table ronde*, finally figuring as an appendix to the new edition of his *Homo viator* (Paris, 1962), pp. 348, 351–353, 364–366, 368.

Sartre's reading of *The Rebel* prompted no such moral fastidiousness. What annoyed him in Camus's work was the way the latter tried to have the best of two worlds—to deliver ethical judgments while remaining personally unengaged. Recalling with nostalgia the Camus whom he once had loved, Sartre dwelt on the meaning his younger friend had had for him in the period of their close association at the end of the war: both résistant and advocate of personal happiness, still more, a man who taught his readers their "duty to be happy," Camus had offered "the admirable conjunction of a personality, an action, and a work," had summed up in his own person the conflicts of the epoch and gone beyond them by the intensity with which he lived them. But such a fortunate equilibrium—such a tenuous reconciliation of contrasts— Sartre lamented, could occur only "a single time, for a single moment, in a single man." The human struggle had progressed beyond the events of 1944 and 1945, leaving Camus far behind. He who had once been the exemplar of a whole generation now sounded like a voice from the past. The ideal for which he stood had become quite simply obsolete.[8]

Pondering what his critics had written, deeply wounded by the virulence of their attacks against him, Camus might well have wondered whether perhaps Sartre was right. The three years following the publication of *The Rebel* were the most difficult of his mature life: ideologically isolated, weakened through a recurrence of tuberculosis, and torn by conflicting emotional attachments, he was unable to make much progress with his writing; between 1951 and 1956 no major work of Camus appeared. He returned instead for spiritual refreshment to his early avocation of theatrical directing.

In 1954 a further torment descended upon him—the revolt of the Algerian Moslems and France's protracted war of repression against them. For most of Camus's fellow intellectuals of the Left, whether democrats or communisants, Algeria presented no serious moral or political dilemma:

8 "Réponse à Albert Camus" (originally published in August 1952), *Situations*, pp. 91–92, 97, 100–101.

personally uninvolved, they found little difficulty in sympathizing with the movement of liberation. For Camus it was quite different: his own people, the Algerian-French with whom he had gone to school, played soccer, and swum in the Mediterranean, the people among whom he felt far more at home than with the Parisian sophisticates he had subsequently come to know, this people was fighting with its back to the wall for a land it regarded as its own. And the irony of the matter was that Camus was one of the small band of Algerian "liberals" who had understood and sympathized with the plight of the Moslems, and who, if they had been listened to in time, might have staved off the worst. Now it was too late. When at the start of 1956 Camus went to Algiers to appeal for a truce to the fighting, he was shouted down by the very people whom he thought he knew so well. Two years later he again proposed a peace of compromise—and again to no avail. After that, he fell into mournful silence, his thoroughly human and understandable refusal to take sides having alienated nearly everyone.

Camus did not live to see the end of the war and Algeria's liberation. But he must have known that he had lost his radiant home forever. As though with a premonition of what was coming, just before the outbreak of the struggle he had published a collection of essays and notes of travel about Algeria entitled simply *L'été*—Summer. In it he announced his joy at the discovery that the "invincible summer" he carried within him was stronger than the spiritual cold which had nearly destroyed him during his years of ideological altercation in Paris. And to underline what he meant—and perhaps to suggest that he had taken his leave of moralizing —in his last novel, *The Fall*, he abandoned the Algerian cities in which his earlier work had been set and plunged into the mists of Amsterdam. From the standpoint of craftsmanship *The Fall* was a tour de force, the finest thing Camus ever wrote. The five-day monologue of a "judge-penitent," a former magistrate turned self-accuser, it was a pitiless, unremitting revelation of man's hyprocrisy, pursued with psy-

choanalytic thoroughness into the depths of a hell that for
Camus was of necessity cold and wet.

The year following the publication of *The Fall*, Camus
received the Nobel Prize for literature; at forty-four he was
the youngest of the nine Frenchmen who had been thus
honored. With the prize money he was able to buy a house
in a village in Provence, where he planned to retire for long
periods of writing. By the end of 1959, his health seemed re-
established and he was hard at work on another novel that
was larger and more ambitious than anything he had written
before. A new life and a new burst of creation were beginning when in January 1960 Camus was killed, with heartbreaking irrelevance, in an automobile crash.

Sartre's reaction to the event was characterisically generous.
Although he and Camus had never been reconciled, the older
man mourned in the former friend, now doubly lost to him,
the "heir of that long line of moralistes whose works . . .
constitute what is most original in French letters. His stubborn humanism, narrow and pure, austere and sensual, waged
. . . dubious battle" against the formless events of our time.[9]
For Sartre, in common with so many of his countrymen,
Camus was primarily that Gallic brand of essayist known as
moraliste—an observer of mankind, detached and emotionally
concerned at the same time. Abroad he was more usually
esteemed as a novelist. Camus himself apparently could not
quite decide in what genre he wrote most comfortably. In
contrast to Sartre, who moved with rapidity and ease from
one kind of writing to another and seemed thoroughly at
home in all of them, Camus never ceased experimenting
with his own talent. Perhaps he was at his most natural in
the combination of journalism, narrative, and reflection with
which he recalled his native land.

As an Algerian, Camus had won his position in French
letters through a severe self-discipline. Like David Hume,

[9] "Albert Camus" (originally published January 7, 1960), *Situations*,
pp. 109–110.

sedulously ridding his English prose of Scotticisms, he wrote
a French which was all the purer for the fact that it was in
part a learned language and not, as with Sartre or any other
Parisian from the educated classes, the speech he had heard
about him as a child. One of the baffling problems in arriving at an estimate of Camus—a problem neglected by most
of his critics, who take his language for granted—is to penetrate the screen of his noble diction to the human being
behind. A man of romantic temper and strong, direct emotions, Camus trained himself to write with classic simplicity.
His literary universe was "stripped to the fundamental"—
thus making it practically impossible for him "to draw upon
the wealth of comedy, tenderness, and infinite variety inherent in human living to which he himself was not insen-
sitive." In each of his novels he created a closed world which
recalled the "self-contained universe of classical tragedy."
Each was a separate and distinct stylistic feat: each was so
perfect as to hover on the edge of monotony.[10]

Camus was only too glad to recognize his debt to his
predecessors among the novelists of heroism. He wrote a perceptive and laudatory introduction to the collected works of
Martin du Gard, and he is reported to have remarked on hearing of his Nobel Prize that he personally would have voted
for Malraux. He was similarly open in his comments on what
he had learned from Greek literature, from the French seventeenth century, from Nietzsche, and from such nineteenth-
century novelists as Melville and Dostoyevsky. But the first
third of his own century passed him by: he had no time for
the psychological refinements of the generation of Proust and
Mann and Pirandello.[11] He was just reaching intellectual
maturity when Hitler came to power, and from then on he
was obsessed by the miseries of the era into which he had
been plunged. A man who had lost his father in the First
World War, Camus seemed destined from childhood to be

[10] Brée, *Camus*, pp. 85, 104, 110.
[11] R.-M. Albérès, "Albert Camus dans son siècle: témoin et étranger,"
La table ronde, No. 146 (February 1960), p. 13.

the voice of the desperate years, whose course exactly coincided with the three decades of his education and glory as a man of letters.

It was virtually inevitable, then, that Camus should have been put on a pedestal and canonized within his own lifetime. His reaction to his fame was predictably ambivalent. At times he reveled in it; more often he was harassed and annoyed by the miscellaneous demands his admirers made upon him, and distressed by the gap between his real personality and his public image. He who in his editorials or in the political debates he conducted with his fellow intellectuals could be haughty and almost priggish, in his moments of relaxation was not ashamed to show his boyish, comical, plebeian side whose existence most people never suspected. Camus knew very well that he was no saint: among the many excellences of his final masterpiece, *The Fall*, was that it closed at last the gulf between an impossible ideal figure and the very human and fallible individual that lay behind.[12]

At all costs Camus wished to remain true to the double lesson his Algerian childhood had taught him. "There is beauty and there are the humiliated," he wrote. "However difficult the enterprise, I should like to be unfaithful neither to the one nor to the others."[13] His effort to maintain a balance between his joy in the glory of creation and the compassion for suffering he had derived from an equally direct experience was doomed from the start to public misunderstanding. Camus was not even spared the ministrations of the well-intentioned religious who searched his writings for hidden traces of Christianity. In fact, Camus was in no sense a Christian. He was proud to be a pagan: the guiding concepts of Christianity—sin, grace, redemption, atonement, and the rest—had no meaning for him.[14] Nor did he fit into the

[12] See the comments of Simone de Beauvoir in *La force des choses* (Paris, 1963), translated by Richard Howard as *Force of Circumstance* (New York, 1965), pp. 53, 349.

[13] "Retour à Tipasa" (written in 1953), *L'été: Essais*, Pléiade edition, p. 875.

[14] Henri Peyre, "Camus the Pagan," *Yale French Studies*, No. 25 (Spring 1960), pp. 21, 23.

other schemas in which his critics tried to confine him. We have noted already that he was far from being an existentialist in the manner of Sartre. Neither was he a hedonist on the model of Gide: sensual enjoyments had come so naturally to Camus that they did not have to be learned or intellectually celebrated. Finally he was no junior Malraux dedicated to the cult of the heroic: for Camus heroism was bitter, unavoidable necessity, not a way of life to be sought out for its own sake.

Thus all the commentators who found an ethical or philosophical system in Camus's work eventually proved to be in error. And every time he himself tried to put his understanding in logical order—as in *The Rebel*—he ended by distorting it. At the center of Camus's moral universe was nothing more complex than a tremendous revelation of light —the power of the sun, "not as a distant purity, but as a fecundating bath . . . the unifying force of the cosmos." This was the primal intuition of his childhood which his reading of Plotinus had subsequently confirmed.

In contrast to the fundamental experience described in most contemporary philosophies, he had a certain happy experience of being which appeared basic to him: he passed it on to us. Around him and in history he sees the consequences of uprooting: he tells us about them. Camus, who is a thinker though not a philosopher, instinctively perceives certain truths. They had escaped minds dialectically better prepared than his own, but minds that did not know how to extract consequences from these truths or . . . did not wish to extract them. He recalls these consequences inexorably, monotonously. He rediscovers the values of life and happiness lost in the tumult and terrors of our age.[15]

For something over a decade Camus's shock and scandal at what he had understood made him seem rigid and preachy.

[15] Serge Doubrovski, "La morale d'Albert Camus," *Preuves*, No. 116 (October 1960), translated by Sondra Mueller and Jean-Marc Vary for *Camus: A Collection of Critical Essays*, edited by Germaine Brée (Englewood Cliffs, N.J., 1962), pp. 73–74, 76–77, 83.

Later, as he saw more deeply into the ambiguities of his own life, his judgments became less categorical. Camus was in fact the exemplary figure his readers took him to be, but not in the way they imagined. He was neither a rigorous thinker nor the agonized symbol of the years of desperation. He was rather a spokesman for sunlight and joy ceaselessly protesting against desperation as a human norm—a stranger arrived from across a mythic sea to expose in unsparing terms the unholy mess that the Europeans, shrouded in mists of hatred and deception, had made of their Mediterranean heritage.

The protagonist of *The Fall* was called Jean-Baptiste Clamence—the name unmistakably suggesting a voice clamoring in the wilderness. And Camus himself was something of a John the Baptist. As a prophet of reconciliation, he came too early: in the 1950's the French, still torn by ideological strife, were not yet ready to listen to the man of good will who told them that their squabbling was a sordid blasphemy against nature. Had he lived into the 1960's, had he been able to see the end of the Algerian War and the beginnings of cordial understanding between France and the Soviet Union, Camus's public torment would have been infinitely mitigated, and his subsequent writing might have been more in tune with the attitudes of his countrymen. As it was—after Camus's career had been cut off in mid-course—it appeared in retrospect that his fame and the flowering of his talent had been premature: within a half decade of his death his prose was already beginning to sound dated.

However the intellectually sophisticated might belittle Camus, the young continued to read him with rapt attention. For them, particularly in the Anglo-American world, his voice was eternally fresh and alive. The young took Camus to their hearts and made him one of their own. And each successive generation read in terms of a renewed understanding the words with which he had accepted the Nobel Prize on behalf of all those who had come of age as he had in the shadow of approaching war:

For more than twenty years of absolutely insane history, lost hopelessly . . . in the convulsions of the epoch, . . . those of my age . . . had to fashion for themselves an art of living in times of catastrophe in order to be reborn before fighting . . . against the death-instinct at work in our history.

Probably every generation sees itself as charged with remaking the world. Mine, however, knows that it will not remake the world. But its task is perhaps even greater, for it consists in keeping the world from destroying itself. As the heir of a corrupt history that blends blighted revolutions, misguided techniques, dead gods, and worn out ideologies, . . . that generation, starting from nothing but its own negations, has had to re-establish . . . a little of what constitutes the dignity of life and death. . . . Perhaps it can never accomplish that vast undertaking, but most certainly throughout the world it has already accepted the double challenge of truth and liberty and, on occasion, has shown that it can lay down its life without hatred.[16]

II. *Pierre Teilhard de Chardin: Vision of the Future*

By calendar reckoning, Teilhard de Chardin belonged with the generation of Febvre and Bloch, Maritain and Marcel, Martin du Gard and Bernanos. Indeed, he was very nearly the oldest of the lot, having been born in 1881, the same year as Roger Martin du Gard. But the slow pace of his intellectual growth and the exceptional circumstances that held up the publication of his writings until after his death made him the contemporary, rather, of Sartre and Merleau-Ponty and Camus. He was almost unknown in France until 1946; his most influential work did not appear until 1955; his tremendous vogue was a posthumous phenomenon of the

[16] *Discours de Suède* (Paris, 1958), translated by Justin O'Brien as *Speech of Acceptance upon the Award of the Nobel Prize for Literature* (New York, 1958), pp. x–xii.

late 1950's. In this context, Teilhard's influence can be treated as post-existentialist, post-Sartrian, impinging on French cultural life at a time when even Camus was past the point of maximum public favor.

Born in the Massif Central of aristocratic lineage, Teilhard de Chardin grew up in a serious-minded provincial household where the Catholic religion went unquestioned. His family was also of the strenuous, outdoors variety, rooted in a region whose extinct volcanoes and bizarre rock formations could tempt the imagination of a curious child. The boy Pierre early discovered a vocation for geology. For the rest of his life the link between science and religion was to be both his torment and his joy.

By the time Teilhard began the long course of training for the Jesuit priesthood, the Church in France was entering on the most difficult period it had known since the eighteenth century. The clergy's obstinate alignment with the cause of reaction and untruth in the Dreyfus Case brought down upon it the revenge of an anti-clerical government and the suppression or exile of the militant teaching orders. And as though this were not trial enough, the condemnation of Modernism by Pius X demoralized the forces of Catholic renovation. The young Teilhard could not fail to be aware of such a stirring and distressing sequence of events; but they found little reflection in his subsequent writings. As a fledgling Jesuit, he seems to have been a docile pupil: throughout his life he was to combine personal and intellectual adventurousness with an uncomplaining obedience to his religious superiors. The chief effect on him of the tumult within the Church in the early twentieth century was that it obliged him to go for part of his training to England, where he acquired a fluency in the English language which subsequently gave him easy access to the world of international science.

It was the First World War, rather, that awakened in Teilhard the vision of his future course. He did front-line service as a stretcher-bearer, giving the comfort of religion to countless soldiers at the moment of death. When offered promotion to the position of divisional chaplain, with the rank of captain, Teilhard characteristically refused: he felt he could be more useful if he remained with the enlisted men. Without question, he saw his full share of the filth and horror of the trenches. Yet he managed to distill from the experience something beyond agonized participation in the suffering of his fellowmen. He who until his early thirties had lived the sheltered life of a scholarly priest was thrust by the war into close, promiscuous contact with humanity in its raw mass. Whatever his personal fastidiousness—and he remained an aristocrat in manners to the end of his life—Teilhard was not revolted by what he saw around him. On the contrary, he found his soul uplifted by a mighty realization, cosmic in scope, that mankind was one.[17]

When the war was over, Teilhard was free once more to pursue his studies. He took his doctorate in palaeontology and began teaching, as Maritain had done a decade earlier, at the Institut Catholique in Paris. By 1926, however, his evolutionary interpretation of the doctrine of original sin had alarmed his religious superiors. Three years earlier he had made an initial trip to China, where he had joined an expedition exploring the Mongolian desert. Now, with teaching forbidden and further residence in Paris inadvisable, Teilhard returned to Asia as to an intellectual refuge. His second period of work in China little by little extended into a twenty-year exile, lasting from his mid-forties to the age of sixty-five. Here he lived most of the time in Peking, where he soon became quite at home, partly pursuing his own researches and partly serving as scientific adviser to the Chinese government. Field expeditions alternated with the quiet work of writing and classifying: Teilhard's greatest discovery was the remains of Sinanthropus, a Neanderthal-type predecessor of Homo sapiens. As the years went by,

[17] For Teilhard's early years, see Claude Cuénot, *Pierre Teilhard de Chardin: les grandes étapes de son évolution* (Paris, 1958), translated by Vincent Colimore as *Teilhard de Chardin: A Biographical Study* (London, 1965), Chapters 1 and 2.

Teilhard's name became respected among palaeontologists, and he himself a familiar, well-loved figure within the international group of scientists who based themselves in China.

Although he was permitted to return to France at intervals, he never stayed there very long, and this absence from his native land proved particularly painful during the Second World War, when he and the small band of Frenchmen stranded in Peking were virtually the prisoners of the Japanese. Hence it was with a sense of tense anticipation that Teilhard finally reached Paris in the spring of 1946 after a seven-year absence. He had grown old in exile: now was his last chance, he realized, to introduce his countrymen to the meditations he had been elaborating during his two decades in China. Thus far his strictly scientific articles had alone been published: his larger, more speculative works had circulated only in typed or mimeographed form among his friends and associates (we have seen that Saint-Exupéry had some of them). During the five postwar years he spent in Paris, Teilhard worked patiently, tenaciously to break down the ecclesiastical barrier which cut him off from his prospective public: he circulated in high society; he lectured to small, selected groups—he was forbidden large meetings—debating on one occasion with Gabriel Marcel himself; and he made a special trip to Rome to plead for permission to publish his most important work, *The Phenomenon of Man.*

Teilhard was disappointed on every score. Despite changes he made in the text, his book remained under ecclesiastical ban. He was similarly not allowed to be a candidate for a chair at the Collège de France, where the faculty was prepared to vote in his favor. In 1951, he was obliged to leave Paris once more. His "underground" popularity had become too much for Teilhard's religious superiors, who intimated that exile was again in order. The last four years of his life he spent in New York, cherished by his American friends, who were both numerous and faithful, and devoting himself to the twin tasks of getting abreast of the latest theories in evolutionary geology while trying to persuade the anthropological profession as a whole to become more conscious of its ties to physics and palaeontology.

When Teilhard died on Easter Sunday 1955, few in either New York or Paris noted the event. But by the end of the year his posthumous fame had begun. An international committee undertook the publication of his complete works. In December 1955 the appearance of *The Phenomenon of Man* produced a literary sensation; within a short time 100,000 copies had been sold. In the next half decade the rest of Teilhard's semi-clandestine corpus saw the light. By 1960, "Teilhardism" had itself become an intellectual phenomenon of major dimensions.

In attempting to assess what mushroomed into an organized cult, with its devotees and special publications, it is necessary to stress at the start that in the strictly scientific sense Teilhard was a geologist or palaeontologist and nothing more. In the two aspects of his work which most engaged the general public, evolutionary biology and Catholic theology, he ranked as an amateur. What we know of Teilhard's reading suggests that little of it was theological. When Maritain first met him, he was surprised to discover that his colleague either had never known anything about Thomism or had forgotten what he had once learned.[18] His intellectual allegiance had gone, rather, to French neo idealist philosophy and more particularly to Bergson, whom he revered as a "kind of saint." References to Bergson crop up constantly in Teilhard's writing, and it is quite apparent that this was the strongest and most persistent influence on his thought. Yet the views of the two men on evolution were far from identical. Where Bergson had seen a divergence between reason and intuition, or matter and spirit, Teilhard found all nature converging in one tremendous synthesis in which such philosophical distinctions disappeared.[19] The

18 Jacques Maritain, *Le paysan de la Garonne* (Paris, 1966), p. 173.
19 Madeleine Barthélemy-Madaule, *Bergson et Teilhard de Chardin* (Paris, 1963), pp. 9, 639.

great novelty of Teilhard's thought was that it totally abandoned the old dichotomy between the material world and the
realm of consciousness, discovering the latter already present
as potentiality for the future within brute matter itself. Little
wonder, then, that Teilhard early fell under the suspicion of
heresy.

From the standpoint of evolutionary biology, Teilhard's
work descended from Lamarck rather than from Darwin. Although at the end of his life he tried to bring his theories
closer to the Darwinian-Mendelian tradition of natural selection and heredity cultivated in Britain and the United States,
he remained at heart a Lamarckian: he was convinced, as so
many French scientists and philosophers had been before
him, that there was an immanent "intention" to the evolutionary process which the human mind could discern. And
he was similarly convinced—and thought it his mission to
persuade others—that this understanding of evolution was
compatible with revealed religion. Thus Teilhard took up
within the ranks of Catholicism a battle which the Protestants had fought out a couple of generations before. Originally—in the third quarter of the nineteenth century—
Catholics had remained calmer than Protestants in the face
of Darwin's *Origin of Species.* Less dependent on "natural
theology" as an argument for the existence of God, Catholic
intellectuals had been inclined to keep their religion in one
compartment of their minds and their scientific work in
another.[20] Through this politic device, evolution had gradually been able to find a place within Catholic education
without kicking up too much fuss. Teilhard, however, scorned
such evasions. He wanted to bring the whole matter into the
open, to prove to the religious that the evolution of the cosmos was by its very nature a manifestation of the glory of
God, and at the same time to lead the unbelievers along with
him in his search for traces of the divine intent.

In pursuit of the latter aim, Teilhard steadfastly insisted

[20] Stephen Toulmin, "On Teilhard de Chardin," *Commentary,*
XXXIX (March 1965), 53–54.

that even his larger speculative works were "purely and simply" scientific treatises. He kept out of them any explicit theological references, introducing the deity solely in the guise of a cryptic "Omega Point." Such was notably the case with Teilhard's most influential book, *The Phenomenon of Man.*

Originally written in China between 1938 and 1940 and revised during its author's residence in France in 1947–1948, *The Phenomenon of Man* was a detailed, highly organized demonstration of Teilhard's central contention that the historical development of the cosmos displayed a rational order.[21] The species known as man, Teilhard observed, was by its very nature the "center of perspective" on the universe. But it was more than that: man was also its "center of construction"—the "axis and leading shoot of evolution" which gave the entire process its final meaning. Even before the appearance of Homo sapiens—or of life itself—there had existed within the "biosphere" enveloping the earth the prerequisites for human consciousness. Thus there was an inherent solidarity to all life on the planet: both structurally and genetically, living things followed a single line of progress which could be defined as a "rise of consciousness."[22]

The decisive step in the evolutionary ascent, then, was the emergence of "reflection." As Teilhard never tired of repeating, an animal only "knows" while a man "knows that he knows." Or—to introduce some of Teilhard's special vocabulary—the jump from instinct to thought or from animality to the potential for civilized society could be defined as a process of "hominization." And with this process, evolution entered the "noosphere," the sphere of the soul in which man could begin to communicate with the divine.[23]

From the strictly biological standpoint, Teilhard recog-

21 *Ibid.*, p. 51.
22 *Le phénomène humain: Oeuvres de Teilhard de Chardin*, I (Paris, 1955), translated by Bernard Wall as *The Phenomenon of Man* (New York, 1959), pp. 33, 36, 72, 96, 142, 148.
23 *Ibid.*, pp. 165, 180.

nized, Homo sapiens had made no progress since the Crô-
Magnon epoch. At the same time man's contemporary situation opened up totally novel perspectives of evolutionary
adaptation. Modern man suffered from anxiety on a cosmic
scale: the new relationship between space and time that
technology had created gave him a sense of desperate vertigo;
the linking together of the continents into one world civilization produced a feeling of compression and heightened intensity. Under these unprecedented circumstances, man had
no recourse except to lie down on the job—which would be
unthinkable—or to press on to the realization of his full
evolutionary potential through a "mega-synthesis." If they
chose the latter, it was incumbent on all men to push forward
together, to advance in pursuit of the complementary ideals
of science and humanity to a "super-consciousness." Then
would be achieved at last a hyper-personal order in which
individual wills would be merged into a wider spiritual unity.
In the conjunction of reason and mysticism, science and religion, mankind would penetrate beyond the barrier of the
phenomenal world to a culminating "ecstasy."[24]

In a series of essays and lectures written over a period of
three decades and published after his death under the title
The Future of Man, Teilhard specified more precisely what
he meant by these predictions and applied them to the harrowing circumstances of his own day. Human progress, he
explained, was not the comfortable and comforting doctrine
its vulgar votaries imagined. It was a strenuous ideal, laden
with peril. Its "source of life" was a steady increase in
scientific knowledge, its social manifestation a growing pressure toward collective existence. Thus regarded, the frightful
events of the 1930's and 1940's in Teilhard's eyes lost some
of their terrors: the Second World War itself figured as the
birth pangs of a new human order; modern totalitarian movements were "neither heresies nor biological regressions" but
"rough drafts" in the direct line of cosmic evolution. Col-
lectivization was inevitable: the question rather was whether

[24] *Ibid.*, pp. 225–233, 244, 251, 284–285, 289.

it would come about through external compulsion or through an inner work of unification in which the value of the individual personality would be preserved. The first process would be merely mechanical, the second a union of souls inspired by fraternal love.[25]

Similar dizzy options faced mankind with respect to its biological future on the planet. A world that had taken ten thousand years to create had changed more in two centuries than in all the millennia which had gone before. What would it be like in another million years? One possibility was that the intense concentration of human life on the globe would create a cosmic explosion in which mankind would disappear utterly. Alternatively—if spiritual values were to come to predominance—the physical cooling of the planet might be matched by a psychic heating-up that would finally lead to a detachment of humanity from the earth and a reuniting of souls in Omega Point itself. Such was Teilhard's vision of the ultimate "ecstasy"—an "eruption of interior life," the merging of man's spirit in the divine toward which the Christian mystics had aspired through two thousand years of contemplation.[26]

To try to epitomize in a few sentences hundreds of pages of prose that leap without warning from a dryly scientific to a visionary tone and back again is to suggest the overwhelming difficulty in arriving at a fair-minded judgment on Teilhard de Chardin. No figure in contemporary French culture has prompted more divergent assessments. For his votaries Teilhard ranks as the most potent intellectual force of the century: his scientific detractors curtly dismiss him as a mystagogue and charlatan. Indeed, some readers may be surprised that he appears in the present study at all. What is the intellectual historian to do with so perplexing a cultural phenomenon?

[25] *L'avenir de l'homme: Oeuvres de Teilhard de Chardin*, V (Paris, 1959), translated by Norman Denny as *The Future of Man* (London, 1964), pp. 19, 46, 54, 74, 117.
[26] *Ibid.*, pp. 71, 122–123, 307–308.

At the very least it is only reasonable to separate the man himself from the movement that gathered around his name after his death. The latter is irrelevant for our present purposes: as a phenomenon of what used to be called middlebrow culture, it has no place in a study of intellectual leadership. We can simplify the problem further by dealing only in passing with the much-vexed question as to whether Teilhard is to be read—as he himself wanted to be—"purely and simply" as a scientist. Whatever Teilhard's scientific merits —and we may recall that he was known in scientific circles exclusively as a palaeontologist—the passages in his works that gripped his readers' attention and that aroused the greatest subsequent controversy were not those in which he was speaking as an expert. They were his predictions about the future, his charting of the unsuspected evolutionary possibilities that were open to mankind. And these could by no stretch of vocabulary rank as scientific in the customary meaning of the word. It was impossible either to prove them or to disprove them by any experimental procedure. One could simply apply them as a stimulus to the scientific or the religious imagination. And the same was true of Teilhard's idiosyncratic vocabulary. How was the reader to understand such terms as "biosphere" and "noosphere"? Was he to think of them as physically existent strata enveloping the earth? Or was he to regard them as spatial metaphors describing successive stages in the ascent of life on the planet? The latter appears the more probable. Teilhard's language as a whole is so heavily metaphorical, so consciously literary, that the scientific origin of his thought soon becomes lost in the mists of prophecy.

We can similarly dismiss as of concern to only a minority of Teilhard's readers the suspicion of heresy which overshadowed the last thirty years of his life. Unquestionably there was much in Teilhard's writings that exposed him to such a charge: passage after passage seemed to echo Spinoza's pantheist identification of God and nature. On the occasion

of his trip to Rome in 1948, Teilhard did his best to reply
to his theological enemies. While accepting the term "pan-
theism" in its "etymological meaning," he argued that his
particular version of it was "legitimate" from the Christian
standpoint. He also reminded his readers that he was dealing
with no more than the phenomenal aspect of nature; believers were free to posit divine intervention as a supplement
to his account.[27] After Teilhard's writings finally appeared
in print, their mounting popularity brought the very real
danger that they would be put on the Index. But when the
Second Vatican Council met, "Teilhardism," either pro or
con, never figured on that body's agenda: the assembled
Church fathers passed it over in silence. And in the wake of
the Council the Index itself for all practical purposes ceased
to function. By the mid-1960's the legacy of Teilhard de
Chardin, whatever the theological doubts it continued to
arouse, was no longer threatened by ecclesiastical censure.

Among Teilhard's contemporaries as thinkers "who were
Catholics," Gabriel Marcel and Jacques Maritain in characteristic fashion fixed on widely contrasting aspects of his
work. The former was deeply suspicious of a theory which
tried to explain away the horrors his generation had witnessed
by ascribing them to the "coming into being of a planetary or
cosmic consciousness," or by depicting them as "in some
sense the price mankind" had "to pay for establishing itself
on a new and superior level." Marcel thought that such a consciousness was a "mere fiction," and he accused Teilhard of
having destroyed his own ability to conceive the "unspeakable
and intolerable reality of the suffering of the single person"
by "thinking in terms of millions and multiples of millions."
When the two held their debate in Paris in 1947, no meeting
of minds occurred. Marcel was obsessed with the "dehumanizing" effect of collective living and the machine. Teilhard had
no fear of technology as such, and he was confident of man's

[27] *Phenomenon of Man*, pp. 169n., 308.

ability to master the forces his ingenuity had unleashed and
to direct them to beneficent ends.[28]

Maritain dealt with Teilhard more charitably. While he
was surprised that the scientist-priest should be so ignorant
of formal theology, and repelled by the intellectual confusion of his popularizers, he found in Teilhard's own career
more matter for admiration than for reproach:

> The solitary, painful, obstinate search of Father Teil
> hard, his patient courage in face of the ignoble obstacles
> raised against him, his passion for truth, his total com
> mitment to a mission he considered prophetic, the pure
> sincerity which shines throughout his work, and the
> extraordinary and entirely personal experience he lived
> through and which might have torn asunder someone
> less steeled against adversity, are things that deserve the
> most profound respect.

At the origin of Teilhard's thought Maritain found a "poetic
intuition" of the sanctity of "created nature." This poem
which he might have written, and which he delivered over
to his readers in a "kind of disguise," was the "true work"
that remained after one had sloughed off the scientific trappings and the popular cult with which it was surrounded.[29]

Maritain's characterization of Teilhard as a poet in scientific disguise comes closer to the mark than any alternative
interpretation and has the advantage of combining critical
rigor with a personal generosity of judgment. Few who encountered Teilhard failed to be attracted by the directness
and charm of his manner. One traveling companion described
him as "vibrant as a flag fluttering under the Asian sky,
energetic, lively, . . . tireless, greeting each day with a burst
of joyous enthusiasm." Another spoke of his being "very
handsome," with a "matchless style of an . . . irresistible

[28] Gabriel Marcel, *Les hommes contre l'humain* (Paris, 1951), translated by G. S. Fraser as *Men against Humanity* (London, 1952), pp.
122, 124, 198; Cuénot, *Teilhard de Chardin* (English translation), pp.
251–253.
[29] *Paysan de la Garonne*, pp. 172, 175, 186.

distinction. . . . There was nothing obtrusively clerical about him; in gesture and deportment he was as simple as could be. He was gracious and obliging, yet . . . as unyielding as a stone wall." Teilhard's fellow-scientists found him splendid company; but under the courtesy and fascination of his manner they felt a "disarming loneness."[30]

In an intellectual sense he was equally alone. In his early and middle years, he was only rarely able to share his cosmological speculations with his colleagues in the priesthood or in the geological profession. Not until the last decade of his life—after his return from China—did he encounter in Julian Huxley a visionary scientist who agreed with him that man was capable of taking over his own evolution. Outside the ranks of natural science Teilhard had a natural affinity to such "meta-historians" as Spengler and Toynbee, both of whom he studied and admired. Like them he sought to find an underlying design in man's adventure on the planet. But he protested against their "barren cyclism," arguing that it was the long-term "drifts" rather than the "rhythms" that were most important in human history. His optimism about the future of mankind—his effort to expand the confines of a cyclical interpretation—put him closer to Toynbee than to Spengler.[31] Similarly—and predictably—he expressed a preference for Camus over Sartre, and for Jung over Freud.

Once one has charted a few such connections, the basic fact remains that most of the leading thinkers—whether in France or abroad—who encountered Teilhard's work, while granting him their personal respect, refused to take his speculations seriously. Again—as in the case of Spengler or Toynbee—his true following was recruited among those of middling education. These found in Teilhard a kind of super-ecumenicism, preceding by only a few years the Johannine revolution in the Catholic Church and reinforcing the great Pope's message. Teilhard's vision of human unity burst upon

[30] Cuénot, *Teilhard de Chardin* (English translation), pp. 130–131.
[31] *Ibid.*, pp. 237, 345. These connections have been charted by Frank E. Manuel in *Shapes of Philosophical History* (Stanford, Calif., 1965), pp. 145–151, 159–161.

the world just as the Cold War was lifting and peace seemed within reach at last. Those who absorbed his teaching could view all mankind's conflicts as ultimately reconcilable, and the antagonism between Europe and Asia or between Communism and Western democracy as capable of being transcended in a higher synthesis. Although Teilhard had only a superficial understanding of Asian religions and never learned the Chinese language, he taught his countrymen and Westerners as a whole to find spiritual value in alien cultures. In similar fashion he urged them to seek out what was positive in Communism—its faith in man and in the future of the world. And the less dogmatic among the French Communists were ready to grasp the hand he had extended to them, stressing Teilhard's agreement with them in his joy and confidence in humanity, in his celebration of action, labor, and the material world, and in his anticipation of a "humanism of the total man."[32]

Such expressions of opinion, however well taken, belonged more to the category of poetry than to that of science or rigorous reasoning. Teilhard's hymn to humanity brought tidings of good cheer to a tormented planet: it seemed to put man back where he felt he belonged—at the center and summit of creation from which the science of a Darwin or a Freud had deposed him. (But at this summit, how many of man's usual attributes would remain, after he had been stripped to his divine core?) For assertions like these, Teilhard's technical credentials appeared more relevant than they actually were: his readers saw in him an expert replying to his scientific predecessors—denying that nature was necessarily "red in tooth and claw" as the late nineteenth century had believed, or that there was an ultimate irreconcilability between that nature and the culture which man had imposed upon it, as Freud had lamented in his *Civilization and Its Discontents*. What Teilhard's readers seldom noticed was

---

[32] *Future of Man*, pp. 191–192; Roger Garaudy, *Perspectives de l'homme: existentialisme, pensée catholique, marxisme*, 2nd ed. (Paris, 1960), pp. 193–194.

that his more far-reaching statements were almost totally without scientific buttressing: when evidence was lacking, his prose simply took off into rhapsody.

As poetic insight, however, Teilhard's writings gave his countrymen something they needed very badly. His work opened vistas on the world outside France, challenging the central assumptions of French ethnocentricity. As a prophet of universal love and reconciliation Teilhard will doubtless continue to be read long after his meta-science has been either refuted or absorbed into a more systematic inquiry concerning the future of man.

III. *Intermezzo: The New France*

Whatever date one selects—the mid-1950's and the beginnings of prosperity, 1958 and the advent of De Gaulle, or 1962 and the end of the Algerian War—it is apparent that sometime around 1960 French society underwent a profound change. In his last published work Merleau-Ponty, with his customary sensitivity for psychological nuances, began to ruminate on the altered ideological climate he found about him. It was an emotional atmosphere, he surmised, in which the old appeals to "history" had lost their force—in which conservatives could concede the innocence of Captain Dreyfus as a "commonplace" and remain conservatives just the same. The verities of the postwar Left, the passionate belief in "revolutionary heroism and humanism," had "fallen into ruin." Merleau-Ponty's own generation was filled with remorse for speaking about such matters "too dispassionately."

> But we should be careful. What we call disorder and ruin, others who are younger live as the natural order of things; and perhaps with ingenuity they are going to master it precisely because they no longer seek their bearings where we took ours. In the din of demolitions, many sullen passions, many hypocrisies or follies, and many

false dilemmas also disappear. Who would have hoped it ten years ago?[33]

Where Merleau-Ponty remained hesitant and reserved, younger observers—and particularly those from the Anglo-American world—were quite sure that the change was for the best. These were happy to find that as old-line Communism sank into irrelevance, the more flexible Socialists were coming into their own as the advocates of economic planning within a pluralist society. And they also had nothing against the ascension of power of a new class of planners: people of this sort were the bearers of "middle-middle" class values which had traditionally been slighted in French social attitudes; the emergence of middle-range technicians and managers was bringing a new directness to interpersonal relations and an emphasis on competence as the criterion of prestige.[34]

In this new atmosphere, the intellectuals themselves were coming closer to the middle-middle norm and differentiating their standards and way of life less sharply from those of physicians, engineers, or administrators. The loosely-organized political associations, like the Club Jean Moulin, which had become a characteristic mark of the Fifth Republic, provided a common ground on which bureaucrats and intellectuals could exchange views as equals. The mandarin, like the revolutionary, was succumbing to irrelevance. In the new France of public optimism and confidence about the future, the apocalyptic rhetoric of the immediate post-liberation era rang hollow; intellectual life had lost both its fervor and its special prestige.

The liberation—as Sartre put it—had been the intellectuals' "perfect moment": with the traditional powers in collapse

[33] Introduction to *Signes* (Paris, 1960), translated by Richard C. McCleary as *Signs* (Evanston, Ill., 1964), pp. 4, 22–23.
[34] George Lichtheim, *Marxism in Modern France* (New York, 1966), pp. 51, 144; Jesse R. Pitts, "Continuity and Change in Bourgeois France," *In Search of France* (Cambridge, Mass., 1963), p. 300.

or disarray, the mandarinate had enjoyed an unexampled public eminence; its every word seemed laden with portentous meaning. Yet it had never succeeded in defining a content for its doctrine of universal responsibility: it had oscillated erratically "between the total liberty of the individual revolutionary and the total constraint of Stalinism." By the 1960's such preachments had lost their vertiginous appeal. The younger French intellectuals—more especially the younger social scientists—were renouncing their "excessive ambitions"; their research was becoming "more positive and cumulative"; no longer claiming "to deal with everything at once," they were far more conscious than before of the relation of their work to practical action. As early as 1954 the brief, abortive premiership of Pierre Mendès-France had given the cue for a new public attitude of sober expertise and of reform through "concrete commitment."[35]

Yet if the old questions had been "too big, too vague, too murderous," there now loomed the danger that there would be no questions at all. If Sartre and his like had sacrificed the present to the future, the younger generation of French intellectuals seemed tempted to make a similar sacrifice of ethical aspiration to the acceptance of existing society as a going concern. The young were interpreting Camus's or Aron's pleas for ideological modesty as an "appeal against intellectual probing."[36] They were very nearly as suspicious of the older generation's ambitions as they were of its rhetoric. In putting so heavy a stress on the concrete and the nonrhetorical, the younger writers and social scientists were inclined to lump together the literary vices of the French tradition and the moral seriousness which had given that tradition its characteristic flavor; in the pursuit of a rigorous nominalism of method, they threatened to abandon the old

[35] Michel Crozier, "The Cultural Revolution: Notes on the Changes in the Intellectual Climate of France," *A New Europe?* edited by Stephen R. Graubard (Boston, 1964), pp. 602, 611, 613, 624–625.

[36] Stanley Hoffmann, "Europe's Identity Crisis: Between the Past and America," *Daedalus*, XCIII (Fall 1964), 1262.

quest for ethical norms and for universal statements about human society.

Once again, then—and at least as acutely as at any previous point in the century—a conflict of generations separated those who thought of themselves as the young from those who in fact were not so many years their seniors. Just as the men coming to maturity in the 1930's had been impatient with the refinements of the "last generation of French classicism," so those who grew up in the 1950's failed to understand their elders' absorption with ideology and revolutionary rhetoric. In this situation of mutual incomprehension, a mediator was required; and it was fortunate that the man who emerged as Sartre's rival and successor as France's intellectual laureate was ideally equipped to perform the role.

Claude Lévi-Strauss was only three years younger than Sartre; but his fame had come more than a decade later than that of the author of *Being and Nothingness* and in an atmosphere in which the attractions of both existentialism and Marxism were already on the wane. In his personal style, Lévi-Strauss combined the rationality and humanism of a philosophe in the great tradition with a thorough grasp of the latest techniques in social science. He was close enough to the familiar pattern of French thought to be able to lead along with him the more adventurous of those who still dwelt in that intellectual universe. Yet in recasting the pattern of thought in a new terminology, he in effect exploded it.[37] And in so doing he accomplished the feat of reuniting his countrymen with the world of social speculation beyond France's borders and of epitomizing in his own person the fact that France had finally produced a social theorist who was universally acknowledged as a master.

IV. *Claude Lévi-Strauss: Structure and Society*

With Lévi-Strauss, contemporary French thought was back where it began—in the sphere of social science, international

[37] Crozier, "Cultural Revolution," p. 628.

in scope, and with Frenchmen taking the lead. Like Bloch and Febvre, Lévi-Strauss was deeply, almost obsessively, concerned with developing a type of study that would render the "human" in all its infinite variety. He differed with them, however, in finding in structure rather than in flow the metaphor best adapted to convey what he had understood; indeed, he pushed the notion of structure further than any of his predecessors in this type of social inquiry. Nor did he limit his work, as Bloch and Febvre had done, to the analysis of Western societies. He took up the challenge with which imaginative writers such as Saint Exupéry and Malraux had already engaged themselves, of combatting French ethnocentricity by an open-minded confrontation with the values of alien peoples overseas. Like Malraux, Lévi-Strauss tried to understand what it meant for non-Western societies to live "without a history." But he went far beyond the novelists of heroism in the rigor of his method and in the thoroughness with which he shared the life and thought of the "primitives" who were to become the protagonists of his subsequent anthropological studies.

Which is all to say that Lévi-Strauss' intellectual antecedents were inordinately complex and reached back both to his immediate predecessors of the 1930's and to the pre-First World War generation of French social theorists. Among the latter Durkheim and Bergson naturally loomed the largest. Toward Durkheim, Lévi-Strauss' attitude was of necessity ambivalent. As a young man he had been in "open insurrection" against Durkheim's precepts or any comparable "attempt to put sociology to metaphysical uses." Yet as his professional career went on, he gradually discovered a lingering affinity to the Durkheimian tradition that set him apart from English and American anthropologists.[38] By 1958— the centenary of Durkheim's birth—Lévi-Strauss was ready to dedicate to his predecessor, in the guise of an "inconstant disciple," the series of essays he had collected under the title

[38] Claude Lévi-Strauss, *Tristes tropiques* (Paris, 1955), translated (and slightly abridged) by John Russell under the same title, Atheneum paperback edition (New York, 1963), p. 63.

Structural Anthropology. And he was frank in recognizing his own debt to the kinship and language studies of Marcel Mauss, the most influential of Durkheim's heirs. Toward Bergson, Lévi-Strauss took a more informal tone. In no sense a Bergsonian himself, he nevertheless made a point of recognizing where the philosopher of the élan vital could come to the aid of the student of primitive societies. With characteristic urbanity—and a hint of patronizing—Lévi-Strauss congratulated Bergson on being an "armchair philosopher" who in certain respects reasoned "like a savage," since "his own thought, unbeknownst to him, was in sympathy with that of totemic peoples."[39]

A second of Lévi-Strauss' major works, *The Savage Mind,* was dedicated to the memory of Merleau-Ponty, who had died in the year before its publication and had been its author's friend and colleague at the Collège de France. In this book, as throughout Lévi-Strauss' later production, one finds echoes of Merleau-Ponty, notably in the concern for man as "speaking subject." Yet the minds of the two friends —who in age were only a few months apart—worked in radically different fashions. Where Merleau-Ponty preferred to leave his thought open and elusive, Lévi-Strauss strove for closed formulations that had the precision of crystal. Each faced the same methodological problem: where was the study of man to go, once it had absorbed the teachings of Max Weber? Merleau-Ponty's choice was to push Weber's work to its logical consequences by "relativizing" still further the relativist implications in the ideal-type method—that is, by recognizing even more radically than Weber had done, the subjective and unverifiable character of the ideal types in question. Hence the floating, unstable intellectual universe of Merleau-Ponty's later thought. For Lévi-Strauss such indeterminacy was intolerable. As convinced as was his friend of the instability of the ideal-type method as currently under-

[39] *Le totémisme aujourd'hui* (Paris, 1962), translated by Rodney Needham as *Totemism,* Beacon paperback edition (Boston, 1963), pp. 98–99.

stood, Lévi-Strauss wanted to redefine and to tighten that method by eliminating its ambiguities.

In so doing, he took up the word "model" that in the meantime had come into currency among American social scientists, equating it with the older term "structure" to which he now gave a more precise significance. For Lévi-Strauss a structure was a model that conformed to several specific requirements:

> First, the structure exhibits the characteristics of a system. It is made up of several elements, none of which can undergo a change without effecting changes in all the other elements.
>
> Second, for any given model there should be a possibility of ordering a series of transformations resulting in a group of models of the same type.
>
> Third, the above properties make it possible to predict how the model will react if one or more of its elements are submitted to certain modifications.
>
> Finally, the model should be constituted so as to make immediately intelligible all the observed facts.[40]

Thus the model (or group of models) had an internal consistency that gave an initial guarantee of its validity. But even this progress over Weber was insufficient to satisfy Lévi-Strauss' thirst for certainty. Despite his agnosticism about the values—whether religious or ideological—ordinarily professed in his own society, he refused to remain in a similar state of suspended judgment about the nature of man: the overriding aim of his career as a social scientist was to dig below every theoretical level yet discovered and to come at last to a basic structure of the human mind which would at once cancel out and reconcile the countless explanations of

[40] "La notion de structure en ethnologie" (originally presented in English at a symposium in New York in 1952), *Anthropologie structurale* (Paris, 1958), translated by Claire Jacobson and Brooke Grundfest Schoepf as *Structural Anthropology* (New York, 1963), pp. 279–280.

their behavior that men had offered through all ages and all types of savagery or civilization.

A breath-taking quest—as ambitious as that of any twentieth-century investigator—and one which a half century earlier would have been totally unfeasible. For Lévi-Strauss enjoyed advantages denied to the generation of Weber or of Freud: in the meantime the study of man had evolved in two new directions which opened up unsuspected vistas of intellectual certainty.

The first was Lévi-Strauss' chosen discipline of anthropology. The latest arrival among the social sciences, anthropology as a clearly delimited field of study was only a quarter century old when he encountered it in the early 1930's. At that time its first great generation of field workers was still alive and active. The leaders of this generation, which included Bronislaw Malinowski in Britain and Alfred L. Kroeber in America, were of an age to be Lévi-Strauss' fathers, as the generation of Freud and Weber ranked as his intellectual grandfathers. Certain of them he treated with filial respect, others with an equally filial combativity. Much of Lévi-Strauss' work was a polemic against the underlying conviction of Malinowski and the British school that the rites and myths of primitive peoples could be understood in terms of a social function. His admiration, rather, went to such Americans as Kroeber and Franz Boas in whom he discovered an optimum combination of empirical method and a gift for synthesis.

By the very choice of anthropology as a field of study, Lévi-Strauss was led in a double sense outside France's cultural fortress. The contact with pre-literate societies was the more obvious of these outlets; equally important was the fact that the discipline as a whole was dominated by the Anglo-Americans (many of whom, however, had Central or Eastern European origins) and employed English as its international language. Thus, as a cursory sampling of his footnotes revealed, Lévi-Strauss worked at two removes from the familiar idea-world of his countrymen: he dealt with exotic peoples whose customs were for the most part interpreted in a Western language that was not his own.

The fact that the only anthropologist since Sir James Frazer to achieve general public renown was a Frenchman rather than an Englishman or American gave Lévi-Strauss' work an extra dimension. He brought to his labors a characteristic French conviction that cultural phenomena obeyed an immanent law. And more rigorously than his English-speaking colleagues, he insisted on a standard of objectivity in anthropological study which set this discipline apart from the other social sciences. Every social scientist, he recognized, strove to be objective in the sense that he tried to rise above his own value system; yet the anthropologist alone went one step further and questioned the entire method of thinking which permeated Western civilization. The anthropologist in effect jumped backward through time to the moment in pre-Socratic Greece when the canon of logical reasoning had first been established, and then took off from this point to a systematic investigation of how the mind of primitive man worked. Only by divesting himself of the methodological prejudices, scientific or philosophical, that were second nature to Europeans and Americans, could the student of pre-literate societies hope to discover the fundamental patterns of human thought that underlay its overwhelming diversity of expression.

In this quest, Lévi-Strauss brought to bear the second—and still more recent—of the new methods of study developed since the time of Freud and Weber, the technique of structural linguistics. Since the original pioneering work of a Swiss scholar, Ferdinand de Saussure, before 1914, linguistics had in a single generation become the most sharply defined of the sciences of man. Having totally separated meaning from sound in their study of language, the structural linguists were free to concentrate their attention on the phoneme, the basic unit of human speech. And once they had done so, they found that the possible combinations of phonemes were finite in number and followed rules which were statistically predictable. Such combinations, since they occurred at the unconscious level and were quite innocent of subsequent policing at the hands of grammarians, had the advantage of being value-free and devoid of meaning. The lesson for anthropology seemed clear:

> If . . . the unconscious activity of the mind consists in imposing forms upon content, and if these forms are fundamentally the same for all minds—ancient and modern, primitive and civilized . . . —it is necessary and sufficient to grasp the unconscious structure underlying each institution and each custom, in order to obtain a principle of interpretation valid for other institutions and other customs. . . .[41]

What Lévi-Strauss learned from the structural linguists was to think of his subject in terms of a net of relationships, all of which, if reduced to their essentials, had something in common. In this view, the task of the anthropologist became one of first drawing up an exhaustive inventory of such relationships and then establishing their necessary connections. And the area in which Lévi-Strauss himself chose to illustrate his theory seemed at first glance the most difficult of all— the realm of myth, where the human imagination was commonly supposed to wander untrammeled. If in *this* domain, he argued, the mind could be shown as "bound and determined in all its operations, a fortiori, it must be so everywhere."[42] If the systematic study of myth would bear out his basic contention, then he could "buckle together" the untidy loose ends in the study of man and forge a new positivism more potent and more sophisticated than the nineteenth-century positivist teachings which the generation of

---

[41] "Introduction: Histoire et ethnologie" (originally published in *Revue de métaphysique et de morale*, LIV, 1949), *ibid.*, p. 21.
[42] "Réponses à quelques questions," *Esprit* (special issue on Lévi-Strauss), XXXI (November 1963), 630.

his intellectual grandfathers had thought they had discredited forever.[43]

Although, as we have seen, Lévi-Strauss was the chronological contemporary of Sartre and Merleau-Ponty, he was
launched onto the French intellectual scene later than these
two, since he abandoned philosophy for the slow and round-
about path of becoming a field anthropologist. His reasons
for so doing epitomized his entire intellectual endeavor:
"With philosophy I had a sense of stopping half-way, of
stopping at certain types of thought . . . which were those
of our Western society, . . . whereas anthropology gave me,
rightly or wrongly, an impression of going to the farthest
limits of what was possible in the exploration of philosophy's
goal."[44]

Like Bergson and Durkheim and Bloch, Lévi-Strauss was
of Jewish origin. But no more than for these three was Judaism a living reality to him. (The eminence of this succession
of names—as influential a quartet as one can find in the
history of twentieth-century French thought—suggests religious agnosticism against a Jewish background as an optimum point of departure for social speculation.) In the case of
Lévi-Strauss, the Jewish tradition was attenuated in the extreme: his only memories of the ancestral religion derived
from the years of the First World War, when, already past
his early childhood, he lived with a rabbi grandfather whose
formal and desiccated practice of his faith was hardly of a
kind to stir the emotions. Ten or fifteen years later, Lévi-
Strauss found his philosophical studies equally unappealing:
although he did everything expected of him, passing the
agrégation at an early age and even beginning the normal
course of academic advancement by teaching in a lycée, he
felt that he was simply playing an established set of rhetorical

[43] Marc Gaboriau, "Anthropologie structurale et histoire," *ibid.*,
p. 595.
[44] Claude Lévi-Strauss, "A contre-courant," interview published in
Le nouvel observateur, No. 115 (January 25, 1967), p. 30.

games which bore little relation to "truth." Even the newer forms of philosophical inquiry held no appeal: Lévi-Strauss was suspicious of the phenomenologists' claim to have found a basis for reality in the minute data of experience and of the "indulgent attitude" of existentialism "towards the illusions of subjectivity."[45] Hence it was with a sense of deliverance that in the autumn of 1934, when he had just turned twenty-eight, he accepted, quite literally on three hours' notice, the chance to go to São Paulo as professor of sociology.

The better part of the following five years Lévi-Strauss spent in Brazil. Although sociology was his designated subject and although he was fascinated by the fast-growing, chaotic metropolis in which he taught, his real purpose in leaving France was to pursue the anthropological interests to which he had already been drawn in amateur and unsystematic fashion. Now he was resolved to make himself a professional: at home base in São Paulo, he read the literature of the field; in vacation time he ventured ever farther into the Brazilian interior to study the Indians at first hand. The last and longest of such expeditions, lasting a full year and unprecedented in its scope and hardship, took him all the way across the center of the continent through endless wastes of scrub growth to the valley of the Amazon. By mid-1939, when he returned to France, Lévi-Strauss had become a seasoned anthropologist.

By the same token he had become a stranger to France and had fallen out of the customary sequence of university promotion. The tumults of the late 1930's had passed him by: perspiring and struggling through the desolation of central Brazil, he had sometimes wondered ruefully whether it was not quixotic to follow so eccentric a course rather than getting ahead in the academic world as a fledgling French intellectual was supposed to do. And these biographical anomalies were reinforced after the outbreak of the war. In early 1941, having finished his military service and feeling threatened (as was only sensible) by the Vichy government's cooperation with

---

[45] *Tristes tropiques* (English translation), pp. 61–62, 215.

German anti-Semitic measures, Lévi-Strauss embarked for the United States, where a group of American anthropologists, to whom his name was already known, were prepared to take care of him. For the remainder of the war years he taught in New York, at the New School for Social Research and at the Ecole Libre des Hautes Etudes founded by other Frenchmen stranded overseas, notably Jacques Maritain. Here Lévi-Strauss acquired the fluency in English and the familiarity with American anthropology that were later to rank among his most valuable assets. But he also remained conscious of his role as a *French* intellectual: it was as cultural counselor of the French Embassy, a position he held from 1946 to 1947, that he presided over a lecture delivered by Albert Camus at Columbia University.

Back in France at last—and this time for good—Lévi-Strauss brought to completion the anthropological studies he had been working on for more than a decade. In 1948 the publication of his first book, a study of family and social life among the Nambikwara Indians, established him as a leader in his profession. A year later the first of his more speculative works, on the "elementary structures of kinship," brought him to the attention of a wider circle of intellectuals. Finally in 1955—the year of Teilhard de Chardin's death and of the posthumous publication of *The Phenomenon of Man*—the appearance of *Tristes tropiques* made Lévi-Strauss almost overnight a celebrated author in the eyes of the general reading public.

Although it was totally different in style and conception from *The Phenomenon of Man*, Lévi-Strauss' book derived its popularity from a similar quality of extending the frontiers of a scientific treatise far beyond the usual professional concerns. Besides giving a systematic account of what he had learned about four different South American Indian peoples among whom he had dwelt, *Tristes tropiques* was at once an autobiography and a philosophical reflection on travel in the manner of an eighteenth-century moraliste. Its tone (more nuanced than Teilhard's) alternated like his between the dryly factual and the lyric. Its underlying mood, as its title implied, was of restrained elegy. Subtle in phraseology, dense in thought, *Tristes tropiques* offered the extended meditation of an ultra-civilized Gallic mind on the ways of "savages" whom he had found to be not nearly so unsophisticated as their nakedness and destitution might suggest.

With the publication of his *Structural Anthropology* in 1958, the theoretical outlines of Lévi-Strauss' position had been established; the following year he received a newly-created chair at the Collège de France. It now remained for him to make fully explicit what he had earlier sketched out and to reply to the impatient critics who stood ready to trip him up. This process he began with a small book entitled *Totemism*, the prologue to the most important of his theoretical writings, *The Savage Mind*, published in 1962.

If *Tristes tropiques* had made Lévi-Strauss famous, *The Savage Mind* made him controversial. As the sharpest expression of his views he had yet set forth, it aroused passionate discussion among social scientists, philosophers, and men of letters. For its combination of ultra-relativism and the new dogmatism of the structural method had something in it to upset or displease almost every French school of social speculation.

The mind of the savage, Lévi-Strauss argued, was neither so simple nor so wayward as it was ordinarily supposed to be. In point of fact primitive man thought in an exceedingly complicated fashion; his logic was merely of a different order from the logic of abstract science to which Western man had become accustomed. Still more, the savage thirsted for objective knowledge and was adept at observing the concrete; the systems by which he classified plants, animals, and natural phenomena were detailed and sometimes even intellectually elegant. The results of his speculations were preserved in a "science of the concrete"—the "memory bank" of techniques in agriculture, pottery, and the domestication of animals which had made possible the beginnings of settled habitation in neolithic times. After that enormous cultural revolution, mankind had stopped in its tracks—and most cultures had remained there. Even in the West, thousands of years had gone by before the advent of modern science: the scientific speculation of classical antiquity and the Middle Ages was still neolithic in temper. The only way to explain this "level plain" of "stagnation" was to postulate "two distinct modes of scientific thought"—"one roughly adapted to that of perception and the imagination: the other at a remove from it." The former—the "primitive" science of the concrete—had to its credit the achievements secured ten thousand years ago which still remained "at the basis of our own civilization."[46]

Having thus established the credentials of the savage way of thought, Lévi-Strauss went on to point out the vestiges of such thinking in contemporary Europe and America. These vestiges were of the sort that the Freudian school of therapy condemned as magical—that is, the conviction of hidden affinities and sympathies between human actions and the world of nature. But the word "magic"—like everything else in the mental universe of primitive man—held no terrors for Lévi-Strauss. Magic too had its logic: it would be better, he maintained, "instead of contrasting magic and science, to compare them as two parallel modes of acquiring knowledge"; the former, unlike abstract scientific thought, postulated a "complete and all-embracing determinism." And once the principles of such determinism had been fully understood, they were found to work rather like a kaleidoscope: they reshuffled bits and pieces of traditional lore into endless variations of basically similar structural patterns; they displayed both "internal coherence" and a "practically unlimited capacity for extension."[47]

The magical—or totemic—way of thinking was by its nature anti-historical. But it did not deny the category of

[46] *La pensée sauvage* (Paris, 1962), translated as *The Savage Mind* (Chicago, 1966), pp. 3, 15–16, 42.
[47] *Ibid.*, pp. 11–13, 36, 217.

time: the savage mind simply could not bring itself to believe that anything really changed. Nor did the lack of a sense for history denote some ineradicable inferiority of feeling: an "obstinate fidelity to a past conceived as a timeless model," Lévi-Strauss argued, "betrayed no moral or intellectual deficiency whatsoever." As opposed to the usual "clumsy distinction" between "peoples without history" and those who thought of themselves in historical terms, he preferred to speak of "cold" societies that tried to stay in equilibrium and "hot" ones that were forever on the move.[48] Thus a thoroughgoing ethical relativism lay at the end of Lévi-Strauss' search for the principles of primitive thought: in their acute understanding of the plant and animal world, in their sense of an overarching cosmic harmony, those who dwelt in the "cold" cultures displayed a nobility of temper that the super-heated West had long ago forgotten.

Finally, the structures the mind of primitive man revealed could be presumed to be universal. Under the lofty scaffolding of modern science, the mental patterns of the contemporary city dweller in the West were much like those of his neolithic ancestor. The task of the anthropologist was to find those patterns—proceeding on the principle that "either everything, or nothing, makes sense." And when they had been sufficiently understood, Lévi-Strauss concluded, "the entire process of human knowledge" would assume "the character of a closed system."[49]

The completion of *The Savage Mind*, by Lévi-Strauss' own account, marked a pause in his thought. But the task he had set himself was far from accomplished. He had affirmed the existence of basic mental structures: now he had to prove it. He had declared that myths were capable of structural analysis: to date he had given only a few scattered examples. The purpose of the four-volume series entitled *Mythologiques* which he launched in 1964 was to show the structural method

[48] *Ibid.*, pp. 233–236.
[49] *Ibid.*, pp. 173, 269.

in action—to derive from an exhaustive "coding" of mythic material a "picture of the world already inscribed in the architecture" of the human mind.[50]

Drawing his data from the Indians of South America whom he knew at first hand, Lévi-Strauss focused his attention on myths dealing with food, tobacco, and the transformations raw meat and plants underwent in being prepared for human use. The first volume analyzed how the practice of cooking had altered man's relations with nature; the second traced the more complex symbolic significance of smoking and eating honey. In the remote past, the mythic material suggested, men had simply laid out their food on stones to be warmed by the heat of the sun: the sun's rays had united heaven and earth in a harmony in which mankind felt itself to be in no way separate from the world of nature. With the change to cooked food, these relations were profoundly altered: the introduction of cooking was the decisive step in the passage from nature to culture; man was cut off both from the gods and from the animals who ate their food raw. In consequence his world became problematic and threatening. Only through the mediation of friendly and helpful animals—the tapirs or jaguars or opossums who were the protagonists of the major myths—could a precarious cosmic order be restored.[51]

In his first volume Lévi-Strauss set up a series of opposites which were simple and tangible: the raw as against the cooked, the fresh as against the rotten, the dry as against the humid. In his second volume—the one which dealt with honey and tobacco—the contrasts were more abstract and equivocal: "empty and full, container and contained, internal and external, included and excluded," plus variants in between.[52] This procedure by pairs was the key feature of Lévi-Strauss' coding: it constituted his method of reducing myth to its component parts, "retaining . . . only a small number

[50] *Le cru et le cuit* (*Mythologiques*, I) (Paris, 1964), p. 346. An English translation, under the title *The Raw and the Cooked*, was published in 1968.
[51] *Ibid.*, pp. 172, 295, 333.
[52] *Du miel aux cendres* (*Mythologiques*, II) (Paris, 1966), p. 406.

of elements suitable for expressing contrasts and forming pairs of opposites." Such codes, he argued, were capable of transformations from one into another. Among them there were no "privileged semantic levels."[53] In a universe of concepts liberated from the "servitude" of "concrete experience" all relationships were equally meaningful—or perhaps equally lacking in significance.[54]

The work of coding and transformation—carried out in meticulous detail—made *Mythologiques* exceedingly difficult to read. It also raised the central problem of meaning in Lévi-Strauss' whole enterprise which will occupy us shortly: what was one to make of an endeavor which the author himself described as a kind of mythologizing of mythic material?[55] Moreover, all question of meaning aside, certain peripheral features of these volumes were sufficiently extraordinary to suggest both the fascination his work exerted, particularly on the young, and his reputation as an elusive and hermetic thinker.

In *Mythologiques* the mannerism that had always been latent in Lévi-Strauss' prose became explicit and obtrusive. The work was quite unnecessarily precious in tone, and the first volume was organized around a labored (and frequently inappropriate) analogy with musical composition, its chapters including an overture, theme and variations, sonata, symphony, cantata, and fugue. Evidently the author enjoyed playing cat-and-mouse with his readers. As one British critic put it, half admiring and half exasperated:

> The prose of Lévi-Strauss is a very special instrument. . . . It has an austere, dry detachment, at times reminiscent of La Bruyère and Gide. It uses a careful alternance of long sentences, usually organized in ascending rhythm, and of abrupt Latinate phrases. While seeming to observe the conventions of neutral, learned presentation, it allows for brusque personal interventions and

[53] *Le cru et le cuit*, p. 347.
[54] *Du miel aux cendres*, p. 407.
[55] *Le cru et le cuit*, p. 14.

asides. Momentarily, Lévi-Strauss appears to be taking the reader into his confidence, . . . making him accomplice to some deep, subtle merriment at the expense of the subject or of other men's pretensions in it. Then he withdraws behind a barrier of technical analysis and erudition so exacting that it excludes all but the initiate.[56]

Thus a writer who ostensibly made no claim to being a literary figure in fact very consciously contrived his work for its effect as literature. And the stance he adopted toward his subject matter was equally ambivalent—stoicism and disengagement alternating with warm human sympathy. If on the one hand he ruthlessly saw through all meanings and directed his attention to structure alone, he was not ashamed to give voice to his own values when his emotions were stirred: he could write with transparent anger of the ravages of a Western technology that converted South Sea islands into "stationary aircraft-carriers" and threw its "filth . . . in the face of humanity"; he could bemoan the irony of his profession that condemned him to hasten "in search of a vanished reality."[57] He loved his métier; yet it brought him to near-despair as he watched how contact with "advanced" societies dissolved his subject matter before his very eyes. To the young French of the 1960's such reflections carried the ring of truth: in France too the achievement of technical modernity was being purchased at a painful psychic cost. In sum, the secret of Lévi-Strauss' immense influence lay in his talent for "carrying out a rigorous and strictly scientific work, while at the same time reflecting on this work, examining its method, extracting the philosophic elements from it, and remaining through it all a kind of Rousseau, both misanthropic and a friend of mankind, who sometimes dreams of reconciling East and West by completing the economic

[56] "Orpheus with his Myths," *The Times Literary Supplement,* LXIV (April 29, 1965), 321.
[57] *Tristes tropiques* (English translation), pp. 39, 45.

liberation inherent in Marxism with a spiritual liberation of Buddhist origin."[58]

The relation to Marx was one central problem that Lévi-Strauss' work raised. The relation to Freud was another. Beyond these lay the question of his attitude toward his own contemporaries—more particularly Sartre—and toward the high valuation they placed on historical understanding. Finally, and most troublingly, loomed the problem of meaning, the ground on which compromise between Lévi-Strauss and his adversaries was next to impossible.

Marx he encountered early in life, when as a boy of about seventeen he met a young Belgian Socialist.

> A whole world was opened to me. My excitement has never cooled: and rarely do I tackle a problem in sociology or ethnology without having first set my mind in motion by reperusal of a page or two from the *18 Brumaire of Louis Bonaparte* or the *Critique of Political Economy*. Whether Marx accurately foretold this or that historical development is not the point. Marx followed Rousseau in saying—and saying once and for all, so far as I can see—that social science is no more based upon events than physics is based upon sense-perceptions. Our object is to construct a model, examine its properties and the way in which it reacts to laboratory tests, and then apply our observations to the interpretation of empirical happenings.

No more than Merleau-Ponty in his final guise, could Lévi-Strauss be called a Marxist in any simple meaning of the term. It was rather that for him, as for so many of his French contemporaries, Marxism remained a source of inspiration and a point of departure for social-science method.

It was comparable, Lévi-Strauss found, both to geology

[58] Jean Lacroix, *Panorama de la philosophie française contemporaine* (Paris, 1966), p. 222.

and to psychoanalysis in that all three tried to reduce an obvious reality to a less apparent one which took care to "evade our detection." In all three cases the problem was the same—"the relation . . . between reason and sense-perception"—as was the goal pursued, which could be defined as a "*super-rationalism*," an integration of sense-perceptions into reasoning in which the former would "lose none of their properties."[59]

Yet if Lévi-Strauss was convinced that Marx had been on the right track, he was less sure about Freud. One senses that psychoanalytic theory was a point of special difficulty for him: of the various "codes" his predecessors had offered, it was the most recalcitrant to the universal relativizing process at which he aimed. Much of what he wrote in *Mythologiques* about the trauma mankind had undergone in tearing itself loose from the world of nature seemed of a piece with Freud's own musings in *Civilization and Its Discontents*. But this was Freudianism in its speculative and quasi-anthropological manner: toward its clinical claims Lévi-Strauss was more severe. He warned against the possibility that psychoanalytic therapy might result in no more solid a "cure" than a conversion on the part of the patient to the particular and limited mental set of the therapist himself. This was substantially what sorcerers and shamans had always done—and in a tone of scarcely veiled patronizing Lévi-Strauss remarked that the psychoanalysts of today might learn something from comparing their methods and goals with those of their "great predecessors."[60] Such tolerance for magical procedures, however, did not extend to the work of Jung. Whatever superficial similarities their common interest in the realm of myth might suggest, Lévi-Strauss found Jung's "obscurantism . . .

[59] *Tristes tropiques* (English translation), p. 61.
[60] "Le sorcier et sa magie" (originally published in *Les temps modernes*, IV, 1949), "L'efficacité symbolique" (originally published in *Revue de l'histoire des religions*, CXXXV, 1949), *Structural Anthropology*, pp. 182–185, 201–204.

quite abhorrent." Still more, the latter had committed the supreme methodological error of directing his attention to the content of myth rather than to its form.[61]

The emotions, Lévi-Strauss argued, explained nothing; they were "consequences, never causes." These latter could be sought only in a biological investigation of the organism, or in the intellect, which was the "sole way offered to psychology, and to anthropology as well."[62] Lévi-Strauss' own method of coping with the emotions was to intellectualize them. He reduced subjectivity to its "intellectual laws," proposing a "sequence of constantly narrower definitions of the unconscious."[63] The result, as the philosopher Paul Ricoeur complained, was an unconscious that was "rather . . . Kantian than Freudian," an unconscious that dealt in categories and combinations—a formulation of his own thought to which Lévi-Strauss in the end was quite willing to assent.[64]

This process of intellectualization, in terms of method and sympathy, put him closer to Marx than to Freud. While the accusation of hostility to psychoanalysis seems to have bothered him very little, he was quick to reply to the Marxist charge that he was a foe of progress.[65] A lingering affinity for Marxism kept him safely within the camp of France's left-oriented intellectuals and helps explain the surprisingly respectful attention he gave to the work of Jean-Paul Sartre.

Lévi-Strauss regarded the *Critique of Dialectical Reason* as a sufficiently important cultural phenomenon to warrant his devoting to it a special and concluding chapter of his *Savage Mind* and to linking up with it his own reflections on the study of history. Sartre was right, Lévi-Strauss agreed, in dis-

[61] George Steiner, "A Conversation with Claude Lévi-Strauss," *Encounter*, XXVI (April 1966), 35.

[62] *Totemism*, p. 71.

[63] Emilio Renzi, "Sulla nozione di inconscio in Lévi-Strauss," *Aut Aut*, No. 88 (July 1965), pp. 57–58.

[64] "Structure et herméneutique," *Esprit*, XXXI (November 1963), 600; "Réponses à quelques questions," *ibid.*, p. 633.

[65] *Structural Anthropology*, Chapter 16; see also Edmund Leach, "Claude Lévi-Strauss—Anthropologist and Philosopher," *New Left Review*, No. 34 (November–December 1965), pp. 17–19.

tinguishing the dialectical from the analytic method, but he refused to accept the former's sharp separation of the two. Rather than being of a different logical order, the dialectic was a prolongation of analysis onto new and risky territory. Moreover, Sartre had muddled his account by equating dialectical reasoning (in its "true" form) with the historical consciousness of the West, while describing such a procedure among "primitives" as a merely repetitive process which was close to the biological level. Nor was this the end of Sartre's confusions. "In his manner of invoking history," he had mixed up three common but quite distinct meanings of the term— the "history men make unconsciously," the "history of men consciously made by historians," and the subsequent interpretations philosophers put on the two previous types of activity.[66]

Most of the time, Lévi-Strauss found, Sartre's work fell within the third definition; he was the architect of a grand historical design in the Hegelian manner. And as such, what Sartre had offered ranked as a "first-class ethnographic document" (again the note of patronizing) which could claim the dignity of myth. Indeed, Lévi-Strauss seemed to suggest, the nobility of Sartre's attitude lay in the intense fashion with which he lived his own myth—the myth of the French Revolution and its thunderous twentieth-century successors. Lévi-Strauss personally had nothing against this way of thinking—as a part-time adherent of the Left he even shared in it —he simply maintained that "in a different register" of their consciousness people like Sartre and himself should recognize that their ideological notion of historical meaning did not constitute eternal truth and that posterity would regard things quite differently.[67] Moreover, they should take care, as Sartre had not done, to distinguish their reflections on history from the second meaning of the word, that is, the history of the historians.

The accusation of anti-historicism lodged against Lévi-

---

[66] *The Savage Mind*, pp. 246, 248, 250–251.
[67] *Ibid.*, pp. 249n., 254–255.

Strauss almost invariably referred to the speculative, Hegelian activity which exerted so strong an attraction on postwar French intellectuals. And in such a form he was perfectly willing to accept the charge: he had no use for historicity as the "last refuge of a transcendental humanism."[68] The majestic type of history with a capital "H" was quite foreign to his own concept of social science. But for what the professional historians did he voiced real sympathy. He referred to it as a type of study complementary to anthropology, which organized its data "in relation to conscious expressions of social life," while anthropology proceeded by "examining its unconscious foundations." Nor could even this division be airtight. "To an increasing degree," Lévi-Strauss found, the historian was calling "to his aid the whole apparatus of unconscious elaborations. . . . Any good history book" was "saturated with anthropology"—Lucien Febvre's study of sixteenth-century disbelief offering an illustrious example.[69] Throughout the inaugural lecture he delivered at the Collège de France in 1960, Lévi-Strauss scattered conciliatory remarks in the direction of his historical colleagues. And six years later in his *Mythologiques*, he repeated the reassurance: far from refusing to recognize the claims of history, structural analysis granted it a position of first importance—the position that belonged "by right to the irreducible contingency without which necessity would not even be conceivable."[70]

So much seemed clear: the contingency that historians studied was the indispensable prerequisite to Lévi-Strauss' own efforts to establish the basic categories of human thought and action. In such a methodological program Bloch and Febvre might well have concurred. Or at the very least they would have been willing to give the new procedure a fair hearing. This was the line their successors on the *Annales* took in assessing Lévi-Strauss' work: as long-time proponents of a unified study of man, they were bound to welcome it—

[68] *Ibid.*, p. 262.
[69] *Structural Anthropology*, pp. 18, 23.
[70] *Du miel aux cendres*, p. 408.

if only as a "cathartic" which forced them to question the very language of their craft.[71] Yet with whatever good will historians might greet Lévi-Strauss' attempt to find structure in history, the type of analysis to which he was inviting them to adjust was not always clear. In his methodological statements—as in his *Mythologiques*—he seemed to be proposing a reduction (or coding) of historical material on a mechanistic model; in the bulk of his published work he proceeded in the more conventional anthropological fashion of trying to understand an exotic society in its own terms.[72] The latter was approximately what the school of Bloch and Febvre had been doing all along. The former was a program so alien to the historian's mentality that he had no choice but to watch its development from a respectful distance.

However polite Lévi-Strauss might be to the professional historians—however carefully he distinguished their work from the ideological exploitation of history which he criticized in Sartre—on one point he refused to compromise: he was unwilling to accord history the status of a privileged order of knowledge that constituted the special cultural superiority of the West. To have done so would have been inconsistent with the radical relativism of his approach and with the equal weighting he gave to the values of "cold" societies as against the "hot." In this final sense there remained an irreconcilable incompatibility between Lévi-Strauss and those who thought in primarily historical terms.

By training and temperament historians were more concerned with the content than with the formal characteristics of their subject. They were similarly inclined to take the values they studied "straight"—rather than trying to convert them into an abstract and universal code. What Lévi-Strauss was after was precisely the opposite: he believed that content in itself had no meaning; it was only the way in

[71] Roland Barthes, "Les sciences humaines et l'oeuvre de Lévi-Strauss," *Annales: économies—sociétés—civilisations*, XIX (November–December 1964), 1085–1086.

[72] Gaboriau, "Anthropologie structurale et histoire," pp. 592–594.

which the different elements of the content were combined
that gave a meaning.[73] But once meaning had been drained
of content, what was left? This was the ultimate question
historians and philosophers and social scientists proposed:
was there in fact any meaning to Lévi-Strauss' infinitely ingenious constructions?

The basic trouble with his method—quite aside from the
closed conceptual universe it presupposed—was that it made
no value distinctions among the coded relationships it established. Nor could it even lay claim to an exhaustive process
of coding: the elements that went into it, as in the performance of a computer, were limited to the small number
that were capable of unambiguous manipulation. The result
was perhaps no more than a glorious cerebral game. Or, in
terms of formal philosophy, it amounted to a "discourse" at
once "fascinating" and "disquieting"—an "admirable syn-
tactical arrangement" that said nothing.[74]

Thus in one guise Lévi-Strauss could be considered the
most extreme and consistent of the students of society who
in the 1940's and 1950's—throughout the Western world—
were inaugurating a new and more sophisticated positivist
method. He was convinced that he had fulfilled—or was
about to fulfill—the social scientist's eternal dream of integrating method and reality.[75] He had re-established the
structure of the mind as basically rational; he accepted the
word "determinism"; he was unafraid of materialist explanations. In so doing, Lévi-Strauss accomplished the extraordinary feat of carrying out a universally-applicable and intellectualist program in the dominant French tradition while
at the same time linking up with the work of other neo-pos-
itivists outside France who were attracted by the rigor and

[73] Steiner, "Conversation with Lévi-Strauss," p. 35.

[74] Paul Ricoeur in "Réponses à quelques questions," p. 653.

[75] *Totemism*, p. 91. This universalist claim provides the point of
attack for Clifford Geertz's expert and ably-reasoned critique: "The
Cerebral Savage: On the Work of Claude Lévi-Strauss," *Encounter*,
XXVII (April 1967), 25–32.

elegance of his method: he broke out of his countrymen's cultural confinement while remaining authentically and recognizably French.

But there was also Lévi-Strauss' second guise as moraliste and philosophe, the heir of Montaigne, Montesquieu, and Rousseau. If his first incarnation was of greater interest to the world of science, the second was the source of his prestige among the general public. For it was here that in true eighteenth-century manner he held up the cultural universe of the "primitives" among whom he had dwelt as a mirror in which the French (and Westerners as a whole) could find a critique of their own society. He grieved over the defenseless savages whose way of life stood condemned by material "progress." In a tone of lyric pathos he had written in his travel notebook of the 1930's a passage on the tiny remnant of the once great Nambikwara people, which he was to publish two decades later and which may stand as a sample and symbol of this elegiac aspect of his thought:

The camp-fires shine out in the darkened savannah. Around the hearth which is their only protection from the cold, . . . beside the baskets filled with the pitiable objects which comprise all their earthly belongings, the Nambikwara lie on the bare earth. . . . When they lie entwined together, couple by couple, each looks to his mate for support and comfort and finds in the other a bulwark, the only one he knows, against the difficulties of every day and the meditative melancholia which from time to time overwhelms the Nambikwara. The visitor who camps among the Indians for the first time cannot but feel anguish and pity at the sight of a people so totally dis-provided for; beaten down into the hostile earth . . . by an implacable cataclysm; naked and shivering beside their guttering fires. . . . Laughing whispers can still make light of the Nambikwara's poverty. Their embraces are those of couples possessed by a longing for a lost oneness. . . . In one and all there may be glimpsed

a great sweetness of nature, a profound nonchalance, an
animal satisfaction as ingenuous as it is charming, and,
beneath all this, something that can be recognized as
one of the most moving and authentic manifestations of
human tenderness.[76]

During his stay with the Nambikwara, Lévi-Strauss had
discovered a "society reduced to its simplest expression"—a
society in which "nothing but human beings" remained. It
was perhaps a "vestigial version of what Rousseau had in
mind" when he spoke of a state of nature. As he had proceeded with his field investigations, Lévi-Strauss' respect for
Rousseau had steadily grown. The author of *Emile* and *The
Social Contract*, he surmised, had seen the necessity of setting up a model—based on an exact correspondence to no
existing social state—which would orient future investigations
by "enabling us to distinguish the characteristics common
to the majority of human societies." And Lévi-Strauss was
"inclined to think" that Rousseau "was right" in believing
that the "image nearest" to this model "was what we now
call the neolithic age." For the author of *Tristes tropiques*,
as for the philosophe he hailed as his "master" and "brother,"
the neolithic was the norm.[77]

We who dwell in "hot" societies, he constantly implied,
could well take lessons from those who have no truck with
change. And in an interview he gave after the publication of
the second volume of his *Mythologiques*, he made this injunction, and with it his own attitude, explicit at last:

I have little taste for the century in which we live. What
seems to me the present tendency is on the one hand
man's total mastery over nature and on the other hand
the mastery of certain forms of humanity over others.
My temperament and my tastes lead me far more toward
periods which were less ambitious and perhaps more
timid but in which a certain balance could be maintained

[76] *Tristes tropiques* (English translation), p. 285.
[77] *Ibid.*, pp. 310, 389–390.

between man and nature, among the various and multiple forms of life, whether animal or vegetable, and among the different types of culture, of belief, of customs, or of institutions. I do not strive to perpetuate this diversity but rather to preserve its memory.[78]

Thus—despite the contradictions he recognized in such an attitude—Lévi-Strauss found that an anthropologist like himself almost inevitably became a "critic at home" and a "conformist elsewhere."[79] Abroad he resented the inroads of "civilization" on his "primitives." In his own country he saw more starkly than his fellow-citizens what was out of the human scale in modern industrial society. The same range of sympathy came into play in both cases. In this perspective it was perfectly consistent for Lévi-Strauss to preserve an attachment to the ideological Left; it was thoroughly understandable that he should have joined Sartre and the other members of the celebrated "121" in their opposition to the Algerian War.

Yet with Lévi-Strauss—whether in his mood of conservation or with his voice of protest—there was a difference of "register," as he would put it, from other intellectuals of his generation. There was a tone of acceptance, of cosmic resignation in the face of nature reminiscent of Buddhism. "The world began without the human race," he declared in one of his most quoted utterances, "and it will end without it."[80] Lévi-Strauss was anything but a doctrinaire opponent of progress; his outlook necessarily made him favor the kind of change that would reduce human want and suffering. But he was far more aware than the run of his contemporaries of the enormous price in ugliness and cultural dislocation which progress entailed. His conception of freedom, alternately elegiac and utopian, was authentically of the late twentieth century in that it looked beyond the liberal or radical or

78 "A contre-courant," p. 31.
79 *Tristes tropiques* (English translation), p. 384.
80 *Ibid.*, p. 397.

Marxist ideology to a time which Saint-Simon had glimpsed
in his prediction that humanity would finally pass "from the
government of men to the administration of things." Lévi-
Strauss yearned for that distant era when the imperative of
progress would have ceased to operate—or better, when
machines would have taken over the task of social improvement—and when the characteristics of the hot and the cold
cultures would be gradually fused, until humanity was
liberated at last from the "age-old curse which forced it to
enslave men in order to make progress possible."[81]

v. *Conclusion: History, Anthropology, and Poetry*

In French intellectual life of the 1960's Lévi-Strauss
found no lack of counterparts or imitators. By the middle of
the decade "structuralism" had become the mode—the word
was discussed everywhere, whether or not those who spoke of
it had any precise idea of its meaning. Most of them probably
did not: the writings of the leading "structuralists" were
austere, hermetic, and difficult to follow. Such was notably
true of the work of Louis Althusser on Marxism and of
Jacques Lacan on psychoanalysis. Both of these emptied the
original teaching of its humanist content and recast it in the
form of a rigorous logic; in both cases the structural interpretation relentlessly emphasized a single aspect of the
theory in question. In an ironic sense, psychoanalysis might
finally be said to have become acclimatized in France since
it had produced in Lacan its own indigenous heretic.

Most broadly, the philosophical turning-point of the 1960's
could be defined as a concerted attempt at the liquidation
of traditional humanism. Lévi-Strauss' successors let drop
the *moraliste* content in his work and devoted their exclusive
attention to his structural method. In this new perspective,
the three decades 1930–1960 began to look like a transition

[81] Collège de France, *Leçon inaugurale faite le mardi 5 janvier 1960
par M. Claude Lévi-Strauss*, pp. 43–44.

era in which a succession of thinkers—often against their announced intention—had tried to salvage whatever items in the classical humanist baggage could still serve the needs of heroism or despair. The structuralists of the 1960's banned both humanism and the starker attitudes that had issued from it: all smacked of a subjectivity that was no longer tolerable. Whether Catholic or Marxist, existential or Weberian, the thought of the previous generation stood condemned as irremediably subjectivist and amateurish. The new stress was on the formal aspects of syntax and of thinking itself. It was symptomatic that the most influential of the younger structuralists, Michel Foucault, composed an "archaeology of the human sciences" delineating the successive abstract categories in which man's reflection on his own works had expressed itself since the sixteenth century.[82]

Language, logic, and coding having become ends in themselves, French thought was undergoing, "with thirty years delay, its crisis of logical positivism."[83] It was experiencing the sort of change that had occurred in Anglo-American philosophy a generation earlier. From this standpoint, structuralism might have been expected to provide a bridge to the world of speculation abroad. But it came too late to perform such a role: by the time the structuralist onslaught hit France, the British and Americans were having second thoughts about logical positivism and linguistic analysis and were becoming more tolerant of other types of philosophical discourse. Furthermore, it came encumbered with characteristically French accretions that made it difficult to export. The writing of the structuralists lacked the literary leanness and colloquial manner of the best English work in analytic philosophy. It was over-argued and over-sophisticated, affected, pretentious, and given to esoteric word-games—"mandarin"

[82] *Les mots et les choses* (Paris, 1966); see also Lacroix's comments in *Panorama de la philosophie française contemporaine*, pp. 8–9, 209.

[83] Lecture by Mikel Dufrenne at the annual congress of the review *Esprit* at Melun, December 4, 1966. For a fuller statement see his "La philosophie du néo-positivisme," *Esprit*, XXXV (May 1967), 784.

in the most unfavorable meaning of the term. In respect to the rhetoric of social thought, the structuralist revolution had had the melancholy effect of reintroducing, under the guise of philosophical rigor, the age-old vices of the Gallic mind. And these weaknesses obscured the richness and originality of what someone like Foucault had to offer.

As the century reached the two-thirds mark, the self-confidence of the French, whether in international affairs or in the realm of the intellect, had quite apparently been regained. But it had been restored at a heavy cost. Although the elections of 1967 seemed to announce the twilight of De Gaulle's regime, the experience of Gaullist rule was likely to leave its mark for a long time to come. In the intellectual sphere the counterpart to the pride—the orgueil—that the General-President had taught his countrymen was the resurgence of a cultural nationalism against which writers as diverse as Camus and Teilhard and Lévi-Strauss had warned in vain.

With the twentieth century two-thirds past, of fourteen leading thinkers of the contemporary era eight were dead. Three more—Marcel, Malraux, and De Gaulle—for a number of years had published little major writing. Of the three remaining, Lévi-Strauss alone—with half his *Mythologiques* still to go—seemed to be in full course. Sartre was evidently pausing for breath: the public was still waiting for a second volume of the *Critique of Dialectical Reason* he had promised.

Maritain was old enough to be the father of these two, and the fact that he felt sufficiently vigorous to publish a substantial work was the great philosophical surprise of the year 1966. From the monastery in Toulouse to which he had withdrawn after the death of his wife, Maritain issued a book of essays in the form of a self-interrogation on his own time. Much of it recalled the militant Thomist of the interwar years—the polemical vigor, the spare style, and the carefully articulated arguments. But there was also a new tone of informality, of indulgent amusement at his earlier incarnations, as when he recalled the time that he had "gently entreated his gray matter" and it had obliged him by producing the "personalist" formula. And in a retrospective passage in which he surveyed his philosophical reading over nearly seventy years, he characterized with generous understanding the masters against whose example he had fought or who had brought him intellectual sustenance: Descartes was an enemy who had aroused his liveliest interest; Hume's "implacable bitterness" had won his admiration; he was even grateful to Comte for the "uncharitable joys" he had given him. Then had come Bergson, who had tried to break off the whole philosophical succession; but he had failed—after him everyone went back to Cartesianism, or on to Husserl, for whom, "despite the catastrophe he caused," Maritain entertained a "great intellectual respect"; even Sartre, who was too "cunning" by far, had "borne witness" to something "which one would be very wrong to neglect."[84]

Thus the "old layman," as Maritain now called himself, ruminating on his illustrious antecedents and successors, suggested that his philosophical track was not so rigidly marked out as his earlier writings might have led his readers to suppose. At eighty-four the senior figure among France's social thinkers, he could afford to grant himself the indulgence of a slackening of intellectual tension. And he could at last give voice to the lyricism in his temperament that he had earlier held in check.

Maritain had always been more of a poet than he had permitted himself to appear. He might well have applied to his own work what he had written of Teilhard de Chardin, that he had clothed his vision of the universe in a "kind of disguise"—a Thomist disguise, where Teilhard's had been scientific. And the same had been true of a succession of younger men. These had done their best to cast off the straitjacket of Cartesianism. But they had not allowed themselves to enjoy their liberty for long: they had hastened to

[84] *Paysan de la Garonne*, pp. 82, 151–152.

embrace the new servitude of Hegelian or phenomenological discourse or of structural method. Still more, they were prone to falling back into the familiar Cartesian formulas. Writer after writer who had at some point experienced a burning intuition felt obliged to discipline that illumination in an accepted philosophical form: the author of *The Plague* went on to write *The Rebel;* the author of *Tristes tropiques* would not rest content until he had begun his *Mythologiques.*

Most of the time between 1930 and 1965 French social thought had had poetry at its core. Writers who had thought of themselves as rigorous theorists had been poets without knowing it. And this "disguise" slowed their coming to full awareness of what they were about. Their problem was not so much one of making contact with the world of discourse in which Anglo-American and Central European thought had fused—although that was part of it—as of extricating themselves from the intellectual confinement of their own tradition. By the 1960's this liberation was still far from accomplished. But a few pathfinders had shown the way.

In the process the French had once more proved to be fearless explorers of the moral universe. Novelists and philosophers alike had probed the mortal anxiety, the bad faith, and the ever-disappointed yearning for human solidarity that had engaged the thoughts and emotions of their contemporaries. In the very act of breaking with the French classic tradition, they had maintained and reinforced the heritage of the moralistes whose work had been an integral part of that tradition. Such explorations, however, were by their nature fragmentary and frequently amateurish. In the more "scientific" aspects of social thought, the originality of the French was not yet apparent. So much of their energy had been absorbed in catching up with methodology abroad that it was not until the 1950's that they began to devise in structuralism a new procedure of their own. A decade later the future of the structural method was still an unknown quantity. It was perhaps just another of those fragile constructions—those untenable syntheses—which had punctuated the years of desperation.

Meantime in the study of history alone—in the discipline which was the closest to poetry of the social sciences—the pre-eminence of a handful of the French had been universally recognized. It was here that what was still viable in the example of both Durkheim and Bergson had produced its finest results. In historical study redefined as retrospective cultural anthropology, the French had pointed the way to a broader and more "human" understanding of the life of man in society. By the 1960's it was symptomatic that Foucault's work, although formally labeled psychology, was in fact a kind of anthropological history which combined the insights of Febvre and Lévi-Strauss—the former's feel for the mentality of past ages and the latter's structural method.

The social thought of the desperate years began with history and ended with anthropology. It was in the dialogue between these two that French speculation of the era just past produced what was most compelling and of greatest interest to the world outside.

Index

The Sea Change

29 August 91

The Great Migration

IN THE PERSPECTIVE of the 1970's, the migration to the United States of European intellectuals fleeing fascist tyranny has finally become visible as the most important cultural event—or series of events—of the second quarter of the twentieth century. Why it took until then to recognize so obvious a phenomenon is something of a mystery. Perhaps it was that the presence of émigrés on the American scene was so much a part of our daily lives that we were unable to see it as "history." Perhaps it required a certain time for the individual aspects of the great migration to sort themselves out: after the passage of three decades and the restoration of European culture, it became apparent that the older generation of the émigrés had died, that those who had returned to their lands of origin had been re-Europeanized, and that the majority who had chosen to remain in their adopted country had been absorbed into American society—in short, that the emigration experience was over.

Some such recognition prompted the almost simultaneous publication of three works on the subject at the end of the 1960's.[1]

1. Laura Fermi, *Illustrious Immigrants: The Intellectual Migration from Europe 1930–41* (Chicago, 1968); Donald Fleming and Bernard Bailyn, eds., *The Intellectual Migration: Europe and America, 1930–1960* (Cambridge, Mass., 1969); *The Legacy of the German Refugee Intellectuals* (special number of the review *Salmagundi*) (Fall 1969–Winter 1970). For an assessment of these studies, see my review article "La grande emigrazione intellettuale," *Rivista storica italiana*, LXXXII (Fasc. IV, 1970), 951–959. One should fur-

From them we have learned a great deal about the scope of the emigration and the activities of its leading personalities. We now have a clear idea of the approximate number and national distribution of the intellectuals who left Europe for the United States. We know that nearly half of them were Germans (or, if one adds the Austrians, two-thirds) and that a corresponding (and overlapping) two-thirds were of Jewish origin. We have had our earlier impression confirmed that French émigrés were comparatively few and that still fewer of them chose to remain in America. And we have discovered—rather more surprisingly—that Italians accounted for only a small percentage of the emigration, their eminence and their success in their new country compensating for the thinness of their ranks.[2]

Beyond the matter of numbers, we have repeated evidence of the intellectual stimulus that emigration provided, of how the experience of living suspended between two cultures fostered rather than confined the flowering of talent. This "creative force of an interstitial situation" was not without precedent.[3] We may think of such illustrious exiles as Thucydides and Dante, or Joseph de Maistre meditating the fate of postrevolutionary Europe in the snows of St. Petersburg. A geographical and emotional displacement has often provided the shock that has set the mind off its familiar course and turned it toward introspection and social or psychological probing. Yet the emigration of the 1930's went beyond any previous cultural experience: in its range of talent and achievement it was indeed something new in the modern history of Western man. The émigrés themselves were "astounded at how much they accomplished" and were "the first to assert that they would not have accomplished as much had they remained in their

---

ther note two earlier, briefer works, Franz Neumann et al., *The Cultural Migration: The European Scholar in America* (Philadelphia, 1953), and Helge Pross, *Die Deutsche Akademische Emigration nach den Vereinigten Staaten 1933–1941* (Berlin, 1955), and the sociological and psychological study by Donald Peterson Kent: *The Refugee Intellectual: The Americanization of the Immigrants of 1933–1941* (New York, 1953).

2. Fermi, *Illustrious Immigrants*, pp. 13, 95, 122. The usefulness of Fermi's statistical analysis of some 1,900 émigrés is limited by the fact that she has cast her net very wide, including, for example, Poles and Russians in addition to her main category of victims of fascism.

3. Editors' introduction to *The Intellectual Migration*, p. 8.

homelands."[4] Of course there were exceptions: older men too weary and disillusioned to adjust to American life, those so wedded to their native languages as to be unable to recast their work in English, the proud and the inflexible who refused to accept positions they thought unworthy of them. Yet the predominant impression they made was one of triumphant achievement in a new land.

How are we to account for this success—and in an America where economic depression and a scarcely concealed anti-Semitism all too often set limits to the welcome the émigrés received? No single explanation or combination of explanations suffices; we have only to recall an Einstein or a Schönberg to realize that the quota of genius among the émigrés was once again unprecedented. Yet there were in addition certain characteristics of America in the 1930's and 1940's that made it receptive of foreign talent to an extraordinary degree. The society was open—far more inclined than that of Germany or Austria or Italy to the recognition of individual merit irrespective of birth or class. Beyond that, it was a pluralist society in which an alien accent occasioned little comment and in which the majority of the citizenry that was not of Anglo-Saxon origin was in these very decades breaking through to positions of leadership. Quite specifically, the institutions of higher learning were more varied and less rigid than the European: in a situation in which individual professors enjoyed little power or prestige, it was comparatively easy to add the foreign born to their number. And when the Second World War broke out, the government itself proved willing to put into positions of trust men whom it might well have considered enemy aliens. Finally, the very anti-intellectualism of so many Americans challenged the newly arrived Europeans to put their thoughts in a form that the wider public could understand: the theologian Paul Tillich has spoken of this experience as having "deprovincialized" him, to which the philosopher Theodor W. Adorno adds that he became "inclined . . . toward critical self-scrutiny" when he saw that "in America . . . no reverential silence in the presence of everything intellectual prevailed."[5]

4. Fermi, *Illustrious Immigrants,* p. 16.
5. "Scientific Experiences of a European Scholar in America," *The Intellectual Migration,* p. 367.

More particularly, those branches of American activity that were on the verge of making a great leap forward could profit to the full from the arrival of the refugees from Europe. Atomic physics and psychoanalysis offer the two major examples of fields of endeavor in which the émigrés came just at the critical moment—when the native-born, already professionally prepared, were eager for the advanced training and direction that Europeans could give them. These two disciplines, in which the center of gravity definitively crossed the Atlantic during the war years, suggest the extent of a shift in intellectual weight that made the former pattern of deference toward the Old World no longer necessary or appropriate.

This much we now know about the great migration. Its general outlines have been established, and its contributions to American culture have been fully recognized. But the other side of the process is less well understood. It is here that the difficulties begin—and specifically in the sphere of the social thought that underlay and buttressed so much of the work of the emigration. We know that the arrival of the émigrés enriched American intellectual life; we know that it meant a loss for Europe from which the Continent took decades to recover. But what of the refugees themselves? If it is true that they accomplished more than they would have if they had remained at home, did this mean an increase in their own understanding or simply a diffusion of that thought to the larger audience their hosts provided? In widening its influence, did Central European sociology or psychology become shallower? Or did its "sea change" give it a bite and specificity that it had lacked before? In short, how did the experience in America alter the character of thought itself? We can approach this range of questions by going beyond chronicle or external biography to a psychosocial analysis of that experience as a major intellectual drama in its own right.

1. *Lands of Origin*

At the end of the 1920's, Benito Mussolini had already governed Italy for seven years. For the last three of them, his power had stood virtually unchallenged. Italian Fascism had won acceptance at home and abroad as a new form of rule, despotic to be sure, but one which seemed suited to the presumed political immaturity of its subjects. Through his agreement with the Vatican in 1929, the Duce had settled to the satisfaction of the vast majority of his countrymen the quarrel of Church and state that had bewildered the Italians and divided their loyalties for two full generations. So popular indeed was this accord that by 1931 the opposition to the regime was growing weary and demoralized. And in that same year, when an oath of Fascist allegiance was demanded of Italy's 1,250 university professors, only a dozen refused.

These latter, however, were almost all scholars of distinction. And among those who took the oath it was an open secret that hundreds had settled their struggles of conscience by putting ahead of abstract principle their duty to support their families. Such behavior was thoroughly in accord with Italian practice. Most of what Mussolini had done was not. "None of the principal concepts and aspects of Fascism was in harmony with Italian traditions and predilections."[6] Its ruthless application of police power threatened ancient habits of indiscipline and tenacious local pride. Its efforts at ideological indoctrination flew in the face of an age-old skepticism about political formulas of all descriptions. Its self-centered national assertiveness vulgarized and perverted the Italians' proudest claim—that they exemplified the values of a universal humanist culture. With so much to his discredit, it is curious that Mussolini succeeded in winning over to his side the greater part of Italy's intellectuals.

The tradition of skepticism itself prompted a disabused acceptance of the latest political novelty that the turn of fortune had brought to a much-tried people. Beyond that, Fascism both profited by and intensified a drawing inward of Italian culture that was already becoming manifest in the immediate postwar years. Italy's participation in the First World War had brought to a halt the effort at "deprovincialization" associated with the work of Benedetto Croce; for Croce and his like, the rupture with Germany marked a cruel hiatus in their closest philosophical affilia-

6. Leonardo Olschki, *The Genius of Italy* (New York, 1949), p. 455.

tions.[7] Similarly in the arts such experimental movements as Futurism and Surrealism by the mid-1920's had spent their force or been diverted into ideological channels. Meanwhile the country's younger poets were turning to a "hermetic" cultivation of an intensely private aesthetic sphere. Even before Fascism had fastened its grip on Italian cultural life, there was becoming perceptible a separation of that culture from wider European currents of thought and expression.

During the first decade and a half of Mussolini's rule Italy's aging culture hero, Gabriele D'Annunzio, lived impotent and pampered in a fantastically decorated villa on Lake Garda. His gorgeous rhetoric now dried up and outmoded, the self-styled Nietzschean superman accepted with princely dignity the bounty of a regime which by plagiarizing his style had cast him into irrelevance. D'Annunzio's brief moment of triumph had come with his seizure of Fiume in 1919. Two years later the challenger had appeared who was to usurp his place as Italy's foremost creative writer.

In just over a month's time in the year 1921 Luigi Pirandello had written the plays that established his international fame—*Six Characters in Search of an Author* and *Henry IV*. By the time of Mussolini's March on Rome Pirandello had emerged from obscurity to the position of his country's most passionately discussed man of letters. It was quite natural that the recently installed Duce should have been eager to make the new luminary's acquaintance and should have proposed a meeting. What is harder to explain is that Pirandello accepted, wrote of Mussolini in laudatory terms, and even became a member of the Fascist party.

The question of Pirandello's relations with Fascism has both pained and perplexed Italy's intellectuals. The course of those relations in itself suggests the ambiguous reaction of most Italian writers to the Fascist regime and the impossibility of making any simple statements about it. Initially Pirandello shared the widespread sentiment that Mussolini had given his country the order it desperately required, along with the illusion that his rule would be milder than it in fact proved to be. Subsequently the dramatist's

7. Benedetto Croce, "La Germania che abbiamo amata," *Propositi e speranze* (1925–1942): *scritti vari* (Bari, 1943), pp. 33–45.

ardor cooled, he insisted more sharply on his own independence, and in the early 1930's he spent much of his time abroad, assuming when at home an attitude of "absent-minded compromise, which relapsed every so often into insincerity and adulation of the Duce," until his death in 1936.[8] In Pirandello's case, self-seeking prompted to only a minor extent his conformist behavior; the official subsidies his theater received were modest and unreliable. It was rather that Fascism had struck a chord in his nature which his public never suspected and which was apparently in radical opposition to the implicit ideology of his own writings.

Ostensibly there was nothing Fascist about Pirandello's plays. Quite the contrary: the emotional universe they depicted—atomistic, dissociated, relativist—seemed to undercut or dissolve the rhetoric of solidarity that the regime propagated. Below the surface, however, Pirandello's behavior suggested fright at what he himself had revealed about his fellow men—and at the success that had greeted it. His victory had preceded Mussolini's by only one year: the two events had become linked in his mind, as he tried to exorcise by a punctilious loyalty to his chief the scandalous act of dissection he had performed on his own class. After the vertiginous period in which he had led his characters to the brink of madness, he appreciated the "normalization" that Fascist rule provided. Of solid bourgeois stock, catapulted to fame in his mid-fifties, Pirandello never lost the ideological timidity, the distrust of democracy and socialism, that betrayed his origins.[9] Nor could he shake off the sense of injury at the hands of better-known writers which his long years of obscurity had left with him. It was symptomatic of his spirit of contradiction and distaste for his peers that he chose precisely the wrong moment to announce his adherence to the Fascist party—the aftermath of the assassination of the Socialist deputy Giacomo Matteotti, when the regime itself was in danger of collapse and when a number of the prominent intellectuals who had at first endorsed it began to have second thoughts.

Chief among those who withdrew their support and against whom Pirandello nursed a particular grievance was Benedetto

8. Gaspare Giudice, *Luigi Pirandello* (Turin, 1963), p. 455.
9. *Ibid.*, pp. 441–448.

Croce. If the former had become Italy's most debated writer, the latter remained its most influential. Paradoxically enough, Croce's conversion to anti-Fascism strengthened rather than diminished his intellectual dominance. For the Neapolitan philosopher—serene, self-confident, and respected by Mussolini as untouchable—had license to say the things his countrymen dared not utter, in part because he did so in a lofty philosophical form that held no active threat for the regime. (And being a private scholar of ample means, he was not obliged to confront the moral dilemma of the oath that vexed the university professors.) With Croce in charge of the literary opposition, intellectual competition lapsed. Younger social thinkers failed to appear; the older ones disappeared or fell silent. In 1930 Vilfredo Pareto had been dead for seven years, carrying with him to the grave the secret of what he really thought of his country's new regime; Antonio Gramsci was wasting away in one of Mussolini's prisons, patiently composing the fragmentary writings that were to lie unpublished for another two decades; Gaetano Mosca had ceased to speak out on political matters, after delivering at the end of 1925 his last address in the Italian Senate—a dignified refusal to vote for the basic law establishing the Fascist dictatorship. Croce had likewise opposed the law; after another half-decade he too decided that it was no longer worth his while to exercise his rights as a senator.[10]

Secure in his Neapolitan *palazzo* or his villa at Sorrento, Croce maintained his hegemony over Italian cultural life. And the character of his influence changed markedly during the interwar years. Before 1914, Croce had raised the level and enlarged the range of Italian thought; even his hostility to social science had acted as a force of liberation, since his target had been a dogmatic "scientism" or positivism in the study of human affairs. After the war, Croce's example had the reverse effect: with a nonpositivist social theory now in the field (as in the case of Weber) or one whose implications extended far beyond its positivist origins (as with Freud) Croce's continued refusal to countenance sociology or psychology, his unrelenting denigration of them as confused and merely practical in aim, discouraged younger men from venturing

10. For a comparative analysis of the work of these four social thinkers, see my *Consciousness and Society* (New York, 1958), Chapters 3, 6, and 7.

into territory which was both philosophically suspect and ideologically dangerous.

Croce disliked social science for his own abstract reasons; Mussolini feared it as potentially subversive. Their double condemnation made its pursuit almost impossible during the Fascist years. The quite accidental convergence of Croce's distaste and the hostility of the regime is apparent in the vicissitudes of psychoanalysis in Italy from a promising start to near-extinction.

As early as 1910 the Florentine literary review *La Voce* had published a special issue devoted to "the sexual question" in which the work of Freud had been discussed with respect. Here and there Italians with inquiring minds were beginning to look into the new theories emanating from Vienna. But it was as philosophy rather than as therapy that psychoanalysis first impinged on the Italian mind—a philosophy loosely associated with the antipositivist views of Henri Bergson or William James. Italy's participation in the First World War ended this phase of tentative inquiry: with Austria the nation's enemy, the intellectual products of the Hapsburg capital were automatically quarantined. And by the time that scientific ties were reestablished with Vienna, the Fascist regime was already on the horizon.

Mussolini and his ideological associates could not fail to distrust a theory of the emotions that at the very least relativized and reduced to human proportions their own ethic of strenuous endeavor. And in this one respect the official verdict echoed the popular attitude: Freudianism struck the average Italian as morbid and foreign to his country's "Mediterranean" health of mind. Such was also the view of the Catholic Church—which had its theological reasons for objecting to the atheist, pansexual, and determinist implications of psychoanalytic theory. As a predominantly Catholic country, Italy proved even more reluctant than France to accept the teachings of Freud. This resistance found sanction in the opposed but mutually reinforcing objections of philosophers and men of science, most of whom were unbelievers in matters of religion.

The medical men and the psychologists remained true to the tradition of Cesare Lombroso, the physician and speculative anthropologist who had figured as one of the most influential

European positivists of the late nineteenth century. To the disciples of Lombroso, a physiological or organic explanation sufficed for the disturbances that psychoanalysis delineated in terms of unconscious emotional conflict; hence, Lombroso had made Freud superfluous. To the idealist philosophers and literary critics, Freud's work smacked of the positivism they loathed; hence, they were inclined to assimilate Freud to the familiar and detested Lombroso. (Croce's attitude was more nuanced, but he too misunderstood psychoanalysis and linked it with a miscellany of intellectual tendencies he scorned.) "On the pretext that there had already been Lombroso, the Italian scientists rejected Freud. . . . On the same pretext, and encouraged by the attitude of the scientists, the men of letters and the critics likewise rejected Freud. With the former, the pretext was disguised as love for Lombroso, with the latter as hatred" for the very same man.[11]

Under these circumstances, it is remarkable that psychoanalysis made any headway at all during the interwar years. Yet in 1925 the Italian Psychoanalytic Society was founded; Trieste and Rome became the centers of modest clinical progress; and in 1931 Freud's most authentic Italian follower, Edoardo Weiss, published a series of lectures that for the first time gave his countrymen a clear idea of psychoanalytic theory. One explanation for this slow but cumulative advance was that the movement was too obscure to attract much unfavorable attention. Another was the relative tolerance of Mussolini himself, who for the most part left psychoanalytic practice undisturbed; in the spring of 1938, at the time of the Nazi annexation of Austria, there was even talk that Freud might take refuge in Italy. The master chose to go to England instead. And later in that same year a misfortune descended upon the psychoanalytic movement that scattered its adherents or drove them underground for the next seven years.

Mussolini's imposition of anti-Semitic laws on the German model had nothing to do with hostility to psychoanalysis. But since the greater part of its adepts, in Italy as elsewhere, were of Jewish origin, its diffusion and practice necessarily suffered. Weiss and most of his colleagues went into exile, where they played only

11. Michel David, *La psicoanalisi nella cultura italiana* (Turin, 1966), pp. 7–8, 18–24.

a minor role in the post-Freudian evolution of psychoanalysis in the Anglo-American world. A few stayed on in Italy, temporarily diverting their professional endeavors into more acceptable channels. Until the mid-1940's, in Italy as throughout Central Europe, psychoanalysis virtually ceased to exist.

Before disappearing from the Italian scene, it had left behind a literary monument that showed a greater familiarity with its theory than any comparable work in French. Some found Pirandello's plays Freudian in inspiration; this the dramatist vigorously denied, alleging quite correctly that he had made his psychological observations on his own. It was Italo Svevo, rather, the Triestino author of *The Conscience of Zeno*, published in 1923, who came closest to being Italy's psychoanalytic man of letters. Living in a city of mixed population and cultural affinities that had only recently passed from Austrian to Italian rule, well acquainted with both James Joyce and Edoardo Weiss, Svevo was attracted to psychoanalysis without ever fully assimilating it. Alternately respectful and rebellious, eventually taking refuge in an ironic detachment from Freudian influence, even Svevo shared the multiple hesitations with which Italy's avant-garde intellectuals approached the psychoanalytic universe.[12]

And on a wider scale, the same hesitancy marked Italian social thought as a whole. After its triumphs of the early twentieth century, it had become conventional; Croce and his followers had drawn its sting. Hence the greater part of its practitioners found themselves able to bypass the Fascist experience. They treated it as little worse than an encumbrance. "In other countries subjected" to such a regime "most writers chose between scornful rejection and fiery involvement: the intellectuals of Italy were more often cautiously and politely indifferent."[13]

In retrospect their timidity has not passed unquestioned. One of the most sensitive and scrupulous of the young professors who took the oath, recalling the incident nearly four decades later, has concluded that he made the wrong choice:

12. *Ibid.*, pp. 58, 66, 371–372, 374–375, 379–380, 385.
13. P. Vita-Finzi, "Italian Fascism and the Intellectuals," *The Nature of Fascism*, ed. by S. J. Woolf (New York, 1968), p. 244. See also Emiliana P. Noether, "Italian Intellectuals under Fascism," *The Journal of Modern History*, XLIII (Dec. 1971), 630–648.

For us professors who . . . did not refuse the oath . . .
people later tried mercifully to find a justification: we saved
the possibility of educating young people, of maintaining the
university at a cultural level that subsequently permitted a
cohort of anti-Fascists to emerge from those indoctrinated by
the regime. . . . One should recognize that the university
climate during the Fascist period was not entirely suffocat-
ing. . . . The most implacable Fascists, the toughest ones,
were unrefined and of limited intelligence, incapable of catching on to the "poison" in a line of reasoning that did not
seem actually to offend the regime. . . . In educated spheres
the tone was set by "converts" who wanted to persuade themselves and others that they had not changed, that they had
not abjured the values of their youth, . . . [and who] . . .
left uncensored an analysis that might stimulate in the young
a judgment on the regime, a historical allusion that invited a
comparison. . . .

While risking scarcely anything, we were able to educate
the alert minority among the young . . . to reason and to
compare. . . .

But having recalled all that, I must add that the justification found for us is worth very little.

Those who chose the right road were those who . . . outside Italy, among the exiles, renounced their university chairs
and bore witness.[14]

In fact, only a small minority emigrated. And these left Italy in
two waves. The first departed in the mid or late 1920's, when the
despotic character of the regime had become clear. The second—
and much larger—exodus came in 1938 and 1939 after the inauguration of Mussolini's anti-Semitic campaign. Parenthetically we
should note that this series of actions once again violated the
traditions of a people which nourished little hostility against the
Jews. Italy's twentieth-century fall into anti-Semitism was to be
only a brief hiatus in its dominant experience of tolerance and
assimilation.

14. Arturo Carlo Jemolo, *Anni di prova* (Vicenza, 1969), pp. 145–146.

Aside from those of Jewish origin—and Italy's Jews were far less numerous than those of Germany—few among the emigration could be counted as primarily intellectuals. Most of the more prominent figures were political activists, intent on overthrowing the regime which governed their country. And at first the militant among them preferred to live in France rather than in Britain or America, since it bordered directly on Italy and was culturally more familiar to them. This activist emphasis, this tarrying on the European Continent as long as possible, distinguished the Italian emigration from the German or Austrian. It meant that among the Italians there occurred no such wholesale transplantation of Old World culture to the New as was effected by the refugees from Central Europe.[15]

Hence it is not surprising that the achievement of the Italian emigration in the field of social thought was largely confined to a critique of Fascism itself. When a prominent literary critic such as Giuseppe Antonio Borgese or a historian like Gaetano Salvemini came to the United States, it was as an analyst of Fascism that he made his mark. The polemical task of passing judgment on Mussolini crowded out his more abstract concerns and gave his writings a severely practical purpose.

North of the Alps fascism had failed in its initial bid for power. The postwar discontents that in Italy had swept Mussolini into office, in Germany had spent themselves in a many-sided struggle that in the end left bourgeois democracy in control. After the collapse of his Munich *Putsch* in 1923, Adolf Hitler required another decade to fight and cajole his way to the chancellorship of the Reich. The years in which Italian Fascism was steadily consolidating its control were the years of Weimar Germany's reprieve—the second half of the 1920's, when contemporaries were lulled into the illusion that economic prosperity and a conciliatory foreign policy had together exorcised the "demonic" in German politics and ideology.

15. On this whole subject, besides Fermi, *Illustrious Immigrants*, pp. 48–51, 116–123, see Aldo Garosci, *Storia dei fuorusciti* (Bari, 1953), and Charles F. Delzell, *Mussolini's Enemies: The Italian Anti-Fascist Resistance* (Princeton, N.J., 1961), Chapters 2–4.

The fact that the advent of fascism in Italy and its progress in Germany were out of phase meant that Europe's intellectuals awoke to the reality of life under such a regime only when it was too late to do anything about it. While the Italians were making their personal adjustments and concessions with little sympathy from abroad, their German counterparts were at the height of their international cultural prestige. The fortuitous circumstance that the Weimar Republic's last years coincided with the zenith of its intellectual achievement made all the more bitter the succeeding experience of barbarism.

Already the turn of the decade had a precarious atmosphere that gave a special intensity to the life of the mind. With anxious clairvoyance Karl Mannheim peered into the future in the series of essays entitled *Ideology and Utopia* with which in 1929 he assessed his predecessors' struggle to define the ideal bases of society. A similar mixture of assurance and trepidation characterized Berlin's new status as the most stimulating metropolis in the Western world. While Paris might be more beautiful and London more urbane, there was in Berlin an appreciation of aesthetic novelty, a sharpness of tone, a quickness of mind, a juxtaposition of contrasting styles, that persuaded men of talent to put up with its lack of outward charm and the abrasiveness of its personal encounters. In the late 1920's Berlin finally became the unquestioned cultural capital of the German-speaking world. Munich, Frankfurt, and the rest kept their former eminence, but the city on the Spree was the place where the young and the gifted preferred to go.[16] Even Vienna found itself outclassed. With the Hapsburg Empire shattered and Austria shrunk to an exclusively German state, its capital was no longer as self-confident or as cosmopolitan as it had been before. Vienna lived on its aesthetic memories and cultivated a distaste for modern technology. It too had to defer to Berlin.

The Austrians in 1919 had expressed a decided preference for union with the Reich. This the victorious Allies had prevented, and the *Anschluss* of the two nations was not to be achieved until

16. For an evocation of Berlin's cultural life in the late Weimar years, see Peter Gay, *Weimar Culture: The Outsider as Insider* (New York, 1968), pp. 128–132.

1938 under the very different circumstances of Nazi rule. Meantime Central Europe had found unity in the cultural sphere. The distinction between Germans and Austrians had become blurred, as large numbers of the latter, discouraged by the depressed economic circumstances and the lack of opportunities in their own country, sought careers in the Reich. With the creation of the Slavic successor states to the Austrian Empire, German-speaking professional men no longer had access to positions they had once nearly monopolized throughout the former Hapsburg domains.[17]

Hungarians encountered comparable difficulties. Hungary's intellectuals, mostly Jewish and leftist, had already begun to suffer from discrimination in the early 1920's—even before the consolidation of Fascism in Italy. Since they generally spoke German with ease, they could readily move to Vienna or Berlin, where they became absorbed in the local intellectual milieu. Hence when they were forced to make a second move—this time across the Atlantic —they were scarcely distinguishable from Germans and Austrians. In the great migration, as in the culture of the 1920's, the Central Europeans shared a common experience. The chief difference was that those in Berlin or Munich were obliged to leave after 1933, while the Viennese could wait another half-decade.

For independent-minded German-speaking intellectuals, the course so many Italians pursued of pretending to ignore their country's new regime was not a realistic option. For one thing, the imposition of the Nazi *Gleichschaltung* was too rapid and rigorous to permit such evasions. For another, the high percentage of Jews among the German and Austrian intelligentsia meant that many who were not ideologically suspect were threatened on "racial" grounds. Yet for the most part Jewish origin and anti-Nazi sympathies paralleled and reinforced each other: those who manifested either or both found themselves automatically barred from the German "folk" community. The decisive reason why German-speaking writers and professors confronted a sterner ethical choice

17. Karl Mannheim, *Man and Society in an Age of Reconstruction*, trans. from the German by Edward Shils (London, 1940), p. 99 n. For a characterization of the Viennese intellectual milieu in the 1920's, see William M. Johnston, *The Austrian Mind: An Intellectual and Social History, 1848–1938* (Berkeley and Los Angeles, 1972), pp. 73–75, 391–396.

than their Italian counterparts was that the predominant definition of Germanism was harsher and more exclusive than that of *italianità*.

During the 1920's a split in German culture had become evident which in fact went far back into the preceding century. In the ebullient, multiform intellectual life of the Weimar Republic the basic cleavage ran between those who adhered to a *völkisch* ideal and those of cosmopolitan sympathies. In retrospect the latter were to seem more typical of Weimar culture—the former, if less eminent and original, were always numerically stronger and surer of their popular backing.

In its simplest form there was nothing particularly sinister about the *völkisch* ideal. Its celebration of rootedness in the soil did not differ notably from the nationalist doctrine propagated by Maurice Barrès in France; the Germanic theorists shared with the French a spuriously naïve admiration for peasants and the rural life. Yet the German notion of harmony between man and nature had racial and metaphysical connotations that were lacking elsewhere:

> The nature of the soul of a Volk is determined by the native landscape. Thus the Jews, being a desert people, are . . . shallow, arid, "dry" . . ., devoid of profundity and totally lacking in creativity. Because of the barrenness of the desert landscape, the Jews are a spiritually barren people. They thus contrast markedly with the Germans, who, living in the dark, mist-shrouded forests, are deep, mysterious, profound. Because they are so constantly shrouded in darkness, they strive toward the sun, and are truly *Lichtmenschen*.[18]

Few leading German intellectuals of the 1920's would have subscribed without qualification to such a set of propositions. But the style of thought was congenial to a majority among them. Moreover, certain ideological corollaries of "Germanic" thinking were embraced by a great many who would not have characterized themselves as *völkisch*. Among these associated ideas was the old distinction—which Oswald Spengler had popularized and to which even Thomas Mann had succumbed in his wartime writ-

18. George L. Mosse, *The Crisis of German Ideology: Intellectual Origins of the Third Reich* (New York, 1964), pp. 4–5.

ings—between Germany as the dwelling place of authentic "culture" and France as the epitome of a "civilization" that was superficial, charming, and merely clever. Along with it went a conviction that what bothered foreigners about the Germans was in reality the source of their superiority: their country's troubled, erratic behavior betokened its spiritual depth, and the outbreaks of ferocity to which it was intermittently subject were signs of a "demonic" force that could be in turn creative and destructive. In short, the Germanic wing of professors and writers were quite happy to recognize and to extol the elements in the national tradition which marked it off from the "civilized" West—for example, its apparent unfitness for parliamentary democracy. They took pride in the very same manifestations of national uniqueness that were a cause of anguish to those of cosmopolitan leanings.

That the Germanic—or *völkisch*-minded—welcomed the advent of National Socialism is a matter of historical record. It is also relevant to add that they got rather more than they anticipated. Here lay the fundamental ambiguity of the Nazi ideological experience. Initially Hitler appeared to be doing no more than what the Germanic theorists had long aspired to: giving strong leadership to a healthy and united people and bringing into the fold those beyond the national borders who shared its speech and its cultural traditions. Few suspected that this was only his minimum program, that hidden within the literal meaning of the Führer's rhetoric lurked a project without precedent in history. The peasant and warrior mentality which the *völkisch* had preached ended in war—this was to be expected. What only a handful of Germans ever fully grasped was that the conflict in question was eventually to lose all semblance of a struggle for recognizable national ends, that it was to become an endless, insatiable succession of acts of pillage and annihilation, with "racial" victory the final and unattainable goal.[19]

As this macabre scenario unrolled, more and more German intellectuals took refuge in what they called "inner emigration." They quietly dropped out of the National Socialist consensus. At

19. This is in substance the line of reasoning in Ernst Nolte's *Der Faschismus in seiner Epoche* (Munich, 1963), trans. by Leila Vennewitz as *Three Faces of Fascism* (New York, 1966), pp. 407–414.

its lowest level, inner emigration meant little more than prudent silence; it was thoroughly familiar to writers and professors who had regarded as another mark of their countrymen's superiority their ability to stand "above" the political battle. An aloof neutrality which in practice meant conformism had in the past been the normal stance of German men of letters. In this cautious guise, inner emigration meant merely reverting to type. There were a few, however, for whom it signified a proud and conscious secession from the national community. After a harrowing stay in a concentration camp, which he was subsequently to narrate in *Der Totenwald*—the forest of the dead—the novelist Ernst Wiechert found no recourse but silence. Similarly, in the stillness of his Munich lodging the Catholic essayist Theodor Haecker composed the *Tag- und Nachtbücher*—the diaries by day and night—in which he set down his anxious musings on the evil he saw around him.

   Thus in its various guises the experience of inner emigration bridged the gap between the Germanic and the cosmopolitan intellectuals. Yet for the most part only the more conservative among the latter were able to fall back on such a course. The rest found the atmosphere of Nazi Germany stifling; they could not bear to witness its brutalities and lies and the indignities it inflicted on their Jewish acquaintances. Besides, they were already marked down as potential dissidents. Some lost their jobs; others departed after receiving official threats or warnings from their friends. In the early years of Hitler's rule, nearly 1,700 scholars and scientists were dismissed from their posts, including more than 300 professors; something over three-quarters of these were of Jewish or partly Jewish origin. And a correspondingly high percentage emigrated. The absorption of Central European thought by Britain and America from the 1930's to the 1950's was to be facilitated by the fact that that thought was transmitted by the heterodox wing of the German-speaking intelligentsia whose vocabulary and conceptual frame were closer than were those of the orthodox majority to the rational-empirical tradition of the West.

   Cosmopolitanism, pacifism, left-wing sympathies—or perhaps a merely generic *esprit frondeur*—these were the marks of a dissidence that dated from the Wilhelminian era and that under the Republic had for a brief period come close to setting the dominant tone. Its foothold in the universities was never extensive or secure. Although there were influential professors such as the historian Friedrich Meinecke who supported the Republic and its democratic institutions, they tended to be sober-minded scholars with few links to the life of active politics; there seem to have been only four academics of any prominence who took a Marxist line—among them Karl Mannheim (whose ancestors were both Jewish and Hungarian!). The real home of the dissident and cosmopolitan-minded was the world of journalism and the arts. Here wit and scorn could range untrammeled by professorial inhibitions.

It has frequently struck foreign observers that the land of the murky Germanic ideology was also the nation that produced Heinrich Heine and Karl Marx and Friedrich Nietzsche—that "so many of the great debunking analysts of modern culture" were "German or Austrian, not English or French." It was as though the arrogance and self-assurance of the majority made fury or irony their opponents' only recourse. "The result was that mild criticisms of conventional notions were very hard to express. To challenge the orthodox at all, the critic almost had to make a leap into a new vocabulary."[20]

The chief of the new vocabularies was that of psychoanalysis—as the greatest of the German-speaking "unmaskers" was Sigmund Freud himself. In the cosmopolitan milieu where Anglophilia or Francophilia or Semitophilia (or combinations of them) reigned, the single clearest sign of membership in the fraternity of dissidence was an acceptance of the psychoanalytic way of thinking. Right up to the Nazi takeover, Central Europe remained the stronghold of psychoanalysis. Vienna, as Freud's home city, was of course its capital. But Berlin had become a close rival: alone among the Psychoanalytic Institutes that of Berlin could hold its own alongside the Viennese. It was here that in 1922 Freud had delivered his last public theoretical utterance. The city where he found his most faithful immediate disciples—Karl Abraham and

20. Fritz K. Ringer, *The Decline of the German Mandarins: The German Academic Community*, 1890–1933 (Cambridge, Mass., 1969), pp. 201, 240–241, 440–441.

Max Eitingon and Hanns Sachs—was also the place where some of
the most imaginative analysts in the emigration received their
training.

While Germany's intellectual dissenters frequently tried to be
classless or "bohemian" in their style of life, its leading social
thinkers remained "bourgeois." This was certainly true of practicing psychoanalysts, whose personal habits—however permissive
their theoretical beliefs—were for the most part conventional. The
same was true of the few but eminent figures who held university
chairs. And it was even the case with a major creative writer such
as Thomas Mann. Yet the dissident intellectuals' adherence to
bourgeois values and a bourgeois life style did not pass unquestioned: it was a constant source of perplexity to men who could not
help asking themselves whether the lack of congruence between
the boldness of their ideas and the cautious way in which they
conducted their lives betokened some hidden inauthenticity. The
question of the viability of "bourgeois humanism" in an apocalyptic era was the first of two nagging and related problems that
such humanists carried with them into exile.

The second was that of *Geist*—of intellect or mind or spirit
(depending on how one chooses to translate a German term
heavily laden with favorable implications). In this respect the
difference between the Germanic majority of the intellectuals and
the cosmopolitan-minded minority was not so great as might be
imagined. Most of the latter spoke of *Geist* in very nearly as awestruck tones as did the conventionally educated among their
countrymen. And the notion of their own roles was correspondingly exalted. As the purveyors of *Geist*, German writers and
professors had claimed the status of "a priestly caste" legislating
"ultimate values to a peasant population." In the 1930's, despite
the buffeting it had received in the world of reality, this claim was
still confidently advanced: even some of those who regarded
themselves as cultural revolutionaries—men like Theodor W.
Adorno, Max Horkheimer, and Herbert Marcuse—remained sufficiently close to the teachings of Hegel to find no inconsistency in
such a stance. The "abstract language of cultivation" was the
common coin of German men of letters.[21] It was bound to clash

21. *Ibid.*, p. 268.

with the vocabularies current in the Anglo-American world—and in so doing to reinforce the doubts that the more self-questioning of the émigrés already entertained about it.

II. *The Literary Precursors: Hesse and Mann*

The émigrés' John the Baptist was Hermann Hesse. When Hitler came to power Hesse had already been living in the wilderness for two decades—if one can refer in such terms to the idyllic village in Italian Switzerland where he had eventually settled. In 1933 his reputation as a novelist rested primarily on the two works in which he had addressed himself to his countrymen's characteristic intellectual vices: *Demian*, of 1919, with its torrential assault on hypocrisy and conformism; and *Steppenwolf*, of 1927, in which he had chronicled his own unavailing efforts to come to terms with bourgeois society and in the process had attempted the infinitely more difficult feat of subjecting to the play of a relativizing irony the values of pacifist-minded intellectuals like himself.

Thus there was something disconcerting about Hesse's role as Germany's literary exile of longest standing. Regarded from afar, his credentials appeared impeccable: those who took flight after 1933 might well have admired the foresight of a man who even before the First World War had sensed where his nation was heading. More closely regarded, however, Hesse had little to teach his countrymen that could be of use during the twelve years of Nazi rule. It was not only that *Steppenwolf* had suggested a withdrawal from daily struggle to the crystal spheres where the laughter of the immortals—Goethe, Mozart, and the rest—echoed in mockery of human self-righteousness. Beyond that, the two novels with which Hesse followed it were still more detached and allegorical. And by 1934, when he published the introduction to what was to be his most ambitious work, *The Glass Bead Game*, Hesse's evolution into a proponent of pure aesthetics and intellectualism seemed complete.

The game that this introduction outlined epitomized the loftiest ideal of *Geist*. "A . . . virtuoso flight through the realms of the mind," it embodied in imaginative form a synthesis of the cultural creations of the Western world:

> The Glass Bead Game is thus a mode of playing with the total contents and values of our culture. . . . All the insights, noble thoughts, and works of art that the human race has produced in its creative eras, all that subsequent periods of scholarly study have reduced to concepts and converted into intellectual property—on all this immense body of intellectual values the Glass Bead Game player plays like the organist on an organ. . . . Theoretically this instrument is capable of reproducing in the Game the entire intellectual content of the universe.[22]

Music and mathematics provided the rules and precedents for its meticulous ritual. Indeed, the Glass Bead Game could most readily be thought of as a theme and variations—or as a series of themes drawn from disparate fields of cultural endeavor that were set in an elaborate contrapuntal relation to each other. Hesse's descriptions of the game were deliberately vague: he evidently wanted to present it "in terms so general that the reader" could "produce his own associations from almost any area of modern intellectual life." Yet it seemed to stand above all "for the tendency toward abstraction and synthesis characteristic of the years between the two world wars—in non-objective art, in atonal music, in symbolic logic."[23] Although Hesse's personal preferences were nostalgic, although he found himself most at home with strict classical music and in the magical world of German Romanticism, he was sufficiently aware of what was going on around him to be able to offer his contemporaries a foretaste of their intellectual future. The introduction to *The Glass Bead Game* delineated with a single complex metaphor the implications of his countrymen's cultivation of disembodied *Geist*.

This was the point that Hesse had reached in the early 1930's.

22. *Das Glasperlenspiel* (Zürich, 1943), trans. by Richard and Clara Winston as *The Glass Bead Game* (New York, 1969), pp. 15, 38. Note that the translators use for *Geist* the word "intellect" rather than "spirit."
23. Theodore Ziolkowski, *The Novels of Hermann Hesse: A Study in Theme and Structure* (Princeton, N.J., 1965), p. 77.

The advent of Hitler could not fail to affect the character of the novel which was to detail the vicissitudes of the game through three centuries of imaginary future history. As Hesse labored over it during the first decade of Nazi rule, its outlines changed by imperceptible but cumulative stages: it gradually ceased to be an exercise in pure cerebration; it moved from the realm of aesthetics and intellectualism to a concern for the public arena and human solidarity. By 1943, when *The Glass Bead Game* was finally published, those who had read the introduction nine years earlier discovered to their surprise that Hesse's protagonist had in the end abandoned his position as a supreme virtuoso of the mind and thrown in his lot with struggling humanity.

Among those who welcomed *The Glass Bead Game* with gratitude was Hesse's closest counterpart among German novelists, Thomas Mann. There was "scarcely another work," Mann wrote, that inspired in him "such warm and respectful feelings of comradeship."[24] When Mann himself had gone into exile in 1933, he renewed with Hesse ties of mutual honor and affection that dated back for more than twenty years—just as the same separation from his national community threw him into closer contact with Freud and made him the spokesman for the German literary world in exile on the occasion of the master's eightieth birthday in 1936.

If Hesse was the original prophet of the emigration, Mann early became its most prominent and representative figure. Such a role would not have come naturally to him in his first years as a novelist, when he had been absorbed in finding his own aesthetic stance to the exclusion of political concerns. But as the 1920's had gone on—as Mann had accepted and defended the Weimar Republic and in his major novel *The Magic Mountain* (1924) and his short story "Mario and the Magician" (1930) had affirmed the power of "goodness and love" against the gathering forces of terror and obscurantism—he had attained almost in spite of himself the status of an enunciator of public values. During the Weimar years, Mann was crossing a double divide: he was passing over from

24. *Die Entstehung des Doktor Faustus* (Amsterdam, 1949), trans. by Richard and Clara Winston as *The Story of a Novel* (New York, 1961), p. 74.

German national to cosmopolitan sympathies, and he was shifting the axis of his work from private sensibility to ideological commitment. Eventually "his old age was taken up with a ceaseless publicist struggle against fascism"—as his fictional characters traveled "from isolation to human and social community." Thus Georg Lukács wrote of the man he admired as the greatest of the twentieth century's "critical realists."[25]

Mann's initial attitude toward his own emigration had been more hesitant. Even when he had found a home that suited him near Zürich in the autumn of 1933, he could derive little satisfaction from an exile which might last the rest of his life. His ties to German culture were too close; he shrank from an irreparable rupture; after toying with the idea of southern France, he chose a city where the German language was spoken. Not until 1936, in response to a Swiss critic's characterization of the writers in exile as Jewish and un-German, did Mann unequivocally align himself with his fellow men of letters who had also left their country. As he wrote to Hesse in explanation, he had felt a need to clear up the "ambiguous, half-and-half notions" that were current about his relationship to the Third Reich.[26] Two years later, when with the annexation of Austria Mann decided to settle permanently in the United States, he had thrown off all doubt about his choice. He now saw his exile as a kind of spiritual ambassadorship in behalf of German culture: "What does it mean to be without a homeland? My homeland lies in the works that I bear with me. Sunk within them I experience all the cosiness of being at home. They are my language, the German language and its form of thought, a possession handed down by my country and people which I have developed further. Where I am, there is Germany."[27]

In America, Thomas Mann the exile came into his own. At first he lived in Princeton, attracted by the university's offer of a special lectureship in the humanities. But two years of this variety of

25. *Thomas Mann*, 5th ed. (Berlin, 1957), trans. and abr. by Stanley Mitchell as *Essays on Thomas Mann* (New York, 1965), pp. 49, 54.
26. February 9, 1936, *Letters of Thomas Mann 1889–1955*, sel. and trans. by Richard and Clara Winston (New York, 1971), p. 249.
27. Quoted from an unpublished portion of Mann's "Tagebuchblätter," dating from early April 1938, in Herbert Lehnert, "Thomas Mann in Exile 1933–1938," *The Germanic Review*, XXXVIII (Nov. 1963), 291.

"jokes," as he put it, amply sufficed. He moved to southern California, where he found a plot of land and built a house in a lemon grove close to the sea. The climate and landscape appealed to him, as did the chance to devote himself to his writing free of academic commitments. Yet his time was never fully his own: he gave of his thought and energy to other refugees less fortunate than he, and he broadcast messages of hope to his countrymen who had remained in Germany. He was well aware of his special position and the responsibilities that went with it: the wealthy and the powerful made a great fuss over him; his fame brought him security and comfort in the form of lecture fees and royalties for his novels in translation. Nor did his public activities reduce his capacities for creative work as some of his friends had feared. The reverse may have been true: Mann's polemical efforts seemed to provide the outside stimulus which his continued artistic production required.[28]

Hence it was not surprising that he should eventually have come to speak of the experience of exile in terms of warm commendation. In a lecture delivered in Washington in November 1942, he characterized the current "diaspora of European culture" as "something very strange and unprecedented" which had assumed "an entirely different significance from that of any former emigration"—it meant nothing less than the possibility of creating a "new feeling of humanism" that might bring unity to the whole world.[29] Never had the hopes of humanity been higher. At the very moment when Mann was speaking, the tide of war was turning in North Africa and at Stalingrad: the defeat of Hitler now loomed as probable, perhaps even as certain. As the emigration's public spokesman, Mann gave voice to the delicious, transitory euphoria that lay between the early trials of adjustment to a new land and the moral perplexities of the cold war that were to follow.

The occasion for the lecture in Washington was the completion of Mann's tetralogy of novels on the biblical theme of Joseph and his brothers. By far the most extended of his works, it had ab-

28. Henry Hatfield, "Thomas Mann and America," special no. of *Salmagundi*, p. 174.
29. "The Joseph Novels," *The Atlantic Monthly*, CLXXI (Feb. 1943), 100.

sorbed the greater part of his energies for a full decade and a half.
It had been his "steady companion," "insuring . . . the unity" of
his life through all his changes of scene and fortune.[30] The first
two novels—*The Tales of Jacob* and *Young Joseph*—had been
written before his exile and could still be published in Germany
during the initial period of Hitler's rule. The third, *Joseph in
Egypt*, whose unfinished manuscript had been recovered by
Mann's oldest daughter from his already confiscated house in
Munich, was completed in Switzerland and appeared in Vienna in
1936. It remained for the concluding volume, *Joseph the Provider*,
to ripen in its author's mind under the appropriately "Egyptian"
sky of California.

The themes of the Joseph novels were as varied as the circumstances of their composition. An enormously expanded version of
the spare account in Genesis, the books proceeded in leisurely
fashion with interspersed digressions and loving attention to detail.
Most obviously they suggested Mann's solidarity with the suffering
Jewish people—as though when he had undertaken his task in the
mid-1920's he had already suspected what was to come. A decade
and a half later he granted that "there were hidden, defiantly
polemic connections" between the novels and "the growing vulgar
anti-Semitism" which he had "always found repulsive. . . . To
write a novel of the Jewish spirit was timely just because it seemed
untimely." More broadly, Mann hoped that his work would depict
the triumph of "crafty goodness" over "stupid . . . slave drivers."
His old theme of humanism was with him still, but it had now
turned "away from the bourgeois toward the mythical aspect."
And to carry these disparate elements, he had settled on an "indirect, a stylized and bantering language" whose humor frequently
failed to penetrate the veil of translation.[31] Mann's readers might
well be puzzled by a set of novels that were at once high comedy
and a deeply felt affirmation of Western civilized values.

The key to such apparent contradictions lay with the contemporary leader who all unsuspecting had offered Mann the half-
mythical type-figure he required. As the cycle of Joseph drew to its

30. *Ibid.*, p. 96; *Story of a Novel*, p. 14.
31. "The Joseph Novels," pp. 93–94, 96; to Agnes E. Meyer, July 26,
1941, *Letters of Thomas Mann*, p. 368.

close, its protagonist little by little took on the attributes of that other "provider," Franklin D. Roosevelt (and the novelist correspondingly began to give his ancient Egyptians the national peculiarities he both admired and mocked in the Americans among whom he dwelt). Mann had a respect for Roosevelt bordering on adulation. He had twice been entertained at the White House and had come away from these visits utterly bewitched. Like the legendary Joseph, the American president seemed to combine cunning and kindness in appropriate measure. While Mann found it "hard to characterize" Roosevelt's "mixture of craft, good nature, self-indulgence, desire to please, and sincere faith," he saw in him "something like a blessing" from on high that made him the "born opponent" to Adolf Hitler.[32]

Sixteen months after *Joseph the Provider* was published in Stockholm, Roosevelt lay dead. And in the meantime Mann's thoughts had turned more somber. The bourgeois humanist ideal that in Joseph himself and in the American president had found such reassuring incarnations had again become doubtful as the Second World War drew to its ambiguous end.[33] The completion of Mann's cycle of biblical novels marked a high point of confidence among the émigrés before the phase of self-questioning began.

iii. *Wahlverwandtschaften*

Just as there was a curious affinity that kept Mann's American readers faithful to him even when his writing was most "difficult"—just as he held on to an audience that knew him only in translation and that eluded comparable writers in exile such as his older brother Heinrich—so we can detect in other realms of thought what the Germans call *Wahlverwandtschaften*. Some styles of thinking prospered, and others withered or barely held their own in the new American setting. And the most important

32. To Agnes E. Meyer, January 24, 1941, *ibid.*, p. 355. On Mann's relationship to Roosevelt see the article by his nephew Klaus H. Pringsheim, "Thomas Mann in Amerika," *Neue deutsche Hefte*, XIII (1966), 29–31.
33. See Chapter 6.

explanation for their success or lack thereof was the extent to which the German idiom in each case could be carried over into English relatively intact.

In this respect the creative writers and the social thinkers among the émigrés faced different problems. The former continued to use their own language and to depend on translators for their American public; the greater part of them, including men as eminent as the dramatist Carl Zuckmayer and the novelist Hermann Broch, passed their years in the United States in almost total obscurity.[34] This was the cruel price they paid for settling in a land where their native tongue was spoken by only a very few and read by no more than a small educated minority—a minority probably smaller than it had been a generation earlier, before the blight of anti-Germanism in the First World War had discredited the study of the German language in a fashion from which it never recovered. The social thinkers, with rare but distinguished exceptions, made the opposite choice: they did their best to write in English—awkwardly at first, then with growing confidence. Yet only the youngest or most adaptable of them fully mastered their new tongue: most were acutely conscious of what they had lost along the way. As a veteran of these linguistic struggles viewed them in retrospect:

> Working in a language which is not the language of one's dreams is to miss many over- and under-tones, ambiguities and poetic notions, the spontaneousness and even the silences. Dimensions of thought and feeling must be replaced by a technique of significations, using spoken words in prefabricated, studied sequences which threaten to impoverish that which they ought to enrich. . . .
>
> Uneducated people quickly learn to make small talk in canned phrases. Intellectuals learn slowly and tend to speak "translatese," painfully aware that it is one flight below the level they would like to inhabit intellectually.[35]

34. For Zuckmayer's experiences, see his *Als Wär's ein Stück von mir* (Frankfurt, 1966), trans. by Richard and Clara Winston as *A Part of Myself* (New York, 1970).
35. Henry Pachter, "On Being an Exile: An Old-Timer's Personal and Political Memoir," special no. of *Salmagundi*, p. 19.

Thus the émigrés found themselves using an English that the classically inclined could equate with what the ancient Greeks termed *koine*. Those whose native languages were German or Italian or Magyar were forced to write in an idiom that was ungracious, narrow in range, and merely serviceable. Yet the Americans were polite about it, far more polite than the British would have been. The editors at the publishing houses did what they could to turn Teutonic English into a passable imitation of the literary language, and the public, accustomed to the slipshod writing of so many American-born authors, did not protest. The result was to convert English into still more of a lingua franca than it had been before. As with Greek in the Hellenistic age, the widening of its sphere of influence was accompanied by the danger that it would lose its fine edge and its ability to convey nuances of thought and expression.

A rare optimist among the refugee intellectuals might find it of advantage to his thought to be obliged to translate it into a language which did not lend itself to verbal bedazzlement. Tillich used to recall with wry self-irony the mixture of pleasure and dismay he experienced at seeing Germanic profundities vanish when put into plain English. The more usual reaction was a sense of linguistic impoverishment. And this impoverishment worked both ways—on the émigrés themselves and on their hosts, whose own grasp of the literary idiom was frequently none too secure. Again and again in the postwar years British scholars would complain of the Teutonic-American jargon in which the social science from across the Atlantic was composed. A generation after the event—when the refugees who had become Americanized might be presumed to think more naturally in English than in their native languages—it was still difficult to weigh linguistic loss against intellectual gain.

So much for the matter of language in the literal sense. In the broader sense of conceptual idiom, one can detect a bifurcation in the intellectual influences that radiated out from Central Europe in the 1930's and 1940's. The more metaphysical current associated with the trio Hegel, Husserl, and Heidegger was welcomed in

France.[36] The more concrete and empirical styles of thought—whether in philosophy or psychology, history or sociology—found a home in Britain or the United States. Three in particular of such *Wahlverwandtschaften* between the German- and the English-speaking worlds deserve closer attention: the approaches deriving from Max Weber, from Sigmund Freud, and from Ludwig Wittgenstein.

1. When Weber died in 1920, he left no organized school behind him. His influence in his own country was in no sense comparable to that of his contemporary Emile Durkheim, whose students and whose methods continued to dominate French social science during the entire interwar period. Even when alive, Weber had been an isolated scholar; after his death, his precepts about a "value-free" study of society were more frequently honored than observed. It was not until it reached the United States that the Weberian inheritance became a major force in social thought.

In part this delayed influence was due to the state of German sociology itself. As much a product of quasi-priestly scholarship as the older learned disciplines, it had in common with them a nostalgia for a simpler world of agrarian relationships. Yet it refused to indulge such yearnings. It had no ideological ties to the landed aristocracy—nor, we may add, to the capitalist middle class, nor even to the proletariat, despite its concern for the "social question" and the fact that a large part of its conceptual apparatus derived from Marx. Though far from being truly neutral in the realm of values, it fostered a stance of detachment and discrimination. The work of the German sociologists was suffused with "a sense of resignation. . . . They proposed . . . to accept some facets of modern life as inevitable or even desirable, while seeking to temper its more accidental and less tolerable aspects. This attitude led them to control their emotional response to their new environment, to uphold a heroic ideal of rational clarification in the face of tragedy."[37]

Thus hovering above the ideological wars of the Weimar era, the sociologists remained insulated from the harsher aspects of their own milieu. Nor did they succeed in finding acceptance

36. See my analysis in *The Obstructed Path* (New York, 1968), Chapter 5.
37. Ringer, *Decline of the German Mandarins*, p. 163.

within the mainstream of German academic life. It was not true,
as has frequently been asserted, that their labors were almost
exclusively abstract or historical. Before the First World War they
had inaugurated a series of quantitative surveys of conditions
among the working class, and some of this interest had carried
over into the postwar period. But such research lacked continuity
and a secure organizational base.[38] It required the move to
America to prod German sociology toward a more consistently
empirical stance.

Moreover, the sociologists and the sociologically minded historians who emigrated to England or the United States tended to
be the less conventional and the more experimentally inclined.
Besides Mannheim and some of his students, they included a
larger number who carried with them the methodology and style
of thought that they had acquired either directly or by derivation
from Weber. And of these many were only too happy to learn
from their American counterparts the techniques whose development had been arrested in their own country.[39] The result was an
initial example of transatlantic synthesis—a merging of sociological
traditions in which the Germans characteristically supplied theory,
the Americans a talent and enthusiasm for empirical research.
Such was the origin of the international discipline of sociology as
we know it today.

In the process the example of Weber made itself felt very
gradually and sometimes imperceptibly—and this is a further
explanation for his delayed influence. The Weberian attitude
permeated social thought by slow capillary action, frequently
through the work of scholars whose connection with Weber himself was either tenuous or not fully conscious. "Handicapped by
. . . discontinuous and incomplete translations," the reception of
his teaching "was bound to be fragmentary." In the end it
achieved recognition through piecemeal appropriation by men
facing "a particular theoretical need or research problem. The
result might be called 'creative misinterpretation' "—a fate not

38. Anthony Oberschall, *Empirical Social Research in Germany 1848–1914*
(Paris and The Hague, 1965), p. 137.
39. See Paul F. Lazarsfeld's engaging account, "An Episode in the History
of Social Research: A Memoir," *The Intellectual Migration*, pp. 270–337.

necessarily damaging to a corpus as wide in range and as tentative in assertion as Weber's.[40] In America Weber, like some mythic deity, underwent a series of transformations whose consistency with one another was frequently hard to detect.

The émigrés who worked in the Weberian tradition illustrated what the implacable dissector of the Nazi system Franz Neumann was to characterize as the optimum solution to the problem of cultural adaptation. They did not abandon their "previous intellectual position and accept without qualification" a new one. Nor did they "retain completely" their "old thought structure" and take upon themselves "the mission of totally revamping the American pattern"—or perhaps withdrawing "with disdain and contempt into an island" of their own. They chose the far more difficult assignment of integrating "new experience with old tradition."[41]

2. In contrast to the legacy of Max Weber, which was subtle and diffused, the other comparable *Wahlverwandtschaften* can be readily documented. Freud and Wittgenstein lived on into the period of emigration, the one until 1939, the other until 1951. Both of them maintained regular contact with disciples and admirers scattered throughout the English-speaking world. And both settled in England rather than the United States—which is in itself a reminder that the British aspect of the emigration requires greater attention than it has usually received.

In the case of Freud, however, despite the fact that his daughter Anna remained in England and continued his work there, the bulk of his most influential heirs crossed the Atlantic. In practical terms, this decision made sense: psychoanalysis was already established on the American scene, and its practitioners who arrived after 1933 or 1938 could adjust rapidly to their new situation. The more important of them were familiar to their hosts through earlier encounters at international congresses; most of the others experienced little difficulty in launching themselves into clinical practice. Indeed, the American milieu was more welcoming than

40. Guenther Roth, " 'Value-Neutrality' in Germany and the United States," *Scholarship and Partisanship: Essays on Max Weber* (with Reinhard Bendix) (Berkeley and Los Angeles, 1971), p. 35.
41. "The Social Sciences," *The Cultural Migration*, p. 20.

the one they had left. In Europe the members of the psychoanalytic movement had lived the life of sectarians walled off by a hostile environment. "They had, as it were, experienced premature training in the psychological condition of being émigrés, and this must have stood them in good stead when they had to become émigrés in the full sense of the term." In the United States minds were less likely to be closed to them, and people were curious about the message they brought. They arrived at an auspicious moment, when with the widespread questioning of the secularized Protestant ethic that had followed the economic crash, the Americans were hungering for an alternative system of thought which would "explain man to himself."[42] In the emotional hesitations of the 1930's, psychoanalysis—at least on the more popular level— found its chance.

Such success also carried dangers. In the relatively benign American setting, Freudian theory ran the risk of being "revised" beyond recognition, of being watered down to the point of extinction. The psychoanalysts who settled in America were obliged to steer a careful course between stubborn fidelity to the lessons of the founder and wholesale acceptance of the blander outlook of their new compatriots. A large number went aground on one or the other shoal. Yet it was in the treacherously propitious atmosphere of the United States that psychoanalysis completed a momentous theoretical change—the development of the ego psychology associated with the names of Heinz Hartmann and Erik H. Erikson. Here too we can find examples of a fortunate integration of new experience with established tradition.

3. Wittgenstein's arrival in Cambridge in 1929 and a visit of his friend Moritz Schlick to the United States in the same year marked the beginning of the major phase of interaction between the logical analysis of Vienna and the comparable philosophies that were already being formulated in Britain and the United States. This exchange antedated, then, by nearly a decade the wholesale flight of philosophers from Austria after the *Anschluss* of 1938. Wittgenstein chose Cambridge because he knew it already and thought it a good place to "do" his sort of philosophy.

42. Marie Jahoda, "The Migration of Psychoanalysis: Its Impact on American Psychology," *The Intellectual Migration*, pp. 429–430, 433.

Rudolf Carnap and other members of the Vienna Circle subsequently emigrated to the United States for similar reasons. The predominantly empirical tone of American philosophy promised a favorable reception; its pragmatic and instrumental approaches paralleled in less rigorous fashion the findings of the Viennese.[43] Precise in method, respectful toward natural science, prizing clarity above all else, the logicians from Central Europe were admirably equipped to address their new English-speaking students. Still more, since they cast their teaching so far as possible in the language of unambiguous symbols, the problems of translation that vexed the other émigrés were reduced to a minimum. Within less than a generation English almost effortlessly replaced German as the lingua franca of logical analysis.

Such was the situation in the United States. In Britain matters were more complex. Wittgenstein's arrival in Cambridge not only reinforced the position of that university as the philosophical capital of the West. It also encouraged a new direction in his own work which he had just begun to stake out. Living in England, teaching in English, but continuing to write in German, Wittgenstein was drawn by force of circumstance to pursue his speculations on the function and characteristics of what came to be called ordinary language. The new concerns that established him as the most influential Central European thinker at work in the Anglo-American world also provided the forum for the crucial intellectual drama immediately preceding the emigration itself. It is fitting to start the analysis of this primarily American experience with an account of the philosophical prologue played out on English soil.

43. Herbert Feigl, "The Wiener Kreis in America," *ibid.*, pp. 643–647.

Philosophical Prologue in England

1. The British Peculiarity

SINCE THE LATE nineteenth century the sequences of British thought had been out of phase with those on the Continent. The English and the Scots had pursued their own course, borrowing from abroad only such concepts as fitted their characteristic and self-defined purposes. Just as in the early part of the century, the reverberations of the French Revolution had occasioned a less widespread questioning of the Enlightenment than had appeared in Germany or in its country of origin, just as the tradition of Bentham and the two Mills had descended in untroubled succession from the pre-1789 world of ideas, so the intellectual battles of the generations succeeding John Stuart Mill took place in a different order and had a different tone from their counterparts across the Channel. In Britain both liberalism and a plain, commonsense brand of positivism were home-grown products that had become second nature in philosophical discourse. Both could claim a legitimate ancestor in John Locke. And the positivist stance had been reinforced by the triumphs of natural science in the Darwinian age.

Against the dominance of this latter attitude, idealist thought could offer only a wavering or intermittent challenge. The full panoply of German idealism did not reach the British universities until a half-century after its best days on the Continent—and

when it did come it was in Hegelian guise. Britain's major encounter with the idealist way of thinking was out of date even in
its own time. At the turn of the century, when Continental
theorists—notably Durkheim and Weber—who had experienced
idealism and positivism alike in their pristine forms were beginning to define a new canon of social thought that would combine
and transcend what they had learned from both, in Britain such
philosophers as F. H. Bradley and Bernard Bosanquet were still
trying to introduce their recalcitrant countrymen to Hegel.[1]

Hegelian idealism—or Absolute Idealism, as it was sometimes
called—figured as "an alien import, . . . an exotic in the English
scene."[2] It was not surprising, then, that its brief preeminence
should have been easily and permanently overthrown. The demise
of the idealist style, and the concomitant definition of Britain's
most pervasive twentieth-century modes of thought, came at the
hands of two distinct sets of writers. The two had in common,
however, besides their distaste for high-flown abstraction, the fact
that they reached back across the period of Hegelian aberration to
a robust and authentically British philosophical past.

The first in time was the pragmatic, nominalist social science
primarily exemplified by Alfred Marshall in economics and
Graham Wallas in sociology. Renouncing nineteenth-century aspirations toward universal theory, men like Marshall and Wallas
concerned themselves with the discrete and the particular. They
were also deeply involved in social reform and in the practical
application of their ideas. More modest in aim than their Continental contemporaries, they refused to worry about the epistemological problems that seemed so urgent to Germans and Frenchmen and Italians around 1900. The British social thinkers preferred measurement to speculation, and solid fact to theories of
knowledge.[3] Their most influential achievement was to come in

1. For a fuller account of this contrast, see my *Consciousness and Society*
(New York, 1958), Chapter 2, and Noel Annan, *The Curious Strength of
Positivism in English Political Thought* (L. T. Hobhouse Memorial Trust Lecture No. 28) (London, 1959).
2. G. J. Warnock, *English Philosophy since 1900* (London, 1958), p. 9.
3. Reba N. Soffer, "The Revolution in English Social Thought, 1880–
1914," *The American Historical Review*, LXXV (Dec. 1970), 1938–1941,
1963; Martin J. Wiener, *Between Two Worlds: The Political Thought of
Graham Wallas* (Oxford, 1971).

the next generation with the new economics of John Maynard Keynes.

The second set of thinkers who overthrew Absolute Idealism were the Cambridge philosophers G. E. Moore and Bertrand Russell. In his *Principia Ethica*, published shortly after the turn of the century, Moore undertook to refute both positivist and Hegelian teaching with his contention that what was "good in itself" was "quite unique in kind"—that it could not "be reduced to any assertion about reality." This separation of the realm of value from the realm of fact (or science) paralleled the almost simultaneous methodological pronouncements of Max Weber: the Englishman and the German had in common their precarious situation of conducting a battle on two fronts. On the one hand they found it necessary to challenge the easy-going positivist practice of moving back and forth between scientific and ethical assertions without giving warning to the reader. On the other hand they assaulted the Hegelian notion that in some realm of the spirit the two types of statement could arrive at a majestic synthesis. As Moore put it, "to search for 'unity' and 'system,' at the expense of truth," was not "the proper business of philosophy."[4]

It is curious that the parallelism between Moore's and Weber's efforts has seldom been observed. Their vocabularies and the subjects they discussed were so different that their underlying intellectual compatibility has remained unrecognized. Yet both were concerned with asking the right questions—that is, those that philosophers had not asked before—and with finding out the meaning of those questions once they had been proposed. In Weber's case, such procedures figured as the preliminaries to an investigation of human society; in the case of Moore and his associates, these initial clarifications became the main business at hand. In the early, quasi-mathematical work of Moore's Cambridge contemporary Bertrand Russell, philosophy found itself reduced and refined to the narrow scope of the logical analysis of language; and this it remained in the practice of Russell's stricter successors. Moore's legacy was more open: his simple, candid, direct style of argument and his respect for "common sense" in no

4. *Principia Ethica* (Cambridge, 1903), pp. 114, 222.

way debarred the two generations of students who fell under his influence from pursuing whatever attracted them. But most in fact stayed within the safe and respectable bounds of logic and epistemology. Of those who had been closely touched by Moore's example, Keynes alone became a social thinker of the first rank.[5]

Thus while Marshall and Wallas in one type of intellectual endeavor, and Moore and Russell in another, revitalized the central British tradition—empirical and nominalist—descending from Locke and Hume, no such philosophically grounded social science as Weber and Durkheim had inaugurated developed at the universities of England and Scotland. Keynes was equipped to play the role of founder, but he chose to devote his energies to public service and technical economics instead. It was rather a man whom Keynes had befriended and even financially aided—Ludwig Wittgenstein—who late in time and in tantalizing fragments gave his British students a glimpse of the possible connection between rigorous philosophical analysis and speculation on the nature of society.

Wittgenstein was not a refugee from political or "racial" persecution. Although of Jewish ancestry, he had never suffered discrimination on account of his origins. Moreover, his definitive move to England preceded by four years the advent of Hitler in Germany. Yet the function he performed among the British was the precise counterpart to—and even surpassed in influence—the work of the émigrés from Central Europe in the United States.

Britain's educational institutions were less receptive to the foreign-born than those of America. Far fewer in number, for the most part literary or classical in their curriculum, the British universities could absorb only a handful of the social scientists who emigrated from the Continent in the 1930's. It was not merely that teaching positions were scarce. It was also that the whole notion of formal graduate education was just beginning to take on in Britain and that a majority of the research students enrolled in

5. For Moore's influence on Keynes, see R. F. Harrod, *The Life of John Maynard Keynes* (London, 1951), pp. 75–81; see also on the wider significance of the two founders of British analytical philosophy, A. J. Ayer, *Russell and Moore: The Analytical Heritage* (Cambridge, Mass., 1971).

the universities were specializing in the natural sciences. Still more, the major discipline of sociology languished in obscurity. In these discouraging circumstances, it was natural that most Central European scholars preferred to cross the Atlantic.[6] And it was also not surprising that the most influential of the Continentals located in England should have been a man at work in the impeccably legitimate field of philosophy and one whose university connections dated back to before the First World War.

In his mid-twenties Ludwig Wittgenstein had studied at Trinity College, Cambridge, for three terms of the year 1912 and two terms of the year following. Here he had known both Moore and more particularly Russell. Lord Russell has recalled his consternation at the young visitor who came to him after one term of study and asked him point-blank:

> "Do you think I am an absolute idiot?" I said: "Why do you want to know?" He replied: "Because if I am I shall become an aeronaut, but if I am not I shall become a philosopher." I said to him: "My dear fellow, I don't know whether you are an absolute idiot or not, but if you will write me an essay during the vacation upon any philosophical topic that interests you, I will read it and tell you." He did so, and brought it to me at the beginning of the next term. As soon as I read the first sentence, I became persuaded that he was a man of genius, and assured him that he should on no account become an aeronaut.[7]

So Wittgenstein settled down in Cambridge to read systematically in philosophy. But this decision did not end Russell's bewilderment at his behavior:

> He used to come to see me every evening at midnight, and pace up and down my room like a wild beast . . . in agitated silence. Once I said to him: "Are you thinking about logic or about your sins?" "Both," he replied, and continued his

6. Helge Pross, *Die Deutsche Akademische Emigration nach den Vereinigten Staaten 1933–1941* (Berlin, 1955), pp. 34–37.
7. *The Autobiography of Bertrand Russell*, II: *The Middle Years: 1914–1944*, Bantam paperback ed. (New York, 1969), p. 133.

pacing. I did not like to suggest that it was time for bed, as it seemed probable both to him and me that on leaving me he would commit suicide.

Apparently Russell's conviction of Wittgenstein's genius—"passionate, profound, intense, and dominating"—enabled him to sustain so taxing a relationship. He even put up with technical criticism from the younger man that gave him "a sense of failure" and for a while convinced him that he "could not hope ever again to do fundamental work in philosophy." Yet years later—and when the end of the war had once again made intellectual exchange between Englishmen and Austrians possible—Russell was the prime mover in the long battle to get Wittgenstein's *Tractatus Logico-Philosophicus* published. The two met in The Hague and "spent a week arguing" the book "line by line."[8] And Russell wrote for it a laudatory introduction.

This introduction marked the beginning of a slow estrangement. Wittgenstein was furious at what he felt was Russell's distortion of his own intentions and even considered withdrawing his work entirely. Their friendship could not survive the strain. After a decade had passed, with the book in question now a modern classic and its author preparing to return to Cambridge, his former teacher's assessment of Wittgenstein's ideas had grown less enthusiastic. While they might "easily prove to constitute a whole new philosophy," Russell wrote, it was unclear whether they were true. "As a logician" who liked "simplicity," the older man added, he preferred to think that they were not. This was the nub of the disagreement, since Wittgenstein for his part had come to the conclusion that Russell's philosophy—and with it his own early work—consisted largely of tautologies. As Wittgenstein's fame spread, his former teacher's distrust of his new style of thought settled into detestation. And one by one the rising luminaries in British philosophy shifted their allegiance from Russell to Wittgenstein. The man who had begun as his pupil, the senior ruefully noted, had "ended as his supplanter."[9]

8. *Ibid.*, pp. 64, 90, 132, 134.
9. Michael Frayn, "Russell and Wittgenstein," *Commentary*, XLIII (May 1967), 73–74; Russell, *Autobiography*, II, p. 288.

With Moore, Wittgenstein's relations had been calmer. At the start the visitor from Austria had been less impressed by Moore than by Russell. Many years later he confessed that he had found the former's lectures repetitious, although he had in fact pleased Moore by looking "puzzled" during them. After his return to Cambridge, Wittgenstein's judgment was more even-handed: he concluded that while Russell might be "bright," Moore was "deep" and particularly adept at destroying "premature solutions" of philosophical problems. In their later years, when Wittgenstein had succeeded Moore as professor of philosophy at Cambridge, the two saw each other frequently. Their minds still worked in different fashions, and Wittgenstein still found Moore "childlike," but he evidently set a high value on their conversations. Indeed he was "extremely vexed" when Moore's wife, solicitous for her ailing husband's health, put a time limit upon them. The old philosopher, Wittgenstein maintained, "should discuss as long as he liked. If he became very excited or tired and had a stroke and died—well, that would be a decent way to die: with his boots on."[10]

This anecdote tells us a great deal about Wittgenstein's attitude toward life and death. It also suggests that he never adapted to the urbane style of the older English universities. One of his closest associates has gone so far as to say that he had a "great distaste . . . for English culture and mental habits in general."[11] While such may well have been the case, it did not limit his intellectual attraction. On the contrary, Wittgenstein's stubborn refusal to be assimilated to Cambridge ways constituted an integral part of his unique role as mediator between the Continental and the Anglo-American philosophical traditions.

II. *Ludwig Wittgenstein and Vienna*

Wittgenstein had been and remained authentically Viennese in his inbred familiarity with "high" culture and the life of the mind.

10. *Ibid.*, p. 133; Norman Malcolm, *Ludwig Wittgenstein: A Memoir* (London, 1958), pp. 66–68, 73.
11. *Ibid.*, p. 28.

The offspring of a wealthy and richly educated family, he had grown up in a milieu in which the fostering of artistic talent and the refinement of aesthetic appreciation had come more and more to rank as the main business of life. His home had been distinguished even in Vienna for the level of its conversation and the discrimination of its taste; Brahms had been a friend of his parents, and Schopenhauer's works a frequent subject of discussion. Jewish in origin like so much of Vienna's high bourgeoisie, the Wittgensteins had no sense of cultural separateness. They were typical, rather, of a society in which an understanding of the representational arts was taken for granted as the single clearest badge of status.[12] Ludwig Wittgenstein acquired by right of birth a cultural endowment that someone less privileged might have struggled a lifetime to obtain; his competence in music and in architecture commanded the respect of professionals. Yet he carried such accomplishments lightly and seldom spoke of them; his self-esteem as an intellectual was concentrated on the perceptions he had wrung from himself by his own unaided efforts.

Both Ludwig and his father Karl had been brought up as Christians. But they were Protestants rather than Catholics, and there was in the family a streak of puritanism that was far from characteristic of Austrian Catholicism. The atmosphere of the household—from which the children seldom ventured forth, since they were educated by tutors—was ultraserious and even somber. With no fewer than three older brothers having committed suicide, it was small wonder that Ludwig took a grave view of life and that he never felt at ease with the brittleness and irreverence of his Cambridge contemporaries. On such a man Oswald Spengler's *Decline of the West* made an immediate and strong impression.

Among his numerous brothers and sisters, Ludwig did not rank in the family estimate as particularly gifted. Rather curiously the Wittgensteins "thought of themselves as entirely Jewish in character"—defining their Judaism as "a tradition of aesthetic idealism." And within this self-definition music apparently held the highest

12. Carl E. Schorske, "The Transformation of the Garden: Ideal and Society in Austrian Literature," *The American Historical Review*, LXXII (July 1967), 1298–1300.

position. As a mere amateur in the field, Ludwig could not approach the virtuoso ability of his brother Paul, who despite the loss of one arm became a concert pianist and for whom Maurice Ravel composed his "Concerto for the Left Hand." In the future philosopher's mind music served rather as an indirect and even mystical form of communication. Following Schopenhauer, he considered it a way of transcending "the limits of representations" and of conveying the deeper matters which formal philosophical language could never express. In his ingrained concern with the nature and scope of the "sayable," Ludwig Wittgenstein was at one with a number of similarly perplexed young Viennese.

Although the son's eventual course diverged sharply from that of his father, the two Wittgensteins shared a personal modesty and dislike of show. An engineer, a highly successful founder of the Austrian iron industry, and the author of influential newspaper articles on economics, Karl Wittgenstein refused an imperial offer of ennoblement and limited the circulation of his collected essays.[13] His son, born in 1889, early showed an even greater talent for self-effacement. His impatience with outward forms— even of ordinary civility—was already apparent during his first stay in Cambridge. It evidently deepened during the First World War, when he quite literally carried the manuscript of his *Tractatus* in his knapsack and shouldered the burden of military life without complaint.

Wittgenstein's attitude toward his wartime service was free of the revulsion and protest voiced by so many of his generation. He accepted the hardships and dangers to which he was subjected as facts of life or as a simple matter of duty to the state. From all accounts he was a model soldier, cool under fire and decorated more than once for bravery. As an enlisted man he was a "good comrade." When he subsequently became an officer, he knew how to calm the men under his command and to get "the best out of them." Torn from the hothouse environment of Viennese high culture, Wittgenstein seems to have experienced the war as a kind

13. Allan Janik and Stephen Toulmin, *Wittgenstein's Vienna* (New York, 1973), pp. 117, 166, 169–177, 191; Paul Engelmann, *Letters from Ludwig Wittgenstein: With a Memoir*, trans. by L. Furtmüller, ed. by B. F. McGuinness (Oxford, 1967), pp. 119–121.

of liberation. Its "harsh circumstances . . . imposed a naturalness and a freedom from artificiality which were congenial" to his nature.[14] When Wittgenstein returned to civilian life in 1919, he had left his adolescence of wealth and privilege far behind him; he had even stripped himself of the large fortune he had inherited from his father. As he turned thirty, his sense of personal independence had become almost total. The publication of his *Tractatus* was the outward and visible sign of the transformation that had gone on within.

It is possible that from the start Wittgenstein's fellow Austrians —the young philosophers of what came to be called the Vienna Circle—misunderstood the deeper-lying drift of the *Tractatus*. Its famous concluding words were susceptible of a variety of interpretations:

> My propositions are elucidatory in this way: he who understands me finally recognizes them as senseless, when he has climbed out through them, on them, over them. (He must so to speak throw away the ladder, after he has climbed up on it.)
> He must surmount these propositions; then he sees the world rightly.
> Whereof one cannot speak, thereof one must be silent.[15]

At first and for a generation thereafter, nearly everyone assumed that Wittgenstein was propounding a radical positivism. This was why the Logical Positivists of Vienna were attracted to his work and why they held him in such great respect. Similarly in England, misled by Russell's introduction, the philosophers of logical analysis found in the *Tractatus* a thoroughgoing rejection of metaphysical or ethical inquiry; in their view, all that Wittgenstein had left standing was epistemology and linguistic exercises. From such an interpretation, the path was clear to the full-scale demolition of speculative philosophical concerns that characterized such influen-

14. *Ibid.*, pp. 73 and (editor's appendix) 140–142.
15. *Logisch-Philosophische Abhandlung* (Vienna, 1921), trans. with parallel German text as *Tractatus Logico-Philosophicus* (London, 1922), p. 189.

tial books as A. J. Ayer's *Language, Truth and Logic*, published in 1936, and Gilbert Ryle's *The Concept of Mind*, which followed thirteen years later. Not until another two decades had passed did an Englishman educated in the analytical tradition venture to assert that Wittgenstein had never been a positivist, that it was incorrect to make a sharp distinction between the early Wittgenstein of the *Tractatus* and the late Wittgenstein of the 1930's and 1940's, and that the puzzling obiter dicta of Wittgenstein the "thinker" were similarly of a piece with his statements as a technical philosopher—in short, that the "80% of the *Tractatus*" which "could, without obvious misrepresentation, be used as a source of forthright, no-nonsense, positivist slogans" was not necessarily the most important part of that work.[16]

The book's conclusion had enjoined a philosophical silence: it was the nature of the silence that was in question. A careful reading of the injunction to "surmount" Wittgenstein's own propositions suggested that they were merely "elucidatory" and in no sense definitive. Beyond them lay what could not be spoken. Already before the *Tractatus* had appeared in print, Wittgenstein had explained to one of its prospective publishers the deeper purpose of his work:

> The book's point is an ethical one. I once meant to include in the preface a sentence which is not in fact there now but which I will write out for you here, because it will perhaps be a key to the work for you. What I meant to write, then, was this: My work consists of two parts: the one presented here plus all that I have *not* written. And it is precisely this second part that is the important one.[17]

Thus Wittgenstein's silence was one not of mockery but of respect. "Far from equating the important with the verifiable, and dismissing the unverifiable as 'unimportant *because* unsayable,' Wittgenstein took exactly the opposite stand. In the concluding section of the *Tractatus*, and repeatedly thereafter, he kept insist-

16. Stephen Toulmin, "Ludwig Wittgenstein," *Encounter*, XXXII (Jan. 1969), 60.
17. Engelmann, *Letters from Wittgenstein* (editor's appendix), p. 143.

ing—though to deaf ears—that *the unsayable alone" had "genuine value."*[18]

For the time being, however, he saw no alternative to leaving the unutterable alone. Declining an invitation to return to Cambridge, he gave up philosophy and turned to pursuits that he apparently regarded as of greater human importance. For more than half a decade he taught elementary school in a succession of Austrian villages; subsequently he worked as a gardener and an architect. In his teaching he felt lonely and isolated: stranded among uncomprehending rural folk, he was thrown back utterly on his own resources. His letters from these years bespeak acute misery; even as a teacher he had a sense of failure. Yet for all his wretchedness he was learning something that would be of infinite value when he returned at last to philosophy. He had learned to know children, to listen to them, and to ask questions. Most of the time he got no clear answers—but the same would be true of his teaching in Cambridge. Working with children, he had begun to pose questions that would strike adults as senseless—questions that could be approached only in a language simpler than the language of convention and that suggested meanings even when they could not be answered at all. Like Sigmund Freud before him, Wittgenstein had learned from children how humanity spoke and thought when it had not yet put on the trappings of civilization. And in so doing he had shifted the axis of his philosophy from the categorical propositions of the *Tractatus* to the Socratic form of his later writings.[19]

At the end of 1924, Moritz Schlick, on behalf of the Vienna Circle that had been informally organized earlier in the year, wrote to Wittgenstein in admiring terms in the hope of arranging a meeting. The *Tractatus* was already well known within the Circle, where, since copies were lacking, it was "read aloud and discussed sentence by sentence." And of the young philosophers who had been captivated by it, Schlick was the one best qualified to approach its elusive author. Kind, modest, and diplomatic, Schlick knew how to reassure the skittish Wittgenstein and persuade him

18. Toulmin, "Wittgenstein," p. 61. These statements reappear almost verbatim in Janik and Toulmin's *Wittgenstein's Vienna*, pp. 219–220.

19. Engelmann, *Letters from Wittgenstein*, pp. 114–115.

to speak of his ideas. Even so the meeting took more than two years to arrange. Not until early 1927, when Wittgenstein had moved to Vienna to design a house for his sister, was Schlick at last able to see him—a meeting to which he went in the "reverential attitude" of a pilgrim and from which "he returned in an ecstatic state."[20]

It was one thing to talk in private with Schlick, another to speak with the rest of the circle and more particularly with its dominating personality, Rudolf Carnap. By the summer of 1927 Wittgenstein had indeed met Carnap, and subsequently there seem to have been a few sessions with the Circle as a whole. But such encounters had to be hedged with careful protocol. Schlick made sure that his friends did not indulge in the uninhibited philosophical give and take that marked their discussions among themselves. Wittgenstein, he explained, was "very sensitive and easily disturbed by a direct question. The best approach" was to let him "talk and then ask only very cautiously for the necessary elucidations." Conforming to this procedure as best he could, Carnap eventually came to the conclusion that Wittgenstein would tolerate "no critical examination by others," once he had gained an "insight . . . by an act of inspiration." And Wittgenstein himself had confessed to Schlick that "he could talk only with somebody" who "held his hand." Evidently the militantly scientific and positivist tone of the Circle was in the end too much for Wittgenstein. In early 1929, shortly before his departure for Cambridge, he declared that he would see Carnap no more and would limit his contact to Schlick and one other. Carnap "regretted" this decision: for all its difficulties, he had found his association with Wittgenstein "interesting, exciting and rewarding."

At the same time he was obliged to admit that his and Wittgenstein's minds were profoundly incompatible. Earlier, when the Vienna Circle had first read the *Tractatus* together, Carnap "had erroneously believed" that its author's "attitude toward metaphysics was similar" to his own. He "had not paid sufficient attention" to Wittgenstein's "statements . . . about the mysti-

20. *Ibid.* (editor's appendix), pp. 146–147; Rudolf Carnap, "Intellectual Autobiography," in *The Philosophy of Rudolf Carnap*, ed. by Paul Arthur Schilpp (La Salle, Ill., 1963), p. 24.

cal." Subsequently he had discovered that the latter's "point of view and . . . attitude toward people and problems, even theoretical problems, were much more similar to those of a creative artist than to those of a scientist; one might almost say, similar to those of a religious prophet or a seer."[21] Between Wittgenstein and his Viennese admirers there had opened up a philosophical chasm that Schlick's diplomacy could never bridge.

Yet for all their ambiguity and eventual collapse, Wittgenstein's encounters with the Vienna Circle had achieved one decisive result—they had led him back to philosophy. The conversations with Schlick and Carnap and the others had shaken him out of his state of intellectual suspension and self-doubt and forced him to confront once more the problems he had intended to lay to rest in his first book. The revelation that he was not *their* kind of philosopher obliged him to begin the slow process of defining just what kind of philosopher he was.

In 1936 Schlick was murdered by a deranged former student. The shock of his death not only snapped the tenuous link with Wittgenstein; it demoralized the remaining members of the Vienna Circle, who were already beginning to scatter. Five years earlier, Carnap had been appointed professor at the German University of Prague, and in the very year of Schlick's murder, he moved permanently to America. In 1938 the Nazi annexation of Austria finished off the Circle in the same definitive fashion in which it broke up the headquarters of Sigmund Freud. Vienna ceased to be a center either of philosophy or of psychoanalysis, and in neither did it regain its preeminence after the Second World War.

With the departure for the United States of Carnap and a number of the other adherents of the Circle, its intellectual affinities with Wittgenstein were weakened still further. During the war years, it was impossible for philosophers living in Britain and those who had settled in America to talk with each other. Still more, the cordial reception that the Viennese (and Viennese by adoption, such as Carnap himself) had received in America rein-

21. *Ibid.*, pp. 25–27.

forced their strictness of method. The analytic current in philosophy, as in the broadest terms it had come to be called, began to diverge on the two sides of the Atlantic. In the United States it remained aggressively empirical and "no-nonsense"; in Britain it took on the more informal tone of the analysis of ordinary language.[22] And while in America neither the émigrés nor the native-born were particularly inclined to extend their investigations into the field of social thought, at the English universities the possibility remained open.

This possibility entailed some clear reckoning with the realm of value. For the members of the Vienna Circle, as for those who followed their example in Britain and the United States, the base point for such a discussion was Hume's classic distinction between "is" and "ought"—in contemporary language, the assertion that normative statements could not be derived from factual descriptions.[23] On so simple and fundamental a delimitation of the field of inquiry there was no divergence of opinion. And it was also natural that most of the philosophers who subscribed to Hume's principle should have chosen to stay on the safe side of the line in the realm of fact or science. Few followed Moore's attempt to define the "good in itself," which, since in his usage the good and the beautiful were nearly identical, amounted to taking up once more the traditional concerns of ethics and aesthetics. The majority not only agreed with Wittgenstein in classifying such matters as unsayable; it dismissed them with the scorn they wrongly attributed to the author of the *Tractatus*.

Yet one at least of the Vienna Circle had sketched the nature of the statements that lay beyond the boundary of the verifiable. In the year following his move to Prague, Carnap undertook to describe what he called the "philosophy of norms" or the "philosophy of value." If this could not be couched in the language of empirical statements, was there another language in which it could properly be expressed? Was there a different method by which a

22. *Ibid.*, pp. 28–29; Herbert Feigl, "The Wiener Kreis in America," *The Intellectual Migration: Europe and America*, 1930–1960, ed. by Donald Fleming and Bernard Bailyn (Cambridge, Mass., 1969), p. 639.
23. A. J. Ayer, editor's introduction to the anthology *Logical Positivism* (Glencoe, Ill., 1959), p. 22.

person could voice his "general attitude . . . towards life"? Usually this had been done in the language that the Vienna Circle characterized as "metaphysical"; and metaphysics, Carnap argued, offered "an inadequate means for the expression of the basic attitude." It was art, rather, that was equipped to convey the philosophy of value. And among the arts, "perhaps music" offered "the purest means of expression" because it was "entirely free from any reference to objects." This Nietzsche alone had understood: "the metaphysician who perhaps had artistic talent to the highest degree . . . almost entirely avoided the . . . confusion" into which the run of philosophers had fallen. When Nietzsche left the realm of "historical-psychological analysis," when he tried to express what others had clothed in the language of metaphysics or ethics, he did not "choose the misleading theoretical form"; he chose "the form of art, of poetry."[24]

Nietzsche had been the most musical of philosophers. Wittgenstein was musically gifted to the point of being able to conduct a chamber orchestra or whistle a full sonata without mistake. The example of Nietzsche was virtually the only one available to him as he embarked on his agonizing quest for the unutterable.

III. *Ludwig Wittgenstein and Cambridge*

In early 1929 Wittgenstein arrived in Cambridge in the anomalous role of a research or graduate student. From the standpoint of the university officialdom, the author of one of the most influential philosophical works of the decade was simply beginning his apprenticeship as a scholar. Apparently the incongruity soon struck those in charge of his studies: it was found possible to give him credit for his prewar residence and to consider the *Tractatus* his doctoral thesis. In June of 1929 Wittgenstein was awarded his degree, and in the following year he became a fellow of Trinity College.

24. "Überwindung der Metaphysik durch Logische Analyse der Sprache," *Erkenntnis*, II (1932), trans. by Arthur Pap as "The Elimination of Metaphysics through Logical Analysis of Language" for *Logical Positivism*, pp. 77–80.

Nine years later he received a professorship, which he held for the better part of a decade thereafter. But it would be quite wrong to assume that this series of administrative steps tamed the restless Wittgenstein or converted him into any sort of "normal" academic. He continued to treat the conventions of university life with the impatience with which he regarded all outward forms; although he lived in Trinity, he refused to dine there, and he neither behaved nor dressed like a professor. "One could not imagine Wittgenstein in a suit, necktie, or hat."

> His face was lean and brown, his profile was aquiline and strikingly beautiful, his head was covered with a curly mass of brown hair.
>
> Whether lecturing or conversing privately, Wittgenstein always spoke emphatically and with a distinctive intonation. He spoke excellent English, with the accent of an educated Englishman, although occasional Germanisms would appear in his constructions. His voice was resonant, the pitch being somewhat higher than that of the normal male voice, but not unpleasant. His words came out, not fluently, but with great force. . . . His face was remarkably mobile and expressive when he talked. His eyes were deep and often fierce in their expression. His whole personality was commanding, even imperial.[25]

For such a man it was sheer torture to conform even in minimal fashion to what was expected of him. There remained something provisional and desperate about Wittgenstein's career as an academic. In the mid-1930's he visited the Soviet Union and thought of settling there. The outbreak of the Second World War gave him another chance to break away from university routine, and his service as a medical technician brought him back once more to the world of physical fact that he had always respected; his earliest subject of study had been engineering, and throughout his life he loved to tinker with machinery. After the war's end, he found two

25. Malcolm, *Wittgenstein*, pp. 23–25 (there are further details in the "Biographical Sketch" by Georg Henrik von Wright included in this volume, pp. 1–22).

more years of teaching all that he could bear; in 1947 he resigned his professorship.

He was still under sixty and looked younger than he actually was. As though suspecting that he had only a few years to live, he decided to devote his full energies to completing the work which he had undertaken in Cambridge. This ultrasensitive, "difficult" man finished his intellectual life as he had begun it—as a lonely wanderer. Never marrying, confined to male friendships that were often troubled and passionate, Wittgenstein lived, like Nietzsche or Weber, close to the edge of madness. Apparently the fear of slipping over that border never left him. Nor did a sense of his own moral uncleanliness. Yet his last words, as he lost consciousness forever, were these: "Tell them I've had a wonderful life!"[26]

Until the posthumous publication of his later writings, Wittgenstein's intellectual situation was anomalous in the extreme. "A philosopher who was known to be one of the greatest, if not the greatest alive, had changed his mind, but the only people who had any direct knowledge of the change were the privileged few who had heard him lecture or had had discussions with him."[27] The change was not so much in the content of his thought—he repudiated the *Tractatus* only in part—as in his view of what constituted "doing" philosophy in the first place. Philosophers, Wittgenstein had learned, ordinarily went about their business in a clumsy way: they behaved like "savages, primitive people, who hear the expressions of civilized men, put a false interpretation on them, and then draw the queerest conclusions from it." They allowed themselves to be seduced by their own reasoning processes into the illusion that the world was fully susceptible of logical explanation. And in succumbing to this particular form of self-deception, they found themselves trapped in a set of problems which appeared insoluble—problems which could "only be removed by turning" the "whole examination round."[28]

26. *Ibid.*, pp. 3, 16–18, 100.
27. David Pears, *Ludwig Wittgenstein* (New York, 1970), p. 40.
28. *Philosophische Untersuchungen*, trans. with parallel German text by G. E. M. Anscombe as *Philosophical Investigations*, 3d ed. (New York, 1958), ¶ 108, 194.

"A person caught in a philosophical confusion," Wittgenstein explained one day to a favorite student, "is like a man in a room who wants to get out but doesn't know how. He tries the window but it is too high. He tries the chimney but it is too narrow. And if he would only *turn around*, he would see that the door has been open all the time!" The imagined incident elaborated on one of Wittgenstein's dicta that became famous after his death: "What is your aim in philosophy?—To show the fly the way out of the fly-bottle." It also suggested his new view of the philosopher as a therapist, a healer of the ills of understanding. "Philosophy"—so ran another of Wittgenstein's most celebrated aphorisms—"is a battle against the bewitchment of our intelligence by means of language." This battle—to change the metaphor—entailed the destruction of most that seemed "great and important" which philosophers had built before, "as it were . . . leaving behind only bits of stone and rubble." But what was destroyed was in fact "nothing but houses of cards," which were knocked down in the process of "clearing up the ground of language" on which they stood.[29]

Language, then, was the terrain on which Wittgenstein chose to do battle. Yet it would be wrong to call his investigation linguistic in a narrow or merely technical sense. His assault on language was part of a wider inquiry into the way in which words functioned in the lives of human beings. More particularly, Wittgenstein was trying to clarify how his own ideas had changed since writing the *Tractatus*. At that time he had maintained that language proceeded from reality—that the structure of the real world determined the structure of speech. Now he had come to believe that the reverse was the case: language, as the vehicle for understanding reality, determined the way in which people saw it. Nor was it true, as Wittgenstein had once thought, that philosophical analysis could reveal an underlying uniformity in the logical structure of language. There was no such uniformity: all that the philosopher could do was to try to get at the deeper nature of language by examining its uses in their infinite diversity.[30]

29. Malcolm, *Wittgenstein*, p. 51; *Philosophical Investigations*, ¶ 109, 118, 309.
30. Toulmin, "Wittgenstein," p. 62; Pears, *Wittgenstein*, pp. 3–4.

"How many kinds of sentence are there?" Wittgenstein asked. There were "*countless* kinds," and with them "countless different kinds of use of what we call 'symbols,' 'words,' 'sentences'." And "this multiplicity" was not "fixed, given once for all; . . . new types of language, new language-games" were coming into existence all the time, as others dropped out of circulation.

Language games are the forms of language with which a child begins to make use of words. The study of language games is the study of primitive forms of language or primitive languages. If we want to study the problems of truth and falsehood, of the agreement and disagreement of propositions with reality, of the nature of assertion, assumption, and question, we shall with great advantage look at primitive forms of language in which these forms of thinking appear without the confusing background of highly complicated processes of thought. When we look at such simple forms of language the mental mist which seems to enshroud our ordinary use of language disappears. We see activities, reactions, which are clear-cut and transparent. On the other hand we recognize in these simple processes forms of language not separated by a break from our more complicated ones. We see that we can build up the complicated forms from the primitive ones by gradually adding new forms.[31]

Such "language games" constituted the core of Wittgenstein's highly unorthodox method of teaching. He held his classes in his own rooms in Trinity and always in the late afternoon. What he called his lectures, but which in fact were closer to informal seminars, met twice a week for two hours. He supplemented them with "at homes" in which he discussed more speculative topics, but the line between these and his regular classes was not as sharp as Wittgenstein supposed. He also invited his students individually to tea. The result was a heavy teaching burden, which was all the greater because of the ruthless intellectual demands that Wittgenstein made on himself and on those who were trying to learn from him.

31. *Philosophical Investigations*, ¶ 23; *The Blue and Brown Books*, Torchbook paperback ed. (New York, 1965), p. 17 (*Blue Book*).

These would sit tightly packed on folding chairs. On one occasion at least their number reached as high as thirty, "wedged together without an inch to spare." Usually, however, the total would shake down to between ten and fifteen, once the "tourists," as Wittgenstein angrily called the more casual students, had had their curiosity satisfied and had given up trying to follow him. For it was a formidable task to understand exactly what was going on: one former student recalled that it took "at least three terms . . . before one could begin to get *any* grasp" of it. Wittgenstein spoke "without preparation and without notes"; when he had tried to proceed in a more conventional fashion, his words had appeared to him like "corpses." Thereafter he simply spent a few minutes before class "recollecting the course that the inquiry had taken at the previous meetings" and starting from there. One problem led naturally and spontaneously into another—although the transition was not always clear to his listeners. "There were frequent and prolonged periods of silence, with only an occasional mutter from Wittgenstein, and the stillest attention from the others. During these silences, Wittgenstein was extremely tense and active. His gaze was concentrated; his face was alive; his hands made arresting movements; his expression was stern."

While thus carrying on "a visible struggle with his thoughts," Wittgenstein associated the class in the battle by asking questions of individual students or engaging them in dialogue. Fear of their teacher kept them ever on the alert. Wittgenstein could be peremptory and crushing with what he took to be a stupid remark or objection—but by the same token he could refer to himself as a fool when he thought that his mind was not in good working order. Two hours of relentless probing left both teacher and students exhausted. After it was over, Wittgenstein himself would frequently ask a friend to go off with him to a film.

The students who became his friends, while they never ceased being frightened of him, were utterly devoted. They bore his severity and his gloom and enjoyed the rare moments in which he was positively merry. They appreciated his unsparing integrity, both intellectual and moral, and the fact that he was harder on himself than on those around him. "In talking about human greatness, he once remarked that he thought . . . the measure of

a man's greatness would be in terms of what his work *cost* him."
(One might compare this with Weber's assessment of his own
scholarly endeavor: "I want to see how much I can endure.") The
students who knew Wittgenstein well had no doubt of the fearful
price he had paid for what he himself regarded as mere glimmerings of understanding in a dark world.[32]

It was to such student friends that Wittgenstein dictated (in
English) the preliminary studies which from the color of their
covers became known as the Blue and Brown Books. The first
dated from the academic year 1933–1934, the second from the year
following. Both circulated quite widely, in typed or in mimeographed form, in British philosophical circles, although neither
was regularly published until more than a half-decade after Wittgenstein's death. There were also in existence a number of notes
taken down by his students—which unlike the Blue and Brown
Books had not been checked over by Wittgenstein himself; selections from these jottings also began to appear in print in the
1960's. The most important from the standpoint of social thought
were lectures on aesthetics and religion dating from 1938 and
conversations about Freud held in the mid-1940's.

The Blue Book differed from the Brown Book in being a mere
set of notes never intended for publication; as such it had a simplicity that made it the most accessible of Wittgenstein's later
works. The Brown Book was a rough draft of what Wittgenstein
had projected as a major philosophical treatise. After trying more
than once to turn it into German—the language he always used
for his finished products—he gave up the attempt in 1936 and set
about writing the *Philosophical Investigations* that were to give
the full measure of his late thought. The first part was finished in
1945; the second remained incomplete at his death in 1951; both
were published posthumously in 1953.

In the preface he wrote to the first part of the *Investigations*,
Wittgenstein explained his purpose in returning to the notion of
publication after having given it up for so many years. His "van-
ity" had been "stung" by the fact that his ideas, "variously mis-

32. Most of the foregoing is derived from Malcolm, *Wittgenstein*, pp. 24–
29, 32, 55, 62, 72.

understood, more or less mangled or watered down," were already in circulation in fragmentary form; it was incumbent on him to set the record straight. Moreover, people were bound to be puzzled by the relation between the "old thoughts" in the *Tractatus* of nearly a quarter-century earlier and the "new ones" he had developed at Cambridge: although he had been "forced to recognize grave mistakes" in his early work, he did not want to discard it entirely; he wished rather to put his new ideas "in the right light . . . by contrast with and against the background of" his "old way of thinking." Yet the very structure of the two books betrayed the magnitude of the change that had occurred. The *Tractatus* had had the beauty of a finished and detached perfection; the *Investigations* was a report on work in progress. His second book, Wittgenstein explained, consisted of "*remarks*, short paragraphs," sometimes running in "a fairly long chain about the same subject," sometimes "jumping from one topic to another." It could be compared to an "album" of pictures, "sketches of landscapes which were made in the course of . . . long and involved journeyings" and which crisscrossed "in every direction."[33]

It was unfortunate that the majority of Wittgenstein's readers were to know the *Investigations* only in the parallel English text which was published, as had been done with the *Tractatus*, alongside the German. But even a casual glance across the page at the original could give some impression of its author's mastery as a stylist. His German was direct and supple; he eschewed involved constructions, literary phrases, and technical terms; he shifted easily from dialogue to aphorism and back again. Underlying the flow of his sentences and the surprising turns of his thought was a musical quality which reminded those who knew him well that his favorite composer was Schubert.[34]

Yet his writing gave him little but agony. After he had resigned his Cambridge professorship, he turned himself wholly to the second part of his *Investigations*. He went to live in Ireland, first in the remote countryside, subsequently in a hotel in Dublin. In 1949 he made his first and only trip to the United States. Here he

33. *Philosophical Investigations*, pp. ix–x.
34. Von Wright, "Biographical Sketch," p. 21.

discovered that he was gravely ill, an illness which was diagnosed on his return as cancer. He had been in a "frenzy" at the thought he might die in America: he was a European, he insisted, and he wanted to die in Europe. A year and a half later he died, as he had wished, in Cambridge close to his friends. Throughout the last period of his life, his work had progressed only intermittently. He was tormented by the thought that his mental powers were waning and by the question of what he should do with his existence if his talent was gone. He may even have feared that what he called "loss of problems" was setting in—a philosophical malady which he attributed to Russell and which made the world become "broad and flat" and writing about it "immeasurably shallow and trivial."[35]

For the task he had set himself had proved even harder than he had believed when he had originally struggled with his thoughts in the early 1930's. At that time he had imagined that his language games could proceed in a cumulative fashion—that it would be possible to "build up the complicated forms from the primitive ones by gradually adding new forms." As early as the Brown Book he had begun to doubt the feasibility of such a work of construction. By the time he was in difficulties with the *Investigations*, he had come to see that his games did not add up to anything—they simply pointed to the "big question" of what language was in the first place. The further Wittgenstein pushed his pursuit, the fewer answers it afforded him. In the end he was obliged to conclude that the various "phenomena" called language had "no one thing in common," only the "relationships" whose crisscrossed paths he had endeavored to follow.[36]

The new view of philosophy that Wittgenstein embodied in his *Investigations* was "empirical, pedestrian, and even homely." Its full effect demanded a "personal involvement"—as had been true between Wittgenstein and his students; it worked itself "into people's lives." Abandoning the high ground on which nearly all

35. Malcolm, *Wittgenstein*, pp. 93–100; Ludwig Wittgenstein, *Zettel*, ed. by G. E. M. Anscombe and G. H. von Wright, trans. with parallel German text by G. E. M. Anscombe (Berkeley and Los Angeles, 1967), ¶ 456.
36. Preface by Rush Rhees to *The Blue and Brown Books*, pp. ix–xi; *Philosophical Investigations*, ¶ 65.

previous philosophizing had been conducted, the author of the *Investigations* had given up *"striving after* an ideal." As early as the Blue Book, he had renounced the "craving for generality" that derived from a "preoccupation with the method of science." It could "never be" his "job," he had insisted, "to reduce anything to anything" or indeed "to explain anything." His job, rather, was to combat "the contemptuous attitude towards the particular case" which had characterized most previous philosophers.[37]

If one focused, then, on the particular case, one soon discovered that even the simplest terms one employed had no single meaning. In a *"large* class of cases . . . the meaning of a word" was "its use in the language"; the very word "meaning," as Wittgenstein had earlier explained, caused "philosophical troubles" by the way in which it did "odd jobs." Precise definition made matters worse: it was only the context (*Zusammenhang*), the circumstances in which a word or phrase came out, that counted. In such a fluid universe of discourse, there were no fixed rules. Yet at the same time there was no disorder. If a sentence, however vague, in practice made sense, then "there must be perfect order" in it. And similarly with the great problems that had vexed philosophers for centuries. The "most important . . . aspects of things" had been "hidden because of their simplicity and familiarity." Philosophy, Wittgenstein asserted, merely put "everything before us. . . . Since everything" lay "open to view," there was "nothing to explain." Eventually one might make "the real discovery"—the one that would enable men to stop "doing philosophy," the one that would make "philosophical problems . . . completely disappear," the one that would give philosophy "peace."[38]

The "extreme anthropocentricism" of such a view left Wittgenstein's readers dizzy. It was hard to grasp a world in which there were "no independent, objective points of support," and in which "meaning and necessity" were "preserved only in the linguistic practices" which embodied them. Yet at the same time, from the standpoint of social thought, Wittgenstein's method offered

37. Pears, *Wittgenstein*, pp. 109, 113–114; *Philosophical Investigations*, ¶ 98; *Blue Book*, p. 18.
38. *Philosophical Investigations*, ¶ 43, 98, 126, 129, 133; *Blue Book*, pp. 43–44.

marked advantages. It reopened old vistas that Russell and the Vienna Circle had threatened to close off. It drew philosophy back to the concrete case and to the actual process of living: "to imagine a language," Wittgenstein surmised, meant "to imagine a form of life." In its tolerance for imprecision of discourse it encouraged the philosopher to discuss everyday human concerns in a way that tried to follow the contours of the concerns in question. While it did not denigrate science, as Carnap and his friends had feared, it did suggest that there were enormous areas of men's thought and conduct which remained relatively immune from what was ordinarily understood as scientific analysis—and were none the less important for that.[39] This was the artistic or mystical side of Wittgenstein's speculations which had disconcerted his Viennese admirers.

Aesthetics, ethics, metaphysics—these matters of value, Wittgenstein agreed, lay in the realm of the unutterable. But it was natural and inevitable that men should speak of them, and much could be learned from the way in which people went about their foredoomed task of trying to say the unsayable. Moreover, it would not be clear where the boundary of sanctioned speech lay until an attempt had been made to cross it and that attempt had failed. Such efforts Wittgenstein regarded with benevolence. He treated them as reconnaissance expeditions, perilous to be sure, but well worth the effort expended on them. His *Investigations* aimed to "retrieve" some portion at least of what his contemporaries had banished from philosophical discourse—and at the price of posing riddles that even he could not answer.[40]

Thus he refused to drop the word "soul" or "spirit" (*Geist*) from his vocabulary. "Where our language suggests a body and there is none: there, we should like to say, is a *spirit*." One of the psychological tricks Wittgenstein detected in his own meditations was observing his "soul out of the corner" of his eye. In his conversation he expressed sympathy for St. Augustine and Kierkegaard—and even Heidegger.[41] Indeed his *Investigations* began

39. Pears, *Wittgenstein*, pp. 179, 193; *Philosophical Investigations*, ¶ 19.
40. Pears, *Wittgenstein*, pp. 22–23, 104, 126–127.
41. *Philosophical Investigations*, ¶ 36, Part II, p. 188; Toulmin, "Wittgenstein," p. 60.

with a quotation from Augustine which indicated his knowledge of the Christian tradition and the peculiar fascination that religion held for him.

Wittgenstein's personal view of religion, like so much else in his outlook on life, was bleak and comfortless. It was Augustinian in its conviction of sin and in its image of God as a "fearful judge." These were the emotional residues that Wittgenstein's puritan childhood had left with him. On the intellectual level, his characteristic reaction to talk of religion was puzzlement. Unable to subscribe to any particular belief himself, he respected those who did believe and kept wondering what the grounds of their faith might be. He was quite sure that it could not be rational argument; religious belief not only was "not reasonable": it didn't even "pretend to be" so. Yet he defended himself against the notion that he was a complete skeptic, and he had two converted Catholics among his loyal followers. Religion he apparently regarded as one of those "forms of life" whose linguistic networks he was endeavoring to trace; it hovered in the back of his mind as a possibility that others might grasp but whose "essence"was forever eluding him.[42] Like James or Durkheim a generation earlier, Wittgenstein saw the need for calling attention to the *fact* of religion that his positivist-minded contemporaries left out of their reckoning.

When it came to ethics, Wittgenstein found a firmer footing. Religion had puzzled him in that it possessed a language of its own whose meaning he could not penetrate. (Yet he could "quite well imagine" a religion in which there were neither doctrines nor speech.) With ethics it was unavoidable that one should "go beyond" language entirely. Indeed, the human "urge to thrust against the limits of language" was what constituted ethics. This expression of "thrusting" or "running" against the boundaries of speech kept recurring in Wittgenstein's lectures and conversation in the period immediately following his move to England. It figured at the start of the only "popular" lecture he ever gave, an

42. Ludwig Wittgenstein, *Lectures and Conversations on Aesthetics, Psychology and Religious Belief*, ed. by Cyril Barrett from notes taken by Yorick Smythies, Rush Rhees, and James Taylor (Berkeley and Los Angeles, 1967), pp. 58, 70. See also Von Wright, "Biographical Sketch," p. 20, and Malcolm, *Wittgenstein*, p. 72.

informal talk on ethics delivered at the end of his first Cambridge year. Ethics, he explained, could be thought of in a wide sense as including "the most essential part" of what was generally called aesthetics; it was an inquiry that extended beyond the "good" into what was "important" or "valuable"—in short, it was an excursion into the realm of value. But these matters could never be defined, as even the intellectually fastidious Moore had supposed. They could be spoken of only in terms of metaphor or simile. Such similes, however, as opposed to the figures of speech in ordinary discourse, had no facts standing behind them. They were "supernatural": they gave evidence of man's "perfectly, absolutely hopeless"—yet deeply respectable—effort to burst the bonds of his "cage." It was impossible to write about ethics "a scientific book, the subject matter of which could be intrinsically sublime and above all other subject matters. . . . If a man could write a book on Ethics which really was a book on Ethics, this book would, with an explosion, destroy all the other books in the world."[43]

There was of course the alternative possibility of writing a "natural" or scientific work about how men behaved. But this would be simply a description or analysis of "facts," which could be subsumed under the heading of psychology. Sooner or later Wittgenstein was bound to make his reckoning with psychology— and with his great fellow Viennese, Sigmund Freud. The two already had something in common in combining what amounted to ethical relativism in the intellectual sphere with a stern view of morality in practice. Freud had said that morality was self-evident. Wittgenstein believed that "relativity must be avoided at all costs, since it would destroy the *imperative*" in ethics.[44] In their dealings with those close to them, both delivered harsh and absolutist judgments; both were convinced that the run of mankind was evil.

Like so many other leading twentieth-century intellectuals,

43. "A Lecture on Ethics," *The Philosophical Review*, LXXIV (Jan. 1965), 4–5, 7, 9–12. This is followed by a translation by Max Black of the key passages on ethics in the notes on talks with Wittgenstein taken down by one of the members of the Vienna Circle: Friedrich Waismann, *Wittgenstein und der Wiener Kreis*, ed. by B. F. McGuinness (Oxford, 1967), pp. 68–69, 115–118.
44. "Lecture on Ethics" (commentary by Rush Rhees), p. 23.

Wittgenstein could well have had recourse to psychoanalytic therapy. It might have mitigated his personal torment and enabled him to come to terms with the dark side of his nature. It was not that Wittgenstein misunderstood his own emotional life; in his capacity for self-awareness he was comparable once again to Nietzsche. But for him, as for Nietzsche, this awareness caused intense suffering. In his lecture on ethics, when groping for an example of what one meant by a term like "absolute good," he came up with "the experience of feeling *absolutely* safe," the sense of safety *whatever* happened. Wittgenstein freely granted that such an expression was "nonsense"; yet the vivid way in which he depicted the experience behind it suggested how rare and cherished a privileged moment of the sort must have been for him.[45] And he was far too stoical to seek professional counsel in his desolation.

Hence it was to be expected that his judgment on Freud should have been ambivalent. Basically he was skeptical of all psychology, characterizing it on the very last page he ever wrote as in a state of "conceptual confusion." (He had earlier noted the difficulty one encountered in dealing with the "unbridgeable gulf between consciousness and brain-process.") Although the similarity of his and Freud's methods was readily apparent, and although he himself in the preface to his *Investigations* described his approach in terms which resembled free association, he angrily dismissed the notion that the two techniques could be equated with each other. Psychoanalysis he called "a powerful mythology"; it was a "way of thinking" which needed "combatting." Yet he spoke of himself as "a disciple of Freud," "a follower of Freud," and ranked him among "the few authors he thought worth reading."[46]

Freud was worth reading because he possessed the rare quality of "having something to say": his "way of thinking" should be opposed because of the "subservience" it fostered. This contrast gave the key to Wittgenstein's divided mind. On the negative side, he found Freud clever but not wise and his claim to scientific validity unfounded. What Freud had given, rather, was "*specula-*

45. *Ibid.*, p. 8.
46. *Philosophical Investigations*, ¶ 412, Part II, p. 232; Malcolm, *Wittgenstein*, pp. 56–57; *Lectures and Conversations*, pp. 41, 50, 52.

tion—something prior even to the formation of an hypothesis."
More specifically Wittgenstein rejected the central psychoanalytic
precept that nothing in the human mind was guided by chance; he
himself was inclined to believe that there was no such thing as a
law governing mental phenomena. And similarly with the unconscious: the Freudians had obscured the whole issue by speaking of
"unconscious thought"; the clearer way to have expressed it would
have been to reserve the word "thought" for what went on in full
consciousness and to speak of the unconscious in terms of "newly
discovered psychological reactions." Wittgenstein's finely honed
mind took offense at the slippery use of language in psychoanalytic
theory—just as his prudishness recoiled from the sexual emphasis,
the "bawdy," in Freud's work. But what annoyed him most was
the role "persuasion" played in the acceptance of psychoanalysis.
To learn from Freud, one had to be critical—and this the psychoanalytic process ordinarily prevented.[47]

Wittgenstein's reading of Freud tended toward reductionism. It
also did not get much beyond *The Interpretation of Dreams.* It
was unfortunate that he had not studied psychoanalytic theory in
its fully developed and more permissive forms, that he was unacquainted, for example, with the work of still another Viennese
and his own contemporary, Heinz Hartmann, whose first statement of what subsequently became known as ego psychology had
been read to the Vienna Psychoanalytic Society shortly after
Wittgenstein himself began writing his *Investigations* and in the
year prior to the Nazi takeover in Austria. Wittgenstein's distrust
of psychoanalytic theory was of a piece with his doubts about the
Vienna Circle of philosophers: they smacked too much of positivism; they seemed to threaten the open universe of discourse
which his own late work was endeavoring to delineate.

Yet when all this has been said, it remains undeniable that
Wittgenstein acknowledged profound affinities between himself
and Freud, not so much as theorists—Wittgenstein, after all, had
discarded explicit theory—as in the human implications of what
they were trying to do. Both were negative and practical in their
aim. Both sought to strip away the illusions—or fantasies or
"pictures"—by which men ordinarily lived and to reveal the

47. *Ibid.,* pp. 23–24, 27, 41–42, 44, 51–52; *Blue Book,* pp. 57–58.

incongruence between avowed statement and the hidden meaning or intention behind it. Both were alert to the slips and tricks of language that could serve as clues in the search. Both argued that mere understanding was useless unless it was accompanied by a change within. In the broadest terms, Freud and Wittgenstein alike rejected the ideal images of man to which earlier thinkers had tried to make the intractable raw material of humanity conform. Freud had shown that a recognition of man's animal nature was essential to comprehending—and accepting—the burden of civilization. Wittgenstein taught that the gift of language which distinguished men from beasts and which offered them everything they really knew of the world about them could be appreciated at its full worth only if it too were accepted in all its ambiguity and imprecision.[48]

It would be incorrect to classify Wittgenstein as a social theorist in the usual sense of the term. His mind was far too nominalist for that. The very word "society" would have had little meaning for him; he would have experienced great difficulty in focusing on so amorphous a concept, since he himself preferred to deal with concrete, particular cases studied in their individual context. And his attitude toward society in practice was not without contradictions: although scorning conventions and hating all humbug, he had nothing but respect for "genuine" or legitimate authority and regarded as "immoral . . . revolutionary convictions of whatever kind."[49]

Yet subsequent social thought could not escape the responsibility of digesting what the young philosophers of Britain and America had learned from Wittgenstein. He himself was far from sure how much he had accomplished, and he chose as the motto for his *Investigations* the remark of the Austrian writer Johann Nestroy that it was "in the nature of every advance" to appear "much greater than it actually" was. The formula neatly embraced

48. For reflections in this vein, see Frayn, "Russell and Wittgenstein," pp. 74–75, and Stanley Cavell, "The Availability of Wittgenstein's Later Philosophy," *The Philosophical Review*, LXXI (1962), reprinted in *Wittgenstein: A Collection of Critical Essays*, ed. by George Pitcher (Garden City, N.Y., 1966), pp. 184–185.
49. Engelmann, *Letters from Wittgenstein*, p. 121.

Wittgenstein's unremitting oscillation between despair and confidence in judging his own achievement. If he frequently doubted the value of what he had written, he at least suspected that he had seen farther than any of his predecessors. If he was almost always dissatisfied with the way he finally put matters into words, he could rest assured that he had brought the meaning of those words into question with unprecedented thoroughness and penetration. If he sometimes thought himself foolish in his teaching, he ordinarily dismissed his fellow philosophers as still greater fools than he. Convinced that he had made an advance—how great, how small, he did not know—he was tortured by the thought that his admirers might propagate a travesty of his intentions.

Thus it would be further incorrect to try to find in Wittgenstein precepts to "apply" to the study of society. It was rather that he offered a new perspective for social thought that was both revolutionary and reconciliatory. His work inaugurated—or better, epitomized—a revolution by undercutting the entire vocabulary in which human beings commonly spoke of their own doings; it relativized not merely the words in ordinary use but, by implication, the more formal language of the sciences of man. And thereby it suggested a way to heal the schism in Western thought that Wittgenstein's own early writing had done so much to bring about.

In his youth, with his *Tractatus*, he had given twentieth-century neopositivism a rallying point. He had played a crucial role in establishing a new type of positivist thinking, more modest in aim than its nineteenth-century predecessor, a type of thinking which based its scientific credentials on logical rigor and a clear delimitation of "facts" rather than on the ascription of causal or lawful relationships to the universe of human affairs. Subsequently Wittgenstein gravitated toward an even more subtle type of positivism, close to the example of Hume and expressing itself in a "naturalistic" attitude to linguistic usage. In this late view, statements of fact retained a privileged position over value judgments. Yet since both were alike seen as mediated by the vast imprecision of language, the line between factual and value discourse became more fluid than most neopositivists supposed. The result of this "leveling" process was a refusal to discriminate "against any of the modes of human thought. Each" was to be "accepted on its own terms and justified by its own internal standards."[50] On the one hand, Wittgenstein repudiated the "destructive" stance toward the realm of value that so many of his early followers had derived from his *Tractatus*. On the other hand, he would have disagreed emphatically with the alternative neopositivist way of thinking, primarily associated with structural linguistics and the anthropology of Claude Lévi-Strauss, which claimed to have discovered beneath the phenomenon of language the immanent structure of the human mind.[51] What Wittgenstein discarded and what he ventured to assert were alike more tentative than was true of the vast majority of his positivist-minded contemporaries.

Once these distinctions had been understood, it became immaterial whether or not one referred to Wittgenstein as a positivist. From the standpoint of social thought, the most valuable aspect of his legacy was the prospect it afforded of putting back into a single intellectual universe the styles of thinking that had split apart in the 1920's—analytical philosophy and logical positivism on the one side, phenomenology and existentialism on the other. A man who was a mystic as well as a logician had shown how it was possible to read Heidegger and Moore with equal respect.[52] Still more, in his attitude toward language, he had suggested that one could readmit into the company of serious thinkers the practitioners of disciplines whose vocabularies were of necessity imprecise. Wittgenstein was not particularly concerned with history and seldom spoke of it; yet in his distrust of exact definition and his emphasis on the full context in which events occurred, he came close to the loose and permissive usage of the practicing historian. His operational notions about language epitomized his appreciation of those who labored in fields of investigation where unassailable rigor of method was out of the question.

For the most part Wittgenstein's contemporaries in the social

50. Pears, *Wittgenstein*, pp. 29, 184–185.
51. See my *The Obstructed Path* (New York, 1968), pp. 270–271, 286, 291.
52. Cf. Janik and Toulmin, *Wittgenstein's Vienna*, p. 194, in which one of his letters is referred to as unifying "Wittgenstein the formal logician with Wittgenstein the ethical mystic."

sciences knew little of his work and went their own way without
reference to him. Once he had been "discovered," however, it
became apparent that he had put in the most plain and general
terms what so many of them had been groping for in their specialized languages.[53] Within a decade of his death, his example was
already established as that of the German-speaking intellectual
who had done more than any other to unite the world of his
origins to the Anglo-American cultural milieu which welcomed
him. Yet there was one linkage that even Wittgenstein could not
forge or prefigure: the bulky inheritance of Hegel fell outside his
scope. And correspondingly the neo-Hegelians of the German
emigration to the United States had no use for Wittgenstein; they
misunderstood his teaching and did their best to maintain the old
distinction between the philosophical tradition of Central Europe
and that of Britain and America.[54]

It is finally noteworthy that Wittgenstein commented scarcely
at all on public affairs or on the events of his day. In this apolitical
stance, as in so much else about his life that he accepted without
question, he remained an authentic representative of the pre-1914
Austrian intelligentsia. Unlike their counterparts in the Reich, the
Austrians had seen no incompatibility between technical and
cultural pursuits, nor had they found anything incongruous in
combining total religious skepticism with an acceptance of
Catholicism as the "normal" religious posture. And their corresponding loyalty to the state that guaranteed their German linguistic heritage had deterred them from revolutionary yearnings.[55]

After the breakup of the Hapsburg Empire, such attitudes had
begun to change and to polarize. But Wittgenstein had stayed
fixed in his earlier views. Although he obviously detested fascism
and became a British subject when the annexation of Austria in

53. For example, Hanna Fenichel Pitkin, *Wittgenstein and Justice: On the
Significance of Ludwig Wittgenstein for Social and Political Thought* (Berkeley and Los Angeles, 1972), p. 328, envisages "a Wittgensteinian political
theory . . . addressed from one citizen to others" rather than delivered in the
customary style from some intellectual eminence.
54. See Chapter 4.
55. See David S. Luft, *Robert Musil and the Crisis of European Culture
1880–1942* (Berkeley/Los Angeles/London, 1980), Chapter 1. Luft notes
striking parallels between the family and intellectual backgrounds of Wittgenstein and of Musil.

1938 would have made him a citizen of Nazi Germany, he limited himself to speaking of the "dark" times in which he lived and to volunteering for civilian service in the Second World War. What was informal and commonplace in his approach seemed to preclude the kind of cataclysmic pronouncements that occurred so readily to people of his generation. It may also have been true that he hesitated to speak of matters of which he had no direct knowledge. The most probing commentary on fascism was to come not from minds of philosophical distinction such as Wittgenstein's but from men of a robust and combative intelligence who knew at first hand whereof they wrote.

CHAPTER

3

The Critique of Fascism

N OT A SINGLE PROPHET, during more than a century of prophe-
cies, . . . ever imagined anything like fascism. There was, in
the lap of the future, communism and syndicalism and what not;
there was anarchism, . . . war, peace, deluge, pan-Germanism, pan-
Slavism . . . ; there was no fascism. It came as a surprise to all. . . ."[1]
Thus Giuseppe Antonio Borgese, musing on the convulsions that
had driven him from his homeland, voiced the bewilderment of
intellectuals before a phenomenon which none had predicted and
which threatened to annihilate the bright anticipations the nineteenth century had bequeathed to its successor.

Europe's intellectuals were at a loss because they could get no
handle on the movements that Mussolini and Hitler led. Writers
and professors were accustomed to deal in words, and with fascism
words gave little guide to what was occurring. Language functioned to deceive or to arouse or to lull rather than to explain; the
gap between rhetoric and actuality went far beyond the normal
bounds of political usage. More particularly, it was unclear
whether fascism was revolutionary or reactionary, whether it belonged on the left or on the right. Most of those who studied it
could see where it derived from the course of contemporary history: they could trace its origins to the delayed and unfinished
character of Italian and German national unity, to the defeats and

1. G. A. Borgese, "The Intellectual Origins of Fascism," *Social Research*, I
(Nov. 1934), 475–476.

disappointments the Italian and German peoples had suffered in the First World War, to the economic dislocations of the immediate postwar years and to the mass unemployment of the early 1930's. Those who probed deeper could note a lack of homogeneity in the societies of Italy and Germany as opposed to those of France and Britain, and a less widespread acceptance of middle-class or democratic values. Yet such fragments of an explanation were patently insufficient: the dynamics of fascism itself eluded any simple formula.

Of one thing, however, nearly everyone—both those who remained in Europe and those who emigrated to America—was sure: what had come to power in Italy in 1922 and in Germany eleven years later deserved to be called by the same name. No doubt it was significant that Mussolini had triumphed a decade earlier than Hitler; no doubt Hitler ran a tighter show and was infinitely more concerned about "race" than the Italian leader who had originally served as his model. But these were matters of timing and emphasis: to contemporaries it went without saying that German National Socialism should be considered a variant— an extreme variant—on the type of rule which the Italian Duce had invented and to which he gave the name eventually applied to his imitators throughout Europe. During the period when fascism was in power, those who had experienced it were scarcely in a position to think of it as some vague abstraction. Its rigors were far too real for that. It would have seemed absurd to indulge in the kind of nominalism—or obscurantism—that a decade or two later was to dismiss the comparative study of fascist regimes as a matter too complex for generalization. It was true that in the meantime, particularly during the Second World War, the term "fascist" had all too often been exploited for purposes of indiscriminate abuse. But this had gone on in the forum of partisan debate rather than at the level of scholarly analysis. The more conscientious students of fascism strove for intellectual rigor: although they had suffered under fascist tyranny and made no secret of their antipathy toward it, they did their best to amass their documentation and to weigh their evidence in accordance with accepted professional standards.

Thus movements and regimes which had mastered the arts of obfuscation and whose ideologies were a maze of contradictions presented a special and very personal challenge to the thought of the emigration. Far from engulfing those who studied it in its own semantic morass, fascism stimulated its critics to heroic efforts at clarification. It served as the precipitant directing social speculation toward immediate issues of a burning actuality. It raised in acute form the question of what should be considered the key features of modern industrial society and the extent to which Marxist or quasi-Marxist theory was appropriate for analyzing them. In the most general terms, the fascist systems posed the problem of whether it was possible to arrive at judgments that could claim any long-term validity, when the prior investigation, by force of circumstance and temperament, had been anything but "value-free."

1. *Initial Perspectives: Borgese, Mannheim, Fromm*

With three of the most influential critics of fascism, their accounts of its nature and prehistory did not rank as their chief literary production or the focus of their intellectual lives. Borgese, Mannheim, and Erich Fromm had in common the fact that study of the fascist phenomenon came at the end or at the beginning of careers devoted to other concerns. What they had to say about it was necessarily tentative. They offered suggestions, beginnings; they did not attempt a full-scale analysis.

Giuseppe Antonio Borgese was not quite fifty in 1931 when, on an American lecture tour, he refused to take the oath demanded of Italian university professors and chose to remain in the United States. Born in Sicily in 1882, he had earned the reputation of an *enfant terrible* of Italian letters, as critic, poet, novelist, and teacher of aesthetics. He had also been a publicist, independent and outspoken, who had broken with the philosophical doctrines of his master Croce and had pursued an isolated and eccentric anti-Fascist course.[2] In America he taught first at Smith College, later

2. For biographical details, see Sarah D'Alberti, *Giuseppe Antonio Borgese* (Palermo, 1971), pp. 25–38, 53.

at the University of Chicago, where he met and married a daughter of Thomas Mann. His father-in-law quickly recovered from his consternation at the thirty-six-year age difference in the bridal pair; Borgese, he wrote his brother Heinrich, was "a brilliant, charming, and excellently preserved man . . . and the bitterest hater of his Duce."[3]

As was to be expected from a writer whose intellectual preparation had been preponderantly literary, Borgese's critique of fascism was vivid and impressionistic. It also made extremely good reading: Borgese had acquired a command of written English that was astounding in a man who had begun to use it so late in life; his work bubbled over with surprise effects, telling anecdotes, and arresting figures of speech. And the same theatrical inclination led him to stress those features of fascism that lent themselves to a consciously artistic presentation—the vicissitudes of its march to power and the cultural-historical context from which it derived. Borgese's experience of Mussolini's rule had convinced him that its acceptance by the Italian people was primarily due to weakness of character; "the specific elements of fascism" were "of a mental and sentimental nature"; it had "happened first in the mind" and only subsequently "found its way into the facts of mass history."[4]

In the year following the advent of Hitler, Borgese published an essay on fascism's intellectual origins. While it dealt primarily with his own country, it made frequent reference to what was going on in Germany and traced to the same cultural sources the movements that Hitler and Mussolini had founded. These sources Borgese discovered in the "ideal and emotional backgrounds" of people with a "middling" education. Fascism had "nothing to say" to "the proverbial peasant." Nor could it appeal to "real minds," which wanted a "critically clean food." But to those suffering from "intellectual starvation," it gave a "daily spiritual meal." Fascism was "first of all a degradation of romanticism, both cultural and political, . . . not a revolution . . . but an involution." As such, it taught that "change" was "substance" and "passion . . . virtue." In its belief that force made right and in its "substitution of

3. November 26, 1939, *Letters of Thomas Mann 1889–1955*, selected and trans. by Richard and Clara Winston (New York, 1971), p. 320.
4. "Intellectual Origins," p. 463.

the idea of power for the idea of justice," it had become "the creed of the lower middle classes."[5]

Why, then, had fascism triumphed first in Italy? Borgese gave no simple answer, but he was inclined to believe that it was because his countrymen had had a spectacularly mixed history of glory and degradation:

> accustomed through two thousand years of world empire and universal church . . . to loftiness of political imagination, and at the same time to the most dejected renouncement of personality in public life, . . . they were prepared to accept anything strange and new, particularly if the novelty promised somehow to revive the hereditary complex of Roman superiority and to check the stubborn . . . complex of modern inferiority.

Borgese's psychological pronouncements did not rise above the clichés available to any educated layman in the 1930's. But they indicated his appreciation of the emotional disorientation that characterized both leaders and led in the fascist movements. Mussolini, he was later to suggest, should be studied in "the perspective of the good novelist." Freud, Borgese added, "would not have very much to say" about the Italian Duce. "He would probably hand over the case to his colleague Jung" (an unlikely event, one may note, to have occurred a quarter-century after the break between the two), a seer whom Borgese thought peculiarly qualified to handle "the all-embracing ego problem."[6]

The book entitled *Goliath* that Borgese published three years after his essay about intellectual origins enlarged on a number of the latter's themes, concentrating this time almost exclusively on the Italian experience. He took pains to refute the Marxian interpretation of fascism, which in the meantime had been gaining currency: "social and economic factors," he contended, explained the phenomenon "as little as the mushrooms crowding at the foot of the tree or the mistletoe clambering on its branches" explained "the tree itself." Borgese had declared fascism to be "an outburst

5. *Ibid.*, pp. 463, 467, 474.
6. *Ibid.*, p. 477; *Goliath: The March of Fascism* (New York, 1937), pp. 171, 195.

of emotionalism and pseudo-intellectualism," and he stuck by the definition: "the sin had been in the mind; and from the mind should have come redemption." Hence he deemed it crucial how his fellow intellectuals had reacted to Mussolini's rule. Most of them, he observed with bitterness, had behaved like cowards. Even Croce, whom the outside world viewed as the symbol of intellectual resistance, had failed to give the guidance that his juniors had the right to expect of him—first, by never repudiating the ethical Machiavellianism of his writings of the prefascist era; second, by appeasing the consciences of the young with the assurance that "working for culture" was an adequate response to tyranny.

"All strongholds of Italian intelligence," Borgese concluded, "were razed to the ground: because they had not been strong at all."[7] We now know that this verdict was unduly pessimistic. But we may also understand the personal reasons why Borgese wrote as he did. Alone in a strange land, unattached to any émigré political movement, and without the training for close ideological or social analysis, Borgese fell back on the intellectual equipment he had, his literary gifts and his thorough knowledge of European cultural history. His *Goliath* was an engrossing human chronicle; the product of a lofty idealism in both the philosophical and the ordinary moral meaning of the term, it scored an immediate popular success. If it did not go very far beyond a spiritual interpretation of the fascist appeal, it at least located those whom that appeal had touched and for whom future investigators were to show a special concern.

In the last two decades of his life, Karl Mannheim never recaptured the intellectual heights he had attained at the end of the 1920's with his *Ideology and Utopia*. His emigration to England in 1933 led him to neglect the theoretical concerns that had made him after Weber's death the most inventive sociologist in Germany. Virtually abandoning his longstanding interest in the sociology of knowledge, he turned to applied and even propagandist pursuits. He persuaded a London publishing house to support his editing of an "International Library of Sociology and Social Reconstruction"—a collection of works, many of them Continental

7. *Ibid.*, 217–218, 289, 299–302, 305.

or American, which ranged from demography, education, and law to anthropology and religion—and he lectured and wrote voluminously in behalf of the "democratic planning" which he was convinced offered the only hope for rescuing Western society from the grip of dictatorship and war.

If the influence of his adopted country was apparent in Mannheim's later writings—if the pragmatic, reform-minded bent of English social thought guided him toward a more direct and accessible presentation of his ideas—there could also be discerned in his new sense of mission a return to his origins. As a young man in Budapest before the First World War, Mannheim had belonged to a coterie of left-oriented writers, a large number of them Jewish like himself, who had followed the lead of Lukács in regarding intellectuals as the future saviors of society. This attitude was thoroughly comprehensible in a situation such as the Hungarian where the ruling aristocracy and gentry remained adamant against every type of change and the educated bourgeoisie was small and lacking in influence;[8] it was to lead Lukács himself into his lifelong association with Communism. In Mannheim's case, the relationship to Marxism and the political left was always more nuanced. And after his move to Germany his view of his own situation as a "free-floating" mind was reflected in a concept of intellectuals as mediators among classes and interests rather than as social innovators in their own right; such had been one of the central contentions of his *Ideology and Utopia*. With Mannheim's second transplantation, however, his old messianic feelings returned: jumping over the aloof, academic stance of his central years in Germany, he arrived at a curious and highly personal combination of his early Hungarian intellectual elitism and an Anglo-Saxon insistence that for a given social or political problem an appropriate remedy must exist.

The book entitled *Man and Society in an Age of Reconstruction* marked the transition from Mannheim's German to his British

8. For Mannheim's Hungarian background, see Zoltán Horváth, *Die Jahrhundertwende in Ungarn: Geschichte der zweiten Reformgeneration* (1896–1914), trans. from the Hungarian by Géza Engl (Neuwied and Berlin, 1966), and for a general biographical sketch, Lewis A. Coser, *Masters of Sociological Thought* (New York, 1971), pp. 441–449, 457–463.

phase. Originally published in German in the Netherlands two years after its author's emigration, it appeared in English in 1940 in revised and enlarged form. At the very start of the work Mannheim explained how the circumstances of its composition had affected its content. As one of "those to whom destiny" had "given the opportunity of living in many different countries and of identifying themselves with various points of view," he had thought it his task to blend these views "in a new synthesis"—and more particularly to reconcile his firsthand, German-based sense of "sitting on a volcano" with the optimism derived from the British experience of "living in a country where liberal democracy" functioned "almost undisturbed." If his stay in England had enabled him "to free himself from his deep-rooted scepticism as to the vitality of democracy" in his own age, he had not changed his former conviction that profound structural changes had eroded the social foundations which democratic apologists ordinarily took for granted.[9]

In trying to define these changes, Mannheim felt that he was "only groping his way"; his work remained incomplete and without any "illusion of finality or absolute proof." Yet in the most general terms he found it undeniable that the "last decades" had witnessed a retreat from "moral and rational progress." In common with the Frankfurt Hegelians Adorno and Horkheimer, Mannheim associated the advent of authoritarian rule with an eclipse of rationality. And the danger of such a lapse, he thought, lay in the very nature of large-scale industrial society. As Weber had already observed, that society had created "a whole series of actions" which were "rationally calculable to the highest degree" and which depended on a corresponding "series of repressions and renunciations of impulsive satisfactions." It had so refined "the social mechanism that the slightest irrational disturbance" could "have the most far-reaching effects"; concomitantly it had produced "an accumulation of unsublimated psychic energies" which threatened "to smash the whole subtle machinery of social life."[10]

9. *Man and Society in an Age of Reconstruction*, trans. from the German by Edward Shils (London, 1940), pp. 3–5, 9.
10. *Ibid.*, pp. 32, 51, 61.

In the fatal antinomy of technical rationality and mass emotion—in the dialectical play between sophisticated equipment and latent barbarism—Mannheim discerned the psychosocial dimension of fascist movements.

"Up till now," he surmised, people had been able to believe that "relatively free competition between different forms of education and propaganda would, by natural selection, allow the rational, educated type of man, best fitted for modern conditions, to rise to the top." The experience of the 1920's and 1930's had proved this confidence unfounded; the "normal mechanism" of choice had failed to operate. There had come about instead a "negative selection of the élites": the "earlier bearers of culture" had begun "to be ashamed of their . . . values" and "to regard them as the expression of weakness and . . . a form of cowardice"; meanwhile "the representatives of local culture" were discrediting the intellectuals' cosmopolitan ideal with appeals to xenophobia and primitive virtue.[11]

Mannheim had never ceased to believe in the association of high culture with aristocratic values. In Britain he found it still possible for the upper orders to assimilate "a gradual influx from the lower classes" while maintaining their own traditional standards. On the Continent, however, he saw the older intellectual groups losing "their assimilative power." They were being submerged by numbers and forfeiting political and cultural leadership to the lower middle class—"the minor employees, petty officials, artisans, small business men, small peasants, and impoverished *rentiers*." And this composite stratum was of necessity reactionary: threatened from every quarter, it was attempting "to rescue itself by using all the political techniques at its command in order . . . to restrict the extension of rationalized industry, and to prevent the development of the modern rational type of man with . . . his humane ideals."[12]

Thus by a very different route from Borgese's, Mannheim arrived at the same social class as his focus of primary concern. Whereas the Italian littérateur had traced from its nineteenth-

11. *Ibid.*, pp. 74, 95–96.
12. *Ibid.*, pp. 101–102, 105.

century origins the neo-Romanticism of the half-educated, the Hungarian-Jewish-German-Englishman-by-adoption followed a Freudianized version of Max Weber in delineating the "negative selection of the élites." But in fastening like Borgese on the lower middle class, Mannheim did not limit himself to trying to understand the fears and resentments that made it fascism's major reservoir of recruits. He peered behind the frightened little people to see who else might be lurking in the shadows. In the turmoil of mass psychic breakdown, he suggested, there must be some who stayed cool and kept their power of rational calculation. Such men of substance as army leaders, large businessmen, and high officials might still hope to turn the general insecurity to their own advantage. And they might also locate and support those better endowed than they with the gift of popular leadership:

> It is not to be expected that the old bureaucracy . . . or the former commercial and industrial leaders trained in the ways of rational calculation will find the secret of symbol-manipulation. They need an alliance with a new kind of leader, and this leader, and the petty leaders, must come chiefly from those holes and corners of society where even in normal times irrational attitudes prevailed and where the catastrophe of unorganized insecurity was most severe and prolonged. Thus the leader must himself have experienced that emotional rhythm which is common to those who have been most exposed to the shocks of a partial dissolution of society.[13]

The fascist leaders had learned at first hand to play upon the mass anxieties of their countrymen. At the same time they were obliged to cultivate their own calculating faculties and to gain the sympathies of those who possessed such faculties to the highest degree. Mannheim merely sketched the alliance of disparate partners that lay behind the garish façade of fascist rule; he held his analysis to the generalized, schematic level of a psychosocial ideal type. The configuration he had marked out was to be filled in by a different variety of scholar, one with an eye for detail and a convic-

13. *Ibid.*, pp. 135–136, 138.

tion that a thorough empirical investigation could alone give the full measure of the fascist phenomenon.

Eleven years younger than Borgese, Mannheim was in terms of historical experience a member of the same generation. Both had come to intellectual maturity before the First World War; both had their base point in the prewar sense of economic security and social deference that the cultivated had enjoyed. The smaller age gap which separated Mannheim from Erich Fromm marked on the contrary a real psychological watershed. Born in 1900, Fromm belonged to the generation that went through the war as adolescents and whose decisive intellectual encounters were to occur in the tormented early years of the 1920's.

A psychoanalyst by training, Fromm had evolved away from Freud. He also broke with the Frankfurt Hegelians with whom he had been associated both before and after his emigration to the United States in 1934. By the time he published his first book in English, *Escape from Freedom*, seven years later, he had worked out a personal blend of a revisionist Freudianism and a similarly diluted Marxism that won him a wide audience in his new country.[14] *Escape from Freedom*, like Borgese's *Goliath*, was easy to read and attuned to the unspecialized; it had in common with Mannheim's work a characteristically German substructure of social and psychological theory.

Dissatisfied with purely psychological explanations and equally unwilling to accept any rudimentary Marxian schema, Fromm sought to combine elements of the two in a long-range historical assessment of fascism's appeal. Disregarding entirely the Italian experience, he found in his own native land the acute and extreme manifestation of a pervasive modern unease. And this in two separate epochs: the most original feature of Fromm's book was the simplistic and anachronistic suggestion that Reformation Germany prefigured the social history of the Weimar and Nazi periods. In each case, the line of reasoning ran, sudden economic change dislocated the traditional structure of society; in each case "the individual's feeling of powerlessness and aloneness . . . in-

14. For Fromm's intellectual autobiography, see *Beyond the Chains of Illusion: My Encounter with Marx and Freud* (New York, 1962).

creased, his 'freedom' from all traditional bonds" became "more pronounced, his possibilities for individual . . . achievement . . . narrowed down," and he felt "threatened by gigantic forces." The result, in the sixteenth century as in the twentieth, was a "compulsive quest for certainty," a "desperate escape from anxiety" into the arms of a religious or ideological leader, a Luther or a Hitler.[15]

Such a flight from a freedom seen as spurious, Fromm argued, characterized the lower middle class in particular. "The isolation of the individual and the suppression of individual expansiveness . . . were true to a higher degree" of this class than of those above and below it. Nazism could appeal to its "destructive strivings" and use them "in the battle against its enemies." For the average member of the lower middle class did not comprehend his own situation: he thought that he was suffering from the defeat and humiliation of his nation rather than from economic obsolescence; he failed to appreciate the extent to which Hitler's rule worked against his own social survival.[16] In short, he offered a classic example of what Marx had labeled false consciousness.

Thus in the end, like Mannheim before him, Fromm arrived at a sociopsychological explanation that hinted at the cleavage between ideology and economic reality in the fascist movements. In delineating the emotional universe of the lower middle class, he was more precise than either of his predecessors. Convinced, as they were, that the little people's vulnerability gave the key to fascism's success, he knew that this was only the first part of the story. But to write the sequel would require a detailed knowledge of events and an economic expertise that Fromm did not possess. Diffuse, hortatory in tone, and replete with banal psychoanalytic explanations, *Escape from Freedom* looked more impressive when it first appeared than it did a few years later. Second thoughts were to suggest that it had stretched its historical parallel too far and put together too tidy an explanatory synthesis.

Those who had acquired the special qualifications for analyzing fascism that Borgese and Mannheim and Fromm in their different

15. *Escape from Freedom* (New York, 1941), pp. 77, 91, 123, 207–208.
16. *Ibid.*, pp. 184–185, 216, 221.

ways all lacked were not necessarily their intellectual superiors. But they were men whose severe intelligence admirably fitted them for the task of making sense out of an incoherent mass of contradictory data. Quite independently of each other, Gaetano Salvemini and Franz Neumann, from their contrasting Italian and German experiences, wrote accounts whose conclusions were mutually reinforcing and whose factual density and critical bite very quickly gave them an authoritative standing. Subsequently, in the 1950's, they were frequently dismissed as "leftist" and subjected to major correction. When a full generation had passed, they were retrospectively restored to honor as the classic examinations of fascism in power.

ii. *Gaetano Salvemini between Scholarship and Polemic*

Gaetano Salvemini has been described as the last of the now "extinct species" of Italy's intellectual "masters." He has similarly been characterized as the ideological spokesman of his country's radical petite bourgeoisie, with a role comparable to Croce's for its grand bourgeois liberals, and Gramsci's for its Marxists.[17] Simply as an intellectual, Salvemini bulks less large than either of these in the culture of his own country or in the history of social thought. His mind was of a coarser grain than theirs, and his expression less disciplined. Yet there fell to him the task that neither Croce nor Gramsci was in a position to accomplish—the job of exposing to the outside world the realities of the despotism under which the Italians lived for two full decades. Croce was both too prudent and too fastidious to grapple with the sordid day-to-day realities of Mussolini's rule; cut off from reliable sources of news, Gramsci was reduced to the cryptic, coded aphorisms of his writings from jail. Neither the eminent untouchable nor the wretched prisoner could speak his full mind. Only an exile could proclaim the whole truth,

17. Gaspare De Caro, *Gaetano Salvemini* (Turin, 1970), p. 425; Massimo L. Salvadori, *Gaetano Salvemini* (Turin, 1963), p. 8. The former, the fullest biographical study, is bitterly hostile to its subject; the latter is briefer but more judicious. See also the laudatory collaborative volume by Ernesto Sestan et al., *Gaetano Salvemini* (Bari, 1959), and Salvemini's own *Memorie di un fuoruscito* (Milan, 1960).

and among the Italian émigrés Salvemini soon emerged, as though predestined for the assignment, in the congenial guise of the Duce's critic-in-chief.

He was just short of fifty-two when in 1925 he left Italy for an absence that was to last more than twenty years, and he had behind him a quarter-century of active involvement in ideological strife. Along the way he had delivered himself of countless misjudgments and had repeatedly been obliged to revise or to disavow positions he had earlier espoused with passion. It has not been hard for critics two generations younger to ferret out the inconsistencies in his voluminous writings and to question the moralizing tone that came naturally to him. Loathing what was merely abstract and forever in search of the "concrete," Salvemini often ended up in his own peculiar form of ethical or political abstraction.[18] His corresponding distaste for industrial society led him to underestimate the dynamic force of Italian capitalism and to champion the egalitarian misery of small peasant proprietorship. In this as in so much else of his stubbornly held set of convictions, he looked like a holdover from the nineteenth century never fully at home in the intellectual world of the twentieth. Yet there was one aspect of Salvemini's character that his detractors could not belittle or deny—his transparent integrity. He spoke the truth as he saw it, and early experience with hardship and tragedy had left him almost without fear and detached from worldly considerations.

These were to be precious assets when it came time for Salvemini to pass judgment on the Fascist regime. Likewise his mistakes of the past could be mobilized and brought to bear in his rigorous self-appointed task. His very failings—his political amateurishness and his moral impetuousness—became sources of strength when his countrymen lost their bearings and when he undertook to piece together from inadequate information the fundamentals of an unprecedented ideological situation. His three decades in Italy's political arena, coupled with his labors as a professional historian, had given him an immense range of knowledge of men and events, a knowledge which made him confident that

18. Salvadori, *Salvemini*, p. 114.

he could finally understand and explain the facts about Fascism, where others were at a loss.

In the biographical elements contributing to a personality that remained disarmingly simple, the earliest and deepest impressions were those stemming from a precarious lower-middle-class origin in the Italian south. Salvemini was born in 1873 in the small Apulian city of Molfetta—one of those white Adriatic seaports that look so charming until one discovers the squalor of the back streets. His family had struggled up from the peasantry into the petite bourgeoisie, only to be reproletarized by the economic depression of the 1880's. As a boy he had known hunger and anxiety, and along with them a meager intellectual diet. An uncle who was a priest had steered him toward an ecclesiastical career—the classic fate of the bright sons of poor southern families from which he was saved by the timely award of a scholarship to study in Florence.

These origins naturally invite comparison with those of Croce and Gramsci—both of whom similarly came from Italy's under-privileged regions. But with Croce the comparison ends there: the latent hostility that marked a half-century of intermittent relations between Salvemini and the Neapolitan philosopher sprang not only from profound differences in intellectual temper; it reflected the social cleavage between a man born into the southern elite and far removed from the poverty of the southern masses and one who early set himself up as the champion of the oppressed peasantry. In this latter course, Salvemini's career anticipated that of Gramsci —whose Sardinian petit bourgeois childhood closely paralleled his own. Indeed Salvemini, who was a half-generation older, saw twenty years before Gramsci the need for Italian Socialism to concern itself at last with the peasants of the south and of the islands. Yet whereas Gramsci settled in Turin—the most advanced of Italy's industrial centers—and preached from there the virtues of an alliance between urban and rural proletarians, Salvemini remained stuck in his loyalty to what was economically retrograde in Italian society. His southerner's resentment at northern domi-nance and at the scorn that northerners heaped upon his people was reinforced by the conviction that the south should and could be spared the horrors of industrialization. It was only the patient persuasion of his mentor, the pioneering student of southern society Giustino Fortunato, that little by little cured him of his illusion that the *cafoni* unaided could "save Italy." And there was something primitive and earthy also in Salvemini's abiding distaste for the complexities of formal philosophy: it made him feel, he complained, like "a *pugliese* peasant who begins to suspect in the streets of Naples that someone is trying to deceive him."[19]

At first sight it might appear odd that such a man should have become at home in Florence and have made it his intellectual headquarters. Yet in fact Florence perfectly answered his requirements: it was there that he received his training as a historian, it was there that he passed his best teaching years, and it was to there that he returned when his exile was over. In Florence from the start people were kind to him; the reigning positivist tone he found congenial to his spirit, and despite his peasant ways, he early won acceptance in some of its more exalted social spheres. Moreover, in Florence he could square the circle of his conflicting needs. He could escape the cultural confinement of the south without selling out to the north. He could live in a highly civilized and advanced community that still remained uncontaminated by the industrial bustle of the larger cities farther north. In the Tuscan capital he found a sobriety and moral seriousness which offered a welcome contrast both to the political trafficking in Rome and to the business values of the triangle Genoa-Turin-Milan.

Hence when he became a Socialist—something which was almost inevitable for a young man in the 1890's with Salvemini's ardor and concern for the poor—he soon saw reason to quarrel with the national leaders of the party. It was not only that these leaders viewed Italy's problems in a northern and urban-industrial perspective which was alien to Salvemini's temper. It was also that he could not abide any sort of political orthodoxy. His encounter with Marx was brief and superficial: in his reading of the Marxian texts he never got beyond the *Manifesto* and the works on con-

19. De Caro, *Salvemini*, pp. 200–201; Enzo Tagliacozzo, "Nota biografica," in Sestan et al., *Salvemini*, p. 216. See also Salvemini's own retrospective comments in his preface to Bruno Caizzi, *Antologia della questione meridionale* (Milan, 1955), p. 10.

temporary French history. As opposed to Croce, who came to his
own measured assessment of historical materialism after years of
careful study, Salvemini rather hurriedly picked up from Marx the
notion of class struggle and left it at that. In the course of his
ideological battles it gradually became apparent that he was far
more a positivistically minded radical than a Marxist. Indeed it can
be argued that the imprint of Christianity upon his thought
remained more profound than anything he had learned from the
classics of socialism. In his childhood he had been struck by the
ethical force and poetic beauty of the Gospels—this was the
earliest source of his moralizing—and in his old age he was to
write with warm sympathy of the mystical tradition in Italian
Catholicism, the spiritual universe of charity and undogmatic faith
that kept itself blessedly unaware of the official pronouncements
issuing from the Vatican.[20]

Salvemini's historical writings illustrate his evolution from a
simple, quasi-Marxist schema of class conflict to a more nuanced
view in which the radical values of the eighteenth-century Enlightenment predominated. The book with which he established
his reputation, *Magnati e popolani a Firenze dal 1280 al 1295*, had
"undeniably a certain mechanical quality," despite the impressive
archival scholarship that had gone into it.[21] In its delineation of
the issues pitting the great against the "little people" in Florence
six hundred years earlier, it betrayed its author's anxiety about the
social struggles that were currently shaking his country. The date
of publication was 1899: at the turn of the century Italy was
tormented by civil strife and official repression. In such a situation,
Salvemini's Socialist comrades were quick to hail his book as
inaugurating a new type of class-oriented history. These hopes
Salvemini disappointed. The works with which he followed
Magnati e popolani, while written for a wider audience, could no
longer be described as Marxist in inspiration. In moving from the

20. *The Origins of Fascism in Italy* (New York, 1973), pp. 155–156. This
work, written in 1942 and based on one of the lecture courses that Salvemini
gave at Harvard University, was published three decades later under the
editorship of Roberto Vivarelli, who had already edited an Italian version entitled "Lezioni di Harvard: L'Italia dal 1919 al 1929," *Scritti sul fascismo*
(*Opere di Gaetano Salvemini*, VI), I (Milan, 1961).
21. Ernesto Sestan, "Lo storico," in Sestan et al., *Salvemini*, p. 13.

Middle Ages to the modern era, Salvemini reversed the usual pattern by becoming more rather than less cautious. His books on Mazzini and the French Revolution, both published in 1905, won their lasting popularity as models of lucid synthesis and reasoned exposition.

Yet they had in common with his earlier and his subsequent writings a point of departure in the controversies of his own day. In his study of Mazzini, Salvemini was clearly trying to distinguish for the benefit of his countrymen what was helpful and what was dangerous in the legacy of the Risorgimento hero: while applauding the man of action, he warned his readers against the dogmatic and the "theological" in Mazzini's thought. Similarly it was characteristic of Salvemini's didactic bent that he should have ended his account of the French Revolution in 1792—*before* the era of terror and foreign conquest. He quite evidently wanted to demonstrate that the permanent significance of the Revolution lay in its reforming phase and its destruction of privilege: what had followed was sound and fury. He also meant to admonish the governing classes of contemporary Italy that they must adapt to democracy and socialism while they still had time.[22] In arguing that there was nothing fated, inevitable, or necessary about the violent phase of the Revolution in France, Salvemini was already anticipating what he was to maintain two decades later about the advent of Fascism in Italy—just as in his study of Mazzini he foreshadowed the role of moral leader in exile that he himself was to assume after 1925.

Here lay a further reason for his strained relations with Croce. While the two might agree that the historian's most authentic and convincing products took their initial impetus from some deeply felt contemporary concern, they went about the historiographic task in very different fashion. Croce tried to free himself from polemical passion by lifting his account to a high level of philosophical generalization; in his work the narration of "facts" and the judgment passed upon them were fused in a continuous line of quietly persuasive prose. Such was the practical manifestation of

22. *Ibid.*, pp. 19, 24–25; Franco Venturi, preface to republication of *La Rivoluzione francese* (1788–1792) in Salvemini's collected *Opere*, II, Vol. I (Milan, 1962), pp. xi, xiv–xv.

his idealist canon in the historian's daily labors. With Salvemini, these successive phases of history writing remained distinct. In his reconstruction of factual sequences, he conscientiously tried to detach himself so far as was humanly possible from the work at hand—hence the crisp, no-nonsense clarity of the expository portion of his writings. But when this duty had been performed, he felt at liberty to indulge in partisan rhetoric. In Salvemini's mind, the historian was entirely justified in expounding his own moral or ideological position, providing he had first established his account with scrupulous accuracy. In thus juxtaposing polemic and historical scholarship, Salvemini remained true throughout his life to the tradition of the Enlightenment and of nineteenth-century positivism. Quite naturally Croce dismissed such a procedure out of hand as methodologically crude and philosophically untenable.[23]

Yet when personal tragedy struck Salvemini in 1908, Croce was among those most deeply affected. In the earthquake at Messina— where seven years earlier he had received his first university chair— Salvemini's wife and five children all perished. As an adolescent Croce had similarly lost his parents in an earthquake: he was in a nearly unique position to understand what Salvemini had suffered. More broadly, to Italians of all sorts the misfortune that had befallen Salvemini ranked as the supreme, the unspeakable disaster. For a society that cherished and honored the family above everything, the fact of having lost wife and children in one blow passed mortal comprehension. In his grief-stricken state his friends feared for Salvemini's sanity: after the Messina earthquake his career was to be marked—and possibly furthered—by the pity and sympathy with which he was surrounded.[24]

Still more significantly, the entire central portion of his life—the quarter-century until his move to America in the early 1930's—was delivered over to a frenzy of activity. Once the first shock was over, and virtually abandoning historical scholarship, Salvemini sought forgetfulness by plunging into the murky eddies of Italian politics.

23. See, for example, Salvemini's lectures delivered at the University of Chicago in 1938 and published under the title *Historian and Scientist* (Cambridge, Mass., 1939), pp. 75, 82–84, 160, and Croce's ironical, condescending review of the Italian edition: *Quaderni della "Critica,"* No. 13 (March 1949), pp. 93–95.
24. De Caro, *Salvemini*, p. 150.

The variety and feverishness of his pursuits are explicable only in terms of the despair that lay behind them. He denounced Italy's liberal parliamentary master, Giovanni Giolitti, as the "minister of the underworld"; he detailed the combination of corruption and threats of violence with which Giolitti's henchmen managed elections in the south; and as though to prove the point, he ran unsuccessfully for the Chamber of Deputies from his native Molfetta. His basic aim—and his great contribution to the understanding and awakening of the south—was to politicize the southern masses. Most of the peasantry were still disenfranchised: at the best their landlords' relations with them remained paternalistic. Universal suffrage alone, Salvemini argued, could mobilize the peasants to stand up for themselves and struggle in their own behalf. And it was for this that he did battle in the years of Giolitti's rule. It was not his fault if the ringleader of Italian politics reduced him to a state of "stupefaction" by granting from on high in 1912 the substance of the universal manhood suffrage that Salvemini had urged the southern peasantry to wrest from Italy's governing classes by their own exertions.[25]

In the previous year, with the foundation of the review *Unità*, he had assumed the role to which he adhered for the remainder of his life—the role of preceptor to his countrymen. Gathering about him a group of contributors drawn from a broad spectrum of political persuasions, Salvemini sought to make the new review a forum for technical, nonrhetorical analysis of Italy's political and social problems. Not surprisingly Croce found Salvemini's writings as editor "half naive and half unjust, and tinged with utopianism,"[26] Others have characterized *Unità* as excessively eclectic. But unquestionably it raised the level of the discussion of public affairs in Italy, and in the range of subjects it dealt with admirably prepared Salvemini for his future task as dissector of the Fascist system. More immediately it occasioned a change in its editor's life that had been long in the making—his withdrawal from the Socialist party.

On the outbreak of the First World War, Salvemini broke

25. *Ibid.*, p. 177; Salvadori, *Salvemini*, p. 51.
26. *Storia d'Italia dal 1871 al 1915* (Bari, 1928), trans. by Cecilia M. Ady as *A History of Italy 1871–1915* (Oxford, 1929), p. 251.

completely with his former comrades by advocating Italian intervention on the side of Britain and France. He joined in the agitation that at length led Italy into the conflict through the street demonstrations of 1915 known to nationalist history as "radiant May." Still more, he served as a volunteer at the front until his health buckled under the strain. No action—or series of actions—of Salvemini's has occasioned more subsequent controversy. Even his most admiring biographer has admitted that the "resolute and aggressive . . . minority" in which he enrolled "succeeded in dragging into the war" a people whose "great majority" were opposed to intervention.[27] And Salvemini himself was subsequently to grant that the Italian masses "asked only to be left at peace in their daily life" and to describe radiant May as a "coup d'état" and dress rehearsal for the extraparliamentary pressure which seven years later brought Mussolini to power.[28] While he never precisely apologized for what he had done, he made it clear that later events had shed doubt on the stand which in 1914 and 1915 had seemed to him—as to so many educated and public-spirited Italians—a simple matter of loyalty to the memory of the Risorgimento and to the embattled forces of Western democracy.

Alongside and reinforcing the growth of Fascism, what had discredited democratically minded interventionists such as Salvemini had been their failure to persuade their countrymen of the virtues of a "Mazzinian" or Wilsonian peace. As interventionists they had always been a minority within a minority: by 1919, their voices were drowned out by those who in the name of "sacred egoism" clamored for Italy's full share of the victors' spoils. In that same year, Salvemini was elected to the Chamber on a nonparty "veterans'" ticket; but he soon learned that his running mates were losing whatever enthusiasm they may once have had for a peace of international reconciliation and were moving toward a protofascist course. In 1921, he did not stand for reelection; in 1922 the March on Rome found him tired and disillusioned, with a sense that age was overtaking him and that his own political

27. Tagliacozzo, "Nota biografica," p. 235.
28. "La diplomazia italiana nella grande guerra" (originally published in 1925), *Dalla guerra mondiale alla dittatura* (1916–1925), in Salvemini's collected *Opere*, III, Vol. II (Milan, 1964), p. 726; *Origins of Fascism*, p. 108.

mishaps and the collapse of Italy's popularly based political movements had borne out the contention of his countryman Gaetano
Mosca that active and determined elites alone knew how to
govern.

When Mussolini came to power, then, it might have seemed
that Salvemini's public career was finished. In fact within two
years he was to launch the third and greatest of his battles—
dwarfing his fights for universal suffrage and for a just peace—the
"implacable" battle he waged from exile against the Fascist
regime.[29]

In common with nearly everyone else of influence in Italy,
Salvemini had misjudged Mussolini. In the prewar years he had
viewed the future Duce as the gadfly the Socialists needed to stir
them out of complacency. There had even been a curious episode
linking Mussolini not only to Salvemini but to the former comrade
he would imprison, Antonio Gramsci. Just before the outbreak of
the war the *torinese* left Socialists with whom Gramsci was associated had proposed that Salvemini run for the Chamber in a by-
election from their city; his candidacy, they explained, would
express the solidarity of the northern industrial workers with the
peasants of the south. Salvemini, although "shaken and. . .
moved" by the proposition, had felt obliged to refuse. And in his
place he had suggested Mussolini.[30]

Subsequently the two former Socialists had been aligned together in the interventionist cause. As the gap had widened
between the Italian nationalists and the advocates of a Mazzinian
peace, Salvemini and Mussolini had gone their separate ways. By
1919 they were clearly enemies. But still Salvemini hesitated to
throw the full weight of his polemic against the approaching dictatorship. His uncharacteristic passivity during Mussolini's assumption of power was a sign of more than weariness: it showed
that he shared the illusion of most of the Italian elite that they
and the Duce lived in the same moral universe. Mussolini was a
familiar figure on the Italian political scene; Salvemini, like Bor-

29. Salvadori, *Salvemini*, pp. 28, 33.
30. For Gramsci's own account of this episode, see his posthumously published *La questione meridionale* (Rome, 1952), pp. 14–16.

gese and so many other critics of Fascism, had known him personally in his double capacity as politician and journalist. On the left
as on the right, there was a widespread conviction that the Socialist leader turned nationalist would remain substantially within
the tradition of Italian public life. This was a mistake that many
fewer German antifascists would make about Hitler, who was
easier to spot from the start.

It took the "great shock" of the murder of the Socialist deputy
Giacomo Matteotti in mid-1924 to convince Salvemini that his
own "inertia" amounted to complicity with an "infamous regime"
and that he "must say a resolute and public no to that regime."[31]
From this point on he hesitated no more: he became the guiding
spirit among the anti-Fascists of Florence, where he had lived
since 1909 and been professor of history since 1916; he edited the
first of Italy's clandestine journals; he was arrested, tried, released,
and then, with his life in danger, crossed the Alps into exile.
Shortly thereafter he resigned his university chair—on the grounds
that freedom of teaching no longer existed in his native land—and
began a wandering life that was to last the better part of a decade.

Shuttling back and forth between France and England, Salvemini labored ceaselessly to collect evidence on what was occurring
in his home country. To give himself any respite, he felt, would be
to let down his friends who had remained in Italy and who were in
far more peril than he. Yet among the emigration that made its
headquarters in Paris, Salvemini stood almost totally isolated. He
did not share the belief of most of his fellow exiles that the Fascist
regime would soon succumb to an internal crisis and that their
energies should be directed toward maintaining contact with the
opposition inside Italy and preparing for an eventual insurrection.
Salvemini foresaw that the job of fighting Mussolini from abroad
was a very long pull indeed, and he was skeptical of plans for
clandestine action. To his mind, the only way to topple Fascism
was to discredit it in the eyes of the great Western democracies. In
France and Britain and the United States, most solid citizens were
taking a benevolent view of Mussolini's rule; they were inclined to
disregard or to remain in ignorance of the Fascist terror. It was

31. *Memorie di un fuoruscito*, pp. 10, 106.

Salvemini's purpose to force them to look at the facts by presenting them with irrefutable proof.

Two myths which were in general circulation summed up the conventional wisdom about Italy: that Mussolini had saved his countrymen from "Bolshevism," near-chaos, and economic distress; and that the strong rule he had given them was precisely what the Italians deserved. This was the line that the Fascist propagandists were peddling and that foreigners were content to swallow. In combating it Salvemini drew on his training and experience as a historian; by applying his ruthless critical technique to the newspapers and official publications that reached him from Italy he tried to expose the truth below the inflated rhetoric of the regime. His preferred method was to let the documents speak for themselves: with biting irony and marvelous comic effect he lined up the Fascist pronouncements in all their intellectual vacuousness and inconsistency.

The first of his books on Mussolini's rule, *The Fascist Dictatorship in Italy*, dealt primarily with the circumstances under which the regime had come to power. It explained that the postwar economic crisis was already past before the March on Rome and that "the so-called Italian 'Bolshevism' of 1919–20 was nothing worse than an outbreak of uncoordinated unrest among large sections of the Italian people, to which the worse elements of the ruling classes replied by an exhibition of cowardice out of all proportion to the actual danger."[32] There had never been any real peril of revolution from the left—the forces of Italian Socialism were far too divided for that. Nor had the Italians accepted the dictatorship as spinelessly as most foreigners believed. The grisly facts of police repression pointed, on the contrary, to the existence of a stubborn internal resistance unknown to the world outside.

It was in its detailing of the crimes of Mussolini's followers that *The Fascist Dictatorship* really hit home. This was its polemical strength, and in this lay its analytical deficiency. From it the Western public learned for the first time the full story of Matteotti's assassination and the acts of official violence that had followed it. As he had earlier done with Giolitti, Salvemini fastened on the scandalous and gangster features of his country's

32. *The Fascist Dictatorship in Italy*, enlarged ed. (London, 1928), p. 54.

new rulers—hence the sensational and episodic nature of his account.[33] Salvemini's first study of Fascism in power was a magnificent polemic; but it failed to reach the inner articulations or to analyze the structure of that power. It would require one further political disappointment and an assurance of continuity in his intellectual labors before Salvemini was in a position to offer to the English-speaking public his definitive critique of Fascism.

When the most dynamic of Italy's oppositionists, Carlo Rosselli, escaped to France in 1929, Salvemini temporarily abandoned his attitude of detachment toward militant anti-Fascist action. Won over by the charm and persuasiveness of a man who had been his student in Florence, he consented to help in the launching of a new political movement, Giustizia e Libertà. Rosselli's notion of fusing the liberal and the socialist traditions fell in with Salvemini's own ideas. For a few years the older and the younger man worked in harmony. But as Giustizia e Libertà, under the influence of its clandestine *torinese* adherents, began to move toward an understanding with the Communists—whom Salvemini always detested—his faith in Rosselli's movement waned. His personal "affection" and "admiration," he subsequently wrote his friend, remained unchanged. As he had witnessed, however, their joint venture "lose its bearings," he had "shut himself up" in his own concerns. He felt "old, . . . mistrustful," and at "the end of all hope."[34]

From this—the third of the shattering blows that had punctuated Salvemini's career—he was rescued in 1934 by the offer of a lectureship in Italian civilization at Harvard. For the decade and a half of his American sojourn, Salvemini lived in Cambridge in austere, sparsely furnished university quarters. His pay was low, but his teaching burdens were correspondingly light. His lectureship gave him what he needed—the minimum financial security he had lacked before and ideal working conditions. His real home was

33. As though to restore the spirits of the flagging opposition inside Italy, a few of its members, among them Benedetto Croce, received copies of the book, suitably disguised beneath a pornographic dust jacket: *Memorie di un fuoruscito*, p. 105.

34. Letter of September 29, 1935, quoted in De Caro, *Salvemini*, p. 388.

Widener Library, the "enchanted island," as he called it, the refuge from political disillusionment where he achieved at last a kind of despairing serenity.

Although Salvemini's own Ph.D. students were few, his indirect influence extended much more widely. The promising growth of American interest in modern Italian history following the Second World War sprang primarily from his example.[35] And it is as an exemplary figure that Salvemini is remembered in the United States. To the young people in his classrooms he was a curiously exotic and almost legendary character. His courses at Harvard avoided the contemporary topics that might have tempted him into controversy—he confined himself to the medieval communes and the Risorgimento—but he lectured with the same verve that marked his political writings. For a man who had learned to speak English when he was over fifty, Salvemini had an extraordinary command of the language. The humor and pungency of his Italian style passed over readily into his new tongue; one of his Italian editors has noted with how little difficulty Salvemini's ideas go from Italian to English and then back to Italian again. This ease of translation suggests a broader compatibility between Salvemini and the Anglo-American world—a *Wahlverwandtschaft* of shared simplicity, matter-of-factness, and distrust of abstractions.[36]

Such were the material and intellectual circumstances contributing to the writing of Salvemini's most important work on Mussolini's system, *Under the Axe of Fascism*. He had followed his account of the advent of the regime with a study of its foreign policy, *Mussolini diplomato*, published in France in 1932. Like its predecessor, it was a witty and devastating polemic. Yet its author must have sensed that in neither work had he risen to the full height of his analytical capacities. As his research deepened, he discovered that a social interpretation alone could bring into conceptual unity the massive bulk of previously scattered evidence he had gathered. The parallel work in this field by such scholars as Louis Rosenstock-Franck in France and Herman Finer in England

35. See my "Gli studi di storia moderna italiana in America," *Rassegna storica del Risorgimento*, XLV (April–June 1958), 274.
36. Roberto Vivarelli, preface to *Scritti sul fascismo*, I, viii.

reinforced his confidence and sharpened his conclusions.[37] His book appeared at the turning point of Mussolini's rule—in 1936, the year of victory in Ethiopia, the alignment with Nazi Germany, and the intervention of the two fascist powers in the Spanish Civil War. Although in fact the beginning of the long slide into defeat, it looked to contemporaries like a year of triumph.

The immediate stimulus for Salvemini's book was the bombastic proclamation in 1934 of the establishment of the "corporations" that were at last to give substance to what Mussolini had long called his "corporate state." Ostensibly these corporate bodies were to end—indeed, had ended—the strife of capital and labor. In actuality, as Salvemini demonstrated with an irrefutable array of facts, the corporations were patently one-sided. The representatives of capital who sat in them were the businessmen themselves; the representatives of labor were delegated by the Fascist bodies that enjoyed a monopoly in the trade union field. This position they had received nine years earlier under the terms of the Palazzo Vidoni agreement of 1925, a scarcely known transaction between the major Italian industrialists and Mussolini's government, which had completed the consolidation of the dictatorship in the social and economic sphere.[38]

Thus, Salvemini maintained, although the corporative institutions themselves were no more than an elaborate deception, they were worth studying for the key they gave to the way in which the Fascist system worked in practice. When one had penetrated behind the barrage of propaganda which enveloped them, one discovered that the beneficent innovations to which the regime laid claim amounted to extremely little. Far from being substantially modified or "transcended," Italian capitalism remained intact. Indeed, within the capitalist framework the position of the larger industrialists had been strengthened—and at the expense of small businessmen, the professional classes, and agrarian and industrial labor. In the corporative institutions the ordinary worker counted not at all; in the Fascist labor organizations the rank and

37. Louis Rosenstock-Franck, *L'économie corporative fasciste en doctrine et en fait* (Paris, 1934); Herman Finer, *Mussolini's Italy* (London, 1935).
38. *Under the Axe of Fascism* (New York, 1936), pp. 15–16.

file had "no greater authority than do the animals in a society for the prevention of cruelty to animals." And continuing with the zoological metaphor, Salvemini quoted Prince Metternich to the effect that in the desired cooperation between rider and horse it was well to "be the man and not the mount. In Fascist class cooperation the employer is the man and the worker is the mount."[39]

What, then, of the state intervention into the affairs of Italian capital that had marked the early years of the depression? This, Salvemini explained, had nothing collectivist or socialist about it. It was in fact no more than a series of rescue operations directed toward saving big business from bankruptcy. "When an important branch of the banking system, or a large-scale industry which could be confused with the 'higher interests of the nation,'" had "threatened to collapse," the government had "stepped into the breach and prevented the breakdown by emergency measures."

> In Fascist Italy the state pays for the blunders of private enterprise. As long as business was good, profit remained to private initiative. When the depression came, the government added the loss to the taxpayer's burden. Profit is private and individual. Loss is public and social.[40]

"Must we conclude from these facts," Salvemini asked, "that Fascism is a capitalist dictatorship?" His answer was more qualified than the reader might have been led to expect from the analysis that had preceded it. Mussolini's Italy, Salvemini explained, was a conglomerate oligarchy whose main components were "army chiefs, high civil servants, big business men, and Party leaders." The interlocking—and mutually reinforcing—interests of these four groups gave the regime its internal coherence and stability. "In this oligarchy the big capitalists" were "far from exercising an uncontested sway. . . . If the capitalists stopped playing the policies of the Party, the Party could easily steer to the left. Thus, although the employers" were "protected," they were "intimidated at the same time."[41]

39. *Ibid.*, pp. 66, 196.
40. *Ibid.*, pp. 379–380.
41. *Ibid.*, pp. 383–385.

Ultimately the Fascist party leaders called the tune. Yet their power—and that of the Duce himself—was limited by the needs and pressures of the other elements in the oligarchy with which they were obliged to work:

> Among these groups, therefore it behooves Mussolini to move warily and watchfully, now sacrificing the big business man to the high civil servant, now the civil servant to the big business man, conciliating them whenever he can with convenient compromises, never sacrificing the military chiefs, taking no unnecessary risks, and always yielding to the strongest pressure or to necessity.[42]

These were imperatives that the Duce forgot when he plunged his country into the Second World War. His desperate gamble failed: the men of substance in Italian society whom he had favored and who in return had given him their support slipped away from him one by one until at last in the summer of 1943 he was overthrown by his own party chieftains. Salvemini had not predicted in detail how the fall of Fascism would come about. But his dissection of its inner workings accorded precisely with the cumulative loss of confidence that ended in the collapse of the regime.

Mussolini's fall, like Giolitti's grant of universal suffrage a generation earlier, caught Salvemini unprepared. He seemed unable to grasp the new realities that emerged from the slow liberation of his country and the exploits of the armed Resistance in the north. He bitterly denounced the unavoidable tactical compromises of anti-Fascist leaders who had once been his friends. When the war ended, Salvemini was more isolated than ever before, boxed in by the stern demands of his own moral rigor.[43] Hence it was understandable that he should have hesitated about returning to Italy, where his old university chair in Florence had been restored to him. A reconnaissance trip in 1947 convinced him to go

42. *Ibid.*, p. 386.
43. For a balanced assessment of Salvemini's writings during the war years, see Gian Giacomo Migone, *Problemi di storia nei rapporti tra Italia e Stati Uniti* (Turin, 1971), pp. 155–156.

back: he was overcome with joy at seeing his native land again—with pride in his countrymen's hard work of material reconstruction and admiration at the beauty of the Italian women. Two years later, at the age of seventy-six, he took up his university teaching once more.

Now, as in the past, he found an unworthy political regime to belabor. For the third time in his life, Salvemini rose to do battle against his country's rulers. Prime Minister De Gasperi's Christian Democrats, with their covert clericalism and fostering of conservative interests, were no more to his liking than Giolitti had been. Toward the latter, however, he had relented· he was now willing to grant that in view of what had succeeded him, the great parliamentary corrupter was not wholly without merit.[44] Nor did he find Christian Democracy's sins to be even remotely on a scale with those of Fascism. Salvemini's last polemics had about them an air of déjà vu. It was difficult for him to maintain his ethical strenuousness when his fellow citizens of all ages and opinions were treating him as a lovable old schoolmaster whose perplexing vehemence had long ago been forgiven or forgotten.

With his health failing, Salvemini finally took refuge in the Sorrento villa of an aristocratic friend of long standing, who had already sheltered him prior to his emigration. Here he died in September 1957, two days before his eighty-fourth birthday. His death was serene and a source of inspiration to those who flocked to visit him. Some found it Socratic, noting as they did so that in physical appearance also Salvemini resembled Socrates. With his snub nose, his enormous bald forehead, his little eyes that radiated a mocking intelligence, he might have passed for some mythical satyr. His broad, stooped shoulders, his squat torso, his heavy step, his indelible *pugliese* accent, recalled his peasant ancestors. Or perhaps one could see in him "the figure of the eternal emigrant from the Italian South," whose capacity for exhausting labor seemed without limit.[45]

44. For the vicissitudes of Salvemini's views on Giolitti, see A. William Salomone, "Ritorno all' Italia giolittiana: Salvemini e Giolitti tra la politica e la storia," *Rassegna storica del Risorgimento*, XLVI (April–Sept. 1959), 174–223.

45. Ernesto Rossi, "Il non conformista," *Il Mondo*, September 17, 1957; Sestan, "Lo storico," p. 5.

As early as 1899 Salvemini had revealed the complicity of northern capitalists with southern landholders in preserving the status quo among the people from whom he had sprung.[46] He had pointed out how it was to the advantage of both that the peasantry of the south should remain in political and economic subjection: with nearly half of Italy reduced to institutionalized inferiority, the northern leaders could keep their hegemony on the national plane, the southern their local preeminence. This down-to-earth approach, this realistic attention to those who profited and those who suffered from policies ostensibly directed toward the general interest, were to serve Salvemini well when he came to unravel the complexities of Fascism. His peasant suspicion that somebody was trying to put something over on him was exactly what was required in exposing the truth about a regime which specialized in mystification; it enabled him to drag out from behind their façade of nationalist pieties the interlocking pressure groups at the center of the Fascist phenomenon.

In such a task Salvemini's intellectual deficiencies—his eclecticism and distrust of theory—no longer figured as handicaps; on the contrary, they left him free to draw on his own long experience in judging an enormously miscellaneous body of data. Even his inveterate moralizing at last became appropriate when it was quite literally a gang of bandits with whom he was dealing. Salvemini's writings on Fascism, for all their fragmentary and polemical character, raised the basic questions. All subsequent students were obliged to begin where he left off—with a class analysis of those who benefited and those who lost out during the two decades of Mussolini's rule.

iii. *Franz Neumann between Marxism and Liberal Democracy*

By the end of the 1960's most American students of sociology, history, or political theory were only dimly aware of who Franz Neumann was. A half-generation earlier, in the late 1940's and early 1950's, he had ranked as a major force in social science, a man who from the start had given leadership to the intellectual

46. Rosario Villari, "Il meridionalista," in Sestan et al., *Salvemini*, pp. 108–109.

emigration from Germany and had subsequently become one of the most respected professors in one of America's most prestigious universities. This contrast epitomizes what we may call in appropriately Germanic fashion "the Neumann problem." If Franz Neumann was enormously influential in his own time and began to suffer neglect very shortly after his death, the explanation lies only partly in the fact that the corpus of his published writing was small and that his powers of persuasion were exerted primarily through the spoken word; the change was also due to the ambiguity of the intellectual inheritance he left behind him. Beneath the force and clarity of his polemical style, his intimates had increasingly detected a profound hesitation and uncertainty. As long as Neumann himself was in charge of his theoretical output, he managed—at least in public—to impose order on his contradictions through the application of an inordinately powerful mind and a strict sobriety of method. After his death, all the ambiguities came to the surface, and it was difficult for his younger readers to find the thread of ideological and emotional consistency that held them together.

Thus the career of Franz Neumann suggests both what was tragic and transitory in the emigration experience and the fashion in which that experience passed into the wider currents of American intellectual life. Throughout the period when his work was neglected, his indirect influence persisted—and persisted largely through the work of men who considered themselves his students, whether or not they were ever formally enrolled under his direction. For this reason it is urgent for one of those in his intellectual debt to set down the record before memories grow blurred. Even in our century of unmanageable documentation, there are some events of the mind that remain almost entirely unrecorded. The influence of Franz Neumann was one of these: it should not be lost to the history of ideas.

The events of Neumann's life can be briefly told. Their relevance to his development as ideologist and theoretician is readily apparent. Born in Kattowitz (now Katowice) in 1900 of Jewish parentage, Neumann grew up in a border area which was contested between German and Pole and was to change from the hands of one to the other on three occasions in his own lifetime. For Neumann's family, as for most of Germany's eastern Jews, the preference for the Reich was clear; they were also more markedly Jewish than their highly assimilated coreligionists in the western part of the country or in Berlin. Neumann was never religiously observant; at the same time he never denied his Judaic origin. The fact that he entertained no doubts about and saw no contradiction in being both a German and a Jew may help to explain the self-confidence with which he adapted to American life and acquired American citizenship. However his external circumstances might change, he always knew precisely who he was.

As an adolescent, Neumann did military service at the end of the First World War, receiving his first ideological education in the Soldiers' Councils which sprang up in the wake of the armistice of 1918. After that he studied labor law in Frankfurt, and in 1927 settled in Berlin as a labor lawyer. Life in the capital evidently suited his tastes: for the rest of his life he spoke both German and English with the harsh tones of a Berliner, to which his increasing deafness gave an even more metallic character.

Had German democracy been preserved, there seems no doubt that Neumann would have attained a position of major political influence. In the last years of the Weimar Republic, he was simultaneously teaching at the Hochschule für Politik and serving as legal adviser to the executive of the Social Democratic party. In the latter capacity, he acted as an ideological gadfly, contemptuous of the routine-mindedness of the official leadership. It was only natural, then, that when the Nazis came to power, Neumann should have been one of the first they deprived of German citizenship and drove into exile.

On the road of emigration, his initial stop was London. Here, with his characteristic practical-mindedness, realizing that a knowledge of German law was of no use to him abroad, he converted himself into a scholar by taking a degree in political science with Harold Laski. Soon, however, in equally practical fashion, he saw that permanent residence in England would not do. He had, as he recalled two decades later, originally gone there "in order to be close to Germany and not to lose contact with her." Yet "it was precisely in England" that he "became fully aware that one had to bury the expectation of an overthrow of the [Nazi] régime from within. . . . The . . . régime, far from becoming weaker, would grow stronger, and this with the support of the major European powers. Thus a clean break—psychological, social, and economic— had to be made, and a new life started." But England, with its tight, homogeneous society, "was not the country in which to do it. . . . One could . . . never quite become an Englishman. . . . The United States appeared as the sole country where, perhaps, an attempt would be successful to carry out the threefold transition: as a human being, an intellectual, and a political scholar."[47]

Neumann arrived in the United States in 1936—at the high point of the New Deal—and he was frank to recognize that after the timidity of English politics, what he called "the Roosevelt experiment" made the same favorable impression on him that it did on Thomas Mann and so many of his émigré countrymen. But his interest or participation in American political life remained marginal to his chief concern. This was to assault Nazism with his lawyer's talents and the new intellectual skills he had acquired in London. Settling down with Adorno and Horkheimer's left-oriented Institut für Sozialforschung which had migrated from Frankfurt to Columbia University, he began work on *Behemoth*, a massive study of Hitler's system, for which he was to be chiefly remembered. After America's entry into the war, he moved to Washington, serving as principal expert on Germany for the Office of Strategic Services and subsequently for the Department of State; in the last years of the conflict his was widely recognized as the most authoritative analysis of the Nazi regime. And in a military sense the war followed the course he had predicted: Nazism was destroyed utterly, by the massed might of the Soviet and Anglo-American forces.

After 1945, however, Neumann's hopes for the postfascist world were disappointed all along the line: the cold war destroyed whatever lingering chance remained for the international order and the German society based on socialist principles which he had sketched in his wartime memoranda. For the West Germany that was emerging under Adenauer's guidance, Neumann never both-

47. "The Social Sciences," in Franz Neumann et al., *The Cultural Migration: The European Scholar in America* (Philadelphia, 1953), pp. 17–18.

ered to conceal his contempt. Toward Berlin, his former home, he
was more indulgent: on repeated trips to the divided city he gave
generously of his advice and encouragement to the Social Democratic leadership, the trade unions, and the newly established Free
University. To the end of his life, Neumann never ceased to feel
the emotional pull of Germany and of traditional European
culture.

In the United States there was only one career that both
appealed to him and was open to him—university teaching. He
disliked his office chores as a State Department expert, and after
shuttling for a while back and forth between Washington and
New York, he decided for the latter without hesitation as soon as a
full-time professorship of political science at Columbia became
available to him. By the late 1940's Neumann seemed to be fully
absorbed in American life: for more than a decade he had made
the United States his home; he was married and had two young
children; he lived in a prosperous suburb, to outward appearance
thoroughly *embourgeoisé*.

Yet the new fit was never complete. Whatever Neumann's
academic success—and it was very great—however warmly he
might speak of the openness of American social and university life,
he remained curiously detached from his surroundings. And by the
same token he became increasingly melancholy. When roused to
action, his old vigor and combativeness would return; when alone
or with his intimates, he would lapse into silent meditation. He
was evidently groping for a new life and a new style of thought—
and he was beginning to think he could find them when on vacation in Switzerland in the summer of 1954 he was killed in an
automobile accident.

A career such as Neumann's cut off in midcourse necessarily
poses the question of what he would have said and done if he had
lived another twenty or thirty years. And in Neumann's case the
problem is complicated by the fact that his natural temperament
was thwarted by events at two decisive points. The first was when
the advent of Nazism forced him to transform himself from a
political activist into a scholar; the second was when the cold war
frustrated the vision which had inspired both his politics and his
scholarship. It is only if we bear these two enormous disappoint-

ments in mind that we can properly assess the writings he left behind him.

Like his Italian counterpart Salvemini—whom he resembled in the verve with which he attacked the fascist system that ruled his homeland—Franz Neumann detested everything which was empty or false. He was first and above all a critic of established institutions and structures. "A conformist political theory is no theory,"[48] he once declared, and this statement—characteristically brief and cutting—might serve as an epigraph for his entire published work.

In *Behemoth*, the book that first established his reputation, such ruthless incisiveness marked the tempo of both the analysis and the marshaling of fact. Neumann remained faithful to the Marxist tradition in his insistence on "unmasking" as the political scientist's primary concern. "In analyzing the structure and operation of National Socialist economy," he contended, "we must never rest content with the legal and administrative forms. They tell us very little."[49] Yet one could not expose the irrelevance of these forms until one had fully understood their complexities. Thus Neumann felt obliged to plunge his powerful lawyer's mind into a morass of legislation and administrative decrees in which someone less endowed with self-confidence and *Sitzfleisch* would soon have foundered, and he emerged triumphantly with what he regarded as a sure key to the workings of Nazi society.

The key, predictably enough, was economic. This was the first and more compelling of two parallel lines of analysis whose connection was not always apparent. Here Neumann aimed to demolish the facile explanations of Nazism currently in vogue—those which described Hitler's regime in terms of a "managerial" society, or, possibly, as one whose anticapitalist intent was evident in its effort to reconcile class antagonisms—by charting the links between big business and the Nazi leadership. Far from being

48. "The Concept of Political Freedom" (originally published in 1953), *The Democratic and the Authoritarian State: Essays in Political and Legal Theory*, ed. by Herbert Marcuse (Glencoe, Ill., 1957), p. 162.

49. *Behemoth: The Structure and Practice of National Socialism* (New York, 1942), p. 227. The second edition, published in 1944, differs from the first only in including an appendix covering the developments of the two intervening years.

directed against business interests, he maintained, National Socialist economics was "an affirmation of the living force of capitalistic society." But it would be wrong to claim, as doctrinaire Marxists were doing, that the regime was merely a front for monopoly capital. The relationship was more subtle than that: "The German ruling class" in fact consisted of "four distinct groups" whose interests were overlapping and mutually reinforcing—"big industry, the party, the bureaucracy, and the armed forces." And among these the relations between the first two gave the clue to the functioning of the entire system:

> National Socialism could, of course, have nationalized private industry. That, it did not do and did not want to do. Why should it? With regard to imperialist expansion, National Socialism and big business have identical interests. National Socialism pursues glory and the stabilization of its rule, and industry, the full utilization of its capacity and the conquest of foreign markets. German industry was willing to cooperate to the fullest. It had never liked democracy, civil rights, trade unions, and public discussion. National Socialism utilized the daring, the knowledge, the aggressiveness of the industrial leadership, while the industrial leadership utilized the anti democracy, anti-liberalism and anti-unionism of the National Socialist party, which had fully developed the techniques by which masses can be controlled and dominated. The bureaucracy marched as always with the victorious forces, and for the first time in the history of Germany the army got everything it wanted.[50]

Within the framework thus established, Neumann subjected each aspect of Nazi society to unsparing dissection. He traced the steady advance in the cartelization of German business and how the officially recognized regional or functional groupings had come to be dominated by the large concerns. He exposed the sham of the German Labor Front and the "atomization" of the working classes; in this, the most expert of his individual analyses, he returned to his old profession as labor's advocate, systematically

50. *Ibid.*, pp. 305, 361.

dismantling the National Socialist showpiece of class reconciliation. He further demonstrated that the so-called party sector of
the economy was the product of little more than legalized "gang-
sterism" on the part of the Nazi chiefs, and that these latter were
more and more entering into a state of symbiosis with the great
capitalists themselves. "The practitioners of violence tend to become businessmen," he concluded, "and the businessmen become
practitioners of violence."[51] Such was the final shape of the
National Socialist ruling class as defeat drew near.

In subsequent years, hasty or hostile readers frequently dismissed Neumann's interpretation as Marxist and simplistic. And it
is true that he had occasionally let fall an expression—such as a
passing reference to an "iron law of capitalistic concentration"—
which showed the hold that his original intellectual allegiance still
exerted over his thought.[52] But in fact Neumann's argument was
far from simple-minded. It was flexible and often hard to follow,
and it spared no variety of Marxist politician—whether Social
Democratic or Communist—in its analysis of how Weimar democracy had gone wrong. It never claimed that fascism was the
sole or necessary political expression of monopoly capitalism.
Moreover, it closely paralleled what Salvemini was simultaneously
writing about the fraudulent character of Mussolini's "corporative" institutions. It is curious that Neumann, who certainly knew
of Salvemini's work, never referred to it in his *Behemoth*.

However complex his view of Nazi society, Neumann did insist
on one clear distinction: that the Soviet Union (even under
Stalin) operated on different principles from those of Hitler's
Germany, and that to lump them together made only for termi-
nological confusion. It was partly for this reason that he pursued a
second line of argument parallel to his major economic and social
one. The subsidiary analysis was implicit in the book's title, with
its Hobbesian reference to an eschatological monster. It was more
formal and legalist than the first—and less relevant to the main
matter at hand. In brief, Neumann maintained that Nazi Germany—as opposed, in their different fashions, to both Soviet
Russia and Fascist Italy—could no longer be described as a state in

51. *Ibid.* (Appendix to 1944 ed.), p. 633.
52. *Ibid.*, p. 272.

the traditional meaning of the term: it had sunk to a level of ethical and legal dissolution in which the distinction between state and society, along with every other customary norm, had been absorbed in a mass politicization of existence.[53]

Although Neumann admired the author of the *Leviathan* and owed much to his influence, the effort to attach his own work to the Hobbesian inheritance was excessively abstract and in part artificial. Here once again the postwar years revealed the shape of reality, and in this case national and middle-class allegiances proved more tenacious than Neumann had imagined. Along with so many of his counterparts in the emigration, he had been generous to a fault in his judgments on the ordinary German. He had depicted the mass of his former countrymen as pulverized by a combination of economic and psychological pressures and incapable of expressing their sentiments of common decency. He had minimized the strength of popular anti-Semitism and had gone so far as to refer to the German people as "the least Anti-Semitic of all." (Even in the second edition of his book, when Hitler's decision to exterminate the Jews had become known in Washington, he had dealt with the "final solution" only in passing.)[54] In similar vein, Neumann had simultaneously branded racist or "social" imperialism as the "most dangerous formulation of National Socialist ideology" and denied that it had seriously infected the German working classes. As his book drew to its close, it was apparent that for all his hard-headedness and skepticism, he retained a faith in spontaneous indignation, a conviction that in the end the Nazi regime would be overthrown not only by the armed power of the victorious coalition, but by the "conscious political action" of Germany's "oppressed masses."[55]

That this was not the scenario which unrolled in the spring of 1945 was enough in itself to explain Neumann's subsequent disillusionment. Still more, the cement that held German society together through the prostration of the next four years was the traditional middle-class ethos whose dissolution *Behemoth* had announced. After the collapse of Nazism, Neumann had pre-

53. *Ibid.*, pp. vii, 470.
54. *Ibid.*, p. 121 and (Appendix), pp. 551–552.
55. *Ibid.*, pp. 215–217, 476.

dicted, the middle classes would have "ceased to exist as a stratum out of which a democratic society" could "be rebuilt."[56] Yet such a reconstruction was precisely what happened during the era in which the spirit of Konrad Adenauer rather than that of the intellectual emigration presided over Germany's return to the Western community.

If *Behemoth* was mistaken in its specific predictions, the fault may be ascribed to the fact that Neumann's method had been either legalist or economic and had left too little room for emotional considerations. It is in this sense and this alone that the charge of narrow-minded Marxism directed against his work can be accepted. Neumann himself was unquestionably aware of the insufficiencies of his analysis, which he never revised for postwar publication. In his years at Columbia University he began to subject his earlier certainties to critical scrutiny. He expressed a new respect for the achievement of Max Weber.[57] He found intellectual refreshment in studying as unlikely a precursor as Montesquieu. Above all, like Mannheim, he reflected on what it meant for his thought to be a citizen of a country where democracy was a living reality rather than the precarious web of compromise it had been in Weimar Germany. Yet Neumann found no substitute for the faith in Marxism and economic explanation that he had lost. Nor did he succeed in writing the comprehensive study of dictatorship that he had projected. Understandably enough, his postwar output was slight and fragmentary. Neumann's scrupulous and self tormenting search for a new vision of the social world can be documented in the collection of essays entitled *The Democratic and the Authoritarian State* which Herbert Marcuse, who was Neumann's closest friend and was to marry his widow, edited for publication after his death.

What most clearly distinguished the Neumann of *Behemoth* from the later Neumann of the postwar essays was a new insistence on liberty as the condition *sine qua non* of all rational or humanist action, as of all political theory. Whereas earlier, no

56. *Ibid.* (Appendix), p. 629.
57. "The Social Sciences," *The Cultural Migration*, pp. 21–22.

different from other Germans in the Marxist tradition, he had been concerned with unmasking the pieties of conventional liberalism, he now quite consciously joined the liberal-democratic current stemming from England and France. He wrote a perceptive and laudatory introduction to Montesquieu's *Spirit of the Laws*, locating the crucial distinction in the French theorist's writings in the "sharp dividing line" he drew "between despotism and all other forms of government," while limiting the celebrated theory of the separation of powers to its "irreducible minimum" of an independent judiciary. He similarly associated himself with John Stuart Mill's "classic formulation" of the doctrine of political liberty.[58] These new—or better, rediscovered—ideological affiliations highlight the dilemma with which he was contending in the postwar years: he never found a way to reconcile the passionate devotion to liberty that his belated Anglo-American education had given him, with the harsh Germanic conviction, which he refused to abandon, that most of what passed for liberty in the contemporary world was a disgusting fraud.

Thus Neumann's "Notes on the Theory of Dictatorship" remained an unfinished and disappointing fragment. And in his published writings he felt compelled to argue that constitutional guarantees, however desirable in themselves, were inadequate to check the abuse of political power. Nor did he discover any formula which would clearly define the citizen's right of resistance to tyranny: the decision to disobey constituted authority, he concluded, was one that each man was obliged to make in the loneliness of his own conscience. Moreover, the remedies commonly proposed for the failings of liberal democracy were in themselves of questionable value: "social rights," corporatism, attempts to "spiritualize" labor—all these palliatives failed to take sufficient account of the fact that modern industrialism was "politically ambivalent." Industrial society, Neumann found, simultaneously intensified "two diametrically opposed trends in modern society:

58. "Montesquieu" (originally published in 1949), *Democratic and Authoritarian State*, pp. 126, 142; "Intellectual and Political Freedom" (speech delivered at Bonn in 1954, trans. by Peter Gay), *ibid.*, pp. 208–209.

the trend toward freedom and the trend toward repression."[59] Much as he might have liked to share the faith of a Sorel or a Veblen in industrialism's potential as a liberating force and a school of cooperation, he was far too conscious of its stultifying effects to harbor any comforting conviction that twentieth-century urban culture contained its own built-in correctives.

The dominant trend, Neumann knew, was toward political apathy and acceptance. And this he combated with all the intellectual weapons at his command. But here again he never found a formula which brought him satisfaction. His unremitting attack on the tendency of professors and writers to remain "above" the political battle suggested how sorely he himself was tempted to adopt what he called an "Epicurean" attitude of detachment. Even more strenuously than Weber, he argued the intellectual's moral obligation to take a stand.[60] Yet he could provide neither himself nor his readers with any fully convincing reason for resuming the ideological battles of his youth in the disappointing and ambiguous circumstances of his middle age.

The cold war exacerbated these doubts and scruples. From the beginning of the confrontation between the United States and the Soviet Union until his death, Neumann never ceased protesting against the distortion of intellectual and moral values that had resulted from it. He assailed in turn the newly fashionable Machiavellianism among American sociologists and political scientists, the perversion of independent thought through propaganda and vilification, and the "loyalty" program in Washington, with the irrational fear and distrust it engendered of those defined as ideological enemies.[61] Neumann's own passionate revulsion was clear to those who conversed with him and who could discern the emotion under the surface of his dry, clipped prose. Yet in his public style he remained restrained and judicious. This was not

59. "Approaches to the Study of Political Power" (originally published in 1950), *ibid.*, p. 16; "On the Limits of Justifiable Disobedience" (originally published in 1952), *ibid.*, p. 159; "The Concept of Political Freedom," *ibid.*, pp. 189–193; "Notes on the Theory of Dictatorship," *ibid.*, p. 251.
60. "Intellectual and Political Freedom," *ibid.*, p. 215.
61. See particularly the statements in "The Concept of Political Freedom," *ibid.*, pp. 161–162, 188, 194.

through any shallow conformism or fear of the consequences of speaking out. It was rather a manifestation of the tragic dilemma of American (and émigré) intellectuals in the half-decade from 1948 to 1953 when the cold war was at its height: how was one to perform one's essential role as a critic of Western democracy without playing into the hand of either Stalinism or political reaction, or possibly of both at the same time? In Neumann's case this agonized self-questioning was raised to maximum intensity by his previous experience of Nazism and his total lack of illusion.

Neumann died too early to find a way out of what had become a classic impasse—in the very year when, with the passing of Stalin and the end of the Korean war, a glimmer of hope for the future was appearing. Meantime he had felt obliged to act as the defender of a democracy of whose weakness and degeneration he was fully and unhappily aware. It was fitting, then, that his last major public appearance should have been a lecture on the political implications of anxiety. In the summer of 1954, only a few weeks before his death, the Free University of Berlin, which he had so notably aided, awarded Neumann an honorary doctorate. He took the occasion to outline a new view of politics that had been slowly maturing in his mind. The lecture, subsequently published under the title "Anxiety and Politics," marked the fact that Neumann had at last caught up with Freud and the psychoanalytic current; by the same token it showed how far he had advanced beyond the boundaries of law and economics within which he had earlier confined his thought; and it demonstrated his thorough understanding of the manipulation by despots such as Adolf Hitler or by demagogues such as Joseph McCarthy of the anguish and the sense of guilt that afflicted the contemporary world.[62]

"Anxiety and Politics" revealed that Neumann had finally recognized and rectified the insufficiencies in his earlier writing. But in itself the lecture was not notably original; at fifty-four Neumann was too old and too well fixed in his intellectual patterns to make a major contribution to the psychoanalytic study of politics and history on which so many others, younger and

62. Trans. by Peter Gay for *ibid.*, pp. 270–295.

better qualified than he, were about to enter. It is far from certain that had he lived a decade or two longer, his new interests would have significantly altered the character of his intellectual legacy.

This legacy was at least as much oral as it was written. The great difficulty in arriving at an assessment of Neumann's career is that his published work gives no adequate sense of his range and influence. Like most of the émigrés from Central Europe, he never learned to write English with literary ease; but he wrote clearly and directly and without the Teutonic portentousness which so many of his countrymen carried with them across the Atlantic. The trouble with Neumann's prose was almost the opposite: it was so compact and schematic, it made so few concessions to rhetoric or anecdote, that it conveyed little of its author's personal power. Moreover, it was burdened with scholarly paraphernalia and historical citations which were unnecessary to his argument and foreign to the very special combination of practical-minded-ness and abstraction that was his natural temperament. To cite merely one example: although a central contention of his *Behe-moth* was that the intellectual rationalizations of National Social-ism could be dismissed as "pure eyewash," he nonetheless felt obliged to rehearse them at tedious length.

Those who had never met Neumann in person could scarcely be expected to find the human being behind the aridity of his prose style. Those who knew him well recognized the familiar figure—the bald head, the metallic voice, the hearing aid which he switched off with a beatific smile when he sensed that someone was about to embark on a pompous or boring exposition, the thick, heavy-rimmed glasses framing a face that was both ugly and radiating sexual attraction. One of his younger friends concluded that Neumann's mind was like an incandescent bulb which, although it had burned away his hair, his sight, and his hearing, continued to exert a fascination on all it encountered. And another who saw a great deal of him during his years at Columbia named Neumann without hesitation as his "most extraordinary teacher":

It was not simply that he was a European intellectual on an American campus. He would have had an equally startling impact on a European university, as in fact I saw him have at the Free University. Nor was it simply his erudition, great and varied though it was. What struck all, I think, was that he embodied in his own person the vitality and the drama of intellectual life. . . . He had a dazzling power of incisive analysis and critical judgment, and students were overwhelmed by the rapidity and certainty with which he imposed logical meaning or order onto a set of facts or problems. His habit of subsuming various phenomena under logical or historical categories and of seeing things as orderly and clear where to others they had appeared ambiguous or blurred might have been Hegelian-Marxist in origin and might have been practiced in lawyer's briefs and political arguments, but the results were always new and strikingly unpredictable. . . . By his own intellect he belied any crude notion of the social determinism of ideas; he communicated to his students his interest in the social origins and relevance of ideas, and he surprised students and friends alike by his precise and intimate knowledge of so much of European literature. Finally what impressed his students—because rare in any age—was his simultaneous and reciprocal function as philosopher and political man. . . .

The students' admiration was aroused by more than a brilliant mind. There was something in this seemingly austere man, with his brusque manners and his relentless seriousness, that awed students. He was often hard on them. His critical comments were likely to be curt and devastating, and it took little acumen to realize that he did not suffer fools gladly. But there was a magnetism of character and intellect that many students could not withstand. They became disciples and critics, admirers and rebels by turn. . . .[63]

Neumann's own estimate of his role was more modest. He saw himself in a mediating capacity, on the one hand telling his German friends that they cared too little for empirical research while simultaneously counseling his American colleagues to balance their empiricist enthusiasm with a greater concern for history and theory.[64] Within his chosen discipline of political science,

63. Fritz Stern, in a letter to the author of August 21, 1967.
64. "The Social Sciences," *The Cultural Migration*, p. 25.

Neumann's advice was rarely heeded: the quantitative and behavioral approaches which became so influential in the United States immediately after his death were in large part responsible for the neglect into which his work began to fall. And the excessive legalism of his own method frequently gave it an old-fashioned air. It was on historians, rather than on political scientists, that Neumann's precepts left their most lasting impression.

During his war years with the Office of Strategic Services, Neumann had gathered about him an informal circle of younger men, all American-born, but concerned with German affairs and destined to receive professorships of modern European history at some of America's most influential universities. Later on, at Columbia, he attracted into his orbit the talented sons of émigrés from Germany. Toward his younger associates, Neumann was in turn an ideological mentor, an initiator into the realities of European society, and a friend who never ceased inspiring a certain amount of awe. In the informal seminars he conducted in Washington or New York—and a conversation with Neumann seldom failed to turn into a seminar—he refrained from trying to impose any formal Marxian concepts on his listeners. And none of the young historians closest to him in fact became a Marxist. What Neumann imparted to them was something less specific and more pervasive: a conviction that the study of history must begin with economic and class relationships, and that one understood little of politics or ideology unless one was aware of the pressure of interest groups that lay behind them.

A decade or two later such precepts became the common coin of graduate instruction in history, but when Neumann first made the acquaintance of his young admirers, his point of view was far from being generally accepted. The study of contemporary European affairs was still dominated by Ranke's notion of the "primacy of foreign policy"—a conviction reinforced by the tendency of so many American scholars in the post-Versailles years to focus their attention on diplomatic history. Neumann took up the challenge that the most talented of Social Democratic historians, Eckart Kehr, had thrown down: he asserted the "primacy of domestic policy,"[65] in the sense that foreign affairs should be understood

65. See the references to Kehr in *Behemoth*, pp. 203–204, 206.

not in terms of an abiding and consensual "national interest," but rather as an expression of the economic and ideological forces currently dominant in a given society, and this interpretation his American friends brought with them into the universities at which they subsequently taught. It was characteristic of them that they gave only passing attention to war and diplomacy. What was more surprising—and suggested how much independence they combined with loyalty to Neumann's memory—was that they directed their attention to intellectual rather than to social history. In the way they defined such study, however, the spirit of their mentor was readily apparent: as opposed to the older "history of ideas" which dealt in abstract terms with great thoughts perceived as protagonists in their own right, Neumann's heirs wrote what one of them has called a "social history of ideas," setting those thoughts in the full context of historical circumstance out of which their creators had given them form.[66]

Thus although Neumann himself did not succeed in resolving his perplexities, his grapplings with them had a clarifying effect on the minds of his younger friends. Never having been sectarian Marxists, they were untroubled by feelings of ideological betrayal when they found Marx in error. And as native-born citizens of the United States or as bilingual Americans who had come very young to this country, they saw no contradiction between a nondoctrinaire socialism and the liberal-democratic tradition. For Neumann it had been a wrench to recognize that political power or deep-running sentiments might on some occasions be divorced from any visible economic base. His young American friends had never been tempted to think otherwise.

Neumann's influence, then, lived on after his death in a diffused form which it was difficult for the noninitiated to recognize. Besides the work of his intellectual heirs, he left behind him a superb series of individual critiques of politics and society. Neumann's "all pervasive conviction," his friend Otto Kirchheimer has written, was that "critical analysis of established social structures and . . . institutions" was "the political scientist's only worthwhile

66. See the preface by Peter Gay to *The Party of Humanity* (New York, 1964), pp. ix–xii, and my own definition in *Consciousness and Society* (New York, 1958), pp. 9–12.

job. . . . His late writings no less than his early ones" were "impregnated with the belief in the rational propensities of man" and in the "feasibility and urgency of a cooperative society."[67] In this sense his work had an underlying unity and coherence. In comparing Neumann's aspirations with his published writings, one might easily conclude that his professional life was a noble failure. But to do so would be to suggest that he eventually succumbed to despair. This Neumann steadfastly resisted. Although the abiding ambiguities in his thought made it harder for him to put his reflections on paper than to deliver them orally, he kept on trying to give rational, persuasive form to what he had understood about modern society. "Throughout Neumann's essays runs the struggle against temptations to surrender; pessimism and Epicureanism were his personal devils."[68] These devils never conquered him.

"There are historical situations," Neumann wrote two years before his death, "where an individual, no matter how honest, intelligent and courageous, is quite powerless to affect the course of history."[69] He might well have been speaking of himself; he could equally well have made reference to Salvemini. Both of the great critics of fascism aspired to play a major role in the public arena; both suffered repeated disappointments; both were ulti- mately far more influential as students of politics and society than as political activists.

In the precarious equilibrium they maintained between scholar- ship and polemic—or between Marxism and liberal democracy— Salvemini and Neumann made their lasting contribution as critical writers. And the very fact that their analyses of fascism were at once meticulous and engagé gave their work the ring of profound intellectual responsibility. The affinities between the two were readily apparent; but few readers noticed them—perhaps because Salvemini's and Neumann's temperaments and styles were so very different. Yet it was of crucial importance that without reference

67. "Franz Neumann: An Appreciation," *Dissent*, IV (Autumn 1957), 386.
68. David Kettler in *ibid.*, p. 392.
69. Review of *Am Beispiel Österreichs* by Joseph Buttinger, *Political Sci- ence Quarterly*, LXVII (March 1952), 141.

to each other they had discerned the same four groups as the central contenders for power in the fascist systems—the army, the civil service, big business, and the party—that they had alike particularly stressed the relationship between the third and fourth, and that they had agreed in recognizing that whatever the limitations under which it operated, the party leadership in the end had the decisive say.

This last consideration should have been enough to give pause to those who labeled *Behemoth* or *Under the Axe of Fascism* as mere leftist interpretations. And in Salvemini's case such a reminder usually sufficed; his reading of Italian Fascism met little serious opposition in the postwar period. Neumann's similar interpretation, however, of the German fascist experience was repeatedly called into question. Subsequent research suggested that the number of German businessmen who remained free of Nazi involvement was greater than he had supposed; and this numerical rectification seemed to cast a retrospective doubt on his whole enterprise. But the same postwar years in which Neumann's work came under assault also demonstrated that the major German capitalists had ridden through the Hitler era virtually unscathed. And it was difficult to see how they could have accomplished such a feat in the absence of substantial accommodation with the regime. This Neumann's critics or the defenders of German big business never satisfactorily explained.

The most general way in which a Marxist or left interpretation of the socioeconomic bases of the fascist systems might be phrased was Max Horkheimer's lapidary formula: "Whoever is unwilling to speak of capitalism should also keep silent about fascism." Any such interpretation presumed a significant connection between the economic structure of the one and the political organization of the other.[70] But in its notion of the tightness of that connection it could and did take three distinct forms. The most extreme asserted that the big businessmen ran the show—that fascist leadership was no more than a façade for the rule of monopoly capitalism. A

70. See the introduction by Kurt Kliem, Jörg Kammler, and Rüdiger Griepenburg to the anthology ed. by Wolfgang Abendroth, *Faschismus und Kapitalismus* (Frankfurt and Vienna, 1967), pp. 5–8.

second and more moderate variant of the thesis argued merely that the system intentionally and systematically worked for the benefit of big business. A corollary of both these variants was that fascism was the appropriate expression of monopoly capitalism and that those major industrial states which had not yet "gone fascist" were in imminent danger of doing so. The third and final variant limited itself to asserting that the big businessmen, after certain initial hesitations, for the most part supported the fascist leaders, once the latter were installed in power, and that they received in return substantial favors from the fascist regimes. This was all that Salvemini ever argued and what Neumann argued *most of the time*.

Neither suggested that fascism was the sole or necessary expression of monopoly capitalism. They simply maintained that in Italy as in Germany big business did very well under fascism, that most of the major capitalists were only too happy to cooperate in fascist rule, that as such regimes went on, there occurred a kind of symbiosis between top leadership in business and top leadership in the party, and that this interaction gave the key to the functioning of the entire system. Thus the greater capitalists—almost alone among their countrymen—were able to emerge from the fascist experience with minimum damage, while the members of the lower middle class who had put their trust in the rhetoric of a Mussolini or a Hitler found themselves sacrificed to the "higher" exigencies of a nation girding for war.

iv. *Hannah Arendt and the "Totalitarian" Threat*

For a half-generation following the end of the Second World War no important general or comparative works on fascism appeared—neither in the former fascist countries themselves nor in the Anglo-American world. At the same time the years 1945–1960 saw the unearthing of a mass of documentation that confirmed or corrected hypotheses at which Salvemini or Neumann had been obliged to guess and the corresponding publication of a host of monographs and articles on individual aspects of the Italian or German experience. Indeed the flood of this material was so great as to daunt scholars from attempting a new synthesis—witness Neumann's inability to revise his *Behemoth* or to write his projected study of dictatorship. In the absence of such a synthesis, the term "fascism" itself began to lapse; the word currently in style among historians and political scientists, as among journalists and makers of public policy, was "totalitarianism."[71]

In retrospect it seems clear that the vogue of "totalitarian" explanations, more particularly in the United States, was a by-product of the cold war.[72] In the late 1940's and early 1950's, the term served to ease the shock of emotional readjustment for Americans or Englishmen—or émigrés—who had just defeated one enemy and were now called upon by their governments to confront another. If it could be proved that Nazism and Communism were very much the same thing, then the cold war against the late ally could be justified by the rhetoric that had proved so effective against the late enemy. And by the same token Fascist Italy ceased to be of much interest: if it was the comparison between Nazi Germany and the Soviet Union that had now become crucial, Mussolini's looser rule could logically be dismissed as nothing graver than a dramatic manifestation of the already familiar phenomenon of pretotalitarian tyranny. A work such as *Behemoth* did not fit the new intellectual conformism: its line of analysis jarred the comfortable convictions of the cold war at its height. Neumann had in fact used the word "totalitarian"; but he had resorted to it sparingly and only when the context was clear.[73] He never exploited it, as the cold war apologists did, to blur the

71. Ernst Nolte, ed., introduction to the anthology *Theorien über den Faschismus*, 2d ed. (Cologne and Berlin, 1970), p. 65; Wolfgang Sauer, "National Socialism: Totalitarianism or Fascism?" *The American Historical Review*, LXXIII (Dec. 1967), 405–407.

72. In Carl J. Friedrich and Zbigniew K. Brzezinski, *Totalitarian Dictatorship and Autocracy* (Cambridge, Mass., 1956), compare the statement in the original edition (p. 7): "The . . . view, that communist and fascist dictatorships are wholly alike, is presently favored in the United States" with that in the revised edition (1965) (p. 19), where the phrase "is presently favored" has been changed to "was during the cold war demonstrably favored."

73. *Behemoth*, e.g., pp. 49–50, 67, 261.

distinction between fascist and Communist society. This was still another reason for the post-1945 denigration of his work.

Both the most erudite and the most emotionally compelling of the books in the new vein, Hannah Arendt's *The Origins of Totalitarianism*, appeared in early 1951 at the zenith of the cold war. A few weeks earlier, the American and South Korean armies had been hurled back from the Yalu River by the Communist Chinese; Stalin was in the grip of the homicidal madness that Alexander Solzhenitsyn was to depict so chillingly in *The First Circle*; never before—or subsequently—had the United States and the Soviet Union seemed so close to war. It was on such a charged ideological atmosphere that *The Origins of Totalitarianism* impinged. Its author, up to then unknown, soon became an intellectual celebrity. Born in 1906 and a favorite pupil of the philosopher Karl Jaspers, Hannah Arendt brought to the study of twentieth-century tyranny, along with the heavily freighted terminology of existentialism, a tone of ethical revulsion that reached a higher pitch than had been true of any of her predecessors.

Her method of attack was threefold. In the late nineteenth century, she argued, three movements, apparently unrelated, were converging to produce the type of mind and political activity which was to evolve into totalitarianism only after the First World War. What these movements had in common was that they all reflected—and accelerated—the collapse of the European class structure and nation-state concept. Class and nation-state had alone given reality to the rights of man. In their default, these rights were reduced to mere abstractions. With the dissolution of the basic institutions of European society, no barriers remained against what "became this century's curse only because it so terrifyingly took care of its problems."[74]

The first of the preparatory movements was anti-Semitism. Refusing to accept the usual explanation that the Jews served as scapegoats for unscrupulous demagogic agitation, Arendt tried to find reasons why they offered the logical target. It was their intimate connection with the nation-state, she found, that marked the

74. *The Origins of Totalitarianism* (New York, 1951), p. 430.

Jews for destruction. As financiers of the European governments, they had incurred the hatred of the political movements which saw in the state the enemy to be conquered. But the irony of the case was that the real growth of anti-Semitism should have come only after the Jews had ceased to be influential. With the flood tide of imperialism in the late nineteenth century, they had lost their near-monopoly of state business. European Jewry, Arendt surmised, had become "an object of universal hatred because of its useless wealth, and of contempt because of its lack of power."[75]

Meantime the second movement, overseas imperialism, had sapped the foundations of the nation-state. As a doctrine of "expansion for expansion's sake," imperialism brought under the control of the nation-state backward areas that could not be integrated into the European political framework. Moreover, the novel experience of confronting vast assemblages of "primitive" and totally alien human beings taught the Europeans to forget their moral scruples, to indulge with a good conscience in mass murder and unspeakable brutality. For the first time in history, racism attained the status of self-conscious doctrine and practice. And it was racism—with its "contempt for labor, hatred of territorial limitation, general rootlessness, and . . . activistic faith in one's own divine chosenness"—that was most deeply to mark the movements of the future.[76]

Overseas imperialism had one saving grace. It at least drew a sharp line between colonial methods and policy at home. With the third movement—what Arendt called "tribal nationalism"— the line disappeared. In Pan-Germanism and Pan-Slavism, the "concept of cohesive expansion" did not "allow for any geographic distance between the methods and institutions of colony and of nation."[77] Under the ostensible aim of uniting all individuals speaking a common language, this new form of nationalism in fact preached the world supremacy of a master race. To those whose national and personal ambitions had been frustrated, it gave the consoling assurance of their own superiority.

Out of these three movements, Arendt concluded, came totali-

75. *Ibid.*, p. 15.
76. *Ibid.*, pp. 131, 197.
77. *Ibid.*, p. 223.

tarianism—the unprecedented madness of the "mob," the "refuse of all classes," which had coalesced at the turn of the century under the leadership of déclassé intellectuals. With the subsequent declassing of entire categories of the population, the "mob" dissolved into the "masses." The masses—the "superfluous men" of the era—had nothing to lose by following their leaders into the most irrational and reckless of ventures. All they sought was to merge with something larger than themselves, to give up their useless individualities to a movement that in the words of Cecil Rhodes "thought in continents and felt in centuries." And their leaders stood ready to offer them a fictitious world which could "outrageously insult common sense" by imposing its own crazy consistency upon a real world in which common sense had ceased to count.[78]

Overwrought, highly colored, and constantly projecting interpretations too bold for the data to bear, *The Origins of Totalitarianism* recalled Borgese's *Goliath* in its historical amateurishness and its striving for shock effect. Yet the intellectual demands it made were far sterner: Hannah Arendt offered no concessions to her readers; they were obliged either to follow to the end the tortuous but relentlessly consistent line of her thought or to give up the effort entirely.

Those who fought their way through her book might not notice how much they had accepted along the way that was either doubtful or positively mistaken. At the very start, for example, she had assured her readers without proof that the great financiers had served both as the leaders and as the symbols of the European Jewish communities, and on this insecure foundation her entire interpretation of anti-Semitism rested.[79] Similarly she never explained the relevance of dwelling at length on British imperialism, when she herself was quite ready to grant that twentieth-century Britain, even overseas, stood for "moderation in the midst of plain insanity." Gravest of all, however, was her insistence on slurring over or belittling the differences between the Nazi and the Soviet

78. *Ibid.*, pp. 309, 342.
79. Benjamin I. Schwartz, "The Religion of Politics: Reflections on the Thought of Hannah Arendt," *Dissent*, XVII (March–April 1970), 154.

forms of the "totalitarian" phenomenon by treating the two as "essentially identical."[80]

Obviously Arendt knew more about Germany than about Russia, and she frequently seemed to be extrapolating from Hitlerian to Soviet experience. For Nazism she provided a full ideological background; in the case of Bolshevism she jumped over a quarter-century from the agitation of the Pan-Slavists to the triumph of Stalin. She confronted her readers with Soviet Communism as the ideological equivalent of Nazism without any adequate account of how it got to be that way. The fate of classic Marxism in Russia, the complex process by which Pan-Slavist elements fused with it in the Stalinist credo—all this she telescoped into a few sentences. Still more, her basic equation of totalitarianism with madness blinded her to the economic rationale of Communist practice; Soviet realities cut across her generalizations by being at once more rational and more totalitarian than Nazi methods. Thus her account lacked any assessment of the distinctions between the two systems that had given Russian Communism its greater resilience and durability.

The basic difference, of course, lay in economic organization and the power relationships deriving from it on which Salvemini and Neumann had put such stress. Hannah Arendt's account, in line with her previous training, was almost entirely innocent of economics—hence her readiness to dismiss Soviet industrial planning as a further example of "insanity." This, like so much else in her book, bore the imprint of the era in which it was published; and, curiously enough, it dated faster than did the analyses of fascism written closer to the event.

In the preface to her work, Hannah Arendt had herself referred to the circumstances of its composition, to the experience of living "in the anticipation of a third World War between the two remaining world powers."[81] Such a catastrophic assessment was not uncommon around 1950; as little as a half-decade later it was already sounding exaggerated. And in a broader sense the same was true of the entire "totalitarian" interpretation. An "ideal type,"

80. *Origins of Totalitarianism*, pp. 221, 429.
81. *Ibid.*, p. vii.

although one that Weber would have found lamentably imprecise, the term began to dissolve as the 1950's came to a close in an ideological situation whose complexities defied any simple scheme of classification. The notion of a bipolar world lapsed; so too did the clear contrast between freedom and totalitarian rule. By the 1960's it was becoming apparent, particularly with reference to the "Third World," that there were infinite gradations between the two and that it was more illuminating to speak of a continuum extending without sharp breaks all the way from the most authoritarian to the most liberal attitudes and practices.

The "totalitarian" interpretation focused on techniques of control—the horrifying surface of life—rather than on underlying social realities. It took at its face value Hitler's or Stalin's claim to complete power over the lives of his subjects, despite the evidence in the concentration camp literature itself that even within those hellish confines one could discover tiny islands of autonomy.[82] In retrospect totalitarianism loomed as an ideal, an aspiration, and not as a historical reality—witness the fact that the term had been coined by Mussolini to describe a regime which never came close to its attainment. The final irony of the study of totalitarianism was that it led to the neglect of its Italian inventor and of the style of rule which rather more than Hitler's had been admired and imitated in the fascist era.

v. *"Radicalism of the Right"*

In the 1960's a new generation of scholars, unscarred by the ideological battles of their elders, returned to the study of fascism with fresh eyes and a willingness to examine without fixed preconceptions both recently discovered data and old interpretations. They not only rehabilitated the term "fascism" itself; they attempted to redefine it in a fashion that would accommodate national variations while maintaining a minimum of conceptual unity. In the former fascist countries these efforts chiefly took the

82. See, for example, Eugen Kogon, *Der SS-Staat* (Munich, 1946), trans. by Heinz Norden as *The Theory and Practice of Hell* (New York, 1950).

form of anthologies of earlier writings;[83] in Britain and America they resulted in a succession of collaborative volumes to which individual scholars contributed essays on some particular feature of the fascist experience.[84]

It was noteworthy, however, that the one major comparative study—Ernst Nolte's *Three Faces of Fascism,* originally published in Germany in 1963[85]—managed to dominate its material only through an exclusion of much that had seemed of critical importance to the investigators of the 1930's. Still more, the attention it received came to it largely by default: its author had at least mustered the courage to make the attempt before which so many others had faltered. And the way he went about it betrayed the well-nigh insuperable difficulties of the assignment: he chose to follow the safe and traditional German practice of delineating political phenomena in terms of the ideas they embodied.

Thus Nolte's work, no less than Hannah Arendt's, was cast in the form of a vast ideal type. Its central feature was a series of splendidly conceived ideological biographies of the major fascist leaders; in contrast, the sociology of the followers remained on the periphery. Moreover, this ideological emphasis led Nolte to place the eccentric, merely protofascist history of the Action Française on an equal footing with the Italian and German movements. For it was Nolte's contention that fascism needed to be understood as an outgrowth of what in the broadest terms could be called anti-modernism, and the Action Française could serve as the ideological bridge from the nineteenth-century counterrevolutionary currents to the twentieth-century parties launched by Mussolini and Hitler. Without question the antimodernist tendency ranked as one of the major components of fascism; it had already engaged

83. Besides the German anthologies ed. by Abendroth and Nolte already cited, one should note the following Italian works: Costanzo Casucci, ed., *Il Fascismo* (Bologna, 1961), which is limited to Italy, and Renzo De Felice, ed., *Il Fascismo: Le interpretazioni dei contemporanei e degli storici* (Bari, 1970), which includes Germany also.
84. See, for example, Hans Rogger and Eugen Weber, eds., *The European Right: A Historical Profile* (Berkeley and Los Angeles, 1965); *International Fascism 1920–1945* (special no. of the *Journal of Contemporary History*) (I, No. 1, 1966); S. J. Woolf, ed., *European Fascism* (New York, 1968) and *The Nature of Fascism* (New York, 1968).
85. *Der Faschismus in seiner Epoche* (Munich, 1963).

the attention of Mannheim, and it was of particular concern to the specialized students of the phenomenon who dealt with the satellite "fascisms" of southern and eastern Europe. But Nolte's almost exclusive stress upon it meant that his book gave little guide to the concrete workings of fascist institutions. Nor did it distinguish adequately among those who led, those who followed, and those who merely profited from fascist rule. Most particularly, Nolte failed to explain how movements that were by definition antimodernist and antirational could so often have fostered economic concentration and the growth of major industry.[86] The absence of such discriminations among different types of class behavior and of any assessment of fascism's economic base suggested how far Nolte had departed from the tough-mindedness of a Salvemini or a Neumann.

With this gap in the only important work of synthesis, it was left for the authors of monographs and essays to ascertain whether the earlier socioeconomic interpretation stood up when tested against the new data now available. In the case of Italy, Salvemini appeared substantially vindicated. Again and again studies of Fascist society drew attention to the crucial role that economic interest played in winning reliable supporters for the regime from among the propertied classes. In the countryside of the north and center it was clear that this support had rallied early: the Fascists alone could give agrarian proprietors—particularly those enriched by wartime and postwar profits—the protection they required against the militance of the landless laborers; the rural struggles of the years 1920 and 1921 figured in retrospect as pitting the propertied who had benefited from inflation against those whose real wages had fallen.[87] Among the businessmen, as Salvemini had already indicated, the rallying to Fascism proved to have been slower and more cautious; large organized industry did not fully accept the regime until it had been in power for nearly three years. And detailed study of the attitudes of the leading industrialists bore out Salvemini's contention that Mussolini was obliged to act

86. See the critique in Sauer, "National Socialism: Totalitarianism or Fascism?" pp. 413–414, and the more sympathetic review by Klaus Epstein: "A New Study of Fascism," *World Politics*, XVI (Jan. 1964), 302–321.
87. Manlio Rossi-Doria, "L'agricoltura italiana, il dopoguerra e il fascismo" (lecture delivered in 1954), in Casucci, *Il Fascismo*, pp. 308–309.

as mediator in keeping at bay the conflicting pressures impinging upon him, and that among the groups to be placated none demanded greater tact than major industry. Fortunately for the Duce, he and the big businessmen cared about different things: "while to the industrialists economics was everything, to Mussolini everything was politics." Each manipulated the other; "each had something that the other wanted."[88]

Thus the picture which emerged of Italian Fascist rule a quarter-century after the fall of the regime was once again that of an alliance of disparate partners who "were never united by positive affinities." While the industrialists did indeed succeed in taming organized labor and in subverting the corporative institutions from the announced goal of class reconciliation, they never liked or really trusted "the political activists of lower middle class extraction" to whose ultimate authority they were obliged to defer. Yet the balance sheet found Italian capitalism intact and strengthened: as Salvemini had already bitingly observed, even the state intervention of the depression years had "relieved private capital of all responsibility for its unprofitable commitments and left it free to concentrate on the development of profitable investments."[89]

In the case of Germany, the postwar critiques of the socioeconomic interpretation eventually coalesced into at least three rectifications of the earlier view. It now appeared that Hitler's rise to power was only marginally aided by the financial contributions of big business; it was also evident that Nazi rule had brought about more widespread social changes than had occurred in Italy under Fascism; and finally it seemed established that politics and ideological leadership exerted a primacy over economic power in the Reich to an extent that never obtained south of the Alps.[90] These

88. Roland Sarti, *Fascism and the Industrial Leadership in Italy, 1919–1940* (Berkeley and Los Angeles, 1971), pp. 38, 75.

89. *Ibid.*, pp. 95–98, 113, 122.

90. On these three questions (in the above order), see Henry Ashby Turner, Jr., "Big Business and the Rise of Hitler," *The American Historical Review*, LXXV (Oct. 1969), 56–70; David Schoenbaum, *Hitler's Social Revolution* (Garden City, N.Y., 1966); T. W. Mason, "The Primacy of Politics—Politics and Economics in National Socialist Germany," in Woolf, *Nature of Fascism*, pp. 165–195.

modifications taken together—more particularly the second and third—suggested that the wartime imperatives with which Neumann had tried to reckon in the second edition of his work had operated more drastically than the author of *Behemoth* had supposed. The big businessmen, it was true, had held on to their factories and their profits; but the siege conditions of war had narrowed their range of decision and imposed a democratization of personal relations and an increase in social mobility which Neumann had omitted from his account.

Yet even the revisers of Neumann's work alike paid their respects to *Behemoth* and took it as their point of departure.[91] And the way in which they differed with him gave the clue to a major distinction between the Italian and the German varieties of fascism which Neumann had appreciated but which he had expressed clumsily and in his characteristic legalist fashion. In his subsidiary or "Hobbesian" argument, he had drawn attention to the fact that in Italy the theoretical bases of the state had remained unchallenged; nor had there occurred any such dissolution of societal norms as had accompanied the rule of Hitler. Neumann had fastened on matters of particular interest to political theory in formulating his sense that there was something peculiar and extreme about the German fascist experience. If he had shifted the axis of his interpretation to focus rather on the individual, microscopic, but cumulative social change that the war had produced—if he had stressed the aspects of Nazi practice that in fact rather than in ideology had revolutionary implications for the future—it might have been clearer why he, in common with most of his contemporaries, saw Nazism as a special case, while continuing to regard the Italian variant as the "normal" form of fascist rule. Here too, in the renewed interest they directed toward Mussolini's Italy, the writers of the 1960's echoed the verdict of a generation earlier.[92]

91. For example, Mason's statement (p. 166 n.), "*Behemoth* remains the best single work on the Third Reich," and Schoenbaum's (p. 272) that Neumann gave "a generally accurate reflection of the basic social situation."

92. For example, Sauer, in "National Socialism: Totalitarianism or Fascism?" p. 421, speaks of "Mediterranean" fascism as the "original" form and of Nazism as a "special form." A similar emphasis is apparent in Renzo De Felice's brief but comprehensive survey: *Le interpretazioni del fascismo*, 4th ed. (Bari, 1972).

In 1969 *Behemoth* was at last supplanted by another closely
packed, single-volume study of the Third Reich which now could
draw on the wide range of new literature that the intervening
three decades had produced. A skilled historian who had already
published a monumental study of Hitler's seizure of power, Karl
Dietrich Bracher wrote a very different type of book from Neumann's. It was judicious and nominalist in tone, and it ventured
few assertions about the nature of fascism in general. Yet its
author apparently regarded the term as still useful, stressing in
brief but telling passages the tension between party leaders and
businessmen as members of the new Nazi elite. Under Hitler, he
concluded, Germany's "economic and social structures" had been
"subject to profound political and administrative encroachment,"
but they had been "neither destroyed nor basically reorganized."[93]
In sum, Bracher offered a synthesis of the post-*Behemoth* revisions
in the assessment of National Socialism along with a reaffirmation
of what Neumann had maintained about the tenacity of Germany's vested interests.

More broadly, a large number of the studies published in the
1960's aimed to bring up to date the analysis of fascism's socioeconomic base that in the previous generation had been nearly
monopolized by Marxists or bourgeois radicals. From such studies
there began to emerge something resembling a new consensus. It
seemed clear that in the case of Italy the revolutionary or anticapitalist rhetoric of Mussolini's movement could be discounted (as
Salvemini had long ago contended) or at the very most treated as
the faith of a minority of true believers. In the case of Germany,
the record looked more mixed; yet even here fascism's revolutionary potential had apparently found its embodiment more in the by-
products of wartime stringencies than in any conscious acts
directed against Germany's propertied classes. In both countries,
the highly charged, ambivalent relationship between industrial and
preindustrial values seemed to give the key to much that was
bewildering or contradictory in fascist practice. Perhaps one could

93. Karl Dietrich Bracher, *Die deutsche Diktatur* (Cologne and Berlin,
1969), trans. by Jean Steinberg as *The German Dictatorship* (New York,
1970), p. 331.

say that fascism took hold "where preindustrial traditions were both strongest and most alien to industrialism and, hence, where the rise of the latter caused a major break with the past and substantial losses to the nonindustrial classes."[94] Such a generalization fitted Italy and Germany equally well, pinpointing what two societies that looked so dissimilar in fact had in common.

In this view, fascism was a movement of those who had lost out to industrialism. "An analysis in terms of economic growth" suggested that the degree of their radicalization "must somehow be related to the degree of industrialization. The more highly industrialized a society, the more violent the reaction of the losers. Thus Germany stood at the top, Italy lagged behind, and Spain and others were at the bottom." The fascist "radicalism of the Right" preached the "rottenness" of modern society and a return to "the good old values." It presented "the intriguing paradox of a revolutionary mass movement whose goals were antirevolutionary." Its reactionary stance was "fundamentalist," as Talcott Parsons had phrased it in an essay contemporaneous with the work of Borgese and Mannheim and Fromm.[95] All these, of course, had correctly seen the lower middle classes as the main proponents of "fundamentalism." Yet they had been unable to explain why such reactionary (or, if one prefers, revolutionary) aspirations had been disappointed, why the fascist leaders had been unable to put into practice the ideology they shared with their most loyal followers. If a return to preindustrial values—if a reconciliation of classes in a restored sense of community—had been one of the basic fascist aims, why had its attainment proved impossible?

Here the simple answer, as Salvemini and Neumann had already proposed, was that the power of large industrial capital could not be broken. It might be bent or curbed, as happened in Germany, but its toughness and resiliency astounded friend and foe alike. After all, if the fascist powers were to gird for war, they needed the economic base that heavy industry alone could supply. And the

94. Sauer, "National Socialism: Totalitarianism or Fascism?" pp. 415, 420.
95. *Ibid.*, pp. 417, 419; Talcott Parsons, "Some Sociological Aspects of the Fascist Movements" (originally published in 1942), *Essays in Sociological Theory*, rev. ed. (New York, 1954), p. 137.

major industrialists were well aware of their own indispensability. Military preparation and a return to preindustrial community values were incompatible goals, and Mussolini and Hitler, in terms of their own hierarchy of aims, had no alternative but to choose the former. In this ultimate sense the primacy of politics over economics in the fascist systems had the curious result of preserving the economic status quo, while systematically sacrificing those who put their faith in the political ideology of the movement.

Fascist Italy and Nazi Germany, then, were doomed to remain industrial powers. The process of modernization proved irreversible—indeed it was notably accelerated in the generation following Mussolini's and Hitler's fall. Thus those scholars, notably Mannheim and Neumann, who had broadened their treatment of fascism to include some assessment of contemporary industrial society were amply vindicated. And an analysis in terms of class relationships was correspondingly confirmed when it became clear to the investigators of the 1960's, as it had been to those of the 1930's, that the major social drama of fascism in power had been the muted, unrecognized, but deadly struggle between two segments of the middle class—between the faithful followers from the old lower middle class, whose fidelity for the most part went unrewarded, and the new industrial upper bourgeoisie, which consolidated its holdings and maintained its profits.

Such a class analysis might further suggest that in the long view the antilabor policy that the fascist regimes pursued did not have as fatal consequences as Salvemini and Neumann had supposed. Organized labor, like large capital, was indispensable in advanced industrial society, and its situation of potential strength began to bring results with the onset of prosperity in the 1950's. In this case the error in the "classic" studies of fascism was the reverse of the one usually charged to them: rather than overstressing the economic factor, as their critics maintained, they had not given it sufficient weight. Or, to put the matter in terms of analytical method, far from succumbing to doctrinaire Marxism, they had not been Marxist enough.

On balance, a broadly Marxist canon of interpretation had worked better in the critique of fascism than any alternative schema. It had adhered more closely to the concrete details of existence under the rule of Mussolini and Hitler than had the method subsequently proposed—the loose ideal type procedure epitomized in the work of Hannah Arendt and Ernst Nolte. Nor had the passion infusing *Behemoth* and *Under the Axe of Fascism* vitiated their conclusions. Since their authors made no claim to being "value-free" and had alerted their readers to their own critical stance, they had given no grounds for a complaint of propagandist distortion. Neither Salvemini nor Neumann ever knowingly juggled his data to fit his argument; both were far too conscientious scholars for that. And the fact that the investigators of a generation later reached conclusions which in so many respects resembled theirs gave further proof that their emotional involvement in their subject matter had not figured as an insuperable handicap.

Yet what there was of Marxism in *Behemoth*—or even more clearly in *Under the Axe of Fascism*—was far from systematic or thoroughgoing. It amounted to little more than a deep-running conviction of the primacy of class and interest-group conflict in modern society. In this working hypothesis the critics of fascism had remained true to the reassessment of the Marxian heritage that had engaged the minds of so many social thinkers, Marxist and non-Marxist alike, at the turn of the century.[96] Subsequently there had come the writings of Lukács and the publication of Marx's own manuscripts of the early 1840's, and with them a new wave of Marxist theory and a reemphasis on the Hegelian concept of alienation. These theoretical rediscoveries had not touched Salvemini at all; they had affected Neumann only marginally through the work of his émigré friends. Both had held to an eclectic and practical definition of social-science method. The neo-Hegelian Marxism of the second quarter of the twentieth century was to put its stamp on the thought of the emigration at a more rarefied level, in a philosophical critique of a phenomenon that was wider and more pervasive than fascism, a critique of what came to be called mass society.

96. See my *Consciousness and Society*, Chapter 3.

CHAPTER

4

The Critique of Mass Society

I N THE COURSE of the 1950's the concept of mass society began to win acceptance among the more speculative American sociologists. The publication of David Riesman's *The Lonely Crowd* at the midcentury had both reflected and stimulated a mood of national soul-searching. What this work and its successors had in common was the effort to locate and define the attributes that distinguished the contemporary United States—and by implication other advanced industrial societies—from the phenomena of fully developed capitalism and clearly drawn class lines that earlier social critics, Marxist and non-Marxist alike, had more or less taken for granted. The American analysis of mass society was not uniformly polemical in intent. Yet the experience of cold war abroad and McCarthyism at home of necessity gave it a tone of moral urgency. At the very least it was prompted by anxiety and a sense of intellectual disorientation.

The term "mass society" was shot through with ambiguities: the ways in which it was used were imprecise, overlapping, and frequently contradictory. Sometimes its emphasis was on undifferentiated numbers, sometimes on mechanization, sometimes on bureaucratic predominance. Yet for all their fuzziness of language, the analysts of mass society agreed on a few defining characteristics: what they saw about them was a situation at once uniform and fluid—a state of social "nakedness" in which the notion of community seemed to be slipping away and the individual lacked a cushion of intermediate groups to protect him against direct and overwhelming pressure from the wielders of political and economic power.[1]

Warnings of the threat from the masses were nothing new in Western social thought. The nineteenth century had seen the forebodings of men as diverse as Burckhardt and Nietzsche, Tocqueville and Henry Adams. The first generation of the twentieth had produced the nostalgic musings of Ortega y Gasset and the more systematic analyses of the Italian trio of Croce and Mosca and Pareto. But these had been aristocrats both in their social position and in their intellectual stance: they had shrunk in fastidious revulsion from the vulgarity or "leveling" of taste and opinion that the enfranchisement of the masses was bringing in its wake. The great novelty in the mid-twentieth-century critique of mass society was its democratic inspiration. Those who wrote of America in the 1950's accepted the transition to highly concentrated industrial conditions as an accomplished fact; they did not suggest that the process of modernization could be either undone or stopped. Their underlying moral purpose was not to preserve what was left of a society based on status and cultural privilege; it was rather to protect the mass men themselves from the fruits of their own liberation by exposing what had been lost in the process.

Such was true for the most part of the native-born Americans. The émigrés were more likely to be skeptical of political democracy—at least in the form in which they saw it around them—and to discover their ideological point of departure in Marxism. But the Marxian doctrine that alone made sense to them was curious in lacking a historical protagonist. It derived instead from a massive disappointment—disappointment in the course of recent history, in the strategy of the political parties that laid claim to the inheritance of Marx, and, most particularly, in the proletariat itself. The class which Engels had celebrated as the "heirs of classical philosophy" had failed to perform in the style expected of

1. Daniel Bell, "America as a Mass Society: A Critique," *The End of Ideology* (Glencoe, Ill., 1960), pp. 21–25; William Kornhauser, *The Politics of Mass Society* (Glencoe, Ill., 1959), pp. 23, 30, 114–115. For a survey of the literature, see also Cesare Mannucci, *La società di massa* (Milan, 1967).

it. It had preferred creature comforts to heroism, and kitsch to the elevation of its intellect.[2]

Thus at the hands of the émigré students of mass society, what had been propounded in the nineteenth century as an *economic* critique of capitalist relationships became transformed into a *cultural* critique of the business civilization that large-scale industry had produced. Implicit in such an analysis was the assumption that mere abundance would never suffice. However close capitalism might come to the century-old socialist aim of eliminating poverty and drudgery—and in the affluent circumstances of 1950 such an eventuality did not yet appear far-fetched—humanity's plight would remain unchanged. As long as men's perceptions of their work (and play) were "alienated" or "reified"—as long as in a world whose quintessence was *Entfremdung* and *Verdinglichung* people acquiesced in their own transmutation into "things"—it was pointless to vest one's hopes in a merely technical shift of ownership in the means of production. The Soviet Union stood as the sobering example: though the critics of mass society offered widely varying interpretations of the realities of contemporary Russian life, they were agreed that the goal of a more authentic human existence was still far from attained.

Some such assessment of the nature of twentieth-century industrial society was presupposed in Franz Neumann's *Behemoth*, more especially in the parts that dealt with the working classes. But Neumann's focus was primarily legal and economic; he touched only tangentially on the issue of mass culture. It remained for men with whom he was once closely associated—Max Horkheimer, Theodor W. Adorno, and Herbert Marcuse—to try to discover the link between technological rationality and the aesthetic and moral values of the contemporary masses. In this latter view, fascism figured not as the polar opposite of liberal democracy but as the "most extreme example" of a trend that was general throughout the industrialized West—a "trend towards irrational

2. Edward Shils, "Daydreams and Nightmares: Reflections on the Criticism of Mass Culture" (first published in slightly different form in *Sewanee Review*, LXV [1957]), *The Intellectuals and the Powers and Other Essays* (Chicago, 1972), pp. 249–252.

domination."[3] As Adorno was to put it, "In the body movements that machines" demanded "of those who served them," there could already be detected what was violent and incessant and unrelenting in "fascist abuse."[4]

Adorno, Horkheimer, Marcuse, and their like had been disturbed by the cultural corollaries of a machine civilization long before their emigration from Germany. But it was the move to America that gave these concerns an immediate relevance. If there was indeed an underlying cultural uniformity in which all the advanced industrial nations shared, how did the democratic United States differ in its essentials from the authoritarian National Socialist Reich? If ideological ignorance and apathy, stereotyped thinking and the cult of "personality," were the predestined political manifestations of mass society, what would prevent the Americans from following where the Germans had pointed the way? Was it possible—even probable—that the same threatening forces which had driven the émigrés from their homeland were now confronting them in a more subdued and disguised form in their country of refuge? These agonizing questions led naturally to an exploration of the features of American society that appeared to hold a "fascist potential"—the blander varieties of social coercion which figured as the functional equivalents of what the Nazis had accomplished through terror and violence. The behavior that Riesman was subsequently to identify as "other direction" could be observed under ideal conditions in the United States. And in California, where Adorno and Horkheimer eventually chose to settle, the practice of taking one's cue from the subtle but overpowering pressure of one's fellow citizens was daily displayed with the naïveté of people who found in it nothing to be ashamed of.

All this would have been enough in itself to give the émigrés pause. To it was added a sense of intense personal exposure. In Europe it had been possible for intellectuals to protect their own

3. Martin Jay, *The Dialectical Imagination: A History of the Frankfurt School and the Institute of Social Research 1923–1950* (Boston, 1973), p. 166.
4. *Minima Moralia: Reflexionen aus dem beschädigten Leben* (Frankfurt, 1951), p. 60.

lives from the inroads of popular culture. Shielded by the ramparts of traditional status and respect, they had been able to keep at a safe distance the grosser and more offensive manifestations of mass taste. With the move to America, these walls collapsed: a flood of vulgarity struck the new arrivals in the face. And correspondingly their mood became more embattled: what in Europe had been no more than "vague disdain" in the United States turned into an "elaborate loathing."[5]

Yet in this respect, as in so many others, Adorno and his friends viewed the combat they were waging as an ambiguous two-front struggle. In the task of subjecting to unsparing criticism the tastes and attitudes of the masses, they found it patently insufficient merely to defend the values of traditional "high culture." For one thing, it was not really the masses' fault if they behaved so disappointingly. It was rather the fault of the economic relationships that dominated their existence or, in more personal terms, of those who systematically manipulated the lives of others. Perhaps it was for this reason that Adorno and Horkheimer did not use the term "mass society"; they preferred to speak of the *verwaltete Welt*— "the world of the administered life." Within such a world, they thought, it would be reactionary to join the run of critics whose conservatism expressed itself in a frantic attempt to cling to bits and pieces of the cultural values of the past. Unaware of the social processes from which true culture sprang, critics of this sort were guilty of a special and insidious kind of "fetishizing": in handling art and literature as prized "goods," they tore them from their spontaneous context and rendered them lifeless. Under such circumstances, the authentic and fully conscious critic could not side with those who made a cult of the mind or spirit. Nor could he enroll in the far more crowded ranks of the enemies of traditional civilized values. Still more, it was questionable whether there was any high culture left to defend: its purveyors had so dressed it up and "neutralized" it as to reduce it to "trash." "Self-sufficient contemplation" would not do; even to speak of what had gone wrong ran the risk of degenerating into mere chatter; "after

5. Shils, "Daydreams and Nightmares," p. 258.

Auschwitz," Adorno concluded, in his most poignant cry of despair, it was "barbaric" to go on writing poetry.[6]

1. *The Return to Hegel*

The major presupposition behind the émigré critique of mass society was a view of the world that to Americans was alien and virtually unknown—a Marxist doctrine renewed by a return to its Hegelian source. Beginning with the appearance of Lukács's *History and Class Consciousness* in 1923, there had occurred within the "ancient Central European heartland of the Marxist tradition" a "revival of metaphysical idealism." Communist party discipline had forced Lukács to repudiate his youthful aberrations. For all practical purposes he had subscribed to the "orthodox" view of dialectical materialism as the mechanical working out of fixed economic laws.[7] But he could not prevent his writings from leading a life of their own; the underground reputation of *History and Class Consciousness* continued to grow; and the publication in the early 1930's of the *Economic and Philosophical Manuscripts* in which the young Marx had gropingly formulated his original conception of human society had given Lukács a retrospective validation—it was now apparent that the Hungarian literary critic turned revolutionary had divined by a process of sympathetic reconstruction what his ideological master had written nearly eighty years before.[8]

Adorno and Horkheimer referred only rarely to Marx's Paris manuscripts. Their relations with Lukács were distant and for the most part hostile. They also denied that they were idealists. Despite their disclaimers, a wider view of their work suggests that

6. "Kulturkritik und Gesellschaft" (originally published in 1951), *Prismen* (Frankfurt, 1955), trans. by Samuel and Shierry Weber as *Prisms* (London, 1967), pp. 22–23, 33–34.
7. See the qualified retraction of his original retraction in the preface to the new edition (1967) of *Geschichte und Klassenbewusstsein*, on which the English translation (Cambridge, Mass., 1971) is based.
8. On this whole topic, see George Lichtheim, *From Marx to Hegel* (New York, 1971), pp. 2, 19–21, 38.

they too exemplified the subjectivist reinterpretation of Marxism which in the four decades from the 1920's to the 1960's gave that doctrine a new and enhanced philosophical standing. In such a view, Antonio Gramsci ranks as an isolated Italian precursor and Maurice Merleau-Ponty as a belated and quasi-liberal French propagator of twentieth-century neo-Marxism—a Marxism stripped of its late-nineteenth-century scientific pretenses and thrown back on its early-nineteenth-century Hegelian base. For ideologists of this stamp, the concept of alienation offered the key to social analysis. It was the guiding term which bound together the most diverse thinkers. (The discussion of alienated labor was after all the centerpiece of Marx's own early manuscripts.) Originally employed by Hegel, with its range expanded through the work of Nietzsche and Freud, the word "alienation" eventually took on universal connotations as an overarching characterization of contemporary existence. It carried the promise that those who had been reduced from "ends" to "means," who had even lost all feeling for the wrong that had been done them, could be restored to full humanity through a laborious process of bringing into consciousness the dismal contrast between men's current behavior and the potentialities that lay within them unused.

Max Horkheimer was the dominating figure in the Institut für Sozialforschung (Institute for Social Research) founded in Frankfurt in 1923. Privately endowed and loosely affiliated with the city's university, which was itself less than a decade old, the Institut insisted on and managed to maintain its intellectual and ideological independence. Marxism—variously understood—was the common denominator that linked the Institut's associates. Indeed, it was for reasons of prudence alone that the word was not included in its title. As the Institut's researches developed, however, and competing intellectual influences impinged upon it, this original identification was to become ever more nuanced.[9]

A second point of common experience was Jewish origin. Nearly all the Institut's leading members came from prosperous, assimi-

9. The early history of the Institut and the biographies of Horkheimer and Adorno are fully detailed in Jay, *Dialectical Imagination*, Chapter 1.

lated Jewish families. Yet as was so often the case with German Jews, they preferred most of the time not to speak of the matter or to speak of it with a certain embarrassment. Not until the advent of Hitler and the Institut's move to America did the question of anti-Semitism come to rank high among their concerns. Meantime they were distinguished as particularly outspoken representatives of the cosmopolitan and freethinking minority within the German academic community—a minority whose tendency to look to France for inspiration dated back to Heine and to Marx himself.

The beginnings of the extraordinary collaboration between Horkheimer and Adorno are difficult to establish with precision. They made each other's acquaintance in 1922—the year before the Institut was founded—but it was not until a decade and a half later that Adorno became formally associated with that body. The coalescence of their minds seems to have been a gradual process which eventually reached a point of such fusion that Horkheimer could flatly refer to their philosophies as "one."[10] A symbiosis of this sort is extremely rare in intellectual history: the parallels that most readily spring to mind are the collaboration between Tocqueville and Beaumont and that between Marx and Engels. But in these earlier cases it was apparent who was the junior partner: both at the time and in the view of posterity one mind clearly dominated the other. Adorno and Horkheimer's relationship was less simple: while the former wrote much more and became far better known, the latter was the man who organized their common projects and the one to whom his partner deferred. The secret of their untroubled friendship—which went as deep personally as it did in the intellectual sphere—apparently lay in a happy contrast of temperaments and a largely fortuitous division of responsibilities.

Horkheimer was eight years Adorno's senior. Born in 1895, the son of a prosperous Stuttgart manufacturer, he had just completed his graduate studies in philosophy when he served as one of the Institut's founding associates. Hence his whole mature life was bound up with that body, and the history of its migrations was identical with his own. It was not until 1930, however, when he

10. Preface to *Eclipse of Reason* (New York, 1947), p. vii.

became its director and was named to a new chair in "social philosophy," that Horkheimer took his place as the Institut's tenured representative on the University of Frankfurt faculty and the leading spirit within the Institut itself. As the title of his professorship suggested, his understanding of philosophy was broad and unconventional. It also involved a passionate commitment to social change. Although Horkheimer lost his ideological model with the murder of Rosa Luxemburg in 1919 and never discovered another political leader toward whom he could feel entire sympathy, his adherence to a Marxist interpretation of events and a Marxist stress on the unity of theory and practice remained unwavering.

As a young man, Horkheimer seems to have been moody and diffident. By the 1930's he had gained a self-confidence which apparently got sturdier as his life went on. Perhaps the change was associated with a brief but apparently helpful psychoanalysis that he underwent in 1928–1929. In any case the personality which came to the fore in exile was that of a strong and even ruthless organizer—what in the United States would be called a promoter—with something of a Mephistophelean manner. As he gained in personal force, however, the matter of putting his thoughts on paper, which had never been easy for him, grew still more troublesome. Thus it was that he increasingly served as the protector and fosterer of the cherished friend who by the same token became the one who usually gave the final form to what they had talked out in common.

"Teddie" Adorno has been described by a younger associate as an "unguarded" human being who was constantly in need of human shelter. "Unguarded," that is, in the sense of never learning to play the game of being an adult and never seeing through the petty stratagems by which others lived and took advantage of him. He joined the Institut late and stayed clear of its organizational struggles. When at the end of his life he became a professor, he did not behave in the accepted academic fashion and seemed ill at ease in his new role. Although he achieved eminence in at least four fields—philosophy, musicology, literary criticism, and sociology—it was only in the last of these that he received full recognition by the professional guild. (When as an elderly man he was chosen president of the German Sociological Association, he was overcome by a childlike joy.) Throughout his career Adorno figured as an "eccentric," on the margin of corporate intellectual endeavor.[11]

In his writings from exile, Adorno more than once referred to the "damaged" (*beschädigtes*) life. But it was not necessarily his own that he had in mind. The offspring of wealthy parents—his father was a Frankfurt wine merchant—he had had a happy childhood and youth in which his every taste was indulged. Music and cosmopolitanism were in the air he breathed. (He was eventually to prefer his mother's exotic-sounding name, that of a Corsican-French army officer who had married a German singer, to his paternal name of Wiesengrund.) Having already studied composition at home and taken his doctorate in philosophy, he was turning twenty-two when he went to Vienna in 1925 to work under Arnold Schönberg's disciple Alban Berg. There he frequented the circle around Schönberg, with whom he was to renew his acquaintance in California many years later. Although Adorno returned in 1928 to Frankfurt and to philosophy, he remained, as had been true of Nietzsche, a philosopher whose life was suffused by music. In this sense the damage wrought him by external events could always find an inner compensation. Never lacking for money, enclosed by the devotion of his great friend and his utterly loyal wife, Adorno managed to live a rare and uncompromisingly intellectual existence right up to the bizarre tragedy with which his life ended.

Horkheimer and Adorno described their work as "critical theory." By this they meant a style of thought that proceeded from negation to negation until its subject matter had been bounded or pierced by a series of devastating cross-fires. Unsystematic by definition and practice (Horkheimer almost invariably preferred the essay form to the organized treatise, and Adorno did so most of the time), critical theory was necessarily hostile to every sort of closed philosophical structure. Thus its debt to Hegel lay more in its method of attack than in its ultimate development. Like most twentieth-century neo-Hegelians, Adorno and Horkheimer

11. Jürgen Habermas in *Die Zeit*, September 12, 1969.

esteemed the author of the youthful, intellectually open, and potentially revolutionary *Phenomenology of Mind* rather than the established Berlin professor who had composed *The Philosophy of Right* and *The Philosophy of History*. In thus discriminating between the early and the later Hegel, they were following in the path of the original Left Hegelians and of Marx himself. But they were not returning simply to the idea-world of the 1840's. Too much, both in social change and in the history of ideas, had happened in the meantime. The moment of consciousness of the European proletariat had come and gone, and a host of new philosophies had crowded Hegel from his erstwhile lonely eminence. Horkheimer's earliest philosophical enthusiasm had been for Hegel's deadly enemy Schopenhauer, whom he was to celebrate nearly a half-century later as the unsparing destroyer of human illusions and the ancestor of psychoanalytic theory. And of course beyond Schopenhauer lay not only Freud but Dilthey and Weber and Mannheim, the whole new German intellectual pantheon, most of whom had had little use for Hegel.[12]

Critical theory, then, found itself obliged to integrate with the Hegelian inheritance the social thought of the succeeding century. In its unremitting process of negation, it was led to employ "the Hegelian method beyond and against Hegel's own system." The result was a new type of dialectic, methodologically still more subversive than that of Marx, a "dialectic without synthesis."[13] In common with Marx, Adorno and Horkheimer detested the abstractions in which German metaphysics and philosophical idealism had veiled the real world; they similarly reproached Hegel with the primacy he had conferred on the thinking subject. But they refused to fall into what they regarded as the opposite error of vulgar materialism or pseudoscience. Their theory hung precariously between a down-to-earth insistence that "things" took priority over one's perception of them and a rarefied form of expression

12. Jay, *Dialectical Imagination*, pp. 41–44; Max Horkheimer, "Die Aktualität Schopenhauers" (originally published in 1962), trans. for *The Critical Spirit: Essays in Honor of Herbert Marcuse*, ed. by Kurt H. Wolff and Barrington Moore, Jr. (Boston, 1967), pp. 64, 71.
13. George Lichtheim, "Adorno" (originally published in *The Times Literary Supplement*, LXVI [Sept. 28, 1967]), *From Marx to Hegel*, p. 140; Gian Enrico Rusconi, *La teoria critica della società* (Bologna, 1968), p. 245.

which was itself abstract in the extreme. In this latter sense they remained in the idealist and metaphysical mold. Moreover, in maintaining even more rigorously than Hegel that nothing could be known directly, that everything in the natural or human universe was "mediated" by something else, critical theory was as many-sided, as elusive, and as bewildering as the thought of the late Wittgenstein.

The two key terms—one favorable and one pejorative—which regularly recurred throughout Horkheimer and Adorno's writings were "reason" and "positivism." The former carried the traditional Hegelian meaning of a quality that subject and object potentially had in common: "a principle inherent in reality"; the latter served as a catch-all for a number of intellectual tendencies which critical theory opposed. If the social thinkers of the turn of the century had already been inclined to lump their dislikes under the word "positivism," Adorno and Horkheimer's usage was looser still. The two Frankfurt philosophers not only dismissed as positivist the materialism and "scientism" that had been the particular targets of the critique of the 1890's;[14] they included along with them the whole nominalist, empiricist tradition. Thus at their hands the logical positivism or logical empiricism of the 1920's and 1930's fared no better than the cruder forms of such doctrines whose errors these twentieth-century philosophies had tried to correct: all figured alike as enemies of "reason," since all of them had reduced it to a merely "subjective faculty of the mind."[15]

Frank irrationalism, one scarcely needs add, stood condemned before critical theory as worse still. And where the self-declared foes of reason had come to power—notably in Nazi Germany—Adorno and Horkheimer's attitude was necessarily one of passionate revulsion. Here once more they found themselves in a war on two fronts: German "thinking with the blood" they loathed with a hatred even mightier than that they directed against Anglo-American empiricism. At the same time they suspected that these two views of the world were not in as total contradiction as was commonly assumed. One was perhaps the historical result of the other. The most original and jarring feature of Adorno and

14. See my *Consciousness and Society* (New York, 1958), Chapter 2.
15. Horkheimer, *Eclipse of Reason*, p. 5.

Horkheimer's thought was the conviction which gradually settled upon them that twentieth-century neobarbarism was the direct heir of the eighteenth-century Enlightenment.

All the foregoing figured in embryo in a programmatic essay entitled "Traditional and Critical Theory" that Horkheimer published in 1937. Here the word "traditional" did service in much the same inclusive fashion in which "positivism" usually made its appearance. In the study of society, Horkheimer explained, empiricists and traditional theorists were only superficially at odds: basically they held to the same theoretical model—a model derived from natural science and primarily from mathematics. This "eternal Logos" determined the way they conducted their own work; they isolated themselves from the life about them, parceling out their investigations as the specialized division of labor dictated. Critical theory, in contrast, tried to understand the human universe "in the context of real social processes"; it was "dominated at every turn by a concern for reasonable (*vernünftig*) conditions of life."[16]

As opposed to the "aimless intellectual game, half conceptual poetry, half impotent expression of states of mind"—which was all that in Horkheimer's view traditional social theory amounted to— he urged his fellow intellectuals to direct their thought toward the emancipation of mankind and "an alteration of society as a whole." "Reason," he explained, could not "become transparent to itself" as long as men acted "as members of an organism" that was lacking in reason. Thus, in terms of critical theory, the distinction between the scholar's "scientific" role and his role as citizen on which Weber had insisted so strenuously made no sense at all. It sundered the human unity of intellectual labor: "in genuinely critical thought," research and value, knowledge and action, were inextricably entangled; here explanation signified "not only a logical process but a concrete historical one as well. In the course of it both . . . social structure . . . and the relation of the theo-

16. "Traditionelle und kritische Theorie" (originally published in *Zeitschrift für Sozialforschung*, VI [1937]), *Kritische Theorie*, II (Frankfurt, 1968), trans. by Matthew J. O'Connell for *Critical Theory* (New York, 1972), pp. 191, 194, 197–199. The translated volume is a selection from Horkheimer's two-volume collected essays.

retician to society" underwent alteration; the explainer changed along with the matter he was explaining.[17]

In another essay published earlier in the same year, Horkheimer had stressed more bluntly the interconnectedness of the thinker's two roles:

> When an active individual of sound common sense perceives the sordid state of the world, desire to change it becomes the guiding principle by which he organizes given facts and shapes them into a theory. The methods and categories as well as the transformations of the theory can be understood only in connection with his taking of sides. This, in turn, discloses both his sound common sense and the character of the world. Right thinking depends as much on right willing as right willing on right thinking.[18]

This activist definition of the intellectual's task condemned as an "evasion of theoretical effort" the sentimental leftism which was "satisfied to proclaim with reverent admiration the creative strength of the proletariat." A "professional optimism," a "happy feeling" of finding oneself "linked with an immense force," might well turn to despair in "periods of crushing defeat" such as that in which Horkheimer himself was writing. It was better for the social critic to face being thrown "back upon himself" in ideological isolation. Nor should the thought which derived from a withdrawal into theory be confused with "an abstract utopia." Whatever it might have "in common with fantasy," it rested on the bedrock conviction that there was "only one truth" and that "the positive attributes of honesty, internal consistency, reasonableness, and striving for peace, freedom, and happiness" could not be ascribed "in the same sense to any other theory and practice."[19]

Such a conviction, Horkheimer recognized, meant that to an important extent mind (*Geist*) was "not liberal." The fact that it was "not cut loose from the life of society," that it did "not hang

17. *Ibid.*, pp. 208–211.
18. "Der neueste Angriff auf die Metaphysik" (originally published in *Zeitschrift für Sozialforschung*, VI [1937]), *Kritische Theorie*, II, trans. for *Critical Theory*, p. 162.
19. *Ibid.*, pp. 214, 219–220, 222.

suspended over it," precluded the notion, dear to the "liberalist intelligentsia," of a "detached" (*freischwebend*) role. The mediating function which Mannheim had assigned to social thought was patently incompatible with the formulations of critical theory. At the same time Horkheimer was prepared to say that mind was indeed liberal in the sense of tolerating "no external coercion, no revamping of its results to suit the will of one or another power."[20] Throughout the next three decades of their intellectual labors he and Adorno were to wrestle with the dialectical relationship between the liberal and the illiberal aspects of their thought, as they stoically accepted the isolation which events forced upon them.

ii. *Max Horkheimer and Theodor W. Adorno:*
The Years in America

When these preliminary definitions of critical theory were elaborated, the Frankfurt philosophers had already been four years in exile. The advent of Hitler had doomed the Institut für Sozialforschung: as a Marxist-oriented body, consisting almost entirely of scholars of Jewish origin, it was doubly anathema to the Nazis. In March 1933 its activities in Germany came to an end; Horkheimer escaped to Switzerland; and in the following month his name appeared among the first batch of university professors whom the new regime had dismissed from their posts.

After a brief sojourn in Geneva, the Institut moved in 1934 to the United States, where Columbia University had offered it hospitality. Here Adorno—who had spent a half-decade in Oxford and London—officially joined its ranks in 1938. The fact that the Institut had its own private endowment (prudently transferred abroad in time to escape seizure by the Nazis) gave it a mobility which comparable organizations lacked. But this ease of travel did not mean a corresponding adaptability to a new environment. On Morningside Heights Horkheimer and his associates remained stubbornly European; indeed a number of the latter tarried across

20. *Ibid.*, pp. 223–224.

the Atlantic until the last possible moment. A branch office continued to exist in Paris, and it was from there that the Institut's publications—still in German—regularly appeared.

The fall of France in 1940 and America's entrance into the war a year and a half later changed all that. Now that the tie with Europe had been severed, Horkheimer and his colleagues reluctantly decided to publish in English. Shortly thereafter the Institut underwent a series of internal crises. High costs and unsuccessful new investments forced it to cut its staff and curtail its activities. Fortunately, the American government's wartime need for expertise on Germany helped to solve the Institut's personnel difficulties. A number of its members left for Washington, first among them Franz Neumann, who had joined the group in the mid-1930's. Although the author of *Behemoth* was a new recruit, he had apparently soon taken a leading role in its discussions. As a man of forceful temperament who differed with Horkheimer in his interpretation of Nazism, Neumann had almost inevitably become the director's ideological and organizational rival. His departure for Washington served to head off the clash of two indomitable personalities.

Meantime Horkheimer himself had felt obliged to leave New York. Persuaded by a heart condition to seek a milder climate, he had moved in 1941 to southern California—more precisely to Pacific Palisades, where Thomas Mann had just settled. Here Adorno loyally followed him, as the rump of the Institut which remained on Morningside Heights slowly withered and died.[21] Hence it was in California, where German culture in exile established its most substantial beachhead, that Horkheimer and Adorno were to write the works for which they would be chiefly remembered.

In view of the tenacity with which they clung to their European inheritance and the virulence with which they assailed American mass culture, one might be tempted to conclude that they regarded their experience in the United States as totally negative. Yet such was not Adorno's final judgment. In a reminiscence

21. On all the foregoing, see Jay, *Dialectical Imagination*, pp. 29–31, 37–40, 113–114, 167–169, 172.

published a year before his death—perhaps tempered by the passage of time—he stressed the things he had learned from his hosts that had corrected an imbalance in his intellectual preparation. Although he had arrived, he recalled, "free from nationalism and cultural arrogance," his previous work had been "thoroughly speculative"—directed exclusively toward interpretation. In America he found that people kept asking him for "the evidence" for what he said, and he in turn began to acquire greater respect for empirical methods. Still more, the first assignment that came his way was a study of jazz which was quite at variance with his own intensely cultivated musical tastes. From it, however, he was able to derive such concepts as "pseudo-individualism" and spurious "personalization" that were later to take a prominent place in his social theory. More broadly he discovered—and here his view paralleled Neumann's—that in the United States, as opposed to Weimar Germany, "democratic forms" had "penetrated the whole of life." Beyond that recognition, he naturally questioned the extent to which these forms mirrored the underlying realities—and this was to be the central concern of his years in exile. Yet when all the negative features had been noted, the intellectual debt remained: it was "scarcely an exaggeration to say that any contemporary consciousness" which had not "appropriated the American experience, even if in opposition," had "something reactionary about it."[22]

The book in which these new concerns surfaced was *The Authoritarian Personality*. Although it was the last in point of composition of Adorno and Horkheimer's major writings in exile, it was the first to come to the attention of the wider American public. It was also the one that clashed least with the American intellectual tradition. Thus it makes sense to analyze these writings in reverse order and to work only gradually toward their most challenging formulations.

22. "Scientific Experiences of a European Scholar in America," *The Intellectual Migration: Europe and America, 1930–1960*, ed. by Donald Fleming and Bernard Bailyn (Cambridge, Mass., 1969), pp. 339–340, 351, 367, 369–370.

Launched in 1944 and published in 1950, *The Authoritarian Personality* formed part of a wider collaborative project entitled "Studies in Prejudice." This sort of venture was already familiar to the Institut's associates: its single largest effort in the 1930's had been a series of extended essays on problems of authority and the family. What was new about *The Authoritarian Personality* was its juxtaposition of American and émigré authorship and of empirical and speculative method. While Horkheimer had been its original moving spirit, he did not participate in the actual research and writing; this devolved, for the quantitative analysis of test and interview material, on a team of native-born psychologists based in Berkeley, California, and, for the "qualitative" interpretation, on Adorno himself. Adorno was later to recall that the "cooperation in a democratic spirit" which characterized the work, "in contrast to the academic tradition in Europe," had been "the most fruitful thing" he had experienced in America, and he paid particular tribute to one of his collaborators, R. Nevitt Sanford, who had painstakingly edited his own English prose.[23]

The basic assumption behind *The Authoritarian Personality* was that there existed in the United States—and presumably throughout the Western world—a "fascist potential" which could be isolated in specific individuals. Such men and women manifested what might be called in psychoanalytic terms an "authoritarian syndrome." Deriving from a "sadomasochistic resolution of the Oedipus complex," this syndrome betrayed an unconscious "hatred against the father . . . transformed . . . into love" for those perceived as the strong and directed against the weak and defenseless. In its psychic economy, the Jew frequently became "a substitute for the hated father." And so, predictably, anti-Semitism figured as its key symptom. Among the others was a tendency to think in stereotypes and to be taken in by the facile "personalizing" of public rhetoric, whether in politics or in advertising, along with a stubborn rejection of any utopian vision.[24]

23. *Ibid.*, p. 358.
24. T. W. Adorno, Else Frenkel-Brunswik, Daniel J. Levinson, R. Nevitt Sanford, *The Authoritarian Personality* (New York, 1950), pp. 1, 664–665, 695, 759–760.

The Authoritarian Personality was widely read and commented upon by the American social-science community.[25] Even those who found fault with its methods and conclusions acknowledged its suggestive power. Yet there was something bewildering about the book that eluded nearly all its readers. It had been six years in the making—and it might have taken still longer had Adorno not decided to return to Germany and thereby obliged his colleagues to hurry it to completion without the overhaul and shortening by which it could have profited. In a quieter period, such a lapse of time would have made little difference. In this case, the book was published in an ideological atmosphere sharply at variance with the one in which it had been projected. As David Riesman complained, it addressed itself to the problem of twenty years ago. Anti-Semitism was no longer the issue. Although *The Authoritarian Personality* appeared in the very year in which Joseph McCarthy launched his campaign of defamation, it dealt only tangentially with the mass fears on which the Senator played with consummate skill: its frame of reference was still a European-style fascism markedly different from what was currently threatening the United States.[26]

From the methodological standpoint critics noted mistakes that the authors had made in sampling techniques, their tendency to disregard the educational level and social situation of those they interviewed or tested, and a certain arbitrariness in the handling of qualitative material. The more discerning surmised that these failings derived at least in part from the "marriage" of two disparate research styles. Although a common allegiance to Freudian categories bound together the émigrés and the native-born who collaborated on *The Authoritarian Personality*, it had not sufficed to close the gap between data gathering and speculation. In the end, Adorno stood out as the intellectual virtuoso of the team. "Quantitative statistical method" was "all too often cast in the

25. See, in particular, Richard Christie and Marie Jahoda, eds., *Studies in the Scope and Method of "The Authoritarian Personality"* (Glencoe, Ill., 1954).

26. David Riesman, *Individualism Reconsidered* (Glencoe, Ill., 1954), pp. 476–477.

role of the stodgy husband" answering " 'Yes, dear' to . . . the bright suggestions made by the wife."[27]

Underlying and overlapping this imperfect fusion of method was an unrecognized divergence in ideology. *The Authoritarian Personality* used the word "democratic" as the antithesis to "fascist"; such presumably was the spontaneous vocabulary of its American-born authors. But the term did not come so naturally to Adorno: he would more likely have spoken of "socialist" or "revolutionary." The Institut für Sozialforschung had always been sparing in its reliance on Marxian expressions. After its transfer to the United States, its tendency to write in "Aesopian" language became even more marked.[28] Impelled by what seems in retrospect an excessive caution, Adorno and Horkheimer and their colleagues tried to conceal their true ideological affiliation. No wonder that American readers found the implicit argument of *The Authoritarian Personality* confusing and had trouble in detecting its latent drift.

The clue, of course, lay in the works in German on which Adorno had been simultaneously working. There was also one other book in English that might have dispelled some of the misunderstanding. In 1947 Horkheimer published under the title *Eclipse of Reason* a revised version of a series of lectures he had given at Columbia University three years earlier. *Eclipse of Reason* went over much of the same ground that its author had covered in his major essays of 1937. But it did so in a flatter and less arresting manner· in passing from German to English, Horkheimer's style lost its verve and its polemical force. *Eclipse of Reason* impressed neither the critics nor the public; its effect on American intellectuals was almost nil.

Perhaps with his new audience in mind, Horkheimer concentrated his fire on those targets which were particularly prominent in the United States. Warning of "the tendency of liberalism to

27. Herbert H. Hyman and Paul B. Sheatsley, "A Methodological Critique," *Studies in the Scope and Method of "The Authoritarian Personality,"* pp. 69–71, 91, 102–104, 114–115.
28. Jay, *Dialectical Imagination*, pp. 226–227.

tilt over into fascism and of the intellectual and political representatives of liberalism to make their peace with its opposites," he
noted that a merely "formal" or "subjectivist" view of reason
could be of no "help in determining the desirability of any goal."
The liberal empiricist, he argued, was at sea in dealing with the
problem of values; under contemporary conditions, people were
"living on the residue of . . . ideas" which had once embodied
"elements of truth" but which were now "gradually losing their
power of conviction." From assertions such as these it was only a
short step to a full-scale assault on pragmatism, America's sole
home-grown philosophy. Pragmatism, Horkheimer alleged, tried
"to model all spheres of intellectual life" on "the techniques of
the laboratory"; it was "the counterpart of modern industrialism,
for which the factory" offered "the prototype of human existence." As the American variant of the pervasive positivist outlook,
it gave "a censorial power" to science, transferring "the principle
of the closed shop to the world of ideas." The open-mindedness
on which it prided itself proved in practice to be no different from
the intellectual absolutism of other positivist philosophies: "in a
way, even the irrational dogmatism of the church" was "more
rational than a rationalism so ardent" that it overshot "its own
rationality."[29]

Thus in its current guise positivism figured rather as a symptom
than as a corrective in a general cultural "failure of nerve." The
"objective mind"—the spirit pervading "social life in all its
branches"—worshiped "industry, technology, and nationality
without a principle that could give sense to these categories"; it
betokened "the pressure of an economic system" that admitted of
"no reprieve or escape." Still more, the world of nature itself was
becoming "the object of total exploitation" which had "no aim set
by reason, and therefore no limit." This emphasis on conflict
between man and nature—on the unprecedented domination of
one species over all the others—was a new element in Horkheimer
and Adorno's thought, an element that suffused much of their
work in America and that received a triumphant vindication two

29. *Eclipse of Reason*, pp. 7, 20, 34, 50, 71, 77–79.

decades later with the widespread awakening to the ecological facts of life toward the end of the 1960's.[30]

Meantime Adorno had been sporadically at work on a book which led an even more obscure existence. Composed in fragments over the years 1944–1947, *Minima Moralia* was to see the light only in 1951—and then only in German. Adorno's immediate occasion for putting his private reflections into some tentative order was Horkheimer's fiftieth birthday and the accompanying realization that their labors in common had been broken off by his friend's organizational responsibility for "Studies in Prejudice." And so it was to Max—using only his first name—that Adorno dedicated his book in "gratitude" and "fidelity." *Minima Moralia* he characterized as a *dialogue intérieur*: the French expressions scattered through it suggested its debt to the Gallic tradition of the short essay or aphorism on which Nietzsche had also drawn. If it had a central theme, it was the "damaged" life referred to in its subtitle. Of this, Adorno explained, the intellectual émigré possessed a knowledge that was peculiarly painful. Whether he knew it or not, every such émigré was damaged and would do well to recognize the fact himself before being taught it "cruelly behind the tight-shut doors of his self respect." However he might come to feel at home in his professional guild or in driving a car, he would always go astray. His sole source of help lay in a "steadfast diagnosis of himself and others"—an analysis that could at least save him from "blindness" to his misfortune. "Where everything is bad," Adorno quoted the English Hegelian F. H. Bradley, "it must be good to know the worst."[31]

As he plumbed the depths of his anguish, a new word had crept into Adorno's vocabulary: "redemption" (*Erlösung*), which carried Christian overtones. It had been prefigured at the very start of *Minima Moralia*, where the author had announced his intention of exploring what had once been the true sphere of philosophy but had since fallen into "disregard" and "forgetfulness," the precepts of "right living." Year after year his search for such precepts had led him through the twisted, broken, and overgrown paths of his

---

30. *Ibid.*, pp. 85, 108–109, 154; Jay, *Dialectical Imagination*, pp. 256–257.
31. *Minima Moralia*, pp. 14, 44–45, 145.

own inner reflections. In the end he had emerged with the conviction that in the face of despair, it was the responsibility of philosophy to present matters "from the standpoint of redemption"—and that in this light "the question of the reality or unreality" of redemption was "almost immaterial."[32]

The task which Adorno and Horkheimer had shared before their conflicting responsibilities separated them was the work entitled *Dialectic of Enlightenment.* Begun in 1941, with their move to California, and substantially completed in 1944, it marked the climax of their intellectual collaboration. No other of their books gave so clear a notion of the farthest reaches of their thought: picking up where their essays of the 1930's had left off, *Dialectic of Enlightenment* mercilessly spelled out the half-concealed assumptions underlying *The Authoritarian Personality* and *Eclipse of Reason*, finally providing the key to what its authors really meant. Yet for the first decade and a half of its existence, the book was known only to small circles of specialists and enthusiasts. Originally published in German in Amsterdam in 1947, it did not become widely available in Germany until its reissue in 1969, and in the United States until an English translation appeared three years later.

From the text itself it was impossible to tell which parts each author had composed. According to their own account, Horkheimer and Adorno "jointly dictated lengthy sections" of it. Yet readers might guess that where the prose came in hammer blows, it was the work of the older man, and where it was more nuanced and involuted, it bore the mark of Adorno's discriminating intelligence. The book's organization suggested a series of linked essays —first a treatment of the concept of enlightenment itself, then an "excursus" on Homer and another on the Marquis de Sade, followed by the detailed examples of the main theme that the "culture industry" and anti-Semitism provided, the whole concluded by a set of "notes and drafts" which might well have found a place in *Minima Moralia*. The argument, while sometimes repetitive, was continuous and cumulative. The authors' view of

32. *Ibid.,* pp. 7, 480–481.

the Jewish question—highly idiosyncratic and the explanation for much that was puzzling about *The Authoritarian Personality*—could be appreciated only in the light of the reasoning which had gone before.

Horkheimer and Adorno's aim was to discover "why mankind, instead of entering into a truly human condition," was "sinking into a new kind of barbarism." More specifically it was to determine why enlightenment had succumbed to "self-destruction." In employing this term, the authors meant something wider than the progressive thought of the eighteenth century: they meant the whole process of rationalization or "disenchantment" in the modern world which Weber had defined in classic fashion. The enlightenment, Horkheimer and Adorno argued, had striven to shatter myths; in the course of so doing, it had in turn become a myth—the myth of "false clarity." "The only kind of thinking . . . sufficiently hard" to break the hold of superstition was ultimately led to direct its weapons against itself. Thus it was incumbent on the contemporary intellectual, if men were "not to be wholly betrayed," to *redeem* "the hopes of the past," through rethinking the concept of enlightenment.[33]

Considered in its broadest contemporary manifestations, enlightenment proved to be the equivalent of manipulation. According to the scientific-positivist vocabulary, knowledge meant the power to manipulate things; in the course of understanding them, "abstraction, the tool of enlightenment," liquidated its objects. Its simple, harsh terminology expressed the realities of domination; it converted the world into "a gigantic analytic judgment," in which the "brute facts" constituted a "sacred . . . preserve" impervious to criticism.[34]

All this could be found elsewhere in the writings of Horkheimer and Adorno. But never before or subsequently was it expressed with greater intransigence. Moreover, the two digressions that immediately followed the introductory statements gave them the living actuality which critical theory so often lacked. The first

33. *Dialektik der Aufklärung*, new ed. (Frankfurt, 1969), trans. by John Cumming as *Dialectic of Enlightenment* (New York, 1972), pp. ix, xi, xiii–xv, 4.
34. *Ibid.*, pp. 9, 13, 27–28.

excursus retold the story of Odysseus sailing past the island of the sirens. At Horkheimer and Adorno's hands, the Homeric legend became a prophetic "allegory of the dialectic of enlightenment." Odysseus, well aware that the charm of the sirens' song was irresistible but wanting to hear it nonetheless, had had himself bound to the mast of his ship; his oarsmen—his "pliable proletarians"—with "stopped ears" and all unknowing had doggedly rowed past the danger. And so it had been in the subsequent experience of humanity: the majority of mankind had been denied the knowledge of beauty and love; the minority who had won the right to leadership had gained it "at the price of the abasement and mortification of the instinct for complete, universal, and undivided happiness." The history of civilization was the history of "man's domination over himself," a "history of renunciation."[35] What Weber had accepted with stoic resignation, what Freud in his *Civilization and Its Discontents* had reckoned as the inevitable cost of curbing men's destructive drives, Horkheimer and Adorno were determined to protest with all the dialectical skill they could muster.

The second excursus introduced the Marquis de Sade, not, as Albert Camus was to do a few years later, in the guise of prefiguring the world of concentration camp torture, but in a more provocative incarnation as "the bourgeois individual freed from tutelage." The eighteenth-century Enlightenment, Horkheimer and Adorno maintained, had been incapable of finding a basis for ethical judgment; while its overall theory might be "firm and consistent," when it came to formulate "moral doctrines," it succumbed to propaganda and sentimentality. Kant himself, despite the care with which he had approached his task and the "sublime and paradoxical" nature of his results, had failed in his effort "to derive the duty of mutual respect from a law of reason." He and his fellow rationalists had bequeathed to the nineteenth-century bourgeois order no ethical sanction beyond convention and fact. This Nietzsche had revealed: he had "trumpeted far and wide the impossibility" of basing on reason as his contemporaries understood it "any fundamental argument against murder." And with it

35. *Ibid.*, pp. 34–36, 54–57.

he had rejected the facile moral optimism of the bourgeoisie, the "assurance" that sought "only to console." Whatever else Horkheimer and Adorno might mean by "redemption"—and the term remained shrouded in obscurity—it was apparent that consolation formed no part of it: they preferred the "merciless doctrines" which proclaimed the "identity" of domination and enlightenment.[36]

After this second excursus had probed the relationship between enlightenment and morality, the main argument resumed with a discussion of the "culture industry" in which enlightenment manifested itself as "mass deception." Horkheimer and Adorno quite consciously chose to speak of mass culture as an industry in order to suggest that what was popular about it was spurious and contrived.[37] Far from being democratic, it too expressed the realities of domination. While the great art of the past had embodied "a negative truth"—while even classical music tested the dictates of a "flawless and perfect style"—the contemporary culture industry reduced art to "absolute . . . imitation." It impressed "the same stamp on everything"; it provided for everyone, discarding tragedy and purveying in "fun" a "self-derision of man" or "parody of humanity."[38] It was here that the mark of their residence in America showed most clearly in Horkheimer and Adorno's work. When they wrote *Dialectic of Enlightenment,* they were living close to Hollywood and associating with fellow émigrés from Germany who had ties to the entertainment industry. In these circumstances, it was only natural that the cinema should offer them their finest examples of the covert coercion which underlay "the world of the administered life."

If the culture industry demonstrated how enlightenment had turned to deception, anti-Semitism betrayed its limits. Horkheimer and Adorno's treatment of this subject was both the most subtle and the most shocking to come out of the emigration; it surpassed even that of Hannah Arendt in its challenge to the comfortable convictions of the liberal intelligentsia. For the Frankfurt philosophers argued in effect that the conventional bourgeois had

36. *Ibid.,* pp. 85–86, 118–119.
37. Jay, *Dialectical Imagination,* p. 216.
38. *Dialectic of Enlightenment,* pp. 120, 130–131, 141, 149, 153.

"good," if unacknowledged, reasons to hate the Jew. By his mere existence the Jew reminded his fellow citizens of what they had lost in the act of self-domination; by his ambiguous marginal status he recalled the possibilities which had been cut off when men had renounced their claim on happiness. "Liberalism had allowed the Jews property, but no power to command." In place of authority it had left them free to indulge the "expressiveness" that others had curbed—"the painful echo of a superior power . . . voiced in a complaint." The Jew's eternal lamentation was like a woman's: as those who had not ruled "for thousands of years," women and Jews, out of "their fear and weakness," had retained an "affinity to nature which perennial oppression" had granted them. They had kept alive the memory of "happiness without power." And to those who were neither Jews nor women the thought of such "true happiness" was "unbearable." Thus when the Nazi derisively mimicked the Jew, he was in fact projecting upon his imagined enemy the longing for a more natural and expressive life that he had tried to stifle in his own soul.[39]

Anti-Semitism, then, was simply the most readily identifiable manifestation of the dehumanizing ideology into which enlightenment had degenerated. It suggested obedience to "social mechanisms in which the experiences of individual persons with individual Jews" played no part. In their all-or-nothing quality, anti-Semitic judgments had regularly "borne witness to stereotyped thought." And herewith came at last the explanation for why hatred of the Jews had figured so prominently in *The Authoritarian Personality*. Anti-Semitism, Horkheimer and Adorno had discovered, offered the clearest possible evidence of the "ticket" behavior—the inclination to accept a program in toto—which characterized not merely those of authoritarian bent but even the ordinary victims of the administered life. Yet the very fact that it occurred "only as part of an interchangeable program" gave "sure hope" that it would "one day . . . die out."[40] It was on this unanticipated note of optimism that *Dialectic of Enlightenment* closed.

39. *Ibid.*, pp. 112, 172, 182, 187.
40. *Ibid.*, pp. 200–201, 207.

When it was republished in 1969, its authors could perhaps have said that they had been right in predicting a waning of anti-Semitism. More broadly they claimed that their "prognosis of the . . . conversion of enlightenment into positivism" and the accompanying "identification of intellect" with what was "inimical to the spirit" had been "overwhelmingly confirmed." Faced with the apparently irresistible "advance toward an administered world," Horkheimer and Adorno could only demand "support for the residues of freedom," even if these seemed "powerless in regard to the main course of history."[41]

iii. *Max Horkheimer and Theodor W. Adorno: The Postwar Polemic*

Despite their hostility to American mass culture and the depth of their European allegiance, Horkheimer and Adorno's decision to return to Germany after the war was not as easy as might be supposed. Their work on "Studies in Prejudice" had finally given them a stake in American-style research, and it proved hard to disentangle themselves from this commitment. Three years passed before Horkheimer made his first postwar visit to his native land. The centennial of the 1848 Frankfurt Parliament provided the occasion: the director of the Institut für Sozialforschung received a warm reception and an invitation from the University of Frankfurt to move that body back to the city in which it had been founded a quarter century earlier. Besides this official recognition, the new generation of students seemed eager to learn about critical theory: the imaginary audience for which Horkheimer and Adorno had continued to write in German had at last become a reality. In 1949 Horkheimer's university chair was restored to him; his lectures quickly became a thunderous success. A year later the Institut—the "Café Max," as the students nicknamed it—reopened in Frankfurt, with Adorno now in the position of assistant director and subsequently professor of philosophy and sociology. Although during the next decade the two friends returned at

41. *Ibid.*, preface to the new ed., pp. ix–x.

intervals to the United States, their center of gravity had definitively shifted back across the Atlantic. Their Institut had successfully accomplished what no other organized German intellectual
group had managed to do—to bridge the gap of exile between the
culture of Weimar and the new post-Nazi culture that was beginning to unfold.[42]

In 1951, Horkheimer was chosen rector of Frankfurt University,
the first Jew ever to have been elevated to such a position. His
election by his colleagues signified something more than a decline
in anti-Semitism. It underlined Horkheimer and Adorno's new
position as "official" ornaments of culture in a Federal Republic
which could as yet boast of few intellectual luminaries. As the cold
war passed its height, their critics found evidence of an unwonted
ideological caution in the critical tone that the Frankfurt philosophers adopted toward the Soviet Union and China. But this was
no real novelty: Horkheimer and Adorno had never equated
Stalinist or Maoist despotism with their notion of Marxist practice
and had long denounced Communist terror in the name of freedom. What was actually new about their writings of the 1950's
and 1960's was that they now focused their generic antipositivism
on specific, concrete problems of social-science method.[43]

Adorno and Horkheimer had always thought of their work as at
the very least a two-front combat. After the midcentury, however,
they began to reckon with a shift in the opposing forces. Abstract
idealism was no longer a potent foe. In the intellectual void left by
the discrediting of conventional German thought, the Frankfurt
philosophers were in an optimum position to teach their postwar
students what they had learned of empirical social science in the
United States. Yet only up to a point—as American techniques
caught on and threatened to sweep the field, Horkheimer and
Adorno found it necessary to call a halt. They felt it incumbent on
them to restate more fully the basic precepts of critical theory and
to delimit the respects in which it was compatible with other types
of social thought and the respects in which it was not. The task

42. For full particulars, see Jay, *Dialectical Imagination*, pp. 281–282, 285–
288, 298.
43. Rusconi, *Teoria critica*, pp. 207–208.

devolved mainly on Adorno: with Horkheimer engrossed in administrative responsibilities and writing even less than before, the younger man was obliged to speak for both of them. And in so doing he became the most prestigious intellectual on the German scene. This last phase of Adorno's life—his two decades of postwar polemic—falls outside the scope of the present study. But a summary treatment of its main features is essential to an assessment of critical theory as it emerged from its period of intellectual obscurity and ideological concealment in the United States.

In 1966 Adorno published what many took to be his philosophical summa—a substantial volume entitled *Negative Dialectics*. But far from being a systematic treatise, it developed once again as a succession of extended essays. It embodied Adorno's final reckoning with his philosophical predecessors and more particularly with the idealist tradition which he had assailed all his life while remaining true to its metaphysical rhetoric and arcane form of expression. Indeed, from the standpoint of style, *Negative Dialectics* was as difficult a book as Adorno had ever written. Its argument did not unfold: it was "hurled at the reader in an unbroken sequence of staccato affirmations whose precise and lucid phrasing" failed to "make up for the absence of a discernible logical skeleton."[44] It offered, Adorno announced, on the model of the "anti-drama" or "anti-hero" of contemporary literature, an "anti-system" that with the "strength" of the subjective itself would "break through the fallacy of . . . subjectivity."[45]

"Philosophy, which once seemed obsolete," lived on, "because the moment to realize it was missed." With these words Adorno said the farewell to Marxist practice that had been in the making ever since the great disappointments of the 1930's. The proletariat had not reaped the inheritance of classical philosophy which Marx and Engels had promised it; what had happened instead had been the advent of the administered life. Thus philosophy was still needed—but a philosophy that would "disenchant" the whole

44. Lichtheim, "Adorno," *From Marx to Hegel*, p. 141.
45. *Negative Dialektik* (Frankfurt, 1966), trans. by E. B. Ashton as *Negative Dialectics* (New York, 1973), p. xx.

process of conceptual thinking. Nor—despite its total lack of fixed concepts—would it resemble the sociological relativism of a Mannheim or the desperate plea for "engagement" of a Sartre. Relativism Adorno dismissed as a "popularized" form of materialist thought. Existentialism in its French guise he found—as Sartre himself had eventually recognized—still "in idealistic bonds." The author of *Being and Nothingness*, in propounding the notion of absolute freedom of choice, had against his own intention condemned his philosophy to irrationality: the Sartrean individual was obliged to make a choice without knowing the reason which determined that choice. It was to Sartre's honor, Adorno added, that in the plays which were supposed to embody his formal philosophy the protagonists behaved not as free subjects but as though they were in chains.[46]

The existentialists, of course, in common with Adorno, had gone back to Hegel, and by preference to the Hegel of the *Phenomenology*. In this last assessment of the Hegelian legacy, Adorno did not repudiate his philosophical debt; but he underscored those aspects of it which confined rather than inspired the course of the dialectic. These he discovered more especially in Hegel's notion of a world-spirit and the "mythical," if secularized, teaching of an immanent "logic of things" that accompanied it. The result, Adorno contended, had been a stress on the general at the expense of the particular—an overemphasis which was eventually to lead to the worship of society itself. By reasoning in similar fashion a positivist such as Durkheim could "overtrump" Hegel in substituting for the metaphysics of the world-spirit the spirit of the human collectivity. The author of the *Phenomenology* had "abhored . . . insipid edification"; but in his *Philosophy of History* he had lapsed into precisely what he had earlier condemned. Through his insistence on the independent status of a "people's spirit" (*Volksgeist*), he had legitimized despotism over individual human beings—just as Durkheim was later to do with his notion of "collective norms" and Spengler with his theory of the "souls" of different cultures. Hegel, in short, had fought the historiographic battle on the side of what was immutable and identical in

46. *Ibid.*, pp. 3, 13, 36, 49–50.

its action, a "totality" in which he had found salvation. For this he stood accused of having fabricated a "mythology of history."[47]

Yet Adorno did not deny that history had a course which the philosophic mind could discern. He simply maintained that Hegel had used categories such as freedom and justice in a generic and potentially reactionary fashion. A speculative philosophy of history Adorno apparently considered an intellectual enterprise worth attempting, but with results quite different from what Hegel had imagined. In a passionate outburst in one of the drafts appended to *Dialectic of Enlightenment,* he and Horkheimer had in fact sketched their own vision of past and future.

> In the sense of . . . serious history, all ideas, prohibitions, religions, and political faiths are interesting only in so far as they increase or reduce the natural prospects of the human race on earth or in the universe. . . . Reason plays the part of an instrument of adaptation. . . . Its cunning consists of turning men into animals with more and more far-reaching powers, and not in establishing the identity between subject and object.
>
> A philosophical interpretation of world history would have to show how the rational domination of nature comes increasingly to win the day, in spite of all deviations and resistance, and integrates all human characteristics. . . . Either men will tear each other to pieces or they will take all the flora and fauna of the earth with them; and if the earth is then still young enough, the whole thing will have to be started again at a much lower stage.[48]

When these words were written, the first atomic weapon had not yet been exploded and the public consciousness of ecological peril was still more than two decades away.

Besides putting his formal philosophy in final order, Adorno also found it necessary to defend and explain his critical theory in the new professional guise of sociologist he had acquired in America.

47. *Ibid.*, pp. 316, 319, 326 n., 337–338, 357. I have altered the translation slightly.
48. *Dialectic of Enlightenment*, pp. 222–224.

His sense of intellectual responsibility led him into the sort of elaborately arranged confrontations that German scholarship delighted in—notably with the philosopher and social-science methodologist Karl Popper—and into assessments of such eminent "positivists" as Weber and Wittgenstein. Adorno's lofty and intensely committed polemic can be followed in a series of essays on the theory of society extending over the years 1955–1969 and published shortly after his death.[49] Here the traces of his stay in the United States were everywhere apparent—and not least of all in the Anglicisms or Americanisms with which his prose was strewn.[50]

It was only natural that positivism, as in the past, should figure as the chief target of Adorno's polemic. But in this respect too, the decade spent across the Atlantic had left its mark: in these essays of the 1950's and 1960's the judgments on individual figures were more nuanced than had been true of the Frankfurt philosophers' earlier programmatic pronouncements. Thus a new respect for Weber accompanied the reiteration of a profound disagreement on the problem of values. The notion of ethical or aesthetic value, Adorno pointedly observed, was modeled on an economic exchange rate. The whole problem could be dismissed as useless "ballast" which sociology had been dragging along with it; the "dichotomy of is and ought" was as "false" as it was "historically constraining"; a judgment about something was "always . . . prescribed" by that thing and did not "exhaust itself in a subjectively irrational decision" as Weber had imagined. The abstract knowledge of society, Adorno predictably added, could "crystallize . . . only around a conception" of what "a correctly-constituted society" might be; it arose from criticism, "from a social conscious-

49. *Aufsätze zur Gesellschaftstheorie und Methodologie* (Frankfurt, 1970). These essays were subsequently republished in Adorno's *Gesammelte Schriften*, VIII (*Soziologische Schriften* I) (Frankfurt, 1972). For the context of the polemic, see George Lichtheim, "Marx or Weber: Dialectical Methodology" (originally published in *The Times Literary Supplement*, LXIX [March 12, 1970]), *From Marx to Hegel*, pp. 200–218.

50. A cursory inspection turns up the following: "healthy sex life," "some fun," "go-getters," "social research," "team," "middle range theory," "trial and error," "administrative research," "common sense," "fact finding," "statement of fact," "case studies," "facts and figures," "nose counting," "likes and dislikes."

ness of contradiction and necessity." Yet despite these strictures, he was ready to grant that when one looked at Weber's own writings, the "disjunction of objectivity and value" appeared "more qualified" than the sociologist's "battle-cry" might "lead one to expect" and that they could serve as a starting point for rethinking categories which had hardened into dogmas.[51]

Similarly in regard to Wittgenstein, Adorno recognized the "pain" that the Viennese philosopher had experienced in trying to meditate on logic with the intellectual tools which logic itself provided. This "most reflective of positivists" had demonstrated his superiority over those of the Vienna Circle by becoming "aware of the limits of logic"—and therewith had reached "the threshold of a dialectical consciousness." What he had not seen, Adorno maintained, was that everything which went beyond pure sense experience had "an aura of indeterminacy," that "no abstraction" was "ever entirely clear," and that every such abstraction was "indistinct . . . through the multiplicity of its possible content."[52] But this last was precisely the purport of Wittgenstein's *Philosophical Investigations*, a work which Adorno apparently never read; the references in his essays clearly indicate that he knew only the early Wittgenstein of the *Tractatus*. If Adorno could speak with such respect of a book which its own author had half-repudiated, how would he have written if he had been familiar with the later works in which so much that was dogmatic or limited in the *Tractatus* was refined and put into a new context? One may conclude that in Adorno's failure to come to grips with the *Philosophical Investigations*, an enormous intellectual opportunity was missed—the chance to associate two of the finest intelligences of the century in the enterprise of bridging philosophical traditions which Wittgenstein's death had cut off in midcourse.

In the absence of a full reckoning with the author of the *Philosophical Investigations*, Adorno was thrown back on the dialectical base that he had maintained intact during his years in America.

51. "Zur Logik der Sozialwissenschaften" (originally published in *Kölner Zeitschrift für Soziologie und Sozialpsychologie*, XIV [1962]), *Aufsätze zur Gesellschaftstheorie*, pp. 122–124.
52. "Der Positivismusstreit in der deutschen Soziologie" (originally published in 1969 as an introduction to a volume with the same title), *ibid.*, pp. 169, 189–190, 228.

Idealism, he explained, "which once glorified speculation," might have "passed away," but the speculative "moment" that critical theory exemplified remained "indispensable." Curiously enough, although it was the positivists who believed they had done the job of discrediting the idealist way of thinking, in their stress on the "perceiving subject" these same positivists remained far closer to idealism than was true of critical theory. His own position, Adorno kept insisting, had a concreteness that the conventional sociology of the midcentury lacked. Its very cast of sentences suggested it: in place of the usual scientific formulation of a law in terms of an eternal "whenever—then," dialectical thinking spoke in historically specific terms which could be expressed as "after this happens—that must follow." Even the critical theorist's stubborn conviction that beneath "appearance" (which was all that positivism recognized) there lay something else which could be called "essence" (*Wesen*)—even this apparently most traditional and abstract category betokened an effort to reach the concrete reality below or beyond the world of surface manifestations. It made a difference, Adorno explained, whether one subsumed human phenomena (as in the sociological tradition stemming from Weber) under such words as "prestige" and "status," or whether one sought as he himself did "to derive them from objective relationships of domination." An ostensibly "value free" debate over selecting a "system of coordinates" in fact went to the heart of conflicting concepts of society: within the "logical-scientific" style of thought, the real social antagonisms could not become visible. As had always been true of Adorno and Horkheimer's polemic, the Hegelian-Marxist notion of a potential truth embedded in the data of economic existence had the last word: "the idea of scientific truth" was "not to be split off from that of a true society."[53]

In 1958 Max Horkheimer retired as director of the Institut für Sozialforschung, thereafter to spend most of his time in Italian Switzerland in a house overlooking Lake Lugano until his death in 1973. Adorno naturally succeeded him—and at a most difficult

53. "Zur Logik der Sozialwissenschaften," *ibid.*, p. 118; "Der Positivismusstreit," *ibid.*, pp. 172, 175, 179, 197–198, 214.

moment when pressure from the German radical left was mounting. The newest student generation had no use and even less understanding for the Frankfurt philosopher's upper-bourgeois fastidiousness and intellectual discrimination. After repeatedly occupying the building of the Institut, in April 1969 the young militants invaded Adorno's classroom; three girl students bared their breasts and mockingly overwhelmed him with flowers and kisses. Thereupon, with characteristic cruelty, they declared him dead "as an institution." For one so vulnerable, the experience must have come as a fearful shock; apparently he never fully recovered. Five months later he died of heart failure.[54]

Not until he was gone did the wider public outside Germany begin to appreciate the loss that Western intellectual life had sustained. And this was in part Adorno's own fault in insisting on a mode of expression which was "mannered, hermetic and remote from ordinary discourse." It was not merely that the Gallicisms of his early work and the Americanisms of his postexile writings raised special linguistic hurdles. It was that he consciously chose "a style refined and formalized to the point of complete artificiality." At least one critic has found in this "density" a necessary expression of Adorno's intellectual "intransigence," characterizing "the bristling mass of abstractions and cross-references" as "precisely intended to be read . . . against the cheap facility" of its surroundings and as "a warning to the reader of the price" he had "to pay for genuine thinking." More commonly, even sympathetic commentators have noted a contradiction in the fact that so musically inclined a philosopher should have written a prose so lacking in music. They have similarly remarked on the discrepancy between Adorno's championship of the ordinary suffering human being and "his inability to cast off a stylistic armature impenetrable to all but an elite of readers." This "discordance between the medium and the message" was the first of two baffling problems that Adorno left behind him.[55]

The second—and here he shared responsibility with Hork-

54. Martin Jay, "The Permanent Exile of Theodor W. Adorno," *Midstream*, XV (Dec. 1969), 66–67.

55. Lichtheim, "Adorno," *From Marx to Hegel*, pp. 132, 137; Fredric Jameson, *Marxism and Form* (Princeton, N.J., 1971), p. xiii.

heimer—concerned the extent to which the Frankfurt philosophers still adhered to the Hegelian style. In their vocabulary and
cast of sentences, they unquestionably remained rooted in the
Hegelian tradition. Moreover, they drew on the best of that tradition in passing effortlessly back and forth from philosophy to
history or aesthetics—while adding to them a more than respectable competence in such newer disciplines as psychology and
sociology. Only in economics did the writings of Adorno and
Horkheimer betray a certain amateurishness. Moreover, in their
application of the dialectical method the Frankfurt philosophers
had tried to cast off what was stiff and schematic in the way it was
conventionally understood. Scarcely less conscientiously than
Wittgenstein, they had striven to think in terms of a universe of
fluid relationships. Yet once more only up to a point. Despite all
that they had renounced in the Hegelian or Marxist tradition—
despite the intricate many-sidedness of their perceptions—one
aspect of their philosophical inheritance they steadfastly refused to
give up: "the conviction that an all-embracing or fundamental
structure of being could be discovered."[56]

This conviction was held even more strenuously by their former
associate Herbert Marcuse, who had made the opposite choice
from theirs in staying after the war in the United States. Whereas
Adorno was utterly serious and uncompromisingly intellectual in
nearly everything he wrote, Marcuse preferred to indulge a play-
fulness of manner. He also stuck more closely than Adorno to
strict Hegelian categories. The question of Adorno and Horkheimer's Marxist-Hegelian allegiance can be further illuminated by
considering the work of a man whose ideological origins were
almost identical with theirs but who diverged increasingly from
them as his life went on.

IV. *Herbert Marcuse's Vision of Happiness*

Born in Berlin in 1898 and thus between Horkheimer and Adorno
in age, Marcuse came as they did from a well-to-do, assimilated
Jewish family. He too had sympathized with the left wing of the

56. Horkheimer, *Eclipse of Reason*, p. 12.

Social Democratic party, from which he had resigned in 1919 following the assassination of Rosa Luxemburg. Thereafter he remained a critic outside the ranks of organized German socialism, in notable contrast to the course pursued by Franz Neumann, who tried to change Social Democracy from within and who in the years of exile was to become Marcuse's closest friend.

When Marcuse joined the Institut für Sozialforschung in 1933 —which by this time meant assignment to its Geneva office—he had behind him more than three years of formal philosophical study at Freiburg with Husserl and Heidegger. The latter in particular seems to have exerted a strong influence on Marcuse's thought, and it was under his guidance that the young philosopher produced his first book, a study of Hegel's ontology. Indeed, it may have been to Heidegger that Marcuse owed his ineradicable hostility to modern technology.[57] But by 1932, with his mentor moving toward collaboration with the Nazis, whose accession to power was now looming, Freiburg no longer afforded Marcuse a congenial intellectual environment. In this precarious situation, the Institut offered a welcome haven.

Marcuse brought into its ranks, besides his exposure to phenomenology and existentialism and a Hegelian expertise surpassing that of any of his colleagues, a difference of temperament which was to become more marked with each passing decade. He took his stand far closer to both utopia and anarchism than did either Horkheimer or Adorno; he tried to envision, as they did not, what the new postrevolutionary society would actually look like. And in so doing he made it his particular province to give substance to the notion of personal happiness—to define what Stendhal and Nietzsche had meant in referring to beauty as *une promesse de bonheur*, a theme to which his co-workers constantly returned but which they preferred to leave in a state of misty abstraction.

In the summer of 1934 Marcuse was among the first of the Institut's members to reach its new headquarters in New York. From here he published—in Paris and in the German language—a series of major essays that remained almost totally- unknown to

57. Martin Jay, "Metapolitics of Utopianism," *Dissent* XVII (July–Aug. 1970), 343.

American readers until their translation into English a full generation later. These essays staked out the lines of thought which were
to bring Marcuse fame in the quasi-revolutionary atmosphere of
the late 1960's; they anticipated most of the argument subsequently developed in <u>One-Dimensional Man</u>. But they did so in a
less uncompromising form and in a style inaccessible to the ordinary reader. As their author himself remarked, in restrospect they
struck him as perhaps "not radical enough."[58]

Most of their themes paralleled what Horkheimer and Adorno
were simultaneously writing—the link between liberal society and
the advent of fascist rule, the alienation of humanity under the
capitalist system, the intellectual deceptions of an ostensibly "pre-
suppositionless" positivism, the status of the dialectic as a privileged mode of thought. Where Marcuse sounded a new note was
in the last essay of the series, "On Hedonism," which appeared in
1938. In this reassessment of a philosophical tradition dating back
to classical antiquity, he discriminated between hedonist ethics,
which he found frequently mistaken, and the liberating aspect of
hedonist teaching. The criterion of pleasure seeking, he maintained, had been "right precisely in its falsehood," since it had
"preserved the demand for happiness against every idealization of
unhappiness." It had acted as a counterweight to the "devaluation
of enjoyment," whether through the cult of work or through the
celebration of an "affirmative culture" that transformed beauty
into disembodied consolation. More particularly hedonism served
as a reminder of the sacrifice of sexual happiness which humanity
had endured in the reduction of sex to a matter of duty, habit, or
emotional hygiene; it contained an unsuspected revolutionary
potential which might one day break loose upon a startled world:

> The unpurified, unrationalized release of sexual relation-
> ships would be the strongest release of enjoyment as such and

58. Foreword to *Negations: Essays in Critical Theory* (Boston, 1968),
p. xvii. This volume includes translations by Jeremy J. Shapiro of the follow-
ing essays originally published in the *Zeitschrift für Sozialforschung:* "Der
Kampf gegen den Liberalismus in der totalitären Staatsauffassung," III (1934);
"Zum Begriff des Wesens," V (1936); "Über den affirmativen Charakter der
Kultur," VI (1937); "Philosophie und kritische Theorie," VI (1937); "Zur
Kritik des Hedonismus," VII (1938).

the total devaluation of labor for its own sake. No human being could tolerate the tension between labor as valuable in itself and . . . freedom of enjoyment. The dreariness and injustice of work conditions would penetrate explosively the consciousness of individuals and make impossible their peaceful subordination to the social system of the bourgeois world.[59]

This was a motif that Horkheimer and Adorno were to touch on a few years later when they inserted in *Dialectic of Enlightenment* their excursus on Odysseus and his "proletarian" oarsmen. Characteristically they left it on the level of metaphor and platonic protest. Equally characteristically Marcuse was eventually to pursue it into a full-scale critique of Freud's *Civilization and Its Discontents*. But that was to wait for nearly two more decades. In the meantime Marcuse was only beginning his education in psychoanalytic theory; he still owed an almost exclusive allegiance to Hegel and to Marx; and in the mature writings of these two the goal of personal happiness was mediated through so much else as to be barely perceptible.

It is curious that Marcuse's essay on hedonism should have come just before his work on Hegel entitled *Reason and Revolution*, the major achievement of his early period in America and the first book that he, or indeed any other leading member of the Institut für Sozialforschung, was to publish in English. When it appeared in 1941, it created little stir. With the United States girding for war, its only immediate relevance seemed to be its defense of Hegel against the accusation of having served as one of the remote progenitors of Nazism. But the fashion in which Marcuse undertook this defense both summed up what he had written before and anticipated his work of the 1950's. In effect, he discovered in Hegel the insight which Marx in his Paris manuscripts had derived from the same source; Marcuse argued that Hegel's use of the term "alienation" was virtually identical to the understanding to which Marx had fought his way in what he believed to be an act of independence from his philosophical master. In thus converting Hegel into a revolutionary, Marcuse was following a tactic similar to the one he was later to pursue in

59. *Ibid.*, pp. 118–119, 162, 173, 186–187.

the case of Freud. "With both he attempted to make his case by disregarding their explicit political pronouncements and turning instead to an analysis of their basic philosophical or psychological conceptions. . . . And in both instances the result was to uncover beneath an apparently conservative veneer the same critical impetus which achieved explicit formulation in the writings of Karl Marx."[60]

Reason and Revolution closed the first phase of Marcuse's intellectual life. The year following its publication, he went to Washington, where he accompanied Franz Neumann into the newly founded Office of Strategic Services. Therewith began a decade of government service, which marks a strange hiatus in his biography. To those who have written on his thought, this second phase has sometimes seemed a "moratorium," in the psychological sense with which Erik H. Erikson was subsequently to invest the word. Alternatively it has figured as a plunge underground in a period of maximum stress, both personal and ideological. Perhaps it can best be viewed in terms of the Freudian concept of latency: the ideas that came to the surface once more in *Eros and Civilization* might be much the same as those Marcuse had expressed in his essay on hedonism, but in the interval between the two they had acquired the explosive force of a long-delayed intellectual maturation.

Again it is curious that during his years in Washington Marcuse should have moved into Neumann's orbit and away from Horkheimer and Adorno, with whom he apparently had so much more in common. Physical distance, of course, played a part: in wartime it was not easy to travel between California and the national capital. But there was also the matter of Neumann's personal magnetism: a diffident Marcuse allowed himself to be dominated by his overpowering friend. In this case once more the man who in the end was to emerge as the better-known of the two began the association in the role of junior partner.

The anomalies of Marcuse's position as a civil servant, which during the war had been papered over by the prevailing mood of solidarity in the struggle against Nazism, became less tolerable

60. Paul A. Robinson, *The Freudian Left: Wilhelm Reich, Geza Roheim, Herbert Marcuse* (New York, 1969), p. 156.

when the conflict ended. Moving, again with Neumann, into the Department of State, he shared the latter's research responsibilities as an expert on Germany. In retrospect—particularly after Neumann's departure for Columbia—it has seemed deliciously incongruous that at the end of the 1940's, with an official purge of real or suspected leftists in full swing, the State Department's leading authority on Central Europe should have been a revolutionary socialist who hated the cold war and all its works. No doubt Marcuse would have left the government much sooner if a suitable professorship had offered itself; denied this option, he stayed on desolately in Washington, as though paralyzed by the painful, lingering death of his first wife and apparently disinclined to return to Germany.

Besides the composition of a number of classified memoranda—which notably simplified his English style—Marcuse produced in these years only one bit of published work, a review of Sartre's *Being and Nothingness*. Most of what he wrote about it was negative: as Adorno was subsequently to do, Marcuse rejected the book's concept of freedom as "idealist" and remote from human reality. Ironically enough, Sartre himself by 1960 was to come around to the same opinion, a fact which Marcuse duly noted when his review finally appeared in German translation; the author of *Being and Nothingness* now received congratulations for his conversion to Marxism and his militant stand in support of revolution in the colonial world. Even the earlier version, however, had had words of praise for Sartre's explicit discussion of the ontological meaning of "the flesh" and the sexual caress—an intimation that Marcuse's essay on hedonism would one day find a sequel.[61]

With Neumann's death, his own remarriage, and his entry into the American academic world, the third and major phase of Marcuse's intellectual life began. After a transition period at Columbia's Russian Institute, during which he lived in Neu-

61. "Existentialism: Remarks on Jean-Paul Sartre's *L'être et le néant*," *Philosophy and Phenomenological Research*, VIII (March 1948), 322, 327–328; Marcuse's revised opinion may be found in the collection of essays entitled *Kultur und Gesellschaft*, II (Frankfurt, 1965), 83–84.

mann's house, Marcuse moved in 1954 to the Boston suburbs and began teaching at Brandeis University, where an attractive professorship had at long last materialized. Not until his mid-fifties, then, did he become a professor, and only then did he acquire the self-confidence that enabled him to speak out after his protracted silence.

A year later there appeared the book—*Eros and Civilization*—which first brought Marcuse to general attention. Subtitled "a philosophical inquiry into Freud," it was the fruit of a decade and a half of pondering on psychoanalytic theory. In it Marcuse undertook to unravel the social riddle that Freud's metapsychology had passed on to his successors—the problem of how Eros, "the builder of culture," could also be the force which needed to be curbed and weakened, through "continuous sublimation," in order for culture to survive. Most readers of *Civilization and Its Discontents* had taken Freud at his word, concluding with him that renunciation, guilt, and self-punishment were and would remain the inevitable emotional cost of life in civilized society. Marcuse refused to leave it at that: he dug below Freud's pessimistic pronouncements about the impossibility of a "nonrepressive" civilization and emerged with "elements" that he believed could "shatter the predominant tradition of Western thought and even suggest its reversal." Freud's work, Marcuse explained, was

> characterized by an uncompromising insistence on showing up the repressive content of the highest values and achievements of culture. In so far as he does this, he denies the equation of reason with repression on which the ideology of culture is built. Freud's metapsychology is an ever-renewed attempt to uncover, and to question, the terrible necessity of the inner connection between civilization and barbarism, progress and suffering, freedom and unhappiness—a connection which reveals itself ultimately as that between Eros and Thanatos.

Marcuse did not argue, however, that Freud himself had shown humanity the way out of its self-imposed imprisonment. On the contrary, in "extrapolating" from what the founder of psychoanalysis had actually said, Marcuse felt obliged to introduce two new terms into the psychoanalytic armory—"surplus repression" and the "performance principle." The first he distinguished as the restrictions required by "social domination," over and above the "basic . . . 'modifications' of the instincts necessary for the perpetuation of the human race in civilization." The second he defined as the "prevailing historical" guise of Freud's reality principle—the injunction to *perform* according to society's expectations, whether on the assembly line or in the marriage bed.[62]

Marcuse's use of the word "surplus" was already a tip to the alert reader that Marx was lurking in the background. In thus combining Marxist with Freudian categories, Marcuse put on a spectacular intellectual performance of his own—more particularly since Marx's name never appeared in his pages. The idea of surplus repression enabled him to graft onto Freud's instinctual-biological trunk of theory a devastating socioeconomic critique of modern industrial society. The performance principle similarly extended Marx's concepts of alienation and reification into the sexual realm. This principle, Marcuse maintained, had instituted a "genital supremacy"; it had concentrated libido "in one part of the body, leaving most of the rest free for use as the instrument of labor." Hence the way to human fulfillment lay through a re-sexualization of the body; the tyranny of the merely genital or procreative must and could be broken by a rehabilitation of the so-called perversions, the "polymorphous-perverse" inclinations of original undifferentiated sexuality, which, Marcuse suspected, offered a *promesse de bonheur* greater than that bestowed by what society conventionally sanctioned as normal.[63]

A program breathtaking in its utopian sweep—but, as a French critic soberly pointed out, one that circumvented Freud's basic categories. Whatever Marcuse might have done to Marx (on which it was difficult to be precise, since a Marxian ghost alone was present), in the case of psychoanalytic theory he drew the extreme implications from Freud's boldest speculative flights with no attention to the clinical "soil" from which these latter had sprung. Thus when he ran up against such a triad of coupled terms as id-unconscious, instinct-drive, repression-suppression, Marcuse

62. *Eros and Civilization* (Boston, 1955), pp. 17, 35, 83.
63. *Ibid.*, pp. 48–49; Robinson, *Freudian Left*, pp. 204–207.

invariably settled on the first of each pair; the second failed to figure in his line of thought. In a treatment dealing almost exclusively with the instincts and their repression, the absence of any clear delineation of the unconscious made it impossible to situate Marcuse's work unambiguously within the context of psychoanalytic speculation.[64]

All this notwithstanding, *Eros and Civilization* ranked as the most original and important of Marcuse's books. It accomplished the incredible feat of fully accepting the pessimistic aspects of Freud's metapsychology—the predominance of sexuality, the determination of future behavior in the emotional events of early childhood, the death instinct (Thanatos), and all the rest—while turning them toward even more "positive" conclusions about human fulfillment than was true of Freud's most optimistic heirs.[65] It likewise reversed the classic psychoanalytic conviction about man's destructiveness by arguing that the release of sexuality rather than its denial was the way to tame humanity and pacify the world. In brief *Eros and Civilization* managed to convert Freud into a still more revolutionary figure than Marx by ascribing to him a sense of cosmic injustice in the thwarting of instinct—an injustice which cried out for radical, but unspecified, social changes.

The process of thinking through these changes was to occupy Marcuse for the next decade. At its end he was to endorse as his own, in the 1966 reissue of *Eros and Civilization,* the slogan of the young militants "Make love, not war" which gave the book a clear political thrust. The faint beginnings of such a shift were already apparent in two lectures he delivered in Germany at a commemoration that Horkheimer and Adorno had organized for the centennial of Freud's birth in 1956. Coming only a year after *Eros and Civilization,* these lectures made more explicit the notion of "domination" as the guiding reality in contemporary society. "In acknowledging it," Marcuse observed, Freud was "at one with idealistic ethics and with liberal-bourgeois politics." The founder

64. Jean Laplanche, "Notes sur Marcuse et la psychanalyse," *Marcuse cet inconnu* (special no. of the review *La Nef,* XXVI [Jan.–March 1969]), 115–116, 126, 128.

65. Robinson, *Freudian Left,* p. 201.

of psychoanalysis, he added, felt justified in combating "the integral claim of the pleasure principle," the organism's constitutional bent toward "fulfillment, gratification, peace."[66] Once Marcuse turned, then, toward specifying the contours of a non-repressive existence, the image of Freud the revolutionary began to recede. By 1963 he had reached the conviction that the Freudian concept of man was "obsolescent" in its emphasis on "private autonomy and rationality." In the contemporary world the best that could be said for psychoanalysis was that it might enable one "to live in refusal and opposition to the Establishment," that it invoked "not only a past left behind but . . . a future to be recaptured."[67]

In the meantime Marcuse had at last come to the point where he could offer his own picture of human happiness:

> a state in which there is no productivity resulting from and conditioning renunciation and no alienated labor: a state in which the growing mechanization of labor enables an ever larger part of . . . instinctual energy . . . to return to its original form, . . . to be changed back into energy of the life instincts. It would no longer be the case that time spent in alienated labor occupied the major portion of life and the free time left to the individual for the gratification of his own needs was a mere remainder. Instead, alienated labor time would not only be reduced to a minimum but would disappear and life would consist of free time.[68]

Some such vision of man's potentialities had hovered on the utopian wing of socialism ever since the young Marx had speculated that in the remote future people might "hunt in the morning, fish in the afternoon, rear cattle in the evening, criticize after dinner," as their inclination might prompt.[69] But Marcuse was

66. "Trieblehre und Freiheit," *Freud in der Gegenwart*, ed. by Theodor W. Adorno and Walter Dirks (Frankfurt, 1957), trans. by Jeremy J. Shapiro and Shierry M. Weber for Marcuse's *Five Lectures* (Boston, 1970), p. 11.
67. "The Obsolescence of the Freudian Concept of Man," *Five Lectures*, pp. 60–61.
68. "Die Idee des Fortschritts im Lichte der Psychoanalyse" (originally published in *Freud in der Gegenwart*), *ibid.*, p. 39.
69. *The German Ideology*, International Publishers ed., p. 22.

almost unique in bringing this vision down to earth and in arguing
for its contemporary feasibility.

With the publication of *One-Dimensional Man* in 1964, Marcuse's decade-long evolution toward ideological explicitness—and
from Freud back to Marx—was virtually completed. This book
reintroduced Marx under his own colors; it also further extended
the circle of Marcuse's readers. For here the revolutionary message
which had previously remained clouded by its Hegelian wrappings
found a clear target in the society of the author's adopted country.
By the early 1960's American minds were ready for a work that
opened vistas of liberating social change; the terrors of McCarthyism lay in the past, and the civil divisions with which the decade
closed were still in the future. On such an atmosphere, *One-
Dimensional Man* could impinge with optimum effect; and it
came as more of a novelty than would have been the case if
Horkheimer and Adorno's *Dialectic of Enlightenment* had already
been in translation.

Marcuse discerned in the United States—as the farthest point
that advanced industrial civilization had reached—"a comfortable,
smooth, reasonable, democratic unfreedom" where technology had
triumphed all along the line; where the "Welfare State" and the
"Warfare State" coexisted in apparently untroubled harmony;
where a universal "flattening out" of values meant that the citizenry failed to notice its lack of any real choice; where the same
people did not believe—or did not care sufficiently to disbelieve—
what their rulers told them, yet acted "accordingly"; where fascism
was no longer required for social discipline, since the status quo
defied "all transcendence"; where Marxism, although still theoretically valid, lacked historical agents; and where one's sole faint hope
for the future must be vested in the anger and the aspiration for a
decent life among the "substratum of the outcasts and outsiders."[70]
Marcuse's catalog of horrors did not go perceptibly beyond the
analysis of society that American-born critics were simultaneously
producing. What gave his work a different and arresting tone was

70. *One-Dimensional Man* (Boston, 1964), pp. 1, 17, 19, 57, 103, 256–
257.

his insistence, in common with Horkheimer and Adorno, that in the culture of the midcentury language and thought were losing their evocative character and becoming, like the reality they reflected, "one-dimensional."

Hence, as Horkheimer had done in *Eclipse of Reason*, Marcuse coupled his social critique with a renewed attack on "positivism"—and this time specifically in the sphere of language. Anglo-American linguistic philosophy naturally offered him a prime target; so too did the later works of Wittgenstein. Marcuse had read the *Philosophical Investigations*, as Adorno had not. But quite evidently he had misunderstood them: by citing the less significant passages in one of the key sections of Wittgenstein's work, he dismissed the matter as a succession of trivia.[71] Marcuse's misreading of the *Philosophical Investigations* put off many Americans who would have been ready to accept the main lines of his social analysis. It also epitomized the curiously bifurcated character of a book that both closed his four decades of philosophical speculation and inaugurated a new phase of political activism.

This last phase of Marcuse's endeavors lies beyond the present inquiry. Stimulated by a combination of outrage at the Vietnam war and friendly contact with the German student movement, it gave to the work he published from 1967 on a sharply polemical character.[72] In the year following the appearance of *One-Dimensional Man*, Marcuse had gone from Brandeis to the University of California at San Diego, and it was there that he assumed his new role as the philosophical idol of militant youth. For a thinker who had lived the greater part of his mature life in almost total obscurity—and who had been known in intellectual circles for scarcely more than ten years—the sudden transition to international fame might well have been disorienting. Marcuse carried it off gracefully: his success did not change him; he could administer

71. *Ibid.*, pp. 173–179 (the part of the *Philosophical Investigations* is ⁋ 97–124).

72. One may note an abrupt shift in tone in the *Five Lectures* between the third, dating from 1963, and the fourth and fifth, which were delivered in 1967.

a rebuke to the young when he felt they deserved it, while remaining true as an old man to the ideological faith he had embraced a half-century earlier.

"Pleasure is, so to speak, nature's vengeance. In pleasure men disavow thought and escape civilization."[73] This aphorism of Horkheimer and Adorno epitomizes their abiding difference from Marcuse. It was not merely that they became more conservative—and in particular more skeptical about revolutionary practice—as they grew older, whereas Marcuse moved even further to the left than he had been before. It was also that despite their yearning for personal happiness, Horkheimer and Adorno retained Freud's original sense of the fateful paradox of civilization—of the inescapable anguish inherent in the clash between men's desire for pleasure and their deeply seated need to build a viable culture or society. Adorno never resolved the dilemma: he remained torn and perplexed—and in deadly earnest—until the end. Marcuse tried to rescue what he could of the element of play that mankind had sacrificed, while insisting on its compatibility with a life of thought.

In so insisting, Marcuse resembled the Young or Left Hegelians rather more than he did the mature Marx. His stress on the alienation of men from their own sexuality and his endeavor to restore to them an assurance of primeval innocence recalled such immediate precursors of Marx as Ludwig Feuerbach.[74] This Left Hegelian—or possibly even Romantic—aspect of Marcuse's writings goes far to explain their popularity in the effervescent atmosphere of the late 1960's. It also suggests the extent to which, despite his transplantation to the United States, he remained rooted in the idea-world of early-nineteenth-century Germany.

The vast majority of his American readers had no inkling of the cultural inheritance that lay behind Marcuse's strictures on con-

73. *Dialectic of Enlightenment,* p. 105.
74. This is the contention of Alasdair Macintyre, *Herbert Marcuse: An Exposition and a Polemic* (New York, 1970), pp. 18–19, 41, 58. On Feuerbach and the rest, see John Edward Toews, *Hegelianism: The Path Toward Dialectical Humanism, 1805–1841* (Cambridge, 1980), Part III.

temporary industrial society. Nor—since their own intellectual preparation was for the most part modest—did they feel obliged to explain the ambivalence in Marcuse's writings between his refined appreciation of literature and the arts and his assaults on traditional or "affirmative" culture. One contradiction, however, could not escape the least attentive: the discrepancy between the activist role he eventually assumed and his passive, nonstriving, tactile-sensuous conception of happiness. Marcuse himself recognized that his "non-repressive . . . order of values" was "in a fundamental sense conservative." He also expressed his dissent from Sartre's notion of human existence as "an eternal 'project' " which never reached "fulfillment, plenitude, rest."[75] There was in Marcuse's life and work an apparently congenital element of passivity—witness the number of years that passed before he resolved to enter the public arena. The fact that he finally did so gave evidence of a quite extraordinary civic courage, since it went against his own inclination.[76]

A hale, elderly man with a puckish grin, looking far younger than his years, his white hair blowing on some sun-drenched beach—such was the picture of Marcuse that lingered with those who knew and loved him. Even the friends who could not follow him into his last phase of activism cherished his mordant turn of phrase, his abounding love of life, and his indomitable independence.

v. *From Marx to Freud and Back*

"In psychoanalysis nothing is true except its exaggerations."[77] In this case an aphorism of Adorno suggests the common element in what he and Marcuse discovered in Freud. Both fastened on the shocking and the culturally subversive. Both tried to determine the ground on which psychoanalytic insight could broaden the range of the philosophical and sociological categories they had derived

75. *Five Lectures*, pp. 23, 41.
76. This courage is stressed in the basically critical analysis by Pierre Masset, *La pensée de Herbert Marcuse* (Toulouse, 1969), p. 183.
77. *Minima Moralia*, p. 78.

from Marx. But the way they went about the job of integration once again betrayed their temperamental differences: Marcuse built an entire theoretical book upon a couple of risky extrapolations; Adorno delivered his opinions in the form of casual comparisons and obiter dicta—plus, of course, his collaboration in *The Authoritarian Personality*.

From the very foundation of the Institut für Sozialforschung, Horkheimer and his associates had been concerned with Freud. They maintained cordial relations with the Frankfurt Psychoanalytic Institute, and a number of their early studies drew heavily on psychoanalytic material. Among them Erich Fromm, the future author of *Escape from Freedom*, was the most knowledgeable; but by the time he wrote his psychological interpretation of Nazism, he had taken leave both of the Institut and of Freudian orthodoxy.[78] Thereafter psychoanalysis seldom emerged very far into the foreground of critical theory: it remained a reference point, a set of injunctions that the social thinker could disregard only at his peril, and, above all, a bulwark against any teaching that aimed to "console" mankind or to reconcile it to its contemporary fate.

Six years after the Institut's return to Germany, the Freudian centennial gave Horkheimer and Adorno an opportunity to specify their own debt to the founder of psychoanalysis. Besides Marcuse, the roster of invited speakers included Erik H. Erikson and representatives of both the "revisionist" and the "existential" wings of psychoanalytic thinking. While these gave regular lectures, the Frankfurt philosophers limited themselves to brief statements designed to situate the centennial in its wider intellectual context. Most obviously they felt it urgent to reintroduce Freud to a German academic public which a half-generation of Nazi rule had denied knowledge of his writings and which even after 1945 had not seemed much inclined to restore those writings to honor. Perhaps it was with his conservative colleagues in mind that Horkheimer referred to Freud as an "enlightenment figure" (*Aufklärer*), using the term for once in a favorable sense, and that he and Adorno sharply rejected the notion that psychoanalytic theory could be dismissed as "out of date." Quite the contrary, they

78. Jay, *Dialectical Imagination*, pp. 88, 98, 101–105.

asserted, Freud's legacy needed to be rescued from those who had embraced it with shallow enthusiasm as "cultural goods" or who had reduced it to a "trivial psychology"; it needed to be viewed once more in the "youthful style" of its "most sublime discoveries."

Yet to see Freud intact meant to see him in dialectical terms. It meant to stress above all the economic pressure that Freud had recognized in the form of *Lebensnot,* or the bitter necessity of life.[79] Hence Horkheimer and Adorno's assessment of Freud's abiding validity was bound to cut both ways: while giving their full endorsement to his unsparing critical acumen, they felt obliged to warn against the undercurrent of resigned acceptance in his writings. Such a warning, they thought, would be particularly salutary when applied to those who attempted facile syntheses between psychoanalysis and Marxism or between the disciplines of psychology and sociology. In an essay prepared for Horkheimer's sixtieth birthday—one year before the Freud centennial—Adorno characterized as an "expression of helplessness" the "war-cry" of intellectual integration. One would succumb to "false consciousness," he explained, if one tried to separate the psyche from the society that conditioned it: it would be equally false, he added, to fail to recognize the difference between one's inner and one's outer life. "The divergence of the individual and society" was "essentially of social origin," was "perpetuated by society," and was "first of all to be explained in social terms." Only in this fashion could one comprehend how under contemporary conditions what pointed to a "higher condition" for mankind was always the "damaged" and not the "more harmonious." And only thus could it be made clear that even a successful psychoanalytic treatment bore the "stigma" of emotional damage and of "fruitless . . . adaptation."

Psychoanalytic therapy, Adorno concluded, in its very origins and not merely in its decline on the intellectual marketplace, fitted the dominant mode of "reification."[80] A decade later, he had not

79. *Freud in der Gegenwart,* pp. ix, xi, 33–34.
80. "Zum Verhältnis von Soziologie und Psychologie" (originally published in *Aufsätze, Max Horkheimer zum 60. Geburtstag gewidmet* [Frankfurt, 1955]), *Aufsätze zur Gesellschaftstheorie,* pp. 10, 16–17, 23, 34, 53.

changed his mind: even more strenuously than before he insisted that while one should "hold fast" to Freud's "strict sexual theory" against the "obscurantism" which was still trying to suppress it, one should also recognize that a therapy which was "installed" in the social mechanism itself strengthened "the functional capacities of human beings within a functional society." The author of *Civilization and Its Discontents*, Adorno added, might not have been fully aware of the ravages that his reality principle inflicted on his fellow men. But it was time to admit the harm that the psychoanalytic "contempt for humanity" could do to a living individual. What Freud had called anxiety and what the existentialists had "ennobled" with the same term was in fact a sense of "claustrophobia in the world." It betokened the chill that had descended on human relations. "In the universal coldness" of contemporary society, anxiety was "the necessary form of the curse" that hung over mankind.[81]

With Adorno and Horkheimer, then, as with Marcuse, the original allegiance to Marx in the end predominated over an infusion of psychoanalytic thinking which was never entirely assimilated. Yet the Marxism of the Frankfurt philosophers was more nuanced and skeptical than Marcuse's and became even further attenuated as their lives went on. Some critics have suggested that after their return to Germany they could be called Marxists no longer. Or perhaps one could say of them—as Merleau-Ponty implied of his own late writings—that the question of whether they were or were not Marxists was simply pointless. That, however, would be a patent exaggeration: virtually all the concrete examples in Adorno's postwar methodological essays derived from the economic substructure of society or the pressure of economic interests and were phrased in the terminology of dialectical materialism. When the Frankfurt philosophers got down to cases, they returned to Marx for inspiration.

This abiding allegiance goes far to explain the curious alternation in their writings—more especially in those of Adorno—between rarefied complexity and brutal assertion. It also helps us to

81. *Ibid.* (postscript of 1966), pp. 58–59; *Negative Dialectics*, pp. 346–347, 351–352 (I have altered the translation slightly).

understand their ineradicable hostility to "positivism" and their bludgeoning use of the term. It finally suggests why their receptivity to intellectual stimulus or their readiness to alter their ideas during their stay in the United States always ran up against impassable if not fully specified limits. It was not merely that they were reluctant to write in English and that they recoiled from the kitsch or middle-brow aspects of American life. It was that their philosophical set remained fixed, that beneath the dazzling variety of their cultural attainments lay a residue of dogmatism of which the casual reader might be totally unaware.

Scarcely less than Marcuse, Adorno and Horkheimer dwelt in the spiritual universe of preindustrial Germany. Despite their efforts to keep up with the contemporary avant-garde, at the deeper levels of their being they felt more at home in the world of Hegel or of Beethoven. The early, the Hegelian Marx was the one they really understood: their passionate protest against the works of capitalism had little of Marx's own subsequent appreciation of capitalist rationality as a necessary stage in the advance of society toward a socialist future; to them the process of economic rationalization figured above all as the overriding (and most grievous) symptom of the degeneration of the enlightenment into manipulation. To a surprising extent, Adorno and Horkheimer echoed the "other" Germany of their ideological enemies—the anachronistic, romanticized Germany of those who preached rural values and community solidarity—an echo epitomized by their longing for a society of warm, direct human relationships and an "organic," shared understanding of high culture and refined taste in literature and the arts.

Yet this nostalgic element in their thought did not necessarily invalidate what they wrote about mass society. It might be responsible for the imprecision and the emotional tone of their strictures on contemporary urban life—as it was for their disorienting blend of revolutionary indignation and intellectual snobbery. It might make them leap to the conclusion that America's "culture industry" was the functional equivalent of fascist terror. But it got to the heart of the quiet, uncomplaining desperation of the midcentury; it articulated what lurked just below the threshold of consciousness among millions of ordinary citizens. And in so doing it kept alive the notion of transcendence in an era when most social scientists—particularly in the United States—were settling for acceptance of the status quo. Adorno and Horkheimer's forebodings about the fascist potential in their host country proved (for the time at least!) excessively alarmist: their delineation of the "administered life" was increasingly borne out by the facts. Still more, in the late 1960's, the smoldering discontent with this kind of existence was to erupt in sterile, uncoordinated violence—and to claim Adorno himself as one of its victims. The wave of interest in Adorno's writings which followed almost immediately upon his death suggested that the "administered life" had been experienced as a clear and present reality by those who labored to decipher them. And by the same token it served notice on the sociologies and psychologies which traveled under the banner of adjustment or adaptation that they had a new and unexpected force to reckon with.

The Advent of Ego Psychology

I SUSPECT that Freud's contempt for men is nothing but an expression of such hopeless love as may be the only expression of
hope still permitted to us."[1] Thus Theodor W. Adorno tried to
embrace in one convoluted formula his full ambivalence toward
the founder of psychoanalysis. Love and contempt, he surmised,
might be two sides of the same coin: Freud's lack of illusions
about humanity anticipated what Adorno himself had learned in
the isolation of exile. Far more than one might suppose, the
Frankfurt philosopher accepted the bleakness of the Freudian perspective on mankind; the two had in common a hatred of sentimentality and an insistence on integrity in personal relations as in
intellectual pursuits. Where Adorno drew the line was at Freud's
Olympian detachment from politics and his "skepticism about all
ideologies except those of the private life."[2] And he argued that
the founder's original error in developing a therapy of social "adaptation" had been compounded by followers who had steadily
"watered down" the basic distinction between consciousness and
the unconscious.

In protesting against the practice he saw about him of convert-

1. Paper delivered in Los Angeles in April 1946 entitled "Social Science
and Sociological Tendencies in Psychoanalysis," cited in Martin Jay, *The
Dialectical Imagination: A History of the Frankfurt School and the Institute
of Social Research 1923–1950* (Boston, 1973), p. 105.
2. Philip Rieff, *Freud: The Mind of the Moralist*, Anchor paperback ed.
(Garden City, N.Y., 1961), p. 278.

ing psychoanalysis into "a superficial ego psychology," Adorno lumped together two distinct tendencies—the revisionism of the "neo-Freudians" and the current closer to psychoanalytic orthodoxy exemplified by the founder's daughter Anna and by Heinz Hartmann. He accused both these tendencies of distortion in interpreting psychologically what was social in origin, although he granted that Hartmann had delineated with greater insight than the revisionists the way in which a given social structure selected out the emotional attitudes which fitted it best. Both, he argued, established an illusionary "harmony between the reality principle and the pleasure principle." Both underestimated the ego's regressive dependence on the primary id and failed to differentiate between the functions of the ego that were individual in origin and those that embodied the claims of society.[3]

Adorno's difficulty in situating the post-Freudian schools was a common experience in the quarter-century following the founder's death. After 1939, there had emerged no uncontested heir to psychoanalytic leadership, although Hartmann came closer than anyone else to that position. Moreover, the Freudian legacy itself was sufficiently rich and bewildering to leave doubt as to where the course of orthodoxy lay—let alone the path of creative renewal. In its completed form, psychoanalytic terminology crisscrossed and overlapped: to the original threefold system of classification within his theory—topographical, dynamic, and economic—Freud had subsequently added the "structural" distinctions among id, ego, and superego, which, as Adorno observed, became the main ground of contention among his heirs.

The status of these four modes of "metapsychological" description varied widely within the practice of psychoanalysis. Nearly all its adepts accepted the structural triad, while reserving the right to reinterpret the three components. Similarly the topographical distinction between the conscious and the unconscious remained the bedrock of theory. But the precise fit of topography to structure was subject to debate: if the id could clearly be located in the

3. "Zum Verhältnis von Soziologie und Psychologie" (originally published in *Aufsätze, Max Horkheimer zum 60. Geburtstag gewidmet* [Frankfurt, 1955]), *Aufsätze zur Gesellschaftstheorie und Methodologie* (Frankfurt, 1970), pp. 25, 39, 42, 49.

unconscious, it was not equally correct to assign the ego to consciousness; indeed, the unconscious aspects of the ego presented a particularly knotty theoretical problem. As for the dynamic category of explanation—the terminology of "drives" (*Triebe*) and the ego's defenses against them—here once more an apparent consensus concealed deep-seated theoretical divergences. While people could agree that it was a vulgar error to confuse a drive with a merely biological instinct, and while virtually everyone granted the usefulness of such words as repression and rationalization, projection, sublimation, or identification, the same people were at odds over whether the dynamics of the mind should be depicted primarily in terms of conflict, as Freud had done, or whether the emphasis should be shifted toward equilibrium and reconciliation.

Freud himself had specified as the minimum tenets of orthodoxy his own earliest discoveries: the primacy of the unconscious and infantile sexuality (plus the Oedipus complex that went along with it). At the very least, then, a topographical and a dynamic way of looking at things constituted a prerequisite for belonging to the psychoanalytic movement at all. The same was not true of the other original explanatory mode—the "economic" terminology which spoke of the storing and spending of psychic energies. This had long ranked as the most doubtful and dated of Freud's interpretative schemata; it had borne most clearly the stamp of mechanistic nineteenth-century assumptions. It was to a large extent responsible for the positivist tone that infused his work; it gave a determinist cast to statements that in fact derived from an elaborately nuanced approach to the limits of mental and emotional freedom. By the end of his life Freud had long outgrown his mechanistic vocabulary; it had become increasingly inappropriate to his later speculative writings. But Freud himself seemed uncertain as to whether he considered these works his crowning achievement or a series of mental lapses. What was undeniable was his inclination to tinker with his own theoretical results as he constantly extended the reach of his metapsychological system.[4]

4. On this whole subject, see my *Consciousness and Society* (New York, 1958), Chapter 4, III.

Perhaps Freud could properly be described as a positivist in his tendency to write as though the mind "really" operated as he had explained it. In his casual remarks on methodology he had sometimes implied that one might treat his terms more modestly as metaphors or heuristic devices. But most of his followers had not thought in this fashion: at their hands psychoanalytic concepts had hardened into a set of unquestioned dicta. The displacement of the movement's center to the United States had encouraged this tendency: American Freudians, like the run of their countrymen, were impatient with epistemological hairsplitting. If the shift across the Atlantic, with the vastly enlarged opportunities it opened up, finally gave psychoanalysis a chance to become the "general" psychology at which the founder had aimed, it also threatened to restrict the movement's philosophical range and depth. Those among the émigrés who continued to explore the status of the abstractions that Freud had left behind him were out of step with the practical-mindedness of their new associates.

The refugees and the native-born could agree, however, on the crucial importance of one problem at least in the Freudian legacy: the individual's relationship to society, and more particularly his vicissitudes in adapting to the circumstances of his group life. While Freud's own therapeutic and theoretical work had concentrated on the individual, it had not totally neglected the social dimension. Less than a decade after the publication of *The Interpretation of Dreams*, he was beginning to speculate on the emotional consequences of a rigidly imposed sexual morality. By 1921, in *Group Psychology and the Analysis of the Ego*, he was trying to define in erotic terms the tie that bound human beings together and led them to identify with a beloved leader. But these speculations never got much beyond the stage of tantalizing suggestions which subsequent commentators have endeavored to piece together.[5] They merely hinted at the possible application of psychoanalytic insight to the study of history or group relations. It was left to Freud's heirs to pick up where he had left off and to develop as best they could a coherent social theory. And the way in

5. Besides Rieff's *Freud* and my *Consciousness and Society* (Chapter 4, IV), see Paul Roazen, *Freud: Political and Social Thought* (New York, 1968).

which they carried out this assignment served to delineate, perhaps more than any other single issue, the conflicting tendencies that separated them.

1. *The Freudian "Left," "Right," and "Center"*

Compared with the clamorous secessions of Jung and Adler before the First World War, the quarrels within the psychoanalytic movement in the 1930's and 1940's were polite and muted. The original dissenters had been sufficiently close to Freud in age—Adler was fourteen years younger, and Jung nineteen—to approach him as a near-contemporary, and their rupture with orthodox psychoanalysis, in particular that of Jung, had left correspondingly deep scars. The subsequent contestants stood in a quite different relationship to the founder. Born for the most part in the 1890's, they were clearly of a different generation. Those who were personally acquainted with Freud knew him only as an old man wracked by illness. A few had had their psychoanalytic training with him; the majority had trained with one of his older followers. In the generational succession of the movement, they ranked somewhere between Freud's "sons" and "grandsons."

A neat, if perhaps arbitrary way to classify them—with special reference to their social philosophies—is in the classic political terms of Left, Right, and Center. In such a schematization, Marcuse unquestionably belonged on the left. But Marcuse figured as an unusual case: without psychoanalytic training himself and in no position to draw on clinical experience, he simply speculated on the implications of the therapy that Freud had devised. Two others, however, both trained clinicians, shared Marcuse's radicalism and engendered an embryo left wing within psychoanalysis itself—Wilhelm Reich and Geza Roheim. In their case, as in Marcuse's, the radicalism was threefold: sexual, political, and stylistic. To an "enthusiasm for sex" and a belief that sexual pleasure was "the ultimate measure of human happiness," they joined the conviction that politics and sexuality were closely linked, that the repression of instinct functioned as a major weapon of political domination. And in stylistic terms, all three indulged in extreme statement, pursuing a given line of argument to its farthest reaches.[6]

Reich, Roheim, and Marcuse worked independently of one another. The same was not true of the neo-Freudian revisionists, who for the most part were bound together by professional ties and were frequently perceived as a constituted school. Here too the interpretation of sexuality was central to the group's definition. If the "Left" went beyond Freud himself in stressing the primacy of sex, the "neos" tried to modify the founder's more categorical statements on the subject and to suggest that nonsexual elements should receive greater recognition in psychoanalytic theory. It is primarily in this sense that they can be classified as a Freudian "Right."

From the political standpoint, however, they were not uniformly conservative. The remote progenitor of the revisionist tendency, Alfred Adler, had regarded himself as just the opposite and had adhered, as had most of his immediate followers, to his own brand of socialism. But the neo-Freudians refused to acknowledge him as their ancestor: one of the most curious chapters of psychoanalytic history is the stubborn denial on the part of men and women whose theories bore the strongest resemblance to Adler's that he had exerted any influence at all upon their work.[7] Adler had stressed the imperatives of the communal life; he had urged the therapist to turn the neurotic back toward human society; and in so doing he had reintroduced a "surface" moralizing which Freud had endeavored to banish forever from psychoanalytic practice. All this the revisionists echoed, but in a blander tone and in a language that stuck closer than Adler's to Freud's original terminology.

The native-born American members of the school, notably Harry Stack Sullivan, entertained few doubts about the society in which they lived. While they sought out, as Adler had, the social origins of individual neuroses, they were more inclined than he had been to suggest adjustment to a milieu they thought of as on

6. Paul A. Robinson, *The Freudian Left: Wilhelm Reich, Geza Roheim, Herbert Marcuse* (New York, 1969), pp. 4–6.
7. Henri F. Ellenberger, *The Discovery of the Unconscious: The History and Evolution of Dynamic Psychiatry* (New York, 1970), pp. 638, 645.

the whole beneficent. The émigrés were less sure: their recent experiences in Berlin or Vienna had not encouraged them to take a favorable view of the political status quo, and they shared some of Adorno and Horkheimer's anxiety about the direction in which their host country might be heading. But most of these too eventually accepted the tenets and practices of American democracy as presuppositions of their psychoanalytic labors. Here once more we may find evidence of a drift toward conservatism.

In a broader sense, the psychoanalytic émigrés' uncompromising rejection of Nazism as irredeemably evil entailed a critique of ethical relativism: in discovering what they were against, they almost found out what they were for. Psychoanalysis, of course, was not necessarily relativist; Freud himself had upheld the sternest standards of personal conduct. But in philosophical terms it had suspended judgment on questions of morality and been skeptical of mankind's capacities for improvement. For a resolute minority among the émigrés, this disabused stance no longer sufficed; in the ideologically open and welcoming atmosphere of the United States, they became militant optimists. Emotional suffering, they began to imply, was not integral to the human condition; beyond Freud's modest goal of alleviating psychic misery gleamed the vision of maximizing man's potentialities in a reordered society.

The most persuasive and popular advocate of such optimism was Erich Fromm. Already in *Escape from Freedom* he had rebuked Freud for accepting the conventional Judeo-Christian view of the human propensity toward antisocial behavior. Six years later he was ready for a full-scale assault on the citadels of psychoanalytic orthodoxy. In *Man for Himself* Fromm undertook a task that Freud had barely sketched out and that Weber and Moore and Wittgenstein had dismissed as impossible of accomplishment —to build an ethical world view on a theory laying claim to the status of science. *Man for Himself* aimed to unite psychoanalysis with the major secular tradition of humanist ethics; it reached back for intellectual support to Plato and Aristotle, to Spinoza and Goethe. "In many instances," Fromm argued, "a neurotic symptom" was "the specific expression of moral conflict" and demanded to be resolved in moral terms. But what Freud, no less

than Jung, had offered in response had been the unacceptable
alternatives of ethical agnosticism or religious faith. A third path—
the path of human values expressed in exclusively human terms—
they had left unexplored. So Fromm set out to inquire into the
nature of man, and more particularly into man's chances for
"productive" living—by which he meant self-love, a sense of
plenitude and autonomy, and the unfolding of human powers, as
opposed to the altruism and self-denial that religion had taught—
in brief, what was "good for man" without any element of
transcendence.

In trying to delineate humanity's full potential, Fromm made a
number of telling observations. He found a covert puritanism in
the near-obsession of classic psychoanalysis with the sexual drive.
He followed—and expanded—Max Weber's concept of inner-
worldly asceticism in showing how the modern capitalist's ostensible
ethic of self-interest in fact amounted to an ethic of self-denial as
punishing as anything that religion had devised.[8] Fromm's critique
of the cult of work and of the anxiety and insecurity which a
highly competitive society had created recalled his early association
with the Institut für Sozialforschung. But there remained little in
it of Adorno and Horkheimer's—and Freud's—tragic sense of
humanity's emotional entrapment. Fromm patently overestimated
man's capacity for autonomy, just as he underrated the devastating
force of sexual and destructive urges. As *Man for Himself* begot
sequel after sequel, Fromm's theoretical substance grew ever
thinner and his reliance on ethical abstractions more intrusive. In
the end—to use Marcuse's term—the "affirmative" elements in his
writing submerged its critical content.

Thus although Fromm, in common with Adler, considered
himself a socialist, his emphasis on productive living gradually
eroded his points of difference with his American-born colleagues.
Like them, he moved away from Freud's fundamental conviction
about the primacy of the unconscious. Like them, he perceived
among his patients and among humanity at large an unmistakable
"capacity for psychic growth" and "drive toward mental health."
Like them, he diverted psychoanalysis toward a celebration of the

8. *Man for Himself* (New York, 1947), pp. vii–ix, 6–7, 20, 45, 135.

humane, libertarian values of the civilized West. "Positive freedom," he had asserted in his first book, consisted of "the spontaneous activity of the total, integrated personality."[9] When these
words were written, they stood for an aspiration toward the far
future; as the years went by, they sounded more and more like a
description of what had already occurred or at the very least was
possible of attainment.

The dissatisfaction with a simple schema of primitive drives
extended beyond the ranks of neo-Freudian revisionism. More
generally the younger analysts in the 1930's and 1940's found it
reductive and began to work their way toward a more complex
theory of motivation. By the 1950's there had emerged something
of a consensus: the dominant tendency was now to speak of a
hierarchy of motives that could account for a "progressive taming"
of the drives and to adopt "a view of personality functioning" that
included "its steady, stable, ordinary, organized, enduring patterns
of behavior and thinking."[10] To do all this while remaining true
to basic Freudian principles required a high degree of theoretical
dexterity. The trick was to hold fast to the unconscious while
elaborating above it a sophisticated explanatory structure—to jettison reductionism while making sure that one did not throw the
baby out with the bath. So much for a brief initial definition of
the Freudian "Center."

Fortunately for the psychoanalytic movement the founder himself had suggested what might be done. Freud had a way of
putting theoretical heresies to good use at the very time he was
casting the heretics themselves into outer darkness. Just as he had
drawn on Jung's anthropological insights to launch his own such
speculations with *Totem and Taboo,* so a few years later he exploited the work of Adler in focusing his mind on the ego.[11] In

9. Martin Birnbach, *Neo-Freudian Social Philosophy* (Stanford, Calif.,
1961), pp. 213, 218; Erich Fromm, *Escape from Freedom* (New York,
1941), p. 258.
10. Merton Gill, "The Present State of Psychoanalytic Theory," *The Journal of Abnormal and Social Psychology,* LVIII (Jan. 1959), 1, 3, 5.
11. Roazen, *Freud,* p. 224; Abram Kardiner, Aaron Karush, and Lionel
Ovesey, "A Methodological Study of Freudian Theory: III. Narcissism, Bi-
sexuality and the Dual Instinct Theory," *The Journal of Nervous and Mental
Disease,* CXXIX (Sept. 1959), 207.

his earlier writings Freud had frequently mentioned the ego's role in psychic conflict. But he disliked the metaphysical overtones with which German idealism had associated the term, and he wanted to be sure that he had nailed down his epoch-making original discoveries about dreams, familiar slips, and their relation to the unconscious before exploring systematically the more conventional realm of self-consciousness. Heinz Hartmann was to see in this "retardation of Freud's interest in the ego . . . a rather fortunate event." "The great superiority of his later ego psychology," Hartmann found, lay "to a considerable extent in the very fact that his work on the unconscious mind and on the drives, and his insights into human development, had preceded it."[12] When in 1923, in *The Ego and the Id*, Freud finally enunciated his structural triad, he assumed a previous knowledge (and acceptance) of psychoanalytic fundamentals on the part of his readers and described the structural hypothesis as a completion rather than a basic modification of what he had written before.

In fact matters were not that simple. In ascribing to the ego an organizing function—or better, system of functions—Freud was running the risk that his followers might interpret this change as an authorization to displace the unconscious id from its original position of primacy. Still more, just three years before unveiling his threefold structure, he had found it necessary to embark on a parallel elaboration of his theory of drives. *Beyond the Pleasure Principle* of 1920, perhaps the most tentative of Freud's theoretical works, had added a new and perplexing element to both the dynamic and the economic modes: in trying to account for the repetition compulsion he had found among his patients—a compulsion that struck him as more elementary and primitive than the impulse toward pleasure itself—Freud guessed at a basic drive toward the restoration of an earlier state, a state in which life did not yet exist. Such was the genesis of the notion of "death instinct," whose lack of clinical confirmation was to plague Freud's successors at least as sorely as any of his feats of theoretical acrobatics. (It was characteristic of Marcuse that he was among

12. "The Development of the Ego Concept in Freud's Work" (originally published in 1956), *Essays on Ego Psychology: Selected Problems in Psychoanalytic Theory* (New York, 1964), pp. 280–282.

the few to find merit in the idea.) And to confuse the outlook further, Freud virtually equated the death instinct with hate or aggressiveness as the polar opposite of Eros, while failing to specify the ends toward which aggression might be directed.[13]

Thus the three works of the early 1920's with which Freud rounded out his theory raised new problems even as they put old ones to rest. If *The Ego and the Id* flashed a permissive signal to the psychoanalytic "Center," *Group Psychology* and *Beyond the Pleasure Principle*, in tantalizingly casual or even playful fashion, drew attention to the booby traps with which the promised path was strewn. Those who ventured on it needed to keep their wits about them; after all, they were writing with a glance over the shoulder to catch the reaction of the aging master. They felt obliged to choose their words with care and to weigh with precision every minute shift in emphasis. To this day it has remained debatable to what extent they were correct in laying claim to the title of Freud's lineal heirs or whether they were subverting his theory without ever quite admitting what they had done.

"Gentlemen, I think we are committing an injustice." The girlish voice that rang out in the stormy international psychoanalytic congress of 1927 was that of Freud's daughter Anna, his youngest child and the only one to work professionally with him. The subject at issue was laden with portents for the future—coercion of the American minority on the question of lay analysis—and the fact that Anna, although only just over thirty, was listened to suggested that she had already won the respect of her father's colleagues.[14] Nine years later she was to emerge as a major and once again a conciliatory force in the psychoanalytic movement.

By the mid-1930's the evidence was mounting that some of Freud's closest followers were ready to take the decisive step toward the ego psychology which their master had sketched out. Although the innovators included several men who were destined to make influential contributions to psychoanalytic theory—

13. Kardiner, Karush, Ovesey, "Methodological Study of Freudian Theory: III," pp. 217–218.
14. Ernest Jones, *The Life and Work of Sigmund Freud*, III: *The Last Phase* 1919–1939 (New York, 1957), pp. 295–296.

notably Edward Bibring, Otto Fenichel, and Hartmann's future collaborator Ernst Kris—it was left to Freud's own daughter to produce the work that was to figure in retrospect as the founding document of the new interpretation. The circumstances could scarcely have been more dramatic: the setting was Vienna itself, the world capital of psychoanalysis, living out its half-decade of precarious independence between the advent of Hitler and Austria's annexation to the Nazi Reich; the protagonists were members of Freud's "family," a child and a cherished pupil; the founder himself, stoically enduring his daily round of pain and apparently too sick to say much about what the younger generation was writing, had only three more years to live; sixteen months before his death he was to be driven into the exile that gave his movement a new language and a new home. The founding of ego psychology ranked, then, as the last great event in the history of psychoanalysis in its original Central European incarnation.

Anna Freud's *The Ego and the Mechanisms of Defense*, published in 1936, had about it a disarming air of simplicity. Its style was flat and direct, with none of the literary turns of phrase in which her father had delighted, and its argument proceeded with the clarity of the self-evident. The study of the ego, Anna Freud explained, far from being the "beginning of apostasy from psychoanalysis" that the orthodox feared, should be thought of rather as an essential further exploration. For if, as now seemed apparent, "large portions of the ego institutions" were "themselves unconscious," an inquiry into the workings of the ego did not entail abandoning fundamental convictions about unconscious processes. Quite the contrary: the only way to "reconstruct the transformations . . . undergone" by the basic drives was to analyze the ego's "defensive operations," most of which lay below the threshold of consciousness.[15]

Having skillfully inserted the thin entering wedge of the ego's protection against self-knowledge, Anna Freud went on to specify the roster of such defenses, some of which, like "identification with the aggressor," were themselves to become classic in psycho-

15. *Das Ich und die Abwehrmechanismen* (Vienna, 1936), trans. by Cecil Baines as *The Ego and the Mechanisms of Defense*, rev. ed. (*The Writings of Anna Freud*, II) (New York, 1966), pp. 3, 25–26.

analytic theory. Gently, persuasively she moved from the unconscious to the conscious level, even venturing along the way the suggestion that her father had overestimated the importance of the superego.[16] As the skilled therapist she was, she kept offering reassurance to her skittish colleagues. She defined her subject narrowly and dutifully cited the approved texts. Her method, as she frankly recognized, was cautious and even conventional. It lacked the "revolutionary" potential she attributed to a man who had entered the Vienna Psychoanalytic Society almost simultaneously with herself and whom she regarded in professional terms as her "slightly elder brother, or half brother," since in this respect they "shared the same father." For three decades Anna Freud and Heinz Hartmann were to advance along parallel tracks, each "immersed" in his or her special field, "respecting each other, quoting each other, but not in active interchange." Indeed Hartmann on occasion suspected that the founder's daughter should be reckoned his "silent critic." That this was far from true was to emerge at last in the mid-1960's, when Anna Freud, joining in the tributes which showered on Hartmann for his seventieth birthday, unequivocally ranked herself as his "eloquent supporter."[17]

II. *Heinz Hartmann and the "Conflict-Free Sphere"*

The theoretician who was to make the critical leap beyond the ego's defenses to an assertion of its substantial autonomy was as authentic a Viennese and as respectful a disciple of Freud as one could ask for. In his family origins Hartmann was the most illustrious of the Central European converts to psychoanalysis, and throughout his life he carried himself with an air of effortless inborn distinction. His paternal grandfather had been both a prolific writer and a deputy to the Frankfurt Assembly of 1848. His father, a historian of Rome and professor at the University of Vienna, served as Austria's ambassador in Berlin after the First

16. *Ibid.*, pp. 57, 116.
17. Anna Freud, "Links between Hartmann's Ego Psychology and the Child Analyst's Thinking," *Psychoanalysis—A General Psychology: Essays in Honor of Heinz Hartmann*, ed. by Rudolph M. Loewenstein et al. (New York, 1966), pp. 18, 26–27.

World War. His maternal grandfather had been called by Freud "the most eminent of all our Vienna physicians," and Hartmann himself was to marry a pediatrician from a leading medical family. Even the tutor who supervised his early education, Karl Seitz, was later to win fame as Social Democratic mayor of Vienna. To his more discerning friends, Hartmann seemed a man "whose major challenge in life must have been to protect his integrity and creativeness against an overflow of good fortune."[18]

Born in 1894, Hartmann grew up without religion or even a sense of its loss. (The Jewish origins that his name suggests evidently lay buried in the past.) This lack of a religious problem—or of the moral torments springing from it—sharply distinguished his adolescent development from Wittgenstein's, whose social and cultural milieu in other respects so much resembled his own. Like Wittgenstein, Hartmann breathed from childhood an atmosphere in which artistic attainments were the stuff of life itself; like the future philosopher, who was five years his senior, he became an accomplished musician and learned through early acquaintance with his parents' prominent friends not to be dazzled by public reputations or to seek such prominence for himself.

After Hartmann settled on psychiatry as a career, he continued to cultivate a wide range of interests. In the spring of 1918 he attended the university lectures in Vienna with which Max Weber resumed teaching after more than a decade and a half of silence; in his subsequent writings Hartmann was to return repeatedly to Weber as a methodological guide. A few years later, a stint of service in his father's embassy gave him a chance to observe politics at first hand. He was also unique among the Austrian psychoanalysts in maintaining contact with the Vienna Circle of philosophers. Even within his profession, he refused to limit himself to one branch or school. Having begun his work under the tutelage of conservative, experimentally oriented clinicians, he did

18. Marie Jahoda, "The Migration of Psychoanalysis: Its Impact on American Psychology," *The Intellectual Migration: Europe and America 1930–1960*, ed. by Donald Fleming and Bernard Bailyn (Cambridge, Mass., 1969), p. 430. The best source for details on Hartmann's life is the "Biographical Sketch" by Ruth S. and K. R. Eissler in *Psychoanalysis—A General Psychology*, pp. 3–15.

not encounter psychoanalysis directly until the mid-1920's, when he underwent a training analysis in Berlin. Meantime, however, he had published an influential paper on the experimental validation of Freudian theory and begun to write a book on psychoanalytic fundamentals, which appeared in 1927. The clue to the respect that Hartmann had already won for himself as a young man lay in his unrivaled combination of rigorous training in experimental psychology, close study of psychoanalytic theory, varied clinical experience, and an ingrained concern for the arts, for social science, and for public affairs.

Such was the man who as he was turning forty received the honor (shared apparently by only one other) of being asked by Freud to undertake a second training analysis with the master himself. By 1934 the founder of psychoanalysis had become too weak to maintain a regular relationship with more than a few carefully selected individuals. His choice of Hartmann proved fortunate: the older man found a superbly qualified successor, the younger a chance to complete his intellectual and emotional preparation at the highest source. During his years with Freud, Hartmann pondered, and published nothing.

This period of turning inward came to an end in 1937 with his reading of the paper entitled "Ego Psychology and the Problem of Adaptation" which little by little was to win its place as the most influential single post-Freudian piece of writing. The audience of analysts who originally heard it has been described as both "stunned" and unaware of its full implications. For Hartmann's presentation was so low-keyed and meticulous as to anticipate the objections of the theoretically inclined and to leave the rest at a loss. His purpose, he announced, was nothing less than to stake out the "*general* psychology," the "*general* theory of mental life," the promised land into which Freud himself, now engaged in his final meditation on the mission of Moses, had been unable to lead his followers.

The basis for such an intellectual program, Hartmann explained, the "meeting ground with nonanalytic psychology," was the ego psychology that the old master and his daughter had already been formulating. But Hartmann ventured far beyond them in the role he ascribed to the ego. In expanding what Freud had called its "organizing" system of functions and in characterizing its work of adaptation as "reality mastery," he markedly reduced the classic psychoanalytic emphasis on inner conflict. "Not every adaptation to the environment," Hartmann argued, "or every learning and maturation process" needed to be thought of as conflict-derived. A host of processes in the development of the individual—"perception, intention, object comprehension," and the like—went on in what he designated the ego's "conflict-free sphere." This sphere constituted the particular domain of "ego strength"—and in speaking of such strength in the traditional moral terms of "character" and "will" Hartmann came perilously close to revisionist vocabulary.[19]

Beyond defining the conflict-free sphere, Hartmann added the hope that its study would "open up the no-man's land between sociology and psychoanalysis and thus extend the contribution of psychoanalysis to the social sciences." But he was not yet ready to specify what that contribution might be. He confined himself to speculating on the "hierarchies of values" which every social structure dictated to the individuals within it and on the ways in which psychoanalysis could help people sort out their relationship to those values. While "the deepening of a man's knowledge," he explained, might "change his valuations" by making him see where his true allegiances lay, it could not lead to an assertion of value itself. It was an illusion to think that such understanding could "provide the goals of action." In vigorously denying the existence of "a 'natural' value hierarchy" applicable to all men, and in rejecting the view that values could be *derived* from psychoanalytic knowledge," Hartmann unequivocally aligned himself with Weber.[20]

The same held true in delineating the bounds of rationality. "The realm of strictly rational action," Hartmann granted, had proved "rather narrower than some of us would expect." But like Weber he refused all "traffic" with those who bemoaned "the

19. "Ich-Psychologie und Anpassungsproblem," *Internationale Zeitschrift für Psychoanalyse und Imago*, XXIV (1939), trans. by David Rapaport as *Ego Psychology and the Problem of Adaptation* (New York, 1958), pp. 4, 6, 8, 15–16, 22, 69.
20. *Ibid.*, pp. 21, 76, 83–84.

mind as the 'adversary of the soul.' " The current task, he suggested, with a bow to Mannheim, was rather to put into perspective the concept of rationality while adhering to rational method:
"the tendency of psychoanalysis to enlighten must of necessity
relativize the rationalistic doctrine of enlightenment."[21] Hartmann was far from sharing Horkheimer and Adorno's despair of
enlightenment itself. Yet he saw as they did that its claims must
be tailored to the bitter ideological realities of the 1930's.

In the year which intervened between the reading of Hartmann's paper and its publication in more extended form, the tide
of irrationality engulfed his homeland. The annexation of Austria
obliged Hartmann, no less than Freud and his daughter, to leave
their native city. But Hartmann hesitated longer than most of his
colleagues to seek refuge in the English-speaking world. It was
only after spending three more years in Paris and Switzerland that
he finally reached New York in 1941.

Here he established himself both in private practice and in
theoretical work with the ease which came naturally to him.
Without striving for primacy, he found it devolving upon him: his
personal enemies were few, and his admirers legion. Apparently his
associates did not hold against him his aristocratic demeanor or his
formidable cultural equipment; they regularly elected him to all
the high offices in the international psychoanalytic movement in
which he would consent to serve. One explanation for this lack of
professional jealousy was his courteous, unpolemical manner of
speaking and writing. Another was the fact that he remained
unknown to the general public; in contrast to the fame which
Fromm or Erikson enjoyed, Hartmann's circle of readers reached
scarcely beyond the psychoanalytic community itself.

The three decades between his arrival in the United States and
his death in 1970 might strike the casual observer as eventless.
Indeed his shift of scene marked no break in his thought, which in
its classic abstraction and conciseness passed easily across the
Atlantic and from German into English. Yet it was in America
and more particularly during his early and mid-fifties that Hartmann's powers of synthesis reached their full development.

21. *Ibid.*, pp. 65, 67–68, 70–72.

Around 1950 he published a cluster of papers—some of them in collaboration with his friends Ernst Kris and Rudolph M. Loewenstein—which together constitute the basic theoretical corpus of ego psychology.

These essays explored three matters that his original paper composed in Vienna had left tentative or uncertain: they spelled out the functions of the ego; they tried to fit Freud's terminology to the new material which the emphasis on the ego had opened up; and they provided at last some specification as to how the findings of psychoanalysis might illuminate the study of society.

The term "ego," Hartmann explained, was "often used in a highly ambiguous way, even among analysts." Hence it could best be defined in negative terms, to distinguish its psychoanalytic meaning from the various other meanings it had acquired in popular or philosophical usage. Viewed from the standpoint of Freudian therapy, it was "not synonymous with 'personality' or with 'individual,' " it did "not coincide with the 'subject' as opposed to the 'object' of experience," and it was "by no means only the 'awareness' or the 'feeling' of one's own self." In analysis, the ego figured as "a concept of quite a different order." It was "a substructure of personality" and was "defined by its functions." These functions were far too numerous to catalog—more numerous than those of the id or the superego. But among the most important one could mention adaptation to reality, action, thinking, and the defenses which Anna Freud had studied. Beyond and less tangible than these lay the set of functions commonly called "a person's character." And at a still further remove from the observable data of experience one could speak of the work of psychic "synthesis" or "organization."[22]

The heterogeneity of these functions already threatened to land Hartmann in multiple complexities: as he listed them, the activities of the ego went on at levels of specificity so different as to be barely comparable one with another. Moreover, he compounded his problem by adopting from one of Freud's last theoretical essays the notion of a congenital element in the ego, the guess that it, no less than the id, had emerged from "the matrix of animal in-

22. "Comments on the Psychoanalytic Theory of the Ego" (originally read in 1949 and published in 1950), *Essays on Ego Psychology*, pp. 114–115.

stinct." To ascribe to the ego so remote and basic a pedigree helped to buttress the newly won conviction of its autonomy. But by the same token it entailed a ramifying definition of its development as the "result of three sets of factors: inherited ego characteristics (and their interaction), influences of the instinctual drives, and influences of outer reality."

> Contrasts in the ego there are many: the ego has from its start the tendency to oppose the drives, but one of its main functions is also to help them toward gratification; it is a place where insight is gained, but also of rationalization; it promotes objective knowledge of reality, but at the same time, by way of identification and social adjustment, takes over in the course of its development the conventional prejudices of the environment; it pursues its independent aims, but it is also characteristic of it to consider the demands of the other substructures of personality. . . .

Such apparent contradictions, Hartmann insisted, became more manageable when regarded "from an intrasystemic point of view."[23] By this he evidently meant to suggest that the ego's widely varying aims derived from its separate functions and that these latter could be seen as fitting together provided one considered them on a sufficiently high plane of abstraction. For those who had learned in elemental Freudian terms to think of the ego as an embattled contestant in its daily struggle for survival against the superego and the id, such a rarefied explanation might offer little more than semantic deliverance.

To enhance still further the ego's newly won status, Hartmann urged his readers to assume that it disposed of "independent psychic energy." Earlier he had taken pains to point out that the energy in question—at least as revealed in analysis—had nothing in common with a "metaphysical" Bergsonian élan vital; it was "rather an operational concept, devised to coordinate observational data." Yet it was also apparent that the whole notion of energy, as a physical term, led ultimately back to biology. And with this recognition, Hartmann found himself in the most doubtful realm of Freud's theory—the question of drives and their

23. *Ibid.*, pp. 119–120, 138–139.

crucial situation at the meeting point of his dynamic and economic modes of explanation. Here Hartmann frankly confessed his puzzlement. Aside from lamenting the fact that Freud's English translators had not seen fit to maintain the distinction between instinct and drive and had used the first expression indiscriminately for both, he treated the whole matter with extreme caution. He refused to "enter into a discussion of Freud's biological speculation." "Assumptions concerning . . . drives toward life or death," he added, facilitated "neither the 'fitting together' of existent propositions, nor the formulation of new ones," if one limited oneself, as he and his closest collaborators did, to hypotheses that could "now or in the foreseeable future be checked against empirical evidence, against data of clinical observation, developmental studies, or experimentation in normal or abnormal psychology."[24] The clear implication was that it was safer to stick with a phenomenon such as sexuality whose reality and force were undeniable.

Yet there was one of Freud's late additions to his energetic theory which Hartmann welcomed in elucidating the ego. The delineation of aggression as an independent drive Hartmann found indispensable to the work of the contemporary analyst. Having separated it out from the "death instinct" with which Freud had left it entangled, he felt free to devote some of his most meticulous pages to elaborating its aims, its derivatives, and its substitutes. For Hartmann the concept of aggression remained among the fundamentals of theory; Freud's duality of sex and aggressiveness passed over intact into his thought.

Hence it was logical that he should reject the course which had been proposed by a number of his colleagues "to confer emeritus status on Freud's concept of instinctual drives, to pay respect to it" in the history of psychoanalysis, "but not to entrust it any longer with active duty in psychoanalytic theory." Hartmann described himself as "in sharpest opposition" to the assertion that the

24. *Ibid.*, p. 130; "Comments on the Psychoanalytic Theory of Instinctual Drives" (originally published in 1948), *Essays on Ego Psychology*, pp. 74, 79; Heinz Hartmann, Ernst Kris, and Rudolph M. Loewenstein, "Notes on the Theory of Aggression" (originally published in 1949), *Papers on Psychoanalytic Psychology* (New York, 1964), pp. 58, 60.

concept in question was "no longer useful."[25] This fidelity to the founder's legacy was central to Hartmann's view of his own professional integrity. It suffused his discussion of the second major issue that he treated in his essays of the 1940's and 1950's—the extent to which orthodox theory still conformed to the findings of ego psychology.

His own starting point, he explained, was to accept "the complexity of psychoanalytic propositions" as Freud had left them—and, he might have added, as he himself had further complicated them. Such complexity, he argued, was "not accidental but necessary." The very term "psychoanalysis" referred to "a set of propositions" that were "internally cohesive, elaborated in some detail, and allowing for predictions of human behavior." Its "validation" constituted "a gradual and slow process" in which one assessed insights derived from many sources and in which multiple types of evidence had "to be taken into account, foremost among them clinical experiences and the study of child development" that Anna Freud had pioneered. "Under these conditions neatness in theorizing" (an apt self-characterization!) figured among the prime qualifications for undertaking to expand or refine the psychoanalytic corpus.

Against the theoretically tidy stood those whom Hartmann viewed, to borrow Jacob Burckhardt's expression, as "terrible simplifiers." Although he himself would never have spoken so categorically, the force of his scorn pierced through the measured politeness of his condemnation. For Hartmann the notion of "dissent" did not depend simply on the extent of agreement of new ideas "with similar ones proposed by Freud" or his heirs. It derived also from the fact that the self-styled innovators forgot that the propositions of psychoanalytic theory were arranged in a hierarchical order and that to disturb this order could lead to impoverishing the entire structure. The dissenters tended "to fragmentize . . . theory, to stress one set of propositions and to neglect others." The result was a "simplified version, reduced to fewer factors, based on fewer concepts," which far from improving that theory put it "in danger of becoming atrophied."

25. Hartmann, Kris, Loewenstein, "The Function of Theory in Psychoanalysis" (originally published in 1953), *ibid.*, pp. 140–141.

Prominent among the abbreviators figured certain well-known students of culture and personality. It was characteristic of them, Hartmann maintained, to fail to reckon with the whole range of psychoanalytic thinking, "to polemicize with insistence against views contained in the earlier writings of Freud and his collaborators" while ignoring the subsequent "reformulations" that ego psychology had devised. This neglect, he thought, was particularly unfortunate in separating natural allies. For ego psychology might "well suggest the most fruitful and pertinent propositions for interdisciplinary cooperation."[26] Such cooperation was already implicit in Hartmann's call to make psychoanalytic theory "general" in its scope. It stimulated his observations on the third problem which his work in Vienna had left unresolved—the relation of psychoanalysis to the study of society.

Rather early in his explorations—as early as 1944—it became apparent to him that anthropology offered a more promising field for cooperative endeavor than either sociology or history. Much of what sociology studied in statistical or quantitative fashion, Hartmann had found, stemmed "from those layers of the personality" which were "not in the center of analytic interest and research." It was above all in explaining "human conflicts" that psychoanalysis could contribute to sociological knowledge. As for history, the full application of Freudian theory could begin only when the historians themselves turned their attention to those "spheres of life" which the analysts regarded as primary. And this sort of data gathering as yet barely existed. Up to now, Hartmann lamented, echoing all-unknowing a plea that Lucien Febvre had made just three years earlier in the silence of occupied France, historical research had unearthed very little about "how, in the Middle Ages, the Renaissance, or the eighteenth century, . . . the feeding, weaning, and toilet training of the infant was managed, or in what way the parents . . . handled the child's sexual and aggressive drives."

With these matters, of course, the anthropologists were already familiar. They were the ones most expert in delimiting "the

26. Ibid. pp. 134–135; Hartmann, Kris, Loewenstein, "Some Psychoanalytic Comments on 'Culture and Personality'" (originally published in 1951), *ibid*., pp. 88–89.

plasticity of the infantile situation"—the degree to which one culture or another could mold a young personality to its own requirements. Such "social compliance," Hartmann observed, helped to determine both the "mobility of the ego" and the "severity of the superego," along with the life roles that individuals fitted themselves to assume.[27] Seven years after this tentative assessment, he was as convinced as ever that "reports on child care and child rearing" constituted "the most fruitful and the most suggestive contact between psychoanalysis and anthropology." But he was becoming more wary of the anthropologists' relativist attitude toward cultural norms and less willing to remain the humble learner.

In his fullest statement on the subject—this time, as so often in his major theoretical essays, writing in collaboration with Kris and Loewenstein—he challenged the anthropologists' assumption that the cultural bent which derived from "institutional regulation" was necessarily primary to both the observer and the people observed. In the observer, he argued, at least in the analytic situation, cultural background might be "of comparatively minor relevance"; it was far from true that an analyst reared and trained in the West was incapable of understanding the emotional disorders of a patient from another culture. For the analyst was "likely to be less impressed by the . . . range of differences in everyday behavior than the anthropologist" and more inclined to view such differences as of diminishing importance as the psychic exploration moved "from the periphery to the center." Beyond that, Hartmann thought it inadvisable to draw sweeping conclusions from evidence on child rearing: "similar experiences in childhood," he had discovered, tended "to produce the most varied results." The social or familial pressures acting upon the child were no more than "initial links in a chain of influences." And among those influences "a decisive point had been insufficiently taken into account: the mother's personal attitude," much of it unconscious, toward her offspring and the fact of her own motherhood.[28]

27. "Psychoanalysis and Sociology" (originally published in 1944), *Essays on Ego Psychology*, pp. 24–25, 27, 32, 35–36.
28. Hartmann, Kris, Loewenstein, " 'Culture and Personality,' " *Papers on Psychoanalytic Psychology*, pp. 102, 105, 107, 109–111.

Thus while still respectful and cooperative in his view of anthropology, Hartmann insisted on two crucial divergences in emphasis. In nominalist vein, he drew attention once more to the uniqueness of individual experience; as a universalist, he stressed what was common to the human condition and transcended the barriers of culture. "Under the impact of cultural anthropology," he observed, "the question how man" behaved "under any given set of circumstances" tended "to be neglected in favor of the question how a member of a specific culture" behaved. The contradiction between Hartmann's two points of difference was only apparent: both derived from his deepest professional and personal conviction. The "autonomy of the ego"—its nurture and its strengthening—united them in an aim that was alike particular to the individual and universal in range. And it was, Hartmann surmised, less esteemed in the "primitive" societies which the anthropologists preferred to call "preliterate" than in a society such as his own in which scientific thinking had for centuries combated the remnants of "magical attitudes."[29]

Hartmann's reflections on anthropology had already led him deep into the problem of values. This problem—which had lurked in the back of his mind for a quarter-century—he finally undertook to unravel in his last sustained piece of writing, a lecture on psychoanalysis and ethics delivered in 1959 and published in extended form in 1960.

With Weber, Hartmann had all along insisted that the notion of reason involved no more than the weighing of means against ends, or of ends against their consequences, and was incapable of establishing the rationality of any particular human goal.[30] If, then, psychoanalysis, as a technique of reason in action, debarred itself from providing "ultimate moral aims or general moral imperatives," if it treated such matters simply as "psychological givens," was there no way in which the theorist or the therapist could offer ethical assistance? Into this treacherous terrain, Hartmann advanced with his characteristic prudence. He rejected most

29. *Ibid.*, pp. 95, 115.
30. "On Rational and Irrational Action" (originally published in 1947), *Essays on Ego Psychology*, pp. 49–50.

of what passed for psychiatric counsel among the uninitiated and the methodologically sloppy: he refused to speak of social or cultural systems as "healthy" or "sick," adding that even the concept of "maturity" had been frequently abused. Yet he did not throw up his hands in despair; he surmised that there were a few things that psychoanalysis could venture to say, and in specifying what these might be he turned once more to the congenial field of anthropology.

With the passage of time he had come to the conclusion that the anthropologists might not be such thoroughgoing relativists as they themselves conventionally supposed. "Common elements shared by different moral systems" had recently begun to appear in their work:

> . . . Murder, unlimited lying and stealing are everywhere valued negatively; also something like a principle of "reciprocity" is recognized everywhere. . . . Some incest regulations are universal; nowhere is cannibalism regular practice. Also, the duty of the adults to take care of the children is generally accepted; a certain respect for private property is, too, and so is respect for the dead of one's own group. The analyst will be ready to accept, he will indeed expect, that there are such commonalities.

Since human beings in all cultures went through comparable experiences in growing up—and more especially in the formation of their superegos—it was only natural that the anthropologist or the analyst should encounter a few virtually universal ethical valuations.[31]

Beyond the common condition of mankind, Hartmann speculated that psychoanalysis itself might offer elements of a moral code. In its attitude toward the two basic human drives, he found it drawing a significant practical distinction: "full discharge of the sexual drives" it considered "rarely as damaging to society" as people had "assumed in the past; the same" could not "be said of the full discharge of aggression." In his relatively "relaxed" stand toward sexuality and in his concern for the social dangers of

31. *Psychoanalysis and Moral Values* (New York, 1960), pp. 60, 73, 78–79, 82–83.

aggressive behavior, Hartmann's view of psychoanalysis recalled what Fromm had argued a decade earlier about its place in the tradition of humanist ethics. But unlike Fromm, Hartmann refrained from spelling out the implications of his moral obiter dicta. He refused to formulate a world view; he recoiled from the role of the psychoanalyst as preacher. Following the example of his master Freud, he kept his own high personal standards to himself. Here once again one can discriminate the nuanced position of the psychoanalytic Center as against the moralizing of the Right wing and the ultrapermissiveness of the Left.

Hartmann similarly cleaved to Freud's own conviction in stressing "self-knowledge" and "intellectual integrity" as central to the psychoanalytic ethic. "In analysis," he suggested, man was "confronted with a more encompassing reach of 'his good' and 'his bad' than he had been aware of before." Facing up to one's "blind spots" could "give to moral awareness a depth dimension" that it would otherwise have lacked. "All great religions," Hartmann added, had "aimed at this confrontation," however they might differ with psychoanalysis in their "postulates," their "tools," and their "intent." Yet to urge acceptance of reality did "not imply . . . passive submission to a given social system."[32] On political ideology as on so much else, Hartmann held to a delicate equilibrium. Like Wittgenstein, he preferred to set the limits beyond which lay the unsayable rather than to specify what could be said within those boundaries. Further than that he would not go.

With his accustomed modesty of manner, but in full consciousness of his magisterial responsibility toward his own profession, Hartmann had tried to chart for his colleagues the future of the theory in which they had been trained. Yet his greatest contribution lay in what he had done to rescue its past. Freud had "left his followers with a terrible dilemma at the very heart of the psychoanalytic enterprise": by defining the ego as the weakest of the structural triad, he had suggested that its chances for victory in its struggles with the superego and the id were slim indeed—and implied that the outlook for successful therapy was correspondingly doubtful. Hartmann endeavored "to lead psychoanalytic

32. *Ibid.*, pp. 88–89, 94.

theory out of this dead end. . . . In the language of Freud's military metaphor," he "placed many more battalions at the disposal of the ego. . . . And he did so tactfully, painlessly, authoritatively and unobtrusively. . . . He accomplished a major piece of theoretical surgery without shedding a drop of blood."[33]

In establishing a conflict-free sphere of ego development and ego functioning, Hartmann delineated processes which were initially unconscious and yet eventually capable of contributing to rational, purposive action; he grounded his ego in the instinctual substratum of the psyche while allowing for its almost infinite elaboration at the conscious level. Those who knew him best found it "by no means accidental" that he had hit on the concept of the conflict-free: it reflected his own self-confidence and "cheerful tranquility."[34] For the run of analysts, however—particularly those tormented by doubts about themselves and the viability of their profession—the serene abstraction of his prose raised unexpected and highly sophisticated difficulties in the very course of dealing with basic and familiar ones. Moreover, it merely hinted at the promised alliance between social science and a psychoanalytic theory which had become "general" in scope. And within the terms of that theory it stubbornly adhered to a vocabulary that had already been stretched far beyond its original context.

Thus despite the precision of Hartmann's mind and the care with which he chiseled his phrases, it was often difficult to determine how his lofty formulations could be applied to the realities of clinical or social research. Or perhaps better, his intellectual refinement itself entrapped him in the delicate web of theory. He lacked the temperament of the ruthless innovator who cuts through a welter of complexities and emerges with a startling new formulation. He hated to let go any precious strand of reasoning in his theoretical patrimony. He loved to demonstrate how two lines of thought that apparently contradicted each other could be woven together in a way which gave each its due. Like the immediate predecessors of Copernicus, he "expended . . . tremen-

33. Daniel Yankelovich and William Barrett, *Ego and Instinct: The Psychoanalytic View of Human Nature—Revised* (New York, 1970), p. 103.
34. Eissler, "Biographical Sketch," *Psychoanalysis—A General Psychology*, p. 13.

dous energy . . . in 'adding epicycles' " to the metapsychology he had inherited.[35]

This metapsychology, of course, consisted of figures of speech and heuristic devices. And as a collection of metaphors it presented the further difficulty of attempting to describe a set of activities—the mind—that by its very nature defied exact delineation. If all scientific language of necessity explains phenomena in terms of something else, more tangible and closer to home, the elucidation of mental events is obliged to operate at a level and in a vocabulary even more remote from verifiable reality than is true of ordinary investigation into the natural or the social world. The figures of speech in which it is couched—whether spatial or energetic—suggest a concreteness utterly foreign to the material at hand.

It would be quite wrong to imply that Hartmann was unaware of these pitfalls. His own mind was far too scrupulous to entertain for a moment the thought that matters "really" went on as Freud had described them. But he wrote as though they did: in his prose, the four classic metapsychological modes figured as near-actualities. And from there it was only a step to relapse once more into dogmatic certainty, a step which simplified life for Hartmann's unphilosophical American admirers. He had gently insisted that Freud's concept of drives ranked along with the distinction between the conscious and the unconscious, and between the ego and the id, among the essentials whose abandonment would reduce psychoanalytic interpretation to a flat meaninglessness. Without it, the inner drama would lack an initial thrust to set it in motion. But there was no such imperative to try to explain what the drives were; as Hartmann himself recognized, this sort of explanation lay in the realm of biology—or possibly of metaphysics.[36] More particularly, retaining as he did the notion of psychic energy—or even units of energy—as their basic characteristic encumbered the theory of drives and severely reduced its plausibility.

35. Yankelovich and Barrett, *Ego and Instinct*, p. 113.
36. Kardiner, Karush, Ovesey, "A Methodological Study of Freudian Theory: II. The Libido Theory," *The Journal of Nervous and Mental Disease*, CXXIX (Aug. 1959), 136.

Hartmann had rescued the human ego and made welcoming gestures to his colleagues in the social sciences. He had notably enhanced the range and the internal consistency of psychoanalytic theory. But he had not solved the problems of vocabulary and epistemology that Freud had left to his heirs. And this was what sympathizers outside the psychoanalytic fraternity were demanding with ever greater insistence as Hartmann's life drew to a close.

III. *Erik H. Erikson and the Sense of "Identity"*

In comparing the career of Hartmann to that of Erik H. Erikson, one starts almost inevitably with a set of contrasts: a clear and early-defined sense of direction as against decades of groping; a quiet, orderly existence with only one major change of scene as opposed to a life of frequent moves and a taste for adventure; theoretical tidiness versus imprecision of method; the self-effacement of one secure in his status and his talents as against a prolonged uncertainty on both these scores that manifested itself in a curious alternation of shy and dramatic behavior. In Hartmann the young man it was already possible to discern the future mentor of the psychoanalytic movement; in Erikson's case a tall, strong, ruddy young "Viking" was only gradually metamorphosed into a dignified, white-haired figure who quite literally exuded charisma and looked "the part of the sage."[37] The one guarded his privacy while working easily and closely with collaborators his own age; the other's unusual life history set him apart from his age mates and steered him toward the public arena and the discipleship of his juniors. Hartmann's influence by imperceptible stages suffused and transformed the theory and practice of psychoanalysis; Erikson's labors remained on the margin of the movement until they suddenly and for the most part unexpectedly became the center of a cult.

Although only eight years younger than Hartmann, Erikson seemed a half-generation behind him. He waited until he was forty before publishing his first significant article. The European phase

37. Robert Coles, *Erik H. Erikson: The Growth of His Work* (Boston, 1970), p. 266.

of his life ranked in retrospect as preparation; his entire mature
career was passed in an American setting, Still more, the period of
Erikson's most intense activity began just as Hartmann was putting the finishing touches on his own theoretical corpus. Hence it
was natural that the references to each other in their work should
appear more often in the writings of the younger man. Hartmann
took note of Erikson only in passing; Erikson, while recognizing a
primary debt to Anna Freud, tried to specify what he owed to the
co-founder of ego psychology. In his Freud centennial lectures in
1956, he credited Hartmann with having built a "bridge to a
psychoanalytic theory of the environment," while characterizing as
"theoretically undeveloped" his own empirical investigations along
corresponding lines. Twelve years later, with the publication of a
second volume of his lectures and miscellaneous papers, Erikson
felt ready at last to set down more precisely what he and Hartmann had in common: in a "Theoretical Interlude"—a rare occur-
rence in writings which were almost exclusively clinical, historical,
or discursive—he aligned himself with the older man's contention
that the technical term "ego" should be sharply discriminated
from the sense of one's own selfhood.[38] This emphasis on the
self—or more usually, of identity—was the core of what Erikson
for more than a quarter-century had been struggling to express.

From the day of his birth in 1902, Erikson's existence had
unfolded in unconventional fashion. His very name gave evidence
of his mixed origin and puzzling family relations. The child of
Danish parents, he "grew up in Karlsruhe in Baden as the son of a
pediatrician, Dr. Theodor Homburger." With the best intentions,
Dr. Homburger and his wife "kept secret" from the little boy the
fact that his "mother had been married previously" and that he
was actually "the son of a Dane who had abandoned her" before
his birth. And as though this national and paternal confusion were
not enough, he had to contend with the further question of his
religious identification. "Blond and blue-eyed," young Erik "acquired the nickname 'goy'" in his "stepfather's temple." To his
schoolmates he "was a 'Jew.'"

38. "Trieb und Umwelt in der Kindheit," *Freud in der Gegenwart,* ed. by
Theodor W. Adorno and Walter Dirks (Frankfurt, 1957), pp. 48–49; *Identity: Youth and Crisis* (New York, 1968), pp. 217–218.

Eventually, of course, the boy found out the truth. But the result was not an unequivocal turning against his stepfather. He kept the latter's transparently Jewish name as his own middle name "out of gratitude . . . but also to avoid the semblance of evasion." And he "came as close to the role of a children's doctor as one could possibly come without going to medical school." In so doing, he "mixed" what he called "an ambivalent identification" with his "stepfather, the pediatrician," with "a search" for his "own mythical father." This resolution of internal strain, however, did not emerge until years later when his "truly astounding adoption by the Freudian circle" provided him a surrogate father in "the then already mythical founder" of psychoanalysis while letting him know that the status of stepson carried advantages as well as liabilities. It made him "take for granted" that he "should be accepted where" he "did not quite belong"; it gave him the confidence to work "between the established fields" and "in institutional contexts for which" he "did not have the usual credentials."

From the very start his mother and his stepfather had had the "fortitude" to let him find his way "unhurriedly." They had not objected to his decision to forgo university studies and to "set out . . . to be a wandering artist." It was thus through rich personal experience that he stumbled upon what later became one of his key concepts—a social and emotional "moratorium" before buckling down to one's life task. After seven years of this free and "romantic" existence, he at last found a regular job that appealed to him: he signed up as a teacher in a small experimental school in Vienna. And here by fortunate coincidence he met Anna Freud, whose psychoanalytic studies of children were then in their own infancy. A training analysis with the founder's daughter followed, along with formal instruction in clinical procedure by such rising luminaries as Hartmann himself. Erikson had arrived in Vienna in 1927 as a young man uncertain of his course; he left in 1933 as a full-fledged lay analyst, married, with two small sons and an ample fund of observation of other people's children.

Thus he was not driven from the Austrian capital, as in the case of the Freuds and Hartmann, by the Nazi takeover. He left five years earlier of his own accord. "After . . . intense training under

. . . complex conditions, the idea of moving on and working independently seemed . . . invigorating." Erikson evidently sensed that in a Vienna teeming with psychoanalytic talent where the founder's heirs were already staking out their advanced positions, an untheoretical mind such as his would feel hemmed in. First, and very briefly, he tried to establish himself in his native Denmark; subsequently, and definitively, he moved to the United States, his way smoothed by his wife's American birth and the fact that child analysis was a new field which aroused interest wherever he went. From 1934 to 1935 he was at the Harvard Medical School and for the next three years at Yale. In the year of Freud's death and the outbreak of the Second World War, he moved once more, this time to the University of California at Berkeley, where he was to spend the decisive decade of his life.

Indeed, the major phase of Erikson's residence in America divided itself neatly by decades: the 1940's in California, the 1950's in the Berkshires, the 1960's at Harvard. Each had its distinctive character and focus. Throughout, however, the base point of his clinical work and writing remained the study of children: in child's play (like Wittgenstein!) he had found the royal road to understanding that Freud had discovered in the world of dreams.[39] Erikson was always at his most convincing when he spoke of children; the farther he got away from them, the more his thought wavered and blurred.

Erikson's move to California—to San Francisco Bay, that is, and not to the Los Angeles area, where so many German-speaking émigrés were to congregate—gave him a feel for American life that he might never have acquired if he had stayed in the East. As opposed to Hartmann's transplantation to a cosmopolitan and Europe-oriented New York, Erikson's decision to go West entailed a far sharper break with the cultural tradition in which they had both grown up. Associating mostly with the native-born, Erikson became fascinated by a people in which he discerned "a strangely adolescent style of adulthood." Tentatively, cautiously he

39. For all the foregoing, see Coles, *Erikson*, pp. 13–25, 30–36, 43, 180–181, and Erikson's own "Autobiographic Notes on the Identity Crisis," *Daedalus*, XCIX (Fall 1970), 735, 739–746.

began to explore the American "national character." At the same time, by another series of lucky coincidences, he found opportunities to observe at first hand the customs and beliefs of two utterly different tribes of American Indians. While he was still at Yale, an anthropologist friend had taken him to a Sioux reservation in South Dakota. At Berkeley he met the senior figure in American anthropology, Alfred L. Kroeber, who introduced him to the Yurok of the north California coast. Once again in contrast to Hartmann, "Erikson did not at first speculate on the conceptual relationship between psychoanalysis and anthropology or history. Instead he made a series of . . . direct observations of specific people living under particular and varying circumstances."[40]

During the early 1940's Erikson's provisional conclusions about both the aboriginal and the white inhabitants of the United States began to take form in a series of papers and drafts that only gradually developed into a book. This book was also to contain a reworking of the first article with which he came to general attention, "Hitler's Imagery and German Youth," published at the height of the war in 1942, and which Hartmann's collaborator Rudolph M. Loewenstein called "a unique and memorable contribution." Four years later, Erikson stopped his incidental publications: rigorously taking off one day a week from his clinical research and private practice, he settled down to complete the book that appeared in 1950 as *Childhood and Society*.[41]

Disarmingly amorphous in structure, *Childhood and Society* was in fact a much more ambitious work than it seemed. Starting with case histories, it progressed through the Sioux and the Yurok to the author's central reflections on the ego and identity until it came at last to contemporary America and Hitler's childhood. Behind this loose essay-type organization, however, lay a fixed and dramatic purpose. His conviction, Erikson explained, was that psychoanalytic method was "essentially a historical method" and that "the history of humanity" was "a gigantic metabolism of individual life cycles"; his aim, then, was to write "a psychoanalytic book on the relation of the ego to society"—something

40. Erikson, "Autobiographic Notes," pp. 747–748; Coles, *Erikson*, pp. 48, 61.

41. *Ibid.*, pp. 85, 113.

that Hartmann never attempted on this scale and with this wealth of clinical detail.[42]

Embedded among Erikson's case histories there now appeared the formulations for which he would later become famous—the "basic trust" that the child learned at its mother's breast, the "source of both primal hope and of doom throughout life"; the "life cycle" or "ages of man," fully spelled out with an "epigenetic diagram" attached; above all, the matter of identity. Erikson's cycle was intended to demonstrate that at each stage of life, from the infant's trust to the old person's "ego integrity," there was a hurdle over which the ego had to jump, a characteristic emotional set which the ego had to acquire in order to fulfill its potentialities; and for every stage there was a corresponding negative term—as, in early maturity (stage six), the "isolation" that made "intimacy" impossible—which marked the risk inherent in each successive turn of the cycle. For youth (stage five) identity versus "role confusion" stood as the polar opposites.[43] Indeed throughout Erikson's account, the maintenance of identity ranked as the ego's crucial and overriding task.

It was typical of him that in this, his first grapple with his most celebrated concept, he should have defined it elusively and for the most part in historical terms. Identity, he explained, could be condensed into a formula of sociopsychological change:

> The patient of today suffers most under the problem of what he should believe in and who he should—or . . . might—be or become; while the patient of early psychoanalysis suffered most under inhibitions which prevented him from being what and who he thought he knew he was.

Who one might be or become: the riddle of identity, Erikson had discovered, thrust itself in particularly bewildering form on the children of an advanced urban society. "Mechanisms of adjustment which once made for evolutionary adaptation, tribal integration, caste coherence, national uniformity" were "at loose ends in an industrial civilization." Having lost the possibility of sharing social rhythms inherited from the past—of a clearly understood

42. *Childhood and Society*, 2d ed. (New York, 1963), p. 16.
43. *Ibid.*, p. 80, Chapter 7.

step-by-step initiation into adult existence—closed off in a specialized environment and separated from "real life," the children
Erikson had encountered were obliged to grope their way toward
self-awareness with little guidance from any usable tradition. In
contemporary America, as opposed to the Europe Erikson had left
behind him, the boy was less likely to fear and hate his father, in
the classic "Freudian" mold; he was more inclined to suffer from
the harshness of a mother who had "abandoned" him, who had
pushed him out into a world for which he felt unprepared. And in
the same breath—as though to balance his strictures against his
host country—Erikson noted with approval the quasi-fraternal
relations between fathers and sons that American conditions fostered and the "democratic" aspects of a family life in which
paternal authority had long been on the wane.[44]

Childhood and Society was an immediate success. It seemed to
fill a need of which the younger psychoanalysts and the more
imaginative social scientists had become acutely aware. Erikson
now emerged as a recognized figure on the American intellectual
scene. Yet ironically enough, just a few months before his first
great achievement, he had become involved in a crisis that was
both public and personal and that was to deflect his career once
more.

When *Childhood and Society* appeared, Erikson had just
turned forty-eight. He had reached the stage of life (number
seven) in which according to his own schema "stagnation" threatened the "generativity"—the work of "establishing and guiding
the next generation"—appropriate to full and late maturity. His
biographer has suggested that at this point in his life he began to
traverse a second "identity crisis": in common with so many men
more ordinary than he, Erikson experienced his late forties as a
period of emotional peril. What occasioned his change of scene,
however, was no inner upheaval but rather the turmoil which
shook the University of California over the non-Communist oath
which the Regents had required of the faculty. While quite
willing to declare for himself that he was no Communist, Erikson

44. *Ibid.*, pp. 238, 279, 296, 312–318.

could not stomach the firing of colleagues who had refused to do so. In June 1950 he resigned the professorship of psychology to which he had only recently been appointed.

Although the author of *Childhood and Society* was welcome at a number of other universities, Erikson chose once more to become a full-time clinician. He evidently felt the need of peace, a rural setting, and a situation conducive to sustained thought. Joining the staff of the Austen Riggs Center in the Berkshires, he settled down in an "ideal place" whose "ideal patients" were young men and women with "severe but not intractable" emotional problems.[45] And in this extraordinary environment where patients and therapists mingled with an ease impossible in a conventional institution, Erikson began to ponder the career of a deeply troubled young man who had set off an epoch-making explosion in human history—Martin Luther.

Seven years after Erikson's move back East, his second book, *Young Man Luther,* was published. As influential as its predecessor, it reached an even wider audience, since the author's focus had now shifted to historical biography, or more precisely to an "ideological" study of the "life history" of a young man destined for greatness. Erikson's sweeping definition of ideology added a new term to the roster of concepts he had spelled out in *Childhood and Society;* so too did his stress on the crucial need for a "moratorium"; finally his delineation of the historical role of a "great young man" both explained his concentration on an individual figure and sanctioned the daring extrapolations that his study of Luther inaugurated in his work.

Ideology, Erikson specified, for his purposes meant "an unconscious tendency underlying religious and scientific as well as political thought: the tendency at a given time to make facts amenable to ideas, and ideas to facts, in order to create a world image convincing enough to support the collective and the individual sense of identity." What Luther had done was to forge in the fire of his own tribulation a new ideology suited to a new era. But he had been able to do so only after "marking time" in a monastery:

45. *Ibid.,* p. 267; Erikson, "Autobiographic Notes," p. 747; Coles, *Erikson,* pp. 156–159, 181.

We will therefore concentrate on this process: how young Martin, at the end of a somber and harsh childhood, was precipitated into a severe identity crisis for which he sought delay and cure in the silence of the monastery; how being silent, he became "possessed"; how being possessed, he gradually learned to speak a new language, *his* language; how being able to speak, he not only talked himself out of the monastery, and much of his country out of the Roman Church, but also formulated for himself and for all of mankind a new . . . ethical and psychological awareness. . . .

A man of this sort, "in the years before he" became "a great young man," could be conceived as "inwardly" harboring "a quite inarticulate stubbornness, a secret furious inviolacy." "Allness or nothingness, then," was the implicit "motto of such men." They truly and totally *meant* what they said.

Ideological leaders, so it seems, are subject to excessive fears which they can master only by reshaping the thoughts of their contemporaries; while those contemporaries are always glad to have their thoughts shaped by those who so desperately care to do so. Born leaders seem to fear only more consciously what in some form everybody fears in the depths of his inner life; and they convincingly claim to have an answer.[46]

This last was only the most extraordinary of the historical extrapolations with which Erikson had widened the range of his account. Along the way he had felt "obliged to accept . . . as half-history" the "half-legend" of Luther's "fit in the choir," of the young monk's having roared out during a reading from the Gospel, like an ox or a bull, his denial of some suspected transgression. Similarly Erikson had conjectured on the scantiest of evidence, or rather as his "clinician's judgment," that "nobody could speak and sing as Luther . . . did if his mother's voice had not sung to him of some heaven." Assertions such as these were bound to raise doubts in the minds of scrupulous historians. The nub, however, of the protracted controversy which Erikson's book aroused lay in its claim to have established a conceptual bridge from the indi-

46. *Young Man Luther: A Study in Psychoanalysis and History* (New York, 1958), pp. 22, 43, 47–48, 83, 109–110, 176.

vidual conscience to that of the masses, to have delineated the process whereby a man "with the sensitivity and the power-drive of a Luther" could "sow ideological seeds into fresh furrows of historical change."[47]

Thus while open-minded historians and historically inclined psychoanalysts derived immense profit from the intellectual vistas that *Young Man Luther* opened up—indeed, it was around this work that the "Erikson cult" first gathered—as the years passed they began to recognize that the presumed bridge from the individual to the mass was not so secure as Erikson's admirers had initially supposed. They remained grateful to him for having dealt with history and social milieu in an incomparably richer and subtler fashion than had been true of a neo-Freudian like Erich Fromm. They were particularly happy that Erikson's stress on the stage of life in which men discovered their ideological allegiances —from the midteens to about the age of thirty—facilitated the researcher's task by shifting the emotional weight from the classic Freudian period of half-forgotten childhood, on which data were usually sparse, to the better-documented years of late adolescence and early maturity.[48] But when those who had been stimulated by Erikson's example tried their hand at what came to be called "psychohistory," they almost invariably produced an individual biography; their efforts to project their interpretations onto a wider group remained tentative and unconvincing. Most of the time, in addressing themselves to mass behavior, they "simply and mistakenly inferred . . . the motivation for this behavior . . . from the motivation of the leader." A methodological "model based on the development of the individual in the family" proved inadequate for explaining the origins of major historical change.[49]

In 1960, after his decade of withdrawal, Erikson returned to a university setting. His appointment at Harvard carried the un-

47. *Ibid.*, pp. 23, 37, 72, 221; Coles, *Erikson*, p. 207.
48. See my *History as Art and as Science* (New York, 1964), p. 59.
49. Fred Weinstein and Gerald M. Platt, *Psychoanalytic Sociology: An Essay on the Interpretation of Historical Data and the Phenomena of Collective Behavior* (Baltimore, 1973), pp. 13, 68. This judicious review of the problem includes (pp. 12–13 n.) a roster of psychoanalytic biographies directly or indirectly inspired by Erikson's example.

precedented title Professor of Human Development, and it was understood from the start that he would not be expected to behave like an ordinary member of the faculty. His teaching load was light: from the time of his arrival to his retirement ten years later, he gave only two regular courses, a lecture course for undergraduates on "The Human Life Cycle" and a seminar for advanced students on the writing of psychoanalytic biography. In Cambridge Erikson quickly became a celebrity: having received all the intellectual recognition a man might desire, he could now afford to point with pride to his total lack of academic credentials.

The Harvard years completed the gradual shift in Erikson's interest from childhood to youth and from occasional moral commentary to explicit ethical assertion. The two miscellaneous volumes he published in this period document his overriding concern with the search for identity by the young; as a consequence and much to Erikson's chagrin, the term "identity crisis" was soon circulating among the undergraduates as a catch-all for emotional distress, however banal its origin. Here he could correctly claim to have been misunderstood. In the matter of ethics, however, there was no room for mistake: Erikson had quite consciously assumed the role of moral preceptor that Hartmann (and Freud before him) had rejected as incompatible with the profession of psychoanalysis. Whereas in *Luther* he had confined himself to characterizing in passing "the mutilation of a child's spirit" as the deadliest "of all possible sins," in the lectures which appeared six years later such ethical statements had advanced to the foreground. Erikson was now ready to employ so familiar and reassuring a word as "fidelity" or even "virtue," while reformulating each to accord with his own category of "ego strength." And "in the light of new insight" he returned to the "Golden Rule" of Christianity. As Erikson understood it, "the Rule would say that it" was "best to do to another what" would "strengthen you even as it" would "strengthen him—that is, what" would "develop his best potentials even as it" developed "your own."[50]

50. *Young Man Luther*, p. 70; *Insight and Responsibility: Lectures on the Ethical Implications of Psychoanalytic Insight* (New York, 1964), pp. 174–175, 233.

The culmination and synthesis of Erikson's new emphases came with the publication of his third major book, *Gandhi's Truth*, in 1969, the year before his retirement from teaching. Another "life history" on the scale of his *Luther*, it marked a striking departure from the model of his earlier work. Most obviously the personal references, which had never been absent in his writings, had vastly proliferated. Erikson's book on Gandhi not only recounted in detail the frustrations and intellectual breakthroughs he had himself experienced on his journeys of orientation to India; it included, halfway along, "a personal word" in which the author wrestled with his own ambivalence toward his protagonist and obliquely took the Mahatma to task for inflicting on others, more particularly on his immediate family, the violence he claimed to have eschewed. Beyond this exercise in self-revelation, Erikson was now prepared to go much further than in *Luther* in attributing to emotional suffering a positive force in the careers of earth-shaking figures:

> This, then, is the difference between a case history and a life-history: patients, great or small, are increasingly debilitated by their inner conflicts, but in historical actuality inner conflict only adds an indispensable momentum to all superhuman effort.[51]

In thus distinguishing between the ordinary victims of emotional misery and the world-historical titans destined for leadership, Erikson seemed to be delimiting, as he had not done before, the sphere of the therapeutic from the sphere of the psychohistorical. But the distinction he drew was coupled with a further change in approach which canceled out whatever clarification might have ensued. In pondering the role of the Mahatma, the author of *Childhood and Society* and of *Young Man Luther* had come to a fresh understanding of his own profession; he had "sensed an affinity between Gandhi's truth and the insights of modern psychology." Subsequently he had hit on a "convergence" between Freud's psychoanalysis and the ideological technique that the Mahatma called Satyagraha or "truth force": "in both encounters

51. *Gandhi's Truth: On the Origins of Militant Nonviolence* (New York, 1969), pp. 252–253, 363.

only the militant probing of a vital issue by a nonviolent confrontation" could "bring to light what insight" was "ready on both sides." Such a convergence, Erikson added, beyond its historical significance, might well have "evolutionary" implications. Based as it was on a "pervasive faith in the brotherhood of man," it pointed "to the next step in man's realization of man as one all-human species, and thus to our only chance to transcend what we are."[52]

Social scientists were quick to spot "in this analogy a rather serious defect." The "enormous force" of "the therapeutic situation" derived from "the stripping away of everything but a common concentration on emotional exploration. . . . With politics it" was "just the reverse: the wider the range of divergent concerns with which it" could "manage to cope the deeper it" cut.[53] Quite apart from their doubts about the notion of congruence between Satyagraha and psychoanalysis, Erikson's more expert readers were taken aback by the transmutation that *Gandhi's Truth* revealed in the author himself. The therapist had become humanity's prophet; diagnosis had yielded to exhortation. In the same period in which Marcuse belatedly won his fame, Erikson too was taken up as an idol by the young. And for reasons that were not totally dissimilar. In contrast to the more fastidious and "private" Adorno and Hartmann, Marcuse and Erikson accepted the perils of the public arena and in so doing risked the vulgarization of their thought and its celebration for propagandist ends.

In the volume of essays and papers he published in 1968, Erikson had defined, but by forecast rather than retrospect, the program he had tried to carry out:

> Psychoanalysis first studied, as if it could be isolated, man's enslavement by the id. . . . Next the focus of study shifted to man's enslavement by seemingly autonomous ego (and superego) strivings—defensive mechanisms which, in order to "contain" an upset libido economy, impoverish the ego's power of experiencing and planning. Perhaps psychoanalysis

52. *Ibid.*, pp. 245, 413, 439–440.
53. Clifford Geertz in *The New York Review of Books*, XIII (Nov. 20, 1969), 4.

will complete its basic studies . . . by investigating more explicitly man's enslavement by historical conditions which . . . exploit archaic mechanisms within him, to deny him physical vitality and ego strength.[54]

The phraseology suggests Erikson's conviction that he was engaged in "completing" the ego psychology which Hartmann and his own therapist Anna Freud had launched. Unquestionably he had deepened and enriched the historical component in their common enterprise. But he had done so with an admixture of extrapolation, ethical obiter dicta, and conjecture which left reservations in the minds of all except his most devoted followers. Moreover, his ventures in the direction of theory, as he himself granted, often produced clumsy and ambiguous results. This was particularly apparent in the two new terms or schemata associated with his name—identity and the life cycle.

Why, Erikson's readers wondered, did he have to specify so concretely the stages of human existence? Though nearly everyone agreed that the course of life fell naturally into a perceptible emotional progression, it was by no means equally clear that each life divided into the same stages and that these must be eight, no more, no less. Why did Erikson insist on reiterating a tight formula so much at variance with his usual discursive method? Even his close adherents provided no convincing answer. To his loyal biographer, the Erikson of the eight stages was "a man struggling to make his case," resorting to the expedient of an "epigenetic" chart and persisting in "developing" that chart, in order to "highlight" views he felt to be peculiarly his own. More detached critics, who had learned a great deal from Erikson along the way, found in his schema an element of the culture-bound. They surmised that a "preindustrial psychoanalyst" might describe the stages of life less in terms of tasks to be accomplished and that he might put his stress on puberty rather than on the protracted adolescence so characteristic of contemporary Western society.[55]

In the matter of identity, Erikson compounded his readers' difficulties by continually coining new definitions which were not

54. *Identity: Youth and Crisis*, p. 74.
55. Coles, *Erikson*, p. 138; Weinstein and Platt, *Psychoanalytic Sociology*, p. 58 n.

always compatible with their predecessors. Here his biographer has offered the helpful suggestion that Erikson was not really interested in defining the concept, that he wanted to let it gradually affirm itself "by using it over and over again and working for years to give it a particular kind of meaning." Indeed the simplest formulation he ever produced he borrowed from William James: "*This* is the real me!"[56] The sense of identity—or lack of it—unquestionably ranked among the basic human experiences. But its status in psychoanalytic theory, as in historical or anthropological interpretation, remained obscure. It was a slippery term which glided back and forth somewhere between the classic ego and an individual's social role; it also came close to such a homespun and traditional word as "character." Perhaps its greatest difficulty derived from Erikson's failure to clarify its relationship to the fundamental Freudian category of the unconscious; one might hazard the guess that in his usage a person's identity became securely established when it finally emerged into the full light of consciousness.

These conceptual difficulties were inherent in Erikson's idiosyncratic style. Whereas the writing in *Childhood and Society* had had the plain, direct quality of a man still uncertain of his command of the English language, Erikson's later work bespoke an author confident that he had won his linguistic struggle and even fancying himself a stylist. From *Luther* on, his prose became increasingly elaborate, evasive, and even coy. In its pretentious and self-consciously "literary" phraseology, it was a far cry from the elegant simplicity of Freud.

Toward the memory of Freud himself Erikson invariably maintained an attitude of respect. Although he had known the founder only at a distance and had never actually "addressed him," he recalled with lively sympathy the uncomplaining fashion in which the old man had borne his suffering. For his own part, Erikson took pains to minimize his departures from standard Freudian practice. What seemed important to him was to "advance" his teaching "by small steps without abandoning" the "unique ideological foundations" he had inherited. His "primary interest," he

56. Coles, *Erikson*, pp. 82, 165; Erikson, *Identity: Youth and Crisis*, p. 19.

explained, "in the flux of phenomena precluded any attempt to find safety in orthodoxy or escape in heresy." Rather than challenging the legacy of the master, he preferred to alter the contours of psychoanalysis through hints and insinuations. Thus he afforded "the curious picture of a prominent . . . theorist who" ignored "four-fifths of Freud's metapsychology" and applied the rest in his own highly personal fashion. To a profession not yet released from an outmoded mechanistic vocabulary, he reintroduced still older words which evoked a prescientific intellectual universe; while all the time protesting his lineal fidelity, he accomplished the unparalleled feat of smuggling "the concept of the human spirit through the back door" of psychoanalytic method.[57]

iv. *The Paths Not Taken*

Hartmann and Erikson shared a reluctance to underline their points of divergence from Freud. In both cases affection reinforced the awe the founder's life and work inspired in them. Moreover, from the strictly professional standpoint, one could view certain aspects of their writings as complementary: both assumed in human beings "an inborn coordination to an average expectable environment"; both traced the unfolding of a "social character" which they took to be part of man's genetic endowment. From this standpoint, Erikson could be seen as extending or particularizing what Hartmann had enunciated in general terms. Yet in the way they went about their task of integrating ego and social milieu—as in their relationship to Freud himself—their procedures contrasted as strongly as their life styles. Hartmann tried "to maintain and repair" the founder's metapsychology. Erikson for the most part disregarded it, while holding to the "biological thrust" that was at the root of Freud's thought. While Hartmann treated the primal drives as springboards for his theoretical elaborations, Erikson returned "again and again to early sexual origins as the grounds of human development"—witness his insistence on

57. Erikson, "Autobiographic Notes," pp. 735–736, 751; *Identity: Youth and Crisis*, p. 228; Yankelovich and Barrett, *Ego and Instinct*, pp. 140, 151–153.

the suckling's "basic trust" (or disappointment therein) as the elemental life experience. In this sense their solutions to the metapsychological problem Freud had left them appeared "exactly opposite."[58]

Both, then, contended with the same dilemma of reconciling loyalty to their common master with what they had discovered on their own. Their perplexities might have been fewer—and their reasoning less tortured—if they had pursued paths which lay open to them but on which they refused to venture, paths taken with apparent ease by native-born American or British clinicians who still regarded themselves as within the psychoanalytic mainstream. One can only speculate on why it was possible for men like Abram Kardiner and W. Ronald D. Fairbairn to redefine more radically than Hartmann or Erikson the concepts which inspired the labors of all of them. Perhaps it was that acceptance in the original Viennese circle around Freud forged links of devotion which a half-lifetime's residence across the Atlantic could not shake; perhaps it was that having English rather than German as a native language afforded greater freedom in employing terms which had passed through the loose meshes of the translator's net. Whatever the reason, simultaneously with the work of Hartmann and Erikson, certain of their contemporaries were proving it possible to delete in explicit terms vast segments of the Freudian metapsychology while faithfully adhering to fundamental psychoanalytic convictions about sexuality and the unconscious.

One of the few native-born Americans to have trained directly with Freud, Kardiner has been characterized as the "broadest" and the "deepest" of the "neos."[59] More properly, however, in the emphasis he placed on the earliest discoveries of psychoanalysis and the infrequency of his ethical affirmations, he belonged with the mainstream or "Center." A decade before Hartmann died— and when his theoretical writings were virtually complete— Kardiner undertook to assess the adjustments that Hartmann had

58. David Rapaport, "A Historical Survey of Psychoanalytic Ego Psychology," *Psychological Issues*, I, No. 1 (1959), 14–16; Yankelovich and Barrett, *Ego and Instinct*, pp. 153–154.

59. Birnbach, *Neo-Freudian Social Philosophy*, p. 127. See also Kardiner's "Freud: The Man I Knew, the Scientist, and His Influence," *Freud and the 20th Century*, ed. by Benjamin Nelson (New York, 1957), pp. 46–58.

made in the Freudian corpus. Hartmann's major mistake, Kardiner
argued, was to have "attempted a synthesis of the new concept of
ego functions with Freud's instinctual and energic hypotheses";
the attempt was bound to fail—the delicate balance between ego
autonomy and psychic "motor power" rested on precarious con-
structs constantly threatened with collapse. Still more, Kardiner
questioned whether it was advisable to distinguish ego from superego as sharply as the structural model dictated. Instead, he suggested that psychoanalysis would do better to scrap this model and
go back to the Freud of *The Interpretation of Dreams*—the
Freud whose original view of the dynamics of unconscious mental
operations had "demonstrated its vitality and usefulness over and
over again."[60]

Did Kardiner mean to deny the force of the basic drives along
with the vocabulary of psychic energy in which Freud had described them? Not necessarily: one might plausibly interpret
Kardiner's critique of ego psychology as a venture in conceptual
clarification that kept the drives as "givens" but discarded as excess
baggage the greater part of the theory which had grown up above
and around them. In Freud's mind the task of taming the drives
had exceeded the strength of the unaided ego; in order to gain
mastery the ego had required as an ally a ruthless tyrant—the
superego—which proved just as overbearing as the amorphous and
amoral id. If the emphasis was now to be shifted to ego autonomy
and ego strength, was it not logical to renounce the attempt to
make fine (or mechanistic) discriminations both among the drives
associated with the id and between the two presumed agencies at
odds with them? To translate Kardiner's terminology into common parlance: the notion of a "superagency" was required to
explain neither the animal in man nor what the moralists called
the voice of conscience.

It was here that Fairbairn's writings intersected with Kardiner's.
A Scot working in almost total isolation from his psychoanalytic
peers, Fairbairn drew attention as Kardiner did to the "most re-

60. Kardiner, Karush, Ovesey, "A Methodological Study of Freudian
Theory: IV. The Structural Hypothesis, the Problem of Anxiety, and Post-
Freudian Ego Psychology," *The Journal of Nervous and Mental Disease*,
CXXIX (Oct. 1959), 351–355.

grettable" fact that "a developing psychology of the ego" had come "to be superimposed upon an already established psychology of impulse." (With his characteristic independence, Fairbairn translated Freud's *Trieb* as "impulse"—which in fact served better than either of the two English words ordinarily used, the misleading term "instinct" and the literally accurate but clumsy "drive.") Again like Kardiner, Fairbairn returned to the early Freud, scrutinizing once more the structural triad of the later period. To Fairbairn the id rather than the superego appeared the concept most in need of criticism and correction. If, as he suspected, no "impulses" could "be regarded as existing in the absence of an ego structure," it would "no longer be possible to preserve any psychological distinction between the id and the ego." It would be better to "split . . . ego-structure . . . into three separate egos— . . . a central ego (the 'I'), . . . a libidinal ego, and . . . an aggressive, persecutory ego" designated "the internal saboteur."

Whatever one might think of Fairbairn's new trinity of terms— and he was frank to recognize their "general correspondence" with what Freud had proposed—it had the advantage of suggesting continuity rather than unrelieved antagonism among the three and to be closer than the old triad to the way in which people actually viewed their own inner processes.[61] Moreover, Fairbairn had undergirded his hypothesis with a theory of personality that put the whole matter of drives in a new framework. It was pointless, Fairbairn maintained, to discuss impulse in the abstract: the crucial question was the "object"—that is, the person—toward whom the impulse was originally directed. And with this theory of "object relation," Fairbairn was back in the world of children's earliest emotions—more particularly their feelings toward their mothers—the realm in which Freud had arrived at his first great discoveries and in which his daughter and her pupil Erikson had made their most important theoretical contributions. He was back to the bedrock of psychoanalysis.

Regarded in this fashion, the whole vast, overelaborated corpus of theory took on new and simpler contours. If "impulse" invariably had an object, then it was "to be regarded as inseparably

61. *Psychoanalytic Studies of the Personality* (London, 1952), pp. 59, 88, 101, 106.

associated with an ego structure from the beginning." By the same token, the dynamic and the structural ways of looking at the mind became one. "Both structure divorced from energy and energy divorced from structure" were "meaningless concepts." Fairbairn's "principle of dynamic structure" conceived all emotional change as "inherently directional." It did away with "conceptions of hypothetical 'impulses'" which bombarded "passive structures, much as if an air-raid were in progress." It dealt with "impulse" not as "a kick in the pants administered out of the blue to a surprised, and perhaps somewhat pained, ego," but as "a psychical structure in action—a psychical structure doing something to . . . somebody."[62]

In short, Fairbairn's set of redefinitions abolished the distinctions among the four classic metapsychological modes. Within the old metapsychology, the "topographical" boundary between consciousness and the unconscious alone stood unaltered. Some such recasting was implicit in Erikson's careful avoidance of the issue—but he refrained from saying so. Hartmann never ventured even that far. Fairbairn's blunt, down-to-earth vocabulary accomplished something that eluded both Hartmann's refined precision and Erikson's multifaceted, shifting insights: it translated psychoanalytic theory into a language which investigators in neighboring fields could understand and further recast for their own purposes. While avoiding the methodological crudity of the neo-Freudians, it marked off what was basic and necessary from what had come perilously close to turning into a dignified intellectual game. By the 1970's Fairbairn had found few imitators—Kardiner had picked up rather more—but he had at least shown his professional colleagues, and social scientists at large, that it was possible to spill gallons of theoretical bath water and still keep the baby intact.

When it came to the application of psychoanalytic theory to the social sphere, it was perhaps natural that someone as permissive in the realm of theory as Kardiner should have been particularly successful in working with anthropologists. Like Hartmann and the Erikson of *Childhood and Society*, Kardiner believed that it was with these that collaboration would prove most fruitful. But

62. *Ibid.*, pp. 89, 149–150.

whereas Hartmann had merely outlined what might be done and Erikson had confined himself to trying his hand in his two early studies of American Indians, Kardiner went on to specify the method of such labors in common. In close partnership with a group of well-established anthropologists, he developed the concept of "basic personality" as the focus of research. In every society, past or present, Kardiner and his co-workers surmised, the early conditioning of children produced emotional "constellations" —constellations which tended "to become fixed and integrative," in the sense that "subsequent reactions" were "based upon them and compounded." This conditioning, this molding of the psyche through "practices and customs," could be viewed as operating on two levels, a "primary" level of "childhood disciplines" and a "secondary" one of "religion and folklore." In psychoanalytic vocabulary, Kardiner explained, what was secondary could be described as a "projective system." As such it came close to the meaning Erikson gave to ideology.

Kardiner and his colleagues were quick to add that "basic personality" did not imply that all "reaction types" were "precisely alike"; they were merely "uniform and consistent within a given range."[63] The concept combined concreteness and flexibility in a way which might have been expected to appeal to Kardiner's émigré contemporaries who were trying to integrate psychoanalytic theory with the study of society. But neither Hartmann nor Erikson chose to do much with it. Hartmann limited himself to a passing reference to its possible usefulness "in some respects."[64] Erikson simply disregarded it.

In Erikson's case this neglect of Kardiner's work doubtless derived from the fact that he had settled—as Hartmann never did—on an alternative path to the understanding of social behavior. Erikson's method of extrapolating from the ideological evolution of great men to the mentality of their followers—or even of their era as a whole—debarred him from pursuing a course which

63. Abram Kardiner (with the collaboration of Ralph Linton, Cora Du Bois, and James West), *The Psychological Frontiers of Society* (New York, 1945), pp. 4–5, 21, 23–25.
64. "The Application of Psychoanalytic Concepts to Social Science" (originally published in 1950), *Essays on Ego Psychology*, p. 97.

began with human aggregates rather than a single individual. It also inclined him away from anthropology and toward collaboration with historians. But to maintain sympathetic relations with history and its practitioners did not necessarily entail a concentration on individual biography or on groups of related life histories. In the 1960's historians, like psychoanalysts, were reaching out to anthropology as possibly offering the long-sought bridge from the individual to the mass. More particularly, they were impressed by the cultural anthropologists' stress on the symbols with which a society defined itself, on shared meanings expressed in verbal or institutional form, and on the ways in which human beings internalized what was expected of them—in Kardiner's words, the "secondary" processes of a "projective system."[65] In this respect, Kardiner's pioneering efforts were bringing results even when—as was true most of the time—he himself received little or no credit.

At the same time, the social scientists or historians who worked most comfortably with psychoanalysts were coming to the conclusion that there was no royal road to collaboration between their two spheres. There was little or no possibility of reaching a consensus on the systematic use of psychoanalytic theory in the study of society. It was rather a matter, as Hartmann had once suggested, of a gradual and cumulative "mutual penetration."[66] Understood thus, the *application* of Freudian theory was not the proper expression at all. Hartmann realized this, but, characteristically, he left his injunction to his colleagues on a level of abstraction too rarefied to be of much use to someone investigating a concrete topic. As for Erikson, his tendency to collect disciples produced a bevy of "Eriksonians" more concerned with following where the master had pointed the way than with questioning or refining on his method.

Perhaps this impossibility of establishing any one-to-one relationship between psychoanalytic theory and social research would

65. See my "The Historian and the Social Scientist" (originally published in *The American Historical Review*, LXVI [Oct. 1960]), *Generalizations in Historical Writing*, ed. by Alexander V. Riasanovsky and Barnes Riznik (Philadelphia, 1963), pp. 54–55; Weinstein and Platt, *Psychoanalytic Sociology*, pp. 16, 88–89.
66. "Application of Psychoanalytic Concepts," *Essays on Ego Psychology*, p. 98.

have been more apparent if people had spent less time and emotional effort in trying to trace their own descent from Freud. The spirit of the founder continued to brood over psychoanalysis —and perhaps even more over enthusiasts outside the profession who were pathetically eager to be accepted as equals by those with impeccable credentials. In both cases, the generation-old question of whether the ego psychologists should be reckoned among Freud's subverters or among his heirs continued to burn on with its accustomed intensity. In the light, however, of the broader possibilities that lay open to psychoanalysis as it little by little suffused and "informed" the entire range of social thought, the question ceased to be of particular interest. If it was advisable, even essential, to rephrase much of Freud's vocabulary and to scrap his more dubious concepts—if one further envisaged a series of different vocabularies roughly translatable one into another— then the problem of lineal fidelity lost its urgency.

Yet such a prospect did not constitute a license to pick and choose among psychoanalytic concepts in an arbitrary or grab-bag fashion. Here Hartmann was correct in criticizing the neo-Freudians for so doing and in insisting on theoretical consistency. Had he lived longer and been more polemically inclined, he might have directed a similar critique against Erikson's later writings. For Erikson—whatever his protests to the contrary—had indeed subverted the Freudian legacy: he had used the founder's terminology in so eccentric and elusive a fashion as to rob it of clear or readily communicable meaning.

Hartmann, in contrast, was not mistaken in putting a claim on Freud's inheritance. He was also unduly cautious in specifying where he had diverged from his master's example. Still more, in his filial piety, he refrained from going as far afield as he might have done while remaining loyal to the half-mythical figure whom he honored quite appropriately as the progenitor not only of his own discipline but of twentieth-century thought in its widest sense. The final irony of Hartmann's ego psychology lies in the fact that its defects derived less from an imagined apostasy than from an inability to take full advantage of the intellectual latitude which *The Interpretation of Dreams* had first revealed.

CHAPTER
6

Conclusion: The Sea Change

1. The Emigration and the Cold War

By the early 1950's, with living and working conditions in Europe restored to something approaching their prewar level, the intellectual émigrés faced the question of "going home." But after a decade or more of residence in the United States, it was often far from clear where home was. In certain cases the choice was apparent: for younger people who had found a secure position in American society and whose English-speaking children felt and behaved like Americans, it made sense to stay on; for the more elderly—particularly for writers who had experienced the agony of being cut off from their native language—the emotional pull of the old country might be irresistible. In between came those who hesitated, who made frequent trips back and forth across the Atlantic before reaching a final decision; and among these were some of the most eminent. Each case was distinct; each individual tried to sort out a different mix of considerations, whether sentimental or practical. In the end, Salvemini and Borgese, Horkheimer and Adorno, returned to Europe; Neumann and Marcuse, Hartmann and Erikson, remained in the United States.

Besides the usual and predictable arguments of cultural loyalty or economic well-being, there was a further and more special situation which impinged on the émigrés at the midcentury—the cold war and the accompanying wave of "McCarthyism." Those

who have written on the emigration have had little to say about
this concatenation of events: perhaps the subject has proved too
delicate and embarrassing for full exploration.[1] Moreover there is
no statistical method of determining how heavily ideological considerations weighed in tipping personal decisions in one or the
other direction. Yet it is unquestionable that fear of an American
brand of fascism gave the final push to a number who had hesitated to go back and that at a time when most native-born intellectuals either supported their government or fell silent, leading
figures among the émigrés who stayed on protested vigorously
against the course of American policy, both at home and abroad.

After the American declaration of war against Germany and
Italy in 1941, the newcomers had shared with their hosts an attitude of solidarity in the antifascist effort; no more than a tiny
minority of either group had taken a pacifist stand. In the late
1940's, this alignment began to fall apart: the émigrés were less
prepared than the native-born to mobilize their energies once
more for an ideological engagement. With a few notable exceptions such as Hannah Arendt, they refused to equate Communism
with Nazism as alike "totalitarian" or to view Stalin as Hitler's
counterpart. And for this reluctance there were compelling psychological reasons. Fascism, after all, had served as the precipitating
force that had dissolved the attitude of ethical relativism or suspended judgment so many of them had entertained in the 1920's;
in presenting them with an image of evil, it had led them to
acknowledge their own sense of what was good. Thus while they
viewed the Nazi record as totally negative, they tended to concede
to Communism—even as deformed by Stalin—some glimmer or
memory of the Enlightenment in its origins and potentialities for
the future.

More broadly, the fifteen years from 1930 to 1945 had given the
émigrés a moral base-point. The threefold combat which those
years had witnessed—against economic depression, internal
tyranny, and "racial" conquest—remained with them for the rest
of their lives as their central ideological experience. Hence their

1. See, however, the brief comments by Laura Fermi in *Illustrious Immigrants: The Intellectual Migration from Europe 1930–41* (Chicago, 1968),
p. 388.

inability to react as sharply to the new threat from the East—frequently accompanied by the conviction that the Western remobilization, this time against Stalinism, lacked the admirable qualities of its predecessor. "Hitler," Thomas Mann wrote, "had the great merit of producing a simplification of the emotions, of calling forth a wholly unequivocal No, a clear and deadly hatred. The years of struggle against him had been morally a good era"—an era followed by a fall in ethical level.[2] By 1947 or 1948 an émigré, whatever his sufferings had been, might recall his immediate past with a peculiar kind of nostalgia. How different the verdict of a native-born critic who could speak of the 1930's as a "low dishonest" time and dismiss such nostalgia as "a sentiment possible only to the very young or the very old!"[3]

Two examples out of many, one of a man who stayed in America, the other of the most famous of those who returned, may suggest the anxieties of the émigrés during the McCarthy years. In 1950, Erik H. Erikson, in throwing his support to colleagues at the University of California unwilling to take the anti-Communist oath—whose roster, incidentally, included a high proportion of Central Europeans—gave moral rather than strictly ideological reasons for his act. While alert like others of German birth to the menacing parallel with familiar events in his original home, he chose to stress the repercussions of compliance on the professors' own students. To "acquiesce in an empty gesture," he conceded, might save "the faces of very important personages." But it would "hurt people"—the students—who were "much more important." "Young people," he added, were "rightfully suspicious and embarrassingly discerning." What older people could "laugh . . . off," he noted, in a striking prediction of the temper of the 1960's, could bring about "a dangerous rift" between the generations—a rift "between the 'official truth' and

2. *Die Entstehung des Doktor Faustus* (Amsterdam, 1949), trans. by Richard and Clara Winston as *The Story of a Novel* (New York, 1961), p. 163.
3. Irving Howe, "The New York Intellectuals" (originally published in *Commentary*, XLVI [Oct. 1968]), *Decline of the New* (New York, 1970), p. 221.

those deep and often radical doubts" which were "the necessary condition for the development of thought."[4]

Thomas Mann's struggles of conscience were better-known and more prolonged. Secure like Erikson in a California where he enjoyed acceptance and respect, Mann reluctantly decided to return to Europe two years after the Berkeley oath controversy. The beginnings of his doubts about the United States dated from President Roosevelt's death. He had been happy, he recalled, to have become an American citizen—with Max Horkheimer serving as one of his witnesses—while the leader he revered was still in command. In this period, the unfavorable remarks he directed at his hosts had been limited to the ironic, veiled references in *Joseph the Provider* and to an occasional witticism about "good-natured barbarians." But by 1946 his mood had grown more somber. He felt it his "task" to oppose the coming of a third world war; and in so doing he lent his name to a number of "front organizations," a stand which in the inflamed atmosphere of the times led to the suspicion that he was pro-Communist. He received abusive mail and phone calls; he feared that his passport would be withdrawn or that he might be summoned before a congressional investigating committee. "Why can't they let me sit in peace in my garden," he lamented, "doing the work for which I am equipped, instead of throwing stones at me and . . . forcing me to interrupt my work and defend myself?" At the midcentury he was close to despair. The cold war, he wrote, was "destroying democracy and leading to general madness." And his "depression" had been "intensified by all the final partings in a single year"—by the suicide of his son Klaus and by the deaths both of his older brother Heinrich and of his youngest brother who had remained in Germany.[5] The variegated circle of talented countrymen in southern California that had earlier sustained his spirits was shrinking: some had died; others had gone home.

4. Statement of June 1, 1950, quoted in Robert Coles, *Erik H. Erikson: The Growth of His Work* (Boston, 1970) p. 157.

5. *Story of a Novel*, p. 82; to Klaus Mann, March 9, 1943, to Agnes E. Meyer, January 7, 1944, March 27, 1950, *Letters of Thomas Mann 1889–1955*, selected and trans. by Richard and Clara Winston (New York, 1971), pp. 416, 433, 597; Klaus H. Pringsheim, "Thomas Mann in Amerika," *Neue deutsche Hefte*, XIII (1966), 28, 32, 36–39.

Among the latter, of course, was Adorno. Mann found it "significant" that the philosopher turned sociologist was "feeling so energetic back . . . in our alien homeland." For precisely here was the rub; Mann was convinced that the Germans had become estranged from him. "An abysmal gulf," he wrote, lay between his "experience and that of the people who remained behind in Germany." His wartime "political" writings he recognized—with a touch of exaggeration—had been "felt as comforting and strengthening only outside" the Reich. How then, he asked, could he "make much of a contribution toward raising up out of their deep abasement" those who had reviled him? By 1947 he was ready to visit Europe: he spent the late spring and summer in Britain and Switzerland and the Netherlands without ever entering his native country. Not until two years later did he venture inside Germany; and by this time the hostile demonstrations he had dreaded were totally absent. The chief criticism he incurred was for having crossed the demarcation line to the Eastern Zone and participated in a Goethe bicentennial celebration at Weimar.[6]

But to return to Germany as a traveler was quite another matter from moving there permanently. This was a prospect which Mann still could not entertain. At the same time, with each successive postwar journey to the Old World—he went back again for long stays in both 1950 and 1951—he felt his early ties to Europe gripping him ever more firmly. In 1952 he took the plunge: the prospect of Eisenhower's election as president, incongruously enough, seems to have tipped the balance.[7] Characteristically Mann left the United States with only his light baggage and with most of his acquaintance unaware that it was a final goodbye.

In Europe the resolution of his dilemma came to him at last. He found a way of living outside Germany in a place where his own language was spoken and whose citizens combined cosmopolitanism with respect for German civilization. For the last three years of his life he made his home near Zürich—the city he loved the best and of which he had written with a sympathy that was

6. To Walter von Molo, September 7, 1945, to Manfred George, March 11, 1947, to Paul Olberg, August 27, 1949, to Theodor W. Adorno, January 9, 1950, *Letters of Thomas Mann*, pp. 479, 522, 582–583, 590.
    7. Pringsheim, "Mann in Amerika," pp. 42–43.

amply returned. A year before his death he enjoyed a final reunion with Hermann Hesse in Nietzsche's celebrated retreat of Sils Maria in the Engadine. Despite Mann's disillusionment after 1945, he had learned in Roosevelt's America, in common with Adorno and Neumann and so many others, to experience democracy as an everyday reality, and in the end, by settling in Switzerland, he discovered how he could combine his democratic loyalty with his abiding attachment to the cultural tradition of the Europe in which he had grown to manhood.[8]

II. *From the Demonic to the Banal: Faustus and Eichmann*

Three months before embarking on his first postwar trip to Europe, Mann had completed the novel that was to embody his final retrospective judgment on his own country. Sixteen years later another émigré, a full generation younger than he, was to offer an equally stark indictment of the nation which had driven them both into exile. In style and content Mann's <u>Doctor Faustus</u> and Hannah Arendt's *Eichmann in Jerusalem* may appear totally unrelated. Yet to juxtapose them is to suggest the urgency of coming to terms with their native land that so many of the émigrés felt without quite knowing how to formulate it and the startling difference that a decade and a half made in the way such an assessment might be drawn up.

The fourth and last of Mann's major novels, *Doctor Faustus* marked the closest he ever came to a literary and intellectual summa. He aimed to compose "nothing less than the novel of" his "era, disguised as the story of an artist's life, a terribly imperiled and sinful artist." This "kind of ideal figure" would emerge as "a 'hero of our time,' a person who bore the suffering of the epoch." The novel's "central idea" combined in a single tormented existence "the flight from the difficulties of the cultural crisis into the pact with the devil, the craving of a proud mind, threatened by

8. Henry Hatfield, "Thomas Mann and America," *The Legacy of the German Refugee Intellectuals* (special no. of the review *Salmagundi*) (Fall 1969–Winter 1970), pp. 184–185.

sterility, for an unblocking of inhibitions at any cost, and the parallel between pernicious euphoria ending in collapse with the nationalistic frenzy of Fascism."[9] The vehicle Mann chose for conveying this overwhelming message was a contemporary reworking of the Faustian legend which Oswald Spengler had not been alone in setting up as the archetype of the insatiable striving in the Western soul.

Begun in May 1943 and completed just short of four years later, *Doctor Faustus* consumed its author's creative powers during a period of thunderous world events—the antifascist victory and Germany's fall, the opening of the cold war and the political reaction in America—and, as he said of his imaginary narrator, his pen must often have trembled at the task. Far from the leisurely, far-off, sunlit serenity of *Joseph the Provider*, Mann had returned to the darkness and cold of his native land. "The only major work that he wrote entirely outside . . . Germany proved to be the most German of all." Time and again, to convey the "demonic" in his theme, Mann resorted to the archaic language of Luther; demonology seeped through the crevices of his account, in his struggle to fathom the centuries-old evil in his own people. Two-thirds through his writing, Mann himself fell dangerously ill and was obliged to undergo major surgery. His "wildest" book, he noted, was taking shape as he was turning seventy; "never before" had "any work so agitated and moved" him. No longer—or only at rare intervals—could he find his accustomed refuge in the emotional distance of irony: he was now at grips with material that plumbed the depths of what he had himself experienced, "a reality that threatened to overwhelm him."[10]

In contriving his protagonist, Mann drew most obviously on the biography of Nietzsche. His Adrian Leverkühn went through Nietzsche's life span—transposed to forty years later—as he re-enacted key episodes or aspects of the philosopher's story: the half-intentional contraction of syphilis in a reckless attempt to extend

9. *Story of a Novel*, pp. 30, 38, 88.
10. Gunilla Bergsten, *Thomas Manns Doktor Faustus* (Stockholm, 1963), trans. by Krishna Winston under the same title (Chicago, 1969), pp. 9, 133–134; *Story of a Novel*, p. 221.

his artistic reach, the inability to love another human being, the end in a decade of gentle, uncomprehending madness under his mother's care. Nietzsche had of course been a musician among philosophers, and behind him in Mann's account there also lurked the memory of another heaven-defying figure who had teetered on the edge of insanity, Ludwig van Beethoven. Mann's "hero of his time" almost of necessity had to be a composer. For in the novelist's mind music had invariably ranked as both the highest and the most dangerous of the arts—the one most characteristic of his fellow Germans and in which their acknowledged superiority over other nations carried the most disturbing implications. All his life Mann had alternately combated and succumbed to his infatuation with Wagner, whose *Ring* remained "at bottom" his musical "homeland."[11] A composer it must be, then, and a German composer, as the novel's subtitle insisted, who bore upon his shoulders the heavy ambiguity of his country's cultural tradition.

Yet to cast in the form of a novel the life of a creator of music meant to make that music real—possibly even audible— to the expert reader. This tour de force Mann carried off with his customary blend of meticulousness and literary piracy—borrowing without giving credit, picking other people's brains, exploiting scraps of information from whatever source came his way. On Adorno, a recent acquaintance, he relied for technical competence in close musical analysis; indeed, without Adorno's help Mann could scarcely have written the elaborate descriptions of imaginary cantatas that marked an innovation in the craft of fiction.[12] From Arnold Schönberg he pilfered the invention of the twelve-tone scale— much to the former's annoyance, which Mann answered with "astonished and grieved" respect.[13] Whatever complaints the composer himself might lodge, it was quite apparent that the Faustian Leverkühn was not Schönberg: he was rather a cold, remote, indefinable figure whose works were molded in a style of deceptive simplicity, of "dynamic archaism," incurring at one and

11. *Ibid.*, p. 95.
12. See the repeated grateful references in *ibid.*, pp. 42–48, 72, 103, 117, 150–156.
13. To *The Saturday Review of Literature*, December 10, 1948, *Letters of Thomas Mann*, pp. 567–569.

the same time "the reproach both of bloody barbarism and of bloodless intellectuality."[14]

To catch so elusive a protagonist, Mann called upon a narrator—a friend of the composer from childhood, transparently his inferior, whom Leverkühn treated most of the time with impatience or condescension. Yet to put down the good Serenus Zeitblom as nothing more than a mildly foolish "humanist of the old school," moved by his friend's music to "a mixture of excitement, enthusiasm, admiration and deepest distrust," would be to mistake the subtlety of the novelist's intent. By confiding the recital to "a harmless and simple soul, well meaning and timid, . . . who could only wring his hands and shake his head," Mann escaped "the turbulence of everything direct . . . and confessional." And in the process he managed to express his own inner division: by splitting himself into two related but contrasting characters, he found a dialectical means of conveying his deep ambivalence about his country's culture and its national fate. If Leverkühn spoke for Mann the artist, Zeitblom voiced the author's sentiments as a responsible citizen of Germany and the world. It was to the latter that Mann assigned the task of tracing the dismal course by which the national qualities that had once aroused the admiration of mankind had succumbed to exaggeration and the demonic. Zeitblom's utterances were in the style of Mann the publicist or propagandist, doing his wartime duty in a more optimistic tone and at a lower intellectual level than when he marshaled his full creative power. In the narrator of *Faustus*— where parody figured prominently as an artistic device—the novelist performed the virtuoso feat of mimicking the aspect of his own personality best known to his American acquaintance.[15]

14. *Doktor Faustus: Das Leben des deutschen Tonsetzers Adrian Leverkühn, erzählt von einem Freunde* (Stockholm, 1947), trans. by H. T. Lowe-Porter as *Doctor Faustus: The Life of the German Composer Adrian Leverkühn as Told by a Friend* (New York, 1948), pp. 374, 377. I have altered the translation slightly.

15. Georg Lukács, *Thomas Mann*, 5th ed. (Berlin, 1957), trans. and abr. by Stanley Mitchell as *Essays on Thomas Mann* (New York, 1965), p. 85; *Story of a Novel*, p. 31; Bergsten, *Mann's Faustus*, p. 163; Hatfield, "Mann and America," p. 182. For examples of this self-mimicry, see *Doctor Faustus* (Eng. trans.), pp. 175, 505.

Beyond what it might do for Mann himself, his narrative technique enabled him to write as he intended a book that "itself would . . . become the thing it dealt with: . . . a musical composition." Just as superimposing Zeitblom's account upon the life of Leverkühn made it possible for the author to introduce his own reflections on contemporary events, so this method of storytelling gave *Faustus* a musical quality in its structure and its organization of themes. Like a complex series of chords, it resounded simultaneously on all the levels of its conception.[16] In temporal terms, the novel recalled or portrayed at least three different epochs. Remotely and through linguistic or atmospheric evocation, the era of the Reformation loomed in the background: in common with Erich Fromm, Mann had discovered in Luther's time the spawning ground of his country's subsequent arrogance and misery. On its second and more ostensible level, *Faustus* recounted the life of Leverkühn himself—born in the mid-1880's, initiating his pact with the devil twenty years later and sealing it shortly before the outbreak of war, producing his finest work in the late 1920's, gone insane in 1930, dead a decade later. Finally, in the narrator's constant asides to his readers, the novel reflected the tragedy of Germany in Hitler's grasp: beginning to write, as Mann himself did, when the bombardment of the Reich was mounting and eventual defeat was becoming a near certainty, the imaginary Zeitblom finished his account nearly two years earlier than the actual author—at the supreme moment in the spring of 1945 when Allied tanks were rumbling unopposed through the countryside and the Second World War was crashing to its close.

Within these three time dimensions, the alert reader could discern how the sequences of Leverkühn's life corresponded precisely with the vicissitudes of his nation's twentieth-century history. His pact with the devil coincided with the point at which Germany's leaders succumbed to the self-assertion that was to lead to the desperate gamble of the First World War. His years of

16. *Story of a Novel*, p. 64. On this simultaneity, see Bergsten, *Mann's Faustus*, pp. 44, 135–136, and Erich Kahler, "The Devil Secularized: Thomas Mann's Faust" (originally published in *Commentary*, VII [April 1949]), *Thomas Mann: A Collection of Critical Essays*, ed. by Henry Hatfield (Englewood Cliffs, N.J., 1964), p. 116.

most intense creativity were those of the zenith of Weimar culture just prior to its extinction. "How strangely the times," Zeitblom commented, "these very times in which I write, are linked with the period that forms the frame of this biography! For the last years of my hero's rational existence . . . were part and parcel of the mounting and spreading harms which then overwhelmed the country and now are being blotted out in blood and flames."[17]

The interweaving of the composer Leverkühn's fate with that of his people could scarcely have been expressed in more explicit terms. In the course of the narrative this theme appeared as early as 1914, when the word "breakthrough" figured in the double sense of military aggression and the perilous quest of the artist facing late in time—as the Germans had come belatedly to world power—the problem of bursting the bonds of mere imitation. ("You will break through time itself . . .," the devil had promised Leverkühn, "and dare to be barbaric, twice barbaric indeed, because of coming after the humane, after . . . bourgeois raffinement.")[18] As the story unfolded, its dual themes gradually merged into one: Leverkühn's collapse anticipated the total defeat of his nation; the "sinful" pride of the artist was mirrored in the behavior of the Nazi chieftains. In the end, German culture itself was called into question by the very novelist who had so often spoken in its behalf. "The nation whose power of abstraction" was "the highest, whose spirituality" was "the most perfectly and perilously detached, the nation of Kant . . .," plunged "ahead of the rest into a subanimal condition."[19] The "good" and the "bad" German proved inseparable.

The final device to which Mann resorted in bringing together all the elements mingled in his account—the "chorus of voices from German intellectual history" that had thundered through it—was to "take back" Beethoven's Ninth Symphony and more particularly the "Ode to Joy" of Schiller which constituted its last movement. It was with these words that Leverkühn cried out his woe at learning of the death of a little nephew—the "marvelous child" who at the very end had lifted the curse of lovelessness which

17. *Doctor Faustus* (Eng. trans.), p. 482.
18. *Ibid.*, pp. 243, 307–308.
19. Kahler, "The Devil Secularized," p. 121.

weighed upon the composer. And it was the same words that Mann made his own in voicing his agonized doubts about the literary and philosophical tradition which had nourished him. What he and his imaginary composer together "took back" was not merely the lofty strains of Beethoven and Schiller; the example of Goethe too became dubious—the Goethe whose succession Mann was proud to claim and with whom he had identified more than once in his own creative endeavors. The last of the symphonic cantatas Mann ascribed to his Leverkühn—"The Lamentation of Dr. Faustus"—like the title of the novel itself, transparently recalled Goethe's masterpiece. Just as its wild grief mocked Schiller's joy and love for mankind, so its "deep diabolic jest" canceled out the salvation which the Faust of German classic literature had at length attained.[20] In recapturing an earlier, more authentic Faustus than that of Goethe, Mann undercut the entire humanist current in his nation's thought over the past century and a half. The demonic had triumphed: the disembodied dreams, the elaborately cultivated *Geist* of the "good" Germans in the end stood revealed as a dangerous illusion.

But not quite. Mann recoiled from the notion of leaving his protagonist and his people in total abandonment. Although Adorno had insisted that he harden his account of the "Lamentation"—that he had been "too kindly, . . . too lavish" in consoling his readers—Mann succeeded in rewriting his conclusion in a tone which still admitted a glimmer of light: a "hope beyond hopelessness," a "transcendence of despair." "God be merciful to thy poor soul," were the narrator's and the novelist's last words, "my friend, my Fatherland!"[21]

The Germans and the Jews, one of Mann's minor characters had observed, could not "help perceiving . . . a striking analogy" between them. "In just the same way" they were "both hated, despised, feared, envied; in the same measure" they alienated

20. *Doctor Faustus* (Eng. trans.), pp. 478, 487–490; Bergsten, *Mann's Faustus*, pp. 91, 186, 191.
21. *Story of a Novel*, pp. 222–223; *Doctor Faustus* (Eng. trans.), pp. 491, 510.

others and felt alienated themselves.[22] The novelist was fully aware of the outrageousness of his comparison. Yet as a cosmopolitan and someone whose German-speaking acquaintance in California was preponderantly of Jewish origin, Mann was in a position to understand, as his countrymen who had remained at home failed to appreciate, that his own nation's tragedy and the tragedy of the Jews were two faces of the same reality. The destruction of European Jewry ranked as the most monstrous of Germany's crimes—the macabre chain of events in which whatever had once figured as life-giving in the demonic aspect of the national tradition had been exposed as irredeemably fraudulent. If the Allied military who devastated the Reich from end to end often did not know or care why they were inflicting such punishment, the literary elite in exile never doubted where the supreme sinfulness of their country lay.

But to reenact on the postwar German stage the evil of the immediate past—to demonstrate to the Germans themselves the full inhumanity of their conduct—seemed beyond the capacity of both victors and vanquished. While the Bonn government made financial restitution to the Jews, the trials of the major criminals did not succeed in teaching a lesson. Within Germany, this was perhaps only to be expected: indifference and moral numbness were the predictable reactions to a horror too vast for the ordinary mind to admit. What was more surprising was that even in the new state of Israel—which owed its existence to Hitler's legacy—it proved impossible to recall demonic history in a fashion that would carry conviction to an observer predisposed to believe the worst.

In 1960, a decade and a half after the war's end, Israeli agents abducted from his refuge in Argentina Adolf Eichmann, who was reputed to have been the architect of the Nazi extermination policy. Flown secretly across the Atlantic, Eichmann was duly tried in Jerusalem the following year and executed in 1962. Among those in the courtroom sat Hannah Arendt—the now celebrated author of *The Origins of Totalitarianism*—whose report of the trial stirred up even more of a furor than had greeted her first

22. *Ibid.*, pp. 407–408. I have altered the translation slightly.

book. For with a new directness of style, she bluntly argued that
the key to the evil of the Nazi period was to be found not in the
cosmic barbarism which Mann had lamented but in the "banality"
of procedures to which apparently normal human beings had given
their assent.

In Hannah Arendt's view Eichmann presented his accusers and
his judges the insuperable problem of dealing—whether on a legal,
a moral, or an intellectual plane—with a man unable to understand his own past deeds. If he could have been depicted as a
"monster," his trial would have been immensely simplified. But
this he transparently was not. What was one to do with a person
to whom thought was alien and who "had at his disposal a different . . . cliché"—every one of which, however it might contradict
another, gave him a sense of "elation"—"for each period of his life
and each of his activities?"[23]

Beyond that, the nature and extent of Eichmann's guilt—for
guilty he certainly was—emerged as less clear-cut than had been
anticipated. For one thing, "his role in the Final Solution, it now
turned out, had been wildly exaggerated—partly because of his
own boasting, partly because the defendants at Nuremberg and in
other postwar trials had tried to exculpate themselves at his expense, and chiefly because he . . . was the one German official
who was an 'expert in Jewish affairs' and in nothing else." Yet
even in this capacity Eichmann's guilt proved to be enmeshed
with that of others. And among the latter could be counted not
merely the top Nazis but "gentlemen" and ostensibly "unpolitical" figures below Hitler or Himmler but above Eichmann in the
chain of command: "the elite of the good old Civil Service" had
been "vying and fighting with each other for the honor of taking
the lead" in these dreadful doings. When Eichmann had discovered the bureaucratic lay of the land, he had "sensed a kind of
Pontius Pilate feeling"; he had "felt free of all guilt." Who was he
"to have [his] own thoughts in this matter"?[24]

Together Eichmann and his colleagues had resorted to a bizarre
reversal of moral scruple. They had succeeded in overcoming their

23. *Eichmann in Jerusalem: A Report on the Banality of Evil*, rev. and
enl. ed. (New York, 1965), pp. 49, 53–54.
24. *Ibid.*, pp. 114, 210.

"animal pity . . . in the presence of physical suffering" by "turning these instincts around. . . . Instead of saying: What horrible
things I did to people!" they were "able to say: What horrible
things I had to watch in the pursuance of my duties, how heavily
the task weighed upon my shoulders!" On the rare occasions on
which he had witnessed atrocities, Eichmann had in fact been
affected by what he saw. But in place of the "normal" reaction of
pity for the victims, he—in common with hundreds of others—
had managed to convince himself that it was rather those in *his*
position who deserved commiseration for the dreadful responsibility they had been obliged to bear.[25]

Whatever their stupefaction at this line of reasoning, Eichmann's judges had to decide to whom such crimes should ultimately be ascribed. And theirs was no simple task. As Arendt
explained in elaborate detail, within the tangled, overlapping
structure of the agencies which had handled the Final Solution, it
was often impossible to determine with precision the source of
orders phrased in euphemisms decipherable by the initiated alone.
Moreover, in the death camps themselves "it was usually the
inmates and the victims" who had actually manipulated the
instruments of extermination. Thus, in Eichmann's case, the
Israeli court found itself trying "a mass murderer who had never
killed (and who in this particular instance probably did not even
have the guts to kill)." To its credit the court met the difficulty
head-on: in its final judgment it laid down the principle that
within the unprecedented series of events it had passed in review,
"the degree of responsibility" increased as one drew "further away
from the man who" had used "the fatal instrument with his own
hands." Those who maintained—quite correctly—that they had
never committed murder were infinitely more guilty than the
wrecks of humanity who had performed the role of killers.[26]

If all this was true—and the major controversy Arendt aroused
raged not over the Final Solution as such but over how the Jews
themselves had faced their own destruction—where did it leave
the question of the evil in Germany's immediate past? If the

25. *Ibid.*, p. 106.
26. *Ibid.*, pp. 215, 246–247.

crimes of the Nazis could be characterized as a vast "banality" in which millions had shared and very few had understood exactly what they had done, did that make the German people more or less guilty than had earlier been supposed? Within the emigration opinions varied almost as widely as within the American intellectual community at large. But as the postwar years had passed, one change of sentiment at least paradoxically bore out a part of Arendt's contention. Back in Germany the banal had come fully into its own. When *Doctor Faustus* was published, an émigré could still feel frightened by Germany and the Germans—this was a further reason for hesitating to return. Fifteen years later the same individual was far less likely to be afraid: anti-Semitism, as Horkheimer and Adorno had predicted, had perceptibly waned; right-wing nationalist movements had again and again failed to win a substantial following. Bonn, a bevy of commentators insisted, was not the same as Weimar. If the new Federal Republic provided a less exciting cultural atmosphere than its predecessor in German democracy, by the same token it was less troubled and precarious. If the men of Bonn seemed almost to give preference to the banal, was this necessarily a cause for regret?

In the decade and a half which had elapsed between the appearance of *Faustus* and that of *Eichmann*, the new Germany of Adenauer and his heirs had taken shape—down-to-earth, complacent, and unpolitical—a Germany in which the middle-class philistine set the tone. The Bonn regime might appear stuffier than that of Weimar, but it was nowhere near so disquieting. It lacked the intellectual and ideological militancy which had pulsated through the years from 1918 to 1933, but it provided a more solid assurance that the worst would not occur. Somewhere along the way the demonic had been exorcised from German culture. Had it expired in the apocalypse of 1945 or from the sheer boredom that had followed?

III. *Centennial Celebrations*

The émigrés who chose to go back to their native lands, whatever their fears that their countrymen might no longer understand them, could at least be confident that they would not be ignored. Germany and Austria and Italy needed all available talent: educational levels had fallen everywhere, and with the majority of intellectuals in their middle years heavily compromised by association with fascism, the young people had no recourse but to turn for guidance to the elders who had preserved a moral equilibrium through the era of tyranny. This special—and temporary—prestige of the prefascist generation was understandably greater in the German-speaking world than in Italy; the latter offered no parallel to Horkheimer and Adorno's triumphant return to Frankfurt.

Intellectually as well as physically, Italy was far less devastated than what had only yesterday been called the Greater German Reich. If both peoples undertook a work of restoration, it was more the Germans who thought of themselves as building upon the rubble of their cultural life; the Italians were inclined rather to speak of a return to normal after the "parenthesis" of Mussolini's rule. The fact that most Italian intellectuals had adopted an attitude of prudent indifference toward Fascism persuaded them that there was little to be changed after its fall. Croce and the Croceans had traversed the authoritarian decades unscathed. What needed to be done, then, beyond giving public endorsement to those who already wielded an unofficial sway over the social thought of the peninsula?

This euphoria of picking up where Italy had dropped its cultural baggage twenty years earlier could not last long. Too much had happened in the meantime beneath the surface of Fascist orthodoxy and Crocean complacency. Since the early 1930's, younger intellectuals throughout the country had quietly but persistently been seeking new models and new styles of thought. In literature the search led them to the stripped prose of the American novel. In social thought it led to Marxism—the subtle, quasi-idealist Marxism of Antonio Gramsci. The publication of Gramsci's prison writings in 1947 ranked as the decisive intellectual event of the immediate postwar era; it inspired a school of historians and social investigators who for the better part of a decade preempted the field.[27] Thus Gramsci after his death accomplished from within

27. See my *Consciousness and Society* (New York, 1958), pp. 102–104, and *The United States and Italy*, 3rd ed. (Cambridge, Mass., 1979), pp.

the country what the émigré critics of Fascism such as Salvemini and Borgese had been unable to effect—a thoroughgoing reevaluation of Italian culture. In this sense the "inner emigration" of Gramsci and his heirs—something more desperate and perilous than what the Germans meant by the term—can be reckoned as the functional equivalent of the work of an Adorno outside his native land.

If neo-Marxism reached Italy with the rush and the enthusiasm of a late arrival, the same was true to a lesser extent of psychoanalysis. Here the vacuum after 1938 left virtually nothing with which to make a new start. In 1945 the whole country counted only seven analysts. Two decades later the number had increased nearly tenfold. Once again aided by an American example, the Italians had done in twenty years what elsewhere had taken two or three generations. But in terms of the educated population at large, psychoanalysis had still not penetrated Italian styles of thought. Its influence remained restricted to a sophisticated urban minority. And its diffusion had come less through writings by members of the profession than through works of fiction—the novels of Alberto Moravia and Elsa Morante, and above all the enormously popular *The Leopard* (1958), the posthumous masterpiece of the Sicilian Prince Giuseppe Tomasi di Lampedusa, whose wife was one of Italy's senior practicing analysts. In novels such as these, the psychoanalytic element was usually veiled and allusive: while sexuality was ever present, the vocabulary retained a classic simplicity uncontaminated by technical terms and neologisms.[28]

Italian postwar writers of fiction took pride in the fact that the origins of the antirhetorical honesty with which they depicted the social universe went back deep into the Fascist years—Moravia's youthful success, *The Time of Indifference*, had appeared as early as 1929—and they correctly saw themselves as constituting for the first time in their country's history a self-confident galaxy of

---

232–235, 238; also Mario Sansone, "La cultura," *Dieci anni dopo 1945– 1955: Saggi sulla vita democratica italiana* (Bari, 1955), pp. 519–522, 533–536, 541–544, 566–573.

28. Michel David, *La psicoanalisi nella cultura italiana* (Turin, 1966), pp. 224, 241, 482–510, 528–529, 539–544.

novelists. In the German-speaking lands the situation was the reverse. Here the twentieth century's major generation was passing from the scene: those who had finally devised a type of novel appropriate to the recalcitrant German language—Mann and Hesse among the Germans, Musil and Broch among the Austrians —were in exile or dead. Moreover, the ultrarefined, ultrapsychological example they offered appeared remote from the demands of a literature that was struggling to rise from the ruins of defeat. The young Germans who first gathered in 1947 to read and discuss their attempts to put on paper what might be said after the catastrophe could find little in the immediate past to serve as a guide.

Gruppe 47, the loose association of younger writers whose annual or semiannual meetings marked the stages of Germany's post-Nazi literary revival, refused to accept Adorno's dictum that after Auschwitz it was barbaric to write poetry at all. But like the Italians they demanded an honesty—both among themselves and with their public—which could be almost barbaric in its brutality. This was a new kind of literary movement: a group that was not a group, an avant-garde only in the sense of "good will," a "shadow government" of culture which was "more shadow than government" and which issued no programs or manifestoes—a group whose goals were "so simple and self-evident" that it seemed "superfluous . . . to formulate them." Its gatherings featured reading and unsparing criticism of its members' own works. This critical ruthlessness drew a sharp line between the younger generation and the established writers, even those with unimpeachable anti-Nazi credentials. The "angry young men" felt at ease among themselves; their delicate-tempered elders could not have endured what the group jocularly called a grilling on the electric chair. Thus although Mann more than once gave encouragement to Gruppe 47, it would have been hard to imagine him undergoing its ministrations.[29] Those who in the 1950's emerged as the younger novelists with reputations extending beyond Germany's frontiers, Heinrich Böll and Günter Grass, were robust figures

29. Reinhard Lettau, ed., *Die Gruppe 47: Bericht, Kritik, Polemik: Ein Handbuch* (Neuwied and Berlin, 1967), pp. 11, 31–32, 261, 279, 282, 315, 355, 379.

who had found a new idiom, with an irony that cut deeper than Mann's, to express what they had learned as adolescents of the cruelty of their countrymen and their subsequent exasperation at the philistinism they saw around them.

In social thought it likewise took a decade for a new generation of German writers to emerge; here, however, the link with the great figures of the past was closer than in imaginative literature. Sociologists such as Hans Albert and Ralf Dahrendorf revived the liberal or Weberian tradition; in Jürgen Habermas, Horkheimer and Adorno found a successor. The reknitting of the younger Germans' ties with the generation of their intellectual grandfathers became fully visible in the centennial celebrations in which the German-born, among whom former or present émigrés played a leading part, joined with eminent foreigners in honoring the memory of Sigmund Freud and Max Weber.

The centenary of Freud's birth came too early to exert a maximum influence. In 1956 Germany and Austria were still in the initial stages of their intellectual revival. Thus it was logical that Horkheimer and Adorno should have given a didactic and even an elementary cast to the proceedings they organized in Frankfurt. As their own brief remarks suggested, they saw their main task as one of refamiliarizing the German-speaking world with a body of thought that had migrated en masse to Britain and America. The same was true of the introductory lecture which had been assigned to Erikson. Quite simply Erikson strove to tell his new and unfamiliar German audience who Freud was and what he had done—to reacquaint the Germans, in his original language and that of the founder of psychoanalysis, with the achievement and self-doubt of a figure who had remained hidden from their view for nearly a quarter-century. And in so doing Erikson stressed Freud's own comparison of his work with Darwin's—it had "turned out to be . . . a true vision and a blueprint for a science" —while defending him from the charge that he had "detracted from the 'dignity' of sexuality."[30]

30. "Sigmund Freuds psychoanalytische Krise," *Freud in der Gegenwart,* ed. by Theodor W. Adorno and Walter Dirks (Frankfurt, 1957), Eng. ver-

The passage of a further decade and a half might perhaps have been expected to suffice for the German-speaking countries to catch up with their Freudian inheritance. But when the International Psychoanalytic Congress met in Vienna in 1971, the Americans and Americans-by-adoption still dominated the scene. If the Congress had been held in Germany rather than in Austria, the difference in weight between the old and the new homes of psychoanalysis would have been less overwhelming; but in the native city which Freud had alternately loved and hated it was painfully apparent that the birthplace of his movement had become a backwater. The Viennese, however astonished to discover that the founder of psychoanalysis might rank even higher than Mozart among the sons of Austria, did their best to be hospitable. Anna Freud danced a waltz in the late-nineteenth-century splendor of the Rathaus: the childless matriarch of psychoanalysis who had worked with children throughout her life reigned for a few days as an intellectual sovereign in the city from which she and her father had fled thirty-three years earlier.

With Hartmann recently deceased, the founder's daughter ranked without question as the greatest of the handful of returning Viennese. But there was also Erikson, who had trained with her in Vienna and who, at the insistence of the younger analysts he had inspired, had been added to the program as originally announced. Protesting against the heavily theoretical tone of the proceedings, Erikson called for a return to clinical evidence—an emphasis which, ironically enough, had not always been apparent in his own recent writings.[31] Freud's heritage, one might conclude, had returned to the lands of German speech, but it had come back in English translation and indelibly altered by its change of residence.

The Weber centennial of 1964, held at Heidelberg, in which Adorno once again played an organizing role, cast its net more

---

sion, "The First Psychoanalyst," in Erikson's *Insight and Responsibility: Lectures on the Ethical Implications of Psychoanalytic Insight* (New York, 1964), pp. 21–27, 33, 35.
31. Edith Kurzweil, "The (Freudian) Congress of Vienna," *Commentary*, LII (Nov. 1971), 80–83.

widely than either of the celebrations in honor of Freud. A greater number of fields of study was represented, and the major participants came from a more varied assortment of nations. The host was the German Sociological Association, and the ostensible aim of the gathering, as the title of its proceedings announced, was to assess the contemporary relevance of Weber's example for the discipline of which he ranked as the most influential founding figure and which was currently experiencing a boom in his native land. Eventually, as could have been anticipated, the discussion veered toward politics. In view of Weber's own polemical involvement—despite his struggle to keep this sort of utterance distinct from his "scientific" work—such a turn of events was not entirely inappropriate. Yet it took on added acerbity from the fact that some of the government officials present could not resist the temptation to enroll Weber among the spiritual progenitors of German democracy and from the choice of a militant non-Weberian—Herbert Marcuse—to give the closing address.[32]

With Adorno content to figure in a minor capacity—he had, after all, already said what he needed to say about Weber—the chief responsibility devolved on visitors from abroad. On each of three successive days in late April, a distinguished foreigner or émigré discussed a key aspect of Weberian sociology, followed by an array of commentators, of whom a bare majority were German. On the first day the man who had done the most to introduce Weber's method to the United States, Talcott Parsons, treated the congenial theme of "value-neutrality" and objectivity. The following day it was the turn of Raymond Aron, who had performed a similar function in France, to speak of Weber's relation to power politics. In the climactic final session Marcuse, presumably picked to balance the favorable presentations of the other two, dealt in astringent terms with the association of rationality and capitalism which had been a cardinal principle of Weber's teaching.[33]

Marcuse argued that Weberian sociology was neither so rational

32. Guenther Roth, "'Value-Neutrality' in Germany and the United States," *Scholarship and Partisanship: Essays on Max Weber* (with Reinhard Bendix) (Berkeley and Los Angeles, 1971), p. 46.

33. These papers and the discussions following them are published in *Max Weber und die Soziologie heute: Verhandlungen des 15. deutschen Soziologentages,* ed. by Otto Stammer (Tübingen, 1965).

nor so value-free as its creator had imagined. The notion of "formal rationality," he maintained, had "changed imperceptibly in the course of . . . Weber's analysis." It had been transformed into "a question of domination, of control"—the control exercised by capitalism through the dynamic of industrialization. This domination Weber had conceived as the "fate" of Western man. But society, Marcuse replied, was not "nature." To the world of economics and human relations, the word "fate," with its connotations of a law "largely independent of individuals," did not apply. Who, he demanded, decreed such a fate? If it was men themselves—and there could be no other answer—then they could abolish the domination they had themselves imposed.

Marcuse aimed his most telling observations at Weber's linkage of bureaucracy with charismatic leadership. If bureaucracy could be reckoned the administrative form of "modern economic rationality," the same could not be said for the character of domination at the very top. If the bureaucracy subjected itself "to an extra- and suprabureaucratic power"—to the power of charisma—then "the Weberian conception of reason" ended in irrationality. Thus "Weber's analysis of bureaucracy" broke "through the ideological camouflage. Far ahead of his time, he showed the illusory character of modern mass democracy." While his analysis of capitalism betrayed the insufficiency of his own value-neutrality—while he had taken into his " 'pure' definitions of formal rationality valuations peculiar" to the phenomenon he was discussing—by the same process he had inadvertently exposed the irrational in modern society. Was there perhaps, Marcuse concluded, "in Max Weber's concept of reason the irony that understands but disavows? Does he by any chance mean to say: And this you call 'reason'?"[34]

Grudgingly, obliquely, Marcuse gave Weber his due. Like Adorno a few years earlier, he recognized in the sociologist's writings ambiguities and nuances which made him something more than the patron saint of value-neutrality. Such a critique, at once hard-hitting and respectful, was what most of the younger

34. "Industrialisierung und Kapitalismus," *ibid.* (pp. 161–180), trans. in revised form by Jeremy J. Shapiro for Marcuse's *Negations: Essays in Critical Theory* (Boston, 1968), pp. 213–217, 219, 223, 226.

generation wanted to hear. But not all. Wolfgang J. Mommsen, who himself had written unsparingly of Weber's successive political stands, refused to accept Marcuse's interpretation of his own work as implying that Weber had ever envisaged an alliance with the German right.[35] And it was left to a young Italian philosopher steeped in German social thought to attempt a sophisticated restatement of value-neutrality in contemporary terms. Weber's formulation, Pietro Rossi maintained, was no longer "tenable." It would be wrong to restrict the value aspect of sociological method, in classic Weberian fashion, to "the preliminary stages," of an investigation or to "the delimitation of the sphere of research. . . . On the contrary, reference to value assumptions" found a place "in all the succeeding steps of the inquiry," whether as "working hypotheses" or as "explanatory models."

Yet this modification and correction, Rossi insisted, did not entail abandoning Weberian fundamentals. One should hold fast to the conviction that the social sciences had "the task neither . . . of proposing norms of conduct nor of pronouncing the values related to these norms; . . . the social scientist—like every other scientist"—had no right "to offer his personal opinion as his research results." The problem was rather one of establishing "from case to case . . . what valuations" were "legitimate for a particular discipline. . . . The exclusion of value judgments" meant banning "only . . . a specific kind of valuation" that was "scientifically illegitimate"; it constituted "no general prohibition of every sort of value statement." Within this new formulation, Weber's teaching still applied: despite its "insufficiencies," the "relationship between value neutrality and objectivity" he had enunciated remained "a basic principle of social-science method."[36]

Rossi's brief remarks rescued Weber from both his detractors and his uncritical apologists. And in so doing they reflected the experience of nearly a half-century of post-Weberian research and theory: while it had proved impossible, as Horkheimer and Adorno and Marcuse had repeatedly argued, to protect the "purity" of social thought from value-entanglement, it was a far cry from such a recognition to the sort of categorical moral dicta in

35. Stammer, *Weber und die Soziologie*, pp. 215–216.
36. *Ibid.*, pp. 91–94.

which the neo-Hegelians indulged. Objectivity had proved even
more difficult of attainment than Weber, for all his scruple and
self-torment, had supposed; but as an intellectual ideal it had not
been superseded.

iv. *Paul Tillich as Paradigm: Fusion, Misunderstanding, Transmutation*

When Marcuse and Erikson went back to their native land to
speak in honor or in criticism of the masters of twentieth-century
social thought, they figured at least as much in their new capacity
as Americans as they did in their old guise as Central Europeans.
Survivors of a generation that for the most part had either died or
returned across the Atlantic, they came to Frankfurt or Heidelberg
or Vienna surrounded by the aura of a popularity which had
eluded their German-speaking contemporaries. Moreover—and
partly in consequence of this public acclaim—they had become
enmeshed in the bitterest controversy their new country had
traversed since the Second World War.

A few months after the Weber centennial, the endemic conflict
in Southeast Asia erupted into full American involvement. These
two events of 1964–1965 marked an intellectual and moral watershed. Both Erikson and Marcuse, who shared an ethical goal of
"pacification," opposed the Vietnam war—Erikson indirectly
through his work on Gandhi's nonviolence, Marcuse in vehement
denunciation of "neo-colonial" inhumanity. In both, the war
intensified and accelerated a basic change in orientation: after the
mid-1960's Marcuse and Erikson alike declared their own values
more explicitly and to larger audiences than they had before; they
figured less as social theorists and more as polemicists or sages.
While this change betokened the extent of their "Americanization"—they no longer hesitated, as an émigré might, to attack the
policy of their adopted country—it masked the ways in which their
thought and action remained in a German mold. The timeliness of
their utterances concealed what was Romantic or nostalgic in the
assumptions from which they spoke.

This rootedness in the values of a rural society—this tug back

toward the spiritual universe of early-nineteenth-century Germany
—also characterized a thinker a half-generation older who died in
that same year 1965 when the violence of the Vietnam war began
to dominate the public consciousness. Paul Tillich had been
Marcuse's friend; Erikson delivered a eulogy at the memorial
service for him at Harvard University. Of all the intellectual émigrés to the United States, Tillich was perhaps the one who
embraced America most whole-heartedly and received most affection in return. Yet in his case also an ambiguity lurked in the
background: he too remained more German than his American
admirers suspected. Tillich's experience in the country he came to
love may serve as a final paradigm for what was assimilable in the
emigration and what held stubbornly true to the values of an Old
World childhood.

> My attachment to my native land in terms of landscape,
> language, tradition . . . has always been so instinctive that I
> could never understand why it should have to be made an
> object of special attention. . . .
> I have always felt so thoroughly German by nature that I
> could not dwell on the fact at length. . . .

Thus Tillich wrote of himself in his autobiographical reflections.
"Nearly all the great memories and longings" of his life, he
recalled, were "interwoven with landscapes, soil, weather, the
fields of grain and the smell of the potato plant in autumn, the
shapes of clouds, and with wind, flowers and woods."[37] The
passage served to explain why the quasi-pantheist nature mysticism
of German Romantic religiosity—the example of Schelling and
Schleiermacher—remained the base point from which he never
strayed. An unlikely figure, one might conclude, to take the path
of emigration and to find acceptance in a new home. Yet there
were in Tillich other *Wahlverwandtschaften*—elective affinities he
discovered in the United States and that struck a responsive chord
among listeners who knew nothing of his intellectual origins.

If the American fancied himself the eternal frontiersman, Tillich regarded his own life as passed forever "on the boundary." For

37. *On the Boundary: An Autobiographical Sketch* (New York, 1966),
pp. 17, 93.

a man so constituted, emigration was only an outward manifestation of what had always been a spiritual tendency to roam.
Profoundly attached to rural life, but irresistibly attracted to the
social and cultural tumult of cities—his thought suspended between philosophy and theology, Marxism and political conformity,
theism and disbelief—Tillich conceived the boundary experience
as his destiny. Born in 1886 the son of a rural Lutheran pastor, he
had managed to combine the teaching of theology with a personal
life untrammeled by convention and in sympathy with an artistic
bohemia. In the early 1930's, as a professor at Frankfurt, he had
maintained congenial relations with left-oriented colleagues of
Jewish origin such as Mannheim and Horkheimer, and it was
along with them that the Nazis deprived him of his university
chair in April 1933. In Frankfurt, he had fitted naturally into the
cosmopolitan *esprit frondeur* of the Weimar avant-garde: "Paulus
among the Jews," his friends quipped, using the Latin form of his
name by which he was invariably called.[38] And it was also natural
that that other eminent "Aryan" who accompanied the Jews into
exile, Thomas Mann, should have turned to Tillich for the information on theological study he needed for his *Doctor Faustus*—a
request with which the latter gladly complied, only to find to his
chagrin that the novelist had transformed into parody the reminiscences he had offered.

In another sense, such a twist was justified. Tillich was never
really comfortable as a professor of theology. Although he taught
for two decades at the Union Theological Seminary in New York,
he preferred the secular atmosphere of Harvard, where he came as
an elderly man in 1954. His basic aim, as he explained it shortly
before his death, was to interpret traditional religious symbols in
such a way that secular men—and he included himself among
them—could understand and be moved. In this respect, he was
the German and Protestant counterpart of Jacques Maritain and
Gabriel Marcel in France, who similarly tried to give Catholicism
a fresh meaning for the irreligious.[39] Far more than the founder

38. For Tillich's Frankfurt years, see the reminiscences of his widow Hannah: *From Time to Time* (New York, 1973), pp. 143–153.
39. See my analysis in *The Obstructed Path* (New York, 1968), Chapter 3.

of Protestant neoorthodoxy, Karl Barth, Tillich reckoned with what was non-Christian or alien to the Christian style of thought. Had Barth, with his fundamentalist austerity, left Germany for the United States rather than Switzerland, he would scarcely have found across the Atlantic the welcome and understanding that greeted Tillich almost from the start.

The substance of Tillich's thought falls outside the scope of the present inquiry.[40] From the theological standpoint, debate over his novel, permissive formulations raged during his lifetime and continued after his death. For some it was "impossible to see . . . the God of revelation" in his redefinition of faith as "ultimate concern." For others such a transcending of "the theistic idea" provided exactly the assurance they required to keep them within the Christian fold. More broadly, it was Tillich's philosophical stance that gave him a central relevance for the emigration. As the only existentialist to thrive on American soil, he suggested what was assimilable in an intellectual current which for the most part met resistance or misunderstanding in the United States. Tillich was so robustly and unashamedly himself that he could afford, as others could not, to disregard the predominant empirical tradition of his new country and the neopositivism or analytic tendency which seemed to be sweeping all before it. Instead of combating the reigning style of thought, he settled for coexistence: "he once asked a logical positivist to listen to him lecture and hold up a finger every time he heard something he could not understand; the logical positivist replied that he would have to hold his finger up from beginning to end."

The explanation for this extraordinary state of affairs lay on the "boundary that Tillich bridged most significantly," the one "between the . . . German idealist tradition of the 19th century and the alienation and anxiety of 20th-century experience. In a peculiarly haunting, improbable fusion, it was Tillich's genius to wed his beloved Schelling to Kierkegaard."[41] In similar fashion he succeeded in linking the disquieting and utterly alien Nietzsche to

40. For a sympathetic and comprehensive treatment, see James Luther Adams, *Paul Tillich's Philosophy of Culture, Science, and Religion* (New York, 1965).

41. Michael Novak, "The Religion of Paul Tillich," *Commentary*, XLIII (April 1967), 53–55, 62.

an authentic American tradition. Those who had been brought up on the New England Transcendentalists could hear comforting echoes in the words of the new arrival from across the sea:

> Philosophical idealism in America had had a definitely Protestant tinge, and the many theologians and the few philosophers who still looked back nostalgically to . . . idealism were not ready to take the leap to Barth or Kierkegaard. Tillich met their needs perfectly. He did not propose a renaissance of idealism; he combined Schelling . . . with the most modern movements, spoke approvingly of everything that was avant garde, and, while acclaimed as an existentialist . . ., excelled in the art of obviating any either-or.[42]

Thus if Tillich's theological formulations frequently jarred his public, his ethics gave hope to people awash in a sea of relativism. His respect for what he named "the courage of despair," his search for "meaning beyond meaninglessness," won the attention of skeptics who would have scorned the reasoning of a conventional theologian. For in effect what Tillich did was to press unbelievers to give an answer to the question why they were not total ethical nihilists and to recognize in their own conduct the grounds of *their* ultimate concern.[43] And he did it in a way that was so liberated from asceticism, so overflowing with vitality and endorsement of the process of living in all its contradictory aspects, that he conquered the hearts of those who could find nothing beyond poetic meaning in his vocabulary. Misunderstanding or half-understanding sufficed for Americans athirst for affirmations and who were only too happy to take the leap beyond the verifiable which Tillich asked of them.

The other intellectual émigrés with concerns extending beyond the boundary of a single discipline had encountered a similar half-understanding in the lands of English speech. Readers thinking exclusively in the English language almost never succeeded in

42. Walter Kaufmann, "The Reception of Existentialism in the United States," special no. of *Salmagundi*, p. 88.
43. More particularly in *The Courage To Be* (New Haven, Conn., 1952), pp. 140, 142, 175, 178.

entering fully into the idea world of men whose deepest reflections continued to go on in the other language they had spoken as children. Even Wittgenstein, whose influence had been the greatest of the German- or Austrian-born of his generation and whose writings were unique in being published in parallel German and English texts—whose experiments with two languages in which he was almost equally fluent might have been expected to bridge, if any human being could do so, the gap between these universes of discourse—even Wittgenstein suffered the fate of transmutation by his adherents into far more of an Anglo-American analytic philosopher than he actually had been or had become.

This matter of language suggests an initial discrimination to be made in assessing the profit and loss to Central European thought from its sojourn across the Channel or the Atlantic. In spheres in which nuance of expression was not crucial—where the major terms employed were conventional or international, and meanings direct and unambiguous—exposure to Anglo-American intellectual life brought almost pure gain. For the natural sciences or for disciplines that approached them in precision of method, it is appropriate to speak of a fusion or symbiosis of thought. And the same is true of particular and empirical studies within a clearly defined range. The critics of fascism, for example, suffered no serious diminution of meaning in finding themselves obliged to publish their works in English. On the contrary, what they wrote became even more biting and specific from being cast in a language that lent itself to plain speaking.

In the speculative type of thinking, however, which the Germans had always considered their peculiar province, the fusion remained incomplete or aborted. When Neumann turned from the study of fascism to a broader investigation of the nature of authoritarian rule, he bogged down in conceptual difficulties consequent on his transitional situation between two incompatible styles of thought. When Erikson discovered his own newly won facility at writing English, the result was a hybrid style that was too elaborate for what he had to say. In contrast, by limiting himself to an austere and meticulous prose, Hartmann overcame more successfully than any of his generation mates the problem of

writing in an unfamiliar tongue. At his hands, ego psychology—
even in its farther reaches—came close to a precision of diction
which rendered the shift from German to English harmless and
possibly benign.

Hartmann was a shining exception. In general the Central
Europeans who aimed at the speculative heights were well advised—as in the case of Horkheimer and Adorno—to stick to their
native language. This is not to say that they derived no benefit
from their stay in America. Far from it—Adorno went home a
wiser person, more persuaded of the value of empirical research,
more inclined to respect his intellectual adversaries. In common
with many lesser men, his understanding had been enriched by an
experience he had temperamentally resisted. And unlike the more
pliant of the émigrés, he had taken to himself what his hosts had
to offer without relinquishing his own philosophical patrimony.

It would be incorrect, then, to say that the sea change of
Central European social thought, in widening its audience, had
made it more superficial. But in altering its tone and its vocabulary, the transmutation did not develop that thought as much as
might have been imagined. At a level of abstraction above the
specific empirical study, it was difficult to detect how and where
the émigré generation had surpassed the generation of their intellectual fathers. Of the major expatriates from Central Europe,
Wittgenstein alone unmistakably "went beyond" the work of
Freud and Weber.

The critics of fascism had never claimed to do so. Salvemini
remained throughout his life untouched by the teachings of
Germans and Austrians a half-generation older than he. Neumann
at the time of his death had just come abreast of Freud. Mannheim and Marcuse and Fromm and a number of others conceived
of themselves as having fused the Marxian and the Freudian
traditions, but the product of such an admixture invariably proved
to be fragmentary or elusive, eccentric or sentimental. Of all the
synthesizers, Adorno put on the most dazzling performance, but
his highest flights were forever being dragged to earth by the
Hegelian ballast he refused to jettison. With a similar devotion,
Hartmann and Erikson hung on to more of the strict Freudian
inheritance than they required: in their sharply contrasting fash-

ions, both oscillated between self-confident independence and fidelity to the founder of psychoanalysis. Their hesitation in this respect goes far to explain their failure to establish a viable canon for the psychoanalytic study of society. Ironically enough, ego psychology was at its best when it returned to early Freudian fundamentals. This was the baffling difficulty that a conscientious theoretician such as Hartmann faced: how was one to refine on a body of teaching whose most persuasive features were at the same time its most elemental?

If not in the elaboration of theory, then possibly in their speculations on language and value, the émigré generation saw farther than their predecessors. By the midcentury it was no longer intellectually feasible to treat human discourse in the summary fashion which had earlier seemed to suffice. The development in the meantime of two new social studies—linguistics and anthropology—had forced the more perceptive workers in other fields to subject their own notions of language to critical scrutiny. An intense focus on the forms of communication linked the achievement of Wittgenstein and Adorno to that of younger figures in France such as Merleau-Ponty and the structuralists. And in this reexamination it became apparent that words did not invariably offer—as in the "talking cure" of psychoanalysis—the path to understanding: music emerged as an alternative or even privileged mode of discourse.

Yet if one had resort to music, one evoked a realm in which meanings were never unambiguous. In such a perspective, the social thinker's aspiration to direct, one-to-one communicability dissolved; he found himself obliged to abandon Weber's conviction that in theory at least he could devise a sociological proof which a different investigator, raised in an alien culture, would acknowledge as correct. And through the same process of self-questioning, he was led to inquire more deeply into value systems at variance with the one he took for granted; he felt the urgency of an unremitting assessment of value—whether his own or another's—pressing against him from all sides. No longer, with Freud, could he dismiss morality as "self-evident" and get on with his "scientific" work; no longer, with Weber, could he entertain the hope of fully isolating such work from contamination by value judgments. His personal experience as an antifascist and an exile had thrust upon him the task of making values explicit in unfamiliar contexts where the methodological precepts of the immediate past provided uncertain guidance. Not the least of the accomplishments of the émigré generation was to have demonstrated to themselves and their successors how to discuss human affairs in a way that combined scholarly scruple with passionate ethical commitment. Intellectual honesty remained the social theorist's supreme ideal; but it was now coupled with the realization that its attainment depended on a self-awareness even more complex and ramifying than the masters of twentieth-century thought had imagined.

Index

Abraham, Karl, 19
Absolute Idealism, 36, 37
Action Française, 126
Adams, Henry, 135
Adenauer, Konrad, 103, 109, 255
Adler, Alfred, 193, 194, 196, 197
Adorno, Theodor W., 3, 20, 77,
    136–70, 205, 229, 257–59, 270,
    271; Freud and psychoanalysis,
    critique of, 183–86, 189–90,
    195, 196; Horkheimer's col-
    laboration with, 141–46, 148–
    63, 186–88; last years and
    death, 168–69; and Mann's
    Doctor Faustus, 247, 251; and
    Marcuse, 171–75, 178, 181–
    83; mass society, critique of,
    136–40, 150–61, 187–88; re-
    turns to Germany, 161 63, 240,
    244, 256; in U.S.A., 103, 148–
    50, 166, 187, 245; and Weber
    centennial, 260–63; *quoted*, 165,
    182, 183, 189
*Aufsätze zur Gesellschaftstheorie
    und Methodologie*, 166
The Authoritarian Personality,
    150–53, 156, 157, 160–61, 184
Dialektik der Aufklärung (*Dialec-
    tic of Enlightenment*), 156–
    61, 165, 173, 180
Minima Moralia, 155–56
Negative Dialektik (*Negative Dia-
    lectics*), 163–64
"Zum Verhältnis von Soziologie
    und Psychologie," 185

Albert, Hans, 259
Alienation, 136, 140, 177, 179, 182
America, *see* United States of
    America
American Indians, Erikson's interest
    in, 221, 237
Anthropology, psychology and, 210–
    13, 221, 236–38
Anti-Semitism, 141; Adorno and
    Horkheimer's interpretation of,
    151, 152, 156–57, 159–60; in
    Germany, 108, 162, 255; in
    Italy, 10, 12–13; and totali-
    tarianism, 121–23
Arendt, Hannah, 121–25, 133, 159,
    241
    Eichmann in Jerusalem, 245,
        252–55
    The Origins of Totalitarianism,
        121 25, 252
Aristotle, 195
Aron, Raymond, 261
Augustine, St., 60–61
Austen Riggs Center, 224
Austria, 256, 258; German annexa-
    tion (*Anschluss*), 14–15, 33, 48,
    68–69, 205; German relationship
    with, 14–15; Hungarian relation-
    ship with, 15; Italian hostility
    to, 9; migration from, to U.S.A.,
    2; Wittgenstein's philosophy
    and, 68
Ayer, A. J., *Language, Truth and
    Logic*, 45

ABOUT THE AUTHOR

H. Stuart Hughes is the author of ten books, including *Consciousness and Society*, to which the present two books are sequels. A graduate of Amherst (A.B. 1937), he received his Ph.D. from Harvard (1940) and enlisted in the army in 1941, serving until 1946. He taught at Stanford University from 1952–1956 and in 1957 returned to Harvard where he taught for eighteen years. Hughes is professor emeritus of history at the University of California at San Diego. He lives in La Jolla, California.

(210 - 239)